CW00673480

OLD TESTAMENT
ETHICS
for the
PEOPLE OF GOD

All the royalties from this book have been irrevocably assigned to Langham Literature (formerly the Evangelical Literature Trust), a programme of the Langham Partnership International (LPI). Langham Literature distributes evangelical books to pastors, theological students and seminary libraries in the Majority World, and facilitates the writing and publishing of Christian literature in regional languages.

For further information on Langham Literature, and the other programmes of LPI, visit the website at <http://www.langhampartnership.org>.

In the USA John Stott Ministries is the national member of the Langham Partnership International. All enquiries may be made through <http://www.johnstott.org>.

Christopher J. H. Wright

OLD TESTAMENT
ETHICS
for the
PEOPLE OF GOD

A fully revised, updated and integrated edition

of *Living as the People of God* and *Walking in the Ways of the Lord*

Inter-Varsity Press

Inter-Varsity Press
38 De Montfort Street, Leicester LE1 7GP, England
Email: ivp@ivp-editorial.co.uk
Website: www.ivpbooks.com

© Christopher J. H. Wright, 2004

Christopher J. H. Wright has asserted his right under the Copyright, Designs and Patents Act,
1988, to be identified as Author of this work.

All rights reserved. No part of this publication may be reproduced, stored in a retrieval
system, or transmitted, in any form or by any means, electronic, mechanical, photocopying,
recording or otherwise, without the prior permission of the publisher or the Copyright
Licensing Agency.

Unless otherwise stated, Scripture quotations in this publication are from the Holy Bible, New
International Version. Copyright © 1973, 1978, 1984 by International Bible Society. Used by
permission of Hodder & Stoughton, a division of Hodder Headline Ltd. All rights reserved.
'NIV' is a registered trademark of International Bible Society. UK trademark number 1448790.

Incorporates material first published in
Living as the People of God (IVP, 1983)
Walking in the Ways of the Lord (Apollos, 1995)
(Fully revised and updated for this volume)

First published 2004
Reprinted 2006

British Library Cataloguing in Publication Data
A catalogue record for this book is available from the British Library.

ISBN-10: 0-85111-784-8
ISBN-13: 978-0-85111-784-3

Set in Monotype Garamond 11/13pt
Typeset in Great Britain by Servis Filmsetting Ltd, Manchester
Printed and bound in Great Britain by Creative Print and Design (Wales), Ebbw Vale

Inter-Varsity Press is the publishing division of the Universities and Colleges Christian
Fellowship (formerly the Inter-Varsity Fellowship), a student movement linking Christian
Unions in universities and colleges throughout Great Britain, and a member movement of the
International Fellowship of Evangelical Students. For more information about local and
national activities write to UCCF, 38 De Montfort Street, Leicester LE1 7GP, email us at
email@uccf.org.uk, or visit the UCCF website at www.uccf.org.uk.

To Liz
Catharine and Andy
Tim and Bianca
Jonny and Emma and Helena
and Suzy

CONTENTS

PREFACE TO *LIVING AS THE PEOPLE OF GOD*

Some authors preface their works with an apology or justification for adding another volume to the literature on their subject. At least I feel I am spared that duty since the subject of Old Testament ethics has scarcely any literature to add to. There are many academic articles and special studies, of course, that bear on the ethical significance of the Old Testament, as the bibliographies show. But I am not aware of any recent attempt to present an overview of the subject as a whole. So, without pretending to have exhausted the subject in depth or detail, I have attempted to provide a comprehensive framework within which Old Testament ethics can be organized and understood. The student should find in the bibliographies sufficient resources to take his study to deeper and wider dimensions.

In the interests of the general reader I have avoided as far as possible the use of technical vocabulary and dense footnotes. The only technical term I have consciously allowed myself is 'paradigm' and its derivative, 'paradigmatic'. I can find no simpler word to express the points I wish to make concerning a method of understanding and applying the Old Testament. The term is fully defined and explained as soon as it rears its head in chapter 2. Likewise, one or two other more familiar items of theological vocabulary are explained as they arise.

Two other points need to be made. First, a glance at the table of contents will show that most of the material is concerned with social aspects of the ethics of the Old Testament. Only in the last chapter do we look at personal or individual ethics. This may be somewhat unbalanced, since undoubtedly a lot more could be said on the personal ethical demands to be found in the Old Testament. The emphasis is, nevertheless, quite deliberate, and based on the conviction that the *primary* ethical thrust of the Old Testament is in fact social. The Old Testament is the story of a people – God's people; and all the morally memorable tales of individuals are part of that wider story. God called a whole society to be 'a people for his own possession', to live before him in the midst of the nations of the earth. So, as the title indicates, the Old

Testament is absorbed with what it means to be the living people of the living God.

The second point relates to the subtitle and the chapters in Part Two. I am convinced that the Old Testament, when properly understood and applied as part of the whole canon of Scripture, has a vital relevance for the whole range of our ethical concerns. My aim in this book is to point out ways in which it can be validly applied, to suggest directions for such applications, rather than to follow those directions through to detailed conclusions in each sphere. I am not an economist, nor a politician, lawyer or sociologist, and claim no special expertise in these areas. But my hope is that Christians who do work in these and other fields will be stimulated by what is offered here to a more coherent and effective application of biblical theology and ethics to the particulars of their own environment.

Many of the ideas of this book were first aired and shared in the congenially critical context of various study groups of the Shaftesbury Project. I am most grateful to the members of those groups for their stimulus over the past years, and also to the Shaftesbury Project itself for permission to modify and revise material they originally published as working papers.

I also wish to record my gratitude to the kind ladies of Tonbridge who typed the manuscript: Sheila Armstrong, Sue Bladon, Kathie Portlock and Frances Weller. My thanks also go to Brian and Megan Adams, Kenneth and Margaret Gubbins, Lawrence and Margaret Pope and David and Clare Wenham, who provided hospitality of various kinds for me during the writing of the book. I greatly appreciated the careful scrutiny of the Revd David Field and Dr Gordon Wenham who read the original typescript and made a large number of very helpful comments. Their suggestions helped me to clarify or improve what I wanted to say at a number of points. The book owes its indexes to the labours of some of my students at All Nations.

Only an author's family shares the full burden of the writing of a book, but my own family has gone beyond such patient forbearance and has turned some of the warmer principles of Old Testament ethics into a living experience of great joy. So with gratitude and affection this book is dedicated to them all.

Christopher J. H. Wright

PREFACE

When *Living as the People of God* came out in 1983, the level of interest (academic or popular) in Old Testament ethics was so low that few people (least of all the author) would have been bold enough to anticipate the book surviving two decades and re-emerging in a revised edition. There had been a long dearth of ethical engagement with the Old Testament. Cyril Rodd tells us that in 1956 he was discouraged from any interest in the subject of Old Testament ethics on the ground that there was no future in it.[1] In 1970 I wrote to my former undergraduate theology supervisor at Cambridge, John Sturdy, to ask if Old Testament ethics would be a good topic for doctoral research. He replied that it could well be, since nobody had written anything on it in English for fifty years. In 1973 when I was struggling to gain some leverage on how to tackle a dissertation on the subject, a distinguished German professor told me he was not surprised at my difficulties, since 'the subject doesn't exist' – a comment that did little to fortify my resolve in researching it.

Well, for a discipline that had no future in 1956, no past in 1970 and no existence at all in 1973, Old Testament ethics is in surprisingly good health. The observation I made in the preface to my own first offering on the subject,[2] that the discipline had 'scarcely any literature to add to', while certainly true of scholarship in English at the time (1983), has become wonderfully out of date in 2003. The past two decades have seen an abundance of monographs, symposia, articles, and even dissertations in the field. I surveyed some of the literature of the 1980s (along with material on New Testament ethics) in an article published in 1993.[3] In chapter 13 I have combined that with a survey of the even greater volume of relevant literature in the 1990s

---

[1] Rodd, *Glimpses*, p. ix.

[2] C. J. H. Wright, *Living*, p. 9. This was not my doctoral dissertation. That was published in 1990 as *God's People in God's Land*.

[3] Christopher J. H. Wright, 'Biblical Ethics Survey'.

and the early years of the present century. Such is the increased interest in the field that, of the approximately four hundred titles in the bibliography of this revised and updated edition, almost 75% are dated between 1983 and the present.

After the publication of *Living*, I continued to reflect and write on the subject. I found constant challenge and stimulation in being asked to speak or write on specific subjects from an Old Testament point of view, and discovered that the 'triangular' structure and paradigmatic method I had put forward somewhat tentatively and intuitively in 1983 was being tested and refined as I gave further thought to it. This resulted in a sequel volume, *Walking in the Ways of the Lord* (1995) – a collection of essays that had been previously published elsewhere. Since that volume is now largely out of print, I am grateful to IVP (through Philip Duce, who has patiently waited for this revision) for agreeing to the inclusion of a substantial amount of its contents (also fully revised) within this present volume. This is one factor in the revised edition being considerably larger than the first. The other factor is that I have expanded some chapters and included chapters on topics I scarcely touched in *Living* (e.g. ecological ethics).

While the book originally was (and still is) intended to be accessible to general readers, it has apparently found a place as a textbook for courses on Old Testament theology and ethics in theological colleges in different parts of the world. I have taken this fact into account in several ways while preparing this revised edition. First, while I trust the main text is still accessible to readers without formal theological training, I have included more footnotes with bibliographical references, referring to some of the scholarly debates that ebb and flow around the topics covered. References in footnotes are in abbreviated form. Full details will be found in the bibliography at the end. Secondly, I have added a further reading section at the end of each chapter (except for chapter 13), to enable students to research the topic in greater depth for themselves. And thirdly, I have included a whole final section, Part Three, dealing with the more academic aspects of Old Testament ethics for those seeking a basic orientation to the discipline.

Part Three, then, with its survey of historical and contemporary scholarship, is the part of the book some readers may wish to read first, and other readers may feel free to ignore altogether. The final chapter, however, is a personal attempt to tackle a double-sided central problem of Old Testament ethics; namely, what methods and assumptions are appropriate for the task of writing Old Testament ethics, and, in what sense and on what basis can we talk about the ethical authority of the Old Testament for Christians?

The appendix, 'What about the Canaanites?', is included simply because I get asked that question so often. Invariably, it seems, hearing or reading the phrase 'Old Testament ethics' arouses in people's minds what they regard precisely as the *unethical* dimensions of these texts. This book, however, was never intended as a book about 'the ethical *problems* of the Old Testament' (as we perceive them). That is a major challenge and needs another whole book if it is to be tackled wisely and well. However, to deflect criticism that I have ignored the troublesome question altogether, I offer (with acute awareness of its inadequacy) a brief survey of some perspectives on the matter that I have found helpful, along with some relevant further reading.

Regrettably, the following books came to my attention too late for discussion in the present work:

Brown, William P. (ed.), *Character and Scripture: Moral Formation, Community, and Interpretation of Scripture* (Grand Rapids: Eerdmans, 2002).

Goldingay, John, *Old Testament Theology: Israel's Gospel* (Downers Grove: InterVarsity Press, 2003).

Lalleman, Hetty, *Celebrating the Law? Rethinking Old Testament Ethics* (Carlisle: Paternoster, 2004).

Parry, Robin, *Old Testament Story and Christian Ethics: The Rape of Dinah as a Case Study* (Carlisle: Paternoster, 2004).

With gratitude and blessing I rededicate the book to my family, whose love and encouragement are enriching beyond measure. *Living as the People of God* was dedicated to them with the words

To

My wife Elizabeth

(in the spirit of Proverbs 31:28–31)

Catharine, Timothy, Jonathan

and Suzannah

who shares her beginnings with this book.

In the intervening years our family has shortened most of the names and expanded by three weddings and a granddaughter (Helena). Meanwhile Suzy, like the book that shared the first year of her life, has now reached the mature age of twenty-one. Unlike the book, however, she stands in no need whatsoever of revision or updating.

Christopher J. H. Wright

INTRODUCTION

The ethical triangle

The best way in to understanding and applying the Old Testament ethically is not by plunging in and seizing on whatever appears relevant to our own ethical agenda. Although people often do exactly that – quoting proof-texts almost at random – it usually means taking texts out of their historical, literary and cultural context. And it rarely produces any agreement, since people can easily quote counter-texts with equal disregard for the way the whole canon of the Old Testament hangs together. What we have to try to do is to put ourselves in Israel's position and understand how Israel perceived and experienced their relationship with God and how that experience affected their ethical ideals and practical living as a community.

Theology and ethics are inseparable in the Bible. You cannot explain how and why Israelites or Christians lived as they did until you see how and why they believed what they did. So my purpose in this part is to outline the broad contours of the worldview that lies behind the wealth of laws and exhortation in the Old Testament, as well as the moral values implicit or explicit in the narratives, worship and prophecy. Old Testament ethics are built upon Israel's worldview.

A worldview is a comprehensive set of assumptions that a person or culture makes in answer to several fundamental questions that face humans everywhere.[1] These questions include the following:

---

[1] The articulation of these four 'worldview questions' comes from J. Richard Middleton and Brian J. Walsh, *Truth Is Stranger*. For a more comprehensive discussion of Israel's worldview as it impacts not only the whole of the Old Testament, but also the New Testament's understanding of Jesus (and indeed his understanding of himself), see N. T. Wright, *People of God*.

1. *Where are we?* (What is the nature of the universe and this planet on which we live? How does it come to be here and has it a future?)
2. *Who are we?* (What does it mean to be human and how, if at all, are we distinct from the rest of the living creatures we live among?)
3. *What's gone wrong?* (What is the cause of the way things are, which we instinctively feel is not the way they should be? Why are we in such a mess?)
4. *What's the solution?* (What, if anything, can be done to put things right? Is there hope for the future, and if so, hope in what or whom and by when?)

The worldview of Israel in Old Testament times answered each of these questions broadly as follows:

1. This world is part of the good creation of one single living God, whom we know as the LORD.[2] It wholly belongs to this God (no part belongs to other gods), and the LORD is sovereign over all that exists 'in heaven above, on the earth below and under the earth'.
2. 'We' in the wider sense are human beings made in the image of the creator God, made for relationship with God and one another.
3. What has gone wrong is that we human beings have rebelled against the creator God, in moral and spiritual disobedience, and this has brought evil consequences into every aspect of human life, including the individual personality, our relationships with one another, with our physical environment and with God.
4. The solution lies with this same creator God who has addressed the problems of the nations of humanity by a historical project of redemption, beginning with the choice of Abraham, the father of our nation Israel. This will eventually extend to include the blessing of all nations and a new creation.

'We' in the narrower sense, therefore (an Old Testament Israelite might have explained), are an elect people in unique relationship with the LORD who is both our covenant God as well as the universal God of all nations. Through a great historical act of national deliverance (the exodus), through the covenant made at Sinai, and through the gift of the land in which we live, the LORD has constituted us his own people. But the covenant with Abraham reminds us that we have been chosen with the mission of being the means by which he

---

[2] See chapter 1, n.1 below.

will bring all nations into blessing. In our daily lives we observe rituals of purity, distinctions of clean and unclean categories, which reflect that separateness from the nations that we believe is required of a people called to be holy, as the LORD is holy. In our behaviour we are governed by a body of customs, laws and exhortation, which as our 'Guidance' (*tôrâ*) shapes our response to the LORD as our covenant Lord. In our worship we acknowledge the LORD alone not only as king over Israel, but ultimately also king of the whole earth, of all nations and all creation.

This, in the tiniest of nutshells, is the theology of the Old Testament: the worldview of Israel as expressed in their beliefs, stories and worship. It is only within this matrix of assumptions that Old Testament ethics makes sense. And it is only as we connect this worldview with its development in the New Testament, when the first followers of Jesus made sense of him in the light of their scriptures (what we call the Old Testament), that we can validly appropriate the ethics of the Old Testament into Christian ethics.

Now within this broad matrix of self-understanding we may pinpoint three major focal points:

- The LORD, as the God of Israel.
- Israel themselves as an elect people in unique relation to the LORD.
- The land Israel believed the LORD had promised and given to them.

God, Israel and the land – these were the three pillars of Israel's worldview, the primary factors of their theology and ethics. We may conceptualize these as a triangle of relationships, each of which affected and interacted with both the others. So we can take each 'corner' of this triangle in turn and examine Old Testament ethical teaching from the theological angle (God), the social angle (Israel) and the economic angle (the land). This will be the framework for the three chapters respectively in Part One.

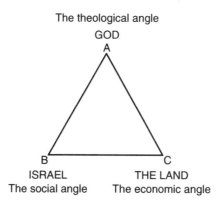

Inevitably, there is something artificial about such a scheme. But it may prove helpful in trying to grasp the complexities of the Old Testament within a relatively simple and comprehensive framework that is nevertheless both compatible with the shape of the canon of the Old Testament, and with the covenantal basis of Old Testament theology.[3]

---

[3] Cyril Rodd summarizes my approach fairly, but complains that this framework, like all other attempts to present ethics 'within a systematic frame distorts the ethics themselves'. It is a pattern that, as he puts it, I have 'imposed' upon Old Testament ethics (*Glimpses*, pp. 2, 316). Obviously, my analogy of a triangle of relationships is nowhere explicit in the texts of the Old Testament. However, even the canon itself was an attempt to present the huge variety of documents within a system or pattern that was in some sense 'imposed' in order to bring to clarity and visibility the theological convictions that informed its creation. My very subjective defence is that I like to imagine that if I could engage one of the Israelite prophets in conversation, or one of the psalmists or historians, and could show them my suggested triangle of relationships between the LORD, Israel and the land, they would recognize something not too far distant from the essential pillars of their faith and tradition.

PART ONE

A STRUCTURE FOR OLD TESTAMENT ETHICS

1. THE THEOLOGICAL ANGLE

A historian of comparative legal systems in Europe was once asked to summarize the essential differences he had observed in different national cultures in their approach to law and ethics. 'It's simple,' he said. 'In Germany, everything is prohibited, except that which is permitted. In France, everything is permitted, except that which is prohibited. In Russia, everything is prohibited, including that which is permitted. And in Italy everything is permitted, including that which is prohibited.'

Ethical systems display a similar variety throughout history and culture. That variety can be seen in relation to the fundamental axiom or assumption taken as the starting point of any given ethical system. Aristotle, for example, spoke of 'the Golden Mean' – popularly summarized as 'all things in moderation'. Utilitarianism advocates the principle of 'the greatest good of the greatest number'. Situation ethics regards love as the governing principle that will be sufficient to guide our choices and behaviour in any given situation. In more postmodern dress this boils down to the 'no harm' criterion – 'It doesn't matter what you do so long as nobody else gets hurt.'

In the Old Testament, however (as in the whole Bible), ethics is fundamentally *theological*. That is, ethical issues are at every point related to God – to his character, his will, his actions and his purpose. So the first angle we must explore as we seek a method for handling the ethics of the Old Testament is the theological angle. How does the Old Testament presentation of God impact its ethical teaching?

God's identity

To say that biblical ethics starts from God is obvious, but doesn't get us very far. Many systems of ethics that have a religious foundation would say the same. So first of all we have to be more specific about the word 'God'. Which god? And how is this god known? As Christians we are so used to using the Anglo-Saxon monosyllable 'god' and investing it with the content of a biblically informed faith that we fail to recognize how much we are packing into it when we decide to promote the first letter to upper case – 'God'. Or, conversely, we may be unaware how much is *not* packed into it by those who have no grounding in the story and worldview of the Bible. For the word 'god' is nothing more than a generic term, which in its linguistic origins was usually plural (gods) rather than singular. It originally referred to the multiple deities of the tribes of northern Europe. So the question, for example, 'Do you believe in God?' means very little (as does any answer given to such a question), unless one specifies what the last word refers to in objective reality. Many who might answer in the affirmative would be in for a surprise if they truly encountered the God of the Bible. And many who would say 'No, I don't believe in God' might be surprised to discover that biblical Christians too do not believe in the 'God' such atheists deny.

In his self-revelation to Israel the living God took no such risks. Monotheism is sometimes said to be the essential distinctive of the faith Israel bequeathed to the world. But that term is also far too non-specific. What were the Israelites to learn from the great acts of God in their history? Did Moses say to them after the exodus and Sinai, 'You were shown these things so that you might know that there is only one God'? If that was all the conclusion they had to draw, the singularity of deity, they would have got no further than what the demons already know, as James said (Jas. 2:19). No, the inference the Israelites were to draw from their history was much more specific: 'You were shown these things so that you might know that the LORD (*YHWH*) is God; beside him there is no other.[1] . . . Acknowledge and take to heart this day that

---

[1] In most English versions of the Bible the words 'the LORD' translate the Hebrew personal name for God. In the original Hebrew text this consisted of the four consonants YHWH. Because of the sacredness of this name, later Jewish custom chose not to pronounce the 'tetragrammaton' ('four letters', as it is called), but to substitute the Hebrew title *adonay* (Lord) in reading the text aloud. The vowel points of *adonay* were added to the consonants YHWH to indicate this practice. It is this combination that gave rise to the Latin form 'Jehovah' used by some older translators. The earliest Greek translation of the Hebrew scriptures, the Septuagint, made about two hundred years before Christ, followed the tradition of replacing YHWH with *adonay* in reading the

the *LORD* is God in heaven above and on the earth below. There is no other'
(Deut. 4:35, 39; my italics).

The acts of *this* God, YHWH, proved who was truly God. It was not the
gods of the Egyptians or the Canaanites. It was YHWH who alone had done
these things, uniquely as God and uniquely for Israel. The issue being stressed
here, then, was not the numerical value of deity (one god or many) – though
that was important and YHWH's unity is affirmed strongly elsewhere (e.g.
Deut. 6:4–5). What mattered was the *identity and character* of the God who had
done these amazing things in their history. This matters greatly when we come
to the ethical teaching of the Old Testament, for it is founded precisely on the
identity of this God. When Israel went after other gods (to use the phrase
most commonly used in Deuteronomy and the history books), the effects
were not just religious but also ethical. Or rather 'unethical' – for idolatry
always has disastrous social and ethical effects, as the prophets saw clearly.
How we behave depends on what or whom we worship – then as now. So for
Israel, ethical behaviour was defined by the identity of this God, their God,
Yahweh, 'the LORD our God', the Holy One of Israel.

God's action

God acts first and calls people to respond. This is the starting point for the
moral teaching of the Old Testament. God takes the initiative in grace and
redeeming action and then makes his ethical demand in the light of it. Ethics
then becomes a matter of response and gratitude within a personal relationship, not of blind obedience to rules or adherence to timeless principals. This
might not always appear so when we read the laws of the Old Testament by
themselves. Dip into a typical chapter of Leviticus or Deuteronomy and it

---

Hebrew text, by rendering the Hebrew divine name YHWH into Greek with *ho kyrios* –
the Lord. Modern convention in the world of biblical scholarship, at least among
Christian scholars, tends to spell the divine name 'Yahweh' (though nobody is entirely
sure how it was originally pronounced). The dominant preference in English translations
of the Bible, however, is to follow the early tradition and render the divine name with 'the
LORD'. In this book I use YHWH where the distinctiveness of the personal name is
important, but also often use the LORD in continuity with this strong historical tradition.
What is important for us to remember is that 'the LORD' is not just a synonym for 'God',
but expresses the personal name and character of the God being referred to. So if we do
use, or read, the name 'Yahweh', it is not just a strange tribal deity of an ancient people,
but the personal name for the living God – used by his ancient people Israel, yes, but also
the God of the whole Bible, the God and Father of our Lord Jesus Christ.

might seem that obedience to the law is all that counts. But 'dipping in', as we saw in the introduction, is always a dubious way to handle the biblical text. It is vitally important that we pay attention to the narrative framework in which the Old Testament laws are set.

It is being increasingly recognized, in fact, that preoccupation with the law of the Old Testament has distorted Christian understanding of the ethical value and values of the Old Testament as a whole. It is somewhat unfortunate that the English expression 'The Law' has been used to translate *tôrâ*, the Hebrew term for the Pentateuch (the first five books of the Bible). The Torah is certainly foundational to the whole canon of the Old Testament (and indeed of the Bible), but equally certainly, the Torah is much more than law, and even the laws within it are more than 'legislation' in a modern judicial sense. Open the Torah at the start and you enter a narrative that goes on for a book and a half before you encounter a single 'code of law'. And that narrative framework is sustained throughout the Pentateuch. The law is given within the context of a story. In that story we meet the God who is creator and redeemer. We read of the wonder of creation, the tragedy of human rebellion, the calling of Abraham and his people. We learn of God's intentions for that people and through them for the rest of humanity. We hold our breath through many moments of suspense and danger and we marvel with Israel at the compassion, patience, anger, judgment and purposes of this God who tangles with them in their historical journey.

Not only is it important to look at this narrative within which the law is set (as we shall do in a moment), we also need to bring into our account of Old Testament ethics the fact that so much of the rest of the Old Testament is also narrative – about half, actually. For there we find the stories through which Israel understood themselves and their God. And it was through these stories that they learned and handed on that accumulated store of revelation and experience, of tradition and challenge, of glowing examples and spectacular failures, that make up the ethical tapestry of the Old Testament. Israel was a community of memory and hope. It was in the remembering and retelling of their past, and in the hope that this generated for the future, that Israel most learned the shape of its own identity and mission and the ethical quality of life appropriate to both. Israel's community was shaped by Israel's story. 'The community is formed . . . by the belief that the narrative witnesses to the reality of the community-shaping encounter with God in historical time and space . . . Israel's character is significantly formed by its remembering and reinterpreting of God's previous actions on its behalf.'[2]

---

[2] Birch, 'Moral Agency', p. 27. The importance of character in ethics, and the

So let us look at the foundational story of the origin of Old Testament law; namely, the exodus and Sinai events described in Exodus 1 – 24. We find the Israelites oppressed and in slavery in Egypt, crying out under intolerable conditions. Their cry is heard by God (2:23–25), and he acts. In a series of mighty acts he delivers (redeems) them from Egypt (chs. 3 – 15), brings them to Sinai (chs. 16 – 19), gives them his law (chs. 20 – 23) and concludes a covenant with them (24). And all of this God does out of faithfulness to his own character and the promises he made to the forefathers of the nation (2:24; 3:6–8):

> Moreover, I have heard the groaning of the Israelites, whom the Egyptians are enslaving, and I have remembered my covenant.
>
> Therefore, say to the Israelites: 'I am the LORD, and I will bring you out from under the yoke of the Egyptians. I will free you from being slaves to them, and I will redeem you with an outstretched arm and with mighty acts of judgment. I will take you as my own people, and I will be your God. Then you will know that I am the LORD your God, who brought you out from under the yoke of the Egyptians. And I will bring you to the land I swore with uplifted hand to give to Abraham, to Isaac and to Jacob. I will give it to you as a possession. I am the LORD.
>
> (Exod. 6:5–8).[3]

The sequence of events in the biblical story is very important. God did not reveal his law to Moses on Mount Sinai when he first met him there at the burning bush. He did not then send him down to Egypt with the message 'This is God's law, and if you keep it fully from now on, God will rescue you out of this slavery.' Israel was not told they could deserve or hasten their own deliverance by keeping the law. No, God acted *first*. God first redeemed them out of their bondage, and then made his covenant with them, a covenant in which their side was to keep God's law, as their response of grateful obedience to their saving God.

This point is made as soon as Israel arrived at Sinai at the start of Exodus 19.

---

importance of narrative as a major means by which character is shaped in biblical ethics, has been particularly focused by Stanley Hauerwas, *Community of Character* and *Peaceable Kingdom*. Waldemar Janzen, *Ethics*, also argues for the priority of narrative over law in formulating an approach to Old Testament ethics.

[3] Notice how God's own identity and character are bound up with the events he here outlines in advance. 'I am the LORD' – YHWH. Israel will not only be delivered in the coming events, they will not only have to make an appropriate ethical response to those *events* as such, they will also know *YHWH*, which is the foundation for Old Testament ethics.

Already there have been eighteen chapters of God's salvation in action. We have not yet reached the giving of the law in chapter 20. First of all God addresses the people in a text that functions like a fulcrum in the whole book, or like a hinge between the story of redemption and the giving of the law. 'You yourselves have seen what I did to Egypt, and how I carried you on eagles' wings and brought you to myself. Now if you obey me fully and keep my covenant, then out of all nations you will be my treasured possession . . .' (Exod. 19:4–5).

God calls attention to his own prior action. Three months previously they had been slaves in Egypt. Now they were not. And the reason lay only in God's combination of compassion, faithfulness to his promise, and judgment on Pharaoh. The Israelites were not told to keep the law so that God might save them and they could be his people. He already had and they already were. He delivered them and made them his people and *then* called them to keep his law. Ethical obedience is a response to God's grace, not a means of achieving it.

Even the Decalogue itself does not begin with the first commandment. There is the vital preface 'I am the LORD your God, who brought you out of Egypt, out of the land of slavery' (Exod. 20:2). With those words God identifies himself ('I am YHWH') and his redeeming activity ('I brought you out'), and then goes on, 'You shall have no other gods before me' (v. 3). The command *follows* the statement, with an implied 'therefore' linking the two.

The relationship between God's command and God's previous actions on behalf of Israel is even more clearly shown in Deuteronomy, where the whole historical prologue, chapters 1 – 4, precedes the Decalogue in chapter 5. It has even been argued that the mainly legal section of the book, chapters 12 – 26, is deliberately reflective of the mainly theological section, chapters 1 – 11. Israel's response to the LORD is meant to be, in broad social terms, a mirroring of the LORD's own actions towards Israel.[4] Certainly, in Deuteronomy 6:20–25, when an Israelite son asked his father about the meaning of, or reason for, all the law his family were observing,[5] the answer was not a curt 'Because God commands it.' Rather, the father was to tell the story, the old, old story of the LORD and his love in action, the story of the exodus. The

---

[4] See J. Gordon McConville, *Law and Theology*.

[5] The question could have several nuances. In Hebrew it is simply '*What* [are] all these stipulations . . .?' It could mean, what are they for? what do they mean? why do we keep them? what is the point of them? etc. The father's answer seems to imply that the son was looking for a rationale or motive, since that is what he offers: 'This is why we do and should keep these laws.'

meaning of the law was to be found in the 'gospel' – the historical events of redemption.

Right from the start, then, Israel's keeping of God's law was meant to be a response to what God had already done. This is the foundation not only of Old Testament ethics, but is indeed the principle running through the moral teaching of the whole Bible. The same order is seen in the New Testament: 'Love each other *as I have loved you*' (John 15:12; my italics); 'We love *because he first loved us*' (1 John 4:19; my italics; cf. Rom. 12:1). There is a fundamental unity between the Testaments on this point. It is a mistake to suggest that the difference between the Old and the New Testament is that the Old Testament taught that salvation came by keeping the law whereas in the New Testament it comes by grace. That is precisely the *distortion* of the Scriptures that Paul was combating. But, as he was keen to demonstrate, grace is the foundation of our salvation and of our ethics throughout the whole Bible. God's grace comes first; human response, second.

As we go further into the story of the book of Exodus we find that not only was Israel's relationship with God founded on his *redeeming* grace; it was sustained by his *forgiving* grace. This is the point of the remarkable and profound narrative in chapters 32 – 34. While Moses is on the mountain, Israel rebels and makes the idol of the golden calf. God declares he will destroy them utterly. But Moses intervenes and pleads with God for the people. First of all he reminds God of his own reputation, which would be lost if, having rescued Israel, he let them perish. What sort of God would they think the LORD was: 'Why should the Egyptians say . . . ?' (32:12). Then Moses reminds God of his earlier promise to Abraham (32:13). At that point God relents somewhat and says he will keep that particular promise: Israel may go and possess the land. But God himself will not go with them (33:3). However, that does not satisfy Moses. He presses on and reminds God of the covenant he has just made at Sinai, in which the LORD had promised to be Israel's God and take them as his people: 'Remember that this nation is *your* people' (33:13; my italics). But how would anyone know this unique YHWH-related identity of Israel, if the LORD did not go with them (33:16)? That prayer goes right to the heart of God. In his mercy he forgives the people, and in chapter 34 the covenant is re-established.

Such a brief outline does not do justice to the depths of this text (Exod. 32 – 34), but it certainly drives home one major point: from such beginnings, Israel knew that the survival of their relationship with the LORD depended totally on his faithfulness and loyalty to his own character and promises, not on their own success in keeping the law. In this text we find one of the clearest definitions of God as the LORD in the Bible, one that is repeated in many other contexts because it spoke so crucially of the nature, character and priorities of the LORD – Exodus 34:6–7. It is a text to which we shall return:

The LORD, the LORD, the compassionate and gracious God, slow to anger, abounding in love and faithfulness, maintaining love to thousands and forgiving wickedness, rebellion and sin. Yet he does not leave the guilty unpunished; he punishes the children and their children for the sin of the fathers to the third and fourth generation.

God's words

Israel's ethical response was not only to what their God, the LORD, had done in their history. It was also to what he had said through the word of revelation they had received. This double mode of God's involvement with Israel – deed and word – is highlighted in that text where we began, Deuteronomy 4:32–40, and it is worth looking at it more carefully. It begins with a rhetorical challenge, which makes the point that what Israel had experienced of God in their recent past was unique, in the sense that it was unprecedented in history and unparalleled in the rest of the world. God had done things for them that he had not done anywhere else or at any other time:

Ask now about the former days, long before your time, from the day God created man on the earth; ask from one end of the heavens to the other. Has anything so great as this ever happened, or has anything like it ever been heard of? Has any other people heard the voice of God speaking out of fire, as you have, and lived? Has any god ever tried to take for himself one nation out of another nation, by testings, by miraculous signs and wonders, by war, by a mighty hand and an outstretched arm, or by great and awesome deeds, like all the things the LORD your God did for you in Egypt before your very eyes?

(Deut. 4:32–34)

The latter part of the reference ('one nation out of another nation') clearly refers to the exodus. But the earlier part ('the voice of God speaking out of fire') equally clearly refers to the great Sinai experience (Exod. 19 – 24; Deut. 5). There, Israel had encountered the living God as the God who speaks. Sinai was a monumental audio-visual experience. But it was the audio that mattered: 'you heard his words from out of the fire' (Deut. 4:36). In fact, in this same chapter it is stressed that Israel saw no *form* of God at Sinai (and so should not be tempted to make idols of him); rather, they heard the *voice* of God. 'You heard the sound of words but saw no form; there was only a voice' (v. 12). Even that was too much for them to bear, so they commissioned Moses to go and listen to God on their behalf, promising (very ironically, in view of their later history), to do whatever he reported back (5:23–29).

THE THEOLOGICAL ANGLE   31

And what Moses reported back were, of course, words – the Ten Words, to be precise, for that is the Hebrew expression for the Ten Commandments, or Decalogue. Along with the rest of the law these were regarded as revealed by God, and therefore to be recorded, kept, stored, read and observed carefully. There is a constant emphasis in Deuteronomy on Israel's ethical response as a response to what God had said – 'all this commandment', as it is sometimes described in a comprehensive singular. They must not add or subtract from it (4:2). They must use it like a map or a path, and not turn aside from it (5:32–33). They must allow its message to impact daily life from breakfast to bedtime, in person, in the home and in the public arena (6:6–9). For Israel, unique among the nations, has the inestimable privilege of having received the revelation of God's law – his own very Word, as guidance for life (Ps. 147:19–20).

One notable effect this understanding had on Israel was that it put ethical living squarely within reach of every ordinary person. Deuteronomy argues passionately against the idea that the commandment of God was way beyond reach – up in heaven or across the sea, attainable only by special elites. God's word is not available only to the privileged few – those who claim special visions from heaven, or those who make arduous pilgrimages to find it. 'No, the word is very near you; it is in your mouth and in your heart so that you may obey it' (Deut. 30:11–14). God's revelation was not a mystic secret for the initiated, but a light to guide every member of God's community. So, not only was the law to be part of the everyday life of every ordinary family, but also, when the law was read in the great seven-year festival, every member of the community – male and female, young and old, Israelite and immigrant – all were to be present (Deut. 31:10–13), for all were called to obedience, and all were deemed capable of obedience.

The revelatory aspect of ethics in the Old Testament is celebrated elsewhere – both as a matter of rejoicing and of rebuke. Rejoicing is certainly the mood of the psalmists when they thought of the law of God. Psalm 19 places the law alongside creation itself as the great 'declaration' of God; just as the heavens declare God's glory, so the law declares God's mind. So the one who learns and obeys God's revealed law gains life and wisdom (v. 7), joy and light (v. 8), value and satisfaction (v. 10), warning and reward (v. 11). Psalm 119, likewise but with greater expansiveness, uses seven different words to speak of God's word (law, statutes, commands, precepts, testimony, words, promises, etc. – the Hebrew terms are translated variously). He finds it to be 'a lamp to my feet and a light for my path' (v. 105) – a strongly ethical metaphor. But the word of God has this very personal and particular relevance and authority precisely because it has a transcendant quality deriving from God himself:

> Your word, O Lord, is eternal;
> it stands firm in the heavens.

(v. 89)

That is what makes it true, trustworthy, righteous and life-giving (to highlight just a few of the things Psalm 119 repeatedly affirms about God's word).

More by way of rebuke, Micah reminded the people of Judah that they had no excuse for not living in a way that would please God. Certainly not the excuse of ignorance. The way to social and personal ethics was not something they had to work out for themselves. Nor could they buy exemption from it by doubling their religious efforts in rituals and sacrifices. No, the matter was plain because God had already revealed it, and it could be summarized simply:

> He has showed you, O man, what is good.
>   And what does the Lord require of you?
> To act justly and to love mercy
>   and to walk humbly with your God.

(Mic. 6:8)

Old Testament ethics, then, while certainly not solely a matter of obeying the words that have come by revelation from God, equally certainly includes that dimension. God had acted and had spoken, and the ethical response of Israel needed to take both into account.

The concept of revelation is problematic, of course, for some scholars and theologians. They have difficulty with the concept at any level, finding that the idea of a God who reveals transcendent truths and laws, which we are then bound to believe and obey, will not fit into their worldview or into their assumptions as to how the God they believe in did or does engage with human beings in history. Some cannot accept a revelatory and thereby authoritative basis for ethics at all, arguing that it infringes on human ethical autonomy or at least on personal maturity (e.g. Rodd, *Glimpses*). Others have difficulty with revelation specifically in an Old Testament context because of the moral difficulties we encounter in any serious engagement with the Old Testament. If God revealed all this stuff, what does that say about him? What does it imply for us now in very different circumstances? What difference does the New Testament make, if it too is revelation from God yet clearly in some places overrides the Old? These are questions I take up in more depth in chapter 14. For now, the important point is that Israelites in Old Testament times certainly believed that their ethical duties and joys were governed not just by the Lord's actions, but also by his revealed words.

God's purpose

We have seen that the dynamic of Old Testament ethics is largely due to the way the Israelites' faith was *historically* generated, grounded and sustained. Their God, YHWH, was believed to have acted, and to be continuously active, in history. Therefore events and sequences of events took on moral significance. Because this was such a live conviction in Israel, there developed a whole genre of literature that we tend, by familiarity, to take for granted; namely, prophetic historical narrative. By this is meant the books of Joshua, Judges, Samuel and Kings (sometimes known as the Deuteronomic History because of the way these books reflect the theological and ethical concerns of the book of Deuteronomy).

The historians of the Old Testament are sometimes called 'moralistic' – as a reproach. Yet the ethical significance of their achievement is enormous. They performed the task of collecting, selecting, editing and commenting on the stories of Israel's past – centuries of it – with consistent theological and ethical criteria and assessment. They were prepared to evaluate boldly events and people in a way that affirmed the ethical significance of both. They wrote a coherent account of several centuries, with a selection of themes, a sense of direction and purpose, and an attempt at explaining events in terms of cause and effect. Some scholars believe that the prize for inventing history as a category of literature should go to the Hebrews, not to the Greeks.

The Hebrew canon's own term for these books was 'The Former *Prophets*' ('The Latter Prophets' were Isaiah, Jeremiah, Ezekiel and the Book of the Twelve). Listing these anonymous authors among the prophets shows that these historians were regarded as writing from a divine perspective. Their ethical assessments were claimed to be 'God's point of view' on the events they narrate. Not that they are forever 'moralizing' – far from it. Indeed, the skill of the Hebrew historians often lies in the tantalizing way they present a story and *refrain* from comment, allowing readers to draw their own ethical conclusions (which are not by any means always straightforward). But the ethical impact remains, precisely because God is at work within the narrative – explicitly or behind the scenes – initiating, reacting, leading and responding to events.

While holding firmly to this conviction, that the LORD was in overall control of events, these Israelite historians managed to avoid two extremes. On the one hand, they did not work with a mechanistic view of God's sovereignty, which would have eliminated human ethical freedom and responsibility. The best illustration of this is provided by the cycle of Joseph stories. Indeed, it is probably part of the narrator's purpose to exploit this very enigma of divine sovereignty and human moral decisions. From a human point of view, the whole story is one of free choices, some evil, some good; at no point does anyone act other than as a free agent according to his own choice. That applies to all the characters – Jacob, Joseph and his brothers, Potiphar and his wife, Pharaoh, Joseph's fellow prisoners, Jacob. Yet at the end of it all, Joseph acknowledges the sovereign control of God, whose redemptive purposes governed the whole story: 'You [his brothers] intended to harm me, but God intended it for good to accomplish what is now being done, the saving of many lives' (Gen. 50:20). This is a wonderful statement of the paradox of divine sovereignty and human freedom. The free and responsible actions of Joseph's brothers were ethically evil and intended to harm. The fact that God 'intended it for good' did not make their actions in any sense 'good' in themselves. Nor did God's ultimate purpose in the whole sequence of events exonerate the brothers from moral blame. But similarly, all their machinations, and all the misfortunes that befell Joseph in Egypt, could not thwart the purposes of God at work behind the scenes. Furthermore, our later discovery, when we read it at this concluding point of the narrative, that God had been in it all the time working for good, does not retrospectively mean that all of Joseph's actions are immune from any ethical inspection. We applaud his resistance to Potiphar's wife. How are we to evaluate the process by which he saved Egypt by bringing the population into a slave status to Pharaoh? It was good that he saved lives. But was the means of doing so not ultimately oppressive? The narrative offers us the simple facts, but refrains from ethical comment.

On the other hand, the belief that these Israelite historians had in human ethical freedom and responsibility did not lead them into ethical relativism, as though everything were determined by the immediate situation, with no objective or prior principles for guidance. They could write stories that show the possible tension between situations that arise and principles that we bring into them. The story of David's encounter with Saul in the cave illustrates this (1 Sam. 24). The circumstances presented David with a perfect opportunity for killing Saul. David knew he had already been anointed as the next king, and his men urged him to see the situation as divinely arranged for the very purpose of disposing of Saul (v. 4). Their argument, with its plausible theology, must have been very tempting. Yet David refrained from killing Saul, checked by the higher principle of the sanctity of one anointed by the LORD, enemy or not (vv. 6–7). The situation by itself was insufficient, even though it was acknowledged as arranged by God (vv. 10, 18). That in itself did not dictate his action, or make it quite as obvious as his men suggested. The moral decision David finally took was guided by prior principle, derived from God's past action.

The two dimensions of Israel's sense of history that had the deepest ethical significance were the past and the future, or, as mentioned earlier, their existence as a community of memory and hope. In theological language we could call these the redemptive and eschatological dimensions of Israel's history.

The redemptive aspect was the belief that God had acted in the past with mighty acts of deliverance for his people and of judgment on his enemies. We have already looked at this feature of the Old Testament, noting how it affects ethics by stimulating the response of gratitude and obedience.

The eschatological aspect was the belief that in those redemptive acts God has a continuing purpose for the long-term future. Israel did not just 'emerge'. They were 'called' into existence on the basis of God's promise to Abraham. And that promise had, as its bottom line, God's intention of bringing blessing to all the nations of the earth. This might also be called the missional dimension of Israel's faith.[6] This generates within Old Testament ethics a *teleological* dimension. Teleology is the study of purpose, ends or goals. Clearly, Israel believed in a God on the move. The LORD reveals himself right from the start as a purposeful God. The very revelation of his identity to Moses launches his great project of redemption – declared in advance and then carried through. We shall consider this dimension of Israel's ethical mission (the mission of being a light to the nations, in other words) in chapter 2 under the distinctiveness of Israel and its implications. For the moment it is sufficient to observe that the context in which Israelites made ethical decisions, and carried on ethical reflection or critique, was the belief that there was both a *past to which* they had to respond (God's redemption of Israel from Egypt) and a *future for which* they were in part preparing (God's blessing to the nations) – and all of it under the sovereign purpose of the LORD as God. That future, in the later vision of some of the prophets, will ultimately bring about the end of present evils such as war and oppression, and will inaugurate an era of peace, justice and harmony within creation, among humanity and between humanity and God. It is striking that Old Testament eschatology – its vision of the future – has a robust ethical core. Old Testament ethics, based on history and bound for a renewed creation, is thus slung like a hammock between grace and glory.

The combination of these two poles of Israel's historical faith, the past and the future, gave immense ethical importance to the present. 'What I do here and now really matters,' an Israelite might have reflected, 'because of what the

---

[6] The phrase '*missionary* purpose' is avoided here, since that term has become almost irretrievably linked to the idea of 'sending out missionaries'. Israel were not 'sent to the nations', in the sense of the Great Commission given by the risen Jesus to his apostles. But they may be said to have had a 'mission' – an identity and a purpose within the overall plan of God for humanity and creation. That 'mission' was fundamentally to 'be a blessing' to the rest of humanity. How that would be so is a major issue which cannot be addressed here. But it is that sense of there being a purpose to Israel's existence which is intended in the use of the term 'missional' here.

LORD has done in the past and what he will do in the future. I am part of the people the LORD has chosen, delivered and blessed beyond measure; therefore my deeds must display my gratitude (Deut. 26). But also I am part of the people called to be a blessing to the nations, among other things by living in a way that stimulates their curiosity and comment (Deut. 4:6–8). Justice and righteousness are not just demands on my immediate present; they are also the means by which God will bring about for Abraham what he has promised him – the blessing of the nations (Gen. 18:19–20). Our holiness is not just a vertical duty towards God, but is also part of what it means to be the LORD's priesthood among the nations (Exod. 19:4–6). And I look forward to the "Day" of the LORD's final intervention, not only wanting to be found among the righteous myself, but also anticipating the praise of the nations for God's salvation (Ps. 67).'

God's way

What shape, then, should Israel's response take? What was to be the substance and quality of their ethical behaviour? Here again, the answer is thoroughly theological: nothing less than the reflection of the character of God himself. What God is like is to be seen in what he does or has done. That was an axiom of Israel's belief about the LORD's self-revelation. It was also reversible, of course: what God as the LORD had done was, and was intended to be, revelatory as to the identity and character of the LORD himself. That is why *knowing God* is such an important theme in the Old Testament. It means more than just knowing what God has done (the stories), or knowing what God has said (the teachings). It means knowing the LORD in person, as a living character; knowing what his values, concerns and priorities are; knowing what brings him joy or makes him angry. And that in turn will mean living in the light of such knowledge.

Jeremiah has two very instructive passages on this point. In Jeremiah 9:23–24 he contrasts some of the best gifts of God (wisdom, strength and wealth) with the counterbalance of actually knowing the LORD. The first trio is not worth boasting about, but,

> 'let him who boasts boast about this:
>   that he understands and knows me,
>   that I am the LORD, who exercises kindness,
>   justice and righteousness on earth,
>   for in these I delight,'
>   declares the LORD.

How, then, should a person behave, who knows the LORD and who knows that the LORD delights in kindness, justice and righteousness? The text does not explicitly say so, but it is surely intended: somebody who boasts about knowing the God who displays these characteristics will want to live in deliberate emulation of those same qualities.

What is implied in this short saying is made quite explicit later when Jeremiah contrasts the ungodly and wicked king Jehoiakim with his illustrious father, Josiah. Of Josiah he writes:

> He did what was right and just, so all went well with him.
> He defended the cause of the poor and needy, and so all went well.
> *Is that not what it means to know me?* declares the LORD.
>
> (Jer. 22:15–16; italics mine)

Combining both texts, then: to know God means to do righteousness and justice; but to know God also means to know that *God* delights in precisely these things. Thus this particular exercise of ethical standards is a direct reflection of the character of the LORD himself.

The phrase 'the imitation of God', or *imitatio Dei*, has increasingly come to be used for this dimension of Old Testament ethics. It needs to be used with some qualification, however, and at least one scholar questions whether it is appropriate or accurate to use it at all for Old Testament ethics.[7] Certainly, it would be misleading to think in terms of mere mimickry – attempting to do *whatever* the LORD did or does, for clearly there are whole areas of the activity of God that are not available or appropriate for human replication. Furthermore, it cannot be used in simple analogy to the imitation of Christ, since the incarnation means that in Jesus we have a human being who, like us, actually lived and acted as a moral agent in the world, and is therefore capable of more direct imitation by ourselves. Nevertheless, the analogy with Christ can help indirectly. For when we speak about Christian discipleship as 'Christlikeness', we do not mean that we are obliged to imitate every detail of Jesus' earthly life in first-century Galilee. Often we work back from the stories of Jesus to a composite picture of his character, attitudes, priorities, values,

---

[7] Rodd, *Glimpses*, devotes a whole chapter to arguing that it is mistaken to speak of 'imitating God' in the Old Testament. In this he follows the earlier caution of Barnabas Lindars, 'Imitation', who argued that the imitation of God did not really surface in Jewish thought until New Testament times, and even then only peripherally. Lindars says it cannot be equated with the New Testament concept of the imitation of Christ, since the latter is, of course, dependent on the incarnation.

reactions and goals. Then we seek to be 'Christlike' by reflecting what we know to have been true of *Jesus* in the choices, actions and responses *we* have to make in our own lives. Paul raises this kind of argument to a very high plane in Philippians 2, to address the need for humility and preferential care for the needs of others: 'Your attitude should be the same as that of Christ Jesus' (Phil. 2:5). The WWJD ('What Would Jesus Do?') expression is a rather simplistic tag, but it does embody a valid ethical stance, even if it usually needs a lot of hard thinking and working out in our very ambiguous circumstances (and usually more than most people are prepared to do). In the same way, the imitation of the LORD, if we use the phrase at all, would have meant that Israelites should work from what they knew of the character and priorities of their God to what they could assume he would want to be done in any given situation. And in a sense their own history was an 'incarnation' of the LORD, for in it he expressly revealed his own identity, character and ethical values. For this reason it would be preferable to speak of the *reflection of God's character*, rather than the imitation of God, if the latter can be confused with merely copying the actions of God.[8]

For example, God had just freed Israel from slavery as proof of his love, compassion and faithfulness. So that same justice and mercy of God was to be reflected in Israel's own treatment of slaves and other vulnerable people in their society: 'Do not oppress an alien; you yourselves know how it feels to be aliens, because you were aliens in Egypt' (Exod. 23:9; cf. Exod. 21:2–11, 20–21, 26–27; Deut. 15:15). This was not just an imitation of a particular *action* of the LORD. Rather, that action (the exodus) illustrated a characteristic trait of the LORD as God: he is the God who 'loves the alien' (Deut. 10:18). Indeed, it could be said that his deliverance of Israel from Egypt was simply the outworking of his character. Deuteronomy 7:7–8 actually does say as much. The LORD had done it out of love, because he is the God who loves to love and Israel needs to know that that is what defines him as the LORD (Deut. 7:9 – a verse that comes the closest the Old Testament ever gets to saying 'God is love').

The most succinct expression of this principle (imitation, or reflection, of God) is found in Leviticus: 'Be holy because I, the LORD your God, am holy' (Lev. 19:2).

Again, this is not so much a call to imitate God, as a call to be like him in character. So what did reflective holiness mean for Israel? What would it mean

---

[8] Scholars who have discussed the ethical importance of this theme in Old Testament ethics include John Barton, 'Basis of Ethics'; *Ethics*; Bruce Birch, 'Moral Agency'; Harry P. Nasuti, 'Identity'; Eryl W. Davies, 'Walking'.

for them, in their earthly, historical and cultural circumstances, to be holy in a way that would reflect the holiness of the LORD? We are inclined to think of 'holiness' as a matter of personal piety or, in Old Testament terms, of ritual cleanliness, proper sacrifices, clean and unclean foods, and the like. Certainly, the rest of Leviticus 19 includes some of these dimensions of Israel's religious life. But the bulk of the chapter shows us that the kind of holiness that reflects God's own holiness is thoroughly practical. It includes generosity to the poor at harvest time, justice for workers, integrity in judicial processes, considerate behaviour to other people (especially the disabled), equality before the law for immigrants, honest trading and other very 'earthy' social matters. And all through the chapters runs the refrain 'I am the LORD', as if to say, '*Your* quality of life must reflect the very heart of *my* character. This is what I require of *you* because this is what reflects *me*. This is what I myself would do.' 'Holiness' is the biblical 'shorthand' for the very essence of God. Holiness has been called 'the Godness of God'. This makes the command of Leviticus 19:2 quite breathtaking. No less breathtaking, of course, was Jesus' own echo of the verse to his disciples: 'Be perfect, therefore, as your heavenly Father is perfect' (Matt. 5:48).

A favourite metaphor used in the Old Testament to describe this feature of Israel's ethics is that of *walking in the way of the LORD*. That is, walking in *the LORD's* way, as distinct from the ways of other gods, or of other nations, or one's own way, or the way of sinners. It is a very common expression especially in Deuteronomy, the Deuteronomic History (Joshua to 2 Kings) and some of the psalms. As a metaphor it seems to have two possible pictures in mind.

One is that of following someone else on a path, watching that person's footsteps and following along carefully in the same way.

> Such imagery implies that Israel was destined to travel on a journey in which God was to lead the way as a guide and example for the people to follow. It also suggests that the moral requirements demanded by God were those which he himself had evinced in an exemplary manner in his dealings with his people. By mirroring the divine activity the people would become a visible exemplar to the nations as to the nature and character of the God whom they worshipped (Deut. 4:5–8).[9]

---

[9] E. W. Davies, 'Walking', p. 103. Interestingly, Davies touches here on a significant aspect of Israel's *missional* significance. The ethical quality of Israel's life was part of their 'witness' to the nations, by being a reflection of the LORD in the midst of the nations. See also, C. J. H. Wright, *Deuteronomy*, pp. 11–14, where this ethical aspect of Israel's mission is discussed.

In that sense the metaphor would have something of the 'imitation of God' concept: you observe how the LORD acts and try to follow suit. 'O let me see thy footsteps and in them plant my own', as the hymn says about following Jesus.

The other picture is of setting off on a path, following the instructions that someone has given you – perhaps a sketch map (if that is not too anachronistic for ancient Israel), or a set of directions to make sure you stay on the right path and do not wander off on wrong paths that may turn out to be dead ends or dangerous. According to Rodd, this second image fits much better with the use of the metaphor in the Old Testament, since the expression 'walking in the way (or ways) of the LORD' is most commonly linked to obeying God's commands, not to imitating God himself. The way of the LORD is simply another expression signifying God's law or commands – his instruction kit for life's journey. Rodd is undoubtedly correct in his analysis of the predominant use of the metaphor,[10] but I think he too rigidly rules out the concept of the imitation of God from the expression. The commands of God are not autonomous or arbitrary rules; they are frequently related to the character or values or desires of God. So to obey God's commands is to reflect God in human life. Obedience to the law and the imitation of God are not mutually exclusive categories: the one is an expression of the other.

One of the clearest model passages for this is Deuteronomy 10:12–19. It begins with a rhetorical flourish, rather like Micah 6:8, summarizing the whole law in a single chord of five notes: fear, walk, love, serve and obey (note that love, the most relational and personal of them all is at the centre of the five). 'And now, O Israel, what does the LORD your God ask of you but to fear the LORD your God, *to walk in all his ways*, to love him, to serve the LORD your God with all your heart and with all your soul, and to observe the LORD's commands and decrees that I am giving you today for your own good?' (my italics).

And what are the ways of the LORD in which Israel is to walk? The answer is given first in broad terms. His was a way of condescending love in choosing Abraham and his descendants to be the special vehicle of his blessing. 'To the LORD your God belong the heavens, even the highest heavens, the earth and everything in it. Yet the LORD set his affection on your forefathers and loved them, and he chose you, their descendants . . .' (vv. 14–15).

That required a response of love and humility in return: 'Circumcise your hearts, therefore, and do not be stiff-necked any longer' (v. 16). But what *specifically* are the 'ways' of the LORD? At last the passage gets down to detail.

---

[10]   Rodd provides a very helpful survey of the usage of the metaphor 'walking with, after, or before' the LORD or other gods (*Glimpses*, pp. 330–333).

'[He] shows no partiality and accepts no bribes. He defends the cause of the fatherless and the widow, and loves the alien, giving him food and clothing. *And you are to love those who are aliens*, for you yourselves were aliens in Egypt' (vv. 17–19; my italics). The concluding line of the verse clearly expresses an ethic of imitation.

It is not only in the law that we find reflection of God's character as a feature of Old Testament ethics. The Psalms constantly exalt the character and ways of the LORD with the clear intention of inculcating not just worship but also a quality of ethical life that reflects the God who is worshipped. Indeed, only those people who mirror the integrity, compassion and purity of God can legitimately come to worship at all (Pss. 15 and 24). Sometimes a psalmist prays for God to teach him those ways and paths of God so that he may walk in them acceptably (Ps. 25). Sometimes the prayer is for a third party, as in the prayer for the king, which explicitly asks that he would be endowed with 'your justice' and 'your righteousness', in order that the king's government may be modelled on the qualities of the LORD's own rule (Ps. 72:1, 4, 12–14). But the clearest example of reflective ethics is the combination of Psalms 111 and 112. Both are acrostic psalms (arranged with verses following in Hebrew alphabetical order). Psalm 111 describes various acts and qualities of the LORD. Then Psalm 112 mirrors many of those qualities in matching verses that describe 'the person who fears the LORD'. Thus he too is righteous (3), gracious and compassionate (4), generous (5). The two psalms are clearly intended to be read side by side, loosely mirroring each other.

Similarly, in the Wisdom literature if the motto of Proverbs is 'The fear of the LORD is the beginning [or, first principle] of wisdom' (Prov. 9:10; cf. 1:7 etc.), it would be appropriate to add that 'the imitation of the LORD is the application of wisdom'. This emerges in the way that so many of the little details of behaviour commended in the book do indeed reflect the character of God himself. There is emphasis on the virtues of faithfulness, kindness, work, compassion, social justice, especially for the poor and oppressed, generosity, impartiality, truthfulness and integrity. All of these reflect the character and concerns of the LORD God.

Finally, the same factor can be seen at work in the Old Testament narratives. The characters who are most commended are those whose closeness and obedience to God lead them to reflect God's nature in their actions and attitudes (at least some of the time – the narratives candidly show the same human actors in much more compromised stances as well). We might think, for example, of Abraham and Moses reflecting God's compassionate love that 'desires not the death of a sinner', back, as it were, to God himself in their intercessions for iniquitous Sodom (Gen. 18:20–33) and rebellious Israel (Exod. 32:11–14); or of Samuel's uncompromising righteousness (sadly, not imitated by his sons, who walked neither in Samuel's ways nor the LORD's, 1 Sam. 8:1–5); or of David's 'kindness of God' (2 Sam. 9:3); or of Ruth's faithful love (Ruth 2:11–12; 3:10); or Abigail's wisdom (1 Sam. 25:32–34).

God's goodness

What God has done, what God has said, what God plans, what God is like – all of these, we have seen, undergird the Old Testament's ethical worldview. But there is another, much more personal, consideration. A major motivation towards ethical living in Israel was the actual personal experience of God's goodness and blessing. It is not simply that 'This is what YHWH has done in the history of the nation; therefore respond appropriately' Or 'This is what Yahweh is like; so follow his example.' Rather, the emphasis in some texts is 'This is what Yahweh has done *for you*. Therefore, out of gratitude, you should do the same for others.' Or, in some of the psalms, 'This is what YHWH has done *for me*, or what I am praying he will do for me, in his goodness and mercy; so this is how I intend to live in obedience to his will and word' (e.g. Ps. 119). Personal experience of God's goodness is turned into motivation for ethical behaviour that responds out of gratitude and love.

We have already seen above how the content of the slavery law in Exodus is motivated by Israel's historical experience of deliverance from slavery. But in the related legislation in Leviticus and Deuteronomy the motive is even more explicitly personalized – in the sense that each generation is addressed as the 'you' whom God had delivered from bondage. Leviticus 25:35–55 has regulations concerning various degrees of impoverishment and the steps to be taken by the better-off kinsman. No fewer than three times the wealthier brother is reminded of the exodus as motivation for fair treatment of the poorer brother (vv. 38, 42, 55; cf. 26:13). Similarly, Deuteronomy 15 urges the Israelite landowner to be generous to the slave who is being released after his six years of service. Why? The familiar national and historical reason is given: 'Remember that you were slaves in Egypt and the LORD your God redeemed you. That is why I give you this command today' (Deut. 15:15). But an even warmer and more directly personal note is sounded in words that could have fallen from the lips of Jesus: 'Give to him as the LORD your God has blessed you' (Deut. 15:14). An Israelite could not have sung the familiar song 'God is so good, God is so good, God is so good, he's so good to me' (though the words echo the Psalms) without being reminded also of its ethical consequence: 'God asks me to show that goodness to others.' In fact, whether in song or in spoken recital, the Israelite did exactly that in

Deuteronomy 26. At the time of harvest the Israelite farmer came into the presence of God to give thanks, not only for the history of his people since Jacob, but also, making it totally personal, for the harvest of 'the soil that you, O LORD, have given *me*' (Deut. 26:1–11). But then, immediately following this celebration of thanks for the goodness of God, worshippers are required to declare that they have kept the laws of God, specifically singling out the law of the tithe, which in the third year was to be stored as a welfare fund for the poor and needy, the landless and the familyless (Deut. 26:12–13). Vertical thanksgiving for God's goodness must be matched by horizontal action for the needy. My thanks to God for his goodness to me is only acceptable when matched by my determination to do for others what God has done for me.

Such direct and often personal motivation for obedience to God's law is one of the most characteristic features of Deuteronomy, which as a whole document sets out to exhort and persuade Israel to be loyal to the LORD and to observe the terms of their covenant relationship with him. In fact, the attaching of motivational clauses to laws is one of the characteristics of ancient Israelite law in general, as has been observed and surveyed by several scholars.[11] We might have thought that, within a worldview in which the LORD was considered the great king and covenant Lord of Israel, that fact alone should be sufficient to require obedience. And yet so many of the laws do actually carry additional phrases that offer reasons why they should be obeyed. These reasons may refer to the character and actions of God, as we have seen, or to the future well-being of the people, or to secure life in the land, or to the deterrence of other potential wrongdoers, or to the fact that other nations were watching. Here, however, we see that one major motivation was perhaps the simplest – personal gratitude to God for his goodness.

The force of this motivation can also be felt in the warnings against *forgetting* the great acts of God. Forgetting, within a personal relationship, is a mark of offensive or tactless ingratitude. It refers not so much to cognitive amnesia (as if one has merely forgotten the other person's name or cannot recognize his or her face), but to a loss of any *personal significance* in the relationship. If someone says, 'You've forgotten me,' it translates, 'I no longer mean anything to you. There is no longer any bond of love, or gratitude, between us. Our shared history no longer matters to you.' In this strongly personal sense, if Israel were to 'forget YHWH' by losing sight of all that he had done for them, it would inevitably lead to failure to obey his law. They would lose both the

---

[11] E.g., B. Gemser, 'Motive Clause'; Greg Chirichigno, 'Motivation'.

model (knowledge of the character of the LORD), and the motive (gratitude for the grace of the LORD). So Deuteronomy devotes the first third of its bulk to sustained historical reminders and repeated warnings against forgetting. Chapter 8 gives the reason:

Remember how the LORD your God led you . . .

(v. 2)

Be careful that you do not forget . . .

(v. 11)

Otherwise, when you eat and are satisfied . . . then your heart will become proud and you will forget the LORD your God, who brought you out of Egypt, out of the land of slavery.

(vv. 12–14)

The prophets attributed Israel's later moral decline and outright disobedience to precisely this failing: they had forgotten the LORD and were no longer motivated by the ethical implications of their own history. It was the ingratitude and inconsistency of Israel's rebellious ways that so hurt and infuriated the prophets. In these samples we can see how they refer back to all that God had done for Israel, and how shocking therefore was Israel's ungrateful, and ethically degraded, response:

I brought you up out of Egypt,
    and I led you for forty years in the desert
    to give you the land of the Amorites.

(Amos 2:10)

But I am the LORD your God,
    who brought you out of Egypt . . .
I cared for you in the desert . . .
When I fed them, they were satisfied;
    when they were satisfied, they became proud;
    then they forgot me.

(Hos. 13:4–6)

My people, what have I done to you?
    How have I burdened you? Answer me.
I brought you up out of Egypt
    and redeemed you from the land of slavery . . .

> Remember your journey from Shittim to Gilgal,[12]
> that you may know the righteous acts of the LORD.

(Mic. 6:3–5).

The same theme of ingratitude producing ethical disobedience is to be found in Isaiah 1:2–4; 5:1–7; Jeremiah 2:1–13; 7:21–26; Ezekiel 16; 20.

We should finish on a positive note, however. If the primary angle of Old Testament ethics is theological (God-centred), then the best place to conclude is with the *worship* of Israel. For here, as in so much else in Israel, their deepest convictions are to be found, not in systematic doctrinal or ethical formulations, but in doxology, the language of worship. Three aspects are relevant at this point.

First, Israel's worship shows the same dynamic as Israel's ethics; namely, that it is based on God's prior action. God had already acted in blessing; therefore Israel was to celebrate that in worship and praise. We may be so used to this idea that we fail to see how distinctive it actually is. In Deuteronomy there is much exhortation to the people to come before the LORD to celebrate the great annual feasts, and to do so with joy and feasting. The reason is always assumed: *the LORD your God has already blessed you.* Worship is presented primarily as a response, not as a negotiation. That is, worship for Israel was not something they did in order to placate or cajole God into blessing them. Worship is a grateful response to the fact that he already had. This feature of Israel's festivals and worship in general was

> in marked contrast to non-Israelite worship, which was conducted as a way of winning a deity's favor so that the deity would bless the worshippers. In Israel's case, worship does not instigate divine blessings; at most, worship contributes to the preservation and perpetuation of blessings by fostering an ongoing recognition of dependence on Yahweh for those blessings.[13]

Secondly, as mentioned above, Israel's worship was to be marked by a deepened commitment to ethical response at the horizontal level. It was to be socially inclusive (the poor, the familyless and the immigrants are specifically to be included, Deut. 16:11, 14). And also it was to have humanitarian implications. Response to God's blessings not only calls for heartfelt joy and celebration but also 'spills over into the everyday lives of the worshippers . . .

---

[12] This refers to the crossing of the Jordan River prior to the conquest of the land of Canaan.

[13] T. M. Willis, 'Worship', p. 285.

In particular, they should "celebrate" their blessing by imitating the way Yahweh provides for them in the way they provide for those who depend on them'.[14]

Thirdly, even coming into the presence of the LORD at all in worship was subject to ethical criteria. At any rate, this is how it is seen in the Psalms. Psalms 15 and 24 make it clear that the worship of the LORD (summed up as dwelling in his sanctuary, living on his holy hill,[15] or standing in his holy place), is acceptable only from those who, in the everyday conduct of their lives, mirror the ethical standards of the God they presume to worship – those, in short with clean hands and a pure heart. By using Psalm 15, Israelites 'identify themselves as a group of loyal worshippers of the LORD God and declare their solidarity in embracing a conscientious and socially responsible standard of conduct . . . In this responsive affirmation the community of loyal Jews declare their own individual commitment to the way of life that shows a wholehearted respect for the *torah* of the LORD God.'[16] Unfortunately, the prophets saw that many Israelite worshippers fell far short of this ideal and castigated those who imagined that religious rites could compensate or even coexist with social wrongs (e.g. Is. 1:10–17; Jer. 7:1–11; Amos 5:22–24).

So, let me sum up what we have seen in this opening chapter. The ethical teaching of the Old Testament is first and foremost God-centred. It is founded on the identity of the LORD, the living God of the biblical revelation. It presupposes God's initiative in grace and redemption; it takes its content from the words of God revealed in the cultural context of Israel; it is framed by the purposes of God, who is sovereign in what he has done and will do in history; it is shaped by God's ways and character; and it is motivated by personal experience of God's goodness in his dealings with his people. Two conclusions follow.

First, this underlines for us the importance of the first commandment: 'You shall have no *other* gods before me.' For any 'other *god*' would result in a different *ethic*. Israel found this when they went after Baal. Did they really want a society based on the ethics of Jezebel? Or, if they truly believed what they

---

[14] Ibid., p. 292.

[15] Clements has shown that these phrases speak not only of coming into the temple to worship, but also symbolize the wider reality of living in the LORD 's land (of which the holy hill and the temple were symbols). See R. E. Clements, *God and Temple*. So the text has a wider ethical implication for Israel in the whole of life in the land, not just in relation to specific occasions of worship.

[16] Clements, 'Worship and Ethics', pp. 85, 90.

protested to Elijah at Mount Carmel, that 'Yahweh, he is God,' then let them strive for a society that mirrored his justice.

Secondly, it underlines for us the importance of deriving our ethical teaching from the *whole* Old Testament. We have seen how the laws are not always sufficient in themselves; we need the narrative in which they are set to understand the principles on which they operate, and we need the later narratives, the prophets, the Psalms and the Wisdom literature to see how they were taken up into the life of the nation. God has spoken in all the Scriptures 'in many and varied ways', and we must use them all in building up our picture of his character, acts and purpose and then work out our ethical responsibilities accordingly.

Further reading

Bailey Wells, Jo, *God's Holy People: A Theme in Biblical Theology*, JSOT Supplement Series, vol. 305 (Sheffield: Sheffield Academic Press, 2000).

Barton, John, 'The Basis of Ethics in the Hebrew Bible', *Semeia* 66 (1994), pp. 11–22.

———, *Ethics and the Old Testament* (London: SCM, 1998).

Birch, Bruce C., 'Divine Character and the Formation of Moral Community in the Book of Exodus', in Rogerson, Davies and Carroll, *Bible in Ethics*, pp. 119–135.

———, 'Moral Agency, Community, and the Character of God in the Hebrew Bible', *Semeia* 66 (1994), pp. 23–41.

Chirichigno, Greg, 'A Theological Investigation of Motivation in Old Testament Law', *Journal of the Evangelical Theological Society* 24 (1981), pp. 303–313.

Clements, R. E., 'Worship and Ethics: A Re-examination of Psalm 15', in Graham, Marrs and McKenzie, *Worship and the Hebrew Bible*, pp. 78–94.

Davies, Eryl W., 'Walking in God's Ways: The Concept of *Imitatio Dei* in the Old Testament', in Ball, *True Wisdom*, pp. 99–115.

Gemser, B., 'The Importance of the Motive Clause in Old Testament Law', in *Congress Volume in Memoriam Aage Bentzen*, Supplements to *Vetus Testamentum*, vol. 1, Leiden: Brill, 1953, pp. 50–66.

Lindars, Barnabas, 'Imitation of God and Imitation of Christ', *Theology* 76 (1973), pp. 394–402.

Mills, Mary E., *Images of God in the Old Testament* (Collegeville: Liturgical Press, Cassells, 1998).

Muilenburg, J., *The Way of Israel: Biblical Faith and Ethics* (New York: Harper, 1961).

Nasuti, Harry P., 'Identity, Identification, and Imitation: The Narrative Hermeneutics of Biblical Law', *Journal of Law and Religion* 4 (1986), pp. 9–23.

Patrick, Dale, *The Rendering of God in the Old Testament*, Overtures to Biblical Theology, vol. 10 (Philadelphia: Fortress, 1981).

Willis, Timothy M., '"Eat and Rejoice before the Lord": The Optimism of Worship in the Deuteronomic Code', in Graham, Marrs and McKenzie, pp. 276–294.

2. THE SOCIAL ANGLE

Biblical ethics, we have seen, flow from the reality of God. They did not, however, flow directly into the consciousness of individuals. Nor did they flow as a complete whole into a single monolithic, dictated rule-book. God chose a much more indirect route, the historical route, a route lined with vistas of immense variety and trodden by people of utterly human fallibility. A route fraught with risk. God created a people and entered into relationship with them. By this means Old Testament ethics could never be a matter of timeless and universal abstract principles, but rather were hammered out within the historical and cultural particularity of this people, this community, this society, this 'house of Israel'. So we must now turn to the second angle of the triangular framework – the social angle.

The social dimension of redemption

The early chapters of Genesis relate the tragedy of humanity's choice of rebellion, disobedience and sin. Faced with the resulting catastrophe, God had, if I may so put it, several options. God could have destroyed the human race and abandoned his whole creation project. The text hints that God considered this possibility (Gen. 6:6–7). But God did not destroy or abandon; God chose instead to redeem and restore.

Again, one could conceive of God redeeming people individually – saving one soul here, another soul there, and conveying them straight to heaven. But neither did God do that. God chose to put into operation a plan of redemption that would encompass the whole of the rest of human history and would involve, as part of that history, the choosing, creating and moulding of an entire nation. No doubt God was aware of the risk involved in such a long-term, massive project. One can imagine the sharp intake of breath among the heavenly hosts when the amazing scheme was unveiled!

As always, we must pay attention to the order of the Old Testament story. Genesis 11 tells the story of the Tower of Babel, bringing us to the climax of the stories about humanity after the fall. The nations were scattered and divided in order to prevent a unified rebellion against God. The effects of sin have now reached 'global' proportions. What can God do next? It is against this background that the story of redemption begins in Genesis 12. God calls Abraham and promises to give him a land and to make his descendants into a nation through whom all the nations on earth will be blessed. The comparison and contrast between the curse at Babel and the promise to Abraham is very striking:

Come let us build ourselves a city . . . so that we may make a name for ourselves . . .
That is why it was called Babel – because there the LORD confused the language of
the whole world. From there the LORD scattered them over the face of the whole
earth.

(Gen. 11:4, 9)

go to the land I will show you.

> I will make you into a great nation
> and I will bless you;
> I will make your name great,
> and you will be a blessing . . .
> and all peoples on earth
> will be blessed through you.

(Gen. 12:1–3)

From the land of Babel the curse of confusion and scattering spread to affect the whole world of the nations. But from the land to be given to Abraham, and through the nation he would become, blessing would spread to the same global extent. God's answer to the international blight of sin was a new community of international blessing, a nation that would be the pattern and model of redemption, as well as the vehicle by which the blessing of redemption would eventually embrace the rest of humanity.

So, then, the social angle of Old Testament ethics recognizes that the people descended from Abraham were not only to be blessed as he was, but also to be a blessing to the whole world of nations. And the key to that role and that mission would be their ethical distinctiveness. The clearest expression of this combined ethical and missional role of Israel is Genesis 18:19, where God, speaking about Abraham, says, 'I have chosen him so that he will direct his household and his children after him to keep the way of the LORD by doing righteousness and justice so that the LORD may bring about for Abraham what he has promised him.'

The context of this verse is God's imminent judgment upon Sodom and Gomorrah. It is, in fact, part of a conversation between God and Abraham while God, with his two angelic deputies, was on his way down, so to speak, to find out the truth about those cities and act accordingly. This makes the ethical heart of the verse even more notable. In the midst of a world characterized by Sodom – whose evil is causing an *outcry* (vv. 20–21; the Hebrew word is *ṣĕ'āqâ*, the technical term for the crying out of those suffering from oppression and cruelty), God wants a community characterized by his own values and priorities – *righteousness* (*ṣĕdāqâ*: one wonders if the wordplay between these two very similar sounding words is intentional here, as it certainly is in Is. 5:7) and *justice*. The presence here in the patriarchal narratives of the two phrases 'The way of the LORD' and 'doing righteousness and justice', both of which would come among the top five of the most used summaries of Old Testament ethical values, shows that Israel's identity as a distinct ethical community comes well before the Sinai covenant and Mosaic law. The demand that Israel should be morally different from Sodom and all it stands for in the Bible was something written into their genetic code, so to speak, while they were as yet in the loins of Abraham. In fact, such ethical distinctiveness is put forward here by God himself as the very reason for the election of Abraham: 'I have chosen him *so that* . . .' The sense of purpose is very strong in the verse. Election means election to an *ethical* agenda in the midst of a corrupt world of Sodoms.

But that ethical agenda is itself only part of a still wider purpose. The goal of the verse moves on into a third purpose clause: '*so that* the Lord may bring about for Abraham what he has promised him'. In the light of the preceding verse that is a clear reference to God's ultimate intention to bring blessing to all nations through the descendants of Abraham. That is God's mission, God's universal agenda. That too was the reason for the election of Abraham. In the structure as well as the theology of this verse, ethics stands as the middle term between election and mission. The distinctive ethical quality of life of the people of God ('keeping the way of the LORD', 'doing righteousness and justice') stands as the purpose of election on the one hand and the means to mission on the other. It is the fulcrum and heartbeat of the verse.

So even before the nation of Israel has come into existence we are given notice of their ethical as well as their redemptive significance. Old Testament ethics is going to be a social affair. It is not simply a compendium of moral teaching to enable the individuals to lead privately upright lives before God. Now, of course, this is not to deny that the Old Testament is deeply interested in the moral choices and behaviour of the individual, as chapter 11 will show. Many Old Testament laws, including the Ten Commandments, are framed in the second person singular, addressing the individual. But they are addressed to the individual as part of the community, and their purpose is not just individual uprightness but the moral and spiritual health of that whole community. For God's purpose, as we have seen, was not to invent a production line for righteous individuals, but to create a new community of people who in their social life would embody those qualities of righteousness, peace, justice and love that reflect God's own character and were God's original purpose for humanity.

The relevance of our 'social angle', then, is that when we seek to interpret the Old Testament text ethically we must not stop short at the question 'What does this text say to me?' In fact, we should not even *start* with that question. We must study the passage within its own social context in Old Testament Israel, asking how this text contributes to our understanding of the social and ethical life of Israel. What is its place in the total shape of that society? Then we might move on at a later stage to ask what it has to say within the present community of God's people; and then, further, what social implications it may have in human society at large. Walter Brueggemann constantly challenges us to see the relevance of the covenantal nature of Old Testament faith for both the church and the world (i.e. to recognize the importance of this social angle of biblical ethics).

> We may re-articulate our covenantal hope for the world. So long as this subversive paradigm [covenant] is kept to God and church, we are safe enough. Its character of surprise and threat becomes clear when the covenant is related to the world beyond the believing community. The covenantal paradigm affirms that the world we serve and for which we care is a world yet to be liberated. A theology of covenanting is not worth the effort unless it leads to energy and courage for mission . . . The three belong together: a *God* who makes covenant by making a move toward the partner (Hos. 2:14, 18–20); a *community* that practices covenant by the new forms of torah, knowledge, and forgiveness (Jer. 31:31–34); and a *world* yet to be transformed to covenanting, by the dismantling of imperial reality (Is. 42:6–7; 49:6).[1]

---

[1] Brueggemann, *Social Reading*, pp. 50, 53 (his italics).

If we have energy left, we will be faced with the challenge 'So what kind of person must *I* be, and what kind of behaviour is required of *me*, if my life is to be shaped by, and be consistent with, such a vision of God's purposes?'

The distinctiveness of Israel

The story struggles on through Genesis. After the suspense of whether Abraham and Sarah would even have a son, let alone give birth to a nation, and then the threat of famine to the whole family a few generations later, the small community survives as a band of refugees in Egypt and then grows to a large nation (Exod. 1:6). After the momentous events of the exodus (to which we shall return later), the nation is established in a covenantal relationship with the LORD at Sinai and sets off for the land of Canaan where the next phase of their history will unfold.

Israel's unique experience

Israel, then, was a nation among the nations. But at the same time they were conscious of being different from the rest of the nations. Even others noticed this about them, as Balaam's reluctant oracles show: 'I see people who live apart and do not consider themselves one of the nations' (Num. 23:9).

This sense of uniqueness is rhetorically captured in Deuteronomy's portrayal of the speech of Moses to Israel on the verge of their crossing into Canaan (Deut. 4:32–40). It is meant as a challenge and encouragement to take seriously the responsibility their unique history laid upon them:

> Ask now about the former days, long before your time, from the day God created man on the earth; ask from one end of the heavens to the other. Has anything so great as this ever happened, or has anything like it ever been heard of? Has any other people heard the voice of God speaking out of fire, as you have, and lived? Has any god ever tried to take for himself one nation out of another nation, by testings, by miraculous signs and wonders, by war, by a mighty hand and an outstretched arm, or by great and awesome deeds, like all the things the LORD your God did for you in Egypt before your very eyes?
>
> (Deut. 4:32–34)

The expected answer to the rhetorical questions is 'No!' At no other time and in no other place had God acted in the way he had done in Israel's recent history. The events described, of course, are the exodus and Sinai experience. And the claim of the text is that these events of the LORD's action on behalf of Israel were unprecedented (they had not happened before), and unparalleled (they had not happened anywhere else). Israel's historical experience of the LORD was unique. They had received revelation that no other nation had,[2] and they had been redeemed as no other nation had.[3] Now we need to be careful to note that this did not mean that the LORD was not involved or interested in the affairs of other nations. Deuteronomy affirms that indeed he was (Deut. 2:9–12, 16–23). The point is that only in and for Israel had God acted with explicit redemptive purpose that had resulted in a covenantal relationship between the LORD and the nation of Israel.

This unique historical experience, however, was not just a wonderful piece of celestial entertainment. It had a powerfully didactic purpose. It was cosmic education. Israel was to learn from it two vitally important things: who really was God (YHWH, the LORD), and how they were now to live (in obedience). There were, in other words, both theological and ethical implications from their history. Our text continues:

> You were shown these things *so that you might know* that the LORD is God; besides him there is no other . . .
>
> Acknowledge [in Hebrew, simply, 'know' or 'learn'] and take to heart this day that the LORD is God in heaven above and on the earth below. There is no other. Keep his decrees and commands, which I am giving you today . . .
>
> (Deut. 4:35, 39–40; my italics)

We observed the first, theological, implication in chapter 1. It was vitally important for Israel to know the true identity of the God with whom they now had to do. Indeed, that was part of the purpose of the exodus itself – 'Then you will know that I am the LORD your God, who brought you out' (Exod. 6:7). For only as they preserved the knowledge of the true and living God would they know how they were to live and thus be of any visible interest to the nations around (Deut. 4:5–8).

The second, ethical, implication is the one we are now concerned with. Notice how seamlessly the text moves to it in Deuteronomy 4:40. If you know and take to heart who God really is, then you go a long way in knowing how you are to live; namely, in responsive and grateful obedience to his will and ways.

So the flow of thought in this rich text (Deut. 4:32–40) is that, first, Israel has had a *unique experience* of God's revelation and redemption. As a result of this, secondly, they now have a *unique knowledge* of the identity of the LORD as God. That in turn means, thirdly, that they now have a *unique responsibility* to

---

[2] The same point is made in Ps. 147:19–20.

[3] The same point is made in Amos 3:2.

live in the midst of the nations in a manner that reflects in their own behaviour the ethical character of the LORD as expressed in the commands he has given them for their own good. So the distinctiveness of Old Testament ethics is not some superior philosophy or higher state of consciousness. It is the distinctiveness of a whole community's ethical response to unique historical events in which they saw the hand of their God. And it is a distinctiveness they regarded as part of their role and witness in the midst of the nations.

Israel's social distinctiveness

But just how distinctive was Israel, in fact, from the surrounding nations and cultures? That is a huge question, and would immediately generate others: Which Israel, at what period of Old Testament history, in relation to what other nations? This is where a full and detailed account of Israel's social history through the centuries of the Old Testament era would be needed, but this is not the place even to attempt to provide it.[4] In some respects Israel was not particularly different. Cross-cultural study of Israel alongside Canaanite and other cultures in the ancient Near East shows that they shared many things in common – as one would expect in such a broad macroculture. We shall consider this in chapter 10. However, there were significant ways in which Israel was markedly different from the nations that surrounded them, or preceded them as the dominant culture in Palestine.

The most obvious difference, of course, was religious. Israel worshipped YHWH exclusively (or were supposed to[5]), and they did so without images or

---

[4] Surveys of recent scholarship and bibliography in the area can be found in R. E. Clements, *World of Ancient Israel*; David J. Chalcraft (ed.), *Social-Scientific Old Testament Criticism*; V. P. Long, D. W. Baker and G. J. Wenham (eds.), *Windows into Old Testament History*.

[5] There is much dispute still over the historical origins of Israel's monotheistic faith, and over the tensions between what might be called the 'official' faith as endorsed by the canon of Old Testament texts on the one hand and popular Israelite religious beliefs at any given period of Old Testament history on the other. For a 1997 survey of critical scholarship and bibliography on this matter, see Robert Karl Gnuse, *No Other Gods*. Bernard Lang, *Hebrew God*, presents a survey of other ancient Near Eastern portraits of gods and their influence on Old Testament presentations of the LORD. Lang's survey is very dependent on a comparative anthropology of religion approach, but he makes the following remarkable statement in his preface: 'The Hebrew God ranks as the most distinguished deity on record in human history . . . No other god can boast a biography comparable to that of the Hebrew God' (p. vii).

statues. But if we imagine that monotheism was merely a matter of quaint religious preference (we just happen to prefer one god rather than many), in the unverifiable sphere of ideas and beliefs (the framework in which discussions of religious difference often take place in a modern context), we could not be more wrong. For Israel, exclusive commitment to YHWH as sole deity was part of a covenantal structure of life that impacted every dimension of their social, economic, judicial and political existence. And in doing so, it made Israel very distinctive indeed. This has been the conclusion of sociological studies of ancient Israel, which have shown that from a very early stage of their historical emergence, Israel had a deliberately articulated sense of national distinctiveness, which was expressed across the whole spectrum of Israelite social life – not just in their religion. Rather, their religion was an integral and sustaining part of that total social objective.[6]

For example, pre-Israelite Canaanite society was organized along 'feudal' lines, with power residing at the elite top end of a highly stratified social pyramid in each of the small city-state Canaanite kingdoms. Israel by contrast was a 'tribal' society. It had a kinship structure based on a threefold division into tribes, clans and households (see chapter 10). The third level consisted of a large number of 'extended-family', landowning households. These units, which were largely self-sufficient economically, performed most of the socially important functions in the villages and localities of Israel – judicial, economic, cultic and military. Early Israelite society, then, as a fabric of such sturdy units enjoying considerable autonomy and social freedom, was socially decentralized and non-hierarchical. It was geared towards the social health and economic viability of the 'lowest' units, not to the wealth, privilege or power of the 'highest'.

The same contrast is seen in economic life in the forms of land tenure. In the Canaanite city-states the king owned all the land and there were feudal arrangements with those who lived and worked on it as tax-paying tenant

---

[6] This perception of the close interrelations between Israel's mono-Yahwistic faith and their social aspirations was most fully worked out by Norman K. Gottwald, *Tribes of Yahweh*. The work of Gottwald has generated many critics. I do not accept either the reconstruction of Israel's historical emergence that he offers (internal revolt of disaffected Canaanite peasants), or the strongly materialist/Marxist theory he brings to his social comment. However, in my view he has adequately demonstrated, across a wide range of social, economic, political and religious factors, that Israelite society had some radically distinctive aspects from other ancient Near Eastern cultures. Further, he has shown that these social distinctives are inseparable from the religious distinctives of Israel's articulation of their faith in the Lord. See also Paul D. Hanson, *People Called*.

peasants. In Israel the land was divided up as widely as possible into multiple ownership by extended families. The division of the land recorded in the book of Joshua clearly intends that the possession and use of the land should be distributed as widely as possible throughout the whole kinship system. The tribal areas were allotted 'according to their clans' (Josh. 15:1 etc.). In order to preserve this system the land could not simply be bought and sold commercially, but had to be retained within the kinship groups (Lev. 25). Furthermore, many of the Old Testament laws and institutions of land use (see chapter 5) indicate an overriding concern to preserve this comparative equality of families on the land. So the economic system also was geared institutionally and in principle towards the preservation of a broadly based equality and self-sufficiency of families on the land, and to the protection of the weakest, the poorest and the threatened – and not to the interests of a wealthy, landowning elite minority. This prominent economic feature of Israelite law is a particularly important sociological indicator of the practical content of Israel's faith. Commenting on this feature of Israel's law, Gottwald says:

> This practical content is of inestimable value for constructing a sociology of Israel's religion, for it gives an unmistakable skeletal structure to the religion of Yahweh as the religion of a particular egalitarian social system. To worship Yahweh, to be an Israelite, meant above all else to practise a specific way of life in separation from and in overt opposition to time-honoured established ways of life regarded throughout the ancient Near East as inevitable if not totally desirable.[7]

The erosion of this distinctive socio-economic system through the inroads of the monarchic state and its beneficiaries, from Solomon onwards, was one of the factors that most aroused the prophetic protest in later Israel.

Turning to Israel's political life (which we shall examine in more detail in chapter 7), we find that the patterns of political activity and power in the Old Testament followed the kinship patterns of Israelite society. They were diffused and decentralized. Power in decision-making within the community, especially in judicial matters, resided in the network of elders. The elders were the mainstay of Israelite sociopolitical life at the broadest level throughout the whole Old Testament period.[8] In the pre-monarchic period this plural and

---

[7] Gottwald, *Tribes of Yahweh*, p. 59.

[8] For a very thorough survey of the identity and role of elders in ancient Israel and the changing role that they played in the different eras of Old Testament history, see Hanoch Reviv, *Elders*. See also J. L. McKenzie, 'Elders in the Old Testament'; C. J. H. Wright, *God's Land*, pp. 78–81, and the bibliography cited there.

corporate leadership was supplemented in time of military need by individual 'charismatic' leaders. These 'judges' were considered as raised up by God and were accepted by the people as mediating the rule of God. However, the stories of Gideon and Abimelech (Judg. 8:22 – 9:57) indicate the difficulties facing any judge who was offered, or who sought, a wider or more permanent, dynastic, rule. Centralized power in Israel seems to have been strongly resisted until the external threat of the Philistines thrust it forcibly upon them. Such centralized 'chieftaincy' seems to have been perceived as directly counter to the basic thrust of Israel towards locating power in the fabric of local households. Even after the monarchy was established, the system of local elders survived at village level and proved resistant to hierarchical and centralized government. Jehoshaphat's judicial reforms established royally appointed judges, but these reforms applied only to the fortified cities (2 Chr. 19:4–11). The administration of justice in town and village communities by their local elders presumably continued unaffected by these royal appointments. Although the Davidic state, and especially the Solomonic state and its successors in the centuries that followed, centralized power in many ways, the narratives and the prophets indicate a steady resistance to such arrangements as being at odds with the more traditional understanding of Israel's covenantal social structure. So there was resistance in Israel to centralized power and a preference for diverse and participatory politics, which tolerated – indeed sought – the voice of criticism and opposition from the prophets, even if some of them paid a heavy price. Such decentralized power stands in marked contrast to contemporary ancient Near Eastern states which had highly stratified and pyramidical political and economic structures.

This very brief sketch of some of the contours of Israelite society, lacking though it is in detailed historical analysis, is sufficient to show that Israel was self-consciously distinctive from surrounding nations, and especially the Canaanites, not just religiously but in their total social system. Israel's determined assertion of religious 'otherness' (holiness) in their exclusive commitment to the LORD was indeed linked to aspirations and some degree of achievement in the social, economic and political spheres. The social angle was inseparably linked to the theological angle. They were to be a different kind of society, because YHWH was unquestionably a different God.

Did it matter?

It may be interesting to see the way Israel linked their social system to their religious faith, but was it really an essential link? Did the link really matter? Was this distinct social shape an essential part of what it meant to be 'Israel' – the people chosen and called by God to be the vehicle of blessing and redemption to the nations? Could they not have been any kind of society in the ancient world but still have carried the flag for the worship of YHWH and his promises to humanity through them? Apparently not.

The problem with imagining that you could have the worship of YHWH and yet be any kind of society is that Israel actually tried it and came rapidly unstuck. The verdict of both their narrative historians and their prophets was that, on the one hand, if you forgot the LORD and went after other gods, then society would quickly disintegrate into injustice and oppression. And, on the other hand, if society had in fact moved in the direction of such rampant social evils, it was clear proof that people had forgotten the LORD, whether or not they protested vigorously that they were still worshipping him with lavish gusto. There was, in other words, an inseparable link between the kind of society Israel was (or was supposed to be) and the character of the God they worshipped.

The most radical change that took place in Israelite society since their emergence in Canaan was the transition from a loose association of tribes to a monarchic state. The process is described with considerable ambiguity in the Old Testament narratives of 1 Samuel. There is great subtlety in the narrative. It begins in 1 Samuel 8 with the miserable failure of Samuel's sons to emulate their father's integrity. They were perverting the very thing they were appointed to uphold; namely, justice (v. 3). The request of the elders for a king thus appears at first sight to be a laudable desire to have a strong figure that would fulfil one of the prime functions of public leadership in the ancient world, the administration of justice. However, their motive is more clearly betrayed at the end of their request: 'appoint a king to lead us, *such as all the other nations have*' (v. 5; my italics). Samuel may have been upset by the personal slight to his own leadership, but God showed him the true essence of the matter. Israel's desire for a king was a rejection of the LORD himself as ruler. So God instructs Samuel to warn the people of the implications of the step they are embarking on. But significantly, Samuel does not harangue them 'religiously' by highlighting their rejection of the LORD. He concentrates on the social and economic consequences such implicit apostasy will bring. They want to be like the other nations? Do they not remember that they were supposed to be different from the nations?[9] And are they not aware of what monarchy has meant in previous and surrounding cultures and what it is most likely to mean if introduced into Israel? Samuel proceeds to show the people that if they become like other nations in having a king, then like other nations they will suffer all the social burdens of a costly monarchy – military conscription, forced labour, confiscation of land, taxation to support a royal establishment, rapacious government:

---

[9]   As, e.g., in the tradition reflected in Lev. 18:1–3.

Samuel told all the words of the LORD to the people who were asking him for a king. He said, 'This is what the king who will reign over you will do: He will take your sons and make them serve with his chariots and horses, and they will run in front of his chariots. Some he will assign to be commanders of thousands and commanders of fifties, and others to plough his ground and reap his harvest, and still others to make weapons of war and equipment for his chariots. He will take your daughters to be perfumers and cooks and bakers. He will take the best of your fields and vineyards and olive groves and give them to his attendants. He will take a tenth of your grain and of your vintage and give it to his officials and attendants. Your menservants and maidservants and the best of your cattle and donkeys he will take for his own use. He will take a tenth of your flocks, and you yourselves will become his slaves. When that day comes, you will cry out for relief from the king you have chosen, and the LORD will not answer you in that day.'

(1 Sam. 8:10–18)

Samuel's account of kingship here is explicit and accurate, both as a description of contemporary non-Israelite monarchy and as a prediction of what Israelite monarchy actually became from the reign of Solomon and increasingly thereafter. 'But the people refused to listen to Samuel. "No!" they said. "We want a king over us. Then we shall be like all the other nations"'(vv. 19–20). And so one facet of their *social* distinctiveness was compromised along with their implied rejection of the LORD's theocratic rule.

A couple of centuries later the great conflict between Elijah and Baal in the northern kingdom of Israel during the reign of Ahab and Jezebel revolved around the very same combination. The crisis in Israel was both a crisis of religion (was YHWH or Baal to be worshipped as God?) and also a crisis of society (was Israel to be a land safe for Naboths to live in, or a land where kings and queens took what they wanted, through murderous injustice?). Elijah addressed both issues in 1 Kings 18 – 19. For the question was not just a matter of which god was to be worshipped. It was a conflict of opposing systems of land tenure – Israelite (sanctioned by YHWH as the owner and giver of the land and guarantor of the rights of Israelite families to their patrimony; see chapter 3) versus Canaanite (sanctioned by Baal and giving royalty unfettered right to a tradable commodity). Choose the wrong god and you get the wrong society. Israel went on proving the point for several more centuries.

They did not necessarily stop worshipping the LORD, of course, or appearing to do so. There were times of great syncretism and apostasy. But even then it is likely that the ordinary people thought they were still giving the LORD his fair share of public acknowledgment. But many a prophet pointed out that if Israel allowed their society to be riddled with injustice, oppression, greed, sexual and physical violence, and the loss of all righteousness and compassion, then whatever or whoever they might have thought they were worshipping, it was not the

LORD. Nor would the LORD accept the worship of such people, however out-wardly orthodox or enthusiastic.[10] Sacred rites could not indemnify social wrongs.

This double reality, this two-sided coin (the character of YHWH as God, on the one hand, and the quality of the society he requires, on the other), is fundamental to the covenantal heart of Old Testament faith. Indeed, it is built into the narratives of Israel's liberation that led up to the making of that covenant. Commenting on Exodus 1 – 15, Walter Brueggemann comments:

> Yahweh is a key and decisive actor in the narrative. There is no doubt that this is a theological report in which Yahweh evokes and legitimates the alternative community of justice . . . Each new generation in Israel is taught to read social reality so that the justice questions, that the issues of social power, social goods, and social access, are made major community issues and major concerns of the God of Israel. Israel thus makes the justice issues central in its narrative of God.[11]

Similarly, Paul Hanson binds together the revelation of the nature of the LORD with the revolutionary nature of the new kind of community envisaged and created through the exodus:

> In essence there was already revealed in this event both the nature of the God Yahweh, and the nature of the community of faith that Yahweh's nature implied . . . In the deliverance from Egyptian slavery, Israel encountered a God whose nature and whose corresponding plan for reality stood in diametric opposition to the gods of the Pharaoh . . . Thus a new notion of community was born with the exodus. In compromising or denying it, as Israel repeatedly would, Israel would compromise or deny its own essential being as a people called by God, a community of freed slaves within which the pyramid of social stratification consigning certain classes to lives of ease and others to relentless suffering and deprivation was to be banned forever.[12]

Norbert Lohfink, commenting on the significance of the exodus and reflecting on texts such as Exodus 19:3–6 and Deuteronomy 4:6–8, makes a similar point about Israel as the LORD's intentional 'contrast-society:

> Yahweh intends that Israel be a nation of sisters and brothers in which there will be no more poor (cf. Deut. 15:4). This in itself makes clear that, according to the bible, the poor of Egypt are to become, through the Exodus, a kind of divinely-willed contrast-

---

[10] See, e.g., Is. 1:10–17; Jer. 7:1–11; Hos. 6:6; Amos 5:21–24; Mic. 6:6–8.

[11] 'Covenant and Social Possibility', in Brueggemann, *Social Reading*, p. 59.

[12] Hanson, *People Called*, pp. 21, 23.

society . . . In fact, the new society that Yahweh creates out of the poor Hebrews through the Exodus is not only in contrast to the Egyptian society they have left behind, but beyond that it is in contrast to all other existing societies in their world [it is thus a task directed not just at Israel's good but to the good of all humanity].[13]

In other words, Israel was what it was as a society, because YHWH was what he was as God.[14] This is precisely the relationship envisaged in Deuteronomy 10:12ff. between the character of the LORD and the social nature of Israel. There, to 'walk in his ways', means to imitate the LORD as the God who 'shows no partiality, accepts no bribes, defends the cause of the fatherless . . .' The kind of society the LORD desires and commands is based explicitly on the kind of God he is. This is supported extensively by the legal, prophetic and wisdom literature, and is reinforced by detailed sociological study.

Does it matter?
We may conclude, then, that, far from the social life of Israel being immaterial or incidental to their theological significance, it is actually through observant study of that social life that a major part of God's self-revelation is to be discerned. This gives critical importance to our getting the social study of Israel right. For the more carefully we understand Israel, the more 'coloured-in' will be our understanding of the God of the Bible. Gottwald makes the point that 'Since the primary manifestation of Yahweh is Israel itself, any misconstruction of Israel entails a misconstruction of Yahweh.'[15]

The question might arise at this point, 'Yes, but where does this get us in the

---

[13] Lohfink, *Option for the Poor*, p. 45.

[14] Gottwald, of course, would complain that in putting it that way I have lapsed into religious idealism (which comes close to the unforgiveable sin in Gottwald's sociology). He himself would put it the other way round; namely, that YHWH was conceived as a certain kind of god because he was the religious symbol of Israel's total social system and its struggle to emerge and sustain itself. YHWH, for Gottwald, was only a 'social servomechanism' (*Tribes of Yahweh*, p. 704), 'Israel's cipher for the enduring human project' (p. 706). It should be clear that in agreeing with Gottwald's observation of the tight structural linkage between the nature of YHWH as God and the nature of Israel's social 'experiment', I do not at all agree with his materialist and reductionist way of explaining that linkage. For Gottwald, the sociology of Israel (as an empirical reality) explains their portrayal of YHWH (as an idealized construct). For me (as, of course, for the Old Testament itself), the reality of YHWH explains the social ideals that Israel struggled to embody.

[15] Gottwald, *Tribes of Yahweh*, p. 688.

task of Old Testament ethics?' It may be interesting, in an antiquarian kind of way, to take note of the social differences of Israel from other nations, but surely that is irrelevant to discovering and applying the message of *the Old Testament text itself* to our context? Surely our authority is 'what the Scriptures say', not 'what Israel was like'? Indeed so, but as we have just seen, the Scriptures of the Old Testament are massively, pervasively, interested precisely in 'what Israel was like' – and for the reasons outlined above. Clearly, it mattered very much indeed. The social shape of Israel was not an incidental freak of ancient history. Nor was it just a temporary, material by-product of their spiritual message. We cannot set aside the social dimension of the Old Testament as a kind of husk, out of which we claim to extract a kernel of spiritual timeless truths. Rather, the social reality of Israel was an integral part of what God had called them into existence for. Theologically, the purpose of Israel's existence was to be a vehicle both for God's revelation and for the blessing of humanity. They were not only the bearers of redemption, but were to be a model of what a redeemed community should be like, living in obedience to God's will. Their social structure, aspirations, principles and policies, so organically related to their covenantal faith in the LORD, were also part of the content of that revelation, part of the pattern of redemption. God's message of redemption through Israel was not just verbal; it was visible and tangible. They, the medium, were themselves part of the message. Simply by existing and being obedient to the covenant law of the LORD, they would raise questions among the nations about the nature of their God and the social justice of their community.

> Observe them [the LORD's decrees and laws] carefully, for this will show your wisdom and understanding to the nations, who will hear about all these decrees and say, "Surely this great nation is a wise and understanding people." What other nation is so great as to have their gods near them the way the LORD our God is near us whenever we pray to him? And what other nations is so great as to have such righteous decrees and laws as this body of laws I am setting before you today?
>
> (Deut. 4:6–8)

Israel as God's paradigm

But that was then, and we live now. How can we get from there to here? How can we step from our observation of the integrated world of Israel's faith and society into the world of our own context and bring anything with us across the gap? Two options seem to me to be closed doors. One is to try to replicate Israelite society in our own age by some programme of heavily literal adherence to Old Testament laws. Such literal imitation is not only practically impossible (because we do not live in the world of an ancient Near Eastern agrarian economy and tribal culture); it is also theologically impossible (because neither the church nor any modern state stands in exactly the same relationship to God as Israel did in the Old Testament). Such claimed literal imitation in our very different circumstances also fails to take account of how God takes history and culture seriously and embedded his ethical requirements of Israel very specifically in their own specific context.[16] And it mistakenly equates Old Testament ethics more or less exclusively with the law codes and their commands and penalties; whereas, as we have seen, the narratives and all the rest of the Old Testament scriptures are of just as much importance. So we cannot just 'do as Israel did', without further ado, or take their laws as binding on us just as written in a literalistic way.

The other option (not open to us, it seems to me) is not even to bother at all with 'what Israel did'; that is, to dismiss the Old Testament as ethically irrelevant altogether. Some people devalue the Old Testament in this way on the grounds that it has all been fulfilled in Christ, or replaced by grace, or relegated to a dispensation now long past. Some do so because they have a very jaundiced view of what they find in the Old Testament; such primitive ethics (as they see them) are best left between the covers of ancient history. Others do so because it is too much like hard work to do anything else. All such neglect of the Old Testament for ethical purposes seems to me impossible to reconcile with either the seal of Jesus' authority on the abiding validity of the law and the prophets (Matt. 5:17–20), or Paul's affirmation that all Scripture (meaning the Old Testament) is not only inspired but also profitable for ethical guidance and written for our instruction (2 Tim. 3:16–17; 1 Cor. 10:1–13). If Israel was meant to be 'a light to the nations', then that light must be allowed to shine. We have to find some way to let the light of Old Testament Israel penetrate the centuries and illuminate our world.

The way that seems to me to have the most potential is to regard the society and laws of Israel as a *paradigm*. A paradigm is a model or pattern that enables you to explain or critique many different and varying situations by means of some single concept or set of governing principles. To use a paradigm you work by analogy from a specific known reality (the paradigm) to a wider or different context in which there are problems to be solved, or

---

[16] Chapter 12 includes a brief survey and critique of the position known as 'theonomism', which believes that the Old Testament law is indeed permanently valid and that the modern church and also the modern state are both at fault for not seeking to embody and execute it within both spheres. That is, theonomists advocate that Old Testament laws should be reapplied through modern legislation.

answers to be found, or choices to be made. Or a paradigm may provide criteria by which you evaluate or critique some set of circumstances or proposals, positively or negatively. So a paradigm may function descriptively or prescriptively or critically. Before explaining further what I mean by this paradigmatic handling of the Old Testament for ethics, let us look again at a key text that seems to hint in this direction – Exodus 19:4–6.

God's priesthood in the midst of the nations

> You yourselves have seen what I did to Egypt, and how I carried you on eagles' wings and brought you to myself. Now if you obey me fully and keep my covenant, then out of all nations you will be my treasured possession. Although the whole earth is mine, you will be for me a kingdom of priests and a holy nation.
>
> (Exod. 19:4–6)

Coming at the hinge between the exodus itself (in chs. 1 – 18) and the actual giving of the law and making of the covenant (in chs. 20 – 24), these programmatic words of God to Israel look both backwards and forwards. First, they point back to the initiative of God's redemptive grace ('You have seen what I have done . . .') as the essential context for obedience to the law (as the Decalogue also does). Then, secondly, they give to Israel an identity and role as a *priestly* and *holy* people in the midst of 'all the nations' in 'the whole earth', which belongs to the LORD. Obedience to the covenant law was thus to enable them to be holy; that is, different, distinctive *from* the nations. But at the same time, as a priesthood, they were to be teacher, model and mediator *for* the nations. Keeping the law, then, was not an end in itself for Israel, but related to their very reason for existence – God's concern for the nations. Deuteronomy 4:5–8, as we have just seen, sets Israel's social righteousness in the same context – the public stage of the world of nations.

If we ask, then, whether the law was given specifically to Israel with unique relevance to them in their covenant relationship to the LORD, or whether it was meant also to apply to the rest of the nations (including eventually ourselves), the answer is 'Both'. But this needs immediate qualification. The law was not explicitly and consciously applied to the nations (as Ps. 147:19–20 says, God had not given it to other nations as he had done to Israel). But that does not mean that Israel's law was irrelevant to them. Rather, the law was given to Israel to enable Israel to live as a model, as a light to the nations. The anticipated result of this plan was that, in the prophetic vision, the law would 'go forth' to the nations, or they would 'come up' to learn it. The nations were 'waiting' for that law and justice of the LORD, which was presently bound up with Israel (Is. 42:4). Israel was to be 'light for the nations'.

Given, then, Israel's role in relation to God's purpose for the nations, and given the law's function in relation to that mission of Israel, we can see that the law was designed (along with all the other aspects of Israel's social reality, as we have just seen) to mould and shape Israel in certain clearly defined directions within their own historical and cultural context. That overall social shape, with all its legal and institutional structures, ethical norms, and theological undergirding, thus becomes the model or paradigm that Israel provides as a priesthood for the nations. And, furthermore, it was a paradigm intended to have a relevance and application beyond the geographical, historical and cultural borders of Israel itself. R. E. Clements draws attention to this broad adaptability of Old Testament law in a way that, though he does not use the term 'paradigmatic', is similar in effect to the point I am making:

> What is remarkable in fact is the way in which the Old Testament has provided a
> system of *tora* – instruction, which has proved to be remarkably adaptable to a vast
> range of human social and political systems. Societies of dramatically different
> economic, political and cultural types have found within the Old Testament a richly
> viable source of social and moral teaching.[17]

The particularity of Israel, then, is not a hindrance to universal application, but rather actually serves it. A paradigm by its very nature is a particular, specific, concrete case that has wider relevance or application beyond its own particularity.

My point here is that this paradigmatic nature of Israel is not just a hermeneutical tool devised by *us* and imposed retrospectively, and therefore anachronistically, on the Old Testament. Rather, theologically speaking, such paradigmatic function was part of God's design in creating and shaping Israel in the first place. When we enquire about the ethical relevance of ancient Israel to our own contemporary context, when we try to see what light the scriptures of Israel shed on our own world, *we are doing what God intended should happen.* That's what we have these scriptures for. They render to us a paradigm, in one single culture and slice of history, of the kinds of social values God looks for in human life generally.

Some further examples of how paradigms work may be helpful.

Paradigms in grammar
When we learn a new language, we often learn paradigm words. For example, *parler* is often used as a paradigm when learning French. If we learn all the

---

[17] Clements, 'Christian Ethics', p. 22.

endings of that verb, we have a paradigm for the other verbs of that type in French – all the regular ones ending in -*er*. Once we know the shape and pattern of *that* paradigm verb, *that* specific example, then we can apply the paradigm to an almost infinite variety of other verbs – or even invent new ones with that ending. They will still conform to the paradigm. Conversely, if we write a sentence beginning *Nous arrivez*, we will be marked wrong: that does not conform to the paradigm. Knowing the paradigm enables us to critique bad grammar as well as speak and write valid grammar. So by learning a certain number of paradigm words (verbs, nouns, etc.), we generate a very flexible capacity for handling a wide range of vocabulary in new situations as we use the language.

Using Israel as a paradigm enables us to move from that known case to multiple contexts where situations will be almost infinitely different, and still find or apply principles that conform to the paradigm we have learned from the Old Testament (and of course, as biblical Christians, from the wider paradigm of the whole Bible). And we shall also be able to use the paradigm to critique situations or proposals to the extent that they do *not* conform to what we know to be the shape of the paradigm God created in Israel. So the paradigm helps us in positive ethical articulation, and in negative ethical critique.

Paradigms in science

In 1970 Thomas Kuhn wrote a book about scientific revolutions which itself revolutionized the way the progress of science is now conceived.[18] Science, according to Kuhn, has not actually followed the classic myth of steady evolution of accumulating theories based on deeper and deeper probing of the evidence. Rather, science has sometimes made huge transitions as one paradigm, which may have stood for centuries, is found to be inadequate and crashes to the ground, to be replaced by another. Thereafter all new experimental work is done within this new paradigm of understanding, until it too is found to be inadequate and is replaced. Such paradigm shifts are relatively infrequent because as they occur they are inevitably disruptive and divisive.

> Research on specific problems always took place against the background of assumptions and convictions produced by previously existing science. In mature science, this background took the form of 'paradigms', a cluster of beliefs, theories, values, standards for research, and exemplary research results, that provided a framework for scientific advance within a whole field.[19]

---

[18] Thomas S. Kuhn, *Structure of Scientific Revolutions*.

[19] Poythress, *Science and Hermeneutics*, p. 43.

Kuhn uses the word 'paradigm' in two senses. On the one hand, it can denote 'the entire constellation of beliefs, values, techniques, and so on shared by the members of a given community'. On the other hand, it designates 'concrete puzzle-solutions' – actual results of experimentation that provide working models for further research by suggesting ways of problem-solving for a large number of unsolved problems. Vern Poythress, commenting on Kuhn, helpfully distinguishes between these two senses by using 'disciplinary matrix' for the first and 'exemplar' for the second. It seems to me that both senses of the word 'paradigm' in this scientific setting (as a matrix of beliefs on the one hand, and as concrete examples on the other) can be fruitfully used in understanding how the Old Testament can function as an ethical paradigm for us.

In the first place, the emergence of Israel introduced a new paradigm of beliefs and values into the ancient Near Eastern world – using 'paradigm' here in its wider sense of an overarching matrix of beliefs. This is not to suggest that somehow Israel was exotic, with no religious or cultural links in its own environment. Vast amounts of comparative scholarship have shown the extent of the interaction between Israel and her contemporary world – as one would expect. Nevertheless, we have shown above that in certain key areas Israel was *different*, consciously and deliberately. And this difference included their whole worldview – the matrix of beliefs and assumptions that governed their social and religious self-understanding and organization. Among the features of this revolutionary worldview – this paradigm – one could include, as a bare minimum list the following:

- Israel's monotheism, emerging first perhaps as mono-Yahwism, but certainly developing into a fully fledged commitment not merely to the uniqueness of YHWH, but also to his sole deity.
- The characteristics of YHWH as the God described above (i.e. one who is Lord of creation and also acts in history).
- The values expressed through YHWH's action in history, made explicit through the exodus and then consolidated in Israel's own law – concern for the vulnerable and oppressed, commitment to justice, rejection of idolatry and its associated social evils.
- A covenantal conception of social structure with remarkable effects in the political sphere – especially the way Israel translated their belief that YHWH was their king into the practical rejection of human kingship for several centuries and a theoretical limit on the king's power when monarchy did emerge.
- A belief in the divine ownership of the land, which produced a drive towards economic justice and inverted the dominant pattern of land ownership.

- A belief in YHWH as creator and sustainer of the natural order, which de-divinized whole areas of life such as sexuality, fertility (of land, herds and wives) and even death.

These are just some of the contours of the paradigm. This was the overall matrix of beliefs, values and assumptions that shaped historical Israel.

In the second place, Israel itself was a paradigm, in Kuhn's second narrower sense. That is, they constituted a concrete model, a practical, culturally specific, experimental exemplar of the beliefs and values they embodied. Now nobody would want to deny what the Hebrew scriptures themselves make clear; namely, that Israel failed to be all they believed themselves called to be in terms of their own covenant, law and social institutions. Nevertheless, it is a simple historical fact that in the transition from Bronze to Iron Age in ancient Palestine a remarkable society emerged with some radically different forms of social, economic and political life, all of which were integrally linked to a very distinctive form of religious belief. They called themselves 'Israel' and 'the people of YHWH', and they succeeded for several centuries to prove, for example, that a theocracy could actually work without a human king; that land could be possessed and enjoyed without being treated merely as a commercial asset, to be bought, sold and exploited through absolute ownership; that a broad equality of families with built-in mechanisms for the prevention or relief of poverty, debt and slavery could be maintained; that the people's spiritual needs could be met without a highly consumptive, landowning, cultic elite. Their whole concrete existence in history is paradigmatic. Of course, as history progressed, this historical experiment went through a lot of change in itself. The people of God from Abraham to the return from exile went through several major metamorphoses, yet in each era there were the constants, the underlying fundamental ideals of what it was to be Israel, of what was or was not 'done' in Israel.[20] In other words, Israel themselves were called to an ongoing self-check against the paradigm of their own 'constitution'.

This second sense of a scientific paradigm is also instructive for our application of it to Old Testament ethics. In scientific research the 'concrete exemplar' provided by the results of scientific experimentation functions as a model for solving other puzzles. That is, scientists working within a certain 'disciplinary matrix' (paradigm in the first sense) assume that a model which successfully solves one problem (paradigm in the second sense) is likely to produce results if applied to other problems in the same general field. This is

---

[20] See Goldingay, *Theological Diversity*, particularly ch. 3, 'A Contextualizing Study of "the People of God" in the Old Testament'. See also chapter 7 below.

another way of looking at what it means to handle Old Testament Israel as a paradigm. By seeing how *they* addressed, within *their* cultural and historical context, problems and issues common to humanity in principle or practice, we are helped to address (if not always to solve) the ethical challenges *we* face in our different contexts. A paradigm has problem-solving power. Historical Israel articulated a comprehensive corporate response to a wide range of economic, social and political issues in their day. We cannot chide them for not solving all the problems of the human race. That is not the purpose of a paradigm. The whole point of a 'puzzle-solution' lies in its specific, concrete nature. John Goldingay stresses the importance of the concrete particularity of Old Testament laws and institutions. They prevent us from being content with abstract generalities:

> Thus either the Bible's statements tell us how to live, or (when they do not do this) these actual statements are the model for and the measure of our attempts to state how we are to live. This means we do not ignore the particularity of biblical commands (and apply them to our own day as if they were timeless universals). Nor are we paralysed by their particularity (and thus unable to apply them to our day at all). We rejoice in their particularity because it shows us how the will of God was expressed in their context, and we take them as our paradigm for our own ethical construction.[21]

Events and stories as paradigms

Another way of approaching the Old Testament through the concept of paradigm was observed by Paul D. Hanson in 1986.[22] He pointed out that in the Old Testament itself certain events and narratives were of such revelatory power that they took on the nature of a paradigm for both how God could be expected to act in future, and also how Israel should act in response. The exodus is the obvious example. In narrative, poetry, law and prophecy the exodus stands as a paradigm of the LORD's faithfulness, justice and compassion, and similarly as a paradigm for Israel's social life in many dimensions. By extension, Hanson argues, what was paradigmatic within Israel in the Old Testament was also paradigmatic for the church as the community of this same God in the New Testament, and for us today.

---

[21] Goldingay, *Approaches*, p. 55. The importance of the particularity of the Old Testament texts is also discussed by J. Barton, *Ethics*, pp. 1–18. Barton similarly argues that what many regard as a weakness of Old Testament ethics (its great detail and variety) is actually its strength.

[22] Paul D. Hanson, *People Called*.

Waldemar Janzen takes this paradigmatic nature of Old Testament narrative somewhat further.[23] Not just the great national epic of the exodus, but also the myriad other smaller narratives functioned within the consciousness of Israel to generate paradigms of behaviour in certain contexts. 'Paradigm' in this sense is more like a mental construct, built up out of the repeated telling of many stories, of what it means to be a good Israelite in different social situations. In similar fashion, much of our own ethical behaviour is subconsciously governed by mental paradigms of what it means to be 'a good father', or 'a good driver', or 'a good friend'. These too are built out of myriad 'stories' – whether actual stories told to us since childhood, or the storied experiences of life in general. So for Israel, paradigms of behaviour were internalized ethical models with narrative foundations. Janzen describes several such major paradigms in the Old Testament: the priestly, royal, prophetic and wisdom paradigms. But he gives pride of place to the familial paradigm, with its major components of life, land and hospitality. Each model of behaviour, each package of expectations, virtues, relationships and priorities, was built out of a wide swathe of narrative, legal, wisdom and worship traditions in Israel.

There is, then, a variety of ways in which the idea of a paradigm is used. I do not see one as more important than another. Each seems to me to add a helpful dimension to what I mean by treating Old Testament Israel as a paradigm, or using a paradigmatic methodology for articulating Old Testament ethics.

Paradigm or principles?

Is there a difference between the paradigmatic method I am advocating here and the familiar idea that, since we obviously cannot simply lift the details of Old Testament laws and apply them in the modern context, what we have to do is 'extract the *principles*' that underlie those laws and apply them? In one sense, there is not a huge difference. To use a paradigm you do have to look for and articulate the principles the paradigm embodies and then see how they can be reconcretized in some other context. However, the problem with the 'look-for-the-principle' approach *on its own* is this: it can lead to the eventual discarding of the specific realities of the Old Testament text, the concrete, earthy history of Israel, the good, the bad and the ugly. Once you have a principle in your pocket, why keep the wrapping? Sadly, this has been how many people have handled the Old Testament (or rather mishandled it).

Yet it is plain that what God has given us is a Bible, not a classified collec-

---

[23]   Waldemar Janzen, *Ethics*.

tion of principles. What he has given us is a wonderfully particular portrayal of a people through many generations. This portrayal comes to us through their narratives, laws, wisdom, worship and visions, their memory and hope, their achievements and failures. It comes to us as a rather untidy and incredibly complex assortment of very complex individuals, over multiple generations, in different nations. Treating all this great collection of texts merely as the expendable container for independent universal principles we can express more simply and tidily denies the character of the Bible as God has given it to us, and might even seem to render Bible reading a waste of time. Regarding the biblical texts about Israel as providing us with a paradigm preserves their historical particularity and forces us to observe all the non-reducible hard edges, all the jarring tensions and all the awkward corners of earthy reality within them.

Providing we keep hold of the total paradigm and make sure we are paying close attention to the texts that render it to us, we can of course articulate the principles built into it. So, taking paradigm in the *broader* sense of a matrix, we may certainly speak of its constituent principles – but the important thing is to see how all those principles hang together as a coherent worldview, the worldview contained in the faith of Israel and the canon of the Old Testament. And taking paradigm in the *narrower* sense of a working model, we can articulate the principles or objectives we believe to be embodied in some particular law or institution, but we must do so in relation to the total package of what it meant to be Israel, socially, economically, politically, internationally and religiously. The paradigm will then govern how we relate the principles to one another, how they are prioritized and their overall direction or thrust.

So my argument is that the concept of paradigm *includes* the isolation and articulation of principles, but is not reducible to them alone. To regard Israel and the Old Testament as an ethical paradigm forces us constantly to go back to the hard given reality of the text of the Bible itself and imaginatively to live with Israel in their world ('inhabiting the text'), before returning to the equally hard given reality of our own world, to discover imaginatively how that paradigm challenges our ethical response there.

In conclusion, this proposed paradigmatic method cannot claim any kind of novelty. It seems to me that it is fairly similar to what we find in the Bible itself in certain examples of ethical argument or challenge. In the Old Testament we have repeatedly observed that Israel's experience of liberation through the exodus functions as a paradigm for a wide variety of social and ethical obligations that were laid upon them. Even in ancient Israel itself this was not a matter of literal imitation or replication: Israel could not recreate an 'exodus, parting of the sea and all' for every social context of need or injustice they encountered. But the exodus was certainly a paradigm, calling for a certain pattern of response to oppression that would reflect in different circumstances what the historical particularity of the exodus had demonstrated about the LORD.

Or consider Nathan's parable to David (2 Sam. 12:1–10). The power of Nathan's rhetoric is that he leads David to believe he is adjudicating a real case of theft. David responds on the basis of known law: the thief (even if the nastiness of what he did makes David exclaim that he deserved to die) must simply compensate fourfold for his theft (Exod. 22:1). But then Nathan slams home the paradigmatic impact: 'If that is what you yourself say on the basis of this case and that law, then how much more does your own behaviour stand judged in the same light? If, as king, you think that a sheep-stealer deserves to die, what do you think a wife-stealer deserves?'

Or consider one of the most powerful narrative paradigms ever created – Jesus' parable of the good Samaritan (Luke 10:30–39). It has entered into the ethical consciousness not just of Christians but of a whole culture affected by the Gospel narratives. But two things are interesting. First, Jesus told the story as a way of modelling the full significance of a particular law, which was the subject of the question raised to him – 'Love your neighbour as yourself' (v. 27). So the narrative, though fictional, embodies the law in a paradigmatic case. But second, Jesus concludes the conversation with the telling phrase 'Go and do *likewise*' (v. 37; my italics). Now that seems to me to be the essence of what I intend by a paradigmatic approach. Clearly, Jesus did not mean that the young lawyer who had asked him the question should hire a donkey, buy some bandages, oil and wine, keep some change for friendly inn-keepers, and set off immediately on the road to Jericho to look for victims of robbery with violence. Jesus' words did not mean 'Go and do *exactly the same*'. They meant 'Go and live your life in a way which expresses the same costly and barrier-crossing neighbourliness that my story illustrates – that is what it will mean to obey the law (since you asked).'

And for us as Christians, the Gospel records of the life of Jesus function in a comparably paradigmatic way too. The Gospels take very seriously the fact that Jesus was a real man who lived, behaved, related, travelled and taught in the way described in their account of his ministry. He called his disciples to 'follow him' and we are commanded in various ways in the New Testament to model our lives on his (e.g. Eph. 5:2; Phil. 2:5; 1 Pet. 2:21 ff.). But rarely in the history of Christian moral thought has that been taken in the sense of literal imitation down to detail (in the way that, e.g., the details of Muhammad's life and habits became obligatory on his followers). We do not feel obliged to practise carpentry, wear seamless clothing, pursue an itinerant and homeless lifestyle, or preach from boats. None of those things, in themselves, would constitute what the New Testament means by being 'Christlike'.

Yet neither, on the other hand, do we feel free to treat the Gospel accounts of the life of Jesus as ethically irrelevant, choosing to pay attention only to his teaching (or worse, the timeless ethical principles Jesus is alleged to have bequeathed to humanity). For it was in part the quality of Jesus' life that authenticated his teaching, confounded his enemies and rendered his execution the travesty of justice it was. Rather, we tend, unconsciously or otherwise, to use the example of Jesus paradigmatically in our ethical decisions, seeking to move from what we know Jesus *did* do to what we might reasonably presume he *would* do in our changed situation. The overall shape and character of his life – comprising his actions, attitudes and relationships as well as his responses, parables and other teaching – becomes our pattern or paradigm, by which we test the 'Christlikeness' of the same components of our own lives. One scholar has described this ethical response to the life of Jesus as a 'concrete universal'.[24] He develops an argument from analogy, which is very similar to what I mean by paradigm:

> The distinctive arrangement of elements in the religious original serves as a paradigm, exemplar, prototype, and precedent to guide the actions and dispositions of Christians in new situations. Because biblical patterns combine a stable core with an indeterminate, open-ended dimension, the moral response can be both creative and faithful. We extend a pattern by *analogy* since we move from the recognizable shape in the first instance to novel situations within certain limitations . . . Analogical imagination requires a creative transfer because, like the exodus and the exile, the gospel events and teachings are *historical prototypes* rather than *mythical archetypes*. A paradigm is a normative exemplar of constitutive structure but it always has an indeterminate, open-ended dimension.[25]

And finally, in the epistles, there are examples of paradigmatic appropriation of Old Testament texts. Paul, for example, can use one aspect of the manna in the wilderness as a way of encouraging equality and sharing among Christians (2 Cor. 8:13–15). Or he can use the law providing for the welfare of the working ox as support for his demand that working pastors and missionaries should be properly provided for (1 Cor. 9:8–12).

Let us then sum up what we have learned in this chapter about the importance of the social angle of Old Testament ethics. When the human race chose to rebel against God and fell into disobedience, arrogance, strife and violence,

---

[24] Spohn, *Scripture and Ethics*, pp. 98–102.

[25] Ibid., p. 100 (his italics).

God's response was not simply to rescue individuals for some disembodied existence at a safe distance from the doomed planet. Rather, God chose to call into existence a community on earth and in history that would be different, and through whom he would eventually bring the blessing of redemption to humanity as a whole. Even in its origins in the book of Genesis, this community was given an ethical agenda. In a world going the way of Sodom they were to walk in the way of the LORD, by doing righteousness and justice. The way of the LORD was made clear to them through his great acts in their history – especially the exodus. This community was further shaped by the law God gave them at Sinai, and by the other great traditions of their faith – prophets, wisdom writers, psalmists, historians and so on. The purpose of all this was not merely for Israel's sake alone, or merely to keep God happy. Rather, Israel as a society was intended from the start to be a paradigm or model to the nations, a showcase of the way God longs for human society as a whole to operate. We are not only justified, therefore; we are indeed expected to make use of the social patterns, structures and laws of Old Testament Israel to help us in our thinking and choosing in the realm of social ethics in our own world.

Further reading

Brueggemann, Walter, *The Prophetic Imagination* (Philadelphia: Fortress, 1978).

————, *A Social Reading of the Old Testament: Prophetic Approaches to Israel's Communal Life*, ed. Patrick D. Miller (Minneapolis: Fortress, 1994).

Clements, R. E. (ed.), *The World of Ancient Israel: Sociological, Anthropological and Political Perspectives* (Cambridge: Cambridge University Press, 1989).

Davidson, Robert, 'Some Aspects of the Old Testament Contribution to the Pattern of Christian Ethics', *Scottish Journal of Theology* 12 (1959), pp. 373–387.

Freedman, D. N., 'Divine Commitment and Human Obligation: The Covenant Theme', *Interpretation* 18 (1964), pp. 419–431.

Gnuse, Robert Karl, *No Other Gods: Emergent Monotheism in Israel*, JSOT Supplement Series, vol. 241 (Sheffield: Sheffield Academic Press, 1997).

Gottwald, Norman K., *The Tribes of Yahweh: A Sociology of the Religion of Liberated Israel 1250–1050 BCE* (Maryknoll: Orbis; London: SCM, 1979).

Hanson, Paul D., *The People Called: The Growth of Community in the Bible* (San Francisco: Harper & Row, 1986).

Hauerwas, Stanley, *A Community of Character: Toward a Constructive Christian Social Ethic* (Notre Dame: University of Notre Dame Press, 1981).

Janzen, Waldemar, *Old Testament Ethics: A Paradigmatic Approach* (Louisville, KY: Westminster John Knox, 1994).

McKenzie, J. L., 'The Elders in the Old Testament', *Biblica* 40 (1959), pp. 522–540.

Meeks, Wayne, *The Moral World of the First Christians* (Philadelphia: Westminster; London: SPCK, 1986).

Pleins, J. David, *The Social Visions of the Hebrew Bible: A Theological Introduction* (Louisville, KY: Westminster John Knox, 2001).

Reviv, Hanoch, *The Elders in Ancient Israel: A Study of a Biblical Institution* (Jerusalem: Magnes, 1989).

Waldow, H. E. von, 'Social Responsibility and Social Structure in Early Israel', *Catholic Biblical Quarterly* 32 (1970), pp. 182–204.

Weinfeld, W., 'The Origin of Humanism in Deuteronomy', *Journal of Biblical Literature* 80 (1961), pp. 241–249.

Wilson, Robert R., 'Ethics in Conflict: Sociological Aspects of Ancient Israelite Ethics', in Susan Niditch (ed.), *Text and Tradition: The Hebrew Bible and Folklore* (Atlanta: Scholars Press, 1990), pp. 193–205.

3. THE ECONOMIC ANGLE

So far in our journey around the triangle of relationships in Old Testament ethics we have looked first at the *theological* angle, and seen how important it is to have a clear understanding of the identity, character and 'biography' of Israel's God, YHWH. Then we moved to the *social* angle and explored Israel's self-understanding as a community in relation with YHWH, set as a nation among the nations. We come now to the third point of our tour, the *economic* angle.

The land in which Israel lived in Old Testament times was a reality of major importance in their relationship with God. It was not merely the place where they happened to live. Nor was it merely an economic asset, essential for agricultural viability. Still less was it considered or handled merely as real estate, property that could be bought and sold commercially. The land, for Israel, was a matter of central theological and ethical importance, and any account of Old Testament ethics must take this angle seriously. This is particularly so for Christian interpreters. Our faith has its centre in a person, not a place; that is, in Jesus Christ, not a holy land or city. And on that basis we are conscious of being a multinational community spread throughout the earth, with no essential ties to any single territory as fundamental to our salvation or our relationship to God through Christ. The result is that much Christian handling of the Old Testament has overlooked the theological centrality of the land within these texts and traditions. Or we have relegated it to the role of 'background scenery' through colourful maps at the back of our Bibles or illustrated articles in Bible encyclopedias.[1]

---

[1] An exception to this, and a fine survey of the land through the whole Old Testament

I shall survey, first of all, the place of the land within the long narrative of Israel in the Old Testament period – a narrative in which the land at times almost takes on the role of a character in the plot. Then I shall look at two major complementary themes in Israel's theology of their land: divine gift and divine ownership. On the one hand, the land was theirs through the promise and covenantal gift of YHWH; and, on the other hand, it was still YHWH's land and he asserted moral rights over how it was to be used. Finally, I shall point out how the land functions as a kind of covenantal thermometer – measuring Israel's relationship with God at any one time. Thus the land at the economic angle functions as a gauge for how things are going at the other two angles – Israel's life as a society, and their relationship to God.

The land in Israel's story

The Bible's story of redemption begins with God's promises to Abraham. Anticipation of God's redemptive intention comes much earlier, of course. The so-called *proto-evangelium* (first announcement of the gospel), in Genesis 3:15, promises that humanity (the seed of the woman) will eventually be victorious over the evil that has injected itself into history (the seed of the serpent). This is a promise Christians traditionally see fulfilled through the man Jesus, who, as a human being (the seed of the woman), defeated the power of Satan (the seed of the serpent). The narrative of the flood also presents both God's judgment on human wickedness and also, through Noah and the ark, God's redeeming grace. Theologically, the flood is a prototype of both sides of God's response to the cursed earth: destruction and renewal. An old sinful world perished. A new world began, as Noah's family and his animal menagerie stepped out onto Mount Ararat. The echoes of the creation narrative are strong in Genesis 8:15–17. It was, of course, still the old world – not yet washed clean of its sin, as the narrative quickly shows. However, the whole story becomes a sign not only of God's commitment to life on earth while it lasts (in the Noachian covenant tied up with its rainbow ribbon) but also of the coming final judgment and renewal – the new creation (2 Pet. 3:3–13).

It is not surprising, therefore, that the covenant promise to Abraham which actually launched the work of redemption in history included land as a

---

period, with many stimulating reflections on its relevance to faith today, is provided by Walter Brueggemann, *Land*. See also my own analysis of the function of the land within the covenantal relationship of the Lord and Israel, with particular emphasis on the centrality of the family, in Christopher J. H. Wright, *God's Land*, especially chs. 1–3.

fundamental constituent of that promise (Gen. 12:7; 15:7, 18–21; 17:8 etc.). In fact, in purely statistical terms land is clearly the dominant note in the ancestral promise. Out of 46 references to the promise in the whole sweep of text from Genesis to Judges, only 7 do not mention the land, while 29 refer solely to it (in Gen. 28:4, for example, the 'blessing of Abraham' means simply possession of the land).[2] The land thus becomes one of the most prominent features of the entire sequel of the Old Testament story.

Once again it is important that we allow the Old Testament to speak to us, not in bits and pieces taken at random, but as a *narrative*. When we do so, it is at once very apparent that the overarching theme of the great history that begins in the Pentateuch, and then runs on through the books of Joshua and Judges and up to the establishing of the territorial limits of the kingdom of David, is the promise and the possession of the land. Conversely, the narrative and prophetic texts that take us through the torrid centuries of monarchy prepare us for the traumatic loss of land in the Babylonian exile. And in the later texts of the canon of the Old Testament the return to the land and its resettlement after the exile, both in prophetic vision and historical description, are dominant themes.

Promise and suspense

The Pentateuch generates tremendous suspense concerning the land. David Clines sees the land promise as the third of the three major elements of the Abrahamic promise: posterity (or descendants), blessing and land. In his proposal for an outline theme for the whole Pentateuch Clines observes how the first of these (posterity – descendants who would become a great nation) is fulfilled by the time you get into the book of Exodus: the descendants of Abraham have become a great people, as promised. The second (blessing, through covenantal relationship with the LORD) is heralded by the exodus and consolidated at Sinai. But the third (land, its promise and possession) is never quite reached within the Pentateuch itself. Thus, Clines argues, the governing theme of the Pentateuch is the partial fulfilment, and partial non-fulfilment, of the promise to Abraham. The promise lies behind and yet still ahead of the people. And this is a posture in which the people of God found themselves towards the end of the exile, and indeed at every point in their pilgrimage with God.[3]

---

[2] A detailed survey of the material is given by von Rad, 'Promised Land', pp. 79–93.

[3] David Clines, *Theme of the Pentateuch*. In the second edition of this book (1997) Clines adds a final chapter in which he deconstructs his earlier position, and confesses that he would no longer now wish to speak of 'the theme' of a complex text such as the

Genesis records the patriarchs (or, to be less gender-specific, the ancestors) wandering in the land with no secure footholds, except for the elaborately achieved purchase of a burial site (Gen. 23), and concludes with the whole family settling down in Egypt. The land was not lost sight of, however, for the book ends with the dying words of Joseph recalling the promise of God and trusting in its fulfilment.

Exodus is launched with God's remembered intention to keep that promise (Exod. 2:24; 3:8, 17; 6:2–8). When, in the course of the momentous events of the first nineteen chapters of Exodus, Israel has been freed, mobilized, organized, and bound to God by covenant at Sinai, the reader would be inclined to think that occupation of the land (the third element in the promise to Abraham) was but a step away. First, however, we must grapple with a detailed description of the tabernacle and its furnishings, not once but twice! The lesson was as clear as the prayer of Moses in Exodus 33:15–16. The presence of the LORD in the midst of his people was even more important than the gift of the land. Without that presence they might as well stay put. And so the book of Exodus ends with the glory of the presence of God settling on the Tent of Meeting and accompanying the Israelites in all their forthcoming travels (Exod. 40:34–38). But Israel is not yet in the land of promise.

Leviticus suspends the story still further as detailed laws are given. But in the latter section of the book, often called the Holiness Code, the land comes back into focus. For many of the laws there are framed from the perspective of life in the land after the conquest. Indeed, the land is personified as the agent of God's blessing or curse, inasmuch as it is described as 'vomiting out' the present inhabitants for their wicked ways, and quite capable of repeating the performance on the Israelites if they imitate them (Lev. 18:24–28; 20:22–24). Such expulsion of Israel is even foreseen in Leviticus 26, but not without another concluding reassurance of the permanence of the promise to the patriarchs (Lev. 26:42–45). And within that final promise in Leviticus, we note how the land functions as a middle term between God's remembrance of his covenant with Abraham and his covenant with the exodus generation.

Numbers brings the suspense to a climax with the stories of the spies, the people's failure of nerve, the abortive first attempt at invasion and the dreary years of a whole generation spent in the wilderness (Num. 13 – 14). Will this

Pentateuch, at least not as some objectively inherent structure. However, in my view, his book in its original form (1978) was immensely helpful in enabling readers to gain an overall grasp of the Pentateuch through what seem to be its own central and dominant categories. Another excellent survey that handles the major themes of the Pentateuch is T. D. Alexander, *Paradise to Promised Land*.

people ever capture Canaan? Can the promise to Abraham ever really be fulfilled? Eventually, however, the painful journeys through hostile territories come to an end with the tribes encamped in the plains of Moab, and only the Jordan to cross. The oracles of Balaam reassure the reader of God's benevolent purpose (Num. 23 – 24). But then the action of the Reubenites and Gadites again raises our suspense (Num. 32). Will they seduce the whole people into accepting life on the wrong side of Jordan? That threat is averted diplomatically and the book of Numbers ends optimistically with the map of Canaan already being redrawn to accommodate the victorious Israelites. But they are still not actually in possession of the promised land.

Surely the final book of the Pentateuch must take us into the land? But no! Deuteronomy begins and ends in Moab. Indeed, Deuteronomy could be said to begin and end in failure – past and anticipated. We are treated to a detailed recapitulation of the story so far, with sustained exhortation to obedient faithfulness to the covenant (Deut. 1 – 11). Then comes the major part of the book, devoted to the law – some old ones modified, some new ones introduced (chs. 12 – 26), but all based on life in the land they have still to occupy. As at the end of Leviticus, the land itself will be both the arena and the agent of God's blessing or curse, depending on the people's obedience or otherwise (chs. 28 – 30). Finally, after the song and blessing of Moses, Deuteronomy brings the whole magnificent structure of the Pentateuch to a close with the moving account of the death of Moses – Moses who had led his people to within a day's march of the land of promise but would not himself set foot in it (ch. 34). So the story of God's people in the Pentateuch ends, as it began, with the promise of the land to Abraham (Deut. 34:4), but with that promise still unfulfilled. Harry Orlinsky summarizes the centrality of the land in the Pentateuch like this:

> From the Exodus on, including the theophany at Mount Sinai (whatever be its date of composition and redaction) and all the laws that were associated with it, the emphasis is on the getting to and into the Promised Land and on the kind of society to be set up there. The laws promulgated in Exod. 21ff., the making of the Tabernacle and its paraphernalia (Exod. 25ff.), the ritual-priestly laws (much of Leviticus and Numbers), the primary purpose of the book of Deuteronomy – regardless of their historical setting and date of composition – all these, for their authors, compilers, and redactors, pertained to the structure and quality of the community of Israel after God had fulfilled His vow to settle them in the Land in which their ancestors had lived as sojourners.[4]

---

[4] Orlinsky, 'Land of Israel', p. 38.

Settlement and struggle

The book of Joshua begins with words the reader has begun to wonder if he would ever hear: 'get ready to cross the Jordan River into the land' (Josh. 1:2). The rest of the book, then, has the land as its principal theme: its invasion, conquest and division. It ends in the same way as Deuteronomy with a renewal of the covenant (chs. 23 – 24), but with one of its promises now an accomplished fact, no longer a future hope. Israel now has possession of the land.

The book of Judges, however, shows how incompletely the initial conquest had been effectively followed up. The land of promise becomes a land of struggle, where long periods of defeat are interspersed with hard-won, short-lived victories. We are in some suspense again, no longer as to whether the people will *enter* the land, but whether they can *survive* within it.

In 1 and 2 Samuel, with the onslaught of the Philistines, the obstacles to secure possession of the whole land seem insuperable. The last and greatest of the judges, Samuel, achieves a victory that holds them at bay during his personal rule (1 Sam. 7). But Israel's first king, who was appointed for the very purpose of leading Israel against the Philistines (1 Sam. 8:20), witnesses at the point of his own death the Philistines achieving their deepest inroad into Canaan, virtually cutting Israel's land in half (1 Sam. 31). What has happened to the promised secure boundaries of the land (Gen. 15:18–19; Exod. 23:31; Num. 34:1–12)? Only with the sustained victories and long rule of David does Israel eventually live at peace within secure borders embracing the territory actually promised (2 Sam. 8; 10). At last the promise had been manifestly and effectively fulfilled.

Abuse and loss

But the land does not then disappear from the continuing story of the Old Testament. The accumulated burden of oppression and injustice in the nation, which had been foreseen and forewarned by Samuel (1 Sam. 8:10–18), began during the reign of Solomon, and became an instrument of state policy under Solomon's son Rehoboam, splitting the kingdom in two in the process (1 Kgs. 12).

In the centuries after Solomon the land becomes the focus of constant struggle between the forces of dispossession, greed, exploitation and land-grabbing on the one hand, and the protest of the prophets on the other. Elijah confronted Ahab and Jezebel over their treatment of Naboth in the ninth century BC (1 Kgs. 21). But in the eighth century Amos shocked the northern kingdom of Israel with a threat that had not featured in the earlier prophets: the LORD would eject his people from the land, hurling them and their king into exile (Amos 5:1–6; 6:7; 7:10–17). These warnings by Amos were fulfilled within about a quarter of a century for the northern kingdom, when it was destroyed by the Assyrians in 721 BC. The people of the ten northern tribes were scattered in a dispersion from which they never fully returned. Southern prophets of Judah in the following century and a half – Micah, Isaiah, Jeremiah – took up the same threat. The LORD could, and would, destroy even Jerusalem itself. Jeremiah was bold enough to make this threat even in the temple (Jer. 7:1–15), citing the historical destruction of an earlier sanctuary at Shiloh as proof of God's ability to do such a thing. Such threats, when set against the cardinal tenets of Israel's faith in God's promise and God's gift of the land, must have sounded like subversive treason (and indeed Jeremiah was regarded as a traitor by some in the Jerusalem establishment). Yet they remained a constant feature of the message of all the pre-exilic prophets right up until the climactic event that vindicated them: the destruction of Jerusalem and exile of the Judaean kingdom to Babylon in 587 BC.

In this event the warnings of the law (Lev. 26; Deut. 28) and the threats of the prophets came true. And in its wake another generation of Israelites learned what it was to live without their own land, under the hand of God's chastisement. The pain of the experience of exile can be felt in passages such as Psalm 137 and Lamentations. Life without the land was scarcely life as God's people at all. In fact, it might as well be death. Ezekiel, who lived in Babylon with the first generation of those who were exiled there from Jerusalem, voiced their own words when he wrote, 'Our bones are dried up and our hope is gone; we are cut off' (Ezek. 37:11). They felt themselves to be in the grave, or like a slain army of bleached bones – dead, unburied and under the wrath of God. That's how Ezekiel addressed them in a vision as realistic about their present condition as it is breathtakingly optimistic about their future – the vision of the valley of dry bones in Ezekiel 37:1–14.

Hope and restoration

Yet Israel was still the LORD's people and, though they were now experiencing the full weight of the curse that had been written into the covenant, he had not abandoned them. The same texts that had spoken of judgment and land loss, also spoke of future restoration – restoration of the people to their God and to their land. For the LORD had not abandoned his promise to Abraham or relinquished his claim to the land.

It was the great achievement of the prophets of this searing period, especially Jeremiah and Ezekiel, to reinforce this hope, with specific reference in both cases to the land. One of the most outstandingly courageous acts of any prophet, in practical demonstration of faith in his own prophetic word, was Jeremiah's purchase of land from his kinsman Hanamel. Jeremiah bought this field (exercising the duty of a kinsman-redeemer) at a time when Jerusalem was in the last throes of its final siege and Jeremiah was cooped up in a dungeon (Jer. 32). Jeremiah himself would never set foot on it. And since he was unmarried, he had no heir to pass it on to. But his legal purchase of a plot of land was a prophetic act. It was a signpost, a tangible token of his faith in God's promise that, after the judgment of exile, 'Once more fields will be bought in this land of which you say, "It is a desolate waste, without men or animals, for it has been handed over to the Babylonians" . . . because I will restore their fortunes, declares the LORD' (Jer. 32:43–44). And so he did. The restoration of the relationship between the LORD and his people was sealed by the restoration of the LORD's people to their land – described in the visionary language of a new exodus (Is. 43:16–21; Jer. 23:7–8). The wheel had turned full circle.

The point of this rapid review of the Old Testament story has been to show that the land is one of its dominant themes. It was *not* just a neutral stage where the drama unfolds. The land, in all its dimensions – promise, conquest, shared possession, use and abuse, loss and recovery – was a fundamentally theological entity. The story of Israel is the story of redemption and we have seen that the *social* shape of Israel was part of the purpose and pattern of redemption. The same can now be said of the *economic* role of the land within the Old Testament story of Israel.[5] The land was part of the pattern of redemption too, because the social shape of Israel was intimately bound up with the economic issues of the division, tenure and use of the land. It follows that anything so important to Israel's theology as the land must be correspondingly important to Old Testament ethics. This is indeed so, as we shall now proceed to discover.

---

[5] Harry Orlinsky argues that the land is *the* primary motif of the whole covenantal relationship between God and Israel in the Hebrew Bible. Speaking about the promise to Abraham, Isaac and Jacob, he says, 'the cornerstone, the essence of the exclusive contract into which God and each of Israel's progenitors voluntarily entered, is the "Land" [ha'arets]' (Orlinsky, 'Land of Israel', p. 34). And further, 'The Israelite occupation of Canaan, then, constituted and fulfilled not just an element, even an important one, but the very heart of the covenant between God and each of the three patriarchs and, finally and for all time, the Israelite nation' (p. 41).

I would not wish to link covenant and land quite so exclusively, since I believe there are grounds even within the Old Testament itself for a vision of Israel that sat more loosely to the land as territory. And of course, a Christian understanding is bound to differ, in the light of the New Testament, from Orlinsky's Jewish theological perspective on this issue. We shall look at this more fully in chapter 6.

As long ago as 1943[6] Gerhard von Rad distinguished between two major concepts of the land in the documents of Israel's faith. He called these the 'historical' and the 'cultic' conceptions. The first was the dominant historical view found in Torah and narratives – that the land was promised by the LORD to Israel and then given to them in the course of their history. This understanding, as we have seen, goes right back to the patriarchal era. The second, which von Rad called the cultic conception,[7] was that the land was the LORD's land; he was its true divine owner. Thus he distinguished between 'Yahweh's land' and 'Promised Land', as the title of his article indicates. The clearest expression of the LORD's ownership is in Leviticus 25:23, 'The land must not be sold permanently, because the land is mine'. The context of this affirmation is the regulations for the sabbatical year and the jubilee year – years in which the LORD's sole true ownership of the land is acknowledged. Von Rad included within this cultic conception of land all the other laws concerning the first fruits of the harvest, tithes, gleanings for the poor and so on. All of these, he said, 'are certainly to be interpreted in the light of the belief that Yahweh is the real owner of the land and therefore claims a recognition of his right of ownership from human beings'.[8]

This dual aspect of Israel's theology of land (divine gift and divine ownership) provides a helpful way of classifying some of the basic principles that affected Old Testament ethics.[9] In the next two chapters we shall look at some of the practical implications in more depth. What we are concerned with here is the broad *theological* perspective on the land found throughout the Old Testament. In terms of *sociological* or *ideological* perspectives within Israelite society, things were doubtless more complex during the changing centuries of Israel's history. Norman C. Habel believes he can identify no fewer than six different ideologies of land in the texts of the Old Testament, and sees considerable conflict between them. He considers that differing theological affirmations and narratives were cherished by certain groups within Israelite society because they constituted ideological 'charters' for their partisan claims in relation to the land. However, it is possible to exaggerate

---

[6] This was the date of the original German essay, translated in English as 'The Promised Land and Yahweh's Land'.

[7] 'Cultic' is used here in the technical sense of the outward expression of religious faith – rituals and practices that people engage in to participate in the religious community.

[8] Von Rad, 'Promised Land', p. 87.

[9] Von Rad argued that the two conceptions had quite separate origins and history in Israel's traditions and texts, but this view has largely been rejected. For a full discussion and bibliography, see C. J. H. Wright, *God's Land*, pp. 5–43.

such differences.[10] Theologically and ethically we can still discern the dominant duality of divine gift and divine ownership exercising major influence throughout many strata of the canon and all eras of Old Testament history. So, to these two linked themes, we now turn.

The land as divine gift

As my rapid survey above shows, the promise of land to the ancestors of Israel and the historical fulfilment of that promise in the gift of the land to their descendants together form the major theme of the Pentateuch and early historical books. Israel had a land to live in because, quite simply, the LORD had given it to them. This strong land-gift tradition had wide implications on Old Testament thinking and practice.

Israel's dependency

In the first place, it was *a declaration of Israel's dependency*. Right at the start Abram was called to leave his native land and go to a country that, in the event, was unspecified until he got there. The patriarchal narratives emphasize the alien, sojourning state of these ancestors of Israel. 'A wandering Aramean was my father' declares the Israelite farmer, referring probably to Jacob (Deut. 26:5). Indeed, it continued to be an abiding thread in Israel's self-consciousness that they had begun and continued their journey through history as 'aliens and strangers'.[11] Israel, therefore, could make no natural, autochthonous, claim to their land. They were not 'sons of the soil'. The land they possessed they owed solely to God's election of, and promise to, Abraham – just as indeed they owed their very existence as a nation to these same two facts. These points

---

[10] Norman C. Habel, *Land Is Mine*. I shall make use of Habel's interesting and nuanced analyses of different land ideologies in subsequent chapters. However, in my view he overstresses the degree to which the different ideologies he presents are in conflict. Sometimes this is due to his assumption that all texts have ideological agendas as bids for power; sometimes it is due to an unwillingness to see certain texts as subject to critique within their own canonical context (e.g. the reports of the Solomonic settlement within the overall perspective of the surrounding Deuteronomic History). Often, it seems to me, Habel reads ideological intention into texts on the basis of an identification of the persons or parties alleged to have produced them – an identification that is sometimes rather speculative.

[11] See Gen. 23:4; Lev. 25:23; Deut. 23:7, 26:5. The same self-perception informs a certain strand of pilgrim mentality in the Christian faith also; e.g. 1 Pet. 1:1; 2:11–12.

were forcefully and unflatteringly impressed upon Israel in Deuteronomy's preparation for the conquest.[12] They must not think they had any claim upon the LORD's acts on their behalf. They had been, and always would be, utterly dependent on the LORD's love and faithfulness. If they owed their land itself to the LORD's gracious promise and gift, how much more did they owe to the same source everything else that depended on it? Let them not, then, boast in any kind of superiority or prior claim.

They could boast no numerical superiority: 'The LORD did not set his affection on you and choose you because you were more numerous than other peoples, for you were the fewest of all peoples. But it was because the LORD loved you and kept the oath he swore to your forefathers . . .' (Deut. 7:7–8). Nor could they boast of self-made wealth, and thus claim economic superiority: 'You may say to yourself, "My power and the strength of my hands have produced this wealth for me." But remember the LORD your God, for it is he who gives you the ability to produce wealth, and so confirms his covenant, which he swore to your forefathers . . .' (Deut. 8:17–18). Least of all could they boast of any moral superiority: 'It is not because of your righteousness or your integrity that you are going in to take possession of their land; but on account of the wickedness of these nations, the LORD your God will drive them out before you, to accomplish what he swore to your fathers . . .' (Deut. 9:5).

Belief in the givenness of the land, then, preserved the right perspective in Israel's relationship with their God. The LORD could not be regarded in the same way as the gods of other nations – a figurehead for their own nationalism or a merely functional protector of their military or territorial claims. Rather, the reverse: without him they would have been no nation and had no land. They and their land depended entirely upon the LORD their God. As they were to discover, on account of their moral disobedience he could bring both nation and territory to the brink of extinction, were it not for the fact that his wider redemptive purpose was unshakeable.

God's dependability

But such dependency was all right because it was placed in a dependable God. For, secondly, the land-gift was a *declaration of the LORD's dependability*. Every

---

[12] The land-gift theme is particularly prominent in Deuteronomy. For a survey of its significance in that book, see P. D. Miller Jr, 'Gift of God'. He writes, 'Here the central theological affirmation about the land is that it is the gift of God to Israel. All descriptions of it, of Israel's relation to it, and of Israel's life in it grow out of this fundamental presupposition . . . Israel's national existence, her existence as a people, depends upon this land and the grace of God' (p. 453).

harvest reminded Israel of this. This land whose produce they now enjoyed had not always been theirs. They had not always even desired it, as the traditions of their wilderness grumblings painfully reminded them. But here it was. The LORD had kept his promise to the ancestors, even in spite of their resistance. The LORD's dependability knew no limits: 'his steadfast love endures for ever' (Ps. 136).

The strength of this proven article of faith is seen not only in worship, but in the almost creedal statement placed on the lips of the farmer bringing the first fruits of his harvest to the sanctuary. It is worth savouring this 'creed' to the full. Having been instructed to place his basket of harvest produce before the altar, he is told:

> Then you shall declare before the LORD your God: 'My father was a wandering Aramean, and he went down into Egypt with a few people and lived there and became a great nation, powerful and numerous. But the Egyptians ill-treated us and made us suffer, putting us to hard labour. Then we cried out to the LORD, the God of our fathers, and the LORD heard our voice and saw our misery, toil and oppression. So the LORD brought us out of Egypt with a mighty hand and an outstretched arm, with great terror and with miraculous signs and wonders. He brought us to this place and gave us this land, a land flowing with milk and honey; and now I bring the firstfruits of the soil that you, O LORD, have given me.
>
> (Deut. 26:5–10)

What is remarkable about this declaration is that, although the occasion of it is the goodness of God in the fruitfulness of *nature*, its total emphasis is on the faithfulness and power of God in control of *history*. And the focus and climax of the recitation is the gift of the land, for the land was the monumental, tangible proof of the LORD's dependability. Here in these few succinct verses an Israelite could recount a history that embraced several centuries, moved through several national and cultural zones, and yet became completely contemporary in the harvest he had just reaped. And he could unify all of this history and harvest under this single theme of the fulfilment of God's promise in the gift of the land. There was no greater visible proof of the qualities of the God of Israel. (Would that our own Christian harvest festivals had any such sense of history and of the faithfulness of God's redemptive purpose!) Morally speaking, therefore, the LORD was a God *worthy* of obedience. The LORD's response to human behaviour would be consistent and dependable, not a matter of arbitrary whim. He could be pleased, but not humoured. The land by its very existence as the backdrop of all Israel's history was a daily declaration that the LORD was the God who kept his promise. The LORD was the dependable, faithful God. Ethics derives enormous stability in the context of such a worldview.

Proof of relationship

Thirdly, in combination of both the above points, the land-gift functioned as *proof of the relationship between God and Israel.* Israel knew they were the people of YHWH because he had given them his land. And that gift ratified the relationship written into both the covenant with Abraham and the covenant made at Sinai with the whole people. As Harry Orlinsky points out, the land was 'the cornerstone of the covenant between God and Israel'.[13]

Another way in which this relationship was expressed was by the use of the term *inheritance* to describe the land. The Hebrew word is *naḥălâ* from the verb root *nḥl.* It speaks of anything that is a rightful share, or entitlement; something legally and properly possessed as one's own. In the Old Testament the terms are used in a kind of triangular set of relationships involving the LORD, Israel and the land. Thus (most commonly) the land is Israel's (Ps. 105:11). But then, sometimes the land is the LORD's (Exod. 15:17; 1 Sam. 26:19; Jer. 3:19). Israel also is the LORD's (Deut. 32:8–9; Ps. 33:12). And occasionally, in a striking reversal, the LORD is Israel's (Jer. 10:16; Lam. 3:24).[14]

In the context of family relationships this term speaks of the inheritance passed on by a father to his son or sons. Thus to speak of the land as Israel's inheritance metaphorically implies a relationship of sonship between Israel and God. It is interesting that in the Exodus narrative God refers to Israel as 'my firstborn son' (Exod. 4:22), for whom he demands release from captivity, with the intention of bringing him to the land of promise. The Egyptian situation was intolerable. What was the LORD's firstborn son doing languishing in a foreign country when his inheritance awaited him? The language of inheritance is not found often in Exodus (cf. 15:17; 32:13), but it comes to the fore in Deuteronomy. The word frequently rendered 'to take possession of' or 'to give possession to' was commonly used in connection with inheritance. In some passages the land is explicitly called an inheritance (e.g. 4:21; 4:38; 12:9; 15:4; 19:10; 26:1), and in others Israel is called God's son or offspring (14:1; 32:5–6, 18–19; and, metaphorically, 8:5). The relational dimension is strong.

Just as the gift of the land was God's act and owed nothing to Israel's

---

[13] Orlinsky, 'Land of Israel', from the title of his article.

[14] See Christopher J. H. Wright, *nḥl,* for a concise survey of these dimensions of the term. See also Habel, *Land Is Mine,* pp. 33–35. Habel queries the popular translation 'inheritance' as too limiting, though appropriate in the family context. 'A *nahalah,* in its primary meaning, is not something simply handed down from generation to generation, but the entitlement or rightful property of a party that is legitimated by a recognized social custom, legal process, or divine charter' (p. 35).

greatness or merits, so with Israel's sonship. Israel belonged to the LORD, not because they had chosen him but because he had brought them to birth (Deut. 32:6, 18).

> What is clear is that it was not by Israel's choice or action that they are Yahweh's son, nor does the status and privilege involved derive in any sense from Israel's own action or merits . . . Israel is the firstborn son of Yahweh for no other reason than that Yahweh brought them as a nation into existence, just as they are the people of Yahweh for no other reason that that he 'set his love upon' them and chose them for himself (Deut. 7:6–7).[15]

The bond between Israel's land theology (the 'economic angle') and their unique relationship with God (the 'theological angle') is here seen at its closest. The one is, as it were, the tangible manifestation of the other.

Property rights

Fourthly, it was the historical land-gift tradition that generated *property rights* in Israel. We have already caught a passing glimpse of this in the harvest declaration quoted above. The Israelite farmer speaks of 'the first fruits of the soil that you, O LORD, have given *me*'. Not 'to *us*', but 'to *me*'. The Israelite did not think only in terms of the whole land given to the whole nation (though he could do, when referring to the national territory; e.g. Deut. 19:3; Ezek. 35:15). That concept of national territory could have been compatible with the whole land being held on the nation's behalf, as it were, by a king as their representative, as in the Canaanite system. Kings owned the land of the small city-states they ruled. But such a notion was strongly resisted among the Israelites. The gift of land percolated, so to speak, down to the lowest social level, so that each individual household could claim that its right to the land it possessed was guaranteed by the LORD himself. Thus inheritance/entitlement language was used of the small portions of land belonging to each household, as well as of the territory of whole tribes or the whole nation. These smaller family entitlements too were held as the gift of God.

This is the principle behind Numbers 26 and 34, and Joshua 13 – 19, which describe the division of the land. This is repeatedly referred to as a division 'according to their clans; that is, the subgroupings of families within the larger unit of the tribe. To us these detailed lists of land allotments may seem tedious and interminable, but for Israel they enshrined a fundamental principle: the

---

[15] C. J. H. Wright, *God's Land*, pp. 17–18. The following pages emphasize the ethical implications of Israel's sonship.

land was intended to be equitably shared out, so that every household had its part in the national inheritance. The LORD's gift of land to his people was to be enjoyed by all the people, through secure property holdings in the possession of the households of Israel. Property rights, then, were not based on natural law, commercial deals or sheer force. They were grounded in the strong land-gift theology. Land holdings were the allotments of the divine giver, and therefore were held in trust from God.

The strength of this belief is seen in Naboth's reaction to King Ahab's suggestion, which at first sight seems innocent enough to us. Ahab proposed that he should purchase Naboth's vineyard, or exchange other land for it. But Naboth's response was vehement: 'The LORD forbid that I should give you the inheritance of my fathers' (1 Kgs. 21:3). The exclamation was literally correct. The LORD did forbid it. This piece of land was not really Naboth's to give, sell or exchange. He held it in trust from the LORD for the benefit of his family. It was not just a question of 'human rights' or 'natural justice'. It was a staunch upholding of the right of a member of the LORD's people to maintain that part of the national inheritance which the LORD had assigned to his personal household. Significantly, the only way Ahab could get the vineyard was by falsely convicting Naboth of blasphemy, an offence by which he forfeited his right to belong to God's people. He was stoned accordingly, and his land confiscated (1 Kgs. 21:11–16). The whole incident shows how closely possession of a share in the land, on the one hand, and personal belonging within the covenant relationship to God, on the other, were bound together.

Prophetic anger

Fifthly, the strength of the conviction that the land was the LORD's gift also lies behind *the prophets' preoccupation with economic exploitation.* The sequel to the Naboth incident just mentioned illustrates this also. Scarcely had the dust of Naboth's stoning settled, before Elijah was bearing down on Ahab as he inspected his ill-gotten possession. Elijah's message was blunt and simple: God is angry at your compound crime and will punish you in like manner (1 Kgs. 21:17–22). YHWH was the God who had given Israel their land to be a place where peasant farmers like Naboth could live in security. Ahab and Jezebel in trampling on Naboth had trampled on that principle and replaced it with a Canaanite ethos in which a monarch could take what he or she wanted. But Naboth's fate became typical of what happened to large numbers of the ordinary populace in the following century. As Samuel had foretold (1 Sam. 8:10–18), kings would confiscate land and give it to their attendants. A wealthy royal elite arose, who made ever-increasing incursions into the traditional Israelite system of inalienable family land tenure. More and more people were deprived of their ancestral land and forced, by debt-bondage and other means, into a state of virtual serfdom on land that had once been their own but was now in the hands of the wealthy, powerful few. And it was the prophets who came to their defence, exposing the corruption and exploitation as mercilessly as it was being practised. Prophets, remember, spoke in the name of the LORD, the God who had given the land in the first place:

> Woe to those who plan iniquity,
>   to those who plot evil on their beds . . .
> They covet fields and seize them,
>   and houses, and take them.
> They defraud a man of his home,
>   a fellow-man of his inheritance.
>
> (Mic. 2:1–2)

> Woe to you who add house to house
>   and join field to field,
> till no space is left
>   and you live alone in the land.
>
> (Is. 5:8)

Everywhere you look in the prophets this vehement indignation at economic injustice is either evident or not far from the surface. In the light of the principles outlined above we can see that this aspect of the prophetic message did not stem from a general concern for human rights, though it would be evident to anyone that what was happening was grossly unfair and iniquitous. It was not even a merely economic issue: it was deeply spiritual. Anything that threatened a household's economic viability or drove them out of secure tenure of their portion of the land of the LORD was a threat to that household's secure membership of the covenant people. To lose one's land was more than an economic disaster: it struck at one's very relationship with God.[16]

And what made this worse, and angered the prophets still more, was that it was *Israelites* who were so viciously oppressing their fellow Israelites, and that they were using the land, the greatest token of God's common blessing on

---

[16] For a detailed examination of the connections between possession of land, membership of a family and belonging within the covenant community, and the practical implications at various levels of Israel's society, see C. J. H. Wright, *God's Land*, pp. 71–109.

them all, to do so. Here was a horrible perversion indeed. One section of the LORD's people was depriving another of what was the LORD's gift and every Israelite's right: freedom and land. Such internal exploitation had been forbidden in the law on the grounds of the equality of all Israelites as God's freed slaves (Lev. 25:42–43, 53–55). But now the defenceless were being devoured by an enemy *within*.

> Lately my people have risen up
>   like an enemy . . .
> You drive the women of my people
>   from their pleasant homes.
> You take away my blessing
>   from their children for ever.
>
> (Mic. 2:8–9)

Economic exploitation is a moral evil that can be condemned on the wide basis of commonly created humanity (as Proverbs does: Prov. 14:31; 17:5). But when those who are the agents and victims of the exploitation are members of the people of God, and when the means of exploitation is a supreme gift of God to his own people, then the evil is seen in all its unnatural perversion, and the vehemence of the prophets' denunciations can be properly understood.

The land under divine ownership

A cynic might be tempted to shrug off the prophets' indignation by saying that, surely, if the land had been given to Israel, they were free to use or abuse it as they pleased. Two responses can be made to this.

Grant under covenant

First, it is insufficient simply to say that the LORD 'gave the land to Israel', without taking into consideration the context of the gift, which was the covenant relationship and its reciprocal commitments. The land was an integral part not only of the LORD's faithfulness to Israel, but also of Israel's covenantal obligations to the LORD. Harry Orlinsky emphasizes this point (though his use of the term 'contract' for covenant imports some unhelpful dimensions).

> In accordance with the covenant between God and each of the patriarchs and with the people Israel, which both parties to the contract vowed to fulfill, God gave Israel the land of Canaan. This is not a gift, 'something that is given voluntarily and without

compensation, a present' . . . The Hebrew Bible regarded the covenant as . . . an altogether legal and binding exchange of obligations and rewards for each of the two contracting parties. If God became Israel's Deity and no other people's, and if He gave to Israel, and to no other people, the land of Canaan, Israel in turn had to accept and worship God alone and no other deity, powerful and attractive as so many of the deities flourishing at the time appeared. This solemn agreement on the part of God and Israel was no gift, with no strings attached – no more on the part of God than on the part of the patriarchs or Israel; on the contrary, it was a normal and valid case of give and take common to every kind of contract into which two parties voluntarily enter.[17]

Furthermore, Orlinsky argues that the verb *nātan*, normally translated 'to give', often has the more technical sense of 'assign, deed, transfer, convey' when combined with the land. As part of the quasi-legal arrangement with Israel that was constituted through the covenant with Abraham and then with Israel at Sinai, God had assigned the land of Canaan to Israel. It was not just an arbitrary and unconditional gift, but a constituent grant that formed part of the total package of their relationship henceforth. Israel's enjoyment of the covenanted *gift*, therefore, demanded their reciprocal obligations to the covenanting *giver*.

YHWH's land

Secondly, Israel could not treat the gift of the land as a licence to abuse it, because *the land was still YHWH's land*. He retained the ultimate title of ownership and therefore also the ultimate right of moral authority over how it was used. This divine ownership of the land of Canaan is hinted at in one of the earliest pieces of Israelite poetry, the song of Moses in Exodus 15. It celebrates the miracle of the exodus and looks forward to the entry into the land, which is described (addressing God) as 'your holy dwelling' (v. 13), 'the mountain of your inheritance' (v. 17) and 'the place, O LORD, you made for your dwelling' (v. 17). In other words, the land of Canaan, into which the LORD was about to bring Israel, already belonged to the LORD (not the gods of the nations resident there). Another early poem refers to 'his land and people' (Deut. 32:43), again expressing the LORD's ownership of the land.

The clearest statement of divine ownership, however, comes in Leviticus 25:23. There the LORD asserts, 'the land is mine and you are but aliens and my tenants'. The description of the Israelites' relationship to God in respect of

---

[17] Orlinsky, 'Land of Israel', p. 42. Orlinsky illustrates his point from Josh. 24; Jer. 3:19ff.; Hos. 2:20–25; and Amos 2:10–12.

the land in this verse is interesting. The terms 'resident aliens and tenants' (*gērîm wĕtôšābîm*), in normal economic discourse, referred to a class of people within Israelite society who did not own any land, being either descendants of the old Canaanite population or else immigrant workers. Such landless people were wholly dependent, therefore, on being able to reside within a landowning Israelite household. As long as the host household retained its land and was economically viable, the position of these dependents was secure. But without such protection they were very vulnerable indeed. That is why they are often mentioned in the law as needing special consideration and compassionate justice.

What happens in Leviticus 25:23 is that the LORD casts himself in the role of the landowner and the Israelites as his dependent tenants. As long as their relationship was maintained and his protection afforded, they were secure. But if they rebelled against his authority and if his protection was withdrawn, they would have to face the consequences: they could become landless aliens again. The implication was clear: 'Be careful what you do on and with my land.' Thus a *socio-economic* phenomenon (dependent labourers in Israelite households) has been taken to describe figuratively a *theological* relationship (between Israel as tenants and the LORD as landlord), in such a way that the ethical implication can be directed back into the socio-economic realm. The LORD is the divine landlord. All Israelites are his tenants. They *possess* the land (they occupy and use it); but the LORD *owns* the land. Like all tenants, therefore, Israelites were accountable to their divine landlord for proper treatment of what was ultimately his property.

Another way of looking at the claim of divine ownership on the land is to compare it with the systems of land tenure in some contemporary cultures. In pre-Israelite Canaan, for example, the king held title to the whole of his land. His subjects lived on it and farmed it as his dependent tenants, usually with a heavy burden of taxation (cf. Samuel's description, 1 Sam. 8:11–17). That whole demand of human authority is now lifted out of the reach of any human individual or group, where it results in inequality and oppression, and claimed by God alone. The whole land belongs to the LORD and therefore the LORD alone has the right to lay claim to his people's dependency. Under a *human* landowning king, people live in the equality of oppression. Under their landowning *God*, Israel lives in the equality of freedom.[18]

---

[18] This levelling feature of Israelite faith and society is found in other social contexts: YHWH is the real king of Israel; the power of human kings is thus reduced and circumscribed. YHWH is the supreme judge; human judges simply deliver his justice. YHWH is the commander-in-chief of Israel's armies; human commanders

Property responsibilities

This equality of redeemed brothers, now slaves of God, is reiterated through-out Leviticus 25. If the LORD alone ultimately owns the land, then no Israelite has the right to treat his own land as if he 'owned' it, in the sense of being able to do as he liked with it. Nor could he lay claim to the land of any other Israelite, except according to the laws of inheritance and kinship. Even a king is but a tenant in the LORD's land! King Ahab is only a fellow tenant with farmer Naboth.

So it emerges that just as, on the one hand, the concept of the land as divine *gift* generated a strong set of *rights* for both the nation and individuals, so, on the other hand, the concept of the land as under continuing divine *ownership* generated a wide range of *responsibilities*. These responsibilities can be classified broadly under three heads: responsibility directly to God; respon-sibility to one's family; responsibility to one's neighbours. Responsibility to God for the land included such things as tithes and first fruits of the harvest, other harvest laws, and the sabbatical legislation as it affected the land – the fallow year, the release of debt-pledges and the jubilee year. Responsibility to the family included the fundamental law of inalienability; that is, that land was not to be bought and sold commercially but preserved within a kinship frame-work. This principle was then buttressed by other kinship responsibilities that related directly or indirectly to land – redemption procedures, inheritance rules and levirate marriage. Responsibility towards one's neighbours included a host of civil laws and charitable exhortations concerning damage or negli-gence to property, safety precautions, respect for integrity of boundaries, gen-erosity in leaving harvest gleanings, fair treatment of employees and, indeed, of working animals. We shall look at some of these laws and their implica-tions for Christian ethics in more detail in chapter 5.[19]

So many of the detailed instructions of the law come into this category of responsibility in respect of the land, directly or indirectly, that it is easily the most comprehensive of the ethical and theological principles governing the law. It is the belief that *the LORD owns the land and demands accountability in the use of it* from his tenants that generates the literal earthiness of Old Testament

---

must fight according to his plans. Norman K. Gottwald sees this as a function of Israel's social egalitarianism. Since all the key functions of authority were assigned to YHWH, human authorities were correspondingly relativized and flattened (see Gottwald, *Tribes of Yahweh*).

[19] Further and more technical treatment of these dimensions of economic responsibility in Israel is found in C. J. H. Wright, *God's Land*, ch. 5, 'Property Owners' Responsibilities'.

ethics. Nothing you can do in, on or with the land is outside the sphere of God's moral inspection. From major issues of the defence of the national territory down to how you prune your fruit trees, every area of life is included. Based on such a principle, so simply stated (the land belongs to the LORD), Old Testament ethics could be both comprehensive and yet deeply practical and particular. This, in turn, gives enormous paradigmatic power to this dimension of the Old Testament texts.

The land as covenantal measuring gauge

Now that I have outlined the main features of the theology of the land in the Old Testament, I shall summarize the function it performed within our basic triangular framework. What is the role of this 'economic angle' in our overall understanding of Old Testament ethics? Its function can be described as a measure or gauge of the effectiveness of the other two angles. That is to say, the economic sphere is like a thermometer that reveals both the temperature of the theological relationship between God and Israel (angle A), and also the extent to which Israel was conforming to the social shape required of them in consistency with their status as God's redeemed people (angle B).

Land and God

As regards the first of these, the theological angle, there appears to have been a prolonged struggle in early Israel to bring them to realize that YHWH, the victorious God of their redemptive history, was also entirely competent in the matter of land use, rain, fertility, crops and herds. The tendency to regard the Baals of the previous occupants of the land as more likely to 'produce the goods' in the economic realm seemed ineradicable, from the conquest to the exile.

This issue is explicitly tackled by Hosea, though it can be seen as early as Elijah and as late as Jeremiah. Speaking of Israel's self-prostitution to the Baals as 'lovers', and condemning the Israelites for attributing to the gods of the Canaanites the gifts they had actually received from the LORD, Hosea declares:

> She said, 'I will go after my lovers,
>   who give me my food and my water,
>   my wool and my linen, my oil and my drink' . . .
> She has not acknowledged that I was the one
>   who gave her the grain, the new wine and oil . . .

(Hos. 2:5, 8)

The irony was that Israel did not apparently perceive this as disloyalty to the LORD, for were they not still worshipping the LORD with all his appointed festivals, sabbaths and so on (v. 11)? But such worship was hollow. Indeed, it was abhorrent to God, because it excluded him from the economic realities of daily life. The LORD was not 'content' to be merely the God of history and festivals. The LORD was God of the land and all that went with it. So the measure of the sincerity and integrity of the nation's acceptance of God's authority over them as his people was the extent to which they would acknowledge God's sovereignty in the *economic*, as well as the *religious*, sphere. Looked at in terms of the geometry of the diagram, the 'theological angle' was not complete unless lines AC and AB converged under the sole authority of the LORD. Failure to honour God in the material realm cannot be compensated for by religiosity in the spiritual realm. Covenantal loyalty required submission across the whole realm of human life on earth, on the farm as much as at the altar.

Not that there was any illusion in the Old Testament that such economic obedience to God was easy. It was one thing to celebrate the victories of God in *past* history. It was another to trust his ability to produce the *future* harvest. It was still another to trust his ability to provide you and your family with sustenance for a year if you obeyed the fallow or sabbatical year laws and did not sow a crop – or for two years if you had a double fallow at the jubilee (Lev. 25:18–22). And could you afford to let your slave, an agricultural capital asset, go free after six years, still less with a generous endowment of your substance, animal and vegetable (Deut. 15:12–18)? Were you not entitled to extract maximum yield from your own fields and vineyards without leaving valuable remainders for others (Deut. 24:19–22)? How could you possibly cancel debts after six years (Deut. 15:1–11)? Would it not ruin your own family if you had to redeem and look after the land or personnel of some incompetent relative (Lev. 25:35–43)?

The whole range of economic requirements in the Old Testament demanded trust in the providential sovereignty of God over nature, and a readiness to obey him in spite of the sorts of questions posed above (of which the Old Testament was well aware, Lev. 25:20; Deut. 15:9).

Land and people

As regards the second angle, the social shape of Israel, this can be seen at its most distinctive in economic terms. We saw in the last chapter that the introduction of monarchy compromised that distinctiveness. But monarchy per se was not utterly incompatible, inasmuch as the king could still live by, and live under, the law of God and lead the nation in the way of God's righteousness. That was the challenge a prophet like Jeremiah could still hold up to the Davidic court even in the late monarchy (Jer. 22:1–5). Indeed, theologically, the monarchy, although its human origins are seen as tainted with sin and apostasy, became a vehicle for a new set of ideas and expectations regarding the LORD's kingly relationship to his people and his future messianic purpose for them (see chapter 7). It was the baleful effects of monarchy in the *economic* realm that so dangerously threatened the distinctive social shape of Israel, as was so perceptively foreseen by Samuel (1 Sam. 8:11–17) and so destructively realized in the centuries that followed.

We have already seen some of those economic effects and the prophets' reaction to them. As they viewed the situation from God's standpoint, the prophets realized the tragedy of what was happening to God's people. A nation that allowed itself to succumb to the same economic evils as the nations around them could not function as a 'light to the nations'. It was no paradigm of the social shape of a redeemed people if it was the same shape as the nations that had none of the advantages of God's covenant and law. Worse still, it lost all moral credibility if it descended below the level of those paradigms of wickedness, Sodom and Gomorrah. Yet that is the comparison drawn by more than one prophet. Ezekiel puts Judah and Sodom in the same family as sisters, and comments, 'Now this was the sin of your sister Sodom: She and her daughters were arrogant, overfed and unconcerned; they did not help the poor and needy' (Ezek. 16:49) – a thoroughly *socio-economic* analysis. He then goes on, breathtakingly, to say of Judah, 'You have done more detestable things than they, and have made your sisters seem righteous . . .' (v. 51). The sisters, remember, include *Sodom!*

So we see that the content of the 'economic angle' in large measure acted as a test of Israel's conformity to the social paradigm of redemption that was God's purpose in calling her into existence. The prophets simply would not allow Israel to get away with claiming the blessing and protection of the covenant relationship for their society while trampling on the socio-economic demands of that relationship (cf. Jer. 7:1–11).

So, then, let me sum up what I have said in this chapter. The story of salvation in the Old Testament is not spiritual, mythical or abstract. Just as God originally created human beings to live on the earth, so he intended for his people, Israel, the vehicle of his promise of blessing to humanity, to have a land to live in. So the land has a prominent role in the whole story of Old Testament Israel. Indeed, the history of Israel in the Old Testament is the story of the land – its promise, gift, abuse, loss and recovery. We have seen that Israel held two fundamental convictions about their land: divine gift and divine ownership. On the one hand, it was the gift of the LORD to them; so they held it securely, provided they remained in covenant relationship with him. But on the other hand, it was still the LORD's land; so he held them morally accountable for their use of the land. Thus the whole realm of Israel's economic life functions as a measurement or gauge of their faithfulness (or otherwise) to the covenant demands of God. There is, therefore, an economic angle to our approach to the ethics of the Old Testament.

Further reading

Brueggemann, Walter, *The Land* (Philadelphia: Fortress, 1977).

Habel, Norman C., *The Land Is Mine: Six Biblical Land Ideologies* (Philadelphia: Fortress, 1995).

Janzen, Waldemar, 'Land', in Freedman, *Anchor Bible Dictionary*, vol. 4, pp. 144–154.

Johnston, P., and Walker, P. (eds.), *The Land of Promise: Biblical, Theological and Contemporary Perspectives* (Leicester: IVP; Downers Grove: InterVarsity Press, 2000).

Miller Jr, Patrick D., 'The Gift of God: The Deuteronomic Theology of the Land', *Interpretation* 23 (1969), pp. 454–465.

Orlinsky, Harry M., 'The Biblical Concept of the Land of Israel: Cornerstone of the Covenant between God and Israel', in L. A. Huffman (ed.), *The Land of Israel: Jewish Perspectives* (Notre Dame: Notre Dame University Press, 1986), pp. 27–64.

Rad, G. von, 'Promised Land and Yahweh's Land', in *The Problem of the Hexateuch and Other Essays* (New York: McGraw Hill; London: SCM, 1966), pp. 79–93.

Weinfeld, Moshe, *The Promise of the Land: The Inheritance of the Land of Canaan by the Israelites* (Berkeley: University of California Press, 1993).

Wright, Christopher J. H., *God's People in God's Land: Family, Land and Property in the Old Testament* (Grand Rapids: Eerdmans, 1990; Carlisle: Paternoster, rev. ed., 1996).

———, 'ereṣ', in VanGemeren, *New International Dictionary of Old Testament Theology and Exegesis*, vol. 1, pp. 518–524.

———, 'nḥl', in VanGemeren, *New International Dictionary of Old Testament Theology and Exegesis*, vol. 3, pp. 77–81.

PART TWO

THEMES IN OLD TESTAMENT ETHICS

4. ECOLOGY AND THE EARTH

In chapter 3 we saw that Israel was not to treat their land any way they liked. Although it was given to them by the LORD their God, it remained YHWH's land. He was the ultimate landlord; they were his tenants. This reciprocal relationship between God and people generated significant rights and responsibilities in the economic sphere in relation to Israel's existence on the land. Divine ownership and divine gift – these are the two fundamental theological assertions that governed Israel's understanding of their land.

Now the paradigmatic understanding of the Old Testament that we are developing in this book invites us to broaden the perspective. It invites us to look beyond Israel to the world of humanity at large, and to look beyond Israel's land to the whole earth. So the inner redemptive triangle – God, Israel and their land – is to be seen in the wider context of the creation triangle – God, humanity and the earth. And the fascinating parallel we discover is that the same two affirmations are made about the earth itself as are made about Israel's land: *divine ownership* (the earth belongs to God, Ps. 24:1) and *divine gift* (the earth he has gifted to humanity, Ps. 115:16). This double claim (that God owns the earth and that God has given the earth to humanity) must therefore be the foundation for our reflection in this chapter on the *ecological dimension* of Old Testament ethics.

But is there, in fact, such a dimension? Ecological concern is obviously high on our contemporary ethical agenda, faced as we are with the terrible effects of massive pollution, ozone depletion, carbon emissions and global warming, habitat and species destruction, deforestation and soil erosion, and all the other ghastly effects of human depredation of our natural environ-ment. The scale of such damage was unknown in the world of ancient Israel. Does the Old Testament, then, have anything to say on ecology as an ethical issue? Biblically minded Christians would wish to affirm that it does. But according to Cyril Rodd, this is just another example of how we so easily read our own ethical agendas back into the Old Testament in a way that is distort-ing and implausible.

Rodd provides an excellent survey of authors who have reflected on the ecological crisis in the light of biblical, and especially Old Testament, teach-ing.[1] He admires their passion and commitment to the cause of caring for the environment, and indeed he claims to share it. However, he does not believe that they are handling the Old Testament itself legitimately. According to Rodd, such concern for the environment was simply not there among ancient Israelites:

> Nearly all these studies . . . have attempted to turn the Old Testament writers into late twentieth-century environmentalists. They were not. It needs to be asserted as forcefully as possible that *the question of safeguarding the environment did not enter into their thinking*. To say this is not to deny that there is a keen appreciation of the beauty and wonder of the natural world in the Old Testament or that it was seen as God's world, or that the fertility of the Promised Land was seen as directly due to God's goodness, idealistic though this is. What I am claiming is that there is no *explicit* demand to *care for* the environment, because it did not occur to anyone in Ancient Israel to make such a plea. Such a demand may be implicit in the creation narratives and the 'cosmic covenant', but hardly ever (if at all) in the Old Testament are human beings urged to take active measures to conserve nature.[2]

Surely, however, it is not just implicit, but clearly explicit in the creation narratives, with their combination of subduing the earth (in Gen. 1) and keeping it (in Gen. 2). Granted, the emphasis falls on the former (subduing

---

[1] These include the following: James Barr, 'Man and Nature'; Walter Houston, 'Let Them Have Dominion'; Sean McDonagh, *Greening of the Church*; Robert Murray, *Cosmic Covenant*; Ronald A. Simkins, *Creator and Creation*; John W. Rogerson, 'Old Testament View of Nature'.

[2] Rodd, *Glimpses*, p. 249 (his italics). I find it somewhat ironic that while Rodd frequently warns us against overconfident assumptions about our ability to understand the cultural ethics of ancient Israel, he has no hesitation in making sweeping a priori statements about what 'did not enter into their thinking', or what 'did not occur to anyone in ancient Israel'. How does he know?

the earth), inasmuch as the agricultural struggle to clear land, provide irrigation and keep wild beasts at bay would certainly have preoccupied Israelite farmers. However, the quantity of material extolling the creation and humanity's role within it surely renders Rodd's very negative assessment too extreme. This further raises the hermeneutical issue of whether our ethical use of the Old Testament scriptures is confined only to those matters about which the ancient Israelites had direct knowledge or expressed active concern. Or whether it is legitimate to take matters that have become important to us, because of the passage of time, and ask what light is shed on them by the moral norms, values and objectives that clearly governed Israel's ethical response to the matters that were important to them. This latter seems to be the route we have to take if we are convinced of the abiding ethical relevance and authority of the Old Testament.[3]

So let us then see what our two broad principles have to say to the ecological issue. What does it mean to affirm that the earth belongs to the LORD, the God of Israel? And what is the responsibility of humanity within creation in view of the affirmation that this creator God has in some sense given the earth into human hands? Then, thirdly, we shall think of the effects of the fall in the natural realm and its effect on the triangle of relationships between God, humanity and the earth. And finally, we shall follow the Old Testament's own gaze into the future and reflect on its eschatology of creation. Where will it all end?

---

[3] Rodd allows for such an approach but deems it a matter of the subjective stance of the reader: 'Whether this [the implicit environmental message of the creation texts] is regarded as showing that the Old Testament writers spoke more than they knew, or whether the opposite view is taken, that it contains no true environmental teaching, probably depends on the temperament of the reader' (p. 249). But one does not have to resort to biblical authors 'speaking more than they knew'. Rather, one can assume that Old Testament writers spoke only about what they knew, but that they did so on the basis of convictions and norms, which have valid ethical claims upon people in ever-changing circumstances that go beyond what they (the Old Testament writers) knew. Without an assumption of such norms that have both longevity (they last longer than just the historical context in which a particular text was written) and fertility (they are fruitful and relevant in relation to fresh issues that could not be addressed or foreseen in the original context), all ethical discourse would have a very limited shelf-life indeed. We would be confined mostly to talking to ourselves, and every other context would indeed be 'a strange land'. This weakness in Rodd's whole approach is further discussed in chapter 14 below.

God's earth: divine ownership

> To the LORD your God belong the heavens, even the highest heavens, the earth and
> everything in it.
>
> (Deut. 10:14)

This bold claim that the LORD, the God of Israel, owns the whole universe is echoed in the familiar assertion of Psalm 24:1, 'To YHWH belongs the earth and its fulness' (my trans.), and in the less familiar claim of God himself, spoken to Job in the context of the grand recital of all his works of creation: 'Everything under heaven belongs to me' (Job 41:11). The earth, then, belongs to God because God made it. Several dimensions of this strong creation faith may be mentioned as having significant ethical implications.

The goodness of creation

That the creation is good is one of the most obvious points of Genesis 1 and 2, in view of its repetition.[4] Six times in the narrative God declares his work to be 'good'. Like a master chef bringing a multicourse banquet before admiring guests, God kisses his fingers with each new delicacy that he brings from his creative workshop, until, after the pièce de résistance, in a seventh and final verdict on the whole achievement, God declares it all 'very good'. The whole wonderful meal has been a triumph of the chef's skill and art.[5] Several things may be said to be implications of this resoundingly simple affirmation.

First, a good creation can only be the work of a good God. This sets the Hebrew account of creation in contrast to other ancient Near Eastern accounts where powers and gods of the natural world are portrayed in various degrees of malevolence, and where some aspects of the natural order are explained as the outcome of that malevolence. In the Old Testament the natural order is fundamentally and in origin good, as the work of the single good God, YHWH. Part of the meaning of the goodness of creation in the Bible is that it witnesses to the God who made it, reflecting something of his character (e.g. Job 12:7–9; Pss. 19; 29; 50:6; 65; 104; 148; Acts 14:17; 17:27; Rom. 1:20). That being the case, it is not going too far to make an analogy to the text 'He who oppresses the poor shows contempt for their Maker' (Prov.

---

[4] Ron Elsdon makes the theme of the goodness of creation the thread running through his survey of biblical material in both testaments on this issue in his book *Green House Theology*.

[5] I owe the culinary metaphor to Huw Spanner, 'Tyrants, Stewards – or Just Kings?' p. 218.

14:31; cf. 17:5 – because the poor person is also a human being made in the image of his or her Creator), along the lines of 'He who destroys or degrades the earth dirties its reflection of its Maker (because the earth is part of the creation that bears the mark of God's own goodness).'

Secondly, creation is good independently of our human presence within it and our ability to observe it. In the creation narratives the affirmation 'It is good' was not made by Adam and Eve but by God himself. So the goodness of creation (which includes its beauty) is theologically and chronologically prior to human observation. It is something God saw and affirmed before humanity was around to see it. So the goodness of creation is not merely a human reflexive response to a pleasant view on a sunny day. Nor is it an instrumental goodness in the sense that the rest of creation is good simply because it exists for our benefit. Rather, this affirmation of the goodness of creation is the seal of *divine* approval on the whole universe at every phase of its creation – from the initial creation of light (Gen. 1:4), to the emergence of continents from the oceans (1:10), to the growth of vegetation (1:13), to the function of sun and moon to mark the days and seasons (1:18), to the emergence of fish and birds (1:21), and of land animals (1:25). All of these were present in all their divinely affirmed goodness before humanity arrived. So the created order, including our planet, Earth, has intrinsic value – that is to say, it is valued by God, the source of all value. It is not just a matter of the value we humans place on the earth. On the contrary, our own value as human beings begins from the fact that we ourselves are part of the whole creation that God already values and declares to be good. There is more to be said about human life, but the starting point is that we take our value from creation, not vice versa.

Thirdly, creation is good in relation to the purpose of God for it, which has clearly included development, growth and change in 'natural history', as well as human history. Of course, the meaning of being 'good' includes the aesthetic sense that the creation is beautiful as a work of stupendous art and craftsmanship. But it also has a functional sense – something is good when it works according to plan, when it dynamically operates as it was designed to. Viewed from this angle, we should not envisage the goodness of creation as some kind of original, timeless or changeless perfection. Time and change are built into the very structure of created reality. And so are decay and death. In whatever way we will wish to articulate the Bible's insistence that death, in the fullest sense that we experience it as humans, is the result of sin, it seems incontrovertible that death in its wider biological sense in the animal and vegetable realms has been part of life on this planet from the beginning. Predation seems built in and there is no evidence that it was ever otherwise in the planet's past. This, along with so many other aspects of the way our planet functions that we find disturbing emotionally and even morally, has to be included within our theology of the goodness of creation. For this is the world as it is, the world God has definitively evaluated as good:

> Thus the ecosphere (indeed, the universe) is valued by the Source of value in all its moral ambiguity – including the predation and prodigality that are inherent parts of the dynamics of evolution and ecology, including the inseparable intertwinings of beauty and ugliness, including the combinations of destruction and construction in floods and quakes, including the ordered chaos in the structure of ecosystems, and including the 'purposive randomness' with elements of creative chance structured into generally predictable processes. But God has a mysterious purpose, and God values the creation in its ambiguous state because it contributes to that purpose.[6]

Fourthly, therefore, the goodness of creation has an eschatological dimension. Creation is not yet all God planned it to be, even apart from the effect of the fall. God built into creation an enormous capacity for procreation: inexhaustible resources of replication, fecundity and diversity. As we experience it, of course, the world is also suffering the effects of human sin, from which it longs to be liberated (Rom. 8:19–21). So Paul locates the double hope of human redemption and cosmic liberation in the glory, the will and the Spirit of God.

> The affirmation of the goodness of creation is also an expression of ultimate confidence in the goodness of God. The world now has an interim goodness. It is not to be despised or rejected or transcended; it is to be appreciated and valued as an expression of the goodness of God. It overflows with marvels and sustains diverse forms of life, for a time. Yet, it is also a world of systemic alienation, in which all life is temporary and destructive of other life. The creation needs liberation and reconciliation. To say with the Nicene Creed that 'all things were made' through Christ is to affirm that the creation as a whole has a redemptive purpose from the beginning. The creation is going on to perfection, ultimately. It is very good because it is being brought to fulfillment by a good God.[7]

We shall return to this eschatological vision in the final section.

Creation is distinct from, but dependent on, God

The opening verse of the Bible, affirming that 'in the beginning God created the heavens and the earth', implies a fundamental ontological distinction

---

[6] Nash, *Loving Nature*, pp. 98–99.

[7] Ibid., p. 100.

between God as creator and everything else as created.[8] The heavens and the earth had a beginning. God was there before the beginning. The two (God and the universe) are different orders of being. This *duality* between the creator and the created is essential to all biblical thought and to a Christian worldview. It stands against both *monism* (the belief that all reality is ultimately singular – all is One, with no differentiation) and *pantheism* (the belief that God is somehow identical with the totality of the universe; altogether, everything is God). The biblical teaching on creation is thus a major point of contrast and polemic with New Age spirituality, which adopts a broadly monistic or pantheistic worldview.

Creation, then, is distinct from God its creator, but it is also totally dependent upon God. Creation is not independent, or co-eternal. Rather, God is actively and unceasingly sustaining its existence and its functions at macro and micro levels (Pss. 33:6–9; 65:9–13; 104). The world is not, in biblical teaching, a *self*-sustaining biosystem. The 'Gaia hypothesis' as originally proposed by James E. Lovelock is a hypothesis about the interconnectedness of the whole biosphere.[9] Lovelock himself, while he suggested that the earth seems to behave like a single organism, a huge living creature, did not personalize nature. That is, he did not speak of the whole biosphere as a sentient or *conscious* being, still less as some kind of *divine* being. Indeed, Lovelock has rejected such popular religious metamorphoses of his work: Lovelock suggests that the Gaia hypothesis represents the scientific recognition of the ancient belief that the earth is a living entity. The self-organizing tendency of Gaia means that Gaia is alive, a kind of immanent mind within the processes and pathways of the earth which may be functionally comparable to the traditional idea of God as sustainer of the life of the cosmos, though Lovelock rejects any theistic interpretations of his hypothesis.[10] Nevertheless, the idea of Gaia (which is the Greek word for 'earth', and also for the goddess of that name in Greek mythology) has certainly been taken that way in popular presentations of New Age thinking. The earth itself is regarded as a goddess, endued with power, intelligence and design. Gaia is fiercely committed to her own self-preservation, and currently (but not forever) tolerates our human

---

[8] 'Ontology' has to do with the nature of being or reality, the essence of things, what anything 'is in itself'. So my statement means that the *being or essence* of God is utterly distinct from the *being or essence* of the universe. God is creator. All else is created.

[9] James E. Lovelock, *Gaia*. For a survey and critique of New Age ecological views and their influence on Christian thought, see Wilkinson (ed.), *Earthkeeping in the Nineties*, pp. 181–199; and Loren Wilkinson, 'New Age'.

[10] Northcott, *Environment and Christian Ethics*, pp. 110–111.

destructive insults. The Bible, however, portrays the whole universe as *distinct* from God (its being is not part of God's being); but yet *dependent on* God for its existence and its sustenance. God is ultimate and uncreated; the universe is created and contingent. This is not to deny that God has built into the earth an incredible capacity for renewal, recovery, balance and adaptation. Lovelock's empirical observations of this amazing capacity of the earth for recovery are undeniable. But the way in which all these systems work and interrelate is itself planned and sustained by God.

Creation de-divinized

The distinctness of creation from God not only rules out monism; it also rules out nature *polytheism*, which was much more prevalent in the cultural and religious environment of Israel. The different forces of nature were regarded as divine beings, and the function of many religious rituals was to placate or persuade these nature gods or goddesses into agriculturally beneficent action. In the faith of Israel, however, the great realities of the natural world, whether forces, phenomena or objects, had no inherent *divine* existence. Such power as they had, which was undoubtedly great, was entirely the work of the LORD and under his command. Thus, on the one hand, the fertility cults of Canaan were rejected, because Israel was taught that the LORD himself provided the abundance of nature for them (e.g. Hos. 2:8ff.). On the other hand, the immensely powerful and influential astral deities of Babylon were unmasked as nothing more than created objects under the LORD's authority (Is. 40:26). In both cases, fertility and astrology, Israel's distinctive belief about creation brought them into severe cultural and political conflict with surrounding worldviews. The Hebrew Bible, therefore, while it certainly teaches respect and care for the non-human creation, resists and reverses the human tendency to divinize or personalize the natural order, or to imbue it with any power independent of its personal Creator.

It is important to distinguish between *personalizing* and *personifying* nature. The Old Testament frequently personifies nature as a rhetorical device, a figure of speech, for greater effect. This is a literary device in which nature is spoken of *as if it were a person*. For example, the heavens and earth are summoned to bear witness to God's address to his people (e.g. Deut. 30:19; 32:1; Is. 1:2; Ps. 50:1–6), they declare his glory (Ps. 19), they rejoice at his judgment (Pss. 96:11–13; 98:7–9). Most vividly, the land itself 'vomited out' the previous inhabitants for their wickedness, and did the same to the Israelites when they followed suit (Lev. 18:25–28). But the point of this rhetorical personification of nature is either to underline the personal character of the God who created it, and who is active in and through it, or to express the personal and moral nature of human beings' relation to God. Such literary usage is not ascribing personhood or personal capacities to nature or natural forces in themselves. In fact, to personalize nature in that way (to attribute ontological personal status to nature itself) results in both depersonalizing God and demoralizing the relationship between humanity and God. To accord to creation the personal status and honour due only to God (or derivatively to humans who bear God's image) is a form of idolatry as ancient as the fall itself (see Rom. 1:21–25), though now given new characteristically twentieth-century dress in the New Age movements.

In the early to mid-twentieth century, many scholars emphasized the historical nature of Israel's faith. This included the affirmation that Israel 'demythologized' the widespread creation myths of the ancient Near East. Israel, it was argued, privileged history over nature; YHWH was the God of history in contrast to the surrounding gods of nature. Thus (according to von Rad, for example) Israel had no independent doctrine of creation; all was subsumed within the dominant redemptive-historical tradition of YHWH and Israel. While these comparisons between Israel and other nations in the ancient Near East are on balance valid, if they are pushed to extreme contrasts they do not fit the evidence. It is now well established that other ancient Near Eastern civilizations believed their gods were active in human history, and not all their gods could be adequately described as merely divinized natural forces. Conversely, it is radically distorting to the faith of Israel to regard all the creation language, metaphors and mythic symbolism we find in the Psalms and prophets as merely a way of talking about history. YHWH is unquestionably the God of the created order as well as the God of Israel's history. However, an unfortunate side effect of the earlier position was the popular view that the Bible 'desacralized' nature. This view implies that Israel had no sense of the sacredness of the created order and regarded it simply as an object to be harnessed for human benefit. This in turn is then claimed as biblical warrant for a scientific, technological and instrumental attitude to the non-human creation as a whole. Such a secularized view of nature is not at all what is meant here by the dedivinizing of nature.[11]

But there is a fundamental difference between treating creation as *sacred* and treating it as *divine* (just as there is a categorical difference between speaking of

---

[11] For a helpful discussion of the effects of this distortion in Old Testament theology, see, Simkins, *Creator and Creation*, pp. 82–88. Simkins shows that, far from creation being subordinated to redemptive history in the Old Testament, God's actions in creation actually provide the paradigm for his compassion, justice and faithfulness in Israel's history, as well as many of the metaphors through which these blessings were experienced by Israel as a whole and by individuals.

the sanctity of human life and regarding any human being as divine). The Old Testament constantly treats creation *in relation to God.* The created order obeys God, submits to God's commands, reveals God's glory, benefits from God's sustaining and providing, and serves God's purposes – including (but not confined to) the purpose of providing for human beings, or functioning as the vehicle of God's judgment upon them. So there is a sacredness about the non-human created order that we are called upon to honour – as the laws, worship and prophecy of Israel undoubtedly did. But to *worship* nature in any of its manifestations is to exchange the Creator for the created. And that is a form of idolatry against which Israel was repeatedly warned (e.g. Deut. 4:15–20; cf. Job 31:26–28), and which Paul links to the whole tragic litany of humanity's wilful rebellion and social evil (Rom. 1:25 and the surrounding context). The radical monotheism of Israel that set itself against all other gods of, or in, nature did not rob nature itself of its God-related sacredness and significance:

> From this perspective of radical monotheism in the doctrine of creation, there are no lesser divinities – not the sun and moon (against the worship of which Genesis 1:14–18 was a reaction), not golden calves and other 'graven images,' not sacred groves or ancient trees, not mighty mountains or volcanoes, not fearsome beasts or demons, not caesars or pharaohs or heroes, and not even Gaia or Mother Earth. In this view, polytheism, animism, astrology, totemism, and other forms of nature worship are not only idolatry, but also, as the prophets regularly suggested, vanity and stupidity (cf. Is. 40:12–28; 44:9–20; 46:1–11; Acts 14:15). The Creator alone is worthy of worship . . . Nevertheless, though only the Creator is worthy of worship, all God's creatures are worthy of moral consideration, as a sign of the worthiness imparted by God and, in fact, as an expression of the worship of God. The monotheistic doctrine of creation does not desacralize nature. Nature is still sacred by virtue of having been created by God, declared to be good, and placed under ultimate divine sovereignty.[12]

The glory and praise of God

'What is man's chief end?' asks the opening question of the Westminster Catechism. It then answers with glorious biblical simplicity, 'man's chief end is to glorify God and enjoy him forever'. It would be equally biblical to ask the same question and make the same teleological affirmation about the whole creation.[13] But even to ask about the end, or purpose, of creation may

---

[12] Nash, *Loving Nature*, p. 96.

[13] 'Teleology' derives from the Greek *telos,* which means *end* – in the sense of purpose or point. So a teleological view of anything enquires regarding the ends or purpose for which it exists.

seem odd, particularly to modern Western minds. For purpose or design pre-supposes intelligence, and intelligence in turn presupposes some kind of rational or personal being. And we have long thought we could do without any such personal rationality in our arsenal of explanations for the way the universe is. 'Why does the universe go to all the bother of existing?' asked Stephen Hawking, but without providing any convincing answer.[14] 'Why is there something, rather than nothing?' asks the philosopher.

Why? is of course the most basic question asked from a very early age by every child, and yet it cannot be answered from within the framework of a sci-entific view of the universe itself. Hence, in its reductionist form as developed within the canons of modernity, science generally abhors teleology; that is, seeking the *purpose* of things. Science is at its best working in the opposite direction, seeking causes and asking how things have come to be as they are. We probe ever further and ever more successfully backwards towards the origins and processes of all things, seeking to complete our knowledge of the great chain of causation. But we almost dare not probe forward to the 'end' of things, or profess to fathom what the universe is *for*. But there is surely a pecu-liar lopsided deformity about a worldview (Western science) that is stagger-ingly brilliant at discovering and explaining *how* things work the way they do, but has nothing to say on *why* things work the way they do, or even why they are there in the first place – and worse, a worldview that decrees that any answers offered to the latter questions cannot be evaluated in the realm of legitimate knowledge. To recycle the familiar analogy, it is like someone pro-viding an exhaustive and accurate account of the mechanisms and dynamics of a watch, but refusing to express a view as to what the watch might be for, and mocking those who cling to the quaint idea that it was actually designed and made by someone for the purpose of telling the time of day.

It is difficult for those of us educated in the canons of modern science to imagine how novel and peculiar is the modern denial of *telos* and purpose in the non-human world. Almost all the people who have ever lived, and most people alive in the world today whose religious and cultural traditions have resisted the secularizing influence

---

[14] Hawking, *Brief History of Time*, p. 174. Hawking's only hope, since philosophy in his view seems incapable of answering the 'Why?' question, lies in some final grand universal physical theory that will explain all the forces we find in the universe. Then, he famously concludes, 'we will know the mind of God' (which presumably is a figure of speech). This seems to me like hoping to answer the question 'Why does this painting exist?' through a comprehensive account of the physical properties of canvas and pigments.

of Western culture, believe that nature is characterized by purposive order and equilibrium which has deep moral, social and spiritual significance.[15]

The Bible suffers from no such reticence as regards its teleological view of creation. The creation exists for the praise and glory of its creator God. As creatures, we humans too share in that reason for existence – our 'chief end' is to bring glory to God, and in doing so to enjoy ourselves because we enjoy God. But that goal of human life is not something that sets us *apart* from the rest of creation. Rather, it is something we *share* with the rest of creation – the purpose of glorifying God. The only difference is that of course we must glorify our Creator in uniquely human ways as befits our unique status as the one creature that has been made in the image of God.

So all creation already praises God and can be summoned (repeatedly) to do so (e.g. Pss. 145:10, 21; 148; 150:6). There is a response of gratitude that befits not just human beneficiaries of God's generosity, but is attributed to the non-human creatures as well (e.g. Ps. 104:27–28).

> This response of gratitude is a fundamental feature of creaturely being which is shared by all the creatures of the earth, humans and animals, landscapes, seas and mountains, earth, wind, fire and rain. The Psalmist charges all things with the first moral duty of the creation, to worship and praise the creator . . . In the Hebrew perspective humanity and the cosmos have moral significance, and both are required to make a moral response to the creator, a response to God which reflects his glory and offers the return of gratitude, praise and worship [Ps. 150].[16]

Eventually, the whole of creation will join in the joy and thanksgiving that will accompany the Lord when he comes as king to put all things right (to judge the earth; e.g. Pss. 96:10–13; 98:7–9).

Furthermore, as we consider the task of bringing glory to God, it is worth noting that several significant texts link the glory of God to the *fullness* of the

---

[15] Northcott, *Environment and Christian Ethics*, pp. 165–166.

[16] Ibid., pp. 180–181. As I have said, humanity is called to praise God in ways unique and distinctive to our status as rational, moral and spiritual creatures made in God's image. Whatever it means to say that the rest of creation praises God is not of the same order. Nevertheless, I do not think we have liberty to reduce the abundant biblical affirmations that creation does praise God into merely a figure of speech (personification) that refers solely to human praise. We may not comprehend *how* creation's praise is expressed or how it is received by God, but that is no reason to deny what the Bible repeatedly affirms – the fact *that* creation praises the Creator.

earth; that is, the magnificently diverse abundance of the whole biosphere – land, sea and sky. The language of fullness is a feature of the creation narrative. From empty void, the story progresses through repeated 'fillings'. So, once the water and the sky have been separated, the fifth day sees the water teeming with fish, and the skies with birds, according to God's blessing and command (Gen. 1:20–22). Likewise, on the sixth day, after the creation of the rest of the land animals, human beings are blessed and commanded to 'fill the earth'. Not surprisingly, then, Psalm 104:24 can affirm 'the earth is full of your creatures'. And Psalm 24:1 can describe this plenitude of creatures as simply 'the earth's fullness'. So does Psalm 50:12, after an illustrative list including animals of the forest, the cattle on a thousand hills, mountain birds and creatures in the fields: 'to me belongs the world and its fullness'. Similarly, that phrase 'the earth and its fullness' becomes a characteristic way of talking about the whole environment – sometimes local, sometimes universal (e.g. Deut. 33:16; Ps. 89:12; Is. 34:1; Jer. 47:2; Ezek. 30:12; Mic. 1:2).

This usage helps us grasp the full significance of the well-known song of the seraphim in Isaiah's temple vision: 'Holy, holy, holy is Yahweh of hosts. The filling (or fullness) of all the earth [is] his glory' (Is. 6:3; my trans.). When we read this in the customary English translation, 'the whole earth is full of his glory', it is easy to think of the earth merely as a kind of receptacle that happens to be filled with the glory of God, like the temple, in verse 1, which was filled with God's robe.[17] Taken that way, only the *earth* and the *glory* are relevant nouns, joined by a connecting verb. But, as we have seen, 'the fullness of the earth' is a way of talking about the whole rich abundance of the created order, especially the non-human creation (when humans are in view, they are often added as 'and all who dwell on it' – as in Ps. 24:1). So what the seraphim celebrate is a recognition of the glory of God *in* the fullness of the earth. That which manifests the glory of God, that which displays his 'weight' or substance or reality, is the teeming abundance of his creation. The earth is full of God's glory because what fills the earth constitutes his glory. Similarly, Psalm 104:31 puts God's glory and God's works of creation in parallelism:

> May the glory of the LORD endure for ever;
> may the LORD rejoice in his works.

Of course, we would have to add that the glory of God also transcends the

---

[17] But in v. 1 there is a participial form of the verb describing what Isaiah saw; namely, 'and his robes filling the temple'. In v. 3 it is infinitive construct, 'the filling/fullness of all the earth [is] his glory'.

creation, precedes and surpasses it. As Psalm 8:1 reminds us, God has set his glory '*above* the heavens'. But the creation not only declares the glory of God (Ps. 19:1); creation's fullness is also an essential part of that glory. The same point is implied by Ezekiel's rather different vision of the glory of God, which included not only the translucent platform and resplendent throne of God, but also the four living creatures, with their four heads representative of all living creatures, of which humanity is one (Ezek. 1). This whole apparition, with its symbolic inclusion of creation, is sometimes referred to by Ezekiel as simply 'The glory of the LORD' (3:23; 8:4, 10:4 etc.). Most of us are relieved that we do not normally experience the glory of God in the way Ezekiel or Isaiah did. But recognizing the link between the fullness of the earth (the totality of all created life on earth) and the glory of God means, as Paul reminds us, that human beings are confronted daily with the reality of God simply by inhabiting the planet (Rom. 1:19–20). What we have done with that experience is another matter, of course.

So, as I conclude this section, what ecological challenges emerge from the affirmation that the earth belongs to God? Where does divine ownership impact our ethical choices? Surely there are ecological implications to regarding the created order as good in itself because of the value it has to God? It is not neutral 'stuff' that we can commodify and commercialize, use and abuse for our own ends. Furthermore, as part of the whole creation, we humans exist not only to praise and glorify God ourselves, but to facilitate the rest of creation in doing so. And if the greatest commandment is that we should love God, that surely implies that we should treat what belongs to God with honour, care and respect. This would be true in any human relationship. If we love someone, we care for what belongs to them. To love God (even to know God at all, Jeremiah would add, 9:24) means to value what God values. Conversely, therefore, to contribute to, or collude in, the abuse, pollution and destruction of the natural order is to trample on the goodness of God reflected in creation. It is to devalue what God values, to mute God's praise and to diminish God's glory.

Our earth: divine gift and human responsibility

> The highest heavens belong to Yahweh,
>   and/but the earth he has given to the sons of Adam/humankind.
>
> Psalm 115:16; my translation

The earth, as we have seen, belongs to God just as much as the heavens do. But unlike the heavens, the earth is the place of human habitation, for God has given it to us. Now, of course, the earth is the place where all God's non-human creatures also have their habitation, as Psalm 104 so evocatively celebrates. Yet the earth is never said to be 'given' to the other creatures in quite the same way as it is given to humanity. So what is it about humankind that makes us the species to whom, in some unique sense, the earth has been given by God?

It is easy to say that human beings are superior, or unique, or special. Undoubtedly so.[18] But the opening chapters of the Bible do not immediately emphasize human uniqueness. On the contrary, it seems that at point after point the Bible tells us that we have more in common with the rest of the animate creation than in distinction from it. Like the rest of the animals (including fish, birds and insects) we are blessed and instructed to multiply and fill the earth (Gen. 1:22, 28). Indeed, they were blessed and busy filling the earth before we arrived. Humankind does not even get a separate day of creation. We share the sixth day with livestock, wild animals and creepy-crawlies. God forms the animals and birds from the ground (2:19) just as he does humans, using exactly the same words (2:7). The only difference is that the man was formed *from the dust* of the ground', 'a distinction which does not obviously mark him out as superior!'[19] Humans and animals alike share the breath of life (Gen. 1:30; 6:17; 7:15, 22; cf. Ps. 104:29–30). If in our case it was breathed into our very nostrils by God (Gen. 2:7), that probably speaks of an intimacy of relationship between humans and God, not an ontological distinction between human and non-human animals (and see 7:22).

Furthermore, it is a hoary misunderstanding of Genesis 2:7 to regard it as the origin of the human 'soul', in the sense of something supposed not to be possessed by the rest of the animals. For the conclusion of the verse, 'the man

---

[18] We do need to be careful, though, in what we claim to be *unique* endowments of the human species in contrast to other species. More and more, biological research indicates remarkable capacities within other species, which we are only beginning to understand – capacities for toolmaking, for communication and 'language', for play and humour, and even, according to some accounts, for gentleness and altruism. For a discussion of the theological and ethical significance of these insights, see Spanner, 'Tyrants, Stewards – or Just Kings?' pp. 219–221. It seems to me there is no need at all to feel threatened by such knowledge. All the commonality we ever discover between humans and other animals has its origin in the fact that we share the same Creator. Our distinctiveness as humans lies not merely in this or that allegedly unique human capacity or even in a list of them. It does not, indeed, reside fundamentally in our biology at all. Biblically, our human distinctiveness resides in the theological truth that we were created by God to be God's image, and as such to rule over the rest of God's creatures.

[19] Ibid., p. 217.

became a living being', uses the same word (*nepeš*) repeatedly used of all the other living beings (1:20, 24, 28, 6:19).[20] Our essential nature as one species of animal among all the rest is highlighted, even after the splendid words of our creation, by the fact that God provides the same food for us as for the rest of the animals (1:29–30). Our commonality with the rest of the creatures is a matter not of anxiety but of wonder and gratitude in Psalm 104. For we, along with all other animals, have the same basic needs of food, water, sleep and shelter – and the Creator provides all these necessities of life in abundance for them and for us as part of his indiscriminate generosity (Ps. 104:10–30). So then, we are animals among animals. We are creatures, earth-creatures – *Adam*, from the soil, *ādāmâ* (or humans from the humus). And as such, of course, we are also a part of that fullness of the earth that is the very glory of God. Createdness is glory, not shame. Our shame lies elsewhere.

The image of God and dominion

But in the midst of all this commonality, where then does our distinctiveness lie? Only two things are said about human beings that are not said about any other creature: that God chose to make us in God's own image, and that God instructed us to rule over the rest of the creatures: 'Then God said, "Let us make man in our image, in our likeness, and let them rule over the fish of the sea and the birds of the air, over the livestock, over all the earth, and over all the creatures that move along the ground"' (1:26). And having done so, God adds to the words of blessing, multiplication and filling (already spoken to other creatures) the unique mandate to 'rule over the fish of the sea and the birds of the air and over every living creature that moves on the ground' (1:28).

At one level, this is a theological expression of what is an obvious fact – the human species is the dominant species on the planet. We have colonized almost all of its land mass and have found ways of controlling and using almost every environment we encounter. But the text affirms that this is much more than a simple biological fact, or an accident of evolution. Rather, our position within the rest of the created order is by divine purpose and mandate. God created the human species with the intention that we should occupy such a position. And by making us in the image and likeness of God, God equipped

---

[20] It is regrettable that the NIV did not take the opportunity of showing the exegetical impossibility of taking Genesis 2:7 as an alleged reference to a divinely in-breathed 'living soul' by using consistent translations in these verses. Instead, it continues to use different English words for the same Hebrew phrase; i.e. 'living creatures' for the non-human animals, and 'living being' for the man. But in both cases the word is *nepeš*. It cannot mean a 'soul' possessed by humans but not by animals, since it is used of both.

us to do so. The two affirmations are so closely linked in the text that there can be no doubt that they are meant to be related. Human beings are made to be like God; human beings are made to rule over the rest of the creation.

It is going too far to identify the two completely; that is, to argue that our dominion over nature is exclusively what actually constitutes the image of God in humanity. For human beings are, and do, very much more than all that is involved in mastering their environment. Much theological ink has been spilled on trying to pin down exactly what it is about human beings that can be identified as the essence of the image of God in us. Is it our rationality, our moral consciousness, our capacity for relationship, our sense of responsibility to God? Even our upright posture and the expressiveness of the human face have been canvassed as the locus of the image of God in humankind. Since the Bible nowhere defines the term, it is probably futile to attempt to do so precisely. In any case, we should not so much think of the image of God as an independent 'thing' that we somehow possess. God did not *give* to human beings the image of God. Rather, it is a dimension of our very creation. The expression 'in our image' is adverbial (it describes the way God made us), not adjectival (as if it simply described a quality we possess). The image of God is not so much something we *possess*, as *what we are*. To be human is to be the image of God. It is not an extra added on to our species: it is definitive of what it means to be human.

Having made that point, we return to the previous one. If having dominion over the rest of creation is not what the image of God *is*, it is certainly what being the image of God *enables*. Among the many implications of being made in God's image, this is the one that Genesis puts in the foreground: having been made by God in God's own image, human beings are instructed and equipped to exercise dominion. Or, to put it the other way round, because God *intended* this last-created species, the human species, to exercise dominion over the rest of his creatures, for that express reason God purposefully created this species alone in his own image.[21]

---

[21] Exegetically, when two 'jussive' clauses (clauses like 'Let something happen' or 'Let us do something') follow one another with a simple conjunction, the overall sense can be to make the second the intended result of the first, or what the first enables to happen. So we might say, 'Let's send Jane to university for a good education, and let her enter a well-paid profession.' There is more to a university education than just getting a good job. But it equips you for it. Similarly, the thrust of God's two statements could be taken as 'Let us make human beings in our own image and likeness, *so that* they may exercise dominion over the rest of creation.' The two are not identical, but the first intentionally enables the second.

So God instructs the human species not only to fill the earth (an instruction given to the other creatures, as we saw), but also to subdue it and to rule over the rest of the creatures. The words *kābaš* and *rādâ* are often noted as strong words, implying both exertion and effort and the imposing of will upon another. However, they are not, as contemporary ecological mythology likes to caricature, terms that imply violence or abuse. The source of this widespread idea that Christianity bears major responsibility for our ecological crisis because of its instrumentalist view of nature, allegedly rooted in Genesis 1:28, goes back to the frequently reproduced and much-quoted article by Lynn White, 'Ecologic Crisis', in 1967. It has been answered by many others since, and has been shown to be based on a misunderstanding of the Hebrew text of Genesis. James Barr, for example, in 1972, showed that

> Man's 'dominion' contains no markedly exploitative aspect; it approximates to the well-known Oriental idea of the Shepherd King . . . The Jewish-Christian doctrine of creation is therefore much less responsible for the ecological crisis than is suggested by arguments such as those of Lynn White. On the contrary, the biblical foundations of that doctrine would tend in the opposite direction, away from a licence to exploit and towards a duty to respect and to protect.[22]

The idea that *kābaš* and *rādâ* could imply violent abuse and exploitation, and the accusation that Christianity is therefore an intrinsically eco-hostile religion, is relatively recent. By far the dominant interpretation of these words in both Jewish and Christian tradition down through the centuries has been that they entail benevolent care for the rest of creation as entrusted into human custodianship.[23] On one level, *kābaš* authorizes humans to do what every other species on earth does – utilize its environment for life and survival. *All* species in some way or another 'subdue the earth', to the varying degrees necessary for their own prospering. That is the very nature of life on earth. As applied to humans in this verse, it probably implies no more than the task of agriculture. That humans have developed tools and technology to pursue their own form of 'subduing' the earth for human benefit is no different in principle from what other species do, though clearly vastly different in degree and impact on the total ecosphere.

The term *rādâ* is more distinctive. It certainly describes a role and function for human beings that is entrusted to no other species – the function of

---

[22] Barr, 'Man and Nature', pp. 22, 30.

[23] For a survey of representative expressions of this view in Christian history, see Nash, *Loving Nature*, ch. 3, 'The Ecological Complaint against Christianity'.

ruling, or exercising dominion. It seems clear that God here passes on to human hands a delegated form of God's own kingly authority over the whole of his creation. It is commonly pointed out that kings and emperors in ancient times (and even dictators in modern times) would set up an image of themselves in far-flung corners of their domains to signify their sovereignty over that territory and its people. The image represented the authority of the true king. Similarly, God installs the human species as the image, within creation, of the authority that finally belongs to God, creator and owner of the earth.

Even apart from that analogy, Genesis describes God's work in regal terms, even without using the word 'king'. God's creating work exudes wisdom in planning, power in execution, and goodness in completion. These are the very qualities Psalm 145 exalts in 'my God the King', in relation to all his created works. There is a righteousness and benevolence inherent in God's kingly power that is exercised towards all he has made. 'These are, of course, royal qualities; without using the word, the author of Gen 1 celebrates the Creator as *King*, supreme in all the qualities which belong to the ideal of kingship, just as truly as Psalms 93 and 95–100 celebrate the divine King as Creator.'[24] So the natural assumption, then, is that a creature made in the image of this God will reflect these same qualities in carrying out the mandate of delegated dominion. Whatever way this human dominion is to be exercised, it must reflect the character and values of God's own kingship. 'The "image" is a kingly pattern, and the kind of rule which God entrusted to human kind is that proper to the ideals of kingship. *The ideals*, not the abuses or failures: not tyranny or arbitrary manipulation and exploitation of subjects, but a rule governed by justice, mercy and true concern for the welfare of all.'[25]

So then, human dominion over the rest of creation is to be an exercise of kingship that reflects God's own kingship. The image of God is not a licence for abuse based on arrogant supremacy, but a pattern that commits us to humble reflection of the character of God:

> This understanding turns our supremacism upside-down, for if we resemble God in that we have dominion, we must be called to be 'imitators of God' (Eph. 5:1) in the way we exercise it. Indeed, far from giving us a free hand on the earth, the *imago Dei* constrains us. We must be kings, not tyrants – if we become the latter we deny, and even destroy, the image in us. How, then, does God exercise dominion? Psalm 145 tells us that God is gracious, compassionate, good, faithful, loving, generous, and

---

[24] Murray, *Cosmic Covenant*, p. 98 (his italics).

[25] Ibid.

protective, not to humankind only but to 'all he has made'. God's characteristic act is to bless, and it is God's constant care that ensures that the cattle, the lions, and even the birds are fed and watered (Ps. 104; Matt. 5:26).[26]

Servant-kingship

What sort of kingship does the Old Testament set before us as a model for human exercise of dominion over creation? Possibly the most succinct statement of the ideal comes from the older and wiser advisors of the young King Rehoboam, when his northern subjects sought relief from the oppressive policies of his father Solomon. This is how they told him to be king: 'If today you will be a servant to these people and serve them . . . they will always be your servants' (1 Kgs. 12:7). Mutual servanthood was the ideal. Yes, it was the duty of the people to serve and obey the king, but his primary duty of kingship was to serve them, to care for their needs, provide justice and protection, and avoid oppression, violence and exploitation. A king exists for the benefit of his people, not vice versa. The metaphor that expressed this, and which was common throughout the ancient Near East and not just in Israel as a metaphor for kingly rule, was that of the *shepherd*. Kings were shepherds of their people. Sheep need to follow their shepherd, but the primary responsibility of shepherds is to care for the sheep, not to exploit or abuse them. The very word 'shepherd' speaks of responsibility, more than of rights and powers. So Ezekiel, in his fierce denunciation of the past kings of Israel describes them as shepherds who had exploited their flock with neither compassion nor conscience. In the process, he gives a superb metaphorical description of what true kingship ought to look like, and says that ultimately only God, and God's appointed Davidic king, will be competent to exercise it (Ezek. 34).

So, human dominion within creation, if it is a form of kingship, must be modelled on this biblical pattern:

> If we have dominion over God's other creatures, then we are called to live in peace with them, as good shepherds and humble servants. We cannot say that we are made in the image of God and then use that as our pretext to abuse, neglect, or even belittle other species, when God does none of those things. As kings, we have the power of life and death over them, and the right to exercise it in accordance with the principles of justice and mercy; but we have the parallel duty, not only to God but to them, to love them and protect them.[27]

---

[26] Spanner, 'Tyrants, Stewards – or Just Kings?' p. 222.

[27] Ibid., p. 224.

It is worth noting that this concept of servant-kingship as the appropriate stance for humans towards the rest of creation is preferable to the more frequently used 'stewardship' model. The teaching that we are supposed to be 'stewards of creation' is very widespread and popular, and of course contains some fundamental biblical truth. Above all it points to the fact that we are not *owners* of the earth. Rather, it has been *entrusted* to our care by the One who truly owns it. However, the concept of stewardship is vulnerable to some misunderstandings and abuse. At the least harmful end is the fact that 'stewardship' is commonly used in Christian circles in some cultural contexts only as a term implying appeals for money ('stewardship campaigns'). At the more harmful end the word is sometimes used in non-Christian circles to give a moral aura to what may be unscrupulous exploitation of resources. It is a word that speaks of the management of things, rather than of caring relationships.

> The problem is that this model [stewardship] does not really challenge the prevailing ethos of our science, which is reductive, and of our technology, which is exploitative. It no more than qualifies the modern idea that the world and its non-human inhabitants are a resource for our use: yes, they are a resource but they belong to God; yes, we can use them, but we must use them with care. Nor does it challenge our supremacism: we think of a steward as other than and superior to the property he or she manages. A king, on the other hand, does not manage things: he rules over living beings. He too must answer to God, but he also has obligations to his subjects.[28]

So let us remind ourselves that the creation mandate was not to be stewards of the earth, but to 'rule over' the other creatures. Our appropriate and biblically authorized model, therefore, is that of kingship, providing we take seriously the full biblical teaching on what kings were supposed to be and do, as servants of those they ruled.

A further dimension of the Old Testament concept of kingship was that it was to be exercised particularly on behalf of the weak and powerless. Psalm 72 prays that God will endow the king with justice so that he can defend the afflicted and the needy. The essential nature of justice as conceived in the Old Testament is not blind impartiality, but intervening to set things right, such that those who have been wronged are vindicated, those who are being oppressed are delivered, those who are weak and vulnerable have their voices heard and

---

[28] Ibid., p. 222. Jim Ball offers a helpful chart of different evangelical approaches to the meaning of 'stewardship', from that which sees the rest of creation as nothing more than a resource for humans that can be exploited to the maximum, to that which emphasizes the servanthood model discussed here. See J. Ball, 'Ecological Crisis', p. 230.

their case attended to. Jeremiah 21:11 – 22:5 holds out these ideals as the criteria by which the Jerusalem monarchy will stand or fall in God's sight. Solomon, at the more optimistic beginning of his monarchy, asked God for wisdom to administer justice as his most urgent need if he was to govern well (1 Kgs. 3:5–12). The narrator goes on to illustrate how effectively God answered his prayer by the story of his wisdom in the case of two prostitutes and their babies – a story of royal power at work for the most vulnerable that was acknowledged by the people as 'wisdom from God to administer justice' (1 Kgs. 3:16–28). And in the climactic chapter of the book of Proverbs the wisdom of King Lemuel's mother holds up the essential challenge of kingship:

> Speak up for those who cannot speak for themselves,
>   for the rights of all who are destitute.
> Speak up and judge fairly;
>   defend the rights of the poor and needy.
>
> (Prov. 31:8–9)

Accordingly, to rule over the rest of creation as king, to act as the image of God the King, is to do biblical justice in relation to the non-human creation. And doing justice must involve particular concern for the weak and defenceless. 'Speak up for those who cannot speak for themselves' is a task of human kingship that could as relevantly describe our responsibility towards the rest of creation as to the human subjects of a ruler.[29] To be the voice of the voiceless is assuredly part of the motivation of Christians involved in ecological action, in protection of species and their habitats, in environmental advocacy, etc.

Indeed, such compassionate justice is to be the mark not only of kings in the Old Testament but of all human ethical behaviour. And at least one text specifically extends the scope of such ethical duties beyond human relations to animals:

> The righteous person knows the 'soul' (*nepeš*) of his cattle,
>   but the compassion of the wicked person is cruel.
>
> (Prov. 12:10; my trans.)

Nepeš here seems to mean the inner, unspoken, feelings and needs of the animal (as it could do for human beings). And it is a mark of biblical righteousness to pay attention to and care for ('to know') that animal *nepeš*, just as

---

[29] For a fuller moral and biblical case for this point, see Linzey, *Animal Theology*, ch. 2, 'The Moral Priority of the Weak'.

much as for fellow humans. On the contrary, the wicked (who in any case do not care about justice, Prov. 29:7) have turned compassion to cruelty.

> The implications of this epigram are profound. Of the Hebrew virtues, the most all-embracing (*ṣedeq*) and the most deeply felt (*raḥămîm*), which are used of God towards humans and of humans towards each other, are here used in speaking of right and wrong attitudes towards animals. Thus animals are brought into the sphere of human ethics.[30]

Finally, moving beyond the Old Testament, to regard our role within creation as that of kingship exercised through servanthood, reflects precisely the pattern established for us by the Lord Jesus Christ. This, of course, is hardly surprising. We are called to act as the image of God within creation, and Christ is the perfect image of God. So we find that his model of lordship was expressed through servanthood. And servanthood for him meant loving generosity and costly self-sacrifice for the sake of those he came to serve. We are familiar, of course, with this as the pattern for Christlike service to our fellow human beings. There is no reason why it is not also applicable to our Christlike exercise of responsibility to the natural world, which was created through Christ and for Christ. The Old Testament already gives us ample teaching about God's generous and loving care for all his creatures (Pss. 104 and 145 are the classic expositions). Jesus even used that characteristic of his Father as an assumption that was so axiomatic that he could build other teaching upon it (Matt. 6:25–34).[31] So we have plenty of biblical ingredients with which to build the contours of a Christlike ecological ethic. Andrew Linzey focuses particularly on Christ's model of self-giving generosity. Reminding us of key 'exemplar' texts such as Philippians 2:5–9 and Matthew 25:35–37, he extrapolates to our relationship with animals:

> It is the sheer vulnerability and powerlessness of animals, and correspondingly our absolute power over them, which strengthens and compels the response of moral generosity. I suggest that we are to be present to creation as Christ is present to us. When we speak of human superiority we speak of such a thing properly only in so far as we speak not only of Christlike lordship but also of Christlike service. There can be no lordship without service and no service without lordship. Our special value in creation consists in being of special value to others.[32]

---

[30] Murray, *Cosmic Covenant*, p. 113.

[31] For a detailed examination of Jesus' teaching and behaviour in relation to animals, see Richard J. Bauckham, 'Jesus and Animals'.

[32] Linzey, *Animal Theology*, pp. 32–33.

Indeed, Linzey argues later, it may well be that our uniqueness as the human species is to be found just here, that we alone of all the species have been endowed with the capacity of giving ourselves to the care of other creatures, reflecting God's own doing so. Linzey suggests that there is even something priestly about that, which enables us to participate with Christ in the redemption of creation. Whether or not that is going beyond the clear affirmation of the Bible (and I rather think it does), it seems a valid point to say that, certainly among other things, 'the uniqueness of humanity consists in its ability to become the servant species'.[33] And such servanthood is a properly biblical dimension of our kingship within creation.

So as we return to the foundational creation narratives, it is again impressive to note the balance that underlies what we have been discussing. On the one hand, in Genesis 1, humankind, created as the climax of the animal creation, is endowed with the necessary capacity to exercise dominion over the rest of the creatures as God's image in their midst. On the other hand, in Genesis 2, the man, created in the context of the surrounding earth and its needs, is put in the garden of Eden, 'to serve and to keep it'.[34] Dominion (ch. 1) exercised through servanthood (ch. 2): that is the biblical balance for our ecological responsibility.[35]

Human priority

It is not quite true to say that human beings were the climax of God's creation in Genesis 1 – 2. The real climax came with God's own sabbath rest, as God entered into the enjoyment of his 'very good' creation. The creation exists for God – for God's praise and glory, as we have already seen, and also for God's delight. To imagine that it all exists *for us* is an absurd arrogance, which cannot be inferred from the role we have been given: to rule over the rest of the creatures. Again, it helps to remind ourselves of the biblical view of kingship. Israelite kings did not 'own' their people, or indeed the land over which they ruled. People and land alike belonged to the LORD. So it was a perversion,

---

[33] Ibid., p. 57.

[34] This is the literal and simplest meaning of the two verbs '*ābad* and *šāmar*. The first involves work and doubtless referred primarily to the task of tilling the soil. But it is still a verb that denotes primarily service.

[35] Perhaps it is worth noting that the same pattern is to be found in the meaning of headship within marriage and pastoral leadership in the church – and both on the same Christological foundations (Eph. 5:22–33; 1 Pet. 5:1–4). In these areas also, that which most reflects the pattern of Christ is the exercise of responsibility through a servant heart and self-giving attitude and actions.

much denounced by the prophets, when kings regarded people and land as their private property and exploited both for their own enrichment. This was something Samuel warned Israel against in his sharp portrait of the corrupt tendency in monarchic rule (1 Sam. 8:10–18). So to imagine that the whole world exists exclusively for our human benefit is an utterly false view of our dominion. 'Gn. 1:26, 28 gives human beings the status of rulers of the world, but it is not a biblical view of government that subjects exist for the sake of their rulers! If anything, the reverse is the case (cf. Matt. 20:25–28).'[36]

So the creation is certainly not *solely* for human benefit. The Old Testament gives it value in relation to God directly, to glorify God and to bring God delight. The Psalms and Wisdom poets celebrate those parts of creation that human beings can scarcely witness, let alone use for their own benefit (e.g. Job 38 – 41). And even to say that God has provided the resources of the earth to feed and shelter humankind is to say no more than that God does for us humans what God equally does for the rest of the animals, birds and fish (Ps. 104).

Missiologically there are two further important points here too. On the one hand, if creation were exclusively for human benefit rather than being primarily for God's glory and pleasure, then caring for creation could be accused of being just another form of human self-serving. Now of course it *is* true that in caring for creation we ultimately also do what is best for humanity, but the task has a legitimacy of its own as well. We care for creation because we love the God to whom it belongs and because we long to see God's glory enhanced through creation and God's pleasure in creation served through our loving care. The task has validity in its own right, not merely as a way of serving our own needs.

On the other hand, some Christians would say that environmental action only has validity as a form of Christian mission if there is some consequential human benefit – preferably of an evangelistic nature. Again, we need not question that Christian environmental involvement can have powerful evangelistic results. But care for creation does not need such consequential justification in relation to humanity. It has its own mandate and validity. We care for creation because God has declared its value to himself, and because we have been instructed to do so as part of our kingly function as the species made in the image of God. Creation care is a fundamental dimension of our humanity, not an optional dimension of our Christianity. In this, as in so much else, to be Christian is to be called to be *more* human, not to behave as if the first great responsibility that God laid on the human race somehow does not apply to us.

However, having said all that, it is nevertheless clear that the Bible does

---

[36] Bauckham, 'Theology of Nature', p. 234.

recognize the uniqueness of human beings, in at least three ways. First, humans alone of all creatures have been made by God in his own image. Secondly, all other creatures have been put 'under his feet' as the creature just a little lower than the angels (or God) and crowned with glory and honour (Ps. 8:5–6). And thirdly, God declares human life to have a particular sanctity – within the general principle that all life matters to God (Gen. 9:4–6). On such texts and their assumptions Jesus could build his familiar exhortations to trust in our heavenly Father on the grounds that we are of more value than other creatures (Matt. 6:26; 10:31; 12:12; Luke 12:7, 24). 'Such sayings do not, of course, mean that other creatures are of no value. Rather, their whole force depends on the fact that animals *do* have intrinsic value to God; otherwise, there would be no point in saying that humans have more value.'[37]

Both accounts of creation in Genesis 1 and 2 point to the priority or pre-eminence of humanity within the rest of God's good and valued creation. The ordered account of chapter 1 leads up to God's decision to create humankind in God's own image, as the penultimate climax of its sequence of days. Genesis 2 puts the human creature at the centre of its whole landscape and discusses the creation of all else in relation to his physical and relational nature. The message of both texts seems clearly to be that human life is supremely important (both climactic and central) to God within the context of whole creation. Creation finds its point and its true head in this human species (a point not contradicted by the New Testament assertion that Christ is the head of the whole cosmos; for, as Heb. 2 reminds so forcefully, it is the *man* Jesus who occupies that role, fulfilling Ps. 8 as he does so).

Indeed, there is a view in science known as 'the anthropic principle'. Proponents of this principle point out that the initial conditions at the very origin of the universe, on a Big Bang understanding of it, had to be very precisely set in order to produce the relatively recent conditions in which human life has been possible on planet Earth in this particular solar system in this particular galaxy. The fact that we humans are here as an intelligent species, with the remarkable capacity to reflect not only on ourselves but on the origins of the universe itself, is the product of some very, very fine tuning at the start. To put it bluntly, if you wanted to end up with the human race, you had to be very particular about how you launched the universe. Allow any minute divergence in any direction and there would have been no universe by now: no stars, no planets, no conditions for life – and no human race. What does that tell us? The biblical Christian will say that it tells us no more than we already knew, or could guess, from the creation narrative – that God had us in

---

[37] Bauckham, 'Jesus and Animals', p. 46.

mind when he first spoke the words 'let there be light'. The scientist who declines such a teleological view of the universe cannot believe in such an anthropocentric explanation.[38]

This 'anthropic' principle need not be derided as that kind of anthropocentrism which regards everything else in creation as at our unfettered disposal and thus gives us licence to abuse, neglect, rape or destroy the natural environment. But it is a principle that resonates well with the biblical affirmation of the priority of human beings within the created order. Rejected as 'speciesism' by some Deep Ecologists, this concept of human priority has to be sensitively maintained by Christian ethics, in relation both to environmental issues and the emotive question of animal rights. The uniqueness of human beings by virtue of their definitive nature as created in the image of God means that wherever a conflict exists between human needs and those of other animate or inanimate parts of creation (*but only when it is a conflict that cannot be satisfactorily resolved by meeting the needs of both simultaneously*), then human beings take priority. Ideally, of course, we should work towards situations where a more holistic and sustainable regime can operate, where environmentally friendly forms of land and water management contribute to human flourishing, and where human benefit is pursued in harmony with the good of the rest of our fellow creatures. As we shall see below, that is part of the eschatological vision of the future, but it can also guide our ecological ethics and objectives in the present.

Cursed earth: human sin and ecological destruction

Nature and the curse

When human beings chose to rebel against their Creator, their disobedience and fall affected the whole of their physical environment. This is immediately clear from God's words to Adam, 'cursed is the ground because of you' (Gen. 3:17), to which we shall return. But in view of the connections between human beings and the rest of creation, it could not have been otherwise. Bauckham expresses the inevitable effects well:

---

[38] Hawking, *Brief History of Time*, pp. 124ff., discusses various versions of the anthropic principle (though he disagrees with them). Simply put, the principle argues, in a rather circular fashion, that the universe exists as it does because we do. If it were different in any way, human beings would not be here to observe it. It is a non-theological, non-purposive way of expressing the theological affirmation that the universe was created in such a way as to prepare ultimately for the arrival of humanity within it.

How does the fall affect nature? Is it only in human history that God's creative work is disrupted, necessitating a redemptive work, whereas in the rest of nature creation continues unaffected by the fall? This cannot be the case, because humanity is part of the interdependent whole of nature, so that disruption in human history must disrupt nature, and since humanity is the dominant species on earth human sin is bound to have very widespread effects on nature as a whole. The fall disturbed humanity's harmonious relationship with nature, alienating us from nature, so that we now experience nature as hostile, and introducing elements of struggle and violence into our relationship with nature (Gen. 3:15, 17–19; 9:2).[39]

All of these things are certainly part of our empirical experience of nature in relation to our own efforts to survive and prosper in the earth. But there is a deeper question that troubles theological minds and receives complex and not very satisfactory answers. Is creation itself fallen? Is there moral evil at work within the processes of the non-human created order, as there manifestly is within human hearts and society? Another way of articulating this is to ask whether God's curse on the earth is ontological (i.e. affecting the very nature of the planet as it now is in itself) or functional (i.e. affecting only our human relationship with the earth).

Some who argue for the former (an ontological understanding of the fall's effect on nature) then go on to attribute destructive natural phenomena such as earthquakes to the curse on the earth. This raises the chronological problem that the natural causes of such events long pre-date the arrival of the human species. Indeed, geology and palaeontology would suggest that the planet was a much more unstable and threatening environment prior to human habitation than since. Others would argue that those features of nature we as human beings find 'unpleasant', such as carnivorous species and the ubiquitous reality of predation, are also morally evil and the result of the fall. Again, the difficulty is that such natural phenomena appear always to have been part of 'the way things were' on the planet, long before humans existed, let alone sinned. Although Genesis 1:30 records God granting vegetation to animals as well as to humans for food, it is difficult to sustain the view that animals only started eating each other within the time span of the existence of *Homo sapiens* and as a result of that creature's moral and spiritual rebellion against God.

My own inclination is to agree with those who see such features of the natural order not as symptoms of sin and evil, or at any rate (in view of the fact that the Bible hints that evil was present within the creation in some form

---

[39]   Bauckham, 'Theology of Nature', p. 240.

before its entry into human life) not as the direct result of human sin, but rather as part of the incompleteness or not-yet-perfect nature of God's good creation.

> Is nature *itself* fallen? Is there, in other words, evil in nature? The fallenness of nature is a concept which has been used to explain various features of nature, such as cruelty and ruthlessness in nature itself, and nature's hostility to humanity in such forms as bacteria which live only by inflicting painful disease or destructive natural events such as earthquakes. No one who has observed the quite gratuitous cruelty of a cat paying with a mouse can be content to believe that nature is as good as it could be, apart from human influence on it. If we can interpret such features of nature as amoral rather than immoral, then we may be able to see them as imperfections, indicative of the incompleteness of the process of creation thus far, rather than as departures from God's creative purpose.[40]

The creation was never meant to be a static, perfect paradise from the beginning, but was always intended to move forward towards future perfection. The garden in Eden was not the whole planet. It was a safe and bounded environment within the earth into which God put the first humans. The implication of this limited location of Eden and the placing of humans initially within it would seem to be that the task of subduing the earth would begin there and extend outwards into a world as yet far from subdued. So it is not really biblical to imagine the whole earth at the dawn of human history as a perfect paradise, or that all the forces of nature that we find threatening or unpleasant are the result of human sin and the divine curse. Furthermore, we should note that God's curse was specifically directed at 'the ground'. The word is *ădāmâ*, which normally does not mean the whole earth (for which *'ereṣ* was more commonly used: what we would now call the 'globe') but usually refers to the surface of the planet – the place of human habitation, the soil itself.[41] This, along with the immediately following explication of the curse in terms of 'thorns and thistles' and 'sweat of the brow' points to a primarily functional curse; that is, the effect of human sin would be felt in the struggle of human existence to wrest our subsistence from the soil. Adam is at odds with the *ădāmâ* from which he was taken. This is its meaning also in the weary longing of Lamech, father of Noah (Gen. 5:29).

---

[40] Ibid., pp. 240–241.

[41] See Christopher J. H. Wright, *"ereṣ"*. On the issue of the relationship between the fall of humanity and apparent evil within creation, see also Stephen Bishop, 'Green Theology and Deep Ecology', and the response by Michael Roberts, 'What on Earth Was the Result of the Fall?' *Themelios* 17.1 (1991), p. 16.

Cosmic covenant

However, while preferring a primarily functional view of the specific curse of God upon the ground, we should not rule out wider cosmic connections between human sin (and indeed all human behaviour) and the rest of the natural order. There is a wide range of biblical material, which we are sometimes inclined to take only in a metaphorical or symbolic sense, that describes what might be called an intricate web of relatedness between God, humanity and the whole non-human creation. Robert Murray coined the phrase 'the cosmic covenant' for this biblical theme, and argues extensively for it in his book by that title. He claims to find in the Old Testament evidence for

> A belief which ancient Israel shared with neighbouring cultures, one well documented especially from Egypt and Mesopotamia: the belief in a divinely willed order harmoniously linking heaven and earth. In Israelite tradition this was established at creation, when the cosmic elements were fixed and bound to maintain order; but the harmony was broken and permanently threatened by disorderly supernatural beings and forces, hostile to God and to humankind . . . [God's promise of] his 'eternal covenant' with all creatures, expressed the belief that the cosmic harmony was the will of YHWH; but for Israel as for her neighbours, it had to be preserved in face of hostile forces.[42]

A primary text for this belief is, of course, the covenant with Noah, which ends the flood and launches a fresh start for creation:

> Then God said to Noah and to his sons with him: 'I now establish my covenant with you and with your descendants after you and with every living creature that was with you – the birds, the livestock and all the wild animals, all those that came out of the ark with you – every living creature on earth. I establish my covenant with you: Never again will all life be cut off by the waters of a flood; never again will there be a flood to destroy the earth.'
>
> And God said, 'This is the sign of the covenant I am making between me and you and every living creature with you, a covenant for all generations to come: I have set my rainbow in the clouds, and it will be the sign of the covenant between me and the earth . . . Whenever the rainbow appears in the clouds, I will see it and remember the everlasting covenant between God and all living creatures of every kind on the earth.'
>
> (Gen. 9:8–12, 16)

---

[42] Murray, *Cosmic Covenant*, p. xx.

This is explicitly a universal covenant with all life on earth, in which God binds himself in covenant commitment to humans and all other life forms simultaneously. It is the covenant within which we stand as a human race and it underpins all other covenantal promises that God will make in the course of biblical redemptive history. Furthermore, it is the covenant within which we stand *alongside* the other creatures on the planet. A covenant relationship binds us both (humans and other creatures) to God our Creator. It is therefore at least a fair assumption that God intended some form of covenantal obligation also to exist between us (i.e. not just between human beings, but between human beings and the rest of the creatures). The analogy of other covenants would suggest this: the vertical dimension of Israel's covenant relationship with God demanded a corresponding horizontal obligation in which individual Israelites were covenantally committed to one another. Genesis 9:1–6 implies some element of reciprocity in human–animal relations, though it is now clearly darkened by the permission to eat meat and the consequent fear of humanity that falls on the animal world. So although the Old Testament never explicitly states the matter in these terms, it seems appropriate to speak of human duties towards animals as covenantal, within the terms of the Noachian covenant. Murray is careful on this point, acknowledging that it is nowhere explicit, but a matter of inference. He refers to the 'eternal covenant',

> which binds humans and animals together as the Creator's partners (Gen. 9:8–17) ... One can only regret that no further implications for the mutual relations of humans and animals are drawn out. Yet it is implicit that God is seen as promising to care for both orders of creatures; and if both are God's covenant-partners, how can they not be in some sense covenantally bound to each other?[43]

This Noachian covenant is also described as 'an eternal covenant'. So it is cosmic in scope and duration. Echoes of this eternal covenant, sometimes also called the 'covenant of peace', inclusive of humans and animals in a covenant relationship with God, are found in Leviticus 26:3–6; Isaiah 54:9–10; Jeremiah 31:35–36; 33:20–25; and Ezekiel 34:25–31.[44]

Two aspects of the case Murray makes are worth noting. First, he notes that in many of the cultures surrounding Israel there was a mythological

---

[43] Ibid., p. 102.

[44] Leviticus and Ezekiel express the hope of peace *from* rather than peace *with* the wild animals, reflecting the fact that wild animals are among the feared threats to human life. However, the underlying belief is that God's intention for his creation is ultimately to remove hostility and danger both from and between animals and humans.

concept of a cosmic marriage between heaven and earth (through their respective deities), which guaranteed the fertility of the earth. In the Old Testament, even though such a view may have been entertained in the popular syncretism that was such a perennial feature of pre-exilic Israel, there was strong resistance to the sexual and fertility aspects that this generated in the religious cult. The LORD was partner to no 'sacred marriage' with any goddess, nor were such cosmic nuptials part of, or necessary to, the fertility of your soil, or your flocks, or your wife. However, Hosea could make use of the sacred marriage symbolism, but in a thoroughly demythologized way. He seems to have been the first to apply such imagery, not to the relationship between the LORD and the earth, but to the historical covenant relationship between the LORD and Israel.[45] Thus Hosea can present Israel's apostasy from the LORD in terms of an adulterous and prostitute wife's desertion of her husband; and conversely, the LORD's restoring love as the costly faithfulness of the injured husband. Hosea's own marriage provided such tragedy and restoration as a life-size model of the cost and commitment involved.

But Hosea has not just borrowed the myth and shorn it of its polytheistic and pagan pollution. For even if the myth had become perverted into the lasciviousness and cruelty of the fertility cults, it nevertheless witnessed to an underlying truth – the intrinsic connection between heaven and earth, and the inseparable links between human behaviour and the order (or disorder) of the rest of nature. So Hosea uses the language of cosmic marriage to describe the future restoration of God's people to obedient relationship and covenant commitment. Hosea 2:14–23 is replete with the imagery of marriage, and includes the technical language of nuptial consent and acceptance; namely, 'respond' or 'answer':

> 'In that day I will respond,'
>   declares the LORD –
> 'I will respond to the skies,
>   and they will respond to the earth;
> and the earth will respond to the grain,
>   the new wine and oil,
>   and they will respond to Jezreel . . .
> I will say to those called "Not my people", "You are my people",
>   and they will say, "You are my God."'
>
> (Hos. 2:21–23)

---

[45] 'Hosea is the key person responsible for harnessing marriage symbolism to prophetic covenantal thinking' (Murray, *Cosmic Covenant*, p. 78).

The metaphor is that of marriage, but the intention is both literal (the recovery of the blessings of fertility and abundance in nature) and theological (the renewal of the broken covenant with Israel). The same use of the marriage imagery of heaven and earth 'answering' each other, with effects in both the natural and social realms, is found in Psalm 85:10–13:

> Love and faithfulness meet together;
>   righteousness and peace kiss each other.
> Faithfulness springs forth from the earth,
>   and righteousness looks down from heaven.
> The LORD will indeed give what is good,
>   and our land will yield its harvest.

Secondly, Murray observes that throughout the ancient Near East, including Israel, there was a special link between the maintenance of the cosmic order and the quality of the rule of human kings. Social justice on earth was closely integrated with harmony in the world of nature. Again, in the polytheistic cultures around Israel, there seem to have been special rituals involving the king, possibly combined with the sacred marriage mythology, designed to ensure the stability of the cosmic order. There is no evidence of such rituals in practice in the texts of Israel, but there is certainly an awareness and affirmation of the link that underlies them.[46] This can be found in positive and negative forms. Psalm 72, for example, positively looks for environmental and economic well-being as a by-product of just and benevolent government. In fact, the psalm rather beautifully interweaves the prayer that the king should do justice (meaning primarily that he should act on behalf of the poor and needy – see vv. 1–2, 4, 12–14) with expectations that there will then be order and prosperity in the natural realm (see vv. 3, 5–7, 16). The same link is expressed in a more eschatological key in Isaiah 32:15–20, and of course in Isaiah 11:1–9, the great vision of the messianic age to come, when righteous government will issue in global environmental concord. So, in Old Testament thought, what the king needed to do to ensure harmony and health in the natural order was not to engage in rituals of sympathetic magic nor to mimic the supposed sexual unions of gods of earth and sky, but to govern with justice and compassion. The living God would then see to the needs of man and beast (Pss. 36:6 [in the context of the LORD's righteousness and justice]; 72; 104) .

---

[46] For more wide-ranging discussion of the use within the Old Testament of vocabulary, imagery and metaphors from the cultural creation myths that were part of the world ancient Israel shared with other nations, see Ronald A. Simkins, *Creator and Creation*.

Negatively, Hosea observes the ecological effects of human sin. He climaxes a damning list of social evils with the observation that nature itself is suffering the consequences:

> Because of this the land mourns,
>   and all who live in it waste away;
> the beasts of the field and the birds of the air
>   and the fish of the sea are dying.
>
> (Hos. 4:3)

In my view this text goes further than a mere personification of nature in response to a broken covenant, and warns its readers that wilful abandonment of the knowledge of God leads to more than merely human consequences.[47] War is especially ecologically destructive. Habakkuk 2, in the midst of a series of woes against the Babylonian excesses, includes gross environmental damage along with the normal human victims of war:

> The violence you have done to Lebanon will overwhelm you,[48]
>   and your destruction of animals will terrify you.
> For you have shed man's blood;
>   you have destroyed lands and cities and everyone in them.
>
> (Hab. 2:17)

The American deforestation of vast areas of Vietnam in the course of that war, and the Iraqi ecological atrocities in the Gulf at the end of the Gulf War of 1991, give the ancient prophetic text a chilling modern relevance.[49]

The apparent simplicity, then, of the narratives of creation and fall contain enormous depths of truth about the triangle of relationships between God, humanity and the whole created order. When combined with other texts such as I have briefly surveyed, it is clear that the Old Testament offers us a very radical assessment of the effects of our wilful rebellion and fall into disobedience, self-centredness and sin. It is not just that every dimension of the

---

[47] On the environmental significance of Hos. 2 and 4, see William A. Dyrness, 'Environmental Ethics'.

[48] 'Lebanon' almost certainly is a figure of speech for the forests that made Lebanon famous, as the parallel with 'animals' suggests.

[49] Elsdon, *Green House Theology*, pp. 102–107, gives some staggering statistics in relation to these two wars alone, in a book that is an excellent survey of the subject.

human person is affected by sin. It is not just that every human person is a sinner. It is also the case that the totality of our economic relationships with each other and of our ecological relationship to the earth itself have all been perverted and twisted. And this is so because not only are we, as humans, an integral part of the created order such that nothing we do can be unconnected with the rest of life on earth, but also because we have been placed by God in a position of dominion within creation. Therefore, just as the behaviour of the kings in Israel affected the totality of society for good or (mostly) for ill, so the way we have exercised our kingly role in creation has had incalculable effects throughout the whole of our 'domain':

> The power imbalance between male and female, the fear between God and humans and the enmity between humans and nature, are all described in Genesis 2 and 3 as originating not in the nature of things as God intended them to be, but rather in the collusion of Adam, Eve and the serpent, who together deny the goodness and sufficiency of the garden and distrust the good intentions of the creator. Even here there are also hints that the moral fall from original goodness is not exclusively a human fall, but involves other orders of being, both angelic and sub-human, for it is the serpent who is the originator of the evil thought which leads Adam and Eve to transgress the command not to eat of the fruit of the tree of knowledge. The relational community between God, humans and natural species is broken by this first act of distrust: pain in childbirth, alienation between animals and humans and the sweated labour of agricultural tillage are all said to be consequences of this original fall from the paradisiacal harmony and fruitfulness of the garden.[50]

So the creation narratives point us back to the beginning, not just to tell us what we already know (that things are not what they should be), but also to explain *why* things are not what they were intended to be and once were. However, if Genesis tells us that sin and evil, suffering and pain, violence and destruction, frustration and loss, did not constitute the first word about our world, the rest of the Bible assures us that they will not be the last word either.

New creation: ecology and eschatology

I began this chapter by pointing out the close analogy between the triangle of redemption (God, Israel and their land) and the triangle of creation (God, humanity and the earth). As we might expect, this interrelatedness is found

---

[50] Northcott, *Environment and Christian Ethics*, pp. 178–179.

not only in relation to ecological issues concerning life on earth now, but also in the Old Testament's expectations of God's redemption. The LORD is both Creator and Redeemer, and so we find the two dimensions of Israel's faith constantly interwoven. This can be seen in three ways.

Historical redemption included the land

The most devastating demonstration of the brokenness of God's relationship with Israel was the loss of their land. Predicted as early as Amos, threatened for forty years right up to the event itself by Jeremiah, the exile to Babylon in 587 BC was the most traumatic episode in the long story of Israel in the Old Testament. Exile from the land of promise seemed to negate everything they took as axiomatic in their worldview. But nothing could ever have so powerfully and effectively proved the seriousness with which the LORD took the covenant that he himself had initiated. The curses for continued and unrepentant rebellion would ultimately include the fate of scattering among the nations and the loss of their land (Deut. 4:25–28; 28:64–68).

So when the prophets, following the lead of the indefatigable hope expressed by Deuteronomy 30:1–10, pointed forward to a more hopeful future, and spoke of a restored relationship with God, it was the land itself that stood at the fulcrum of their message. Nothing could speak more eloquently of a restoration to God than a restoration to the land (though the latter would be of no use without the former). Thus, in Jeremiah 30 – 34, Isaiah 40 – 55 and Ezekiel 36 – 48, to name just the major text blocks, the promised restoration of Israel after the exile is expressed in terms of return to the land. There are many new dimensions to this fresh promise, but it never 'evaporates' into the spiritual stratosphere. Land was still part of God's redemptive package for Israel in the centuries before Christ. Renewal of their covenant relationship meant restoration to their promised land. And so it transpired through the edict of Cyrus in 538 BC.

Creation provides the paradigm for redemption

However, one feature of these and other texts (e.g. Amos 9:13–15) is the vision not merely of a return to the land as it was (that in fact turned out to be a tough new assignment for the tiny post-exilic restoration community, fraught with many disappointments), but of a renewed nature, echoing Eden itself in abundance and beauty (e.g. Jer. 31:12; Ezek. 47:1–12). In other words, as Israel's eschatology sought to express its conception of God's *ultimate* purposes, it found its most helpful resource in God's *original* purpose; namely, a good and perfect earth available for human enjoyment and blessing.

This is not surprising, for it was the characteristic way in which Israel celebrated the acts of God's redemption in their history. The exodus, as the prime example, included a literal 'defeat' of the sea in Israel's liberation from Pharaoh's army. But Israel connected this back to the widespread creation myth of the defeat of the great chaotic sea monster, sometimes named Rahab. This ancient cosmogonic myth has been historicized by Israel in referring it to the actual event of the exodus.[51] But the historical reference has not removed the creation analogy. What God had done to Pharaoh was to be understood from the paradigm of what God had done in creation, in bringing order out of chaos. So the Song of the Sea in Exodus 15 celebrates the historical event using the poetic language of the LORD's victory over the sea itself. And in the historical event God *uses* the sea as his agent of victory over Pharaoh, who exalted himself as the enemy of the LORD and Israel. 'In this manner God demonstrates a kingship and supremacy over creation and thus redeems the people of God.'[52] But since the exodus enters into Israel's whole understanding of God's redemption, past, present and future, the use of the creation paradigm to describe it is very significant. 'God's acts of redemption for the people – their deliverance from the control of the Egyptians, the guidance to the promised land, and establishment there – typically viewed as "historical" acts, are presented according to the paradigm of creation. These events are thus given cosmological significance. Israel's redemption is part of God's new act of creation.'[53]

So, when Israel later came to pray for God to repeat the performance and deliver them again from new enemies, the same appeal to the LORD as creator as well as redeemer is voiced. Psalm 74, for example, written in the appalling aftermath of the destruction of Jerusalem and its temple, appeals to the God whose power split the sea, crushed Leviathan, created the sun and moon, and established the seasons. This is the God you need when human enemies are gloating over their victory. 'According to this psalm, God's activity in creation is not only the paradigm of God's redemption of Israel, it is also the basis by which God can redeem and the reason for which God should redeem.'[54]

Almost as a direct echo of this psalm, the prophet summons God to awake and act in precisely this way again (Is. 51:9–11), binding together creation (v. 9), historical redemption (v. 10) and eschatological hope (v. 11). The prophecies in Isaiah 40 – 55 oscillate continuously between the LORD's greatness and power as creator and his faithful promises of redemption. What God will

---

[51] 'Cosmogony' refers to stories and myths that account for the origins of the cosmos – a common feature of most cultures.

[52] Simkins, *Creator and Creation*, p. 111.

[53] Ibid., pp. 111–112.

[54] Ibid., p. 114.

do for his *people* will mirror what God had done in *creation*. And God's faithfulness to his covenant promise to his people will reflect the dependability of God's existing covenant with nature (Jer. 31:35–36; 33:20–26). Also, ultimately, what God will do for his people will result in cosmic blessing and rejoicing in creation. To that point I now finally turn.

Redemption will ultimately include all of creation

I have already mentioned the glorious composite vision of Isaiah 11:1–9, in which the just rule of the messianic king will issue in harmony and shalom within the created order. Similarly, transforming expectations for the created order attend the return of the redeemed to Zion in Isaiah 35. However, the climax of Old Testament eschatological vision regarding creation is found in Isaiah 65 – 66. The words 'Behold, I am creating new heavens and a new earth' (Is. 65:17) introduce a wonderful section that has to be read in full:

> 'Behold, I will create
>   new heavens and a new earth.
> The former things will not be remembered,
>   nor will they come to mind.
> But be glad and rejoice for ever
>   in what I will create,
> for I will create Jerusalem to be a delight
>   and its people a joy.
> I will rejoice over Jerusalem
>   and take delight in my people;
> the sound of weeping and of crying
>   will be heard in it no more.
>
> 'Never again will there be in it
>   an infant who lives but a few days,
>   or an old man who does not live out his years;
> he who dies at a hundred
>   will be thought a mere youth;
> he who fails to reach a hundred
>   will be considered accursed.
> They will build houses and dwell in them;
>   they will plant vineyards and eat their fruit.
> No longer will they build houses and others live in them,
>   or plant and others eat.
> For as the days of a tree,
>   so will be the days of my people;

> my chosen ones will long enjoy
>> the works of their hands.
> They will not toil in vain
>> or bear children doomed to misfortune;
> for they will be a people blessed by the LORD,
>> they and their descendants with them.
> Before they call I will answer;
>> while they are still speaking I will hear.
> The wolf and the lamb will feed together,
>> and the lion will eat straw like the ox,
>> but dust will be the serpent's food.
> They will neither harm nor destroy
>> on all my holy mountain,'
> says the LORD.

(Is. 65:17–25)

This inspiring vision portrays God's new creation as a joyful place, free from grief and tears, life-fulfilling, with guaranteed work-satisfaction, free from the curses of frustrated labour, and environmentally safe! It is a vision that puts most New Age dreams in the shade. This, and related passages are the scriptural foundation for the New Testament hope, which, far from rejecting or denying the earth, or envisaging us floating off to some other place, looks forward likewise to a new, redeemed creation (Rom. 8:18ff.) in which righteousness will dwell after purging judgment (2 Pet. 3:10–13[55]), because God himself will dwell there with his people (Rev. 21:1–4).

This gloriously earthly biblical hope adds an important dimension to our ecological ethics. It is not just a matter of looking back to creation, but of looking forward to the new creation. This means that our motivation has a double force – a kind of 'push–pull' effect. There is a goal in sight. Granted, it lies only in the power of God ultimately to achieve it; but, as is the case with other aspects of biblical eschatology, what we hope for from God affects how we are to live now and what our own objectives should be:

---

[55] At the end of 2 Pet. 3:10 I prefer the textual reading that the earth 'will be found' to the emendation reflected in several English translations 'will be burned up'. I also find Bauckham's interpretation of this convincing; namely, that the earth will be 'found out': i.e. be exposed and laid bare (cf. NIV) before God's judgment so that the wicked and all their works will no longer be able to hide or find any protection (Bauckham, *Jude, 2 Peter*, pp. 316–322). The purpose of the conflagration described in these verses is not the destruction of the cosmos per se, but rather its purging and new creation.

The role of apocalyptic and prophecy in the Bible is not just to predict the future but to encourage and prove change and moral fulfillment in the present. The physical and ecological character of biblical visions of redemption offers hope that the restoration of ecological harmony does lie within the possibilities of a redeemed human history: this does not remove the need for social and moral effort in responding to the ecological crisis, but rather affirms that human societies which seek to revere God and to mirror his justice, will also produce the fruits of justice and equity in human moral order and harmony in the natural world. According to Ezekiel, even the driest desert can spring to life again, and the dry bones will rise up again to praise their creator.[56]

Finally, as Francis Bridger points out, this eschatological orientation protects our ecological concern from becoming centred only on humanity and reminds us that, ultimately, the earth always has and always will belong to God in Christ:

The primary argument for ecological responsibility lies in the connection between old and new creation . . . We are called to be stewards of the earth by virtue not simply of our orientation to the Edenic command of the Creator but also because of our orientation to the future. In acting to preserve and enhance the created order we are pointing to the coming rule of God in Christ . . . Ecological ethics are not, therefore, anthropocentric: they testify to the vindicating acts of God in creation and redemption . . . Paradoxically, the fact that it is God who will bring about a new order of creation at the End and that we are merely erecting signposts to that future need not act as a disincentive. Rather it frees us from the burden of ethical and technological autonomy and makes it clear that human claims to sovereignty are relative. The knowledge that it is God's world, that our efforts are not directed toward the construction of an ideal utopia but that we are, under God, building bridgeheads of the kingdom serves to humble us and to bring us to the place of ethical obedience.[57]

We might finish, however, with a poem more in the genre of the prophets and psalmists:

The groans of Nature in this nether world,
Which Heaven has heard for ages, have an end,

---

[56] Northcott, *Environment and Christian Ethics*, p. 195.

[57] Bridger, 'Ecology and Eschatology', p. 301. This article was a response and addition to an earlier one by Donald A. Hay, 'Global Greenhouse'.

Foretold by prophets, and by poets sung,
Whose fire was kindled at the prophets' lamp.
The time of rest, the promised Sabbath comes!

. . .

Rivers of gladness water all the earth,
And clothe all climes with beauty. The reproach
Of barrenness is past. The fruitful field
Laughs with abundance; and the land, once lean
Or fertile only in its own disgrace,
Exults to see its thistly curse repeal'd.
The various seasons woven into one,
And that one season an eternal spring,
The garden fears no blight, and needs no fence,
For there is none to covet, all are full.
The lion, and the libbard and the bear,
Graze with the fearless flocks . . .

. . .

One song employs all nations; and all cry,
'Worthy the Lamb, for He was slain for us!'
The dwellers in the vales and on the rocks
Shout to each other, and the mountain tops
From distant mountains catch the flying joy;
Till, nation after nation taught the strain,
Earth rolls the rapturous Hosanna round.[58]

To summarize this chapter: is there, then, an ecological ethic to be derived from the Old Testament? Is there an ecological dimension of Christian mission? In view of my survey in this chapter, I believe the answer has to be 'Yes.' We have seen that the two major theological pillars of Israel's faith regarding their own land were extended to include the whole earth. Thus the whole earth is both the gift of God to humanity, but the whole earth is also still held in God's ownership. These twin perspectives generate a rich variety of themes concerning human relationships with the rest of creation – both inanimate and also (especially) with the rest of the animals. To these two major perspectives I have added the impact of the fall on the rest of the natural creation, on the one hand, and the inclusion of the rest of creation in

---

[58] William Cowper, 'The Task', book 6, lines 729–733, 763–774, 791–797. From H. Stebbing, AM, *The Complete Poetical Works of William Cowper, Esq.* (New York: D. Appleton, 1856), pp. 344–345.

the eschatological hope of redemption, on the other. Ancient Israel may not have been anxious or fearful about the plight of the physical planet in the way we are, for the very good reason that we have made a far greater mess of it than the ancient world ever did. So to that extent many aspects of what we would now regard as urgent ecological ethical issues were not explicitly addressed within the Old Testament. Nevertheless, the theological principles and ethical implications that they *did* articulate regarding creation do have a far-reaching impact on how biblically sensitive Christians will want to frame their ecological ethics today.

Further reading

Ball, Jim, 'Evangelicals, Population and the Ecological Crisis', *Christian Scholars Review* 28 (1998), pp. 228–253.

Barr, James, 'Man and Nature – the Ecological Controversy and the Old Testament', *Bulletin of the John Rylands Library of the University of Manchester* 55 (1972), pp. 9–32.

Bauckham, Richard J., 'First Steps to a Theology of Nature', *Evangelical Quarterly* 58 (1986), pp. 229–244.

———, 'Jesus and Animals i) What Did He Teach? ii) What Did He Practise?' in Linzey and Yamamoto, *Animals on the Agenda*, pp. 33–60.

Bishop, Stephen, 'Green Theology and Deep Ecology: New Age or New Creation?' *Themelios* 16.3 (1991), pp. 8–14.

Bridger, Francis, 'Ecology and Eschatology: A Neglected Dimension', *Tyndale Bulletin* 41.2 (1990), pp. 290–301.

Dyrness, William A, 'Environmental Ethics and the Covenant of Hosea 2', in Robert L. Hubbard Jr, Robert K. Johnson and Robert P. Meye (eds.), *Studies in Old Testament Theology* (Dallas: Word, 1992), pp. 263–278.

Elsdon, Ron, *Green House Theology: Biblical Perspectives on Caring for Creation* (Tunbridge Wells: Monarch, 1992).

Gnanakan, Ken, *God's World: Biblical Insights for a Theology of the Environment* (SPCK International Study Guides, London: SPCK, 1999).

Hay, Donald A., 'Christians in the Global Greenhouse', *Tyndale Bulletin* 41.1 (1990), pp. 109–127.

Houston, Walter, '"and Let Them Have Dominion . . ." Biblical Views of Man in Relation to the Environmental Crisis', *Studia Biblica* 1 (1978), pp. 161–184.

Janzen, Waldemar, 'The Theology of Work from an Old Testament Perspective', *Conrad Grebel Review* 10 (1992), pp. 121–138.

Kraftson-Hogue, Michael, 'Toward a Christian Ecological Ethic: The Lesson of Old Testament Israel's Dialogic Relations with Land, History and God', *Christian Scholars Review* 28 (1998), pp. 270–282.

Linville, Mark D., 'A Little Lower Than the Angels: Christian Humanism and Environmental Ethics', *Christian Scholars Review* 28 (1998), pp. 283–297.

Linzey, Andrew, *Animal Theology* (London: SCM, 1994).

———, *Animal Gospel* (London: Hodder & Stoughton; Louisville, KY: Westminster John Knox, 1998).

Linzey, Andrew, and Dorothy Yamamoto (eds.), *Animals on the Agenda: Questions about Animals for Theology and Ethics* (London: SCM, 1998).

Lovelock, James E., *Gaia: A New Look at Life on Earth* (Oxford: Oxford University Press, 1979).

Marak, Krickwin C., and Atul Y. Aghamkar (eds.), *Ecological Challenge and Christian Mission* (Delhi: ISPCK, 1998).

McDonagh SSC, Sean, *To Care for the Earth: A Call to a New Theology* (London: Geoffrey Chapman, 1986).

———, *The Greening of the Church* (Maryknoll: Orbis; London: Geoffrey Chapman, 1990).

McKenzie, J. L., 'God and Nature in the Old Testament', *Catholic Biblical Quarterly* 14 (1952), pp. 18–39, 124–145.

Moss, R., *The Earth in our Hands* (Leicester: IVP, 1982).

Murray, Robert, *The Cosmic Covenant: Biblical Themes of Justice, Peace and the Integrity of Creation* (London: Sheed & Ward, 1992).

Nash, James A., *Loving Nature: Ecological Integrity and Christian Responsibility* (Nashville: Abingdon, 1991).

Northcott, Michael S., *The Environment and Christian Ethics* (Cambridge: Cambridge University Press, 1996).

Petrie, Alistair, *Releasing Heaven on Earth* (Grand Rapids: Chosen Books, 2000).

Rogerson, John W., 'The Old Testament View of Nature: Some Preliminary Questions', *Oudtestamentische Studien* 20 (1977), pp. 67–84.

Simkins, Ronald A., *Creator and Creation: Nature in the Worldview of Ancient Israel* (Peabody: Hendrickson, 1994).

Spanner, Huw, 'Tyrants, Stewards – or Just Kings?' in Linzey and Yamamoto, *Animals on the Agenda*, pp. 216–224.

White, Lynn, 'The Historical Roots of Our Ecologic Crisis', *Science* 155 (1967), pp. 1203–1207.

Wilkinson, Loren, 'New Age, New Consciousness and the New Creation', in W. Granberg-Michaelson (ed.), *Tending the Garden: Essays on the Gospel and the Earth* (Grand Rapids: Eerdmans, 1987), pp. 6–29.

———, (ed.), *Earthkeeping in the Nineties: Stewardship of Creation*, rev. ed. (Grand Rapids: Eerdmans, 1991).

Zimmerli, Walther, *The Old Testament and the World* (London: SPCK, 1976).

5. ECONOMICS AND THE POOR

'Where there's muck there's brass (or money)' goes the old country saying. Its earthy simplicity contains the truth that all human wealth depends ultimately on what God has entrusted to us in the immeasurable riches of the earth's crust. In the end, all the complexities of economic science go back to what grows on, feeds on or is dug out of the soil of our planet. We have, of course, scarcely begun to tap the resources of the oceans and their floors, or to harness the energy of the wind and the waves. The Old Testament, with its rich theology of the land (see chapter 3) and its even more foundational theology of creation and the earth (see chapter 4), is therefore bound to have plenty to contribute to Christian economic ethics. In this chapter we shall look first at the economic implications of its teaching on creation and the economic effects of the fall. Then we shall see how Israel's historical experience of redemption deepened and amplified these creation principles in the form of a comprehensive system of economic relationships. And in particular we shall explore how Israel understood and responded to the pervasive phenomenon of poverty.

Economic ethics in creation perspective

In the previous chapter we observed that the earth belongs to God, and as such it is good, valued by God, and shares with us the purpose of giving God praise and glory. Then we saw that God has given this earth into the delegated dominion of the human species, who have been made in God's own image in order to be equipped for this kingly responsibility. Placed thus on the earth, a creature among the creatures, yet a creature above all other creatures while subject to God, the human race has a God-given task. What is involved in this human task? Putting together some of the key verbs in the Genesis narratives, we are to fill the earth, subdue it, rule the rest of the creatures with the benevolent justice that reflects God's pattern of kingship, work/serve the earth and care for it. On these conditions, and with these expectations, the earth with all its resources has been entrusted to us. As we explore the texts further, the following four principles seem to emerge to govern our ethics for ecological and economic activity.[1]

Shared access to natural resources

Since the earth was given to all humankind, its resources were meant to be shared and be available to all. Access to, and use of, the resources of the whole planet constitute the legacy bequeathed to the whole human race. The creation narratives cannot be used to justify privatized, individually exclusive claims of ownership, since it is to humanity as a whole that the earth is entrusted. This is *not* to say that there can be no legitimate private ownership of material goods; we have already seen how in Israel legitimate property rights were grounded in the belief in God's gift of the land, and in its distribution to the household units. It *is* to say that such individual property rights, even when legitimate, always remain subordinate to the prior right of all people to have access to, and use of, the resources of the earth.[2] In other words, the claim 'I (or we) own it' is never a final answer in the economic moral argument. For, ultimately, God owns all things and I (or we) hold them only in trust. And God holds us answerable to himself for others who might

---

[1] 'Ecology' and 'economy' are, of course, closely related words. Both derive from the Greek *oikos*, 'home' or 'household', and have to do with the way we care for and govern our human 'home' – the planet Earth and all its resources.

[2] It is important to note that I am not suggesting that some kind of communal ownership, in opposition to any form of private ownership, is the biblical ideal. Nor am I resurrecting hoary anthropological myths about communal ownership being the norm in more primitive societies (among which Israel was once, erroneously, numbered). The pattern in Israel was certainly more geared to family and clan ownership of land than to privatized individual ownership. But even this is a long way from communal ownership. For a critique of earlier theories (occasionally still recycled) on Israel as a primitive, communal society, see C. J. H. Wright, *God's Land*, pp. 66–70.

have greater need of that which is in our possession. Ownership of land and resources does not entail an absolute right of disposal, but rather responsibility for administration and distribution. The right of all to *use* the resources of the earth seems to be morally prior to the right of any to *own* them for exclusive enjoyment.[3] Note also Robert Gnuse's comment at the end of his survey of the Israelite laws and institutions relating to property: 'Laws and moral imperatives about loans, interest, debts, slaves, land, wages, and justice in general indicate that the first concern of Israel was for human need, not ownership . . . The maintenance of property and possessions must come second to human need. Israelite law favored persons over property and possessions.'[4]

The right and responsibility of work

The command to 'fill the earth and subdue it' inescapably entailed human work. Work itself is not a result of the fall, though it was certainly affected by it. Rather, work is part of the image of God in humankind, for God, as presented to us in the creation narratives, is a worker. To be like God is to reflect God's activity as we see it in the story of creation. There we find God at work, thinking, planning, deciding, executing, evaluating, and then resting from work. Work is thus an essential, constitutive part of our God-imaging humanity. So it is our responsibility and right to be engaged in productive economic work with the material resources of the world. This means not only that we ourselves have the moral duty to work, such that voluntary, deliberate idleness is a sin (cf. 2 Thess. 3:6–13), but it surely also means that we have a responsibility to enable or allow others to work. To prevent other persons working, or to deny them work, is to offend against their humanity and the image of God in them, as well as failing in one's responsibility to God for them. Work, in this creation context, has the widest possible meaning, and certainly has to be distinguished from our modern tendency to limit its significance to paid employment.[5]

---

[3] An interesting illustration of the claimed exercise of this moral right was reported in the *New Internationalist* 107, January 1982, as 'The Campesinos' Story'. Impoverished farmers in the hills of Honduras, frustrated by government delay in implementing the Agrarian Reform Bill under which they should have received land, peacefully 'invaded' unused parts of huge estates in the valleys, owned by absentee wealthy cattle owners, and claimed them by clearing and cultivating them. The case was presented that the moral claim of their need to use the land outweighed the legal claim of private ownership of land lying unused.

[4] Gnuse, *You Shall Not Steal*, p. 48.

[5] For a very full discussion of the theological and ethical dimensions of work, see Waldemar Janzen, 'Theology of Work'.

The expectation of growth and trade

The words 'Be fruitful and increase' were, of course, spoken to human beings with reference to their own offspring and growing population. Growth in numbers, however, requires growth in material production and provision. God provided for that need, on the one hand, through the astounding and incalculable riches of the legacy God put at human disposal in the earth's crust, and, on the other hand, through the equally incalculable endowment of ingenuity and adaptability God gave to human beings themselves. So although the greatest part of human labour – in the ancient world certainly and still in much of today's world – is geared to meeting subsistence needs, humanity has always had a built-in potential to produce material goods beyond what is needed for immediate survival. Alongside this human potential is the wide variety of natural resources, climate, vegetation and soil types. If human beings were to 'fill the earth and subdue it', this was bound to lead to surplus of some products in some places and scarcity of some in others. This seems to be a natural result of the way God has enabled the planet to evolve to its present configuration of climatic regions and distribution of minerals and so on. Thus it seems that exchange and trade of commodities are natural conse-quences of human growth in all its dimensions. Being set within the context of creation commands, however, all such economic activity at every level comes within the sphere of God's concern and moral scrutiny. The resources we share, exchange and trade belong to God in the first place, and so there-fore does all the increase of them even when produced by human effort (see Deut. 8:17–18).

Fair sharing of the product of economic activity

Just as the right of access to, and use of, the *resources* of the earth is a shared right that sets moral limitations to the right of private ownership of resources, so too the right to consume or enjoy *the end product* of the economic process is limited by the needs of all. We are as responsible to God for what we do with what *we* produce, as we are for what *God* has given us 'raw'. There is no mandate in the creation material either for private *exclusive* use, or for hoarding or con-suming at the expense of others. Private dominion over some of the material resources of the earth does not give a right to consume the entire product of those resources, because dominion always remains trusteeship under God and responsibility for others. There is no necessary or 'sacrosanct' link between what one owns or invests in the productive process and what one can claim as an exclusive right to consume as income in return. There is a mutual respon-sibility for the good of the whole human community, and also for the rest of the non-human creation, which cuts across the idea that 'what's mine is mine and I am entitled to keep and consume whatever I can get out of it'.

Much more could be said on each of the four points above, of course, and much more needs to be said when specific issues in the contemporary national and global economic scene are brought into Christian debate. But these principles and their implications form a basic framework within which a biblical Christian will want to work. They lock together to form the creation stage, which supports the shifting sets and scenes of human economic history. However, to continue the metaphor, the play has not proceeded as the Author intended and even the stage itself is under threat. We now have to take account of the effect of the fall and the inroads of sin and evil on the whole network of human relationships with the earth.

Economics in a fallen world

The biblical description of the entrance of sin and evil into human life signifi- cantly includes its effect in the realm of the human relation to the earth, and par- ticularly to the soil. The event described in Genesis 3 is portrayed as having radically distorted and fractured our relationship with the earth itself, and also, as Paul points out (Rom. 8:20–21, echoing probably Ecclesiastes), as having frustrated the creation's function in relation to God. The essence of the fall was humanity's arrogant desire for autonomy, a rebellion against the authority and benevolence of the Creator. The havoc caused by this attempted reversal of status, along with the curse it brought, affected not only our spiritual relation- ship with God and our personal and social relationships with one another, but also our whole economic and material environment. I surveyed this in chapter 4. As regards our economic ethics, we can see that each of the four creation princi- ples set out above was corrupted and violated, to our own incalculable cost.

Conflict over resources
Thus, first, instead of shared and equitable access to the earth's resources, land and its resources have become the greatest single cause of strife and warfare. Some resources are hoarded by a few and denied to others. Some are squandered, polluted or abused. Possession of resources, instead of being used as an opportunity for mutual sharing, as of an unmerited gift, has become a matter of conquest and seizure, a tool of oppression, greed and power. And even land simply as territory, with little or no agricultural or mineral benefit, becomes the bone of contention in some of the bloodiest and lengthiest wars that disfigure human history. The Old Testament even portrays the arrogance of kings and emperors who claim the right of owner- ship over their resources as if they themselves had created them. Here is God's response to one absurd boast:

I am against you, Pharaoh king of Egypt,
> you great monster lying among your streams.
You say, 'The Nile is mine;
> I made if for myself.'

(Ezek. 29:3)

Corruption of work

On the one hand, this means that work in itself became toilsome and frustrating because of the curse on the earth. Work is no longer simply part of the joy and privilege of our human nature, but has become a bondage and necessity: 'By the sweat of your brow you will eat your food' (Gen. 3:19). What was given to us as a means of *subduing* the earth has now become for most people merely the agonizing struggle of *surviving* in the earth. This feature of work in the fallen world has been aggravated by changes in the very nature of work in modern times, changes caused by factors that may not *in themselves* be sinful. Industrialization and technological advance may be regarded in some senses as inevitable and not intrinsically evil, except inasmuch as they share in the fallenness of all human enterprise. But the resulting mechanization of work, with fragmented specialization, dull repetition, and alienation from the final product or its users, simply intensifies our experience of the curse of frustration that attaches to a greater or lesser degree to all human work in a fallen world.

On the other hand, it also means that human relationships in the sphere of economic work are corrupted. Work becomes a commodity to be bought and sold with little care or responsibility for the working human being. Work becomes a slave of greed, a tool of oppression, a means of replacing God with one's own ambition. Or work, originally a good gift of God to those created in God's own image, can become an idol when we try to find in it our identity and significance, or some ultimate meaning and purpose for life.

The book of Ecclesiastes has some of the sharpest insights in the Old Testament into the paradoxical nature of human work. On the one hand, it is still the gift of God, and there is no better alternative for a man than to find satisfaction in his work (Eccles. 2:24–25; 5:18; 9:10). But on the other hand, it can be fruitless and frustrating (2:4–11), wasted in the end (2:18–23), riddled with evil motives (4:4), or empty of any purpose (4:8), and is finally reduced to vanity by death (9:10). There is no more perceptive exposition of the outworking of God's curse upon the earth and its effect on human life than these observations of Ecclesiastes on the paradoxes of the human worker.

Uncontrolled growth

In our fallen state, greed and discontent mean that economic growth becomes pathologically obsessive. For those who live in obedient relationship with

God, increase of material goods is seen in the Old Testament as a blessing to be received as a gift and enjoyed responsibly; but never is it seen as a guaranteed 'reward' – indeed, some of God's most faithful servants remained materially poor. For those who live in alienation from God, however, growth in prosperity becomes an end in itself. The desire to accumulate more and more leads to social and economic oppression and violence, as Micah and Isaiah especially observed (Mic. 2:1–2; Is. 5:8). Paul was not the first to teach that covetousness is tantamount to idolatry, which is as much as to say that to break the tenth commandment is to break the first. Deuteronomy is well aware of the danger that the very blessings of God, when they increase, can usurp God's place so that God is forgotten. Having described the abundant natural resources of the land (Deut. 8:7–9), it then immediately describes the symptoms of complacent, growth-obsessed materialism: 'when you eat and are satisfied, when you build fine houses and settle down, and when your herds and flocks grow large and your silver and gold increase and all you have is multiplied, then your heart will become proud and you will forget the LORD your God' (Deut. 8:12–14).

But again, Ecclesiastes observes the insatiable thirst for more, even though wealth is so fickle:

> Whoever loves money never has money enough;
>> whoever loves wealth is never satisfied with his income.
>> This too is meaningless.
> As goods increase,
>> so do those who consume them.
> And what benefit are they to the owner
>> except to feast his eyes on them?

(Eccles. 5:10–11; cf. 5:13–17; 6:1–2)

Unjust distribution

Finally, the end product of the economic process is also manipulated unjustly. Claims of ownership are privatized and regarded as absolute, unfettered by any sense of transcendent responsibility for others. 'Am I my brother's keeper?' has become the selfish abdication of responsibility on a global scale. Resources are extracted from some countries over centuries in a way virtually tantamount to robbery. Then manufactured products, including foodstuffs, are sold back to the same countries at a subsidized cost that undercuts and eventually destroys local industry and agriculture. These grossly unfair trading arrangements are then compounded by the morally horrendous phenomenon of international debt, which contrary to all natural and historical justice, is said to be owed by the poor and plundered to the rich and rapacious. The problem is now global; but it is not new, for it was observed by the sage of Proverbs. Simply being in possession of resources is not enough. Even working hard to produce what you need from those resources is not enough. In the end, injustice can deprive you of both. Millions in our world today would testify to the simple truth of these words, which are expressed in the generic singular, but have a global relevance today:

> A poor man's field may produce abundant food,
>   but injustice sweeps it away.
>
> (Prov. 13:23)

So evil has woven its way into every aspect of humanity's economic life. Furthermore, the Old Testament hints at the extra dimension of the problem; namely, that the whole realm of the material, economic order has become prey to demonic forces, which both incite human sin and amplify and solidify its effects. The narrative of the fall portrays the personal force of evil approaching the first humans by means of the material creation and using the same material creation as a means of enticement to unbelief, disobedience and rebellion. The struggle of the prophets with oppression and injustice was not merely economic but closely linked with their struggle against the spiritual power of Baal worship. For they saw clearly how rejection of the liberating service of the LORD led instead to the service of the gods of selfish greed and cruel oppression. The battle waged by Elijah and the choice he put before the people – YHWH or Baal (1 Kgs. 18:21) – was not merely spiritual or religious. He was fighting on behalf of the victims of greedy *economic* callousness linked to religious apostasy. The tragic case of Naboth demonstrated this. It was as true in Elijah's day as it was when Jesus said the words, and is still true today: 'You cannot *serve* both God and Money' (Matt. 6:24; my italics). For it is indeed a question of which god you will serve. And idolatry will always generate injustice and oppression.

So the Christian involved in any branch of this vast and complex economic sphere of human life needs to remember that the issues are not merely material or physical. Here, as elsewhere, 'our struggle is not merely against flesh and blood' (Eph. 6:12), nor merely against the 'sweat' and 'thistles' of a cursed creation groaning in frustration. Our struggle is against spiritual powers and forces which, by their invasion of and influence over human economic relationships, structures and ideologies can wield an oppressive tyranny over humankind in this sphere, just as they hold people in the slavery of mental and spiritual darkness. Thankfully, the redemptive acts of God also operate in this sphere of human life; and so I now turn to examine the economic implications of the Old Testament's theology of redemption.

Economic dimensions to Israel's story of redemption

Already in chapter 3 we have seen the centrality of the land of Israel in their historical journey through the pages of the Old Testament. Recalling those points, we can now appreciate further their foundational significance for economic ethics.

The covenant with Noah: guarantee of this creation and prototype of new creation

Noah got his name (with its echoes of 'comfort' and 'rest') because of his father Lamech's longing for God to lift the curse from the earth (Gen. 5:29). This is a clue to the earliest biblical understanding of what God's salvation should mean. If the effect of sin had been to blight and belabour human existence in the earth by laying it under a curse, then this antediluvian ancestor points to the answer: let God remove the curse from the earth. Not, it should be noted, let us human beings escape to heaven somewhere, leaving the earth behind. The consistent biblical hope, from Genesis to Revelation is that God should do something with the *earth* so that we can once again dwell upon it in 'rest', in sabbath peace, with him. The Bible speaks predominantly of the need for God to come here, not of the wish for us to go somewhere else. This earth is to be the place of God's judgment, and also the place of God's saving power. So the flood story and its sequel becomes the sign not only of God's commitment to life on earth while it lasts (in the covenant tied up with its rainbow ribbon[6]) but also of the coming final judgment and renewal – the new creation (see 2 Pet. 3).

The significance of the 'cosmic covenant' between God and all life on earth for human economic activity is enormous. Indeed, it is foundational to economics as a science, as an activity and as an ethic. For it roots the permanence and dependability of all natural processes, including the basic cosmological phenomena of what we now know as the rotation of the earth on its axis (day and night), and around the sun (summer and winter), and the whole realm of human productive intervention (seed-time and harvest), in the covenanted faithfulness of God as creator, judge and saviour. So although we take seriously the economic effects of the theological affirmation that we live on a *cursed* earth, we also welcome the stability and hope that comes from knowing that we also live on a *covenanted* earth.

---

[6] On the wider dimensions of the cosmic covenant and its initiation in the story of Noah, see chapter 4 above.

The covenant with Abraham: particular land, universal earth

So, with the strong emphasis on the divine and human relationship with the earth itself in Genesis 1 – 11, it is entirely consistent that when God initiates the historical narrative of redemption through the call of Abraham, land forms a constituent part of the promise made to him. God did not whisk Abraham and Sarah off to heaven the moment they put their faith in God's promise and were thereby 'counted righteous'. Yes, Hebrews tells us that there was a longer-term goal in view beyond either the land they had left behind or the one they arrived in. However, God's purpose for them was not some ethereal paradise, but life in the land of his choosing and promise. And that would in turn become a symbol of life in a redeemed creation, the ultimate goal of God's redemptive work.

There is thus a continuity and consistency in the total biblical story. Genesis 1 – 11 shows humanity in God's earth, but living in a state of alienation from it and longing for restoration and the removal of the curse from the land. The concluding vision of Scripture in Revelation 21 – 22 looks to a new creation in which God will once again dwell with redeemed humanity. The foundational redemptive covenant of grace with Abraham, therefore, includes land in order to make particular and local what will ultimately be universal – blessing not only to all nations but also to the whole earth itself.

It follows from the above point that the land of Israel in the Old Testament has to be viewed in the light of the universality of the Abrahamic covenant as well as its particularity. That is, while God's faithfulness to his promise to Abraham resulted in the historical gift of the land of Canaan to the tribes of *Israel*, that promise had as its ultimate scope the blessing of *all nations*. The other two main ingredients of the Abrahamic covenant certainly have that universal perspective in view: *posterity* (the fact that Abraham would become a nation, which would be the vehicle of God's blessing to the nations) and *relationship* (the special covenant relationship between God and Israel, which the Old Testament envisages being ultimately extended to the nations). Israel became a nation for the sake of all the nations. Israel was blessed by God so that all nations would be blessed by God. The land element of the promise to Abraham, then, has to be viewed consistently in this same universal context. Israel possessed its land as part of its mission in relation to the rest of the *nations*, and as part of God's redemptive intention for the whole *earth*. That is a vitally important point concerning the concept of election.

But it is also important in relation to the task of building biblical economic ethics. Here we must recall the argument in chapter 2 for a *paradigmatic* understanding of the relevance of Old Testament Israel to other cultures and societies. Israel was created and commissioned to be 'a light to the nations'. There was, therefore, a sense in which everything connected with them was exemplary in principle. The gifts of land to live in and law to live by were intrinsic to the way God shaped Israel to be a 'model' people. So, yes, the promise of land to Abraham's descendents certainly issued in a very particular and culturally conditioned economic system, but because of the universal dimension of the promise itself, that system carries wider significance than its own historical and cultural boundaries. It is this understanding that rescues our study of Israel's economic system from being merely an exercise in ancient history or historical sociology, and releases its potential for our ethical reflection, objectives and choices today in the field of economics. When we grasp the structures and objectives of Old Testament Israel's economic system, we are in touch with God's thinking as to how human economic life in general on the planet should be conducted.

The exodus: liberation for economic independence

The prototype and paradigm of all God's redemptive work in the Old Testament, of course, was the exodus. One outstanding feature of the redemption achieved at the exodus was its comprehensiveness. In that one sequence of events God gave to Israel a fourfold freedom: (1) politically, from the tyranny of a foreign autocratic power; (2) socially, from intolerable interference in their family life; (3) economically, from the burden of enforced slave labour; and (4) spiritually, from the realm of foreign gods into the unhindered worship of the LORD and covenant relationship with him. Once again, it is remarkable how closely bound together are the economic and the spiritual realms. The thing that awakens God's concern for his people is their outcry under economic oppression and injustice (Exod. 2:23–25). The purpose of his intention to deliver them is to fulfil his covenant promise to Abraham by giving them the economic blessing of a land of their own (Exod. 3:7–8; 6:4–8). So, the paramount salvation event in the whole Old Testament scripture and history, the exodus, has economic oppression as one of its key motivational triggers, and economic freedom as one of its primary intentional objectives. Economics is written into the very fabric of Israel's redemption story.

Creation values restored in Israel's economic system

Economic life in Israel was carried on within a worldview shaped not only by creation principles such as outlined in the last section, but also by their status as a people in covenant relationship with the creator God who was also their redeemer, the LORD. What we shall see in this section is the way in which the demands of covenant relationship with God and one another affected Israel's economic system. In broad terms, covenant-based economics called for economic relationships to be based on love and mutual support, not just on self-interest. Indeed, some of the economic regulations of Israel called for the sacrifice of self-interest in favour of the needs of a fellow Israelite. And all this was placed within a more fundamental call to trust their creator-redeemer God, even in the face of economic 'common sense'. We can see this in relation to each of the four creation principles outlined above. They provide a convenient and comprehensive structure on which to set out the economic laws and customs of Israel.

Shared access to natural resources

In Israel this was worked out in the first instance by a system of land division intended to be as equitable and as widespread as possible. This stands in stark contrast to the Canaanite system of land tenure that Israel replaced. As far as we know, under the Canaanite system, all land was owned by the local kings or lords in each city. The rest of the population lived as peasant-tenants on land not their own, paying taxes and serving in the king's army. Israel was to be different. Even before they took possession of the land, Numbers 26:52–56 portrays a system of dividing up the land so that every tribe would have an amount proportionate to their numerical size. Subsequently, the account of the land division in Joshua 13 – 19 repeatedly records that land was divided not only by tribe, but 'according to their families'. The purpose seems clear: that each tribe, clan and family should have sufficient land according to its size and needs. Land tenure was to be fair and distributed – not concentrated in the hands of a king or a wealthy few. Given the variety of Palestinian geography, this did not mean that everyone should have the *same*, but that every family should have *enough* – enough to be economically viable.[7] Here is a creation principle operating in a redemption context.

However, the economic effects of sin, such as greed, dispossession, political displacement, coupled with natural disaster, warfare and others, resulted in large numbers of people existing without land of their own. Such people would survive by selling themselves into the service of landed households. The Hebrew slaves of Exodus 21:2–6 and Deuteronomy 15:12–18 belonged

---

[7] For fuller details on the system of Israel's land tenure, and its distinctiveness from Canaanite practice, see Norman K. Gottwald, *Tribes of Yahweh*; Christopher J. H. Wright, *God's Land*; and Robert Gnuse, *You Shall Not Steal*. But for a more cautious view, which raises questions over the alleged sharp distinction between Canaanite and Israelite economies, see John Andrew Dearman, *Property Rights*.

to this landless class of people.[8] Israelite law, therefore, took a special interest in protecting them, as it did other groups of landless people, such as widows and orphans, immigrant aliens and Levites. Economic generosity to ease their plight was commanded, and reinforced by a mixture of theological and economic arguments in Deuteronomy 15:14–18. So those who technically owned no land were still to find provision from the land's bounty. This principle is expressed in Deuteronomy through the phrase 'eat and be satisfied'. On the one hand, this will be the blessing experienced by the Israelites when they take possession of the land and settle on it. 'When you have eaten and are satisfied, praise the LORD your God for the good land he has given you' (Deut. 8:10). But on the other hand, this too will be the blessing of the homeless and landless (the widow, orphan and alien), when they benefit from the distribution of the triennial tithe. They too, though they have no land of their own, 'may come and eat and be satisfied' (Deut. 14:29). The same phrase is to apply to the landed and the landless.

Ultimately, however, generosity was not enough in itself. The eschatological vision of the prophets looks forward to the day of God's redemptive transformation. Then '*every* man will sit under his own vine and under his own fig-tree' (Mic. 4:4; my italics), and those who are now landless will have secure tenure and share in the 'land' of God's new creation (Ezek. 47:22–23). Here is the restoration by God's redemptive act of the first principle of 'creation economics'.

The right and responsibility of work
This, the second creation principle, applied as much to the redeemed community in the Promised Land as to humankind in the Garden of Eden. Even the idyllic descriptions of God's blessing on his people if they lived obediently in

---

[8] It is now widely (though not universally) agreed that the word 'Hebrew' is linked to the word '*apiru*, which is found in a wide range of Mesopotamian and Egyptian texts. The term described a certain social stratum common throughout the ancient Near East; namely, a class of landless people, which might include political refugees, displaced people, outlaws and others. The Israelites were appropriately called 'Hebrews' while in Egypt. The word later became an ethnic name equivalent to Israel. But in the early legal texts the term 'Hebrew slave' almost certainly refers not to native-born Israelites but to landless people, the dispossessed Canaanites and immigrants who survived by selling themselves and their labour into the service of landed Israelite households. Full technical details of the debate over the identity of the '*apiru* and their possible links with the biblical Hebrews can be found in Gottwald, *Tribes of Yahweh*, pp. 401–409 (and elsewhere; see index), and in Niels Peter Lemche, 'Habiru'.

the land presupposed the normal work of agriculture. But in view of the corruption of work and of working relationships by sin, as we have noted, the law made certain explicit demands on the redeemed people in this sphere also. Old Testament laws in relation to work may be classified as follows:

- *Conditions.* 'Hebrew' slaves were to be given the opportunity of freedom (which in practice amounted to a change of employer) after six years, and the terms of their service and release were clearly laid down (Exod. 21:1–6). The owner of slaves was placed under clear legal restraint in his physical treatment of slaves (Exod. 21:20–21, 26–27), while those who had voluntarily entered the service of a creditor because of inability to support themselves were not to be made to work in oppressively harsh conditions (Lev. 25:39–40, 43).
- *Payment.* The wages of hired workers were to be paid fully and promptly (Lev. 19:13; Deut. 24:14–15). The prophets condemn the oppression and exploitation of labourers, specifically on the matter of pay (Is. 58:3; Jer. 22:13).
- *Rest.* Sabbath rest, a principle and privilege since creation, was made mandatory on employer, employee and even working animals, not only on the basis of God's example in creation (Exod. 20:11) but also on the grounds of his redemptive act (Deut. 5:15). In addition to this regular weekly total rest, slaves and other residential and hired workers were to be allowed to enjoy all the benefits of the great festivals and cultic occasions, which added several days' break from work throughout the agricultural year (cf. Deut. 16:11, 14). In an agricultural life of long, hard, physical labour, such regular relief would have been invaluable.

Disastrously, however, the laws governing working life and conditions were ignored from the king downwards, from the time of Solomon and in increasing measure thereafter (cf. 1 Kgs. 5:13–17; 9:20–23; 11:28; 12:3–4, 10–11). This is one of the factors that lay behind the exile, that could only be interpreted as divine judgment in the light of Leviticus 26. In that chapter the judgment is repeatedly related to the people's failure to observe the sabbaths. Now, in the context of Leviticus 25, that includes the sabbatical legislation concerning the *land.* Land sabbaths included the seventh year fallow (explicitly for the benefit of the poor); the release of pledges taken for debt (cf. Deut. 15:1–3; 'pledges' probably included dependants of the debtor, who were working off his debt by their labour); and the jubilee release of those whose land and labour were mortgaged to their creditors. All of these sabbatical institutions were concerned with the interests of *workers*, especially those whose *only* asset was their labour. Neglect of the 'sabbaths', in this sense, corresponds to the accusations of injustice and exploitation of the poor that are so common in the prophets. Similarly, economic exploitation is linked to violation of the sabbath day for greedy motives, by Amos (8:5–6), Isaiah (58:3–14) and Jeremiah (17:19–27; cf. 7:5–11).

So then, from the laws themselves and from the prophets' reaction to their neglect, we can see that there was a deep and detailed concern in the Old Testament with work and employment, in respect of conditions and terms of service, adequate rest and fair pay. And this concern applied across the whole spectrum of the working population – employers, free hired workmen, slaves. Indeed, the principles of fairness and compassion extended even to working animals, such as the laden donkey and threshing ox (Exod. 23:4–5; Deut. 25:4; cf. 22:1–4).

This concern, while it falls within the context of Israel as God's redeemed people, has paradigmatic relevance to Christian ethical concern and action within this economic sphere of work and employment. For what still remains true, as Biggar and Hay express it, is 'the more general Biblical insistence that work is part of human nature, an important element in human dignity, and a source of self worth'.[9] Obviously, there is a vast difference between the nature of employment within a comparatively simple agricultural economy such as ancient Israel's and the complex industrialized economies of modern developed countries. But the constant quest for satisfactory and dignified conditions of work and fair pay shows no signs of receding. On the matter of 'rest', the problem in developed countries has been inverted, since the combination of endemic unemployment and the microchip revolution has made the pressing problem not one of a surplus of work, but of its absence or scarcity. We are being forced to realize afresh that 'work' is not synonymous with 'paid employment' and we are having to rethink the meaning and uses of leisure. At the same time we face the immoral distortion that many people in Western societies are overworked, driven by a combination of tyrannical companies and their own greed, while others have no worthwhile work at all. Overwork for some and unemployment for others is just one of the more curious and absurd results of our human fallenness in the realm of work.

Nevertheless, there are still vast areas of the so-called developing world, or Majority World, where the nature of human labour has changed little from the ancient patterns found in biblical times. And there are societies where the conditions of allegedly 'free' employees are pitiably more harsh and oppressive than those of slaves in Israel. In such situations the paradigmatic relevance of

---

[9] Biggar and Hay, 'Bible and Social Security', p. 62.

the Old Testament economic laws concerning work and employment can be taken almost as they stand. To introduce statutory rest days and holidays, statutory terms and conditions of employment, statutory protection from infringement of personal rights and physical dignity, statutory provision for fair wages promptly paid (to list just some of the Old Testament regulations for workers' rights), would revolutionize the face of economic life for multitudes of workers in some parts of our world. And all of these are drawn from the economic legislation of God's redeemed people, Israel.

Therefore, although we may rightly wish to advocate the simple principles and ideals inherent in the *creation* ordinance of work, the effect of the fall is such that we cannot do so adequately without reverting to the principles and concrete models provided in the *redemption* context of God's people. Incidentally, this remains the case even if we choose also to bring the New Testament to bear on our ethic of work and employment. For the instructions to employers and their slave-employees and the warnings against deliberate idleness are clearly given within the 'redemptive context' of Paul's letters to Christian churches. In the one 'prophetic' blast against exploitative employers, who (presumably) stood outside the community of the redeemed whom he is addressing, James does precisely what we have seen cannot be avoided: he draws on the language and concepts of the covenant law of Old Testament Israel: 'Now listen, you rich people, weep and wail because of the misery that is coming upon you . . . Look! The wages you failed to pay the workmen who mowed your fields are crying out against you. The cries of the harvesters have reached the ears of the Lord Almighty' (Jas. 5:1–6; cf. Exod. 22:22–23; Lev. 19:13; Deut. 24:14–15).

Furthermore, work has its place in the eschatological visions of the new creation. The removal of the curse on the earth and the abolition of human wickedness will not leave humankind in Elysian idleness. The prophets envisage redeemed humanity as humanity at work, but in the joy afforded by the absence of warfare, the reign of righteousness and peace, and the cooperation of nature:

> 'The days are coming,' declares the LORD,
> 'when the reaper will be overtaken by the ploughman
>   and the planter by the one treading grapes.
> New wine will drip from the mountains
>   and flow from all the hills.'

(Amos 9:13)

> They will beat their swords into ploughshares
>   and their spears into pruning hooks . . .

Every man will sit under his own vine
and under his own fig-tree,
and no-one will make them afraid . . .

(Mic. 4:3–4; cf. Is. 11:1–9; Hos. 2:18–23)

Here again, we see that the *new* creation restores God's *original* purpose for humanity. The eschatological vision, alongside the creation ordinance, is thus an incentive for our social ethic, while the redemption ordinances provide principles and models for the present that take account of our fallenness.

The expectation of growth and trade

The third creation principle was the expectation of *economic growth* through exchange and trade and the increase of material goods as humankind spread and diversified their dominion over nature. The effect of the fall was that the desire for growth became obsessive and idolatrous, the scale of growth became excessive for some at the expense of others, and the means of growth became filled with greed, exploitation and injustice. A dilemma arose, therefore, in legislating economically in this matter for God's redeemed people. How were economic growth and material productiveness to be allowed for and encouraged in line with God's creative purpose and explicit desire to grant abundance as a blessing, while at the same time the evils of illegitimate growth were prevented or mitigated as far as possible?

It is in this area that Old Testament economic ethics and laws are, in my view, at their most radical and subtle. They are also at this point most vulnerable to the misinterpretation of two opposite extreme views. On the one hand, some press the texts that refer to material prosperity and increase of goods as God's blessing into a virtual carte blanche benediction on all forms of private enterprise and capitalistic growth-orientated economics. On the other hand, some extend the legal and prophetic antipathy to excessive and unjust accumulation of wealth into a malediction on any form of private property or wealth creation. Both views are mistaken and miss the balance of the Old Testament.

Sufficiency

The guiding ethos of Old Testament economics could be said to be summed up in the tenth commandment: 'You shall not covet.' Addressed in the second person singular to the individual, and including among its specific objects a neighbour's economic assets, this fundamental commandment locates the source of all sinful forms of economic growth where they truly originate – the greed of individual human hearts. The prophet Micah saw behind the socio-economic evils of his day to the private covetousness of individuals who 'plot evil on their beds' (Mic. 2:1). The antidote to 'covetousness which is idolatry' (Col. 3:5, RSV) is that 'fear of the LORD' which engenders the wisdom of contentment. The Wisdom tradition certainly accepted growth and prosperity as divine gifts (cf. Prov. 3:9–10; 10:22). But it was equally as aware of the dangers of excessive wealth as of the temptation of acute poverty:

> give me neither poverty nor riches,
>   but give me only my daily bread.
> Otherwise, I may have too much and disown you
>   and say, 'Who is the LORD?'
> Or I may become poor and steal,
>   and so dishonour the name of my God.
>
> (Prov. 30:8–9)

Deuteronomy 8 is another very balanced commentary on this point. The first part of the chapter anticipates Israel's arrival in the land where, in contrast to the minimal provision of the wilderness, they will find themselves blessed with sufficiency of everything they need: 'a land where bread will not be scarce and you will lack nothing; a land where the rocks are iron and you can dig copper out of the hills' (Deut. 8:9). Such sufficiency should lead to praise (v. 10).

However, the text is well aware that sufficiency will eventually build up to surplus, 'when all you have is multiplied', and then surplus will lead to pride and forgetting God (vv. 12–14). The hinge of the chapter seems to be verse 11 (note the balance of 'eat and be satisfied' on either side of it) with its strong warning against forgetting God. Only when God is properly honoured and praised can we preserve the fine line between *sufficiency and praise* on the one hand, and *surplus and pride* on the other.

Land not on the market

When we come to actual laws and institutions designed to embody this principle, the most important are the regulations concerning the inalienability of family land, and the supporting procedures of redemption and jubilee, in Leviticus 25. The combined effect of these regulations was to take the land itself right off the market as a commodity. Speculation in land or amassing huge private estates by permanent land purchase were *technically* impossible in Israel. Land could not be sold permanently (v. 23). The seller himself could redeem his land later, or the sale could be pre-empted or redeemed by a kinsman (cf. Jeremiah's pre-emption of his kinsman Hanamel's sale of land, Jer. 32:6–12). In any case, if neither happened, the land returned to its original owner or his descendants in the jubilee; that is, within a generation at most.

Any exchanges of land that did take place, therefore, were not really sales of *land* at all, but only of the 'usufruct', or expected *yield* of the land until the next jubilee. The price of land, therefore, actually *decreased* yearly as the jubilee approached (Lev. 25:14–17)! The purpose, to check the unscrupulous 'growth' of some at the expense of others, is made clear twice: 'Do not take advantage of each other' (vv. 14, 17).

Limits on debt

The jubilee also functioned as a safeguard against another kind of 'taking advantage'; namely, abuse of the legal redemption procedure. A prospering kinsman by operating his right of pre-emption or redemption on behalf of his poorer relatives within the clan could end up quite legally possessing most of their land, with the poorer kinsmen reduced to virtual serfdom on his estate (vv. 39–40). The jubilee set a limit to that kind of charitably disguised expansionism by ordering the release and 'return' of all households to their original inheritance.[10]

Thus the combination of an originally widespread, multiple division of the land to families, the inalienability principle, the redemption option and the jubilee statute amounts to an economic system that started from a position of broad equality, but recognized the fallen reality that some would prosper while others fell into poverty. It tried accordingly to set limits and safeguards on the worst effects of that process by regulative and restorative economic measures. The Old Testament was well aware that such measures run counter to the 'natural' economic tendencies of selfish people. That is why in Leviticus 25 there is an insistent appeal to the experience of redemption from Egypt and the covenant relationship with the LORD as sanction and motivation for the economic demands being made (vv. 17–18, 23b, 36, 38, 42–43, 55). These are economic regulations that reflect creation principles, but they are worked out within a covenantal framework among people who know what they owe God.

Limits on accumulation

Around this central core of Old Testament economics we might also list some other injunctions designed to prevent or limit the growth of private wealth at the cost of injustice or oppression.

First, there was the prohibition on removing *boundary stones* that marked out family land (Deut. 19:14). The seriousness of this offence is registered in its inclusion among the curses of Deuteronomy 27 (v. 17). It is used as a byword

---

[10] A fuller discussion of the jubilee law follows in chapter 6.

for injustice by Hosea (5:10) and was a concern to the Wisdom tradition also (Job 24:2–3; Prov. 23:10).

Secondly, the taking of *interest* for loans was prohibited between Israelites (Exod. 22:25; Lev. 25:36–37; Deut. 23:19–20). This did not refer to interest as we understand it in a commercial investment. Deuteronomy's permission to charge interest to a 'foreigner' probably has that kind of commercial trading in mind. But the other laws clearly specify that the loan is required because of *need*, primarily for the annual necessities of agricultural life; for example the loan of seed corn. The ban on interest is thus not concerned with economic growth in itself, but with growth achieved by taking unscrupulous advantage of another's need. A significant effect of the ban on interest among Israelites was that 'since loans from a kinsperson can be obtained without interest, the extended family gains an advantage by keeping such transactions within the kin group rather than going outside'.[11]

Thirdly, there was control over the use of *pledges* taken in security for loans. This ranged from plain humanitarian considerateness (e.g. the return of a cloak by night-time, Exod. 22:26–27; not to take a millstone in pledge, Deut. 24:6; not to invade privacy for a pledge, Deut. 24:10–11) to major sabbatical legislation. The 'release' prescribed for the seventh year in Deuteronomy 15:1–3 probably meant that pledges taken as security for a loan were to be returned to the owner and the loan suspended for the year (or perhaps cancelled altogether).[12] The pledge might be land mortgaged to the creditor, or it might be human dependants of the debtor working off his debts. The releasing of such pledges would bring substantial relief to the debtor and effectively check the rapacious expansion of unscrupulous creditors. Again, the law was well aware of the tendencies of the human economic heart and therefore, like Nehemiah, appeals to the redeemed conscience (Deut. 15:9ff.; Neh. 5:1–13).

Fourthly, the law prohibits excessive economic aggrandizement to the one person who might be expected to be allowed it, *the king*. Surely the king should have his private pile to prove his elevated status. But no, whether horses, wives or gold and silver, 'He must not accumulate large amounts' of them (Deut. 17:16–17). Horses, of course, were the engines of the chariot force. Wives would be kept in a harem – symbol of oriental royal grandeur. Weapons, women and wealth – that is what made a king in popular perception

---

[11] C. J. H. Wright, *Deuteronomy*, p. 252. On the interest ban in Israel, see further Paul Mills, *Interest in Interest*.

[12] For a fuller discussion and bibliography on the laws of debt release in general, see C. J. H. Wright, *God's Land*, pp. 143–148, 167–173, 249–259.

(not a lot has changed for the powerful of the earth today). But God said the kings of Israel were to be countercultural and avoid all such trappings of arrogance and greed. The fact that from the example of Solomon onwards this law was ignored by kings and royal favourites does not negate the point that it was a standing rebuke to that accumulative urge that pursues growth by injustice and oppression, a rebuke delivered in less legally muted tones by the prophets.

Finally, as we might expect from the previous two sections, the eschatological vision of the new creation, when God's people will dwell in a new and perfect relationship with God and one another, includes the fulfilment of the creation ideal of productive growth and fruitful abundance. Jeremiah 31 – 33, chapters that include outstanding prophecies of the new covenant and the everlasting age of God's blessing and bounty, include imagery drawn from the economic realm of the restoration of economic trade, produce and prosperity after the exile. While the outworking of God's ultimate purposes of redemption will certainly include the judgment and destruction of economic oppression and injustice (see the oracles against Tyre and Babylon in Is. 13 – 14; 23, and their echo, economics included, in Rev. 18), it will not ignore the economic dimension of human life and achievement on earth.

Fair sharing of the product of economic activity

The fourth principle of creation economics held that we are accountable to God not only for how we share the raw resources of the earth, but also for what is done with the product at the other end of the economic process. Our responsibility to God for one another means that we can claim no exclusive or unqualified right of disposal, even over what we have produced ourselves. The claim 'It is wholly mine for I made it' can be attributed only to God (cf. Ps. 95:4–5). In any human mouth such a claim is countered by the fact that both the resource and the power to use it are alike gifts of God. 'You may say to yourself, "My power and the strength of my hands have produced this wealth for me." But remember the LORD your God, for it is he who gives you the ability to produce wealth' (Deut. 8:17–18). Naturally, therefore, he holds us morally accountable to himself for *justice, compassion and generosity* in sharing the wealth he has enabled us to produce.

Justice was to govern all of Israel's social life, of course (as we shall consider more fully in chapter 8). But justice was particularly pressing in economic relationships. The marketplace itself, small or large, was the place of economic exchange of goods and services, and justice was to govern its operation. The law calls for accurate weights and measures, to prevent cheating in buying and selling (Lev. 19:35–36). Simple honesty in commercial dealings is a fundamental principle of economic justice:

Do not have two differing weights in your bag – one heavy, one light [depending on whether you were buying or selling produce]. Do not have two differing measures in your house – one large, one small. You must have accurate and honest weights and measures, so that you may live long in the land the LORD your God is giving you. For the LORD your God detests anyone who does these things, anyone who deals dishonestly.

(Deut. 25:13–16; cf. Prov. 11:1)

Justice also extends to those whose work you depend on in order to produce wealth. So prompt payment of wages due to workers (as we saw), is a demand of the law (Deut. 24:14–15), a moral claim by the righteous (Job 31:38–40), and a social issue for the prophets (Jer. 22:13; Is. 58:3b). Even the ox whose rotating labour grinds out the grain for your daily bread deserves the justice of eating from what the beast works to produce for you (Deut. 25:4).

Biblical justice, however, goes beyond a calculus of rights and deserts. Because it is fundamentally relational it always blends into *compassion* for those who are vulnerable. So, in biblical economics, wealth that God has enabled us to produce must always be held and used with a compassionate heart and hand. Compassion is, of course, a matter of the heart and emotions, but it is also a covenantal duty and can therefore be commanded. The important thing is not whether you *feel* compassion, but whether you *act* with compassion. So, whatever you may feel, you are to avoid reaping your fields, vineyards or orchards to the very last grain, grape or olive. There are those whose needs are more urgent than your rights of ownership and on whose behalf God commands very practical compassion (Lev. 19:9–10; Deut. 24:19–22). Compassion is also to govern how you 'view' the poor in the community. Attitudes of the heart govern the use of our hands, so they matter:

If there is a poor man among your brothers in any of the towns of the land that the LORD your God is giving you, do not be hard-hearted or tight-fisted towards your poor brother. Rather be open-handed and freely lend him whatever he needs. Be careful not to harbour this wicked thought: 'The seventh year, the year for cancelling debts, is near,' so that you do not show ill will towards your needy brother and give him nothing. He may then appeal to the LORD against you, and you will be found guilty of sin. Give generously to him and do so without a grudging heart; then because of this the LORD your God will bless you in all your work and in everything you put your hand to. There will always be poor people in the land (*or in the earth*). Therefore I command you to be open-handed towards your brothers and towards the (*your*) poor and (*your*) needy in your land.

(Deut. 15:7–11)

Compassion, then, as this text observes, leads to *generosity*. And the immediately following verses speak of generosity that goes above and beyond the demands of what is technically legal in the release of the debtor-slave after six years of service. Furthermore, it urges generosity precisely on the basis of the generosity of God, which the Israelite is told to imitate: 'Supply him liberally from your flock, your threshing-floor and your winepress. Give to him as the LORD your God has blessed you' (Deut. 15:14). Indeed, grace and compassion, justice and generosity, are the prime qualities of the LORD mirrored by 'the one who fears the LORD'. See especially the mirrored effect of Psalms 111:4–5 and 112:4–5.

Responding to poverty

So far in this chapter, then, we have seen the creational foundation of Old Testament economics, the distortions arising from human sin and disobedience, and the efforts made within Israel's economic system to make creation principles come to life within the arena of Israel's redeemed, covenant community. How was all of this brought to bear on the issue of poverty? Is there, even, an 'issue of poverty' in the Old Testament? Cyril Rodd includes a chapter on 'The Poor' among those issues where he believes that modern ethical problems have been imported into Old Testament ethics (Rodd, *Glimpses*, ch. 14). While characteristically providing a very fine survey of both biblical and scholarly literature on the vocabulary and handling of poverty in the Old Testament, he agrees with T. R. Hobbs who argues that poverty in itself was not a moral problem to Israel (it was simply part of the way things are in this world). The problems for Israelites were rather the loss of status and the shame that poverty entailed. Poverty was a misfortune, not a moral problem. Rodd himself argues that material poverty in itself is rarely the issue for Old Testament writers, but rather the injustice or oppression in society that reduced some, while others prospered. This seems to me a fair point, but it does not remove poverty from the realm of authentic Old Testament ethics in the way Rodd suggests. For Old Testament ethics are characteristically *relational*, not just abstract or quantifiable. It is indeed what poverty implies for human relationships (their abuse, distortion, exploitation etc.) that constitutes the ethical problem. Poverty cannot therefore be addressed merely as an economic or material issue without at the same time addressing the relational issues of social injustice and exploitation.

We shall note, first, some of the causes of poverty recognized and commented upon in the Old Testament. Then we shall survey the responses to poverty that are found in the major sections of the canon.[13]

Causes of poverty

Poverty can come upon a person, family or community for a wide variety of reasons, and the Old Testament recognizes the complexity of the matter.

First, there are what we would call *natural causes*, the result of living in a fallen world in which things go wrong for no reason apparent to us. Such things as blight on crops and invasions of locusts can devastate a local economy. Sometimes such events may be attributed to divine judgment (e.g. Joel), but at other times they are simply recorded without any explanation. Stuff happens. We might think of the famine that drove Jacob's family to Egypt in Genesis, or the one that drove Elimelech to emigrate to Moab from Bethlehem (ironically meaning 'House of Bread'), in the book of Ruth. Illness and disaster can reduce a man to the rubbish tip (Job); bereavement and widowhood can reduce a woman to bitter emptiness (Naomi). Attributing such things to the hand of the LORD (rightly or wrongly) does not mitigate the pain of such reversals. No explanation or rationalization seems to be available.

Then, secondly, the Old Testament recognizes that some poverty may be the direct result of *laziness*. This is particularly the observation of the world of the wise in the book of Proverbs. For that reason, some scholars portray the authors of that book as rather cynical representatives of the well-to-do, urban elite, who saw the poor not so much as a moral challenge as a political eyesore, and felt it necessary to blame the poor for their own poverty.[14] This seems to me an exaggerated ideological interpretation of Proverbs. The point Proverbs

---

[13] There are some very detailed scholarly studies of poverty in the Old Testament, some of which are listed in the further reading list at the end of the chapter. For studies of the rich vocabulary of poverty that is characteristic of the Old Testament, see J. David Pleins, 'Poor, Poverty'; and Mignon R. Jacobs, 'Concern for the Underprivileged'. A full survey of the poor in every part of the Bible is provided by Leslie J. Hoppe, *Being Poor*. An account that claims to find a wide variety of ideological and social perspectives within the different sections of the Hebrew canon is argued in considerable critical detail in J. David Pleins, *Social Visions*.

[14] This is the case argued in several works by David Pleins. See J. David Pleins, 'Poverty in the Social World of the Wise'; and *Social Visions*, pp. 452–483. Less negative accounts of how the Wisdom tradition viewed poverty and wealth can be found in Norman C. Habel, 'Wisdom, Wealth and Poverty'; and R. N. Whybray, *Wealth and Poverty*.

makes, within its own limits, seems to be valid, and it is complementary to the more dominant note of the law and the prophets (as we shall see). For the fact is that laziness and squandering can indeed lead to impoverishment, and hard work is often conducive to economic prosperity (e.g. Prov. 12:11; 14:23; 20:13; 21:17 etc.). Proverbs itself is well aware that these are generalizations, not rules without exception (e.g. Prov. 13:23).

Thirdly, however, *oppression* is by far the major recognized cause of poverty. The Old Testament asserts, as all modern analyses demonstrate, that only a tiny fraction of poverty is 'accidental'. Mostly, people are made poor by the actions of others – directly or indirectly. Poverty is caused. And the primary cause is the exploitation of others by those whose own selfish interests are served by keeping others poor:

> The prophets . . . did not regard poverty as the result of chance, destiny or laziness. Poverty was simply the creation of the rich who have broken the covenant because of their greed. The wealthy used their abilities and resources not to enhance the community but to support their own purpose. In this way they violated the covenant, they destroyed the unity of Israel and called forth divine judgment.[15]

Such oppressive exploitation takes various forms, and the Old Testament offers a remarkably nuanced understanding of this variety:

1. *Exploitation of the socially weak.* There are those whose lack of status in the community makes them vulnerable. This is classically the case with those who have lost either family or land or both: widows, orphans, aliens. Naomi and Ruth illustrate the potential struggle, and 2 Kings 4:1–7 presents a typical case. Loss of family leaves a person defenceless, unless strong defenders take up their cause (as Boaz did, and as Job claimed to have done before his own calamity: Job 29:12–17).

2. *Exploitation of the economically weak.* Debt accumulates, leading to loss of land, and drives people into deepening cycles of poverty. The charging of interest exacerbates the problem (Exod. 22:25). So do royal taxation, confiscation and conscription (1 Sam. 8:10–18). Economic and social powerlessness go together in the situation graphically described in Nehemiah 5. Debt (even apparently trifling debts) could lead to slavery (Amos 2:6). On the other hand, the mechanisms to relieve debt could be abused, or people could be refused loans because of the imminence of the date of cancellation (Deut. 15:7–9). Lenders could abuse their power by unscrupulous demands

---

[15] Hoppe, *Being Poor*, p. 61.

(Deut. 24:17–18). Employers could exploit the most vulnerable section of the workforce – the casual day labourers – by delayed payment of wages (Deut. 24:14–15).

3. *Exploitation of the ethnically weak.* The Israelites themselves, of course, began their national history as an ethnic minority in Egypt, suffering all the horrors of political, economic and social oppression, culminating in state-sponsored genocide (Exod. 1). For that reason they were told to pay particular attention to the vulnerability of ethnic minorities in their midst (Exod. 22:21; Lev. 19:33). Again, the story of Ruth illustrates the potential danger that immigrant foreigners could be exposed to. And one might point out that two of the Old Testament's major figures, Abaham and David, stooped to their lowest in episodes of appalling treatment of ethnic foreigners (Hagar and Uriah).

4. *Royal excess, corruption and abuse of power.* The Old Testament includes some vividly trenchant critique of the violent corruption of power and the gaining of wealth at the expense of the poverty of others. Solomon, of course, is the prime example as his later reign degenerated into naked exploitation of the northern tribes in a way that doubtless contributed to his legendary wealth and splendour, but equally clearly sparked the revolt that tore the whole northern section of the kingdom away from his son Rehoboam (1 Kgs. 11–12). Later kings followed suit to one degree or another. Ahab's greed smashes a Naboth (1 Kgs. 21). Jehoiakim's greed builds his own conspicuous affluence on the backs of unpaid workers (Jer. 22:13). Ezekiel summarizes the whole abusive history of the monarchy in Jerusalem thus: 'See how each of the princes of Israel who are in you uses his power to shed blood . . . There is a conspiracy of her princes within her like a roaring lion tearing its prey; they devour people, take treasures and precious things and make many widows within her.' Not surprisingly, ordinary people follow the examples of their political masters: 'The people of the land practise extortion and commit robbery; they oppress the poor and needy and ill-treat the alien, denying them justice' (Ezek. 22:6, 25, 29).

5. *Judicial corruption and false accusation.* The case of Naboth was not just one of royal greed; the means used to get rid of him (1 Kgs. 21:7–16) was a blatant manipulation of Israel's own legal system by Jezebel (with Ahab acquiescent). Amos 5:7, 11–12 spotlights the terrible corruption of the courts that turned justice to poison for the poor. The powerful could then legislate poverty by decree (Is. 10:1–2)! This is a common cause for complaint in the Psalms, when the poor who are 'righteous' (legally in the right as against wicked opponents) find no human redress in the assembly and can appeal only to God. The failure of the judges to do their job will arouse God's fury and their eventual destruction (Ps. 82).

Responses to poverty

'From the oldest of the Old Testament documents to the most recent, the cause of the underprivileged is upheld.'[16] We should not imagine that Israel's concern for the poor was unique. It certainly had unique features, but Israel was part of a wider ancient Near Eastern macroculture that paid attention to the realities of poverty and wealth. This is not to say that Old Testament responses to poverty were mere borrowings. It is rather to agree with Calvin that 'the common society of the human race demands that we should not seek to grow rich by the loss of others'.[17] Our common createdness, along with the universality of God's common grace and moral demand, makes it unsurprising that concern for the poor is found beyond the borders of the covenant people. Norbert Lohfink shows in detail that 'many biblical statements, motifs and formulations are simply participation in the thought and feeling of the whole environment in which the Bible arose'. He goes on to make the following points, illustrated from many extra-biblical texts: 'In the ancient Near East the rich were brought up to care for the poor . . . Care for the rights of the poor was a special obligation of the king . . . The basis for the lofty ethic of care for the poor was the common con-viction that the gods themselves, particularly the sun god, have a special love for the poor.' Lohfink goes on, however, to point out the limitations of this ancient Near Eastern 'option for the poor'. There was a massive dissonance between theory and practice (an accusation that would apply, of course, to Israel's later monarchy); it did not challenge the social systems that produced the poverty, since the very gods who were said to care for the poor were the same gods who guaranteed the social structures that preserved the power of the wealthy; and thus this palliative approach only served to obscure the real problem.[18] What *is* distinctive about the Old Testament response, according to Lohfink, is the unique and prototypical event of the exodus as an act of liberation and removal of the poor from the system that oppressed them.[19] Let us, then, survey a selec-tion of the documents as we find them in the different sections of the canon.

In the Law

1. The law insists that *poverty must be addressed*, and redressed, whatever its causes may be. The series of clauses in Leviticus 25 beginning 'If one of your

---

[16]   Englehard, 'Lord's Motivated Concern', p. 5.

[17]   From Calvin's observations on the matter of usury, in *Four Last Books of Moses*, pp. 125–133.

[18]   Lohfink, *Option for the Poor*, pp. 16–32.

[19]   For further discussion of the ancient Near Eastern context and its documented perspectives on poverty, see Englehard, 'Lord's Motivated Concern', pp. 11–14.

countrymen becomes poor . . .' (vv. 25, 35, 39, 47) give no hint as to possible causes. It is not a matter of assigning blame. The question is, what is now to be done if a brother is in danger of sinking into poverty? If there were injustices or oppressive practices causing the impoverishment process, that is a matter for another day, or for prophetic rhetoric. Those who are required to take action are not necessarily those responsible for the problem (in the sense of being guilty of causing it). But they are responsible under God for those in danger of falling through the cracks of society. Such persons at risk must be restored one way or another.

2. The law emphasizes *the kinship/family structure of society* as the key factor in preventing poverty and restoring people from it. As we have already seen, Israel's economic system included such family-supportive principles as the equitable distribution of land through the broad network of clans and families (Num. 26:52–56); the inalienability of family land (Lev. 25:23); redemption and jubilee practices, to restore families to participation in the community (Lev. 25); the ban on interest between Israelites (Deut. 23:19); the levirate marriage arrangement (Deut. 25:5–10).

3. Israel's law included a range of measures which, taken together, formed an impressive and systemic *welfare programme* for those who were truly destitute; that is, mainly the landless and familyless.[20] Thus there was the right of annual gleaning in the various harvests (Exod. 23:10–11; Deut. 24:18–22); the triennial tithe, during which 10% of all produce was stored to create a social fund for the support of the needy (Deut. 14:28–29);[21] and the sabbatical year arrangements, which included the availability of what grew of itself on the fallow land (Exod. 23:10–11), the cancellation (or suspension) of debts (Deut. 15:1–11), and the freeing of Hebrew slaves (Deut. 15:12–18). The combination of all of these would have meant that something was available every year for the benefit of those who truly had no means for their own economic support.

4. The law insisted that the poor be treated with *judicial equality* in the whole legal process. This meant neither being treated with an unjust favouritism, nor (the more likely reality) being denied justice altogether because of the social and economic power of the wealthy (Exod. 23:3, 6–9; Lev. 19:15).

---

[20] Stephen A. Kaufman, 'Social Welfare Systems', offers a less than satisfactory account of Israel's welfare system, which is confused in its handling of the provisions in Leviticus and Deuteronomy. For greater detail, compare C. J. H. Wright, *God's Land*; and Hoppe, *Being Poor*, chs. 1, 2.

[21] 'From being an obligatory gift to the gods the tithe has become an obligatory gift to the poor.' Hoppe, *Being Poor*, p. 27.

5. The law typically addresses not the poor themselves but *those who wield economic or social power.* Whereas it is common to see 'the poor' as 'a problem', and to blame them or lecture them on what *they* must do to redeem their situation, Israel's law puts the focus instead on those who actually have the power to do something, or whose power must be constrained in some way for the benefit of the poor. Thus the law addresses the creditor, not the debtor (Deut. 24:6, 10–13); employers, not day labourers (Deut. 24:14); slave-owners, not slaves (Exod. 21:20–21, 26–27; Deut. 15:12–18).

> Deuteronomy makes the alleviation of the suffering of the poor a matter of obedience to the divine will. If Israel would abide by the law, there would be no poverty. Because people have failed to be obedient, poverty is a reality that needs to be handled. Deuteronomy speaks to the prosperous, to judges, to owners of bond slaves, to creditors, to all who are in a position to either mitigate or worsen the situation of the poor . . . [asking] that people of means relinquish some of their 'rights', act against their economic self-interest and treat the poor as members of their own families which, in reality, they are.[22]

6. The law builds around its whole system of legislation on poverty a broad *moral and emotional ethos.* This includes the familiar Old Testament emphases on gratitude to, and imitation of, God as a motivation (see chapter 1), and compassion and generosity as key virtues (see above).[23]

7. The law makes care for the poor *the litmus test of covenant obedience* to the whole of the rest of the law. This is the remarkable thrust of Deuteronomy 26:12–15. The Israelite worshipper, bringing his offering in gratitude for the gift of the land and the harvest, is to declare that he has given the sacred portion to the LORD, and also to the poor and needy, as required by the triennial tithe law (Deut. 14:28–29). Only on that basis could he claim to have 'not forgotten' any of God's commands.

> Thus, giving to the needy is not only a sacred duty to God, but it also is the defining point for any claim to have kept the law. *The law is kept only if the poor are cared for.* Only when Israel responds to the needy by enabling *everyone* in the community to eat and be satisfied can they affirm I have done *everything* that you commanded me. This shows . . . how the enacted love for the poor and needy is the practical proof of genuine, God-honoring love for the neighbor. The Torah itself thus agrees with the way the

---

[22] Hoppe, *Being Poor,* p. 32.

[23] On the distinctiveness of Old Testament motivational material on this issue, see David H. Englehard, 'Lord's Motivated Concern'.

prophets later pinpoint and prioritize care for the poor as somehow definitive or paradigmatic of Israel's response to God as a whole.[24]

In the narratives

1. The constitutive narrative of Israel's redemptive history brings them from slavery in Egypt to freedom in the land of promise. It is true, as Rodd points out (*Glimpses,* p. 183), that the words for poverty are not used of the Hebrews in Egypt, and the situation is described in terms of oppression, not poverty. Nevertheless, Deuteronomy makes much of the anticipated goal of the whole experience, which was the abundance of the land of promise in stark contrast to the minimal subsistence of life in Egypt and the wilderness that preceded it (Deut. 8 and 11). Certainly, the Egyptian oppression included economic exploitation, inasmuch as all the forced labour of the Hebrews was going towards the wealth and grandeur of the Pharaoh, not for their own benefit.

2. This liberating narrative forms the basis of celebration around the theme of this characteristic action of YHWH as God. Hannah sings of God's power of economic reversal (1 Sam. 2:5–8). The psalmists do likewise (Ps. 146).

3. The narratives also provide examples of both negative and positive behaviour in relation to poverty. As we have seen, our Old Testament narrator paints the glaring contrast between the sumptuous wealth of Solomon and the growing oppression of parts of his kingdom, and notes with depressing regularity the succession of kings who followed his example. But we are also given more encouraging stories of what was probably regarded as the true Israelite ideal of justice, compassion and generosity towards the vulnerable and needy – Boaz being the prime hero in this regard.

In the prophets

1. It would be difficult to exaggerate the extent of the prophets' engagement with the struggles of the poor in Israel. Rodd is right to say that the major issue was not purely the fact of material poverty alone, but *primarily one of injustice and oppression.* It was the imbalance in a society that was supposed to be based on covenantal equality and mutual support that most angered the prophets. Donald Gowan eloquently expresses this dimension of Old Testament ethics regarding the injustice that is at the root of most poverty:

> For Old Testament writers the cause of poverty which produced the most concern and true indignation was not what the poor do or do not do but what others have

---

[24] C. J. H. Wright, *Deuteronomy*, pp. 271–272 (italics original).

done to them . . . There were ways to deal with the problems of being hungry and ill-clothed and homeless; but all of them could be thwarted by injustice, and it is that against which the Old Testament rages. Those people who do not have the power to insist on justice for themselves are thus held up as a special concern for the whole community . . . Nowhere does the Old Testament hold up as an ideal a complete equality in the distribution of wealth. It assumes throughout that there will always be some with relatively more possessions. This is no scandal, for wealth is to be prized as one of the good gifts of God (Prov. 22:4). What is a scandal, as many texts have shown us, is when those who do not have so much are deprived of what is rightfully theirs by those whose consciences do not bother them.[25]

But the material aspect cannot be overlooked. That the victims of exploitation were also becoming materially destitute is clear from the way Amos, for example, contrasts their plight with the affluent lifestyle of those he refers to as wicked (e.g. Amos 4:1; 6:4–6); or Isaiah contrasts the accumulating estates and mansions of the wealthy with those who have no place left to live (Is. 5:8). Jeremiah contrasts the exploitative greed of Jehoiakim with the justice and generosity of Josiah towards the poor (Jer. 22:13–17). Micah surely has material suffering in mind when he luridly paints the ruthless rich as those

> who tear the skin from my people
> and the flesh from their bones;
> who eat my people's flesh,
> strip off their skin
> and break their bones in pieces;
> who chop them up like meat for the pan,
> like flesh for the pot.

(Mic. 3:2–3)

2. Perhaps the major contribution of the prophets, and the major lesson we can learn from them in terms of the prophetic responsibility of the church today, lies simply in the fact that *they saw what was going on*. They were the mouthpiece of the God who sees – as Israel should have known ever since Exodus records that God had seen their suffering in Egypt, heard their cries of pain, and intervened on their behalf (Exod. 2:23–25; 3:7). A major part of the problem is that poverty becomes invisible and the poor inaudible. But not to the God of Israel. 'I have been watching! declares the LORD' (Jer. 7:11). So the prophets first notice, then expose the grievances, then challenge

---

[25] Gowan, 'Wealth and Poverty', pp. 349–350.

those in power (kings and judges especially), who would prefer to look the other way. No wonder, then, that Ahab called Elijah 'you troubler of Israel', even though Ahab himself was the source of the trouble (1 Kgs. 18:17–18). A government capable of doing what Jezebel and Ahab did to the family of a peasant farmer, Naboth, needed to be severely troubled, and Elijah did not shirk the task.[26]

In the Psalms

1. Like the prophets, the psalmists affirm unambiguously that *the LORD is the God who hears the cry of the poor*. They are utterly dependent on God when human help fails, and their plight matters to God profoundly (Pss. 145; 146; 147 etc.). There is thus often an oscillation between a material and a spiritual meaning of 'the poor' in the Psalms. It seems misguided to insist on one or the other exclusively. The materially poor are thrown in spiritual dependence on God. 'Poverty' thus serves both as a literal description for the destitute, and as a metaphor for spiritual humility. Sue Gillingham urges that the mission of the church needs to preserve this holistic double focus:

> We cannot feed and clothe the poor without recognizing the spiritual poverty in the world around us – perhaps particularly the poverty of the affluent West; nor can we preach a Gospel which fulfils our deepest spiritual needs without allowing this to challenge our attitude to every aspect of material well-being. This, to my mind, offers a theology of poverty which is both biblical and contemporary.[27]

2. Israel's worship also, like the law and the prophets, is clear about where *the prime responsibility* lies in the matter of addressing the needs and the just cause of the poor; namely, with political and social authorities – kings (Ps. 72) and judges (Ps. 82).

3. The psalter also builds a strong connection between the *claims and criteria of worship acceptable to God,* on the one hand, and practical social concern and economic justice on the other. Among the marks of the righteous worshipper who may dwell in God's holy mountain is the willingness to lend without

---

[26] 'Naboth was not poor in purely economic terms: he was a small landowner. A man who had a vineyard of such high quality that a king coveted it could hardly be considered destitute! . . . The point is that although he was not poor, yet he was powerless to resist the wicked scheming of Jezebel, who, with the tacit approval of the king, contrived to deprive him not only of his property but also of his life' (Weir, 'Poor Are Powerless', p. 14).

[27] Gillingham, 'Poor in the Psalms', p. 19.

demanding interest – a major plank in Israel's economic ethic (Ps. 15:5). And if it is true that you become like the object of your worship, then not surprisingly the one who worships and fears the LORD will reflect him in justice, compassion and generosity (Pss. 111:4–5; 112:4–5).

In the Wisdom literature

1. There is a strongly *creational base for the social ethics* of the Wisdom writers, which contrasts (though in a complementary way) with the way the Torah and the prophets grounded their ethical motivation in the great historical-redemptive tradition. Thus, for Proverbs, the poor should be treated with the dignity that reflects the fact that they too are created by the same God. Indeed, what we do to or for them we do to or for God (in a remarkable anticipation of the teaching of Jesus):

> He who oppresses the poor shows contempt for their Maker,
> but whoever is kind to the needy honours God.
>
> (Prov. 14:31; cf. also 17:5; 19:17; 22:2, 22–23; 29:13)

The created equality of slave and master also governed Job's insistence on his own fair handling of his workers' grievances (Job 31:13–15).

2. As with so many other matters, the Wisdom writers were gifted with *observation and insight on the realities of poverty* – not only in its economic debilitation, but also in its disabling social embarrassment (Prov. 10:15; 19:4, 7). Job is eloquent in his description of destitution (Job 24:1–12). Ecclesiastes observes the impoverishing effect of bureaucracy (Eccles. 5:8–9), and also the speed with which wealth and poverty can change places (Eccles. 5:13– 6:6).

3. Based on this careful observation, the Wisdom writers all advocate the same ethos of *compassion, generosity and justice* that we find elsewhere (Job 31:16–23; Eccles. 4:1). Such an attitude is in fact characteristic of true righteousness, as its lack is characteristic of the wicked. For

> The righteous care about justice for the poor,
> but the wicked have no such concern.
>
> (Prov. 29:7)

However, just caring is not enough. Job, who complained that God seemed to do nothing about the plight of the poor and oppressed, overlooked the fact that he himself had been an instrument of God's justice in action in his own daily work as an elder in the gate, defending the weak and confronting the oppressor (Job 29:7–17; 'confronting' is actually a weak word in comparison to Job's own metaphor 'I broke the fangs of the wicked / and snatched the victims from their teeth'). Addressing poverty that has been caused by the abuse of power inevitably brings conflict with those who are the abusers.

4. Like the law, prophets and Psalms, the Wisdom tradition put its finger on the spot in pointing to *the key role of political authorities* in taking responsibility for the needs of the poor. Thus the final chapter of Proverbs, before its portrait of the ideal wife, has some advice for an ideal king. Adding some colour to the Deuteronomic law that limited the perks of royalty, King Lemuel's mother urges him to avoid profligacy with women, wine or beer. This advice, however, was not for the good of his own health, but so that he would have a clear head to obtain justice for the oppressed. The prime job of the king, according to the wise queen mother, was to

> Speak up for those who cannot speak for themselves,
>> for the rights of all who are destitute.
> Speak up and judge fairly;
>> defend the rights of the poor and needy.
>
> (Prov. 31:8–9)

An end to poverty

In conclusion we may note that the same eschatological hope that concluded the last chapter (the ecological hope for our earth and the whole environment) also strongly flavours Old Testament economic ethics. In the here and now of our fallen world the Old Testament presents to us a sensible balance. On the one hand, it holds up ideals and goals (there need be no poverty if people would live according to the principles and systems God has provided for human flourishing). But, on the other hand, it is realistically aware of the endemic nature of human greed and violence and the perpetuation of poverty that results. Deuteronomy provides the classic expression of both these perceptions in chapter 15. On the one hand, 'there should be no poor among you, for . . . the LORD your God . . . will richly bless you, if only you fully obey the LORD your God and are careful to follow all these commands (vv. 4–5). But, on the other hand, 'There will always be poor people in the land. Therefore I command you to be open-handed towards your brothers and towards the poor and needy in your land' (v. 11).

But the time will come when poverty will be no more. Micah's glorious vision of the messianic era adds to its parallel in Isaiah the proverbial picture that 'every man will sit under his own vine / and under his own fig-tree' (Mic. 4:4; cf. Is. 2:1–5). Both prophets envisage an end to war and armaments as a major contributor to such economic revival. As we saw at the end of chapter 4, the vision of the new creation in Isaiah 65:17–25 is not one of effort-free wealth, but it is one of a society without poverty and oppression, in which work will be satisfying, rewarding and safe, freed from the frustrations of disease and dispossession. As with our ecological ethic, then, our economic ethic is built around the first principles of creation, the realism of the fall, the paradigmatic detail of Israel's systemic response to economic problems (especially poverty caused by oppression), and the eschatological hope of a new world that is as certain as God's own character and promise.[28]

Further reading

Biggar, Nigel, and Hay, Donald, 'The Bible, Christian Ethics and the Provision of Social Security', *Studies in Christian Ethics* 7 (1994), pp. 43–64.

Blomberg, Craig L., *Neither Poverty nor Riches: A Biblical Theology of Material Possessions* Downers Grove: InterVarsity Press; (Leicester: Apollos, 1999).

Brueggemann, Walter, *The Land* (Philadelphia: Fortress, 1977).

Carroll R., M. D., 'Wealth and Poverty', in Alexander and Baker, *Dictionary of the Old Testament: Pentateuch*, pp. 881–887.

Dearman, John Andrew, *Property Rights in the Eighth-Century Prophets: The Conflict and Its Background* (Atlanta: Scholars Press, 1988).

Englehard, David H., 'The Lord's Motivated Concern for the Underprivileged', *Calvin Theological Journal* 15 (1980), pp. 5–26.

Fager, Jeffrey A., *Land Tenure and the Biblical Jubilee*, JSOT Supplements, vol. 155 (Sheffield: JSOT Press, 1993).

Fensham, F. Charles, 'Widow, Orphan and the Poor in the Ancient near Eastern Legal and Wisdom Literature', *Journal of Near Eastern Studies* 21 (1962), pp. 129–139.

Gillingham, Sue, 'The Poor in the Psalms', *Expository Times* 100 (1988), pp. 15–19.

Gnuse, Robert, *You Shall Not Steal: Community and Property in the Biblical Tradition* (Maryknoll: Orbis, 1985).

Gottwald, Norman K., *The Tribes of Yahweh: A Sociology of the Religion of Liberated Israel 1250–1050 BCE* (Maryknoll: Orbis; London: SCM, 1979).

---

[28] This eschatological perspective is part of the narrative nature of the biblical worldview. In that sense it is also a major aspect of the uniqueness of the Old Testament's understanding of poverty. Lohfink points out that, in addition to the exodus as its foundational and unparalleled framework for all social and economic thought, Israel was unique in the ancient Near East in setting its response to poverty within the narrative of God's long-term purposes for the earth and humanity, which are ultimately to lead both to abundance, blessing and prosperity. 'God's interest in the world unleashes a drama' – the biblical drama that encompasses not only the history of Israel, but the whole of humanity. Lohfink, *Option for the Poor*, pp. 12–13.

Gowan, Donald E., 'Wealth and Poverty in the Old Testament: The Case of the Widow, the Orphan, and the Sojourner', *Interpretation* 41 (1987), pp. 341–353.

Habel, Norman C., 'Wisdom, Wealth and Poverty: Paradigms in the Book of Proverbs', *Bible Bhashyam* 14 (1988), pp. 26–49.

———, *The Land Is Mine: Six Biblical Land Ideologies* (Philadelphia: Fortress, 1995).

Hanks, Thomas D., *God So Loved the Third World: The Biblical Vocabulary of Oppression* (Maryknoll: Orbis, 1983).

Hobbs, T. R., 'Reflections on "the Poor" and the Old Testament', *Expository Times* 100 (1988–9), pp. 291–293.

Hoppe OFM, Leslie J., *Being Poor: A Biblical Study* (Wilmington, DE: Michael Glazier, 1987).

Hughes, Dewi, *God of the Poor: A Biblical Vision of God's Present Rule* (Carlisle: OM Publishing, 1998).

Jacobs, Mignon R., 'Toward an Old Testament Theology of Concern for the Underprivileged', in Kim, Ellens, Floyd and Sweeney, *Reading the Hebrew Bible for the New Millennium*, pp. 205–229.

Kaufman, Stephen A., 'A Reconstruction of the Social Welfare Systems of Ancient Israel', in W. Boyd Barrick and John R. Spencer (eds.), *In the Shelter of Elyon* (Sheffield: JSOT Press, 1984).

Lohfink SJ, Norbert F., *Option for the Poor: The Basic Principle of Liberation Theology in the Light of the Bible* (Berkeley: BIBAL Press, 1987).

Pleins, J. David, 'Poverty in the Social World of the Wise', *Journal for the Study of the Old Testament* 37 (1987), pp. 61–78.

———, 'Poor, Poverty', in Freedman, *Anchor Bible Dictionary*, vol. 5, pp. 402–414.

———, 'How Ought We to Think about Poverty? Re-thinking the Diversity of the Hebrew Bible', *Irish Theological Quarterly* 60 (1994), pp. 280–286.

———, *The Social Visions of the Hebrew Bible: A Theological Introduction* (Louisville KY: Westminster John Knox, 2001).

Rad, G. von, 'The Promised Land and Yahweh's Land', in *The Problem of the Hexateuch and Other Essays* (New York: McGraw Hill, 1966), pp. 79–93.

Waldow, H. E. von, 'Social Responsibility and Social Structure in Early Israel', *Catholic Biblical Quarterly* 32 (1970), pp. 182–204.

Weir, J. Emmette, 'The Poor Are Powerless: A Response to R. J. Coggins', *Expository Times* 100 (1988), pp. 13–15.

Whybray, R. N., *Wealth and Poverty in the Book of Proverbs*, JSOT Supplements, vol. 99 (Sheffield: Sheffield Academic Press, 1990).

Wright, Christopher J. H., *God's People in God's Land: Family, Land and Property in the Old Testament* (Grand Rapids: Eerdmans, 1990; Carlisle: Paternoster, rev. ed., 1996).

———, *Deuteronomy*, New International Biblical Commentary, Old Testament Series (Peabody: Hendrikson; Carlisle: Paternoster, 1996).

6. THE LAND AND CHRISTIAN ETHICS

In chapter 3 we saw how central the land is to the Old Testament story and also the major role the theology of the land plays in the overall faith of Israel. In the last two chapters we have seen the ways in which this theological centrality worked out ethically in the form of ecological perspectives and economic laws and institutions. What we shall do in this chapter is to ask how these various threads can be drawn through into Christian ethics. What hermeneutical methods are available to enable us to use Old Testament teaching regarding the land within a Christian framework that is, of course, governed by the New Testament?

Two ways of interpreting the Old Testament in this respect have already been noted, because they arise from within the Old Testament itself. They are the *paradigmatic* and *eschatological* methods of interpretation. To these we must add a third, from a New Testament perspective, the *typological*. Let us first of all remind ourselves of the first two, with the aid of our triangular diagram, and then explain the third in more depth. Then we shall test our method on a particular case study, the biblical jubilee, to see what it can yield to us in Christian theological and ethical terms when we examine it from our three different angles and at three different levels of interpretation.

It should be emphasized that these levels (paradigmatic, typological and eschatological) are three *complementary* ways of interpreting and applying Old Testament ethical material. They are not mutually exclusive, nor are they all relevant in every case. The land, however, does provide a particularly interesting example, because it can be taken up into Christian reflection and application in all three ways. So we should not think that if we speak of the land in the Old Testament having significance for the eschatological new creation, we thereby exclude it from economic relevance in the present social order. Or that if we speak of it as finding typological fulfilment in Christ, we thereby 'spiritualize' it out of any paradigmatic relevance to earthly issues of peoples and territories today. Each level can be meaningful and valid without excluding the others.

Paradigmatic interpretation

This approach rests on the belief that God's relation to Israel in their land was a deliberate reflection of God's relation to humankind on the earth. Or, to be more precise, God's involvement with Israel in their land was God's redemptive address to the fracturing of his creative purpose for human beings and the earth. Humanity has rebelled and lives on an earth under God's curse. Israel was redeemed and lived in a land God promised to bless. We can visualize this dual pattern through the following diagram:

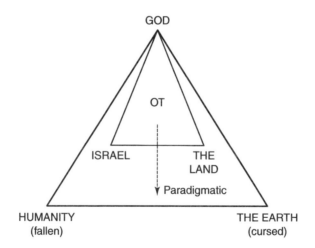

This is not just a case of squeezing complex material into a convenient geometric pattern. We have already clearly seen in chapter 2 how Israel as a society (the social angle) was chosen as a nation for the sake of all the nations of humanity and that her social system was intended to be a part of her theological message of 'light to the nations'. And at the beginning of chapter 4 we observed the correspondence, around the twin themes of divine ownership and divine gift, between the land of Israel (the economic angle) and the whole earth.

We are justified, therefore, in taking the social and economic laws and institutions of Israel (the base line of the inner triangle) and using them as models for our own ethical task in the wider world of modern-day secular society (the base line of the outer triangle). In the economic sphere the Old Testament paradigms provide us with *objectives*, without requiring a *literal* transposition of ancient Israelite practice into twentieth-century society. But at the same time the paradigmatic approach compels us to wrestle seriously with the texts themselves in order to understand fully the models we are seeking to apply.[1]

Eschatological interpretation

This approach rests on the conviction, solidly based in the Old as well as the New Testament, that God's redemptive purpose, initiated through Israel and their land, will ultimately embrace all nations and the whole earth, in a transformed and perfect new creation. Returning to the diagram, if we can think in dynamic terms while using a static figure, this means that the redemptive triangle will ultimately 'transcend' (break through) the triangle of fallen creation:

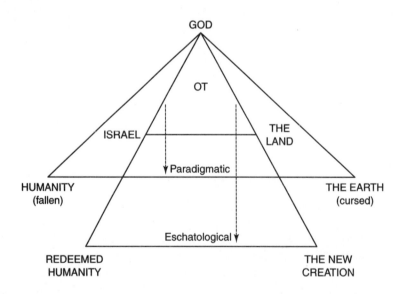

---

[1] An interesting example of such paradigmatic handling of Old Testament economic systems is provided by Nigel Biggar and Donald Hay, 'Bible and Social Security', in relation to the British welfare state.

The Old Testament looks forward not only to the world of nations turning to acknowledge the God of Israel and living at peace under his rule (see chapter 7), but also to the world of nature being transformed by God's miraculous power (as we saw in chapter 4). There is a serious 'earthiness' about the Old Testament hope. God will not just abandon his creation, but will redeem it. And the land of Israel functioned as a prototype of that redeemed earth. Hints of this are to be found in those descriptions of the land that contrast starkly with the cursed earth. It is the land of promise, whereas the earth was the arena of threat and judgment. It abounds in milk and honey (Exod. 3:8, etc.), not thorns and thistles (Gen. 3:18).[2] The descriptions of the land in Deuteronomy recall some of the paradisiacal features of Eden: a 'good land' (8:7ff.), well watered, full of vegetation and rich in resources (cf. Gen. 2:8ff.). In short, 'It is a land the LORD your God cares for; the eyes of the LORD your God are continually on it from the beginning of the year to its end' (Deut. 11:12). Indeed, if only God's redeemed people would wholly obey him, it would be a land of such blessing as to be a veritable 'paradise restored' (Deut. 28:1–14). The same theme is echoed in Leviticus 26:12, where God promises to 'walk among' his people, using the same unusual form of the verb as is used to describe God walking with the couple in the Garden of Eden.[3]

Israel, however, though redeemed and brought into covenant relationship with God, was still part of fallen humanity. And their land was still part of the cursed earth. The historical people and land were part of the *process* of God's redemptive purpose, not its final, perfected *product*. The theological function of both people and land together, therefore, is rather like a prototype, or a sign, pointing to something that lay beyond their present empirical reality. As Israel looked to the future completion of God's redemptive purpose, they did so in terms drawn from their experience of the past and the present. Thus just as they could not conceive of the new covenant without *law*, even though it would be law that transcended the reach of any legislator, for it would be

---

[2] In a wide variety of contexts in the ancient world 'milk and honey' were the Elysian food of the gods. 'What we have here, then, is an image of the plenitude of paradise' (Lohfink, *Option for the Poor*, p. 43). Lohfink's point is that Israel were being invited to live as humans on a diet fit for the gods – by living in obedience to God in the land he was giving them. My point is that the metaphor points on beyond itself to God's intention to restore the creation to the place where redeemed humanity lives in perfect fellowship with God – a hope the New Testament also portrays under the metaphor of banqueting.

[3] It is the hithpa'el form of *hālak*, which means 'to stroll around for one's own pleasure'.

written on the *hearts* of God's people (Jer. 31:33), so they could not conceive of God's future multinational redeemed people without *land*, even though it would be land that transcended the imagination of any geographer or even zoologist! The transformation of nature in passages such as Isaiah 2:2; 11:6–9; 35:1–10; Jeremiah 31:1–14 and Hosea 2:18–23 is clearly not intended literally. Yet neither should it be simply spiritualized, or taken as *merely* metaphorical. God's redemptive purpose for his creation may be beyond our imagination, but not beyond the eye of faith.

This, then, is another important function of the land of Israel within the total sweep of biblical theology. It points eschatologically to that 'new heaven and new earth' in which righteousness will dwell, because God will dwell there with his people (2 Pet. 3:13; Rev. 21:1–3). The identification is explicitly made in the New Testament with the use of 'the new Jerusalem' as a figure for the new creation to come (cf. Rev. 21:4–5; Heb. 12:22).

The biblical vision of the future, however, is not to be regarded as psychological escapism from the problems of the present. The prophets' use of their future vision, just as their use of the historical past, was designed to effect response and change *in the present*. Biblical eschatology is not just a utopian dream of what *might* be, a wistful 'if only . . .' Such dreaming can lead to despair and cynicism regarding the present. It is rather a vision of what *will* be, because God will do it. Therefore it is frequently coupled with urgent moral challenge and the incentive of positive expectation (cf. Ps. 97:10; Is. 2:5; Mic. 4:5; Matt. 25; Rev. 21:8, 27; 22:11). Thus an eschatological interpretation of any Old Testament theme, such as the land in this case, rebounds back into the present world with an ethical thrust. If this is how the story ends, what kind of ethical objectives should shape our behaviour as we live in the midst of the story here and now?

This eschatological dimension of biblical ethics does not add materially to the specific *content* of our ethical imperatives in social or personal terms, in either Testament. That content is already present in the known commands of God and in the examples, paradigms and teaching provided through God's revelation. What it does do is to lend urgency and incentive to those imperatives, on the one hand (as is the case in Rom. 13:11–14; 2 Pet. 3:11–14; 1 John 3:2–3), and, on the other hand, to give us the confident certainty that the vision of fulfilling those imperatives will be achieved. Our work, in the economic or any other sphere, will ultimately be 'not in vain in the Lord' (1 Cor. 15:58), as Paul concluded his affirmation of our future hope of the resurrection of the body.

Typological interpretation

One important question remains. What happens to the land in the New Testament? There can be no doubt that the New Testament writers regarded Jesus as the Messiah who fulfilled and embodied the mission of Israel. Consequently the Christian church, as the messianic community of those who are 'in Christ', stands in spiritually organic continuity with Old Testament Israel. The Messiah is the embodiment of the people of God, the fulfilment of the Old Testament people of God and the foundation for the New Testament people of God. Whether Gentile or Jew, the believer in Christ is the spiritual seed of Abraham, and heir to the covenant and promise (Gal. 3:26–28). But now, that promise made to Abraham had the land as a major constituent. If all the great themes of Old Testament faith and ritual converge typologically on Christ, where does the land fit in? For, as we have seen, the land is one of the most important theological realities in the faith of Old Testament Israel.

No longer holy territory

In one sense the land is almost completely absent from the New Testament. The *physical territory* of Palestine is nowhere referred to with any theological significance in the New Testament. The land as a holy *place* has ceased to have relevance. The vocabulary of blessing, holiness, promise, gift, inheritance and so on is never used of the territory inhabited by the Jewish people anywere in the New Testament as it so frequently is in the Old. This is partly because the Christian churches rapidly spread beyond its borders to other lands throughout the Mediterranean and beyond. But much more importantly it is because the holiness of the land, and indeed all its other attributes in Old Testament thinking, was transferred to Christ himself. The spiritual presence of the living Christ sanctifies any place where believers are present. This transference of the holiness of the land to Christ is well presented by W. D. Davies, who points out how Christianity reacted to all the concrete details of Judaism, including the land, 'in terms of Christ, to whom all places and all space, like all things else, are subordinated. In sum, for the holiness of place, Christianity has fundamentally . . . substituted the holiness of the Person: it has Christified holy space.'[4] The promise of Jesus to be present wherever his people meet, effectively universalizes the Old Testament promise of God's presence among his people in their land, for now the people of Jesus are everywhere:

---

[4] W. D. Davies, *Gospel and the Land*, p. 368.

Jesus where'er thy people meet
There they behold thy mercy seat
Where'er they seek thee, thou art found
And every place is hallow'd ground.[5]

Furthermore, the geographical land of Israel has no place in New Testament teaching regarding the ultimate future of God's people. Even in key passages where the relation between Jew and Gentile Christians is discussed, and especially in Romans 9 – 11 where Paul speaks of the future of the Jewish nation, no mention whatever is made of the land. Nor is there any indication that Paul, himself a believing Jew, believed that the land as physical territory still had *theological* importance for the *Jewish* Christians. No doubt Paul would have included the land among the great gifts that the Jews had enjoyed from God; but the whole context and drift of his argument shows that he regarded all that Israel had received from God as being focused, fulfilled and surpassed in the person of the Messiah, Jesus (cf. Rom. 9:4–5; 10:4). That, indeed, was his personal creed when he compared all he had had in his former identity with what he now had 'in the Messiah' (Phil. 3:3–11). And in his remarkable allegory in Galatians 4 he relegates the present earthly city of Jerusalem to the rank of Hagar in comparison with the city of the free children of God, applying prophecies originally spoken about Jerusalem to the messianic community of believers in Jesus.

Of course, since Paul does not tackle the subject of the land directly as a theological issue, we cannot be dogmatic about what his views on its theological significance may have been. His silence on the matter, however, seems eloquent, given the depth he does go into on some other Old Testament realities he regarded as theologically significant. My own feeling (I put it no stronger) is that if Paul had been faced with questions over the land as he was over the matter of *circumcision*, he would have handled them in a similar way. We know he would not allow that physical circumcision had any further *theological* significance within God's redemptive work. People's salvation and membership of the covenant community no longer required that they submit to this badge of ethnic identity with the Jewish people. *In Christ* there was neither circumcision nor uncircumcision. On this Paul was utterly unyielding. But once that point was conceded, he regarded circumcision as a matter of moral neutrality: it was of no theological importance whether you chose to circumcise or not (Gal. 5:6; 6:15). He had no objection to Jewish Christians continuing the practice as

---

[5] William Cowper wrote this hymn for his congregation when they had to move to a new building for worship and prayer, to reassure them that the universal presence of Christ was a matter of personal relationship rather than physical place.

a cultural custom, and indeed had Timothy circumcised because of the cultural environment of his work (Acts 16:3).

Similarly, we could imagine that he might have argued that the land *as territory* had no further theological significance in God's redemptive purpose, for that was now fully bound up with the atoning work of the crucified, risen and indwelling Messiah. The promise of salvation through Jesus was available to anyone living anywhere in any land; there was no special privilege or advantage to those living in the particular land of Israel's Old Testament inheritance. Provided that point was established, Paul might have seen no reason why Jews and Jewish Christians should not continue to feel an emotional and cultural bond with the land of their ancestors. But their *faith*, their *hope* and their *worship* must no longer be localized there, but on Christ alone. The Messiah himself had taught this same point when he had directed the attention of the Samaritan woman away from the debate over the proper territorial *place* for worshipping God to the only proper *person* through whom to worship God; namely, himself, the Messiah. Jesus, not the land, from now on was to be the focus of the spiritual worship of God (John 4:20–26).[6]

The significance of the land for Old Testament Israel

The New Testament, then, gives no theological significance to the territorial land of Palestine. However, in the Old Testament the land was never *merely* a piece of territory, any more than the temple was merely a building or Jerusalem merely a city. Like both of those, the land was the focus of major theological and ethical traditions. As we have seen, the land embodied many aspects of the covenant relationship between the LORD and Israel: its promises, blessings and demands. These traditions of the land can hardly have just vanished from sight in the New Testament, especially since they were connected with the covenant with Abraham, which had a prominent place in Paul's theology. Elsewhere we can certainly see how themes and symbols connected with the temple and Jerusalem were taken up and used spiritually in the New Testament. So again we come back to our earlier question and ask, what has become of the land in the New Testament?

---

[6] Christian theological presuppositions and conclusions regarding the land of Israel, both in biblical terms, and in relation to the modern state of Israel, are, of course, horrendously complicated and controversial. My own perspective stands alongside others in P. W. L. Walker (ed.), *Jerusalem Past and Present*. A fuller survey of the theme with a wide range of perspectives, is also to be found in P. Johnston and P. W. L. Walker (eds.), *Land of Promise*. An earlier work, now updated, is Colin Chapman, *Whose Promised Land?* See also Gary M. Burge, *Whose Land? Whose Promise?*

To answer that question we must first recall the *function* of the land in *Israel's* life and faith, and then ask what aspect of *Christian* life and faith has absorbed or fulfilled that function in the New Testament. What did the land signify for an Old Testament Israelite? What bears a corresponding significance for the Christian? Defining this analogy is what is meant by a typological approach. What the land meant for Israel's relationship with God is 'typical' of certain realities in the Christian's relationship with God through Christ. So let us see what this typological correspondence points us to.[7]

We have already seen that, for an Israelite, the land was above all else *God's gift*. It had been given in fulfilment of his promise to Abraham, and received in the course of their redemptive history. The land was therefore a huge, symbolic, tangible proof to every Israelite householder that he, his family and his people had a special covenantal relationship with the LORD. Deuteronomy links the land repeatedly with the assurance of their election in Abraham. They were the LORD's people because they lived in the LORD's land, which he had given to them. The individual enjoyed his personal share in the land through the kinship network and his inalienable family inheritance – his 'portion' in the land. Deuteronomy also speaks of the land repeatedly as Israel's inheritance, which invokes family images. Israel was, as Exodus 4:22 stated, the LORD's firstborn son, and the land was again tangible evidence of that relationship of sonship. Thus to belong to an Israelite household living in God's land was to experience secure inclusion within the covenant relationship: the land was the place of *life* with God. But it also meant to accept the demands of that covenant relationship: the land was also the place of a specific moral and spiritual *lifestyle* before God. To possess the land was to share in the inheritance and responsibility of all God's people. The land, in short, for an Israelite meant security, inclusion, blessing, sharing and practical responsibility.

Alongside all this, however, there was also in the Old Testament an awareness that Israel's relationship with God, while undoubtedly grounded in and experienced through this socio-economic realm of land and kinship, transcended that realm, and was not permanently or exclusively bound to it. God had called Israel his 'firstborn son' while they were still in Egypt (Exod. 4:22), and had sealed his covenant with them before they actually entered the land. Likewise, they remained God's people even while undergoing the punishment of exile from the land. Loss of land was a massive fracture in the relationship of God and Israel, but, as the prophets of that era repeatedly insisted, it was not the *end* of the relationship. The LORD was alive and well in Babylon, and

---

[7] I have explained more fully my understanding of a biblically balanced view of typology in C. J. H. Wright, *Knowing Jesus*, pp. 107–116.

could call his people back to repentance and life through an Ezekiel in Babylon as much as through a Jeremiah in Jerusalem. God is not bound by territorial boundaries and, in a growing awareness, neither could God's people be.

More significant, as we move towards the New Testament, is the fact that in the eschatological visions of the prophets we can discern a loosening of, almost a dispensing with, the ancient land–kinship basis of the covenant, in visions of the future constitution of the relationship between God and his people. The restored people of God will have an all-inclusiveness, in which categories of people who, on the old land–kinship criterion, would have been excluded or were in a very uncertain position will be brought into a full and assured relationship with God as an integral part of 'Israel'. Thus, for example, in Isaiah 56:3–8 the doubts of the foreigner (who had no stake in the *land*) and of the eunuch (who could have no *family* or posterity) are alike allayed by the promise of permanent security in the new covenant. And in Ezekiel 47:22–23 the idealized picture of the future 'land tenure' of Israel makes a point of explicitly including those who had previously been excluded or only tolerated as dependants – the *gērîm*, the aliens, immigrants and refugees who previously had no permission to own a share in the land. In this vision of the future their share in the inheritance of God's people will no longer depend on charity or good fortune but will be permanently guaranteed. In other words, the theological themes of security, inclusion, sharing and responsibility, which were once linked to the land, remain valid; but they are loosened from their literal, territorial moorings, as the scope of salvation is widened to include non-Israelites.

'In Christ' as 'in the land'

The New Testament sees this eschatological vision of the extension of redemption beyond the nation of Israel as being fulfilled in the inclusion of the Gentiles in the people of God, through the work of the Messiah, Jesus. The Gentile mission of the early church was, and was explicitly perceived to be (e.g. Acts 15:12–18), a clear fulfilment of Old Testament prophecies regarding the restoration of Israel.

Paul's classic exposition of this new, all-inclusive dimension of the Christian gospel, Ephesians 2:11 – 3:6, is significantly rich in Old Testament imagery. Paul begins by summarizing the previous position of the Gentiles *outside* Christ in terms equivalent to the position of those who, in the Old Testament, had had no share in the land–kinship membership of Israel: 'excluded from citizenship in Israel and foreigners to the covenants of the promise' (2:12). Then, having described the work of Christ on the cross as breaking down that barrier, making peace and providing access to God for the believing Jew and Gentile alike, Paul returns to Old Testament imagery to

192 OLD TESTAMENT ETHICS FOR THE PEOPLE OF GOD

describe the new position of the Gentiles *in* Christ: 'Consequently, you are no longer foreigners and aliens [words that translate *gērîm* and *tôšābîm* – the landless dependants in Israel's economy], but fellow-citizens with God's people and members of God's household' (2:19). This speaks of permanence, security, inclusion and, as he soon points out, practical responsibility. In the climax of this outline of 'his gospel' Paul sums up the new position of the Gentiles in the three words of 3:6 (one of which he invented). They are now joint-heirs (*synklēronoma*), a joint-body (*syssōma*) and joint-sharers (*symmetocha*) with Israel in the promise, in Messiah Jesus, through the gospel. The message is crystal clear: through the cross of Christ, those who were *out* are now *in*; those who were *far off* are now *near*; those who *were excluded* now *belong*. All of this strongly Old Testament language of inheritance evokes the pattern of relationships between God, Israel and their land, within which the Israelites of old had found their security. But now that security is enjoyed by all in Christ: believing Gentiles as well as believing Jews. What Israel had through their land, all believers have through Christ.

Thus, by incorporation into the Messiah, people from all nations are enabled to enter into the privileges and responsibilities of God's people, privileges and responsibilities that, in the Old Testament, had been focused on life in the land. Now Christ himself takes over the significance and the function of that old land–kinship qualification. To be *in Christ*, just as to be *in the land*, denotes first, a status and a relationship that have been *given* by God; second, a position of inclusion and security in God's family; and third, a commitment to live worthily by fulfilling the practical responsibilities towards those who share the same relationship with you. This is what is meant by the *typological* understanding of the significance of Israel's land. It simply means treating the land as we do other great features and themes of the Old Testament, by relating it to the person and work of the Messiah, and through him to the nature of the community of those 'in Christ', messianic Israel.[8]

So far I have used Paul mainly as our theological guide. But Hebrews is arguably even more significant. Paul, on the one hand, was writing mainly to Gentile believers to assure them of their new standing in Christ, in relation to the promises of the Old Testament. The writer to the Hebrews, on the other hand, was writing to mainly Jewish believers, to reassure them that in Christ they have lost nothing of what was theirs under the old covenant, but rather

---

[8] For a similar reading of the land as speaking (among other things) of life and lifestyle in Christ, see also Martens, *God's Design*, pp. 114–121, 243–254. For a somewhat different focus on the symbolism of the land within New Testament and Christian thinking, see Brueggemann, *Land*, chs. 10–11.

now have it in even greater measure by having Christ. The sustained argument of Hebrews is that we now have in Jesus all that was real for Israel. The author's reference to 'shadows' (Heb. 10:1) does not imply that all the great elements of Israel's life in the Old Testament (land, law, temple, priesthood, sacrifice etc.) were unreal, or only a charade. No, they were substantive and significant factors in the relationship between God and Israel as it obtained at that time. But because of God's promises concerning what he planned to do for and through Israel, these original realities would be filled with even greater meaning in God's future relationship with his people. Hence to affirm, as Hebrews repeatedly does, that what we have in Christ is 'better', is not (as it is sometimes disparagingly called) 'replacement theology'. It is rather 'extension', or 'fulfilment', theology. In the same way, the multinational community of believers in Jesus the Messiah is not a 'new Israel' (as if the old were simply discarded). It is rather God's original Israel but now expanded and redefined in relation to Christ through the inclusion of the Gentiles – as God had promised ever since Abraham.

The affirmations in Hebrews of what 'we have' are surprisingly comprehensive, and obviously intended to be so, in order to reassure Jewish readers. We *have* the land – described as 'the rest', which even Joshua did not finally achieve for Israel, but into which we can enter through Christ (Heb. 3:12 – 4:11). We *have* a High Priest (Heb. 4:14; 8:1; 10:21). We *have* an altar (Heb. 13:10). We *have* hope through the covenant (Heb. 6:19–20). We *have* confident access into the Holy Place, so we have the reality of tabernacle and temple (Heb. 10:19). We have come to Mount Zion (Heb. 12:22). We *have* a kingdom (Heb. 12:28). Indeed, according to Hebrews, the only thing we do *not* have is an earthly, territorial city (Heb. 13:14). In the light of all the other positive 'haves' this clear negative stands out all the more significantly. There is no 'holy land' or 'holy city' for Christians. We have no need of either – we have Christ.

Hebrews, then, insists that Jews who believe in Jesus lose nothing of what they had before, but now have it in eternally greater reality through Christ, and that includes all that the land stood for. Paul insists that Gentiles who believe in Jesus gain nothing less than the full inheritance that had belonged exclusively but temporarily to Israel before. Both Jews and Gentiles, then (those who had the land, and those who had nothing; those who were near and those who were far off), now together and alike have everything if they are in Christ. For in Christ all are equal: no-one loses and everyone gains.

Land and the demands of Christian fellowship

But what has become of the *socio-economic* dimension of the land, which we found to be of such importance to Old Testament Israel? Has it all just been transcended, spiritualized and forgotten? By no means! It feeds through precisely into that realm of corporate sharing and practical responsibility, which is just as much a feature of the New as of the Old Testament.

Before glancing at what that meant in practice, let us return to the passage we have just considered, Ephesians 2. Twice in that context Paul refers to the role of the Holy Spirit in the incorporation of Jew and Gentile together into God's new community in Christ (2:18, 22). Elsewhere, indeed, Paul regards the gift of the Holy Spirit as itself the fulfilment of the promise to Abraham, also in the context of the extension of salvation to the Gentiles (Gal. 3:14). In the same context he also relates the *oneness* of believers in Christ to their status as seed and heirs of Abraham (Gal. 3:28–29). Now this oneness of believers in Christ and their shared experience of Christ through the Holy Spirit is no mere abstract, 'spiritual' concept. On the contrary, it has far-reaching practical implications in both the social *and* economic realms. Both realms (social and economic) are included in the New Testament understanding and practice of 'fellowship', and both have deep roots in the soil of Old Testament land ethics.

Fellowship is the usual English translation of the Greek *koinōnia*, which is itself part of a rich complex of words. A study of the *koinōn-* root in the New Testament reveals that a substantial number of the occurrences of words formed or compounded from it either signify, or are in contexts that relate to, actual social and economic relationships between Christians. They denote a practical, often costly, sharing, which is a far cry from that watery 'together-ness' that commonly passes as 'fellowship' in our churches. In the New Testament, fellowship touches our relationships and our possessions.

Some examples will make the point. The first consequence of the outpour-ing of the Spirit at Pentecost was a new community who, in 'devoting them-selves to . . . the fellowship' (*tē koinōnia*), shared everything in common (Acts 2:42, 44), and ensured that nobody was in need (Acts 4:34). In Romans 12:13 believers are urged to share hospitality with the saints (*koinōnountes*). In 1 Timothy 6:18 the rich are to be commanded to be 'generous' (*koinōnikous*). The same duty is laid on all Christians in Hebrews 13:16. Paul refers to his financial collection among the Greek churches for the aid of the Judaean Christians as 'an act of fellowship' (*koinōnian tina*, Rom. 15:26). He justifies this financial collection on the grounds that if the Gentiles have shared (*ekoinōnēsan*) *spiritual* blessings from the Jews, they owe it to them to share *material* blessings (v. 27). The same reciprocal principle applies in the relation-ship between the teacher and the taught in Galatians 6:6 – the one taught must 'share with' (*koinōneitō*), that is, financially support, the teacher. Indeed, in commending the Corinthians for their eagerness to share in the financial col-lection (*koinōnia*, 2 Cor. 8:4; 9:13), Paul describes it as proof of their *obedience to the gospel*, implying that such concrete economic evidence of fellowship was of the essence of a genuine Christian profession. How best could the Jerusalem Jewish Christians be convinced that the Gentiles had really become true believers in the gospel? When they saw the fruit of their obedience to the gospel in bags of hard cash on their table. Is it, then, coincidental that when Paul's own gospel was accepted as authentic in Jerusalem by means of 'the right hand of *koinōnia*', he was immediately asked 'to remember the poor', as if in proof (Gal. 2:9–10)? His Gentile collection did indeed bear out his professed eagerness to honour that gospel fellowship. Likewise, when Paul thanks God for the Philippians' 'fellowship in the gospel' (Phil. 1:5), the rest of the letter makes it clear that he is thinking concretely, not just spiritually. They had been partners (*synkoinōnoi*) with Paul (1:7) in practical financial support for his ministry (4:15ff.).

The extent of this kind of language in the New Testament understanding of fellowship leads me to the view that it has deep roots in the socio-economic ethics of the Old Testament. There are so many similarities which show that the experience of *fellowship* – in its full, rich, 'concrete' New Testament sense – fulfils analogous theological and ethical functions for the Christian as the possession of *land* did for Old Testament Israelites. Both (land in the Old Testament, fellowship in the New) must be seen as part of the purpose and pattern of redemption, not just as accidental or incidental to it. The explicit purpose of the exodus was the enjoyment of the rich blessing of God in his 'good land'; the goal of redemption through Christ is 'sincere love for your brothers' (1 Pet. 1:22), with all its practical implications. Both are linked to the status of sonship and the related themes of inheritance and promise. Both thereby constitute a proof of an authentic relationship with God as part of his redeemed community. For fellowship, like the land, has its boundaries; so that the person who departs permanently from it or refuses to accept it shows that he has no real part in God's people (cf. Matt. 18:15–17; 1 John 2:19).

Above all, both land and fellowship are *shared* experiences: the land, by the nature of the Israelite economic system as outlined above; fellowship, by very definition of the word *koinōnia*. This gives to both that deeply practical mutual responsibility that pervades both Old and New Testament ethics. There is the same concern for the poor and needy (cf. 1 John 3:17), the same ideal of equality among God's people, both economically (cf. 2 Cor. 8:13–15 with its Old Testament allusion) and socially (cf. Jas. 2:1–7). There is even the same prophetic indignation at those whose sin deprives or defrauds fellow members of God's people of their rightful share in what God has given for the enjoyment of all his people. The Old Testament prophets condemned the unjust oppressors who drove fellow Israelites off their land; compare with that Jesus' strictures on those who refuse to forgive a brother (Matt. 18:21–35), Paul's horror at the factionalism and lack of love at Corinth and the priority he gives in his various lists of sins to those that harm the fellowship (e.g. Eph. 4:25ff.; Phil. 2:1–4, 14; Col. 3:8ff.), and John's refusal to accept as a child of God at all the man who hates his brother (1 John 2:9–11; 4:7ff.).

So then, the typological interpretation of the land, which relates it to the person and work of Jesus the Messiah, does not come to a 'dead end' with Jesus himself. Rather, it carries the social and economic thrust of Old Testament ethics onwards into the ethics of practical relationships within New Testament Israel, the Messianic community. Citizenship of the kingdom of God most certainly has a social and economic dimension. This is a dimension that has transcended the land and kinship structure of Old Testament Israel, but not in such a way as to make that original structure irrelevant. This transference of the socio-economic bond of Old Testament society to the Christ-centred bond of the New Testament is recognized by the Jewish scholar Raphael Loewe: 'The sociological basis on which Christianity rests is not the tie of kinship, as in the case of Judaism, but that of fellowship – fellowship in Christ.'[9] In this, as in so many other ways, Christ and the kingdom he proclaimed and inaugurated 'fulfil' the Old Testament, taking up its socio-economic pattern and transforming it into something that can be the experience not just of a single nation in a small slice of territory but of anyone, anywhere, in Christ.

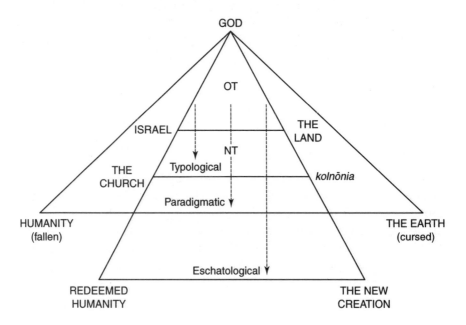

---

9 Loewe, *Women in Judaism*, p. 52.

Our diagram, then, must acquire yet another triangle. At one corner we can place the Christian church – the messianic community of believing Jews and Gentiles – as the spiritual heir and continuation of Old Testament Israel. And at the other corner we can place Christian fellowship, in its fullest, practical New Testament sense, as fulfilling similar theological and ethical functions to the land of Israel. Both together then form the context of a typological interpretation of Old Testament ethics in relation to the church.

Summary

Now that we have looked at the matter from each of the three perspectives, we need to remind ourselves again that these are complementary and mutually reinforcing ways of making Christian ethical sense of Old Testament Israelite economics. It may help to clarify things further if we make a conceptual distinction between interpreting the land in terms of *principles* and in terms of *promise*. From that point of view, the paradigmatic method deals with *principles*; while the typological and eschatological methods are both handling the Old Testament land at the level of its inherent *promise*.

So, when approaching Israel's economic system of land tenure paradigmatically, we are seeking to identify and articulate those principles upon which it was based, the objectives it was aiming to achieve, its rationale, motivations and practical outworkings. Once we have done that, then we are in a position to ask how such a paradigm impacts the context in which we ourselves live. We look for ways of applying the range of economic principles that will authentically reflect the totality of the biblical paradigm itself.

When we approach Old Testament theology of the land from the perspective of its inherent promise, however, we are led to see the fulfilment of that (as of all Old Testament promises) in the coming of Jesus of Nazareth, the Messiah. The New Testament, it seems to me, leaves us no other option than to make that clear link. But this 'promise–fulfilment' motif in relation to the land divides in two, rather like the dual presentation of the kingdom of God in the New Testament. There is an already and a not-yet. Already we have in Christ and in fellowship with the whole household of God in him the reality the land gave to Israel – the tangible blessing of our redeemed, covenantal relationship with God and one another (our typological interpretation). But there is yet to come the ultimate fulfilment of all the land promised the people of God; namely, the restoration of all things in a new creation, a new heaven and a new earth (the eschatological interpretation).

These different levels of interpretation are not, however, independent of one another. For, as we have seen, if we affirm a typological relationship between the land of Israel and the fellowship of Christians, then it is our paradigmatic understanding of the responsibilities of Israelites in the land that helps to shape and deepen our understanding of the social and economic responsibilities of Christian fellowship. And if our eschatological interpretation gives us hope and assurance of the ultimate victory of God over all that spoils his creation, then that in turn feeds into our determination to advocate and apply biblical economic and ecological paradigms in the world today.

This threefold framework of interpretation, then, paradigmatic, typological and eschatological, releases the potential and power of Old Testament ethics into the whole range of Christian concerns for the church, for the world and for the ultimate future of both. It is a framework that we have arrived at in our study of Old Testament economics in particular, but it is valid, I believe, for the whole range of ethical principles operating in and from the Old Testament, as we shall see in the following chapters.

The jubilee: a case study

In order to see how these different angles and levels might work, let us look in some detail at one Old Testament institution deeply rooted in Israel's theology and practice of land tenure – the year of jubilee. First of all we shall study it within its own context, ensuring we have a good grasp of its background, rationale and objectives. For this purpose we shall work our way around the three angles of our basic triangle – the social, economic and theological angles – viewing it from each in turn. This will necessitate a certain amount of brief repetition of points made earlier in the study, for the sake of giving a complete overview of the method used. Then we shall do a brief exegetical survey of Leviticus 25 so as to have a grasp of the whole piece of legislation. Then, finally, in order to reflect on its potential within Christian ethics, we shall work down the three levels of interpretation – typological, paradigmatic and eschatological.

The jubilee (*yôbēl*) came at the end of the cycle of seven sabbatical years. Leviticus 25:8–10 specifies it as the fiftieth year, though some scholars believe it may actually have been the forty-ninth; that is, the seventh sabbatical year. And some suggest it was not a full year, but either a single day as an event within the fiftieth year, or an intercalary month after the forty-ninth year, with the same calendrical effect as our system of leap years. In this year there was to be a proclamation of liberty to Israelites who had become enslaved for debt, and a restoration of land to families who had been compelled to sell it out of economic need sometime during the previous fifty years. Instructions concerning the jubilee, and its relation to the procedures of land and slave redemption are found entirely in Leviticus 25. But it is referred to also in Leviticus 26 and 27. It is an institution that has inspired much curiosity in ancient and modern times, and in recent years it has come to prominence in the writings of those committed to radical Christian social ethics.

The jubilee was in essence an economic institution. It had two main points of concern: the *family* and the *land*. It was rooted, therefore, in the *social* structure of Israelite kinship and the *economic* system of land tenure based upon it. Both of these, however, also had *theological* dimensions in Israel's faith. So we must look at the jubilee now from all three angles of our ethical triangle.

The social angle: Israel's kinship system

Israel had a three-tier pattern of kinship, comprising the tribe, the clan and the household. Gideon's modest reply to his angelic visitor shows us all three: 'Look at my *clan* – it is the weakest in the *tribe* of Manasseh; and I am the least in my *father's house*' (Judg. 6:15, my trans.). The last two smaller units (household and clan) had greater social and economic importance than the tribe in terms of benefits and responsibilities relating to individual Israelites. The father's house was a place of authority, even for married adults like Gideon (Judg. 6:27; 8:20). It was also the place of security and protection (Judg. 6:30ff.). The clan was a larger grouping of a number of father's houses and an important subunit of the tribe. The clans were named after the grandsons of Jacob, or other members of the patriarchal family tree (see Num. 26 and 1 Chr. 4 – 8). This makes visible the fact that they were units of recognizable kinship. But sometimes the clan name was attached to the territorial area of their settlement, such as a village or group of villages. So the clan had the dual constituents of kinship and territory. The clan had important responsibility in the preservation of the land allotted to its constituent households.[10] The jubilee was intended primarily for the economic protection of the smallest of these units – the father's house, or the extended family. However, in Leviticus 25, it is interwoven with the economic practice of the redemption of land and persons, and those redemption procedures were primarily for the protection of the clan, and also a major functional responsibility of the clan. The two sets of provision (jubilee and redemption) were complementary, as we shall see.

The economic angle: Israel's system of land tenure

Whatever may have been the process by which Israel emerged in Canaan, once they were able to establish control over the land (which was not everywhere, of course, for quite a long time – especially in areas of Canaanite city

---

[10] For further information on Israel's kinship system, see chapter 10 below, and also C. J. H. Wright, *God's Land*, ch. 2; 'Family'; Gottwald, *Tribes of Yahweh*, pp. 237–341; Leo G. Perdue, J. Blenkinsopp and J. J. Collins, *Families in Ancient Israel*.

domination), they operated a system of land tenure based on these kinship units. Thus the territory was allotted to tribes 'according to their clans', and within the clans each household had its portion or 'heritage'. Judges 21:24 describes the Israelite soldiers returning each to his tribe, his clan and to his (household) inheritance. This system had two features that stand in complete contrast to the preceding pattern of Canaanite economic structure:

- *Equitable distribution.* In Canaan the land was owned by kings and their nobles, with the bulk of the population living as tax-paying tenant farmers. In Israel the initial division of the land was explicitly to the clans and households within the tribes, under the general rubric that each should receive land according to size and need. The documentary evidence for this is to be found in the tribal lists of Numbers 26 (especially note vv. 52–56) and in the detailed territorial division of land recorded in Joshua 13 – 21. In Joshua the repetition of the phrase 'according to their clans' indicates the intention that the land should be distributed throughout the whole kinship system as widely as possible.
- *Inalienability.* In order to protect this system of kinship distribution, family land was made inalienable. That is, it was not to be bought and sold as a commercial asset, but was to remain as far as possible within the extended family, or at least within the circle of families in the clan. It was this principle that lay behind Naboth's refusal to sell his patrimony to Ahab (1 Kgs. 21), and it is most explicit in the economic regulations of Leviticus 25.

The theological angle: God's land, God's people

> The land shall not be sold permanently, for the land belongs to me; for you are 'guests' and 'residents' with me.
>
> Leviticus 25:23, my trans.

This statement, at the heart of the chapter containing the jubilee, provides the hinge between the social and economic system described above and its theological rationale. Having stated the inalienability rule, it goes on to present the two basic factors in the theological context of the jubilee and related laws: the theology of the land and the status of the Israelites.

God's land

Briefly to repeat and summarize what we saw in chapter 3, one of the central pillars of the faith of Israel was that the land they inhabited was the LORD's land. It had been his even before Israel entered it (Exod. 15:13, 17). This theme is found often in the prophets and Psalms, as part of Israel's cultic tradition. At the same time, although ultimately owned by the LORD, the land had been promised and then given to Israel in the course of the redemptive history. It was their inheritance (Deuteronomy passim), a term that points to the relationship of sonship between Israel and the LORD.

This dual tradition of the land (divine ownership and divine gift) was associated in some way with every major thread in Israel's theology. The promise of land was an essential part of the patriarchal *election* tradition. The land was the goal of the exodus *redemption* tradition. The maintenance of the *covenant* relationship and the security of life in the land were bound together. Divine *judgment* eventually meant expulsion from the land, until the *restored relationship* was symbolized in the return to the land. The land, then, stood like a fulcrum in the relationship between God and Israel (see its position in Lev. 26:40–45). It was a monumental, tangible witness both to that divine control of history within which the relationship had been established, and also to the moral and practical demands which that relationship entailed. For the Israelite, living with his family on his allotted share of the LORD's land, the land itself was the proof of his membership of God's people and the focus of his practical response to God's grace. Nothing that concerned the land was free from theological and ethical dimensions – as every harvest reminded him (Deut. 26).

God's people
The Israelites are described in two ways in Leviticus 25:

1. '*You are guests and residents* (RSV), *aliens and tenants* (NIV) *with me*' (*v. 23*). These terms, *gērîm wĕtôšābîm*, describe a class of people who resided among the Israelites in Canaan, but were not ethnic Israelites. They may have been descendants of the dispossessed Canaanites, or immigrants. They had no stake in the tenure of the land, but survived by hiring out their services as residential employees (labourers, craftsmen etc.) for Israelite landowning households. Provided the Israelite household remained economically viable, its resident alien employees enjoyed both protection and security. But otherwise, their position could be perilous. Hence they are frequently mentioned in Israel's law as the objects of particular concern for justice because of their vulnerability.

The Israelites were to regard their own status before God as analogous to that of these residential dependents to themselves. Thus they (the Israelites) had no ultimate title to the land – it was owned by God. The LORD was the supreme landlord. Israel was his collective tenant. Nevertheless, the Israelites could enjoy secure benefits of the land under the LORD's protection and in dependence on him. So the terms are not (as they might sound in English) a denial of rights, but rather an affirmation of a relationship of protected dependency.

The practical effect of this model for Israel's relationship with God is seen in verses 35, 40 and 53. If all Israelites share this same status before God, then the impoverished or indebted brother is to be regarded and treated in the same way as God regards and treats all Israel; that is, with compassion, justice and generosity.

2. '*They are my slaves whom I brought forth out of the land of Egypt*' (*vv. 42, 55*). Three times in this chapter the exodus is mentioned, and twice more in the following chapter (26:13, 45). It was regarded as an act of redemption in which God had 'bought' Israel for himself. Freed from slavery to Egypt, they were now slaves of God. Therefore nobody could now claim as his own private property a fellow Israelite who belonged by right of purchase to God alone. The exodus redemption thus provided the historical and theological model for the social and economic practice of redemption and jubilee. Those who are God's freed slaves are not to make slaves of one another (25:39, 42).

This weight of theological tradition concentrated into 25:23 gives great moral seriousness to the economic measures outlined in the rest of the chapter. In order to understand these, we need to do an exegetical outline of the chapter.[11]

Exegetical outline of Leviticus 25

1. *Verses 1–7*. The chapter opens with the law of the sabbatical year on the land. This is an expansion of the fallow year law of Exodus 23:10–11, which was also further developed in Deuteronomy 15:1–2 into a year in which debts (or more probably the pledges given for loans) were to be released.

2. *Verses 8–12*. The jubilee is then introduced as the fiftieth year to follow the seventh sabbatical year. Verse 10 presents the twin concepts fundamental to the whole institution; namely, liberty and return. *Liberty* – from the burden of debt and the bondage it may have entailed; *return* – both to the ancestral property if it had been mortgaged to a creditor, and to the family which may have been split up through debt-servitude. It was these two components of the jubilee, freedom and restoration that entered into the metaphorical and eschatological use of the jubilee in prophetic and later New Testament thought.

---

[11] Leviticus 25 is a complex chapter in which several different economic practices have been thrown closely together, along with parenthetical sections and exceptive clauses. Source critics have come to no kind of consensus over alleged documentary division of the material, and the multiplicity of theories is little help in understanding the chapter. However, in its present form the text has some definable paragraphs (as can be seen in the RSV and NIV), which guide us through its provisions.

3. *Verses 13–17.* The financial implications of a recurring jubilee are then spelt out. The apparent sale of a piece of land really amounted only to a sale of the use of the land. So an approaching jubilee diminished the cost for the purchaser, inasmuch as he was buying the number of harvests until the jubilee restored the land to its original owner.

4. *Verses 18–22.* At this point some exhortation is inserted to encourage the observance of the sabbatical regulations, by promising special blessing in the preceding year. The theological principle was that obedience to the economic legislation of Israel would require not prudential calculations but faith in the ability of the LORD to provide through his control of nature as well as history.

5. *Verses 23–24.* These central verses in the chapter constitute a heading to the remaining paragraphs, which are primarily concerned with the economic redemption of land and persons, interwoven with the jubilee. We have already noted the major theological traditions embodied in them.

6. *Verses 25–55.* We come now to the practical details of redemption and jubilee. In these verses there are three descending stages of poverty with required responses, interrupted by parenthetical sections dealing with houses in cities and Levite properties (vv. 29–34) and non-Israelite slaves (vv. 44–46). The stages are marked off by the introductory phrase 'If your brother becomes poor' (vv. 25, 35, 39, 47). Probably this phrase introduced an original series of redemption procedures, unconnected with the jubilee. The addition of jubilee regulations complicates matters in places, but, as we shall see, functions as a necessary complement to the effects of redemption.

a. Stage 1 (vv. 25–28). Initially, having fallen on hard times (for any reason: none is specified), the Israelite landowner sells, or offers to sell, some of his land. To keep it within the family, in line with the inalienability principle, it was first of all the duty of the nearest kinsman (the *gō'ēl*) either to pre-empt it (if it was still on offer), or to redeem it (if it had been sold). Secondly, the seller himself retains the right to redeem it for himself, if he later recovers the means to do so. Thirdly, and in any case, the property, whether sold or redeemed by a kinsman, reverts to the original family in the year of jubilee.

    (i) Exception (vv. 29–31). The above rules did not apply to dwelling places in the walled cities. This was probably because the primary intention of the redemption and jubilee provisions was to preserve the economic viability of families through the secure possesion of their inherited land. City houses were not part of that productive economic base, and so need not be subject to indefinite redemption rights or jubilee return to seller. However, village dwellings were treated as part of the rural scene, and therefore were included.

(ii) Exception (vv. 32–34). This is a rider to exception i. Since the Levites as a tribe had no inherited share in the land but were allotted certain towns, their dwellings in them were to be subject to normal redemption and jubilee provisions.

b. Stage 2 (vv. 35–38). If the poorer brother's plight worsens and he still cannot stay solvent, presumably even after several such sales, it then becomes the duty of the kinsman to maintain him as a dependent labourer, by means of interest-free loans.

c. Stage 3a (vv. 39–43). In the event of a total economic collapse, such that the poorer kinsman has no more land left to sell or a pledge for loans, he and his whole family sell themselves to (enter the bonded service of) the wealthier kinsman. The latter, however, is commanded in strong and repeated terms, not to treat the debtor Israelite like a slave, but rather as a resident employee. This undesirable state of affairs is to continue only until the next jubilee; that is, not more than one more generation. Then the debtor and/or his children (the original debtor may have died, but the next generation were to benefit from the jubilee, vv. 41, 54) were to recover their original patrimony of land and be enabled to make a fresh start.

(iii) Exception (vv. 44–46). This is a reminder that the redemption and jubilee provisions applied to Israelites and not to foreign slaves or resident aliens. This reinforces the point that they were primarily concerned with the distribution of land and the viability of Israelite families, neither of which applied to non-landowning persons.

d. Stage 3b (vv. 47–55). If a man had entered this debt-bondage *outside* the clan, then an obligation lay on the whole clan to prevent this loss of a whole family by exercising their duty to redeem him. The list of potential kinsman-redeemers in verses 48–49 shows how the responsibility moved outwards from the nearest kinsman to the extent of the clan itself ('family' in RSV v. 49 is misleading; the Hebrew is *mišpāḥâ* – 'clan'). The whole clan had the duty of preserving its constituent families and their inherited land. It also had the duty to see that a non-Israelite creditor behaved as an Israelite should towards an Israelite debtor, and that the jubilee provision was adhered to eventually.

From this analysis of the chapter it can be seen that there were two main differences between the redemption and jubilee provisions. First, *timing*. Redemption was a duty that could be exercised at any time, locally, as circumstances required, whereas jubilee was twice a century as a national event. Secondly, *purpose*. The main aim of redemption was the preservation of the land and persons of the *clan*, whereas the main beneficiary of the jubilee was the *household*, or 'father's house'. The jubilee therefore functioned as a necessary override to the practice of redemption. The regular operation of redemption over a period could result in the whole territory of a clan coming into the hands of a few wealthier families, with the rest of the families in the clan in a kind of debt-servitude, living as dependent tenants of the wealthy; that is, precisely the kind of land-tenure system Israel had overturned. The jubilee was thus a mechanism to prevent this, and to preserve the socio-economic fabric of multiple-household land tenure with the comparative equality and independent viability of the smallest family-plus-land units.[12]

Typological interpretation of the jubilee

This approach asks how the institution of jubilee was taken up by Jesus and applied in the New Testament to the age of fulfilment he inaugurated. How,

---

[12] The inevitable question arises, of course, did it ever historically happen? The fact is that there is no historical narrative recording a jubilee. But then, there is no historical record of the Day of Atonement, either. Silence in the narratives proves almost nothing. More divisive is the question whether the jubilee was an early law that fell into disuse, or a late piece of utopian idealism from the time of the exile. Many critical scholars affirm the latter, but others, especially those with in-depth knowledge of the ancient Near East, point out that such periodical amnesties for debt and restoration of land were known in Mesopotamia for centuries before the establishment of Israel, though nothing on such a regular fifty-year cycle has been found. My own preference is that it makes sense to see the jubilee as a very ancient law, which fell into neglect during Israel's history in the land. This neglect happened, not so much because the jubilee was economically impossible, as because it became irrelevant to the scale of social disruption. The jubilee presupposes a situation where a man, though in severe debt, still technically holds the title to his family's land and could be restored to full ownership of it. But from the time of Solomon on this must have become meaningless for growing numbers of families as they fell victim to the acids of debt, slavery, royal intrusion and confiscation, and total dispossession. Many were uprooted and pushed off their ancestral land altogether. After a few generations they had nothing to be restored to in any practicable sense (see Mic. 2:2, 9; Is. 5:8). This would explain why the jubilee is never appealed to by any of the prophets as an economic proposal (though its ideals are reflected metaphorically).

For bibliography of earlier works, see C. J. H. Wright, *God's Land*, pp. 119–127; 'Jubilee, Year Of'. More recent works include Jeffrey A. Fager, *Land Tenure*; Hans Ucko, *Jubilee Challenge*; and Moshe Weinfeld, *Social Justice*. A good, recent and balanced survey is provided by P. A. Barker, 'Sabbath, Sabbatical Year, Jubilee'.

in other words, did jubilee relate to the wider sense of Old Testament *promise* that Jesus fulfilled? Jesus announced the imminent arrival of the eschatological reign of God. He claimed that the hopes of restoration and messianic reversal were being fulfilled in his own ministry. The 'Nazareth manifesto' (Luke 4:16–30) is the clearest, programmatic statement of this, and quotes directly from Isaiah 61, which is strongly influenced by jubilee concepts. Robert Sloan observed that Jesus' use of the word for 'release', *aphesis*, carries both the sense of *spiritual* forgiveness of sin and also literal and *financial* remission of actual debts. Thus the original jubilee background of economic release has been preserved in Jesus' challenge concerning ethical response to the kingdom of God.[13] Sharon Ringe traces the interweaving of major jubilee images into various parts of the Gospel narratives and the teaching of Jesus (e.g. the Beatitudes, the response to John the Baptist [Matt. 11:2–6], the parable of the banquet [Luke 14:12–24], various episodes of forgiveness, teaching on debts [Matt. 18:21–35 etc.]).

The evidence is broad, and conforms to the pattern already set in the Old Testament. The jubilee functions both as a future hope and also as an ethical demand in the present.[14] Likewise, in Acts the jubilary concept of eschatological restoration is found in the otherwise unique idea of 'complete restoration'. The unusual word for this, *apokatastasis*, occurs in Acts 1:6 and 3:21, related to God's final restoration of Israel and all things. It seems Peter has taken the core of the jubilee hope and applied it, not just to the restoration of land to farmers, but to the restoration of the whole creation through the coming Messiah. Significantly, the early church responded to this hope at the level of economic mutual help – thus fulfilling the sabbatical hopes of Deuteronomy 15. Acts 4:34 with it's simple statement that 'there were no needy persons among them' is virtually a quotation of the Greek Septuagint translation of Deuteronomy 15:4, 'there will be no needy person among you'. The new age of life in the Messiah and in the Spirit is described in terms that echo the fulfilment of the hopes of jubilee and its related sabbatical institutions.[15]

Paradigmatic interpretation of the jubilee
This approach, we recall, has to do with identifying the coherent body of principles on which an Old Testament law or institution is based and which it

---

[13] R. B. Sloan Jr, *Favorable Year of the Lord*.

[14] S. H. Ringe, *Jesus, Liberation, and the Biblical Jubilee*.

[15] A full and helpful account of the way Jesus and the rest of the New Testament related to the rich scriptural traditions of the land is given by Holwerda, *Jesus and Israel*, pp. 85–112.

embodies or instantiates. To do this it is helpful once more to move around our three angles and consider how Israel's paradigm speaks to us.

Economically, the jubilee existed to protect a form of land tenure based on an equitable and widespread distribution of the land, and to prevent the accumulation of ownership in the hands of a wealthy few. This echoes the creation principle that the whole earth is given by God to all humanity, who act as co-stewards of its resources. There is a parallel between the affirmation of Leviticus 25:23, in respect of Israel, that 'the land is mine', and the affirmation of Psalm 24:1, in respect of all humanity, that

> The earth is the LORD's, and everything in it,
> the world, and all who live in it . . .

The moral principles of the jubilee are therefore universalizable on the basis of the moral consistency of God. What God required of Israel reflects what in principle he desires for humanity; namely, broadly equitable distribution of the resources of the earth, especially land, and a curb on the tendency to accumulation with its inevitable oppression and alienation. The jubilee thus stands as a critique not only of massive private accumulation of land and related wealth, but also of large-scale forms of collectivism or nationalization that destroy any meaningful sense of personal or family ownership. It still has a point to make in modern Christian approaches to economics. The jubilee did not, of course, entail a redistribution of land, as some popular writing mistakenly supposes. It was not a redistribution but a restoration. It was not a handout of bread or 'charity', but a restoration to family units of *the opportunity and the resources to provide for themselves* again. In modern application that calls for creative thinking as to what forms of opportunity and resources would enable people to do that, and to enjoy the dignity and social involvement that such self-provision entails.[16]

Socially, the jubilee embodied practical concern for the family unit. In Israel's case this meant the extended family, the 'father's house', which was a sizeable group of related nuclear families descended in the male line from a living progenitor, including up to three or four generations. This was the smallest unit in Israel's kinship structure, and it was the focus of identity, status, responsibility and security for the individual Israelite. It was this social unit that the jubilee aimed to protect and periodically to restore if necessary.

---

[16] Interesting and creative applications of the jubilee and other aspects of Old Testament economics are found in John Mason, 'Assisting the Poor'; and Stephen Charles Mott, 'Economic Thought'.

Notably it did so, not by merely 'moral' means – that is, appealing for greater family cohesion or admonishing parents and children – but by legislating for specific structural mechanisms to regulate the economic effects of debt. Family morality was meaningless if families were being split up and dispossessed by economic forces that rendered them powerless (see Neh. 5:1–5). The jubilee aimed to restore social dignity and participation to families through maintaining or restoring their economic viability.[17] Debt is a huge cause of social disruption and decay, and tends to breed many other social ills, including crime, poverty, squalor and violence. Debt happens, and the Old Testament recognizes that fact. But the jubilee was an attempt to limit its otherwise relentless and endless social consequences by limiting its possible duration. The economic collapse of a family in one generation was not to condemn all future generations to the bondage of perpetual indebtedness. Such principles and objectives are certainly not irrelevant to welfare legislation or indeed any legislation with socio-economic implications. And indeed, taken to a wider level still, the jubilee speaks volumes to the massive issue of international debt. Not for nothing was the worldwide campaign to see an ending of the intolerable and interminable debts of impoverished nations called Jubilee 2000.

An interesting, and in my view convincing, paradigmatic handling of the jubilee institution is suggested by Geiko Muller-Fahrenholz in a chapter entitled 'The Jubilee: Time Ceilings for the Growth of Money', in Ucko (ed.), *Jubilee Challenge*. He comments on the powerful theology of time implied in the sabbatical cycles of Israel, and its contrast with the commercializing of time in modern debt- and interest-based economies. Time is a quality that belongs to God, for no created being can make time.

> We enjoy time, we are carried along in the flow of time, everything is embedded in its time, so the very idea of exploiting the flow of time to take interest on money lent seemed preposterous. It does so no more because the sacredness of time has disappeared, even before the sacredness of the land vanished from the memories of our modern societies. Instead capitalist market economies have been elevated to global importance; they are enshrined with the qualities of omnipotence that border on idolatry. So the question arises: does it make sense to attribute to money qualities that no created thing can ever have, namely eternal growth? Every tree must die, every house must one day crumble, every human being must perish. Why should

---

[17] A thorough attempt to apply the relevance of the Old Testament patterns regarding the extended family to modern Western society is made by Michael Schluter and Roy Clements, *Reactivating the Extended Family*.

immaterial goods such as capital – and its counterpart, debts – not also have their time? The capital knows no natural barriers to its growth. There is no jubilee to put an end to its accumulative power. And so there is no jubilee to put an end to debts and slavery. Money that feeds on money, with no productive or social obligation, represents a vast flood that threatens even large national economies and drowns small countries . . . But at the heart of this deregulation is the undisputed concept of the eternal life of money.[18]

Theologically, the jubilee was based upon several central affirmations of Israel's faith, and the importance of these should not be overlooked when assessing its relevance to Christian ethics and mission. Like the rest of the sabbatical provisions, the jubilee proclaimed the *sovereignty of God* over time and nature, and obedience to it would require submission to that sovereignty. This Godward dimension of the matter is why the year is deemed holy, 'a sabbath to the LORD', and why it was to be observed out of the 'fear of the LORD'. Furthermore, observing the fallow year dimension would also require faith in *God's providence* as the one who could command blessing in the natural order. Additional motivation for the law is provided by repeated appeals to the knowledge of *God's historical act of redemption,* the exodus and all it had meant for Israel. And to this historical dimension was added the cultic and 'present' *experience of forgiveness* in the fact that the jubilee was proclaimed on the Day of Atonement. To know *yourself* forgiven by God was to issue immediately in practical remission of the debt and bondage of *others.* Some of the parables of Jesus spring to mind, and the inbuilt hope of the literal jubilee, blended with an *eschatological hope* of God's final restoration of humanity and nature to his original purpose. There is a strong theological pulse beating in this chapter of Leviticus.

To apply the jubilee model, then, requires that people obey the sovereignty of God, trust the providence of God, know the story of the redeeming action of God, experience personally the atonement provided by God, practise God's justice and put their hope in God's promise. The wholeness of the jubilee model embraces the church's evangelistic mission, its personal and social ethics and its hope.

Eschatological interpretation of the jubilee

Our interpretation of the jubilee will be incomplete unless we also allow it to give content to our hope. Even for Israel it had a built-in future dimension.

---

[18] Ucko, *Jubilee Challenge*, p. 109. There are some other creative interpretations of the jubilee in the same book.

Anticipation of the jubilee was supposed to affect all present economic values and set a limit on unjust social relations. It was proclaimed with a blast on the trumpet (the *yôbēl*, from which its name derives), an instrument associated with decisive acts of God (cf. Is. 27:13; 1 Cor. 15:52). We have seen that the jubilee had two major thrusts: *release/liberty* and *return/restoration*. Both of these were easily transferred from the strictly economic provision of the jubilee itself to a wider metaphorical application. That is, these economic terms became terms of hope and longing for the future, and thus entered into prophetic eschatology. There are allusive echoes of the jubilee particularly in the later chapters of Isaiah. The mission of the Servant of the LORD has strong elements of the restorative plan of God for his people, aimed specifically at the weak and oppressed (Is. 42:1–7). Isaiah 58 is an attack on cultic observance without social justice, and calls for liberation of the oppressed (v. 6), specifically focusing on one's own kinship obligations (v. 7). Most clearly of all, Isaiah 61 uses jubilee images to portray the one anointed as the herald of the LORD to 'evangelize' the poor, to proclaim liberty to the captives (using the word *děrôr*, which is the explicitly jubilary word for 'release'), and to announce the year of the LORD's favour (almost certainly an allusion to a jubilee year). The idea of *redemption and return* are combined in the future vision of Isaiah 35, and put alongside a transformation of nature. Thus, within the Old Testament itself, the jubilee had already attracted an eschatological imagery, alongside its ethical application in the present. That is, the jubilee could be used to portray God's final intervention for messianic redemption and restoration; but it could also support an ethical challenge for justice to the oppressed in contemporary history.

This is the jubilee vision and hope that inspired prophetic passages such as Isaiah 35 and 61, with their beautiful integration of personal, social, physical, economic, political, international and spiritual realms. Our use of the jubilee must preserve a similar balance and integration, preventing us from keeping asunder what God will ultimately join together. And, in all our endeavours, the Old Testament jubilee holds before us the light of its own, as yet future, perfect fulfilment. For the day has yet to come when, in glorious jubilee celebration,

> the ransomed of the LORD will return.
> They will enter Zion with singing;
>   everlasting joy will crown their heads.
> Gladness and joy will overtake them,
>   and sorrow and sighing will flee away.

(Is. 35:10)

Further reading

Barker, P. A., 'Sabbath, Sabbatical Year, Jubilee', in Alexander and Baker, *Dictionary of the Old Testament: Pentateuch*, pp. 695–706.

Biggar, Nigel, and Hay, Donald, 'The Bible, Christian Ethics and the Provision of Social Security', *Studies in Christian Ethics* 7 (1994), pp. 43–64.

Brueggemann, Walter, *The Land* (Philadelphia: Fortress, 1977).

Burge, Gary M., *Whose Land? Whose Promise? What Christians Are Not Being Told about Israel and the Palestinians* (Carlisle: Paternoster; Cleveland, OH: Pilgrim, 2003).

Chapman, Colin, *Whose Promised Land?* Rev. ed. (Oxford: Lion, 1989).

Davies, W. D., *The Gospel and the Land: Early Christianity and Jewish Territorial Doctrine* (Berkeley: University of California Press, 1974).

Fager, Jeffrey A., *Land Tenure and the Biblical Jubilee*, JSOT Supplements, vol. 155 (Sheffield: JSOT Press, 1993).

Holwerda, David E., *Jesus and Israel: One Covenant or Two?* (Grand Rapids: Eerdmans; Leicester: Apollos, 1995).

Janzen, Waldemar, 'Land', in Freedman, *Anchor Bible Dictionary*, vol. 4, pp. 144–154.

Johnston, P., and Walker P. W. L. (eds.), *The Land of Promise: Biblical, Theological and Contemporary Perspectives* (Leicester, Downers Grove: IVP, InterVarsity, 2000).

Mason, John, 'Biblical Teaching and Assisting the Poor', *Transformation* 4.2 (1987), pp. 1–14.

Mott, Stephen Charles, 'The Contribution of the Bible to Economic Thought', *Transformation* 4.3–4 (1987), pp. 25–34.

Ringe, S. H., *Jesus, Liberation, and the Biblical Jubilee: Images for Ethics and Christology* (Philadelphia: Fortress, 1985).

Schluter, Michael, and Clements, Roy, *Reactivating the Extended Family: From Biblical Norms to Public Policy in Britain* (Cambridge: Jubilee Centre, 1986).

Sloan Jr, R. B., *The Favorable Year of the Lord: A Study of Jubilary Theology in the Gospel of Luke* (Austin: Schola, 1977).

Ucko, Hans (ed.), *The Jubilee Challenge: Utopia or Possibility: Jewish and Christian Insights* (Geneva: WCC Publications, 1997).

Walker, P. W. L. (ed.), *Jerusalem Past and Present in the Purposes of God*, rev. ed. (Carlisle: Paternoster, 1994).

Weinfeld, Moshe, *Social Justice in Ancient Israel and in the Ancient near East* (Jerusalem: Magnes; Minneapolis: Fortress, 1995).

Wright, Christopher J. H., *God's People in God's Land: Family, Land and Property in the Old Testament* (Grand Rapids: Eerdmans, 1990; Carlisle: Paternoster, rev. ed., 1996).

——, 'Jubilee, Year Of', in Freedman, *Anchor Bible Dictionary*, vol. 3, pp. 1025–1030.

——, *Knowing Jesus through the Old Testament* (London: Marshall Pickering; Downers Grove: InterVarsity Press, 1992).

7. POLITICS AND THE NATIONS

Israel lived as a nation among the nations in the centre of a crowded and frequently convulsed international stage. Accordingly, substantial portions of the Old Testament are concerned with political relationships – both the internal political struggles of Israel, and Israel's political relations with their neighbours. However, if we are to deal adequately with the political significance of the Old Testament for Christian theology and ethics, we have to go beyond regarding politics as a kind of accidental but temporarily necessary feature of the fact that God chose to pursue the first phase of his redemptive purpose for humanity through a national entity. Politics, on such a view, is just the unfortunate by-product of the fact that Old Testament Israel was a nation. The reality goes much deeper than that and in fact redefines what politics means for biblically faithful people. For Israel, politics was not something extraneous to their theological or spiritual faith. Rather, 'the entire vocabulary in which Israel spoke of its relationship with Yahweh was derived from the realm of politics'.[1] The heartbeat of Israel's relationship with the LORD was the covenant. The term for this in Hebrew was *běrît*, which was also the ordinary word for 'treaty'. Treaties were made between individuals and nations, and always involved commitments and obligations. This was the sociopolitical reality through which Israel perceived and articulated their relationship with their divine Lord and King, YHWH.

But then, also, many of the other significant concepts in Israel's faith were

---

[1] Walsh, *Mighty from Their Thrones*, p. 61.

clarified and given substance through the realm and history of political relationships. This is true for concepts such as salvation, loyalty, deliverance, peace, justice and righteousness, trust and faithfulness, obedience, the reign of the LORD and so on. Israel's understanding of all of these was rooted in their political history. And these were the terms that then flow through into the prophetic ministry of Jesus of Nazareth and provide the vocabulary with which the New Testament explains Christ's saving achievement. 'Israel's knowledge of God's blessing was, from beginning to end, a political knowledge; and it was out of that knowledge that the evangelists and apostles spoke about Jesus.'[2] So we should not imagine that the political dimensions of the Old Testament, relevant no doubt for some aspects of our political ethics, will be left behind once we breathe the more rarified spiritual air of the New Testament. For the New Testament sees the significance of Jesus as the completion of the story of Israel, and sees both that story and its fulfilment in radically political terms with universal political consequences for humanity.

> The hermeneutic principle that governs a Christian appeal to political categories within the Hebrew Scriptures is, simply, Israel itself. Through this unique political entity God made known his purposes in the world. In relation to the crisis facing this unique entity, the church proclaimed those purposes fulfilled. Or, to express the same point differently: the governing principle is the kingly rule of God, expressed in Israel's corporate existence and brought to final effect in the life, death and resurrection of Jesus.[3]

We are stepping well ahead of ourselves, however. In this chapter on the political ethic of the Old Testament I shall follow a similar pattern to when we looked at its ecological and economic impact. That is, I shall first set the subject in the light of the creation and of the fall. Then I shall survey the wide range of ways in which Israel as a redeemed community either *was* a state, or was compelled to *relate to* an external state. Finally, I shall survey Israel's eschatological view of the future of the nations in the purposes of God.

Perspectives from creation and the fall

Ethnic and cultural diversity created by God
The rich diversity of the economic resources of the earth has its counterpart in the wide ethnic diversity of the human race and its ever-changing

---

[2] O'Donovan, *Desire of the Nations*, p. 23.

[3] Ibid., *Desire of the Nations*, p. 27.

kaleidoscope of national, cultural and political variations. The Bible enables us to see the one as just as much part of God's creative purpose as the other. Speaking as a Jew to Gentiles in an evangelistic context, Paul takes for granted the diversity of nations within the unity of humanity, and attributes it to the Creator: 'From one man he made every nation of men, that they should inhabit the whole earth; and he determined the times set for them and the exact places where they should live' (Acts 17:26). Although he goes on to quote from Greek writers, Paul's language in this verse is drawn from the Old Testament, from the ancient song of Moses in Deuteronomy 32:

> When the Most High gave the nations their inheritance,
>   when he divided all mankind,
>   he set up boundaries for the peoples . . .
>
> (Deut. 32:8)

So the ordering of relationships between the different groupings of humankind forms part of human accountability to our Creator God, just as much as the accountability of one person for another, as the story of Cain and Abel shows. The same can be said of the structuring of social relationships within any such group, whether it is a small local community or a whole nation. This social nature of humanity, with the sociopolitical organization that flows from it, is a part of God's creative purpose for his human creation. And it is linked to the creation of human beings in God's own image. For God is 'social' as God. The decision to create human beings is introduced as a sudden, contrasting, switch to the plural: 'Let *us* make man in *our* image, in *our* likeness' (Gen. 1:26). And the first fact about this 'image of God' that the text immediately notes is our sexuality, that complementary duality in unity, from which flows the rest of our social nature: marriage, parenthood, family, kinship and outwards in widening circles. So, human beings were created in relationship and for relationship.[4]

Now, of course, the human author of Genesis 1:26 did not have in mind what we, with the broader light of the whole biblical revelation, refer to as the doctrine of the Trinity. Nevertheless, in the light of that wider teaching, we can legitimately discern in the plural forms he used a greater significance than would have been apparent to the original human author. Genesis 1:2 had already spoken of the Spirit of God involved in creation (though, again, we cannot assert that the author would have understood that term in the devel-

---

[4] See Mott, *Political Thought*, ch. 3, on the importance of understanding groups as well as individuals in biblical political thinking.

oped sense of a distinct person in the Godhead, but more likely as the dynamic, effective 'breath' of God), and the New Testament emphatically exalts Jesus Christ as the agent and goal of creation (John 1:1–3; Col. 1:15–17; Heb. 1:1–3).

God, therefore, in the mystery of the Trinity, lives in the harmonious relationship of equal Persons, each of whom possesses his proper function, authority and relatedness to each of the others. Human beings, therefore, made in God's image, were created to live in the harmony of personal equality but with social organization that required functional structures and patterns of relationship. The ordering of social relationships and structures, locally, nationally and globally is of direct concern to our Creator God, then. But such ordering is precisely the stuff of politics. The Bible, therefore, makes no unnatural separation between 'politics' and 'religion', though neither does it identify them. Both are essential dimensions of what it is to be human. To worship the true God is to be committed to God's ways of social relationship. The political task of maintaining a just social order is a human duty under God.

Furthermore, we can see that ethnic and cultural diversity is part of God's creative intention for humanity from the eschatological vision of redeemed humanity in the new creation. The inhabitants of the new creation are not portrayed as a homogenized mass or as a single global culture. Rather, there is the continuing glorious diversity of the human race through history: people of every tribe and language and people and nation will bring their wealth and their praises into the city of God (Rev. 7:9; 21:24–26). The new creation will preserve the rich diversity of the original creation, but purged of the sin-laden effects of the fall.

The fall: disordering of human society

The fall, however, has wrought its evil havoc in this as in every sphere of human life. The Genesis narratives rapidly portray the corrupting of all the social relationships around which human life is structured. The fundamental relationship within marriage is twisted. Instead of husband and wife finding the fulfilment of their own created purpose in enabling the other to fulfil his or hers (Gen. 2:18–24), the relationship degenerates into one of harsh domination and lust (Gen. 3:16b). All derivative relationships are correspondingly debased, by spirals of jealousy, anger, violence and vengeance (Gen. 4), until the whole race is characterized by wickedness and evil (Gen. 6:5).

Violence and vengeance: Cain and Abel

This familiar story and its sequel in the descendants of Cain illustrate the accumulating disorder within human society, starting at the very place where love and support should be strongest – between brothers. As Paul Marshall points out, the story of Cain and Abel portrays not only the consequences of jealousy, anger and violence, but also gives us the prototype of a legal structure. Cain is charged by God as his divine accuser, while the blood of his murdered brother cries out as the plaintiff, the victim of injustice. However, even after Cain is pronounced guilty and sentenced, he is put under divine protection lest he himself become the victim of spiralling violence. The mark upon Cain is not punitive but protective:

> In the story of Cain we see a legal order appearing. Penalties are established for Cain's murder of Abel but Cain in turn is not left to suffer anarchy. A legal order is established with penalties and this order incorporates Cain and anyone who seeks private revenge on him. The 'mark of Cain' is not merely particular to Cain as an individual: it is a sign that God has appointed an order to maintain justice . . . The story of Cain shows us that just as ploughing, hunting, city building and music-making appeared on the earth in the earliest generations, so also appeared a judicial, a legal order, what we would call now some sort of political order, separate from anarchy. Humankind has been given responsibility to maintain the just relations that God decrees.[5]

Arrogance and division: Babel

The effects of the fall upon the international sphere are portrayed in the deceptively simple tale of the tower of Babel (Gen. 11:1–9). There we see that there is a double cause behind the divisions, barriers and misunderstandings between nations (symbolized in the confusion of language), as well as behind the alienation and the sense of being mutually foreign (symbolized in the scattering over the face of the earth). On the one hand, these things are the result of human arrogance and presumptuous ambition. But, on the other hand, they are also portrayed as the divine response to the threat of humankind's unified rebellion in sin.

It is worth emphasizing this latter point. God's deliberation before acting is not about punishment but about prevention: 'If as one people speaking the same language they have begun to do this, then nothing they plan to do will be impossible for them' (Gen. 11:6). It is the horrendous and limitless potential for evil of a *unified* and fallen human race that stirs God to 'divisive' action. The sin of a divided human race will at least be limited by the sheer frustration of never being able to 'get it all together', even in wickedness.

Something of the paradox of evil and God's sovereignty is contained here.

---

[5] Marshall, *Thine Is the Kingdom*, p. 41.

The same proud sin that prevents the whole human race from living in unity for good, also prevents the whole human race from uniting in evil. Thus behind the sin, which has turned God's created diversity into human strife-ridden divisiveness, one can see the mercy and grace of God, which uses that very effect of sin as a dyke to save the human race from being engulfed in the self-destruction of unified evil. Indeed, it is the outworking of this combination of judgment and hidden grace in God's response to Babel that enables human history to continue, so that, in the ebb and flow of its sociopolitical tides, God can pursue his redemptive purpose. And when that purpose is complete, Revelation shows the dyke removed and the human race allowed to create a horrific global unity of deception and rebellion, an apocalyptic Babel that will be the precursor of the final judgment.

At the more local or national level the effect of sin on political life is seen in the lust for power. Like wealth, power becomes something to be grasped, defended, selfishly used and accorded that absolute status due to God alone.[6] The first Middle East war the Bible brings to our attention was caused by political subjugation and its inevitable violent backlash (Gen. 14:1–4).

Political geography

These early chapters of Genesis thus present us with God's passionate concern for, and sometimes direct involvement in, the political life of the nations, from the sphere of international relationships to the local politics of petty kingdoms in the Jordan valley. So it is no surprise, when the story of redemption gets under way in Genesis 12, that it takes place on the stage of the real human world of political geography and history, and not in some supraterrestrial, mythological realm. Again, we must pay attention to the order of the biblical narrative and its theological significance. Both the Babel event, with its implications for fallen, alienated, scattered humankind upon a cursed earth (in Gen. 11), and the call of Abraham, with its promise of redemption and blessing for

---

[6] It is only when power is abused in this way that it becomes evil and idolatrous. Power in itself is neutral – the ability to accomplish any goal. Mott cautions us against a totally negative view of power; its positive aspects include '(1) a legitimate defence of one's created being, (2) the limitation on rebellious freedom and the maintenance of mutuality and community, the healing powers of justice, and (3) the dispersing of power to the powerless, bringing them into the mutuality of power, that creates community'. It is lust for power that corrupts and leads us into oppression and violence. 'Power is exactly what the worst part of us wants to use. Power is not sin in itself, but sin regularly expresses itself in the desire for power' (Mott, *Political Thought*, p. 33).

all nations starting from a new land (in Gen. 12), are set against the background of the table of nations in Genesis 10. What is the purpose of this slab of ancient ethnic geography?

Whatever the purpose for which it was originally recorded, its inclusion at this crucial point between the flood and the beginning of the redemptive history leaves the reader in no doubt about the nature of the biblical narrative that follows. This is not a mythical, prehistorical world of gods and monsters, but the sober 'classifiable' world of nations, territories, cities, kingdoms and languages – a thoroughly recognizable, political, human world. Both the outworking of the baleful effects of the fall and the redemptive activity of God take place side by side in the real world of people and nations. And the story of redemption takes place not only *in* this world, but also *through* it. That is, God acts redemptively in and through all those acts, events, relationships and structures we deem political. To borrow a picture from Jesus, the weeds and the wheat are in the same field, and 'the field is the world'.

Spiritual powers

We must not overlook the Bible's teaching on the spiritual battle that lies behind the historical work of redemption, the conflict between the rule of God and the usurped rule of Satan, 'the Prince of this world' and all the demonic forces at his command. The Old Testament does not have, of course, a developed 'satanology'. But there are hints in the Old Testament of an awareness of a world of spiritual, invisible powers that lies behind the institutions and 'personifications' of states, that lies behind the overwhelming force of political power, that lies behind the distinctive 'character' of different social systems. It is not a question of polytheism or dualism, for these powers, though sometimes called 'gods',[7] are known to be 'no-gods', but, if anything, created beings. Hence Isaiah's stinging debunking of the astral 'gods' of Mesopotamia: 'Who *created* all these?' (Is. 40:26; my italics). Whatever they are, they are subject, like men, including men who have exercised unbridled power under their influence, to the final judgment of God:

---

[7] As in Ps. 82, which may refer to fallen angelic powers ('gods') supposed to rule nations with justice, but that manifestly failed to do so, in view of the universal reality of injustice and oppression among the nations. All such powers will fall under the LORD's judgment. For a fascinating study of the relationship between the LORD as the liberating God of justice and the kind of politics he demanded on the one hand, and the Canaanite gods and myths and the kind of politics they sanctioned, on the other, see Walsh, *Mighty from Their Thrones*, chs. 2–3.

In that day the LORD will punish
the powers in the heavens above
and the kings on the earth below.

(Is. 24:21)

God's people and the state: perspectives from Israel's history

We turn now to the most substantial part of our study in this chapter. If, as
we saw in chapters 3 – 6, Israel had an economic system from which we can
learn much for our Christian ethical reflection, what kind of political system
did Israel have and what can we learn from that? Precisely at this point,
however, we must face up to the historical nature of the Old Testament
canon – and indeed, the historical nature of the revelation of God that it
contains. For if we ask, what was Israel's view of the state, we must also ask,
which Israel and when? Do we take our political theology of the state from the
young revolutionary federation of tribes in the years after the settlement in
Canaan? From the institutional and imperial state of Solomon and his successors? From the persecuted remnant preserving religious distinctives in a
hostile environment of giant empires? To focus too narrowly on any one of
these will produce distortions of what the Hebrew Bible *as a whole* has to contribute to Christian political ethics. We have to be comprehensive and draw
our raw material for reflection from all the major periods of the story of
Israel. This will undoubtedly throw up some apparently contradictory viewpoints on the political nature of the people of God and their relationship
with the state, whether they themselves were a state or had to relate to external states. But, on the other hand, by seeing all of these perspectives together
within the framework of canonical authority we shall avoid elevating one perspective only to a place of exclusive relevance. This in turn should help us to
discern where particular political applications of the Old Testament are
imbalanced or extreme. Oliver O'Donovan makes the same point and turns it
into a major caution:

> If political theologians are to treat ancient Israel's political tradition as normative,
> they must observe the discipline of treating it as *history*. They may not plunder the
> Old Testament as though it were so much raw material to be consumed, in any order
> and in any variety of proportions, in the manufacture of their own theological
> artefact. They are dealing with a disclosure which took form in a succession of
> political developments, each one of which has to be weighed and interpreted in the
> light of what preceded and followed it . . . We may not appeal to the Exodus for the
> deliverance of the poor and then avoid mention of the conquest of Canaan . . . [W]e

may not appeal to the tribal period for the decentralized republican spirit of the amphictyony and then avoid mention of the monarchy, and so on.[8]

Our procedure will be to look at Israel as the people of God in five different phases of their Old Testament history. In each context we shall discuss the nature of the people of God themselves at that time, the nature of the state as portrayed in that context, and the role or concept of God that dominated the consciousness of God's people. Where relevant we shall also observe what kind of influence this particular era of Israel's history has had on the political thinking of Christians throughout the history of the church.[9]

The pilgrim family: the patriarchal period

Though Israel as a nation had its historical origin at the time of the exodus and settlement in Canaan, it is right to begin our survey with the patriarchs,[10] since Israel's sense of national unity is always related to them. Though the Old Testament does acknowledge the diverse elements included in the formation of Israel, there was a strong sense of genetic oneness stemming from the belief that they were all the seed of Abraham. Accordingly, the reality of 'Israel', in essence or potential at least, could be seen to be there in the wandering patriarchal families.

The people of God

In the patriarchal context the people of God is primarily a community called out of the sociopolitical environment and given a new identity and future by the promise of God. They are a people only by this act of God's election. It was not that God elevated an existing people to a chosen status, but that God called Israel into existence as his people, as an entity distinct from the surrounding nation states from their beginning. This went along with a form of life that included maximum independence from the sociopolitical and economic structures of their day. They did not own land, and regarded themselves

---

[8] O'Donovan, *Desire of the Nations*, p. 27 (his italics).

[9] John Goldingay takes the changing nature of Israel as the people of God as a case study when discussing a contextual or historical approach to the theological diversity in the Old Testament. My own survey of the matter here is deeply indebted to his helpful outline: Goldingay, *Theological Diversity*, ch. 3.

[10] The term 'ancesters' would be better, since the narratives in question pay almost as much attention to the female characters as to their husbands and their devious ways. However, the continuing common use of patriarchs and patriarchal to describe the history contained in Genesis 12 – 50 makes this term more readily recognized.

(and were regarded) as resident aliens, sojourners, in the land of their movements. Not that they were socially isolated. Genesis records plenty of occasions of social and economic intercourse between the patriarchs and their contemporaries. But they remained a pilgrim people, called out and called onward.

Corresponding to this given status, there was the requirement of faith in the promise of God and obedience to God's command. Here again a note of distinctiveness emerges with the surrounding peoples. The most illuminating text on the ethical character of Israel from the patriarchal tradition is Genesis 18:19: 'For I have chosen him, so that he will direct his children and his household after him to keep the way of the LORD by doing what is right and just, so that the LORD will bring about for Abraham what he has promised him.' The context of this declaration is God's imminent act of judgment on Sodom and Gomorrah, whose wickedness had caused such an outcry that God must intervene. In contrast to that kind of society, the world in which Abraham lived, God required that the community now emerging from Abraham himself was to be characterized by totally different values. They were to be a people who would imitate the character of the LORD himself ('the way of the LORD') by their commitment to 'righteousness and justice'. These are unquestionably social-ethical values, with economic and political implications. It is clear, therefore, that while God's intention for God's people was to be called out from the surrounding environment, that did not mean an abdication from the sociopolitical process itself. Rather, that sphere, as all spheres of their corporate life, was to be governed by justice, because that is precisely God's own way.

So then, the people of God in this context

- are called into existence by God's act of sovereign election;
- live in the light of God's promise, which enables them to
- sit loose to the surrounding sociopolitical power centres while not losing contact with the communities among which they live;
- are committed to an ethical obedience specifically characterized by God-imitating justice.

The state

The portrayal of *the state* in the patriarchal context as it is represented by the various political power centres and cities of the ancient Near Eastern world varies from neutral to negative. They are not portrayed as excessively oppressive, in anything like the same way as the Egypt of Moses or the Babylon of the exile. Yet when Abraham first appears, in Genesis 12, it is in the context of a society already marked by the story of the tower of Babel in chapter 11. Indeed, it is the land of Babel out of which Abraham was called. As the story indicates, it was a culture of immense self-confidence and pride. At the very least, Abraham's God-required departure relativized it. Human salvation was not to be found in the state per se. The ultimate redemptive purpose of God lay elsewhere, invested in the tenuous human vessel of the ageing husband of a barren wife. The calling of Abraham out of his country and his people (Gen. 12:1) was 'the first Exodus by which the imperial civilizations of the Near East in general receive their stigma as environments of lesser meaning'.[11]

On the other hand, as well as being portrayed in this relativized fashion, the external city-state can be seen as a place of moral rebellion against God and thereby a source of threat to the pilgrim people of God. Sodom and Gomorrah are obvious cases. God was aware of an 'outcry' against them (Gen. 18:20–21: twice). The word $\check{s}\check{e}^{\epsilon}\bar{a}q\hat{a}$ is virtually a technical term in the Old Testament for the cries of those who are suffering from oppression, cruelty and injustice. It is the word used of Abel's blood crying out against his murderer and it is also prominently used in the story of Israel's groaning in bondage in Egypt. People were crying out in Sodom and Gomorrah because of the pain of cruelty and oppression. Genesis 19 catalogues the violence and perversion found there. Isaiah 1:9–10, seen in the light of the rest of the chapter, links the twin cities with innocent bloodshed. Ezekiel 16:49 lists the sins of the cities of the plain as arrogance, affluence, callousness and failure to help the poor and needy (a very modern sounding list, which helps to explain why Sodom and Gomorrah stand as proverbial prototypes of universal human wickedness). For these reasons, these city-states stood in the blast path of God's judgment. The response of the people of God, as represented by Abraham, was intercession.

The portrayal of God
The portrait of God in these narratives is of one who is in sovereign control, as much in Mesopotamia, as in Canaan, as in Egypt. Alongside that is the dominant fact that the LORD is the God of redemptive purpose, whose ultimate goal is the blessing of all nations. In initiating a special relationship with a people of his own creation and possession God actually has in mind the best interests of the very nations out of whom they are called but among whom they continue to live. The promise of blessing for the seed of Abraham is a promise of blessing for the nations.

This means that although we understand from the rest of Scripture that the whole world stands under God's judgment, and although we know from books such as Daniel and Revelation that that judgment is especially directed

---

[11]   Voegelin, *Israel and Revelation*, p. 140; quoted in Goldingay, *Theological Diversity*, p. 61.

at human states in their rebellious condition, nevertheless, the very existence of the people of God *in the midst of* those states is a sign of God's wider and final purpose. That purpose is nothing less than the redemption of humanity, and the transformation of the kingdoms of the earth into the kingdom of God. The interesting thing in the story referred to above, from Genesis 18 – 19, is that it was precisely on his way to deliver the fires of judgment on a particular human community, Sodom and Gomorrah, that God reminded himself of that ultimate universal purpose of redemption for all nations. And he did so while having a meal with the couple in whom he saw that purpose embodied; namely, Abraham, Sarah and their as yet unconceived (and to them inconceivable) son. God, the judge of all the earth, is also the God committed to bless all the nations – a paradox that seems to have fuelled Abraham's persistence in prayer.

The influence of patriarchal narratives
The influence of the patriarchal material on Christian views of church–state relationships has been strong, particularly via the use made of it in Hebrews 11, with its emphasis on the independence of the patriarchs from both the land they left and the land they moved around in. Negatively, stressing this material can result in a world-denying attitude, in which believers are discouraged from *any* participation in the affairs of this world, since, like Abraham we are to be seeking a city not made with hands. On the other hand, the *pilgrim* nature of the patriarchs should make us remember that however much we believe, from the rest of the Scriptures, that the people of God have a mission of giving practical down-to-earth expression to the love-justice of God in human society, we do so still as a people called out, looking for the fulfilment of God's promise of redemption, but not expecting our hope of salvation to be found in the state itself. This world *is* our home, but in its present rebellious state it is not our final home.

The liberated nation: the exodus to judges period
The designated period here may seem enormous, but it hangs together as the period during which Israel was a theocracy in reality, not just in theory. Some scholars regard it as the time when Israel was most markedly a liberated and liberating people, different from the world around them.[12]

---

[12] It is the period slung between the poles of what Walter Brueggemann called the 'alternative and energizing consciousness of Moses' (at the time of the exodus), and the 'royal consciousness of Solomon' (in the early monarchy), a development that 'countered the counter-culture'. Brueggemann, *Prophetic Imagination*, chs. 1–2.

The people of God

God's people, the descendants of Israel, known disparagingly as 'the Hebrews', begin this period as an oppressed ethnic minority within a very powerful imperial state. The demand of YHWH confronts Pharaoh: 'Let my people go that they may worship/serve[13] me.' A state that denies freedom to those who wish to worship YHWH, quickly finds itself YHWH's enemy. The God who in the patriarchal narratives has shown himself to be transcendent, in the sense that he is neither bound to nor impressed by the greatest of human imperial civilization, upholds the right of his people to freedom of worship in the midst of a state with other gods, including the Pharaoh himself.

YHWH's demands on Pharaoh's state go much further than the spiritual right of freedom of worship. Egypt was engaged in civil discrimination against Israel as an ethnic minority, on the grounds of political expediency. The Pharaoh was cynically playing on public fears dressed up as public interest. His government was engaged in economic exploitation of this pool of captive labour. And Pharaoh's people were guilty of gross violation of normal family life through a policy of state-sponsored genocide. On all these fronts, political, economic and social, as well as religious, YHWH demands and then achieves the liberation of his people. In the course of events the state, which had professed ignorance of who YHWH is (Exod. 5:2), learns his identity and his power in no uncertain terms. Indeed, the tale of Egypt's progress from feigned ignorance of YHWH to devastating acknowledgment of his power is undoubtedly a major subplot of the narrative. (Notice the train of ideas through the following texts: Exod. 5:2; 7:5, 17; 8:10, 22; 9:15, 29; 14:18, 25.) The claims of Pharaoh and the other gods of the state must bow to the fact that YHWH is God as much over Egypt as over Israel. Indeed, the claim is lodged that YHWH is God over the whole earth. The climax of the song of Moses, after the sea has sealed the reality of Israel's deliverance, is that YHWH and not Pharaoh is king for ever (Exod. 15:18).

Moving from the exodus of the people of God out of an imperial state, Egypt, we come to their arrival in the midst of a city-state culture in Canaan. At this point it could be said that the people of God have become not merely

---

[13] There is possibly a deliberate play on words in the fact that the Hebrew verb *'ābad* and its noun *'ăbōdâ* can mean both 'serving as a slave' and 'worshipping'. This is undoubtedly intended to echo the fact that in these early chapters of Exodus, Israel was being forced to *'ābad* with harsh *'ăbōdâ* to the Pharaoh. God is demanding both freedom from bondage to a usurping god-king, and freedom to worship the living God in the freedom of covenantal service.

a liberated people, but also a liberating people, though it might well be thought invidious, in view of recent history, to describe invaders as liberators. Nevertheless, the arrival or the emergence of Israel in Canaan produced a most remarkable social, political, economic and religious transformation there.[14] Israel, the people of YHWH, not only thought of themselves as different – they *were* different (see chapter 2).

The main feature of the people of God at this stage is that they were a theocracy in reality. That is to say, they had no human king but placed all key forms of authority ultimately in YHWH. And the rule of YHWH was bound up with a commitment to certain societal objectives embodied in the Sinai covenant and law – objectives characterized by equality, justice and kinship obligation. Furthermore, these objectives were applied through the whole of Israel's corporate life, including the cult (religious rituals). Being the people of God at this stage was a task to be worked out. It was an alternative vision, requiring 'detailed obedience in the ethical, social and cultic spheres [which] . . . establishes the notion of the people of God as an ethical principle. In their behavior the people of God are bound to one another. Yahweh being their overlord, they have no human overlords. Theocracy and socio-political equality (radical theology and radical sociology) go together.'[15]

This point underlines the importance of Sinai, which we might be in danger of overlooking, having jumped straight from Egypt to Canaan. Israel's route was less direct. Sinai stands significantly midway between liberation from Egypt and settlement in Canaan. Liberation was not an end in itself. The newly free people constantly fell prey to the disintegrating forces of licence, rebellion, dissent and failure of nerve. At Sinai God provided the bonding and moulding institutions and laws by which they were to progress from a mass of freed slaves to an ordered and functioning society. It is there, in the Torah, that we find the bulk of those features of Israel's polity that made them so distinctive: the kinship rationale of land tenure, the jubilee and sabbatical institutions, the ban on interest, the equality of native and alien before the law, the civil rights of slaves, the diffusion of political leadership and

---

[14] The question of how and when Israel established itself in Canaan (by conquest, infiltration, revolt, or a mixture of these) is still a much debated area among historians of the period. For recent surveys of the issues, including the controversial interpretation of archaeological evidence, see William G. Dever, *What Did the Biblical Writers Know?*; V. P. Long, D. W. Baker and G. J. Wenham (eds.), *Windows into Old Testament History*.

[15] Goldingay, *Theological Diversity*, p. 66, with references to the work of Mendenhall, Gottwald and other sociologists of early Israel.

authority among the elders, the limitation on the economic power of cultic officials. Israel at this period, though not strictly speaking a state, did not lack social institutions with consistent goals and a coherent rationale. This also shows us the realism of God. Having purposed to create a nation as the model and vehicle of redemption, but set within and still part of fallen humanity, God gave to that nation a framework of social, economic and political institutions designed to preserve the freedom and moral values implicit in their redemption. The goal of redemption is freedom. In Israel's case not only freedom *from* the sociopolitical oppression of Egypt, but freedom *to be* the people of God, a 'priestly kingdom', a 'light to the nations'.

The state

The state in this period is represented by Egypt, on the one hand, and Canaan on the other. Egypt was a large empire, exercising its power in blatant oppression of the people of God, in its own interests. Canaan was a patchwork of small city-state kingdoms with pyramidical forms of political and economic power, which were oppressive and exploitative of their peasant populations. Both are presented in the text also as idolatrous in nature, as enemies of the LORD and as a threat to his people. In both cases the stance of the people of God towards the state when it displays such idolatrous hostility is one of confrontation, challenge and conflict.

The exit and entry of the people of God, out of Egypt and into Canaan respectively, spells judgment on both opposing human states. Egypt was opposed primarily because of its oppression; Canaan was opposed primarily because of its idolatry and 'abominable practices', which are catalogued in Leviticus and Deuteronomy. The state, then, in this particular context, stands over against the people of God as something to be opposed, defeated, dismantled and finally replaced by a wholly distinctive kind of human society under the direct rule of God. There is something about the narratives of the defeat of Pharaoh and the conquest of Canaan that stands like a signpost pointing to the final judgment of God on those who insist on remaining his enemies.

The portrayal of God

The God we encounter throughout this whole context is exclusively *YHWH*, the name that bursts on the scene to herald the exodus itself, and that goes on to become the primary identity of the people of Israel. Thereafter, they are simply the 'tribes of YHWH'. And YHWH is the God who sets himself against injustice and oppression, initiating the exodus expressly to put it right. In so doing, God as YHWH enters into history, and specifically political history, in a way that was not so apparent in the patriarchal narratives. YHWH's transcendence injects itself into Pharaoh's empire and blows it open. Brueggemann comments forcefully on the double significance of the Mosaic 'alternative': what it announced about God, and what it announced about human political possibilities.

> The radical break of Moses and Israel from imperial reality is a two dimensional break from both the religion of static triumphalism and the politics of oppression and exploitation. Moses dismantled the religion of static triumphalism by exposing the gods and showing that in fact they had no power and were not gods. Thus, the mythical legitimacy of Pharaoh's social world is destroyed, for it is shown that in fact such a regime appeals to sanctions that do not exist. The mythic claims of the empire are ended by the disclosure of *the alternative religion of the freedom of God*. In place of the gods of Egypt, creatures of the imperial consciousness, Moses discloses Yahweh the sovereign one who acts in his lordly freedom, is extrapolated from no social reality, and is captive to no social perception but acts from his own person toward his own purposes.
>
> At the same time, Moses dismantles the politics of oppression and exploitation by countering it with *a politics of justice and compassion . . .* his work came precisely at the engagement of the *religion of God's freedom* with the *politics of human justice . . .* Yahweh makes possible and requires an alternative theology and an alternative sociology. Prophecy begins in discerning how genuinely alternative he is.[16]

YHWH, the LORD, the liberating God of justice, is next perceived as king. The heart of theocracy lies here – that Israel initially acknowledged no king but the LORD. That Israel regarded the LORD as king from the earliest period of their settlement (and not just from the time of her own monarchy) is clear in several very ancient texts (e.g. Exod. 15:18; 19:6; Num. 23:21; Deut. 33:5). Belief in the kingship of a deity is not at all unique to Israel, and existed in the ancient Near Eastern world long before Israel emerged.[17] But if theocracy in the general sense of a nation regarding its god as a king was not unique, Israel's particular manifestation and experience of it certainly was. For in Israel theocracy excluded, for several centuries, a *human* king.[18]

---

[16] Brueggemann, *Prophetic Imagination*, pp. 16–17 (his italics).

[17] 'Yahweh was regarded as political leader both of Israel and of the world, a concept which in itself was not unique, however, as the rule of divinity was a belief held by all ancient Near Eastern peoples.' Lind, 'Political Power in Ancient Israel', p. 4.

[18] 'While the kingship of Yahweh as such is paralleled in the ancient mythologies of the Near East, this exclusion and polemic against the human institution is unparalleled, and gives to Yahweh's kingship a new dimension . . . The remarkable point is that the kingship of Yahweh excluded human kingship.' Lind, 'Political Power in Ancient

The reason why the LORD's kingship was incompatible at this time with human kingship is that the LORD took entirely to himself the two major functions and duties of kings in the ancient world; namely, the conduct of war and the administration of law and justice. Indeed, in the exercise of these two functions, human kings in the ancient Near East were at their most sacral; that is, acting on behalf of the god they represented (or embodied). But in Israel, the LORD himself took over these roles. The LORD was supreme military commander and the LORD was supreme judge. This meant that corresponding human political leadership in these spheres was decisively demoted and relativized. Instead, Israel was a covenant nation, with the LORD as Lord of the covenant responsible both for their protection and for the just ordering of their social life in every aspect. And when necessary the LORD would raise up 'judges' with either or both of these two main tasks – military leadership or judicial authority. Judges could come and go – they were not kings – but the LORD's rule went on.

So there was, then, in this period of Israel's history, a truly radical and alternative political option being launched on the stage of human history. And this radical political option was effected in the name of YHWH, in such a way that the religion of YHWH was inseparable from the social objectives of Israel. For Israel was not just the people of *God* (many nations would claim that in one form or another), but specifically the people of *YHWH*, and that in itself meant a covenant commitment to a certain kind of society that reflected YHWH's character, values, priorities and goals.

What this amounts to is that 'theocracy' is not an ideal aim for the people of God in their political dreams. It all depends on who or what is the *theos* who will do the ruling. Only the vision of YHWH, as the God he was truly revealed to be, initiated and sustained Israel's particular form of theocracy. But sadly the state, like humans, tends to make its god in its own image. As Israel itself moved from the radical, alternative, surprising theocracy of YHWH to the institutional state of the monarchy, it did just that, in spite of being reminded by the prophets of its true identity and calling.

The influence of this material

The influence of the exodus paradigm and the story of the conquest on social and political history has been simply incalculable. In Israel itself it became a

---

Israel', pp. 12–13. He points to Gideon's resistance to proffered kingship (Judg. 8:22–23); Samuel's critique of monarchy as an essentially enslaving burden (1 Sam. 8:10–18); and Jotham's fable (Judg. 9:7–15), in which monarchy is mocked as 'a socially useless, even harmful institution'.

model and a point of appeal at all times of suffering and oppression in biblical history. And of course for Jewish people throughout their post-biblical history the celebration of the Passover has kept the story alive and relevant especially in the all-too-frequent times of persecution. Through Christian history it has fired hopes and imagination, sometimes fruitfully, sometimes disastrously. The confrontational stance of the people of God vis-à-vis the state, perceived as evil, satanic, godless and so on has fuelled many varieties of Christian utopianism, millenarianism and radical nonconformity. Such movements often end up in 'unreal expectations, fanatical devotion, irrational behaviour, dictatorial regimes and ruthless repression or elimination of the enemy'.[19] They were usually also fuelled by apocalyptic beliefs that set their whole agenda in a kind of trans-historical mode. By contrast, the exodus itself and the events that followed it were very much within the boundaries of historical reality, and, astounding though they were, they were *limited* by the possibilities of history. Things were not perfect for Israel after the exodus, either in the wilderness or in the land of promise. But within the limitations of history an unparalleled act of justice and liberation *did* take place and a radically different kind of society *was* brought to birth.[20]

This latter use of the exodus paradigm has provided much of the backbone of Liberation Theology. It is also a major factor in Black and Feminist Theologies, as well as in the less sophisticated biblical encouragement that many groups of suffering believers have clung to in patience, longing and hope.

The institutional state: the monarchy period
By the time of Samuel the strain of living as a theocracy was proving more than the people felt able to bear in the face of external pressures. In their feelings of anxiety and vulnerability in the face of Philistine aggression they wanted to rely no longer on the seemingly ad hoc nature of the LORD's protection through randomly raised judges. Paradoxically, then, out of fear of the nations around them, they chose to adopt the ways of the nations around them – centralized and militarized government. They opted for monarchy.

---

[19] Gregory Baum, referring to a historical study of such movements in Europe, by Norman Cohn, *The Pursuit of the Millennium* (London, 1957), in his own article, Baum, 'Exodus Politics', p. 110.

[20] This reading of the exodus paradigm has been explored by Michael Walzer, who lays much greater emphasis on the achievement of attainable goals within history, goals that fit the objectives and values of the exodus paradigm: Michael Walzer, *Exodus and Revolution*.

Having made that fateful turn, they then survived Saul, served David, suffered Solomon, split into two warring kingdoms, both of which finally sank respectively into oblivion and exile. Such, in a nutshell, was the not terribly glorious story of the monarchy in Israel.

People of God and nation state

During this period (from Saul, or at least from David, to the exile), the people of the LORD were unmistakably an institutional state, with central leadership, boundaries, organized military defences, government departments and so on. Yet the identification of people of God with political state was never wholly comfortable. Within the Old Testament itself there are hints of a conscious distinction between the two realities, even while there is formal and apparent identity.[21] So there is the problem of the relationship of people of God and state *internally* to Israel itself. Furthermore, the narratives of the establishment of monarchy give us an ambivalent picture in which the development can be seen to have both negative and positive aspects. Because the narrative of the monarchy, along with the prophetic texts chronologically interwoven with it, is the most explicitly political part of the Old Testament, we must devote considerable space to entering into its subtle and complex perspectives.

1. *Human origins.* One thing that stands out clearly in the emergence of monarchy in Israel is how characteristically human, ambivalent, even squalid at times, were the factors that gave rise to it. There was no divine command or initiating sanction to monarchy. The law in Deuteronomy refers to 'the king the LORD your God chooses', but only as a secondary, limiting, condition to a situation brought about by the people's desire: 'Let us set a king over us' (Deut. 17:14–15). And this is certainly the way the Deuteronomistic historian records the story in 1 Samuel 8 – 12. The demand for a king sprang from a mixture of motives, some apparently good (the desire for justice and non-corrupt leadership, in the context of the embarrassing failure of Samuel's sons to provide it), others unquestionably retrograde (the desire to be like the rest of the nations). And the story unfolds with the continuing ambiguity of Saul, chosen yet rejected by God; raised to power in a wave of popularity, but enraged to jealousy and self-destruction by the fickle shift of that popularity; starting with promise, ending in tragedy.

This utter humanness of the story of Saul is very important precisely

---

[21] E.g. at the time of Elijah a distinction is made between the state authorities of Ahab and Jezebel, on the one hand, and the beleaguered community of faithful believers in the LORD, on the other – the 'seven thousand who had not bowed the knee to Baal'.

because of the glory of his successor David. David generated in Israel a whole new thread of theology, a new way of expressing the link between God's kingship and the king of Israel, a new eschatology of a coming messianic king descended from David. But the memory of Saul kept both the political institution of monarchy itself and its human occupant at any one time firmly in perspective. Monarchy in Israel was not in itself sacred or divine. Kings in Israel could not trace their ancestry back to legendary gods or heroes of the prehistoric past. The historical, human origins of the institution and the all-too-human failings of its first holder, and indeed of his illustrious successors, were of great significance. For they kept Israel free of that kind of royal mythology, which in neighbouring cultures gave unchallengeable sacrosanctity to social stratification and 'pyramid' power-politics.

A further effect of this human origin is that monarchy as a political institution was provisional, and, when seen within the total sweep of the history of Israel in the Old Testament period, transient. Israel had lived for several centuries in the land before opting for a king, and they survived without one from the exile onwards. Furthermore, if the beneficial effects of the monarchy were weighed against its detrimental effects, the scales would almost certainly come down on the debit side. It was kings who split the nation, kings who infringed the traditional pattern of the land tenure, kings who accelerated the economic forces of oppression and inequality, kings whose pride cost the nations dear in the game of political alliances and wars, kings who introduced, or did little to prevent, recurring popular apostasy and idolatry. There were, of course, notable exceptions. But in broad terms it can be said that the course of monarchy in Israel ran closer to the fears and warnings of Samuel (1 Sam. 8:10–18) than to the hopes of the people. The fallen humanity of even the redeemed people was nowhere more evident than in these upper levels of their political life.

2. *Divine involvement.* Yet the remarkable fact is that it is on this stage, crowded with the sordid scenery and personnel of Israel's royal politics, that the major Old Testament historical narratives describe God at work. The great paradox of the monarchy is that, though human in origin and infected from its very conception by tendencies to apostasy and corruption, God nevertheless took up monarchy and wove it into the heart of his redemptive purposes. Israel's king became the focus of new dimensions of God's self-revelation. The king represented God's rule over Israel in the present, and became the symbol of the hope of God's ultimate perfect, messianic rule over all nations. Such is the wonder of the interplay between human freedom and divine sovereignty.

There is an interesting tension here between the theocratic ideal and the attributes and functions accorded to human kingship. As we noted above, the practical effect of reserving all royal prerogatives to the LORD was to reduce the human differentials within Israelite society, socially, politically and economically. But the desire for a king was really an expression of dissatisfaction with theocracy, as the LORD himself warned, 'it is not you they have rejected as their king, but me' (1 Sam. 8:7). But the LORD was the God who stood behind the whole social and economic structure of their society in its distinctiveness from Canaanite inequality and oppression. The LORD was the God of liberation from slavery and justice on the land. Reject the LORD as king and you forfeit those benefits of his rule as well. It was entirely reasonable, therefore, for Samuel to argue that if they wanted a king 'like the other nations', they must be prepared for a society like the other nations as well. The picture Samuel paints in 1 Samuel 8:10–18 was not difficult for him to predict, given the kind of kingship Israel was familiar with in the cultures that surrounded them. Adoption of monarchy would lead to confiscation, conscription and taxation, and would produce a social and economic stratification in Israelite society that would be unjust, burdensome and irreversible. And, in the course of history, that is exactly what monarchy in Israel did produce. The portrayal of Solomon's later reign by the historian is an unmistakeable 'I told you so' from the grave of Samuel. All very negative. So much so that Brueggemann can speak of the whole spirit, ethos and accomplishment of Solomon as a reversal of the Mosaic alternative, a return to the values and management mentality of the empire, a countering of the counterculture of Sinai.[22] Thus the very existence of the king was in one sense a denial of theocracy. Indeed, the earliest attempt to establish a royal house had foundered on this very point. Gideon refused a crown, saying, 'I will not rule over you, nor will my son rule over you. The LORD will rule over you' (Judg. 8:23).

Yet paradoxically, in another sense, *the king became the focal point of theocracy.* Israel's king was certainly not regarded as divine in himself, but was called upon to manifest divine qualities as a paragon of that 'imitation of God' that we saw in chapter 1 to be a major dimension of Old Testament ethics. The king was not to be a 'super-Israelite', revelling in the prestige of status (Deut. 17:20). Rather, he was to be 'model Israelite', setting the highest standard of adherence to the law (Deut. 17:19). For this task he received special gifts of God's grace. He was anointed, which symbolized a special mission for God and the power of God's spirit. He was 'adopted' as God's son (2 Sam. 7:14; Ps. 2:7), thus uniting in his person both the status of sonship and the

---

[22] Brueggemann lists the features of the Solomonic era as 'an economics of affluence (1 Kgs. 4:20–23), politics of oppression (1 Kgs. 5:13–18; 9; 15 – 22) and a religion of immanence and accessibility (1 Kgs. 8:12–13)'. Brueggemann, *Prophetic Imagination*, ch. 2.

responsibility of obedience it entailed, a status and responsibility that belonged to the whole nation.

These high expectations placed on the Israelite kings were summed up in the term 'shepherd' that was applied to them, a term also applied to God, as we know (Ps. 23:1 etc.). At the human level, shepherds had very responsible and arduous jobs but a comparatively lowly social status. Applied to kings, the comparison was a powerful reminder of the duties, not the glories, of kingship. The king was to see that justice was done among his people – God's idea of justice (see Ps. 72:1), which operated especially on behalf of the poor and downtrodden. It was the failure of generations of kings precisely in this area that brought Israel's 'shepherd-kings' under the wrath of the prophets: 'Woe to the shepherds of Israel who only take care of themselves! Should not shepherds take care of the flock? . . . You have not strengthened the weak or healed the sick or bound up the injured . . . You have ruled them harshly and brutally' (Ezek. 34:2–4; cf. Jer. 22:1–5; 23:1–4). Interestingly, Ezekiel sees the ultimate solution to the problem of wicked and callous rulers as a reassertion of theocracy. The LORD declares, 'I myself will search for my sheep and look after them; I myself will tend my sheep . . . I will shepherd the flock with justice' (34:11–16).

Yet even in this eschatological vision, the reign of the LORD remains a mediated theocracy; the Zion-David theology cannot be jettisoned: 'I will place over them one shepherd, my servant David, and he will tend them' (34:23). Only the advent of the messianic king, who was the son both of David and of the LORD God himself, enabled both aspects of the vision to be united. Not that all Israelite kings failed wholly in their duty to mediate and reflect the character of God. Some of them at least achieved a reputation for being merciful beyond the usual standards of their age (1 Kgs. 20:31ff.). And Josiah proved that he truly knew the LORD by doing what the LORD characteristically demands – righteousness and justice for the poor and needy (Jer. 22: 15–16; cf. 9:23–24; 2 Kgs. 23:25).

If the king was genuinely to pursue justice among his people, defending the afflicted, saving the children of the needy, crushing the oppressor' (see Ps. 72:4), then he had to be available and approachable, just as a shepherd is to his sheep. And this indeed is a noteworthy feature of Israelite monarchy, at least in its early period. The king could be approached and implored by ordinary individuals or by prophets on their behalf. Examples include Nathan's parable on behalf of Uriah (2 Sam. 12:1–10), Joab and the wise woman of Tekoa's parable on behalf of Absalom (2 Sam. 14:1–24), the prostitute's appeal to Solomon (1 Kgs. 3:16–28) and the Shunammite woman's appeal to King Joram (2 Kgs. 8:1–6).

This feature of Israel's human kings also has its theocratic counterpart.

A people who cherished the privilege of 'drawing near' to God in worship and prayer (see Deut. 4:7) could hardly accept an unapproachable human king. If God, who inhabited eternity, condescended to dwell with the humble and hear the request of a Hannah, it was not for human political authority to exalt itself beyond approach or criticism. Even when later kings of Judah and Israel grew increasingly autocratic, the vital voice of prophecy could not be silenced. In political terms, the prophets fulfilled a role comparable to 'His Majesty's opposition', compelling political authority to listen to criticism, holding before it its inescapable accountability to God and to the people.

The parabolic approach of Nathan and Joab is interesting and suggestive as a means of confronting political authority. The first was provoked by blatant injustice, the second by an unpopular policy – but both had a similar effect. They gained the attention and involvement of the king as one who *ought* to act: morally and politically they implicated him by getting him to pass judgment on the specific case brought before him. Both were practical, ad hoc interventions related to immediate events, not abstract political theory. Both were successful in their intended effect, to bring about a change of heart and mind in the king. Both called for repentance: moral in the first case, political in the second.

These parabolic appeals to authority serve as a motive and model for Christian involvement in politics. As 'salt' and 'light' Christians should persistently present to political authorities moral arguments with persuasive force and practical relevance. This should characteristically be on behalf of the weak, powerless and those wronged by injustice or callous neglect, as in Nathan's and Joab's action. And such persuasion is most likely to be effective at the level of specific issues and achievable, limited objectives.

The prophetic portrayal of God's attitude to the monarchy

The perception of God at this period has to be sought primarily in the voice of *the prophets*. From them we discover the conditional and qualified nature of God's acceptance of the monarchy as a political form of his people. One could summarize the view of the prophets towards the monarchic state of Israel (in both northern and southern forms) by saying that they accepted its *God-givenness*, but refused its *God-surrogacy*. It is significant, for example, that at the point of the secession of the northern tribes away from Judah, one and the same prophet, Ahijah, both encouraged Jeroboam before the event with a word from the LORD that his secession was divinely willed as judgment on the house of Solomon (i.e. God was giving him a kingdom), and also later severely criticized him for the idolatry into which he had led the northern tribes (his kingdom was usurping the place of God) (1 Kgs. 11:29–39; 14:1–16).

1. *Double sin*. It is interesting to compare the sin of the two protagonists in the narrative of the division of the kingdom; namely, Rehoboam and Jeroboam.

The *sin of Rehoboam* was the oppressive abuse of power for personal wealth and prestige. He inherited, of course, from his father, Solomon, an already overloaded empire that depended on an oppressive burden of taxation and forced labour. But Rehoboam *deliberately* chose the path of oppression and rule by force as a declared policy of state (1 Kgs. 12:1–14), even when offered an alternative. In doing so he rejected the advice of the elders, who reminded him of the authentic Israelite concept of political leadership – mutual servanthood: 'If today you will be a servant to these people and serve them . . . they will always be your servants' (1 Kgs. 12:7). Rejecting that advice cost Rehoboam more than half his kingdom, but did not deter him or his royal successors, north or south, from exploiting the temptations of power. The shepherds plundered their own flocks. But Rehoboam rejected more than human advice. He also rejected the clear covenantal demands of the LORD, that justice and compassion should characterize all dealings within Israel, and especially be the mark of those in political authority.

The *sin of Jeroboam* was to subordinate religious practice to political ends – the survival and bolstering of his own infant state. The idolatry of the northern kingdom was focused on the golden calves at Bethel and Dan. But we need to see carefully what these meant. From 1 Kings 12:26ff. we see that Jeroboam did not apparently intend the worship of false gods as such. The calves were probably meant to represent the presence of the LORD, who brought Israel up out of Egypt. In that sense it was a breaking of the second commandment more than the first. But the real thrust of Jeroboam's idolatry lies in the motives of his action and the additional religious rituals and offices he initiated. His intention was clearly to protect his own nascent kingdom from any popular hankering after the splendour of Jerusalem (vv. 26–27). To make completely sure, he elaborated an alternative cultic system for the northern kingdom, totally designed, appointed and run by himself, and all to serve the interests of his state (vv. 31–33). In effect, the LORD had become a figurehead for his state. The state in itself had become idolatrous. The worship of the LORD was merely a tool for the higher goal of preserving the state, or, to be more precise, to ensure the survival of its new king (v. 27).

That this was in fact the case is shown with ironic clarity in the angry words of Amaziah, the high priest at Bethel under Jeroboam II (nearly two centuries later), against Amos: 'Get out, you seer! . . . Don't prophesy any more at Bethel, because *this is the king's sanctuary and the temple of the kingdom*' (Amos 7:12–13; my italics). Amos, however, like Ahijah at the very start of the northern kingdom, and also like his anonymous fellow Judaean who came to speak for God at Bethel (1 Kgs. 13:1–6), refused to be silenced by the surrogate divine authority of the new political regime. God may have permitted this kingdom to come into existence, but that did not bind God to serve that kingdom's self-interests. The prophets refused to allow the authority of God or God's prophetic word to be hijacked to legitimize human political ambitions – sometimes a costly opposition.

One prophet who certainly could not be hijacked to serve the interests of the state was Elijah. His ministry took place in the ninth century in the northern kingdom during the reign of Ahab and Jezebel, when the whole state became virtually apostate. Nevertheless, there were a faithful seven thousand who had not capitulated to the palace-imposed worship of Baal (1 Kgs. 19:14, 18). The origins of the idea of a faithful remnant probably go back as far as this. It was not the state of Israel itself that constituted the true people of God, but a minority of 'true believers' within it.

2. *Dubious legitimacy.* In the view of the Old Testament historians the northern kingdom, of course, was lacking in legitimacy from the start. But in the southern kingdom of Judah, in spite of all the theological legitimation of the state and its monarchy, the prophetic voice of the LORD could still stand out in conflict with it and challenge the moral validity of any given incumbent of the throne of David. The throne of David had a legitimacy grounded in God's covenant promise (2 Sam. 7). But the specific government of any individual occupant of the throne of David could be subjected to searching scrutiny and, where appropriate, deemed illegitimate. And the criterion of assessment was the covenant law. Unequivocally the prophets subordinated Zion to Sinai.

The law in Deuteronomy that permitted (not commanded, as we noted) monarchy laid down strict conditions for it, including the requirement that the king should know, read and obey the law. He was to be not a super-Israelite but a model Israelite among his brothers and equals (Deut. 17:14–20). As one entrusted with the law, the king was committed to the maintenance of justice in a spirit of compassion (see Ps. 72). Even in the late monarchy Jeremiah proclaimed this strong tradition of the legal, covenantal requirement on the Jerusalem line of kings, at the very gates of their palace in Jerusalem. His words are really a statement of the conditions for the legitimacy, and indeed for the survival, of the Davidic monarchy. Zion must conform to Sinai, or face ruin:

> Hear the word of the LORD, O king of Judah, you who sit on David's throne – you, your officials and your people who come through these gates. This is what the LORD says: Do what is just and right. Rescue from the hand of his oppressor the one who has been robbed. Do no wrong or violence to the alien, the fatherless or the widow,

and do not shed innocent blood in this place. For if you are careful to carry out these commands, then kings who sit on David's throne will come through the gates of this palace . . . But if you do not obey these commands, declares the LORD, I swear by myself that this palace will become a ruin.

(Jer. 22:2–5)

On this basis, Jeremiah then goes on, on the one hand, to commend with approval the reign of Josiah, who lived by the standards of covenant law, which is what it means to know the LORD (22:15–16), and, on the other hand, utterly to reject Jehoiakim, whose actions and policies included forced labour without pay, personal aggrandizement, dishonesty, violence and oppression. The legitimacy or illegitimacy of the two kings is evaluated respectively on the grounds of their treatment of the poor and needy, the workers and the 'innocent'. That is, the king in Zion was judged precisely according to the dominant concerns of the Sinai law.

Thus, even when the sociopolitical contours of the people of God had changed radically from the early theocracy to the institutionalized royal state, the controlling paradigm for political government was still that of the law and the covenant. This meant that the monarchic form of Israel's theocracy could never be rightly regarded as 'the divine right of kings' per se. Being 'the LORD's anointed' was not an unconditional guarantee. The king was subject to, and correctable by, the covenant law. Ultimately, the monarchy itself was as subject to the covenant threats (its curses) as the whole nation.

Moral evaluation of external states

The same moral criterion applies in the prophetic perspective on the authority of *external*, non-covenantal, rulers. For whatever their nationality they too rule by the LORD's authority. As early as the ninth century Israelite prophets claimed to anoint the kings of outside nations in YHWH's name (1 Kgs. 19:15). In the eighth century Isaiah regarded Assyria and its tyrannical sovereigns as no more than a stick in the hand of YHWH (Is. 10:5ff.). Most explicitly of all, Jeremiah could announce, in a seventh-century international diplomatic conference hosted by Zedekiah in Jerusalem, that YHWH had delegated to Nebuchadnezzar supreme, worldwide authority and power – for the foreseeable future. Nebuchadnezzar, says the LORD startlingly, is 'my servant' (Jer. 27:1–11; note especially vv. 5–7).

Now if Israelite kings were subject to evaluation by the moral standards of the LORD and his law, so too were the pagan ones. The clearest example of this is Nebuchadnezzar again. Daniel had clearly absorbed the point of Jeremiah's assertion about Nebuchadnezzar, for he repeats it, almost verbatim, to his face (Dan. 2:37–38). Nevertheless, on another occasion Daniel the civil servant

dons the authentic prophetic mantle when he goes beyond the requested interpretation of a dream to give Nebuchadnezzar some 'advice'. And that advice is
really a warning: unless he pays attention to the injustice on which his boasted
city has been built, by lifting the oppression of the poor and needy in his
realm, he will face inevitable judgment. The boldness of Daniel's prophetic
word in Daniel 4:27 should not escape us, hidden as it is in the midst of an otherwise somewhat weird story. The one to whom the LORD has given all authority and power, far beyond what any Israelite king ever wielded, is here weighed
in the balance of the standards of justice, but is found wanting (to anticipate a
metaphor drawn from the next chapter, Dan. 5).

All this must have some bearing on interpretations of Paul's view of state
authority in Romans 13. The Old Testament would wholly endorse the view
that all human authorities exist *within the framework of God's will*. It would
wholly reject the view that that position gives them a legitimacy regardless of
their *conformity to God's justice*, as revealed in the covenant law.

So, then, the historical experience of the people of God in actually *being* a
state generated enormous tensions. There was never complete ease with the
monarchy, even in Davidic Judah, as the continuing existence of a group like
the Rechabites in the late monarchy showed (Jer. 35). There was always the
feeling that Israel was really meant to be something different. Nevertheless, it
is from the prophetic critique of the kings and institutions of this period (in
both narrative and prophetic books) that we learn most in the Old Testament
concerning God's radical demand on political authorities.

The influence of this material
The influence of the model of Israel as an institutional royal state can probably be seen most comprehensively in the 'Christendom' idea in the centuries
during which Christians seem to have succumbed to the collective delusion
that the best way to save the world was to run it. The Constantinian transformation of Christianity and its dubious effects have often been compared to
Israel's adoption of monarchy and statehood.[23] Certainly, what we have seen is
that the transformation of the people of God into an institutional state generated both approval and rejection, both in the heat of the historical process
itself, and also in theological and canonical assessment. Nevertheless, it happened. And hypothetical reconstructions of what might have happened if

---

[23] For some perceptive comparisons between the various stages of Israel's political
development and the history of the Christian church from its familial origins to its
present 'post-exilic' (post-Enlightenment) tensions, see Goldingay, *Theological Diversity*,
p. 83.

they had listened to Samuel in the first place are as fruitless here as elsewhere. There was, as Goldingay puts it, 'a historical inevitability about the transition from (nominally) theocratic nation to monarchic state. The alternative to such a development was to cease to exist.'[24]

Goldingay goes further and sees God's acceptance of the monarchy, in spite of its dubious origins, as a case of God's making allowance for human inability to live by God's ideal standards – even in his own redeemed and liberated people: 'Being an institutional state means that God starts with his people where they are; if they cannot cope with his highest way, he carves out a lower one. When they do not respond to the spirit of Yahweh or when all sorts of spirits lead them into anarchy, he provides them with the institutional safeguard of earthly rulers.'[25] One might take from this the view that the institutional state, like certain other human conditions that the law permits, is a concession to human 'hardness of heart': permitted but transient.

The suffering remnant: the exile
In 587 BC the institutional, monarchic state of Judah vanished under the rubble of Jerusalem, devastated by the armies of Nebuchadnezzar. The northern kingdom of Israel had long since disappeared, scattered by the Assyrians in 721 BC.

The people of God
Thrown into exile, the people of God were not only no longer a state: they were scarcely even a nation. As a tiny remnant they learned once again to live like their forefathers, as strangers in a strange land, in the very land indeed from which their earliest ancestors had departed in obedience to God's call. Now they were back there under God's judgment.

But Babylon was not just strange. It was also an enormous, hostile and threatening environment, in which the people of God were now a small, uprooted, endangered species – exiles. At this point in their history, then, the people of God were a persecuted remnant, while the state was an ambient, hostile power, within which they had to survive and somehow continue to live as the people of God. The danger at such a time was twofold: (1) they might lose their identity by compromise and assimilation into their new environment, and thus cease to be distinctive; or (2) they might stand out as so intractably different that they would bring destructive fires of persecution on themselves that might finally consume them. The same dilemma has faced the

---

[24] Ibid., p. 70.

[25] Ibid., pp. 85–86.

people of God at many times in history, when they have been a suffering minority in a hostile environment. And in this case also we have a variety of responses from the Hebrew Bible to such a situation. We shall quickly look at four – two positive and two negative.

Responses to the external state

1. *Prayer.* First, there was the advice to *pray for Babylon*. This was the astonishing message sent by Jeremiah in a letter to the first group of exiles, recorded in Jeremiah 29. Contrary to those who were predicting a short exile or proposing a quick rebellion to end their exile, Jeremiah forecasts a long stay of two generations, and therefore counsels a policy of settling down to that. The exiles must realize that Babylon had done what it had done by the LORD's permission, and for that reason to pray for Babylon would put them in line with the purposes of God again. The shalom of the people of God was bound up with the shalom of the pagan nation among whom they now resided.

There is surely more here than merely a pragmatic policy to ensure survival. This advice of Jeremiah echoes the authentic mission of Israel to be a source of blessing to the nations. Indeed, since prayer was a duty of the priests, this is an example of Israel's priestly function among the nations. And since the nation in question was at that time the enemy and oppressor of Israel, it is not going too far to find here an Old Testament anticipation of Jesus' stark command to 'love your enemies and pray for those who persecute you' (Matt. 5:44).

Though coming from an earlier period, it is interesting to compare Jeremiah's advice to the exiles with the stories of Abraham's intercession for Sodom (Gen. 18:20–33) and Jonah's mission to Nineveh. The compassionate quality of Abraham's 'priestly' intercession, though its outcome was not precisely what he had asked,[26] contrasts strongly with the prophetic mission of Jonah. In Jonah's case the outcome was precisely what he had *not* wanted, but had shrewdly suspected would probably happen. The comparison is interesting because Nineveh was just as notorious for wickedness and oppression as Sodom and Gomorrah. But there the similarity ends. Abraham jumped unbidden to intercession; Jonah, though bidden, jumped the other way. Abraham failed to win a reprieve for the cities of the plain; Jonah, reluctantly, brought Nineveh to repentance and thereby to suspended judgment. Abraham interceded because he knew God to be righteous; Jonah tried to escape his mission because he knew God to be compassionate – embarrassingly so (Jonah 4:1–3)!

---

[26] He did not ask God to judge the cities but to spare his relatives. He asked God to spare the cities for the sake of any righteous who might be there.

Together all three stories, of Abraham, Jonah and the letter of Jeremiah, set before us the priestly duty of the people of God in a wicked world. We are to intercede even for those we know are facing God's judgment. We are also to proclaim that judgment, but in the hope of repentance and reprieve. And we are to do so in the spirit of Abraham and not of Jonah.

We can also add that Jeremiah here anticipates the New Testament's command to pray for those in secular authority, out of obedience to God who rules over them. The grounds are the same; namely the redemptive desire and purpose of God: 'I urge, then, first of all, that requests, prayers, intercession and thanksgiving be made for everyone – for kings and all those in authority, that we may live peaceful and quiet lives in all godliness and holiness. This is good, and pleases God our Saviour, who wants all men to be saved and to come to a knowledge of the truth' (1 Tim. 2:1–4).

Prayer puts all things, including all human authorities, in perspective. Prayer seeks the good of the state, while refusing to absolutize it, since the very act of prayer appeals to a higher authority than the state (which is why prayer is also a political action). To pray for Babylon is to relativize Babylon. For as Daniel (a man of prayer) would remind Nebuchadnezzar, Babylon's 'head of gold', 'there is a God in heaven' and 'heaven rules' (Dan. 2:28; 4:26).

2. *Service.* Secondly, there was the response of Daniel and his friends, who went beyond praying for Babylon and were willing to *serve* the young imperial state of Nebuchadnezzar. The book of Daniel is a fascinating analysis of the extreme dangers, as well as the unique opportunities, of such a decision. There are parallels with the story of Joseph. Both were able to witness to the living God in the midst of a pagan and idolatrous state; both were able to influence the state's policies; both were able to benefit the people of God by their 'secular' career positions. The stories of Daniel 1 – 6 are a powerful study of the challenging possibilities of living as a believer at the highest levels of pagan political authority, and remaining faithful and uncompromised in doing so.[27]

Again, we might notice other examples within the Old Testament. There were times when the state of Israel itself was so apostate that it was virtually an 'external' hostile power to faithful Yahweh worshippers. Certainly, with kings like Ahab, the issue of the relationship between loyal followers of the LORD and state authorities who were anything but loyal to him became critical and costly. We are familiar with the response of Elijah. Elijah exhibits implacable opposition, a declared position of allegiance to the LORD above and

---

[27] I have reflected on this dimension of these chapters in Christopher J. H. Wright, *Tested by Fire.*

beyond the state authority. That was the significance of his remark in the very presence of Ahab 'As the LORD, the God of Israel lives, *whom I serve*'; that is, 'I serve *him*, not *you*, Ahab' (1 Kgs. 17:1; my italics). But another response in the same circumstances is represented by *Obadiah*. We are told that he was a 'devout believer in the LORD' (1 Kgs. 18:3). Yet he chose to remain in high political office, serving in the court of Ahab and Jezebel. Not only was he serving the state, but he was able to use the access of his position to preserve the lives of a hundred other loyal prophets in the midst of fierce persecution (18:4). Both responses, of Elijah and of Obadiah, to a hostile state took great courage. But it could be argued that Obadiah's was the more difficult in the long term. Certainly the hundred prophets owed their lives to Obadiah's courage 'on the inside', not to Elijah's stand 'on the outside' of the political lions' den. Later, Jeremiah owed his life to another 'inside' official, Ebed-Melech (Jer. 38:6–13).

3. *Judgement*. Coming again from the pen of Jeremiah is the response of wholesale declaration of *judgment* on Babylon. This shows the astonishing paradox of Jeremiah's advice to the exiles to pray for Babylon. Virtually in the next diplomatic postbag as the letter of chapter 29, Jeremiah also sent the massive tirade against Babylon recorded in Jeremiah 50 – 51. The scroll was to be read out publicly, and then dropped with a stone in the river Euphrates, there to sink as mighty Babylon was destined to do. This shows clearly that the letter in chapter 29 was not a piece of rosy-eyed quietism based on a naive faith in Babylon's benevolence. Jeremiah told the exiles to pray for the shalom of Babylon with his eyes wide open to the realities of Babylon, and especially to the fact that all it stood for was destined to be destroyed in the blast-path of God's judgment.

In this context we should include those much-neglected parts of the books of the prophets, the oracles against the nations. We tend to pass over them as outdated predictions of the fall of empires long consigned to the bin of history, or to the ghostly splendour of museums. But the message of these prophetic messages concerning the nations is powerful. They speak of the sovereignty of God exercised throughout the changing scenes of history. They speak of the accountability of all human empires to the living God of the whole world. And they speak chillingly of the transience of even the most powerful nations on earth at any given time. These are affirmations that the people of God continue to need in any age, and increasingly in our own, when it is not just nations and states that wield such gigantic power, but brands and corporations and phenomenally (obscenely) wealthy individuals.[28]

---

[28] I have reflected on the theological and ethical implications of Ezekiel's oracles against

4. *Mockery*. Finally, there was the response of deliberate *mockery* and the unmasking of Babylon's imperial pantheon and sophisticated 'scientific' civilization. The importance of Isaiah 46 and 47 can be missed if we fail to see their links with each other and the context. Here is a prophet seeking to energize his depressed people to believe that the LORD can again do something great; that their present condition is not final; that they can actually get up and get out of Babylon. The people of God must again claim their identity in the world – an identity of servanthood, but now universalized to be of saving significance for all nations. But a paralysing awe of Babylon stands in the way of Israel making such a response. So even before the armies of Cyrus dismantled Babylon's empire militarily, the poetry of Isaiah was already dismantling it psychologically and spiritually in the perception of the exiles. There is therefore a profoundly political significance to the mockery of idolatry and the deflating of cultural arrogance in these chapters. Brueggemann captures this point with his usual pithiness:

> The poet engages in the kind of guerrilla warfare that is always necessary on behalf of oppressed people. First, the hated one must be ridiculed and made reachable, then she may be disobeyed and seen as a nobody who claims no allegiance and keeps no promises. The big house yields no real life, need not be feared, cannot be trusted, and must not be honoured.
>
> When the Babylonian gods have been mocked, when the Babylonian culture has been ridiculed, then history is inverted. Funeral becomes festival, grief becomes doxology, and despair turns to amazement. Perhaps it is no more than a cultic event, but don't sell it short, because cult kept close to historical experience can indeed energize people. For example, witness the black churches and civil rights movements or the liberation resistance in Latin America. The cult may be a staging for the inversion that the kings think is not possible . . . We ought not to underestimate the power of the poet. Inversions may begin in a change of language, a redefined. perceptual field, or an altered consciousness.[29]

Yet, having said all this, the future of the people of God still depended on Cyrus, who was as much a pagan king of a pagan empire as Nebuchadnezzar and the Babylonians had been. The state Isaiah was mocking was the one that had earlier been described as God's servant, executing his judgment on Israel

---

Egypt and Tyre in C. J. H. Wright, *Message of Ezekiel*, pp. 255–272. Sharp insight on the Old Testament's perception of the nations under God's authority and judgment is also provided by Brueggemann, *Theology of the Old Testament*, pp. 518–522.

[29] Brueggemann, *Prophetic Imagination*, p. 75.

(Jer. 25:9; 27:6). Isaiah avoids using the term 'servant' for Cyrus, since it has special significance in his prophecy as applied to Israel and the one who will fulfil Israel's mission. But he does describe Cyrus as the LORD's 'shepherd' and his 'anointed' (Is. 44:28; 45:1). These were terms normally applied to Israel's own kings. So, while the prophet certainly declares that the deliverance of Israel from exile will be a triumphant work of the LORD, he looks to the newly rising external state to accomplish it. *The new exodus will have a pagan for its Moses!*

Once again we see how fully the Old Testament puts all human political authority and military power under the sovereign will of the LORD. The external empire state may be oppressive and enslaving, as an agent of God's judgment; or it may be more enlightened and liberating, as an agent of God's redemption. Either way, it is the arm of the LORD at work.

The distinctive community: the post-exilic period

The people of God

After the return from Babylon to Judaea the people of God were not an institutional state again. But neither were they the tiny dislocated group of captive exiles. They were scarcely a nation, in any sense of national independence. But they were a community with a clear sense of distinct ethnic and religious identity. As a subprovince within the vast Persian Empire they remained politically insignificant. Yet at the same time they had a much-enhanced view of their own significance as the people of God in the world, with a continuing role as his servant and a mixture of hopes as to how God's purpose for them and through them would ultimately be accomplished. So they were a restored community, a community of faith and promise, a community of memory and hope.

Goldingay identifies four main features of the post-exilic community. (1) They were *a worshipping community*, going back to the original conception of the Israelite *'ēdâ*, the assembly gathered for worship. Ezra laid the foundations of this, and the Chronicler provided its validation in his narrative history. (2) They were *a waiting community*, looking forward with varieties of apocalyptic expectation to a new future from God. (3) They were *an obeying community*, with a new devotion to the law, fired by the realization that it was neglect of the law that had led to the catastrophe of exile. Thus the law, even more than the covenant of which it had originally been the responsive part, becomes the heart of the new community of faith, which eventually became known as 'Judaism'. And (4) they were *a questioning community*. The tensions of faith posed by their own history produced doubts and uncertainties which some strands of the Wisdom literature wrestle with. Not all the questions found answers within the limits of the old faith.

The state

During this period there were enormous fluctuations in the extent to which the external imperial state impinged upon the life of God's people. Under Persia they experienced a comparatively benevolent policy of religious freedom and considerable local autonomy, without independence, of course. But this could be used against them by unscrupulous enemies within the system, as the book of Esther shows. The stories of Nehemiah and Ezra repay study from the angle of how they made use of state sponsorship, protection and authority both in building up the infrastructure of the community and in resisting its enemies. In the later years of the Greek control of Palestine under the Antiochene rulers, however, the community came in for extreme pressures. Some of these pressures threatened to split the community, between those who could accept and accommodate to Greek culture and ways and those who would preserve the faith and its distinctives at all costs. If it was for people facing such dilemmas that the book of Daniel was written or preserved, then the response therein was one of patience, fortified by apocalyptic hopes, and the assurance that all was still in God's control. Neither an exodus nor a Cyrus were expected. Only endurance is called for until God himself intervenes.

Conclusion: applying the material today

There is, then, in the Old Testament, no single 'doctrine of the state', but a variety of responses to an ever-changing human institution. External political authority is to be respected, and can be served legitimately, but Joseph and Daniel show that there are limits beyond which compromise becomes impossible. For the state is not absolute; the king is not divine. But they have a tendency to regard themselves in that way, and those of God's people who enter the political service of such human authorities must accept the possibility of persecution and suffering. Having observed, then, the great range of material available to us for reflection on the relationship between the people of God and the state, what are we to do with it?[30]

---

[30] One thing, in my view, we should not do with it is to assume multiple contradictory ideologies within the variety of materials. There is a tendency among some scholars to exercise a never-ending hermeneutic of suspicion that finds ideological interests under every narrative, law, proverb or prophecy, and then purports to identify the competing social groups within Israel that produced the said text for its own political ends. This procedure, which can become somewhat obsessive, seems to me to vitiate the otherwise magisterial collection of social perspectives in J. David Pleins, *Social Visions*. See further the discussion in chapter 14 below. See also the trenchant critique of such sceptical presuppositions in O'Donovan, *Desire of the Nations*, p. 28.

Acknowledging the diversity

1. We must make careful correlations between the facts of any situation in which a community of God's people today finds itself in relation to a modern secular state and the features of specific periods of Israel's history. This needs careful thought and the avoidance of blanket assertions that may be more romantic than real. Not all Christians, for example, are living under oppression. Nor are all Christians who live under oppression necessarily living in circumstances parallel to the Israelites in Egypt. Babylon may have closer parallels and more important challenges. Some Christians may be living in a time of nation-building after great political changes in their country, in which they can potentially affect the contours of the nascent state according to values drawn from the Sinai and theocracy paradigm. Others may be living as a tiny minority in a moderately benevolent state, but with little chance of influencing it. So we need to think through the diversity of Israel's experience to see when and where it matches our own and what lessons it has to teach.

> Exodus politics [for example] demands that one does *not* designate every situation of injustice as Egypt . . . In the biblical account, a sober analysis justifies the use of the categories, 'oppressor' and 'oppressed'. It seems imperative to me that in every single situation, in every existing social conflict in history, a rational investigation must decide whether the *oppressor/oppressed category is analytically appropriate* or whether it is necessary to look for another sociological paradigm.[31]

2. We need to avoid making an arbitrary selection that may entice us to have a twisted view of the response of the people of God to the state. If we merely conform to the image of Israel in a given period we may well fall prey to the same temptations as Israel did in that period. Even if we find that a particular period has most to say to our situation, we need the corrective and balance of an awareness of the other periods also. For the great thing is that Israel 'found' God in all of them, and learned and coped within them:

> It is a genuine encouragement to find within the scripture itself the people of God coping with different modes of being with the ambiguities that we ourselves experience. God has said yes to each of these. The monarchy was part of God's will, even though it had its earthly origin in an act of human rebellion. The community

---

[31] Baum, 'Exodus Politics', p. 115 (his italics). He goes on to suggest paradigms such as reconciliation between estranged brothers; e.g., as a more helpful and equally biblical way of looking at conflicts such as Northern Ireland and Israel–Palestine.

has to find ways of living with the experience of God's promises not being fulfilled. [But] . . . The danger is that our choice of a perspective from the various ones the Old Testament offers us may be an arbitrary one. A predetermined understanding of what it means to be God's people may be bolstered exegetically by appeal to biblical warrants which support a stance chosen before coming to the Bible.[32]

Finding the norm

If we ask whether any particular period or event in Israel's Old Testament history has prime significance as setting a paradigm for the rest, then I think we have to come back to the normative significance of the covenant and law at Sinai, and the attempts of the early theocracy to initiate a community that embodied those social objectives. We have already seen in detail that the prophets exercised a critical function during the monarchy on precisely that basis – the covenantal 'constitution' of Sinai.

Another good example of the normative stature of the covenant law, even in a pagan situation, would be Daniel again. Living in the midst of exile, when his people were an oppressed minority in a pagan state, Daniel had visions of the empire as essentially 'beastly' in character. Like Jeremiah, Daniel was fully aware of the state as ultimately an enemy of God, indeed a kind of God-surrogate, destined for God's final destruction. Nevertheless, he not only chose to serve the state at the civil-political level, but also took the opportunity to challenge that state in the name of the 'God of heaven' to mend its ways in line with a paradigm of justice derived from Sinai (4:27).

The subtlety and mature balance of Daniel's stance is remarkable. On the one hand, knowing that it was God himself who had given Nebuchadnezzar all authority and dominion, he nevertheless did not feel bound to obey Nebuchadnezzar in every particular. Rather, he set limits on the extent of his submission to the state because there were no limits on his submission to God. *Daniel's doctrine of the divine appointment of human authority did not make him a passive pawn, giving uncritical obedience to the particular authority under which he lived.* But, on the other hand, knowing that Babylon was one of the 'beasts' of his visions, an agent of evil and destruction with spiritual dimensions, he nevertheless continued his daily political duty at his office desk, maintaining his integrity and his witness at the top level of national life. *Daniel's doctrine of the satanic influence on human powers did not make him withdraw as an escapist from political involvement.* Christians need a similarly balanced understanding of their political and social responsibilities within states that may not acknowledge God but are still part of God's world.

---

[32] Goldingay, *Theological Diversity*, pp. 91–92.

Locating authority

The nature and source of authority is obviously a key issue in any discussion of politics. I would make three points here from our survey of Israel's political theology.

First, all authority is the LORD's. The Old Testament affirms this as strongly as the New Testament affirms that all authority is Christ's. And God's authority applies to the totality of human existence on earth. Therefore, any human authority is secondary and derived. Our tendency to absolutize our own human authorities has to be constantly unmasked and decisively relativized. This, of course, ought to be as true of human authority exercised within the people of God as in the sphere of political authority in the state. All human authority is relative to, accountable to, and addressable by, God. Hence the importance of the prophetic gift and ministry.

Secondly, political authority comes from God and not only from the people. This is affirmed in different periods. The people want a king, but it is God who gives one. Nevertheless, the role of the people is important, and legitimacy in the eyes of the people is important. Even in the history of the divinely appointed Davidic kings it is interesting how often the people play a decisive part in the making or breaking of kings (e.g. 2 Kgs. 11:17ff.; 14:19–21). But since the authority comes in reality from God, this sets a limit on the exercise of power by the appointed or elected authority, and indeed on the choices and behaviour of the people also. A majority has no more divine right than a monarch, in Old Testament terms. That is why the division and dispersion of power is a good thing, since it prevents a single individual or group from exercising the kind of total authority that properly belongs only to God.[33]

Thirdly, the model of political authority is servanthood. 'Moses was faithful as a servant in God's house' is not an Old Testament text (Heb. 3:5), but the Israelites would have agreed with it (see Exod. 14:31). Though an outstanding *leader*, among the greatest in human history, Moses could be soberly described as 'the most *humble* man on earth' (Num. 12:3; my italics). Not surprisingly, then, the Deuteronomic law of kingship strictly forbids a king from exalting himself above his brothers; he should rather set an example in embodying the demands and values of the law (Deut. 17:14–20). In fact, this remarkable text more or less says that whatever a king in Israel is to be, he is not to be like any usual earthly king, who enjoys weapons (military prestige), wealth (silver and gold) or wives (harem). In the context of the day it might

---

[33] On these points, the limits of government, the importance of plurality of leadership, and the derivative nature of human authority from the final authority of God, see Marshall, *Thine Is the Kingdom*, pp. 56–61.

have been wondered whether it was worth being king at all on such terms. Israel's was a very different model of kingship indeed, a model that sadly even David scarcely adhered to, and Solomon forgot altogether.

The pattern of true political leadership in Israel is nowhere more succinctly expressed than in the advice given to Rehoboam by his older advisors, already noted above in 1 Kings 12:7, 'If today you will be a servant to these people and serve them . . . they will always be your servants.' Kingship meant mutual servanthood. The same thought is inherent in the common metaphor of shepherd applied to political leadership. As we have noted, a shepherd had a responsible job, but a lowly status. He existed for the sake of the sheep, which were not his own, but for which he was accountable to their owner. So when Jesus not only claimed to be the model shepherd but also affirmed that true greatness is a matter of servanthood, not status, he was recovering an authentically Old Testament perspective on leadership and authority.

God and the nations: Israel's universal vision

I began this chapter with the diversity of nations as part of God's *creational* order, and now return to the nations again in *eschatological* conclusion. How did Israel contemplate the future of the nations in the purposes of God? How, indeed, did they perceive the present relation of the nations to Israel as the covenant people of the LORD? The subject is massive, since it is an issue that surfaces again and again, so I can only very briefly survey some major points here.[34]

---

[34] Israel's theology of the nations has not received the attention it deserves in many works of Old Testament theology. Walter Brueggemann is one of the few major Old Testament theologians to tackle it thoroughly in a way that ties it in with Israel's understanding of the LORD and themselves, Brueggemann, *Theology of the Old Testament*, pp. 492–527. See also Robert Martin-Achard, *Light to the Nations*; Moshe Greenberg, 'Israel and the Nations'; Norbert Lohfink, *God of Israel and the Nations*; C. H. H. Scobie, 'Israel and the Nations'; Eckhard J. Schnabel, 'Israel, the People of God, and the Nations'; G. I. Davies, 'Destiny of the Nations'. For the wider ancient Near Eastern concept see Daniel I. Block, *Gods of the Nations*. More attention has been given to the theme of the nations in *missiological* studies of biblical theology, but these often view the matter retrospectively in relation to the New Testament theology of the Gentile mission of the early church – a valid perspective biblically, but not geared to contextual and exegetical understanding of the texts about the nations in Israel's own understanding. Johannes Blauw, *Missionary Nature of the Church*; Richard R. de Ridder, *Discipling the Nations*; David Burnett, *God's Mission*; Walter C. Kaiser Jr, *Mission in the Old Testament*.

The nations as spectators

In some texts Israel thought of the nations as 'spectators' of all God's dealings with Israel – whether positively or negatively. Israel lived on an open stage and the nations would witness what happened to them. So, whether Israel was enjoying acts of God's deliverance or was on the receiving end of blows of God's judgment, the nations would observe and draw their conclusions, rightly or wrongly (Exod. 15:15; 32:12; Num. 14:13–16; Deut. 9:28; Ezek. 36:16–23). The observation of the nations was also a significant incentive to Israel's moral response to God. This too could be positive (Deut. 4:6–8) or negative (Deut. 29:24–28)

The nations as beneficiaries

Eventually, however, and rather mysteriously, the nations could be portrayed as the beneficiaries of all God had done in and for Israel, and even be invited to rejoice, applaud and praise YHWH the God of Israel. What God did for Israel, even including the defeat of the nations who were their enemies, would ultimately be a matter of gratitude and praise among the nations, so it must finally be for their redemptive good (1 Kgs. 8:41–43; Pss. 47; 67).

The nations included within Israel

Most remarkable of all, Israel came to entertain the eschatological vision that there would be those of the nations who would not merely be *joined to* Israel, but would come to be *identified as* Israel, with the same names, privileges and responsibilities before God (Ps. 47:9; Is. 19:19–25; 56:2–8; 66:19–21; Amos 9:11–12; Zech. 2:10–11; Acts 15:16–18; Eph. 2:11 – 3:6).

These texts are breathtaking in their universal scope. This is the dimension of Israel's prophetic heritage that most profoundly influenced the theological explanation and motivation of the Gentile mission in the New Testament. It certainly underlies James's interpretation of Christ's life, death and resurrection, and the success of the Gentile mission in Acts 15 (quoting Amos 9:12). And it likewise inspired Paul's efforts as a practitioner and theologian of mission (e.g. Rom. 15:7–16); and provided the theological shape for the Gospels, all of which conclude with their various forms of the Great Commission – the sending of Jesus' disciples into the world of nations.

The diversity of the nations preserved in their unity

So the Old Testament has the ultimate vision of the inclusion of all nations in God's *redemptive* purpose, the promise of blessing first given to Abraham. What was an implicit reversal of the scattering and confusion of Babel, in the call of Abraham, becomes explicit in the prophetic vision of Zephaniah for the nations – they will again be united. For after the consuming judgment of God's anger on the wickedness of the nations,

POLITICS AND THE NATIONS 251

Then will I purify the lips of the peoples,
that all of them may call on the name of the LORD
and serve him shoulder to shoulder.

(Zeph. 3:9)

But this eschatological unity in the worship of God will not mean the dissolving of diverse national identities. Rather, the glory of the future reign of God will be the influx of the rich variety of all peoples. This is the throbbing joy of Isaiah 60, and the more sober warnings of Zechariah 14:16ff. Furthermore, not just the peoples, but all their achievement, wealth and glory will be brought, purified, into the new Jerusalem of God's reign.[35] This Old Testament vision is found in Isaiah 60:5–11; Haggai 2:6–8; and in the astonishing conclusion of an oracle against Tyre (Is. 23:18), where it is envisaged that all the profits of that archetypal trading empire will be 'set apart for the LORD', for the benefit of his people.

This is not blatant chauvinism or covetousness. Rather, it is the realization that, since God's ultimate purpose is the creation of a people for himself, a new humanity in a new earth, then all that humankind does and achieves can only, under God's providential transformation, contribute in the end to the glory of that new order. The same vision is taken up in Revelation, when 'the kingdom of the world has become the kingdom of our Lord and of his Christ' and 'the kings of the earth will bring their splendour into it' (Rev. 11:15; 21:24).

Further reading

Bauckham, Richard, *The Bible in Politics: How to Read the Bible Politically* (London: SPCK; Louisville, KY: Westminster John Knox, 1989).
Baum, Gregory, 'Exodus Politics', in van Iersel and Weiler, *Exodus*, pp. 109–117.
Brueggemann, Walter, *The Prophetic Imagination* (Philadelphia: Fortress, 1978).
——, *A Social Reading of the Old Testament: Prophetic Approaches to Israel's Communal Life*, ed. Patrick D. Miller Jr, (Minneapolis: Fortress, 1994).
——, *Theology of the Old Testament: Testimony, Dispute, Advocacy* (Minneapolis: Fortress, 1997).
Gerbrandt, Gerald Eddie, *Kingship According to the Deuteronomistic History* (Atlanta: Scholars Press, 1986).
Gimsrud, Ted, and Johns, Loren L. (eds.), *Peace and Justice Shall Embrace: Power and*

[35] For an excellent exposition of this great eschatological hope for the nations and for creation, see Richard J. Mouw, *When the Kings Come Marching In*.

Theopolitics in the Bible: Essays in Honor of Millard Lind (Telford, PA: Pandora, 1999).

Goldingay, John, *Theological Diversity and the Authority of the Old Testament* (Grand Rapids: Eerdmans, 1987).

Houston, Walter, 'The King's Preferential Option for the Poor: Rhetoric, Ideology and Ethics in Psalm 72', *Biblical Interpretation* 7 (1999), pp. 347–368.

Knight, Douglas A., 'Political Rights and Powers in Monarchic Israel', *Semeia* 66 (1994), pp. 93–117.

Liechty, Daniel, 'What Kind of Political Power? The Upside-Down Kingdom in Millard Lind's Reading of the Hebrew Bible', in Gimsrud and Johns, *Peace and Justice Shall Embrace*, pp. 17–33.

Lind, Millard C., 'The Concept of Political Power in Ancient Israel', *Annual of the Swedish Theological Institute* 7 (1968–9), pp. 4–24.

Marshall, Paul, *Thine Is the Kingdom: A Biblical Perspective on the Nature of Government and Politics Today* (Basingstoke: Marshall, Morgan & Scott, 1984).

Mason, Rex, *Propaganda and Subversion in the Old Testament* (London: SPCK, 1997).

Mettinger, Tryggve N. D., *King and Messiah: The Civil and Sacral Legitimation of the Israelite Kings* (Lund: Gleerup, 1976).

Mott, Stephen Charles, *A Christian Perspective on Political Thought* (Oxford: Oxford University Press, 1993).

Mouw, Richard J., *When the Kings Come Marching In: Isaiah and the New Jerusalem* (Grand Rapids: Eerdmans, 1983).

O'Donovan, Oliver M. T., *The Desire of the Nations: Rediscovering the Roots of Political Theology* (Cambridge: Cambridge University Press, 1996).

Plant, Raymond, *Politics, Theology and History* (Cambridge: Cambridge University Press, 2001).

Reventlow, Henning Graf, Hoffman, Yair, and Uffenheimer, Benjamin (eds.), *Politics and Theopolitics in the Bible and Postbiblical Literature*, JSOT Supplement Series, vol. 171 (Sheffield: JSOT Press, 1994).

Schnabel, Eckhard J., 'Israel, the People of God, and the Nations', *Journal of the Evangelical Theological Society* 45 (2002), pp. 35–57.

Scobie, C. H. H., 'Israel and the Nations: An Essay in Biblical Theology', *Tyndale Bulletin* 43.2 (1992), pp. 283–305.

Voegelin, E., *Israel and Revelation* (Baton Rouge: Louisiana State University, 1956).

Walsh SJ, J. P. M., *The Mighty from Their Thrones: Power in the Biblical Tradition*, Overtures to Biblical Theology vol. 21 (Philadelphia: Fortress, 1987).

Walzer, Michael, *Exodus and Revolution* (New York: Basic Books, 1985).

Wogaman, J. Philip, *Christian Perspective on Politics*, 2nd ed. (Louisville, KY: Westminster John Knox, 2000).

Wright, Christopher J. H., *Tested by Fire: Daniel 1–6 in Today's World* (London: Scripture Union, 1993).

———, *The Message of Ezekiel*, The Bible Speaks Today (Leicester: IVP; Downers Grove: InterVarsity Press, 2001).

8. JUSTICE AND RIGHTEOUSNESS

Follow justice and justice alone. (Deut. 16:20)
For I, the LORD, love justice. (Is. 61:8)

The concern for justice pervades the entire Old Testament. It is found in the
historical, legal, prophetic, and wisdom literature, and in the Psalms as well. It is
found throughout the entire history of the Old Testament literature . . . The evidence
shows that the concern for justice was one, if not the central, factor by which ancient
Israel's multifaceted societal life was united throughout its historical changes . . . No
sphere of Israel's life was exempt from concern for justice, and the LORD was known
to be at work in all its spheres.

Ralph P. Knierim, *Task of Old Testament Theology*

Few themes are more central to any discussion of social ethics than justice.
Wherever human beings in any culture consider primary ethical concepts,
justice will be to the fore. So much else seems to hinge upon it if human
society is to function with any semblance of civil order, security and harmony.
When justice is pervasively trampled upon, then the very foundations of live-
able society crumble. The Old Testament would go further. If justice perished, the foundations of the whole cosmic order would disintegrate, because
justice is fundamental to the very nature of the LORD, the creator of the universe and to the core of God's government of history.

The LORD reigns, let the earth be glad . . .

> righteousness and justice are the foundation of his throne.
>
> (Ps. 97:1, 2; cf. 89:14)

For Israel, then, justice was no abstract concept or philosophical definition. Justice was essentially theological. It was rooted in the character of the LORD, their God; it flowed from his actions in history; it was demanded by his covenant relationship with Israel; it would ultimately be established on the earth only by his sovereign power.

So, then, although the main focus in this book is on the social ethics of Israel, here is one place above all where the point of chapter 1, that Old Testament ethics is fundamentally theological, is borne out. Justice on earth flows from justice in heaven. So rather than approaching the topic in terms of a systematic analysis of Israel's concept and practice of justice (about which there is an overwhelming amount of excellent literature: see the selection at the end of this chapter), we shall keep God at the centre and reflect on three points: first, justice as God displays it; secondly, justice as God demands it; and thirdly, justice as God will ultimately deliver it.[1]

Justice as God displays it

Out of all the array of material in the Old Testament that declares or celebrates that the LORD is the God of justice, it is helpful to focus attention on one rich text and work outwards from there. Psalm 33 includes the bold affirmation

> The LORD loves righteousness and justice;
>   the earth is full of his unfailing love.
>
> (Ps. 33:5)

---

[1] There is some correspondence between the structure I have adopted here and the suggestive outline in the preface to Moshe Weinfeld's comprehensive survey of the theme:

'Justice and Righteousness' appear in the divine sphere in the following cases:

   a) When God created the world and established justice in the universe.
   b) When God revealed himself to Israel to give them Justice (= Law), at Sinai.
   c) When God will reveal himself in the future to judge the nations with 'Justice and Righteousness.'

(Weinfeld, *Social Justice*, p. 5)

The vocabulary

The phrase 'righteousness and justice' in Psalm 33:5 brings together two of the 'biggest' words in the Old Testament. Each of them individually, in various verbal, adjectival and noun forms, occurs hundreds of times. Found together as a couplet (either righteousness and justice, or justice and righteousness), they form what is technically called a *hendiadys* – a single complex idea expressed through the use of two words.[2] The two words in Hebrew are well worth knowing:

1. The first is the root *ṣdq*, which is found in two common noun forms, *ṣedeq* and *ṣĕdāqâ*. There is probably no significant difference between these two forms.[3] They are usually translated 'righteousness' in English Bibles, but that rather 'religious-flavoured' word does not convey the full range of meaning that the words had in Hebrew. The root meaning is probably 'straight': something fixed, and fully what it should be. So it can mean a norm – something by which other things are measured, a standard. It is used literally of objects that are or do what they are supposed to be or do: for example, accurate weights

---

[2] Other examples of hendiadys in English include 'law and order', 'health and safety', 'board and lodging'. Each word in a hendiadys has its own distinct meaning; but when put together in a commonly used phrase, they express a single idea or set of circumstances.

[3] If there is much difference it is probably that *ṣedeq* is more conceptual, while *ṣĕdāqâ* is more dynamic:

> In general, *ṣedeq* refers to the abstract principle of righteousness, while *ṣĕdāqâ* refers to the concrete act. *Ṣedeq* as an abstract ideal is thus personified; it is said to 'look out from heaven' (Ps. 85:12; cf. Isa. 45:8); peace and *ṣedeq* are said to kiss one another (Ps. 85:11); *ṣedeq* and *mišpāṭ* are considered the foundation of God's throne (Ps. 89:15, 97:6) ... By contrast, *ṣĕdāqâ* is bound up with actions (see Isa. 56:1, 58:2; ... did *ṣĕdāqâ*, i.e. acted righteously), and later it became the Hebrew word for giving alms to the poor (Dan. 4:24).
>
> (Weinfeld, *Social Justice*, p. 34)

See also J. N. Schofield's observation:

> In justice there was more mercy than we recognize, and in righteousness, justice and mercy were not opposed terms. So strong was this element of mercy or benevolence in 'righteousness' that in later Hebrew the word becomes the usual term for almsgiving (cf. Matt. 6:1 f.) – that is, for gifts to needy members of the group, which cannot legally be demanded, but are an obligation.
>
> (Schofield, '"Righteousness" in the Old Testament', p. 115)

and measures are 'measures of *ṣedeq*' (Lev. 19:36; Deut. 25:15). Good paths for the sheep are 'paths of *ṣedeq*' (Ps. 23:3[4]). So it comes to mean 'rightness', that which is as it ought to be, that which matches up to the standard. When applied to human actions and relationships, it speaks of conformity to what is right or expected – not in some abstract or absolute generic way, but according to the demands of the relationship or the nature of the situation. '*Ṣdq* terminology indicates right behaviour or status in relation to some standard of behavior accepted in the community.'[5]

Ṣedeq and *ṣĕdāqâ* are in fact highly relational words. So much so that Hemchand Gossai includes a whole section on them in his definition of the term 'relationship'.

> In order for an individual to be *ṣaddîq* [righteous], it means that of necessity he or she must exist and live in a manner which allows him or her to respond correctly to the values of the relationship [which may include relationships of spouse, parent, judge, worker, friend, etc.] . . . In essence then *ṣdq* is not simply an objective norm which is present within society, and which must be kept, but rather it is a concept which derives its meaning from the relationship in which it finds itself. So we are able to say that right judging, right governing, right worshipping and gracious activity are all covenantal and righteous, despite their diversity.[6]

  2. The second is the root *špṭ*, which has to do with judicial activity at every level. A common verb and noun are derived from it. The verb *šāpaṭ* refers to legal action over a wide range. It can mean to act as a lawgiver; to act as a judge by arbitrating between parties in a dispute; to pronounce judgment by declaring who is guilty and who is innocent respectively; to execute judgment in carrying out the legal consequences of such a verdict. In the widest sense, it means 'to put things right', to intervene in a situation that is wrong, oppressive or out of control and to 'fix' it. This may include confronting wrongdoers, on the one hand, and, on the other hand, vindicating and delivering those who have been wronged. Such action is not confined to a court of law, but may take place in other ways; for example through battle. That is why the figures in the

---

[4] The phrase here probably has a double entendre: in the metaphor, the sheep needs to be led along a path that really is a path ('proper paths'), or a path that will lead to safety and good pasture ('right paths'); in the human application, 'paths of righteousness' probably has a more ethical flavour, as traditionally understood.

[5] Reimer, '*Ṣdq*', p. 750. See also the detailed discussion of the word in Gossai, *Justice*, ch. 1.

[6] Gossai, *Justice*, pp. 55–56.

book of Judges have that name. They 'judged' Israel by putting things right –
militarily, religiously, legally – with Samuel being the model of all three.

The derived noun *mišpāṭ* can describe the whole process of litigation (a
case), or its end result (the verdict and its execution). It can mean a legal ordinance, usually a case law based on past precedents. (Exod. 21 – 23, known as
the Covenant Code or Book of the Covenant, is simply called in Hebrew the
mišpāṭîm.) It can also be used in a more personal sense as one's legal right, the
cause or case one is bringing as a plaintiff before the elders. The frequent
expression 'the *mišpāṭ* of the orphan and widow' means their rightful case
against those who would exploit them. It is from this last sense in particular
that *mišpāṭ* comes to have the wider sense of 'justice' in the somewhat active
sense, whereas *ṣedeq/ṣĕdāqâ* has a more static flavour.[7] In the broadest terms
(and recognizing that there is a great deal of overlap and interchangeability
between the words) *mišpāṭ* is what needs to be done in a given situation if
people and circumstances are to be restored to conformity with *ṣedeq/ṣĕdāqâ*.
Mišpāṭ is a qualitative set of actions – something you do. 'As it is frequently
used in biblical texts justice is a call for action more than it is a principle of
evaluation. Justice as an appeal for a response means *taking upon oneself the cause
of those who are weak in their own defense* [cf. Is. 58:6 Job 29:16; Jer. 21:12].'[8]
Ṣedeq/ṣĕdāqâ is a qualitative state of affairs – something you aim to achieve.

Here in Psalm 33:5 the two words are paired, as they frequently are, to form
a comprehensive phrase. Possibly the nearest English expression to the
double word phrase would be 'social justice'. Even that phrase is somethat too
abstract for the dynamic nature of the pair of Hebrew words. John Goldingay
emphatically points out that the Hebrew words are concrete nouns, unlike the
abstract nouns which English normally uses to translate them. That is, they
are actual things that you do, not concepts that you reflect upon.[9]

The context
Psalm 33 celebrates the LORD as redeemer, creator, judge and saviour. Thus its
whole concept of justice is set firmly within the covenantal framework of the
LORD's historical relationship with Israel. It was from that history that they
understood what it meant to say that the LORD loved justice. But it was also
from that history that they universalized the affirmation and turned it into a
statement about 'the whole earth' (v. 5b).

---

[7] On *mišpāṭ*, see Gossai, *Justice*, ch. 3.

[8] Mott, *Political Thought*, p. 79 (his italics).

[9] See John Goldingay, 'Justice and Salvation'.

The surrounding phrases in Psalm 33:4–5 add colour and flavour to the bald statement that God loves righteousness and justice. They show us the context in which Israel thought of justice. I can only sketch them in here.

There is first, the *word* of the LORD (*dābār*, v. 4). This is God's relational communication, through which he not only enters into dialogue with human beings but also accomplishes his purposes in history. It is the powerful word of God that is redemptive, but putting things right and declaring the truth, in a world of wrongs and lies (v. 4a). It is the powerful word of God that is creative, in bringing the whole universe into being out of nothing (vv. 6, 9), and then goes on to govern the history of nations on the face of the planet (vv. 10–11).

Then there is, secondly, the *faithfulness* ('*ĕmûnâ*, v. 4) and *love* (*ḥesed*, v. 5) of the LORD. These are the covenant characteristics of the LORD: his loyal commitment to his people, in keeping his promises and acting out of grace and love. The word *ḥesed* is often translated 'kindness' or 'love', but it is more 'solid' than those words suggest in common English. It means his abiding loyalty to his covenant, his unshakeable will to keep his gracious promise. What he has decided and established in his righteousness he stands by with fixed purpose. The translation '*steadfast* love' (RSV), or '*unfailing* love' (v. 22, NIV), gets nearer the true meaning. Frequently, *ḥesed* and *ṣĕdāqâ* are paired off as parallel terms, both as qualities of *God's* action (Ps. 36:10) and as requirements of *human* ethical response (Hos. 10:12; Mic. 6:8).

Elsewhere God's justice is paired with his grace and compassion; indeed, in Isaiah 30:18 God's justice is the *reason* for his compassion, which sounds odd in ears accustomed to thinking of justice only in terms of punishment and judgment:[10]

> Yet the LORD longs to be gracious to you;
> he rises to show you compassion.
> For the LORD is a God of justice.
> Blessed are all who wait for him!

Thus it is clear that for Israel the whole idea of justice was wrapped up with the qualities and characteristics of the LORD, their God, and especially

---

[10] Stephen Mott cites this verse among others to counter the argument that love and justice are separate moral realms. Not in the Old Testament, he argues. 'Not all benevolence is justice, but love that responds to unmet basic material needs legitimately calls forth justice. Such a loving, benevolent type of justice is not a confusion about biblical justice. It is the meaning of distributive justice in the Scriptures' (Mott, *Political Thought*, p. 87).

connected to the covenant relationship between Israel and the LORD. Justice is essentially relational and covenantal.

The roots: Israel's story

How did Israel know this? On what basis could they make such a comprehensive affirmation as Psalm 33:5? The answer is, of course, from their own story. Psalm 33 does not dwell much on the history of Israel, but it is implicit in several phrases, such as 'faithful in all he does' (v. 4), 'the plans of the LORD' (v. 11), 'the nation whose God is the LORD, / the people he chose for his inheritance (v. 12). So we could highlight some of the key episodes in Israel's history, observing the elements of God's justice manifest in them.

The ancestors

The earliest traditions present the LORD as the God who does justice and who wants justice. Genesis 18:19 makes the remarkable affirmation (in the mouth of God in conversation with Abraham) that the creation of a community of righteousness and justice was the immediate purpose of the election of Abraham. The ultimate purpose was the blessing of the nations ('what he has promised him'):

> Abraham will surely become a great and powerful nation, and all nations on earth will be blessed through him. For I have chosen him, so that he will direct his children and his household after him to keep the way of the LORD by doing what is right and just (*ṣĕdāqâ* and *mišpāṭ*), so that the LORD will bring about for Abraham what he has promised him.
>
> (Gen. 18:18–19)

The context of this comprehensive statement of divine purpose is the wickedness of Sodom and Gomorrah and God's planned judgment upon those cities. However, what the text focuses on is not just that God has observed their wickedness, but that he has seen and heard the suffering of the oppressed – 'the outcry has reached me' (v. 20). 'Outcry' is *ṣĕʿāqâ*, almost a technical word for the cry of pain from those who are oppressed or violated.[11]

---

11 For a full and detailed discussion of this word, including its use in the Psalms and prophets, see Richard Nelson Boyce, *Cry to God*. Boyce gives a whole chapter (ch. 3) to the use of this term (and its associated verb *ṣʿq*, or *zʿq*) in the legal setting of the 'cry for help' addressed to the authorities by the needy. It would certainly sharpen our understanding of Gen. 18:20 if what God heard from Sodom was not just 'an outcry' but specifically 'a cry for help' addressed to himself as the ultimate 'Judge of all the

Almost certainly there is an intentional contrast between the *ṣě'āqâ* (outcry against injustice) that God hears from Sodom, and the *ṣědāqâ* (righteousness/ justice) that he wants from Abraham's community.[12] The justice of God is the justice of the God who sees and hears the cry of the weak and oppressed, cares about them and takes action on their behalf. That is the essential meaning of *šāpaṭ* – to take action on behalf of the wronged and put things right. Two chapters earlier Hagar had experienced this quality of the LORD, and she, a foreign slave woman and the victim of appalling treatment, became the first person in the Bible to give a name to God – 'the God who sees me' (Gen. 16:13–14).

So this is the context in which we need to read the famous question of Abraham, when, horrified by the warning of what God intended to do to Sodom and Gomorrah, he fell to intercession for them, asking that God would spare the cities for the sake of any righteous who might be there. 'Will not the Judge of all the earth do right?' (*mišpāṭ*, Gen. 18:25). It is in the form of a question, but the point is surely a rhetorical affirmation. It was unthinkable that the LORD should do otherwise, since his very character was definitive of what is right and just.[13] It is possible to read into this question severe philosophical problems: is Abraham subjecting God to some standard of rightness above God himself? If so, is God subject to some external criterion: a criterion Abraham is bold enough to appeal to, even over against God? This then leads to the famous dilemma: is something right because God wills or does it; or does God will and do things because they are right?[14] My view is that such questioning is not really apposite to the text. It seems that Abraham is appealing to God, *on the assumption* that God must and will act justly. And in the context of the use of the phrase *righteousness and justice* in verse 19 it is clear that the LORD himself must surely act in accordance with what he requires of Abraham and his household. This is not God being subject to some external

---

earth'. In this case, God's intervention to destroy the cities would be seen as breaking their power over the poor and oppressed in the surrounding area – an act of biblical justice.

[12] The same play on these two words is used to very powerful effect in Is. 5:7.

[13] This indeed, was how Elihu put it in the book of Job: 'It is unthinkable that God would do wrong, / that the Almighty would pervert justice' (Job 34:12, answering Bildad's rhetorical question to the same effect in Job 8:3). Doubtless Elihu drew the wrong conclusions from his theology specifically in relation to Job, but he was certainly expressing orthodox Yahwistic faith.

[14] These are some of the questions Cyril Rodd wrestles with (Rodd, *Glimpses*, ch. 6, 'Abraham's Question').

or superior 'law'; it is simply God being true to the internal integrity of God's own character.

The exodus

For Israel, the exodus was the paradigmatic demonstration of the LORD's justice in action, in both senses – judgment and salvation. It was God's self-revelation, since the name of the LORD itself was inextricably linked to the narrative of God's intervention on behalf of the oppressed Hebrew slaves in Egypt. Several aspects of the episode mark it out as, above all, an act of God's justice:

- The explicit trigger for God's action is his concern for the suffering of the oppressed. Their situation, as described in Exodus 1, had become intolerable, as they suffered the effects of political servitude, economic exploitation and social genocide. God saw, heard, cared and went into action (Exod. 2:23–25; 3:7–10). This, as we have seen, is of the essence of the role of the 'judge' who does *mišpāṭ*.
- God's action was decisively *against* the oppressor and *for* the oppressed. This is celebrated, for example, in Deuteronomy 6:20–25; 26:1–11. On the one hand, the Egyptians were guilty of violating the rights of Israel – their right to freedom, to the product of their own labour, to worship their own ancestral God, even to unhampered reproduction and family life. The events preceding and accompanying the exodus, therefore, were an act of righteous judgment upon Egypt (Exod. 9:27). On the other hand, it all happened because God saw and heard the 'wronged' condition of Israel under oppression, and in the exodus he gave freedom to a captive people, rescuing them out of injustice, restoring them to a situation of 'right' or justice, which eventually issued in secure possession of the land as a place to enjoy and protect that 'right'. For Israel it was vindication and salvation of the most direct and tangible kind.
- God's action of justice, characteristically, was based on love for his people and faithfulness to his promise. These, as we saw, are the relational components of justice as displayed by God.
- God's act of historical justice established both a new relationship between the LORD and Israel within which they 'knew' him as the LORD (i.e. as the God of liberating justice, Exod. 6:6–8), and also established Israel from the start as a community of righteousness, founded on the justice of God. This leads us (as it did Israel) to Sinai and the law.

The Sinai covenant and law

Justice was the social foundation of Israel not only because the initiative of God's redeeming power was an act of righteousness, but also because it called forth a response of imitative righteousness and justice among the Israelites themselves. Having been put 'right', so to speak, the Israelites were to maintain righteousness. Having experienced justice, they were to 'do justice'. What God had anticipated in his conversation with Abraham (Gen. 18:19), while the people of Israel existed only by faith in the loins of Abraham, God now confirmed in the covenantal constitution of the newly established nation.

1. *The Decalogue.* It will help us to focus this point more clearly if we look at the Ten Commandments in this light, taking them as the foundational charter or policy statement of the rest of the covenant law. The Decalogue was a formula for responsible freedom. The Ten Commandments can be seen as given in order to preserve the rights and freedoms gained by the exodus, by translating them into responsibilities. Let us take them more or less in order from this point of view.

- God had given the Israelites the right and freedom to worship God as the LORD alone, the God of their fathers. This had been the express purpose of the demand for release from Egypt (Exod. 4:23); so now they must worship the LORD exclusively (first commandment).
- By his mighty act the LORD had shown himself to be a living and incomparable (jealous) God; therefore, any lifeless image or idol was an insult (second).
- The exodus had involved a powerful demonstration of the meaning of God's personal name Yahweh, the LORD; so they must not use that name selfishly, maliciously or foolishly (third).
- God had freed them from relentless forced labour, enabling them now to work as free people; so they must preserve the right of regular sabbath rest for themselves, their families, employees and even their animals (fourth).
- God had freed them from Pharaoh's intolerable violence against their family life, so they must protect the family as regards its parental authority (fifth) and sexual integrity (seventh).
- Freed from the infanticide and murdering terror of Egyptian oppression, they must respect life and not tolerate murder in their own society (sixth).
- Now that they would no longer be aliens in a foreign country, but possess a land of their own, they were not to steal or covet what was God's gift to all (eighth and tenth).
- With the example of God's justice before them they were not to betray one another by the malicious injustice of perverted testimony in court (ninth).

When we look at the Decalogue from this perspective, we can see it as a kind of 'Bill of Rights', human and divine, expressed in the form of responsibilities, responsibilities that were necessary to preserve and enjoy their freedom as a redeemed people.

2. *The law.* The rest of the law in the Pentateuch presents itself as witness to the LORD's justice. Deuteronomy celebrates this aspect of the LORD as the foundation of the behaviour that is to characterize Israelites when they are observant of his laws and decrees. Thus the wonderfully rich text of Deuteronomy 10:12–19 urges upon all Israelites the simple, fivefold message: all the LORD requires is that they fear him, walk in his ways, love him, serve him and observe his commands. In case there may be any uncertainty about what it means in practice to walk in the ways of the LORD, the text breaks into a double doxology in verses 14 and 17, but then funnels all the majestic superlatives of those verses (the LORD is the God who owns the universe and rules it) down to the poor, weak, needy and marginalized. The LORD is the God of integrity, who cannot be corrupted or bribed. More, the LORD is the God of love for the alien, feeding and clothing him. Then come the key words, translating this characteristic of the LORD into ethical imperative, 'And you are to love the alien . . .' (and presumably follow God's example in all the other aspects mentioned).

No wonder, then, that Deuteronomy, in one of the oldest pieces of poetry in the Bible, the song of Moses in Deuteronomy 32, compares the LORD to a Rock, in the strength of his trustworthy justice:

> He is the Rock, his works are perfect,
>   and all his ways are just.
> A faithful God who does no wrong,
>   upright and just is he.
>
> (Deut. 32:4)

3. *The psalmists and the law.* The psalmists celebrate this revelatory function of the law. Psalm 19 rejoices that the created order declares the glory of God, but immediately goes on to affirm that the law reflects far more of the personal qualities of God, including his trustworthiness, righteousness and justice (Ps. 19:7–9). The law embodies all of these things – and much more, of course. The author of Psalm 119 is utterly obsessed with the wonders of God's law – managing to use some synonym for it in almost every verse of his carefully constructed alphabetic poem. But although the object of attention all through is the law of God, the addressee of the psalm is the LORD himself: in the second person singular, 'you'. This is a highly relational psalm. Its point is that the writer finds in the law the surest way in to knowing the giver of the law. And through the law he comes to know all the rest of God's character – God's love, promises, faithfulness, truth, righteousness, life-giving power, protection, vindication, guidance and so on. So the psalmist's dogged determination to

walk in the paths of justice flows from his intimate relationship with the God he knows so thoroughly as a result of his saturation in God's law.

The continuing story

The rest of the history of Israel in the Old Testament narrates the dealings of the LORD with Israel *and* the nations. The conquest of the land is, like the exodus, presented as an act of judgment/justice upon the wickedness of the Canaanites (see the appendix) (Deut. 9:4–6). Subsequent victories are described as the 'righteous acts' or 'justices' of the LORD (Judg. 5:10). But as Israel's history unfolded they could be 'judged' in apparently opposite ways. God, in his justice, could judge them for their sin, by punishing them at the hands of their enemies. But again, on their repentance and crying out from oppression, God could again judge them through delivering them from their enemies. As we have seen, both dimensions are consistent with the meaning of *šāpaṭ* – God acting in his justice to punish the wicked and vindicate the oppressed.

> God's 'judging' (*saphat*) does not mean an abstract, neutral, judicial act, but an active, saving rearranging of broken relationship. In the context of justice, this means 'to save from oppression', to liberate, to rescue. This means that in the Bible we should not associate the words 'judging', 'justice', 'righteousness' with the Greek and Roman traditions, i.e., with either judicial institutions or abstract virtues of individuals but rather with God's community-building and protecting power.[15]

So it was consistent, in terms of Israel's vocabulary and thought, for them to speak of the LORD 'judging them' when he punished them for their sin, as well as when he vindicated and delivered them from their enemies.

At the other end of Old Testament history the exile and the return from exile are both interpreted in relation to the LORD's justice. And since his righteousness is most evident in his saving work, the nations are invited to turn around from their rebellion and idolatry and find salvation only in the righteousness of the LORD (Is. 45:21–25).

The leap to universality

Coming back to our original text, Psalm 33, it seems that the Israelite worshipper made a remarkable leap in the logic of faith. The argument seems to have gone something like this. If the LORD is like this for Israel, as proved in our history (i.e. the LORD is the God of justice, faithfulness and love), and if the LORD is in truth the only God 'and there is no other' (Deut. 4:35, 39), then

---

[15] Duchrow and Liedke, *Shalom*, p. 78.

ultimately *the* LORD *must be like this for all.* His justice must be universal. His love must be global. And so they could arrive, in the imagination of faith and worship, at the astonishingly comprehensive claim of Psalm 33:5, 'The whole earth is full of his unfailing love' – and, we may be sure from the parallelism of the verse, full of his righteousness and justice also. And this universality is then underlined in the summons of verse 8, 'let all the earth fear the LORD; let all the people of the world revere him', and the mind-stretching affirmation of verses 13–15, that the LORD sees, knows and holds morally accountable every human being on the planet.

All this is part of the certainty of faith and the imagination of worship. This, like Psalm 96, is a 'new song', offering a world-transforming vision. Neither we nor the psalmist can proclaim Psalm 33:5 on the basis of empirical observation, but only as the language of hope and confidence in the redemptive power of God, and the ultimate saving universality of his justice. Nor is this an isolated example. The same kind of universalizing logic is found in other psalms that move from the LORD's sovereignty in the history of Israel to the acknowledgment of his global, rather cosmic,[16] justice and his care for all human beings (e.g. Ps. 36:5–8: notice the same combination of God's love, faithfulness, righteousness and justice; and Ps. 97:1–6: 'the heavens proclaim his righteousness, / and all the peoples see his glory').

To say such things is to lay claim to the character of the living God, revealed as the God of justice through the history of Israel, and destined to be the universal testimony of humanity.

Justice as God demands it

Justice as God's demand on all Israel

Just as I took Psalm 33 as a guiding text for our first section, we might take Micah 6:8 as the text for this section:

> He has showed you, O man, what is good.
>   And what does the LORD require of you?
> To do justice (*mišpāṭ*), and to love mercy (*ḥesed*),
>   and to walk humbly with your God.

---

[16] 'At the beginning of the Creation, [God] prepared his throne *with justice and righteousness, with kindness and truth and uprightness* (Ps. 96:10, 93; cf. Ps. 33:5–6; 89:3, 6, 12–15). This refers to the imposition of equality, order and harmony upon the cosmos and the elimination of the forces of destruction and chaos' (Weinfeld, *Social Justice*, p. 20; his italics).

The inclusive term 'O man' (*'ādām*) indicates that this is something common to all Israelites. Micah 6:8 only crystallizes what Israel had always known – that the whole nation, having been founded on God's redemptive and constitutional justice, was to reflect that throughout society in the exercise of relational love-justice.

We might as easily have taken for our text Isaiah 5:1–7. Isaiah's song of the vineyard is a parable of the whole history of Israel, under the figure of a friend (God) who planted a vineyard (Israel) and then spent great effort and patience in tending and protecting it. Now the purpose of planting a vineyard is to produce grapes for wine. What, then, was God's purpose in planting Israel? Had God not already spelled out his intention clearly in Genesis 18:19? 'I have chosen him (Abraham) *so that* he may teach his children and his household after him . . . *to do righteousness and justice.*' The long-term goal (in the last clause of the verse) was the promised blessing of the nations, but the immediate objective was the creation of a community of justice. This was the point and purpose of Israel's election and redemption and the whole of their history. 'The entire history of Israel under God is subordinated to one purpose – righteousness expressed in justice.'[17]

Accordingly, just as the vineyard owner comes to his vineyard in season expecting to find a goodly harvest of grapes and the promise of quality wine to follow, so the LORD comes to the community he has created, expecting to find a society committed to that righteousness and justice which reflect God's own character, a society that fulfils all his hopes in having planted them in the first place. But the vineyard owner is disappointed – indeed, surprised. How has it happened that such careful planting and nurture has produced only sour and worthless grapes? The thing is as unnatural as it is unexpected. So, in the powerful climax of Isaiah's parable (5:7):

> The vineyard of the LORD Almighty
>   is the house of Israel,
> and the men of Judah
>   are the garden of his delight.
> And he looked for justice (*mišpāṭ*), but saw bloodshed (*mišpāḥ*),
>   for righteousness (*ṣĕdāqâ*), but heard cries of distress (*ṣĕ'āqâ*).

One could go on to list many other texts that make the same basic point – the LORD required his whole people to be as committed to justice as he had proved himself to be. Some texts apply the challenge specifically at an individual level also.

---

[17] Mays, 'Justice', p. 146 (commenting on Is. 5:7).

Jeremiah 9:23–24 is a beautifully crafted small poem. Three of the best gifts of God (wisdom, strength and wealth) are weighed in a kind of verbal scales, and deemed to be not worth boasting about *in comparison* with knowing the LORD. But knowing the LORD means being committed to the things he most delights in – another balancing triplet, kindness (*ḥesed*), justice (*mišpāṭ*) and righteousness (*ṣĕdāqâ*). Knowing God is not a matter of mere inner spirituality, but a matter of transformation of values and resulting practical commitment.

Ezekiel, in his powerful case study of righteousness and wickedness, and God's response to both, paints his portrait of the prototype 'righteous individual' (Ezek. 18:5–9).[18] He gives a comprehensive list of model behaviours, negative and positive, all under the general heading of 'he does what is right and just'. Ezekiel's list includes many different spheres of life within that definition: both private and public, sexual and social, 'religious' and 'secular'.

In the Psalms a similar listing occurs in the criteria for acceptable worship. The one who would dare to come into the presence of God for worship must be the one whose life manifests the character of the God to be worshipped:

> LORD, who may dwell in your sanctuary?
> Who may live on your holy hill?
>
> He whose walk is blameless
> and who does what is right (*ṣedeq*) . . .
>
> (Ps. 15:1–2; cf. Ps. 24)

True to this criterion the prophets insisted that those who lived in ways that denied or trampled on justice were not acceptable to God in their worship. Worse, the worship of such people was an abomination to God (see, e.g., Amos 5:21–24; Is. 1:10–17; 58:2–7; Jer. 7:1–11).

Righteousness expressed in justice is the indispensable qualification for worship – no justice, no acceptable public religion.[19]

The duty of justice to the afflicted is so central that if it is not fulfilled, God will not even accept the divinely ordained sacrifices and worship. When they fail to carry out justice, people do not have the true God as the object of their worship and devotion (Jer. 22:15–16).[20]

---

[18] See further on the function of Ezek. 18, chapter 11 below.
[19] Mays, 'Justice', p. 146.
[20] Mott, *Political Thought*, p. 79.

When we feel the impact of so much material emphasizing the necessity of doing justice, as a requirement from God, and when we put it alongside the obvious fact that, for God, doing justice means particularly attending to the needs of the weak and poor, it makes us question whether the traditional understanding of justice as 'strict impartiality' is really at all appropriate in the biblical context. On the contrary, it is so clear that the LORD is especially attentive to the needs of the marginalized (see Deut. 10:18–19) that it would seem to be the very nature of justice, on God's terms, for humans also to have such a prioritized concern.

This is clearest in the prophets. The prophets uncompromisingly adopt an advocacy stance in favour of the poor, the weak, the oppressed, the dispossessed and the victimized, claiming to speak for the God of justice as they do so. Even before the great writing prophets we find Nathan confronting David on behalf of Uriah, and Elijah confronting Ahab on behalf of Naboth. This is as true of courtly prophets like Isaiah, who stood close to the pulse of regal power, as it is of rustic outsiders like Amos. In this aspect, of course, the prophetic representation of God is wholly in line with the voice of the law itself (see Exod. 22:22–24, 26–27; Deut. 10:18–19), with the worshipping voice of the Psalms (e.g. Ps. 146:7–9) and with the voice of wisdom (e.g. Prov. 14:31; 22:22–23).

However, this undoubted fact of God's active concern for the weak and the poor needs to be expressed carefully. It is not a case of biased or arbitrary partiality on God's part. The expression 'God is on the side of the poor' can rather imply a kind of favouritism in God, which the Bible denies. Nor is it that God turns a blind eye to the sins of the poor themselves, as if poverty and oppression render their victims spotless and innocent. Indeed, Isaiah (Is. 9:14–17) includes even the fatherless and the widow, stock epitomes of the poor and powerless, in his detailed description of the total corruption of the nation. Sin, like God, is no respecter of persons, and the poor are also sinners. Rather, what is being stated is this. The poor as a particular group in society receive God's special attention because they are the ones who are on the 'wronged' side of a situation of chronic injustice – a situation God abhors and wishes to have redressed. For God's righteous will to be done requires the execution of justice on behalf of the poor. Therefore God takes up *their* cause, or case, against those who are doing the injustice. God, through his prophets, and ideally also through godly judges, puts himself on the side of 'the righteous' – meaning, not the morally sinless, but those who are 'in the right' in a situation of social conflict and abuse.[21]

---

[21] 'The most striking characteristic of biblical justice is its bias toward the weak. "Bias" does not mean that God loves the poor more or that they should receive more than

In proclaiming this fact so vehemently the prophets actually vindicate the *impartiality* of God. For in championing the cause of the oppressed in this way the prophets exonerate God from the suspicion of being on the side of the wealthy and powerful. The oppressors in Israel may well have pointed to their wealth and power as apparent evidence of God's blessing on them and their activities.[22] Amos's rhetorical device of reversing this popular assessment – by attaching the judicial verdict 'righteous' (i.e. in the right) to the *poor and dispossessed*, but applying 'wicked' (i.e. in the wrong) to the *wealthy landowners* – was a highly effective and emotive way of *disassociating* God from the claims of the wealthy wicked. Those who imagined God was on their side (the wealthy) were told in no uncertain terms that God most certainly was not. For their wealth was gained through wickedness and oppression, and YHWH was not the God to bless, sanction or reward such behaviour. On the contrary, God was on the side of 'the righteous' – those being wronged and in need of vindication. Such a perspective reasserted God's sovereign independence as the righteous Judge, the One who could not be fooled by outward appearance or pious claims:

> The eyes of the LORD are on the righteous
> > and his ears are attentive to their cry;
> > the face of the LORD is against those who do evil . . .
>
> > > > > > > > (Ps. 34:15–16)

Justice as God's primary demand on human authorities

Leaders in Israel, at all levels, were charged with the primary function of maintaining or restoring righteousness and justice, in their various senses. In the account of the delegation of Moses' authority to different levels of local leadership in Deuteronomy 1:10–18 the main task laid upon these 'wise, understanding and respected men' was that they should exercise justice with integrity and impartiality, recognizing that they were in fact 'earthing' the judgments of the LORD (v. 17). The point is made even more emphatically and rhetorically later in the book: 'they shall judge the people fairly. Do not pervert justice or show partiality. Do not accept a bribe, for a bribe blinds the eyes of the wise and twists the words of the righteous. Follow justice and

---

their just claims. It means that in the raging social struggles in which the poor are perennially victims of injustice, God and the followers of God take up the cause of the weak.' (Ibid.)

[22] They would not have been the last to do so, as some forms of 'prosperity gospel' say much the same.

justice alone, so that you may live and possess the land the LORD your God is giving you' (Deut. 16:18–20).

Judges

Those who were called 'judges' in pre-monarchic Israel were not only involved in judicial arbitration ('judging' in our legal sense) like Samuel, the prototype circuit judge (1 Sam. 7:15–17). Indeed, some of them appear to have had no such function, but were, perhaps solely, military deliverers. But inasmuch as the latter role involved restoring Israel again from oppression and setting them back 'in the right' with God, it was an exercise of dynamic righteousness as Israel understood it. The military judges also 'earthed' the righteous acts of God in the form of national or tribal salvation. Such is the combined exultation of Deborah, the judicial judge (Judg. 4:5), and Barak, the military leader, after the great victory of Megiddo:

> They recite the righteous acts of the LORD,
> the righteous acts of his warriors in Israel.

(Judg. 5:10)

Kings

The duty of maintaining justice was even more clearly laid on the shoulders of Israel's kings. In some of the regal psalms their military and judicial roles are closely linked. The expectation was that if the king was faithful in his duty of executing justice and imitating God's own protection of the afflicted and needy (see Deut. 17:18–20), then God would grant him success and prosperity in other spheres also. The best example of this is Psalm 72. It is a prayer for the king, which begins by acknowledging the true source of all righteousness and justice:

> Endow the king with *your* justice, O God,
> the royal son with *your* righteousness.

(v. 1; my italics)

The psalm then mingles descriptions of his practical execution of justice for the poor and needy with the expectation of material blessing on the land. A stirring account of his international military prestige in verses 8–11 is linked by an explanatory 'for' to a further reference to his judicial activity – again highlighting the primary objective of such justice; namely, the deliverance of the weak, needy and oppressed in verses 12–14 (cf. Ps. 45:4–6; and in contrast Ps. 58). It is particularly noticeable that this judicial activity of the king will contribute to the good order and peace of the nation, by freeing it from 'oppression and violence'. Violence as an accompaniment to injustice is a noticeable theme in the Old Testament. Those who perpetrate oppression rely on violence to sustain their grip, but they also foster violence on the part of their victims.[23] However, the role of political authority, exercised justly under God, is not only the care of the needy but also the overthrow of those who do them wrong. The king, his intervention on behalf of the weak, not only saves them from their oppressors, but also acts to abolish evil and suppresses the oppressors and tyrants: "May he save the needy, and *crush the oppressor*" (v. 4).'[24]

Jeremiah, courageously stationing himself at the very gate of the royal palace in Jerusalem, declared what God required of the Davidic kings, if their legitimacy on the throne was to continue. If they failed in the following tasks, then they would be swept aside. In putting matters in this way, Jeremiah uncompromisingly subordinated the Zion theology to the Sinai covenant. As we saw in chapter 7, there could be no legitimacy for rulers who trampled on the covenantal structures of social justice:

> Hear the word of the LORD, O king of Judah, you who sit on David's throne – you, your officials and your people who come through these gates. This is what the LORD says: Do what is just and right. Rescue from the hand of his oppressor the one who has been robbed. Do no wrong or violence to the alien, the fatherless or the widow, and do not shed innocent blood in this place. For if you are careful to carry out these commands, then kings who sit on David's throne will come through the gates of this palace . . . But if you do not obey these commands, declares the LORD, I swear by myself that this palace will become a ruin.
>
> (Jer. 22:2–5)

There is a similar emphasis on the requirement of social justice on the part of kings in the Wisdom literature (see Prov. 29:4, 14), such that King Lemuel's mother warned him against drunkenness for this very reason:

> It is not for kings, O Lemuel –
> not for kings to drink wine,

---

[23] A very helpful study of the connections between oppression and violence in the Old Testament, including a word study of *ḥāmās*, is provided in Hendrickx, *Social Justice in the Bible*, ch. 4, 'Oppression and Violence'.

[24] Weinfeld, *Social Justice*, p. 49 (his italics). Weinfeld discusses in depth several of the texts mentioned in this section, under the chapter title 'Justice and Righteousness as the Task of the King'. He particularly draws comparisons with similar texts in the ancient Near East (especially Mesopotamian), where the duty of kings to ensure justice is declared.

> not for rulers to crave beer,
>   lest they drink and forget what the law decrees,
>   and deprive all the oppressed of their rights.

(Prov. 31:4–5)

On the contrary, it is the duty of the king as the *most* powerful to champion the cause of the *least* powerful:

> Speak up for those who cannot speak for themselves,
>   for the rights of all who are destitute.
> Speak up and judge fairly;
>   defend the rights of the poor and needy.

(Prov. 31:8–9)

Ideals, of course, are one thing; the reality is usually different. A more pessimistic voice in Israel, also from the Wisdom tradition, has this very modern-sounding observation to make on the oppressive results of hierarchy and bureaucracy: 'If you see the poor oppressed in a district, and justice and rights denied, do not be surprised at such things; for one official is eyed by a higher one, and over them both are others higher still' (Eccles. 5:8).

Critique of leaders

Many texts in the Old Testament critique leaders (whether judges or kings) precisely over how they have handled this matter of social justice in the exercise of their public office. As we might expect, this is frequently negative, but there are shining examples of positive evaluation also:

1. Negatively, Psalm 82 is a trenchant condemnation of those to whom God had entrusted the duty of carrying out divine justice (such that they could even be called 'gods'). The text may be referring to angelic beings exercising their rule over human affairs, but doing so in a state of fallen corruption and perversion; or to human judges effectively doing the same. Either way the message is clear – God holds such authorities (whether celestial or human) accountable and will ultimately destroy those who refuse to do justice as God requires. The psalm closes with the characteristic combination of the call to God to act as judge (destroy the wicked and vindicate the oppressed), and the universalizing tendency we have already noticed:

> Rise up, O God, judge *the earth*,
>   for *all the nations are your inheritance*.

(Ps. 82:8; my italics)

Isaiah, who of all the prophets possibly walked most often in the corridors of royal power, condemned the authorities in Jerusalem as 'rulers of Sodom' (Is. 1:10). The reason follows close behind: like Sodom, Jerusalem had become a place of suffering, oppression, robbery, corruption and violence – instead of the justice and righteousness that used to dwell in her (Is. 1:21–23). Later Isaiah pillories the judicial authorities for being better judges of their cocktails than of their court cases (Is. 5:22–23). They were even legislating oppression by decree; that is, they were passing laws that would make their exploitative practices technically legal (Is. 10:1–2).

Jeremiah scathingly denounced Jehoiakim for his unjust exploitation of unpaid labour, and describes him as a man whose eyes and heart were 'set only on dishonest gain, on shedding innocent blood and on oppression and extortion' (Jer. 22:13–14, 17). What an epitaph (for epitaph it virtually was, since the same passage predicts Jehoiakim's ignominious demise).

Ezekiel had no specific king to accuse, stuck as he was among the exiles in Babylon, so he generalized his attack on all 'the shepherds of Israel' – meaning their past line of kings. All he could see was a history of rapacity, plundering, greed and a lack of care for the needs of the people (Ezek. 34:1–8).

2. On the positive side, however, are some shafts of light. Although it was a claim he made for himself, Samuel's apologia was fully accepted by the people. His discharge of public administration had not been self-serving or corrupt. His rhetorical questions and the people's consent to the claim expressed through them indicate the primary nature of this demand that leaders are there to see that justice is done, and to be people of integrity themselves.

> 'Here I stand. Testify against me in the presence of the LORD and his anointed. Whose ox have I taken? Whose donkey have I taken? Whom have I cheated? Whom have I oppressed? From whose hand have I accepted a bribe to make me shut my eyes? If I have done any of these, I will make it right.'
>
> 'You have not cheated or oppressed us,' they replied. 'You have not taken anything from anyone's hand.'
>
> (1 Sam. 12:3–4)

Of the kings, a few are singled out for commendation for their efforts to restore social justice. The most ambiguous was Solomon. In his early reign he asked precisely for the gift of wisdom in order to be able to administer justice (1 Kgs. 3:9, 11). And among his first acts as king the decision he gave in the matter of the two prostitutes quarrelling over a living and a dead baby is recorded (quite remarkably, one has to say) as a prime proof 'that he had wisdom from God to administer justice' (1 Kgs. 3:28). Sadly, however, as his power and wealth increased he fell into ways of oppression, which, when amplified by his son Rehoboam, ended up splitting the kingdom asunder. The ironic streak of the narrator comes out through the words he puts into the mouth of the Queen of Sheba. At the very point when she is breathless with awe at the wealth of Solomon (which, we are soon to learn, would be his downfall along with the religiously compromising but politically expedient marriages that accompanied his international empire building), she reminds him that 'because of the LORD's eternal love for Israel, he has made you king *to maintain justice and righteousness*' (1 Kgs. 10:9). Quite so. But that is exactly what Solomon was increasingly failing to do, and by the end of the same chapter it is clear that Solomon is living in flagrant disregard of the basic law of the king, in Deuteronomy 17:14–20. The royal rot beneath the royal splendour is exposed in the immediately following chapter (1 Kgs. 11).

Only two kings seem to stand out with an A+ on their ethical report card as regards justice. One was Jehoshaphat (whose name, appropriately, means 'Yahweh is judge'). Second Chronicles 19:4–11 records his efforts at social, educational and judicial reform in ninth-century Judah. The emphasis on how human judicial procedures must reflect divine justice is particularly striking. The other was Josiah, of whom Jeremiah famously wrote (in stark contrast to his godless successor, Jehoiakim):

> 'Did not your father have food and drink?
>> He did what was right and just,
>> so all went well with him.
> He defended the cause of the poor and needy,
>> and so all went well.
> Is that not what it means to know me?'
>> declares the LORD.

(Jer. 22:15–16)

This, after all, was what Deuteronomy had said that the LORD himself does and what he most wants. Josiah, then, simply imitated what the LORD is like, did what the LORD wants to be done, and cared for those whom the LORD loves. And that, says Jeremiah, is 'to know the LORD'. It is a challenging definition. The historian's verdict on Josiah is similarly positive, and Deuteronomic in flavour. 'Neither before nor after Josiah was there a king like him who turned to the LORD as he did – with all his heart and with all his soul and with all his strength, in accordance with all the Law of Moses' (2 Kgs. 23:25).

Finally, we should not ignore the claim of Job about his conduct of judicial affairs in the halcyon days before calamity struck. Like Samuel's it is a moral self-defence, but it does highlight in a very helpful way the ideals honoured in

Israel in the matter of how public duty should be administered by those in positions of leadership in society. In chapter 29, Job is describing how once he had been a respected elder within the community, taking his seat in the public square, as one of those who exercised judicial administration in the local community:

> I rescued the poor who cried for help,
>   and the fatherless who had none to assist him.
> The man who was dying blessed me;
>   I made the widow's heart sing.
> I put on righteousness as my clothing;
>   justice was my robe and my turban.
> I was eyes to the blind
>   and feet to the lame.
> I was a father to the needy;
>   I took up the case of the stranger.
> I broke the fangs of the wicked
>   and snatched the victims from their teeth.
>
> (Job 29:12–17)

In conclusion, then, we can affirm that the matter of whether and how human authorities at every level exercise and administer justice in society is a matter of priority for the LORD, the God of Israel who is also, as repeatedly proclaimed, the God of all the earth, of all nations, and of all humanity. Where such concern for social justice comes on the scale of our human values in any given context is the measure of how much or how little we are in tune with the heart of this God, the God of the Bible.

Justice as God will deliver it

One king whom we did not mention in our discussion of justice as the primary task of kings was David himself. Yet David functioned, idealistically no doubt to some extent, as the model for future kings in this respect, as in many others. In 2 Samuel 5 – 8 there is a connected account of the events through which David became king over all the tribes of Israel and established his capital in Jerusalem. It opens with a summary statement that he became king over all Israel and Judah, and it concludes with a summary statement to the same effect, including the list of his major departments of state (similar texts are found in 2 Sam. 20:23–26 and 1 Kgs. 4:1–6). The climactic statement about David's reign, however, is 2 Samuel 8:15, 'David reigned over all Israel, *doing what was just and right for all his people.*' A better translation of the second clause would be 'and he began to establish justice and righteousness for all his people'.[25] For that indeed was the goal to which all authentic monarchy should aspire, not only in Israel, but according to the common ideals (if not the actual practice) of kingship throughout the ancient Near Eastern world. So David models what the future kings who succeed him *ought* to have done. As we saw, his son Solomon managed it initially – long enough at least for the Queen of Sheba to flatter him about it. Future kings who failed in this regard were said *not* to walk in the ways of David their father, while those few who did engage in social reform, the abolition of idolatry and re-establishing justice,[26] were positively compared to him.[27]

The failure of so many of the historical kings to deliver the justice that was their mandate led, within Israel, to the growing longing for, and predictions of, a *future* coming son of David. This expected, eschatological king would achieve what the historical kings had failed to – the establishment of justice and righteousness, and by that means alone the reign of genuine peace. So the messianic hope, found in various strands of the prophetic literature, sees the ultimate achievement of social justice on earth as the work of the eschatological king, the one who would come finally to 'earth' the cosmic justice of the LORD.

The climax of the great vision of the 'child' who would be born to shoulder the government of God envisages him as 'great David's greater Son', doing for all and for ever what David had 'begun' to do in his own day:

---

[25] Ibid., p. 46.

[26] Although the historical texts tend to major on the efforts of the good kings to eradicate idolatry, we should not disconnect this from the social injustice that idolatry always engenders or justifies. The two go hand in hand throughout history – biblical and contemporary. Biblically, idolatry is not confined to some spiritual or religious sphere of life, unconnected to the realities of the social, economic and political order. Rather, the identity and character of the god or gods you worship will profoundly affect the kind of society you advocate (or tolerate). 'There is no wrong-doing without worship of false gods and there is no worship of false gods without wrong-doing' is the stark crystallization of this point by Ulrich Duchrow. Commenting on the combination of social, political and religious dimensions in the clash between Yahweh and Baal at the time of Ahab and Elijah, he adds, 'A starving people and a wealthy king is a result of the law of the accumulation of riches and power, and happens when Ba'al reigns and not Yahweh' (Duchrow, *Shalom*, pp. 79, 81).

[27] E.g. Jehoshaphat (2 Chr. 17:3 and ch. 19); Hezekiah (2 Kgs. 18:3, 5–6); Josiah (2 Kgs. 22:2; 23:25; Jer. 22:15–16).

He will reign on David's throne
and over his kingdom,
establishing and upholding it
with justice and righteousness
from that time on and for ever.
The zeal of the LORD Almighty
will accomplish this.

(Is. 9:7)

The matching vision of the 'shoot from the stump of Jesse' likewise includes emphatic words about the messianic king's reign of justice:

with righteousness he will judge the needy,
with justice he will give decisions for the poor of the earth . . .
Righteousness will be his belt
and faithfulness the sash round his waist.

(Is. 11:4–5)

Jeremiah and Ezekiel both declared their hope for a Davidic king, raised up by God, and even (in Ezekiel's case) embodying the theocratic rule of the LORD himself. Jeremiah even named him 'Yahweh our Righteousness' (Jer. 23:5–6; Ezek. 34:23–24).[28] And Psalm 72, although originally written as a prayer for the Davidic king, came in time to be seen as a messianic longing for the king who would truly represent the answer to its prayers for justice, an end to oppression, the blessing and worship of the nations, the fruitfulness of the earth, the global reign of peace, and the universal glory of the LORD.

Though not so strongly linked to the Davidic figure,[29] the Servant of the LORD in the various passages in Isaiah 40 – 55 also has the establishment of justice as a key element of his mission. The first time he is introduced, in Isaiah 42, justice is the first thing he is mandated to deliver, through the power of the Spirit of the LORD with which he is endowed. Furthermore, he will

---

[28] The sense of the name is clear in the text. It includes both the achievement of social justice *and* liberating salvation: he will be 'a King who will reign wisely, / doing righteousness and justice in the land. / In his days, Judah will be saved / and Israel will dwell in safety' (Jer. 23:5–6; my trans.). Doubtless Jeremiah would have regarded the name given to this coming one ('Jesus', 'Jehoshua', meaning 'Yahweh is Salvation'), as an appropriate fulfilment of his prophecy.

[29] Except at Is. 55:3–5, which some see as a way of identifying the Servant figure of the preceding chapters with David and the universal extent of his eschatological reign.

bring justice not only to Israel, but also to the nations. The language of the extension of the LORD's law and justice to the ends of the earth is a repeated theme in Isaiah 42:1–9.

> Here is my servant, whom I uphold,
>   my chosen one in whom I delight;
> I will put my Spirit on him
>   and he will bring justice to the nations.
>
> (Is. 42:1)

However, the hope that God would ultimately deliver the justice he displays and demands was not confined to such Davidic echoes in texts that came to be seen as messianic and eschatological. It simply existed as an unquenchable hope based on the known character of the LORD as God. If it was unthinkable that the Judge of all the earth should not do right, how much more unthinkable was it that this same God should not eventually intervene to judge the accumulated wrongs of humanity and put things right once and for all. Only God can finally 'get things sorted'. Only God *can*, but God assuredly *will*, is the unshakeable affirmation of many Old Testament texts. Isaiah sees such a day as the powerful work of the Spirit of the LORD. In his beautiful meditation on what it will be like when 'a king will reign in righteousness and rulers will rule with justice' he looks forward to the time when

> the Spirit is poured upon us from on high . . .
> Justice will dwell in the desert
>   and righteousness live in the fertile field.
> The fruit of righteousness will be peace;
>   the effect of righteousness will be quietness and confidence for ever.
>
> (Is. 32:15–17)

The final word, however, must go to those great forgers of the faith of Israel – their worship songwriters. For it is indeed in the Psalms that we find this great, heart-bursting anticipation of the LORD as *the God who comes*. And the fact that *God* is coming, inexorably coming, is a summons to rejoicing and praise, not only among his own people, but throughout all the earth, and indeed in all creation. Why? Why is it a matter of cosmic rejoicing that God is coming? Because when God comes, things will be put right. God comes to judge – in the authentic Old Testament sense of that word – to right wrongs, destroy wickedness, vindicate the righteous and finally establish justice, right relationships between God and people, among people, and between people and the created order.

No wonder, then, that the whole of creation is invited to join the song of joy. This again, like Psalm 33, is a world-transforming vision, setting before the faith-imagination of the worshipper not a dream of what *might* be but a vision of what *will* be. And this future is such a reality even now to the eyes of faith that it can be celebrated in advance, and proclaimed to the nations as the good news of the kingdom of God. For this is what it will be like when God, YHWH, the biblical LORD God, finally establishes his reign:

> Say among the nations, 'The LORD reigns.'
>> The world is firmly established, it cannot be moved;
>> he will judge the peoples with equity.
> Let the heavens rejoice, let the earth be glad;
>> let the sea resound, and all that is in it;
>> let the fields be jubilant, and everything in them.
> Then all the trees of the forest will sing for joy;
>> they will sing before the LORD, for he comes,
>> he comes to judge the earth.
> He will judge the world in righteousness
>> and the peoples in his truth.

(Ps. 96:10–13; cf. Ps. 98:7–9)

Further reading

Boyce, Richard Nelson, *The Cry to God in the Old Testament* (Atlanta: Scholars Press, 1988).

Brueggemann, Walter, *A Social Reading of the Old Testament: Prophetic Approaches to Israel's Communal Life*, ed. Patrick D. Miller Jr. (Minneapolis: Fortress, 1994).

Duchrow, Ulrich, and Liedke, Gerhard, *Shalom: Biblical Perspectives on Creation, Justice and Peace* (Geneva: WCC Publications, 1987).

Englehard, David H., 'The Lord's Motivated Concern for the Underprivileged', *Calvin Theological Journal* 15 (1980), pp. 5–26.

Gossai, Hemchand, *Justice, Righteousness and the Social Critique of the Eighth-Century Prophets*, American University Studies, Series 7: Theology and Religion, vol. 141 (New York: Peter Lang, 1993).

Hamilton, J. M., *Social Justice and Deuteronomy: The Case of Deuteronomy 15*, Society of Biblical Literature Dissertation Series, vol. 136 (Atlanta: Scholars Press, 1992).

Hendrickx, Herman, *Social Justice in the Bible* (Quezon City: Claretian Publications, 1985).

Knierim, Rolf P., *The Task of Old Testament Theology: Substance, Method, and Cases* (Grand Rapids: Eerdmans, 1995).

Malchow, Bruce V., 'Social Justice in the Wisdom Literature', *Biblical Theology Bulletin* 12 (1982), pp. 120–124.

————, 'Social Justice in the Israelite Law Codes', *Word and World* 4 (1984), pp. 299–306.

Mays, James L., 'Justice: Perspectives from the Prophetic Tradition', in David L. Petersen (ed.), *Prophecy in Israel: Search for an Identity* (London: SPCK; Philadelphia: Fortress, 1987), pp. 144–158.

Mott, Stephen Charles, *A Christian Perspective on Political Thought* (Oxford: Oxford University Press, 1993).

Muilenburg, J., *The Way of Israel: Biblical Faith and Ethics* (New York: Harper, 1961).

Reimer, David J., '*Ṣdq*', in VanGemeren, *New International Dictionary of Old Testament Theology and Exegesis*, vol. 3, pp. 744–769.

Schofield, J. N., '"Righteousness" in the Old Testament', *Bible Translator* 16 (1965), pp. 112–116.

Stek, John H., 'Salvation, Justice and Liberation in the Old Testament', *Calvin Theological Journal* 13 (1978), pp. 112–116.

Weinfeld, Moshe, *Social Justice in Ancient Israel and in the Ancient near East* (Jerusalem: Magnes; Minneapolis: Fortress, 1995).

Willis, John T., 'Old Testament Foundations of Social Justice', in Perry C. Cotham (ed.), *Christian Social Ethics* (Grand Rapids: Baker, 1979), pp. 21–43.

9. LAW AND THE LEGAL SYSTEM

The law of the LORD is perfect,
  reviving the soul.
The statues of the LORD are trustworthy,
  making wise the simple.
The precepts of the LORD are right,
  giving joy to the heart.
The commands of the LORD are radiant,
  giving light to the eyes.
The fear of the LORD is pure,
  enduring for ever.
The ordinances of the LORD are sure
  and altogether righteous.
They are more precious than gold,
  than much pure gold;
they are sweeter than honey,
  than honey from the comb.

Psalm 19:7–10

I will walk about in freedom,
  for I have sought out your precepts . . .
I delight in your commands
  because I love them . . .
Oh, how I love your law! . . .

> I love your commands
>> more than gold, more than pure gold . . .
> All your words are true;
>> all your righteous laws are eternal.
>
> Psalm 119:45, 47, 97, 127, 160

The least one can say about people who express such enthusiastic sentiments for the law is that they were not grovelling along under a heavy burden of legalism. They were not anxiously striving to earn their way into salvation and a relationship with God through punctilious law-keeping. They were not puffed up with the claims of self-righteousness or exhausted with the efforts of works-righteousness. They did not, in short, fit into any of the caricatures that have been inflicted upon the Old Testament law by those who, misunderstanding Paul's arguments with those who had *distorted* the law, attribute to the law itself the very distortions from which Paul was seeking to exonerate it.

On the contrary, people who could frame such paeans of praise for the law knew that it was a national treasure greater than any museum could boast. Such devout Israelites delighted in the law as a gift of God's grace and token of God's love, given to them for their own good (Deut. 4:1, 40; 6:1–3, 24 etc.). They saw it as a blessing in itself, and the means of enjoying God's continued blessing (Deut. 28:1–14). They recalled that the revelation of the law to Israel was a unique privilege, granted to no other nation (Deut. 4:32–34; Ps. 147:19–20). They urged one another to obey it, not in order to get saved, but because God had already saved them (Deut. 6:20–25). They delighted in it as the road to life (Lev. 18:5; Deut. 30:15–20) and as the river of fruitfulness (Ps. 1:1–3).

So then, as we approach this daunting subject of Old Testament law, asking how it can or should relate to Christian ethics, the first thing we must do is to determine to read it within its own Old Testament context and seek to understand its dynamic, its motivations, its theological foundations and social objectives – as far as possible *from within*, from the perspective of an Old Testament Israelite (in so far as we will ever be able realistically to enter his or her world). Postpone, at least for the moment, the problems of a later era that Paul tackles in arguments over the law with Jewish opponents of his Gentile mission. Postpone (preferably further still) the dogmatic and denominational obsessions with this or that way of perceiving the relationship between law and gospel.[1]

---

[1] But when you can postpone it no longer, some help will be found in the survey of different historical approaches to Christian understanding of the law in chapter 12 below, and much more in the comparison of five representative viewpoints in Wayne G. Strickland, *Law, Gospel*.

Our psalmists were not Judaizers, nor were they Calvinists, Arminians, Theonomists, Dispensationalists, Legalists or Antinomians. They were worshipping believers, members of a people who knew themselves to be in a unique covenant relationship with the LORD their God, redeemed by God's saving grace, and privileged to have been given a land to live in and a law to live by. Let us, then, do our best to understand and appreciate the law through their eyes.

The first thing we will realize as we do so is that 'the law' meant more for an Israelite than the word normally means for us. First of all, the term for all this material in the first five books of the Old Testament is *tôrâ*, which means, not just law in the sense of legislation or statute law, but 'Guidance', 'Instruction'. The Israelite saw in all the materials that came to form what we call the Pentateuch (or five volumes; the books from Genesis to Deuteronomy) God's guidebook to life. And this Guidance included not just the great collections of laws found in the second half of Exodus, Leviticus, parts of Numbers and Deuteronomy, but also all the narratives in which they are embedded, along with many other kinds of writing – songs and snatches of ancient poetry, travel journals, genealogies, blessings, geographical notes, census lists, obituaries and so on. The *tôrâ* is a rich tapestry of many threads. The narrative framework is of particular importance in gaining a right perspective on the law, and we shall return to that later.

However, within all this variety are several major blocks of laws in the generally accepted sense. There are also, of course, laws and references to laws outside these major sections, sometimes in a way that indicate a greater universality of God's law than can be confined to the Sinai revelation alone.[2] But my concern here is with the large blocks within which the bulk

---

[2] This is particularly so with the remarkable affirmation of Gen. 26:4–5, in which God renews with Isaac his promise originally made to Abraham, saying that 'through your offspring all nations on earth will be blessed, *because Abraham obeyed me and kept my requirements, my commands, my decrees and my laws*' (my italics). This is usually dismissed by critical scholars as an anachronistic retrojection of later Israelite obsession with the law (probably inserted by the Deuteronomists). But taken with proper theological seriousness (and crediting the editor of Genesis with being just as aware as we are that his text was located chronologically before the giving of the Sinai law) this text suggests that the basic content and thrust of the law, though not yet given in detail as it was at Sinai, was in principle available to and observed by Abraham. Obedience to the law was not merely a matter of the detail of the Sinai codes, but a matter of faith in God's promise and perseverance in the fear of the LORD in the whole orientation of one's life. See also James K. Bruckner, 'Creational Context of Law'.

of Old Testament law is contained. And it is to these legal sections of the Pentateuch that I shall normally be referring when I use the term 'the law' from now on.

The main legal blocks

Most of the pentateuchal laws are contained in three major collections, in addition to the Decalogue itself, with which I begin.

The Decalogue: Exodus 20:2–17; Deuteronomy 5:6–21

'Decalogue' comes from the Greek rendering of the literal Hebrew expression *the ten words* found in Exodus 34:28; Deuteronomy 4:13; 10:4. In the narrative of the events that took place at Sinai (Exod. 19–20; repeated in Deut. 5) the Decalogue is presented as having been given to Israel by God. Although they are described as given through Moses, his role in respect of the Ten Commandments was minimal. They were believed to have been spoken and inscribed in stone by God himself. There was something 'self-contained' and final about them, captured in the Deuteronomic observation 'These are the commandments the LORD proclaimed . . . and he added nothing more' (Deut. 5:22).[3] That unique quality of direct divine speech, along with the awe-inspiring, earth-shaking phenomena that accompanied their promulgation at Sinai, guaranteed the Ten Commandments a special place in Israel's traditions. This simple but comprehensive summary of essential stipulations of the covenant relationship provided a 'boundary fence' around the kind of behaviour that could be seen as consistent with covenant membership. Step beyond these boundaries (by breaking these commands), it implies, and you step out of the sphere of covenantal relationship and obligation. It provided also (particularly, in the view of some scholars, for Deuteronomy[4]) a 'policy statement', a list of strategic

---

[3] In view of the way Deuteronomy goes on to present many other laws given by God through Moses this verse cannot mean that only the Ten Commandments actually came from God or that they alone carried God's authority. Rather, the phrase seems to be a way of articulating the unique and complete nature of this particular set of 'ten words'. God added nothing more *like this*, nothing more in this category.

[4] Some have argued, fairly convincingly, that the order of the Ten Commandments is loosely reflected in the sequence of themes in the book of Deuteronomy; i.e. for the author/editor of that book the Decalogue provided some level of organizational structure (among others). For a survey of this view, see C. J. H. Wright, *Deuteronomy*, pp. 4–5.

values that determined the ethos and direction of the rest of the detailed legislation.

Because of its importance the Decalogue has been the object of a vast quantity of scholarly scrutiny and argument, a selection of which is listed in the bibliographical notes. The debate has swung from questions of authorship and date of origin to what kind of law the Decalogue is and how it functioned in Israelite life and worship. The plethora of scholarly viewpoints is still untroubled by any general consensus, except on the fact itself of the importance of the Decalogue in Israel. 'Whatever one thinks about the authorship, the fact that the Decalogue early held a central position in Israelite life remains as the most important result of recent research . . . [It] stood in association with the review of the Sinai events as the binding charter expressing the will of the divine Lord of the Covenant.'[5]

The Book of the Covenant: Exodus 20:22 – 23:33

This is the name given to the section of laws immediately following the Decalogue. The actual phrase comes in Exodus 24:7: 'Then he [Moses] took the Book of the Covenant and read it to the people. They responded, "We will do everything the LORD has said; we will obey."' This is usually taken to refer back to the preceding section, substantially Exodus 21 – 23. The response of the people then became the basis for the ceremony of covenant ratification recorded in the rest of chapter 24.

After a prologue that underlines the uniqueness and holiness of the LORD (Exod. 20:22–26), this section of laws opens with the title 'These are the *mišpāṭîm* . . .' (21:1); that is 'judgments' or 'precedents'. The laws that follow are mainly case laws (see below). They describe typical situations involving disputes over property, damage, assault, negligence and so on. There is also an important section on social responsibilities for the weaker members of society (22:21–27), regulations concerning judicial procedure (23:1–9), and a section of cultic law (see below) to do with offerings and festivals (23:14–19). The collection then concludes with an epilogue looking ahead to the invasion of Canaan and reinforcing the exclusiveness of the LORD's demand upon his people (23:20–33), thus returning to the theme of the prologue.

This collection of laws, as already mentioned, has been subjected to enormous scholarly study, particularly in view of the many points at which it has features in common with other collections of laws in the great ancient Near

---

[5] Stamm and Andrews, *Ten Commandments*, p. 39. For a more recent survey of Decalogue scholarship, see J. W. Marshall, 'Decalogue'.

Eastern civilizations. It is widely agreed that the Book of the Covenant is the oldest of the legal collections in the Old Testament.[6]

The book of Leviticus

Leviticus consists almost entirely of laws and regulations, with only brief sections of narrative.[7] These snatches of narrative include the opening address to Moses and closing statements (1:1; 26:46; 27:34), the descriptions of the ordination of Aaron and the work of the priests (chs. 8 – 9) and the tragic deaths of Nadab and Abihu (ch. 10). Even these brief indications of the narrative context of the law, however, are important. For, as we shall see, they remind us that even this extensive block of law must be seen in the specific context of the Sinai covenant and all that went before it.

The first seven chapters contain regulations for the various sacrificial offerings, while chapters 11 – 15 list clean and unclean foods and give detailed instructions on hygiene and cleanliness, both personal and domestic. The duties of a priest in Israel seem to have combined the skills of a butcher, a doctor, a teacher and a public health inspector. At the centre of the book stands chapter 16 with instructions for the Day of Atonement.

The section from Leviticus 17 – 26 has been regarded by scholars for over a hundred years now as a separate law collection, which has been given the title *the Holiness Code* (H for short), because of its repeated reference to, and demand for, holiness. Whether or not it was ever a separate document as such is impossible to prove one way or the other, but its emphasis on holiness is certainly clear. But, as we saw in chapter 1, holiness for Israel was far from merely ritual or pious. These chapters are full of very practical laws for the regulation of family life sexually (18 and 20) and of social life generally (especially 19), as well as additional rules for the priestly work and the various festivals (21 – 24). Chapter 25 contains important laws concerning the sabbatical and jubilee years, redemption procedures and general economic compassion, while chapter 26 concludes the collection with characteristic promises of blessing for obedience and threats of judgment for the disobedience that was all too foreseeable. Chapter 27, with its regulations on the redemption of vows, seems to be an appendix. Holiness is thus a very comprehensive concept indeed. It is, really, not so much a religious aspiration, or even just a

---

[6] For a helpful survey of scholarship on the Book of the Covenant, see T. D. Alexander, 'Book of the Covenant'.

[7] The book is so called because substantial portions of it relate to the work of the priests who were of the tribe of Levi. Its name in the Hebrew canon is simply its opening word *wayyiqrā'*, 'and he [Yahweh] called'.

moral code. Holiness is rather a way of *being*: a way of being *with* God in covenant relationship, a way of being *like* God in clean and wholesome living, a way of being God's people in the midst of an unholy and unclean world. Preserving that holy cleanness among God's people – ritually, morally, physically, socially, symbolically – is the primary thrust of the laws in the book of Leviticus.

The Deuteronomic collection

The setting Deuteronomy paints for itself in its opening verses is that of Israel encamped in the plains of Moab, some forty years on from the great events of the exodus and Sinai, when the people of Israel were on the verge of entering Canaan at last. It is, therefore, a 'book on the boundary': historically and geographically. And, indeed, it sets Israel on the boundary of the choice they must now make: would they or would they not move forward with God in faith and obedience? Would they or would they not remain loyal to the LORD, their unique living God beside whom there is no other (Deut. 4:35, 39), when they were confronted with the ambient and enticing idolatry of Canaan?

The whole book has the form of a 'covenant renewal' document (see Deut. 29:1). The covenant had been ratified at Sinai itself (Exod. 24). Now Deuteronomy portrays Moses as renewing it with the succeeding generation before they move into the land of promise. As was common in such documents, there is a historical prologue in which some of the notable experiences of Israel are recounted, both to arouse their shame and to encourage their faith and obedience (chs. 1 – 3). This is followed by a rousing section calling for gratitude, loyalty, wholehearted obedience and total rejection of idolatry – a choice sharpened by the declaration of blessings or curses (chs. 4 – 11). Then comes the central section in which most of the detailed laws are found (chs. 12 – 26). This is followed by the customary list of blessings and curses (chs. 27 – 28, as in Lev. 26). Renewed exhortations to observe the covenant follow, along with warnings of what the future holds if Israel fails (chs. 29 – 31). Finally, the Song of Moses (ch. 32), the Blessing of Moses on the tribes (ch. 33) and the account of the death of Moses (ch. 34) bring the book to a climax and conclusion. So when we speak of the Deuteronomic laws, it is mainly the detailed chapters 12 – 26 that are being referred to.

The word 'Deuteronomy' is a Greek construction meaning 'a second law'. Although not a very accurate Greek translation of Deuteronomy 17:18 (where the Hebrew means 'a copy of this law'), it is a reasonably apt description of the legal section of the book (chs. 12 – 26). The sense intended is not that this is a *new* law, but that it reiterates and amplifies the earlier laws. Thus we find that many of the laws of the Book of the Covenant in Exodus 21 – 23 are found again in Deuteronomy. But usually we will observe slight changes, expansions, explanations or added motivation. In almost every case where there is a law in common between Exodus and Deuteronomy the Deuteronomic version is longer. Deuteronomy has been described as 'preached law', and indeed that is what Deuteronomy 1:5 says Moses was doing: 'Moses began to *expound* this law'. So, as is typical of a preaching style, Deuteronomy's way of presenting the laws makes much use of repetition, patterned structure, exhortation, pleading, coaxing, motivating and warning. Clearly, in the passionate rhetoric of Deuteronomy, the law was much more than a dry crust of legalism: it was the very bread of life. 'They [the laws of the LORD] are not just idle words for you – they are your life' (Deut. 32:47).

The different kinds of law

When we are trying to discover the ethical relevance of Old Testament law as a whole, the traditional hope of being able to lay bare a distinct category of 'moral law', as opposed to 'civil law' and 'ceremonial or cultic law', is not very fruitful. In his exegesis and ethical study of Leviticus 19 Elmer Martens comments:

> One must conclude that the distinctions between cultic, moral, and civil regulations are, if not artificial, certainly extraneous to Hebrew thought. In this single speech the stipulations about refraining from image-making (cult), insisting on truth-telling (moral), and prescribing compassionate treatment for aliens (civil) tumble about in chaotic confusion. As a grid for sorting out the way Christians deal with Old Testament law, the classification of 'cultic, moral, civil' is not helpful.[8]

Rather, we need to study and classify the laws of the Old Testament against their own social background in ancient Israel, and then discuss what significant moral features or principles emerge within *every* kind of law they had. Thus the following attempted classification of Israel's laws is not designed to answer the question 'Which laws are, and which laws are not, still binding on us (or at least ethically relevant to us)?' Rather, we are trying to classify in order that we may discern the ethical relevance of the whole range of Israel's law by first understanding its function and purpose in its own context. This is really nothing more than an application of a fundamental principle of biblical hermeneutics; namely, that the first step towards understanding any biblical

---

[8] Martens, 'Old Testament Law', p. 201. See also J. Daniel Hays, 'Old Testament Law Today'.

text is to ask what it meant within its own historical context, in so far as we can determine what that was.

One of the best-known classifications of Old Testament law in critical scholarship is the twofold division proposed by Albrecht Alt.[9] Alt distinguished between 'apodeictic law' (laws that usually begin simply, 'You shall' or 'You shall not', and proceed to make an absolute command or prohibition, usually without specified penalty) and 'casuistic law' (laws that describe cases, usually beginning with 'If . . .' or 'When . . .', followed by instructions as to what is to be done, what penalties, if any, apply, etc.). While this distinction has been fruitful and widely followed, it is also probably too simple to cover all the variety of laws we find in the Pentateuch. A more nuanced classification was proposed by Anthony Phillips.[10] Although there are weaknesses in the simplicity of Phillips's categorization of criminal law in particular,[11] the basic functional division of the laws he offers seems broadly convincing and I have developed it further in the discussion below.

Criminal law

A 'crime' is any offence a particular state regards as contrary to the best interests of the whole community. The specific legal definition of particular crimes will therefore vary from one state to another, according to historical, social and cultural trends and perspectives. Accordingly, a 'criminal' is punished on behalf of the whole community in the name of the highest authority within the state. Criminal law is therefore distinct from civil law. Civil law is concerned with private disputes between citizens, in which the public authorities may be appealed to for adjudication, or may even judicially intervene. But in civil cases the state or national community is not itself the offended party. So there can be many civil cases where no crime has been committed.

Now Israel was a 'state'.[12] But they believed that they owed their national

---

[9] Albrecht Alt, 'Origins of Israelite Law'. For a good survey of the many approaches to Pentateuchal law, and recent bibliography, see M. J. Selman, 'Law'.

[10] Anthony J. Phillips, *Ancient Israel's Criminal Law*.

[11] Some specific points where I have critiqued Phillips's arguments, particularly in his handling of adultery, theft and coveting, are found in C. J. H. Wright, *God's Land*, pp. 89–92, 131–141, 200–221.

[12] I am using the term here in the loose sense of a named national community, bound together by recognizable ties of ethnicity, religion, language and territory, with some degree of sociopolitical structuring and authority. In this looser sense, even the tribes of Israel formed such a national community (at least ideally) before the formation of the more centralized monarchic state that emerged with David and Solomon. I am not

existence to the historical redemptive activity of YHWH, the LORD. It was the LORD who had called them into existence through his choice of Abraham, the LORD who had redeemed them out of Egypt, the LORD who had constituted them his own people through the covenant at Sinai, the LORD who had given them the constitution and laws under which they were to live, the LORD who had given them the land of Canaan. Accordingly, and in line with the full implications of the covenantal form in which they articulated the relationship between the LORD as 'Great King' and themselves as his vassal people, Israel accorded to the LORD the supreme authority within the state. That is the meaning of 'theocracy' in its Old Testament covenantal form. All the key functions of social authority were placed in the hands of the LORD: the LORD was supreme lawgiver, supreme judge, supreme landowner, supreme commander of the armies. The LORD, in short, was king in Israel.[13]

Israel also believed that this covenantal relationship to the LORD was their very *raison d'être*; that is, they existed as a nation only because of that relationship, so that their survival and security were bound up with maintaining it. Therefore any act that was a fundamental violation of that covenant relationship was a threat to the very security of the whole nation. An offence against God was an offence against the state that depended on God. An offence against God and the covenant relationship threatened to bring the wrath of the LORD upon the whole community (and several narratives record notable instances of just such calamities). Such offences were treated, therefore, as 'crimes' and dealt with in an appropriately serious way. Because Israel regarded the LORD as king, and intended that his kingship should be 'earthed' in every aspect of their national life, the social and theological realms fused into one in the matter of delineating the substance of what constituted 'crime' in Israel.

In the light of this understanding we can see once again the central importance for Israel of the *Decalogue*. It was a summary of certain fundamental kinds of behaviour either required or prohibited on the authority of the God by whose grace and power Israel existed as a people. I am not suggesting that the Decalogue in itself was a 'criminal law code' in my sense of that phrase. For one thing, it contains no specific penalties within the list of 'ten words'.

---

using the term in the more advanced sense of the modern nation state that developed in post-Renaissance Europe as one of the manifestations of modernity.

[13] The remarkable extent to which all the forms of social, political, economic and religious power were focused on YHWH, and the effect this had in relativizing all human exercise of power in these same realms, is explored in great depth in Norman K. Gottwald, *Tribes of Yahweh*.

But it does set out the boundaries and obligations of the covenant, and thus it defined the nature and extent of what, for Israel, would constitute serious 'crime' – crime against the LORD, against the covenant and against the whole covenant community. Other laws spell out the legal details and consequences in relation to specific cases of breaching the different commandments.

It is significant that all the offences for which there was a statutory *death penalty* in Old Testament law can be related, directly or indirectly, to certain of the Ten Commandments.[14] In the light of the nature of 'crime', as just described, these instances of capital punishment should not be thought of as merely primitive or fanatical. They are, however, an eloquent testimony to the seriousness attached to the covenant and the importance of protecting it from violation that would endanger the whole community. The national interest was bound up with preventing and punishing crime against the covenant in a sufficiently serious manner. There was an explicit element of deterrence in such maximum penalties, designed to preserve the life of the whole community by the combination of deterring people from committing such offences and purging the community of those who did.[15]

On the other hand, although all death penalty offences can be linked to the Decalogue, the reverse is not true: not all of the Ten Commandments were sanctioned by the death penalty. The tenth (prohibiting coveting) was by its very nature not open to *any* judicial penalty, least of all death. But that in itself is ethically important, since it shows that a person could be thought of as morally guilty before God without having committed an external, judicially punishable, offence. Jesus applied the same principle to other commandments (Matt. 5:21–24, 27–28). The eighth (prohibiting stealing) concerns property,

---

[14] E.g. worshipping other gods, making idols, misusing the name of the LORD (e.g. in false prophecy), breaking the sabbath, cursing or striking parents, murder, adultery, false testimony (if the false charge would have resulted in the execution of the accused).

[15] An interesting study of the death penalty and the various forms of law that include it in the Old Testament is offered by Erhard Gerstenberger, 'Life-Preserving Divine Threats'. He points out the irony that an explicit reason for imposing these divine death threats is actually the preservation of life, rather like the warning posted at electrical installations – 'Warning: Danger of Death' (my own example). 'Divine threats of death against potential trespassers are counteracting likely catastrophes. Death injunctions or death threats alert us to the gravity of transgression; they are intended to preserve the basis of human life, but they must not be understood in legal terms. They are not "law" in the accepted sense of the term, but rather an anticipatory deterrent' (p. 49).

and no property offence carried the death penalty in normal Israelite legal procedures (see below). However, because of the importance of a family's land and substance, theft was nevertheless a serious matter, and therefore included within the core of covenant law.

Case law

Very many of the laws in the Pentateuch begin with 'If' or 'When', then go on to describe a situation, and conclude with provisions or penalties to cover the circumstances described. This is 'case' law or, as it is sometimes called, 'casuistic' law. Some of the best examples are in the Book of the Covenant, where there are cases of damage, negligence, assault, accidental injury, disputes over loaned or hired property and so on (read, e.g., the list of typical case laws in Exodus 21:18 – 22:15). This kind of civil law, covering disputes between citizens, is of course a common feature of most societies, and there are many points of comparison between Israel's law and other ancient Near Eastern legal collections, especially from Mesopotamia (e.g. the Code of Hammurabi).

However, sometimes the *differences* between Israel's laws and those of other nations are significant. One striking difference in Israel's civil law can be seen in the laws on slaves. Three Old Testament civil laws are quite unparalleled in any other ancient Near Eastern code. Exodus 21:20–21 and 21:26–27 take up the case of slaves injured or killed *by their own masters*, and Deuteronomy 23:15–16 grants asylum to a runaway slave.[16] No other ancient Near Eastern law has been found that holds a master to account for the treatment of his own slaves (as distinct from injury done to the slave of another master), and the otherwise universal law regarding runaway slaves was that they must be sent back, with severe penalties for those who failed to comply.

There can be no doubt that this 'swimming against the stream' in Israel's slave laws is the result of the theological impact of Israel's own historical experience. The action of God on their behalf when they had been in slavery transformed their attitude to slavery into something quite distinctive from contemporary custom. This further shows up the inadequacy of the 'moral–civil' distinction. That distinction is sometimes said to rest on the assumption that the so-called 'moral law' reflects the permanent moral character of God, whereas the 'civil law' was entirely contingent on Israel's historical context and ethically irrelevant to us. But in this case it is by careful study of the *civil* law that we find powerful theological forces at work, applying the character and action of God to the civil realm. We do not find a section of 'moral law' denouncing slavery, not even in the Ten Commandments. But we do find a

---

[16] Each of these laws is discussed further in chapter 10 below.

moral *principle* operative within the civil law, which, when put alongside other Old Testament passages on the subject (e.g. Lev. 25:42; Neh. 5:1–12; Job 31:15; Jer. 34; Amos 2:6), puts a question mark over the whole institution and also sowed seeds that would eventually bear fruit in a radical rejection of slavery per se.

Family law

In ancient Israel the household had a major judicial role. This was one aspect of that social centrality of the family and larger kinship groupings, which I shall discuss in more detail in chapter 10. The head of a household had the primary responsibility for, and legal authority over, all his dependants. That would include his married sons and their families while they resided within the patrimonial estate. A good example of this is the way Gideon, though himself a married man with teenage sons (Judg. 8:20), was afraid of his 'father's house' (Judg. 6:27), and yet was effectively protected by his father Joash (6:30–31) from a possible lynching. Gideon lived within the judicial authority and protection of his wider family and particularly of its head, Joash.

On many routine matters, and some larger ones, the head of the household could act on his own legal authority without recourse to civil law or the external authority of a court of elders. Family law took precedence in some things over civil law. Such matters included parental discipline, which extended beyond childhood. Such discipline stopped short, however, of the right of life and death over a member of one's family (sometimes called *patria potestas*, from Roman law).[17] If the circumstances grew as serious as that, then family law gave way to civil law and both parents were required to bring the matter to the court of elders (see Deut. 21:18–21). Marriages were also arranged within family law and did not involve the public authorities, except where there had been a prior offence (e.g. intercourse with the unbetrothed daughter of another man, in which case the civil law specified clear obligations: Exod. 22:16–17, modified in Deut. 22:28–29), or if a dispute arose between the husband and the father of a bride concerning her premarital chastity (Deut. 22:13–21). Divorce, too, fell within family jurisdiction. The civil law in relation to divorce (Deut. 24:1–4) was concerned only with regulating the post-divorce circumstances; the divorce itself would have taken place within family law, though probably (as in later Jewish law), before a few witnesses. We have seen

---

[17] The idea that fathers in Israel had the right of life and death over their children is one of those old myths from a bygone era of anthropological theorizing about the Old Testament, which had virtually no real basis in the text. Refuting arguments will be found in C. J. H. Wright, *God's Land*, pp. 222–238.

that the civil law took an interest in the fair treatment of slaves, but the ceremony by which a slave might voluntarily accept permanent attachment to one
household, instead of freedom after six years, was possibly also a domestic
ceremony – another case of internal family law (Exod. 21:5–6;[18] Deut.
15:16–17).

As well as these domestic matters (marriage and divorce, discipline of children, certain aspects of slavery) there were laws and institutions designed to
protect the family and its land inheritance. These included levirate marriage
(Deut. 25:5–10), inheritance laws (Deut. 21:15–16), redemption of land and
persons, and the jubilee (Lev. 25). Then, too, we must remember that the
family was the chief educational agency, within which the rest of the laws
were taught and explained (Deut. 6:7–9, 20–25).

Now under the old 'moral-civil-ceremonial' scheme all this family law
would presumably have to be included under 'civil law'. But clearly it needs a
separate category, for sociologically it was a different kind of law. It is distinct
inasmuch as it was a category of legal authority and legal action that did not
involve the public civil arena of the court of elders. Its importance arises
from the legal dimension it gives to the social, economic and theological centrality of the family, which I shall discuss in more detail in chapter 10. As we
explore these aspects of Israel's family law, showing how important the family
was in their society, it gives depth and texture to our own ethical reflection on
the family, which is sometimes otherwise suspended solely from the fifth
commandment to honour parents.

Cultic law

I am using the term 'cultic' here in the technical sense of the outward forms
and rituals of religious life – the *cultus*. It should not be confused with the
more recent use of the term in relation to 'cults'; that is, strange religious sects
that exert oppressive and often secretive power over their adherents. 'Cultic',
as used here, is a neutral word that simply refers to the visible forms of religious practice. Now, under the old threefold division, this 'cultic' or (in older
versions) 'ceremonial' category is that which is said to prefigure the work of
Christ and therefore to have been fulfilled and rendered obsolete by him. For
this reason many people's concept of the ceremonial law of the Old
Testament is controlled by the Letter to the Hebrews and limited to the blood

---

[18] The translation 'before the judges' (NIV v. 6) is in my view a misinterpretation. The
expression, as in the NIV marginal note, is literally 'before God', and probably refers to
a ceremony in the home that took place while invoking the name of the LORD as
witness to the slave's explicit preference.

sacrifices, priestly ordinances and the ritual of the Day of Atonement. All of these were assuredly vital parts of Israel's cultic law, but by no means the whole of it. For an Israelite, cultic life also embraced such matters as dietary regulations with their division between clean and unclean animals and foods; the holy calendar of sabbaths and annual festivals, as well as sabbatical and jubilee years; and also a whole range of practical, material requirements that had important social effects, such as tithes, the first fruits and gleanings of harvest. Although for Israelites these were all part of a total system that expressed their faith and their worldview, for us it may be helpful to observe three main areas of cultic law and practice.

Sacrificial laws

These are primarily what was meant by 'ceremonial law'. Israel's whole system of worship revolved around the extensive range of sacrifices brought for a variety of reasons and purposes. This is not the place to go into them in depth, since many studies exist that do so. Clearly, for Christians, in the light of the death of Jesus and the way it is interpreted in the New Testament as the full and final sacrifice for sin, there is no longer any *redemptive* significance in these Old Testament blood rituals. However, even as we affirm that the sacrificial laws have no further theological claim upon us other than as a pointer to the meaning of the cross, we can discern other features of Israel's laws of sacrifice that embody ethical principles worthy of ongoing reflection.

There was, for example, a remarkable equality of all Israelites in relation to sacrifice. There was no grading of the value of a sacrifice according to the status of the worshipper. The sacrifice of a king was of no greater efficacy than that of an ordinary peasant. Indeed, adulterer and virtual murderer David knew that, king or not, no sacrifice of his was adequate to erase his sin – only God's mercy could do that. On the other hand, those in positions of leadership were required to bring greater offerings reflecting their greater responsibility (Lev. 4). And yet, at the same time, allowance was made for those who were too poor to bring the prescribed blood sacrifice. Sin-offerings could be brought according to what a person could afford – even to the remarkable extent that someone too poor to bring an animal or a bird could bring 'a tenth of an ephah of fine flour' and it would still be counted as if it were a blood sacrifice – a sin-offering (Lev. 5:5–13). This surely made clear that the atonement declared by the priest depended on the mercy of God, not on the intrinsic value of the sacrifice itself. An Israelite who knew that he could come in poverty of spirit as well as of substance with nothing more than a few handfuls of flour to offer to God, and yet go away with the words of forgiveness from the priest ringing in his ears, was learning something about the grace of God and the ethical power of repentance.

Sacred calendar laws

There was a rhythm about Israel's worshipping life. First of all there was the weekly sabbath (Exod. 20:8–11; Deut. 5:12–15). Then there were the recurring annual festivals at the different seasons of the year (Exod. 34:22–23; Deut. 16:1–17). There was the annual Day of Atonement (Lev. 16). There were annual offerings of first fruits and tithes, and a special tithe in the third year (Deut. 14:22–29). Then there was the sabbatical (seventh) year, with various social and economic aspects (Exod. 23:10–11; Lev. 25:3–7; Deut. 15:1–6). And finally, there was the jubilee year (after the seventh sabbatical year – Lev. 25:8–55). All of these in their different ways proclaimed the sovereignty of the LORD over time itself, and his claim on Israel's apportioning of time. All of these events or institutions were 'sacred', in the sense that they were to be observed as a matter of duty and obedience to the LORD himself. But some of them had clear social and economic dimensions also, and a strong ethical rationale.

The sabbath day, for example, was to be kept holy as a sign of the covenant and one of the most sacred defining marks of what it meant to belong to Israel. But the explicit benefit of the weekly day of sabbath rest was for the working population – at every social level. In Israel work was not divided horizontally along class lines, such that slaves and peasants did all the work while the more privileged could enjoy leisure. Rather, it was divided vertically in time, by the rhythm of the sabbath.[19] All should work, and all should enjoy rest, including slaves. It was a form of employee protection and it is clear from the prophets that neglect or willful disregard for the sabbath went along with (indeed was motivated by) blatant exploitation of the poor (Amos 8:4–6; Is. 58).

Similarly, the major economic institution of the sabbatical year – which included regulations for leaving land fallow (Exod. 23:10–11) and later, under Deuteronomic law, an accompanying release of pledges held for debts (Deut. 15:1–2) – had a cultic rationale. It was based on the concept of divine owner-ship of the land (Lev. 25:23), and was described as 'a sabbath *to the LORD*' (Lev. 25:4; my italics) and '*the LORD's time* for cancelling debts' (Deut. 15:2; my italics). So the material obligations involved in keeping this sabbatical institu-tion were thought of as obligations to *God* himself. Yet the intended practical effect of them was *humanitarian* help for the impoverished and the debtor. This is spelt out explicitly in each of the three occurrences of the law (cf. Exod. 23:11; Lev. 25:6; Deut. 15:2, 7–11). The point was that you honoured God by keeping a law that benefited your poorer neighbours. Here again,

---

[19] See Norbert F. Lohfink, *Great Themes*.

then, in this unlikely looking corner of Old Testament *cultic* law, we come upon a basic *moral* principle that pervades biblical ethics; namely, that serving God and caring for other people are inseparably bound together. God will not be worshipped acceptably by those who neglect justice and compassion. This ancient Israelite sabbatical institution, which might otherwise be deemed quite outdated and culturally (and even agriculturally) irrelevant, presents us with a concrete, economic paradigm of a fundamental principle of biblical ethics – the principle that we go a long way towards fulfilling our duty to God when we display responsible, sensitive and sacrificial care for our fellow human beings. Echoes of this could be multiplied.[20]

Finally, we might point out the small but significant point urged upon the Israelites in relation to their festivals: that they had to make sure that they were socially inclusive. The major annual festivals of Israel were primarily times of family rejoicing and feasting, with particular focus on the fruit of the soil. But what about those who had no family nor soil? They too were to be included and not neglected in times of festival and were particularly remembered through the tithe. This is a marked feature of Deuteronomy's generous humanitarianism (see Deut. 14:27–29; 16:11,14).

Symbolic laws

There is another category of law in ancient Israel that seems much more difficult to grasp by those of a modern and especially Western mindset (though more traditional cultures have less difficulty entering into Israel's world at this point). These are the regulations that express Israel's symbolic universe, giving tangible expression to their understanding of the varying 'graded' relationships between God, themselves, other nations and the rest of creation. In Israelite thinking all reality was divided into that which was holy and that which was ordinary (or 'profane' – a word in biblical usage that does not mean necessarily sinful or sacrilegious, but merely common). God, of course, was the ultimately holy reality, and all things or people specially dedicated to God participated to some degree in God's holiness. Most of the rest of life was common. But the realm of the common was further subdivided into the clean and the unclean. Most things in their ordinary state were clean. But sin, pollution of various kinds, sickness and some bodily functions and, worst of all, death, made things or people unclean. Apart from God (the ultimately holy at one end of the spectrum) and death (the ultimately unclean at the other end), most of reality in between could be in a state of flux in either

---

[20] See Deut. 24:10–15; Job 31:13–23; Ps. 15; Prov. 19:17; Is. 1:10–17; 58:1–7; Jer. 7:4–11; Zech. 7:4–10.

direction. Sin and pollution rendered the holy profane and made the clean unclean. But through the blood of sacrifice and the variety of rituals associated with it that which was unclean could be cleansed, and that which was clean could be sanctified and be made holy. A great deal of Israel's cultic activity operated in this constant dynamic of counteracting the profaning and polluting effects of everyday life with the cleansing and sanctifying power of sacrificial blood.[21]

However, there was another aspect of this symbolic world. Just as within Israel itself there was a distinction between the priests (who were holy), and the rest of the Israelites (who were ordinary), so there was a further distinction between Israel as a whole (who, as a whole people, were supposed to be holy and clean before God) and the rest of the nations (who were not in covenant relationship with the LORD and were regarded as ritually unclean). This fundamental distinction between Israel as the people called by God to be a holy people in covenant relationship and the rest of the nations who were not (yet) in that position was to be reflected *symbolically* in the whole complex framework of laws about clean and unclean animals and foods. Just as the LORD had made his selection of Israel from among all the nations, so Israel must observe his selection of the clean from among all the animals. This apparently arbitrary choice (in both cases) did not make the unclean animals any less the good creation of the good Creator, or the non-elect nations any less human beings made in the image of their Creator either. The clean–unclean distinction was symbolic of the distinctiveness of Israel among the nations in the purposes of God.

This is most clearly expressed in Leviticus 20:24–26:

> I am the LORD your God, *who has set you apart from the nations.*
>
> You must *therefore* make a distinction between clean and unclean animals and between unclean and clean birds. Do not defile yourselves by any animal or bird or anything that moves along the ground – those which I have set apart as unclean for you. You are to be holy to me because I, the LORD, am holy, and *I have set you apart from the nations to be my own.* (my italics)

Now once we grasp this essentially symbolic nature of these laws it helps in a number of ways. First, it explains why these laws no longer apply to us as

---

[21] For excellent explanations of Israel's symbolic world in relation to these categories of holy, common, clean and unclean, and further explanation of the 'graded' nature of Israel's concept of holiness in relation to holy space, persons and objects, see Gordon J. Wenham, *Leviticus*; P. Jenson, *Graded Holiness*; John G. Gammie, *Holiness in Israel*.

Christians. The simple reason is that in Christ the distinction that pertained in the Old Testament between ethnic Israel and the nations no longer exists. It is, indeed, abolished through the cross and the way is opened for a new redeemed humanity of believing Jews and Gentiles to be reconciled together to God (Eph. 2). This was the stunning realization that Peter's vision induced (Acts 10:9–15), and that Paul expounded so classically in Galatians 3:26–29. So since there is no longer any distinction between Jew and Gentile *in Christ*, there is no longer any need *as far as Christians are concerned* for the tangible food distinctions that symbolized it.

Secondly, however, it encourages us to expect that other laws and regulations in the Old Testament that may puzzle us may possibly fall into this same category; that is, they may have had symbolic significance in relation to Israel's distinctive faith, even if some aspects of their symbolism may be obscure to us now, being dependent on a very different worldview and symbolic universe. This is probably what lies behind those laws that forbid mixing of seeds, textiles and animals (Lev. 19:19). Similarly, puzzling laws about certain forms of cutting the hair or beard, or marking the body, may have to do with keeping well away from the practices of other nations and religions (Lev. 19:27–28).

Now, we have seen that these symbolic laws no longer apply to us in relation to the distinctions they originally signified. Nevertheless, the concept of the distinctiveness of God's people from the rest of the world, and the need for God's people to strive for holiness, cleanness and purity in a world marked by ungodliness and moral filth are far from irrelevant or outdated. On the contrary, the New Testament urges upon believers an even greater degree of moral seriousness about these things, even if the symbolism and outward expressions have changed:

> What can Christians learn from these laws? First, the importance of the distinctiveness of being the people of God in the midst of the world. Even for Old Testament Israel, ritual cleanness, from the kitchen to the sanctuary, was meant to symbolize God's greater requirement of moral integrity, social justice and covenant loyalty. In fact, as the prophets (and Jesus) vigorously pointed out, if these latter things were lacking, then ritual cleanness of the most scrupulous kind at every level was worthless. If Christians were as serious about moral distinctiveness as Israel was about ritual cleanness, then our 'salt' and 'light' might have greater power in the world.[22]

---

[22]   C. J. H. Wright, 'Leviticus', p. 139.

Compassionate law

Here we have a category that we would not regard strictly as law at all, in the legislative sense. Indeed, the injunctions that we can gather together under this heading could not have been regarded as enforceable legislation in Israel either. Yet such is the compassionate drift of the moral principles we have discerned in other categories of actual law, and such is the degree of penetration of Israel's theological beliefs into the practicalities of legal life, that it comes as no surprise to find hosts of these charitable and humanitarian instructions scattered throughout the legal codes.

The breadth of situations covered by this category of law is very impressive. It includes protection for the weak, especially those who lacked the natural protection of family and land (namely, widows, orphans, Levites, immigrants and resident aliens); justice for the poor; impartiality in the courts; generosity at harvest time and in general economic life; respect for persons and property, even of an enemy; sensitivity to the dignity even of a debtor; special care for strangers and immigrants; considerate treatment of the disabled; prompt payment of wages earned by hired labour; sensitivity over articles taken in pledge; consideration for people in early marriage, or in bereavement; even care for animals, domestic and wild, and for fruit trees. Again, it would be well worth pausing with a Bible to read through the passages in the footnote, to feel the warm heartbeat of all this material.[23]

The practical outcome of this material, as I have said, is humanitarian. But the origin and motivation are theological, and this is what is ethically most significant about it. It is here that we see the clearest illustration of the point made in chapter 1; namely, that a wholehearted covenant commitment to God requires that God's people reflect God's character, as revealed in God's actions on their behalf. The primary, compelling and repeated reason why, if you had been an Israelite, you were supposed to observe this compassionate law towards the weak, the enslaved or the impoverished was that this is the way God had actually behaved towards you, when you were in similar conditions. 'Remember that *you* were slaves in Egypt and the LORD your God redeemed *you* from there. *That is why* I command you to do this' (Deut. 24:18; my italics).

Now that I have outlined the different kinds of law operating in ancient Israel, we can see how futile it is to think of isolating a separate category of 'moral law'. Rather, it is clear that there are moral principles to be found in all the

---

[23] Exod. 22:21–27; 23:4–9; Lev. 19:9–10, 13–18, 33–34; Deut. 14:28–29; 15:7–15; 20:5–7; 21:10–14; 22:1–4; 23:24–25; 24:5–6, 10–15, 17–22; 25:4; 27:18–19, 25.

different categories of law as they functioned in ancient Israel. So the task of interpreting the laws for our own ethical instruction requires careful thought. We need to see how any particular law functioned in its own Israelite context and what moral principles it embodied or exemplifies. Then we can move from the specifics of Israel's laws to the specifics of our own constructive ethics. I shall suggest some guidelines of how we might do that below, after further reflections on Israel's judicial system itself.

The administration of justice

To have admirable laws is one thing, but what really counts in practice for the ordinary person in everyday life is how those laws are actually administered. The process of justice is an urgent human concern in every age and society. Therefore, it is of interest to reflect on what the Old Testament has to say about the administration of law, as well as the actual content of the laws.[24]

Family-focused justice

In ancient Israel, as mentioned above and I shall reflect on further in chapter 10, the family played a significant role in the way legal affairs were conducted. This refers not only to those kinds of legal action that took place within the framework of family law, but also to the fact that members of families themselves had recognized legal duties in wider society. For example, in cases of murder the responsibility for punishing the criminal lay with the *gō'ēl* – the *kinsman* 'avenger of blood' who was a relative of the victim's own family – not with a 'public prosecutor'. The civic elders of a village or city fulfilled only an assisting role to the *gō'ēl* (Deut. 19:1–13), to enable him to carry out the responsibility recognized to be his. The family thus had the primary duty to enforce justice in such a case. The elders of a town acted independently only in a situation where a murderer could not be identified and brought to justice; their task was to conduct a ceremony that purged the blood-guilt from their town (Deut. 21:1–9). This kinship responsibility extended to clan level as well, as the case described in 2 Samuel 14:5–11 shows. That case also shows, however, that appeal could be made beyond the jurisdiction of the clan to the civil authorities, even as high as the king himself. So there was a fluidity between families acting to administer justice and public authorities acting to

---

[24] For a more detailed survey of this theme, see Hans-Jochen Boecker, *Law and Administration of Justice*.

do so. And, in any case, it is most likely that the public authorities (the elders) occupied that role by virtue of being the senior figures in the network of families that made up any particular village or town.

This familial nature of the process of law in ancient Israel had several significant results, which need to be taken into account if we seek to relate Israel's model of justice to contemporary ethical concerns in this area. First, it encouraged a climate in which law was supposed to be known. A child's basic education was substantially education in the *tôrâ*. Now, of course, as I have said, the *tôrâ* included all the narratives and poetry we find in these books – not just lists of laws. Nevertheless, in a devout and observant Israelite home the expectation was that God's law was being taught to children (Deut. 4:9–10; 6:6–9), in such a way that questions would naturally arise and be answered in terms of the great story of redemption (Deut. 6:20–25). Added to this was the teaching of the law that was supposed to be the role of the priests (Lev. 10:8–11; Deut. 33:10; Mal. 2:6–7). They were a kind of Citizens' Advice Bureau. And on top of that there was the public reading of the law, at which everyone, including children, was expected to be present (Deut. 31:10–13). Since all this was supposed to take place and thereby ensure that the law was known, one can understand Hosea's bitter complaint that the moral decline of the nation stemmed from lack of knowledge (Hos. 4:1–6), for which he blamed the priests.

Local administration

Also, the administration of justice was largely local. Most disputes, accusations, trials and cases took place in the local village assembly, literally 'in the gate' (the public square where all public business took place).[25] It was a matter of local people arbitrating their own affairs through their own elders. Justice was not something remote, bureaucratic and imposed from above. On the contrary, it had a local, almost 'democratic' nature, through the plurality of elders. Even the reforms of Jehoshaphat, by which judges were appointed by the king himself, applied only to the fortified cities and therefore probably left the local village courts largely unaffected (2 Chr. 19:5). Such a system of local and fairly unsupervised courts could work well in the circumstances of a broad social equality of families and a wide distribution of land and wealth, which the land-division texts and other laws presuppose. Provided most families were economically viable (possessed their own inheritance of land) and

---

[25] Hence, the instruction to write the law 'on your gates' (Deut. 6:9) meant that God's law was to govern life in the public arena – just as much as in the home ('on the doorframes of your houses'), and in one's personal affairs ('hands . . . foreheads', v. 8).

thus qualified to have their senior males sitting among the local body of elders, there would be a broad base for social justice. But when families began to be deprived of land and driven instead into a kind of dispossessed debt-slavery, control of the courts and other forms of social power fell into the hands of the small class of wealthy landowners. The administration of justice was thus vulnerable to corruption and exploitation. The prophets saw clearly this link between the shift of balance in economic power and the accelerating corruption and denial of justice. It began to happen from the reign of Solomon onwards and provoked the major prophetic protest of the eighth century. The ideal, however, was local justice through local elders acting on behalf of the needy and seeing that the cases of even the weakest (the widow and orphan) were heard. This kind of ideal is portrayed in Job's description of how he had functioned as an elder in the courts in the days when he had family and substance, before he lost both and was himself driven to the margins of society (Job 29:7–17).

This local nature of justice in Israel also meant that the initiative in court procedures was mainly private. As we have seen, it began as a family respon-sibility, and outside that, in any dispute, it was often a matter of self-help aided by the courts if necessary. There were no Director of Public Prosecutions, police force nor an official intermediary profession of barristers and solici-tors. This meant that a judge or group of elders sitting in judgment on a dispute would have been much more directly involved with the plaintiff and defendant than in our society. This could be so even if the judge was the king (as was the case in 1 Sam. 14). And in a village society the judges might be rel-atives or workmates of the persons involved in the dispute or in the case to be settled (as in Ruth 4).

Procedural guidelines

Against this background the careful instructions on applying the law with rig-orous fairness and the warnings against bribery and favouritism are all the more pertinent. We have a remarkably instructive list of such instructions in Exodus 23:1–9. It appears to have been constructed in a systematic order, addressing in turn all three categories of people involved in a court case:

1. *The witnesses.* They are to act with integrity, honesty and independence:

> Do not spread false reports. Do not help a wicked man by being a malicious witness. Do not follow the crowd in doing wrong. When you give testimony in a lawsuit, do not pervert justice by siding with the crowd, and do not show favouritism to a poor man in his lawsuit.

> (Exod. 23:1–3)

2. *The parties in dispute.* This is the meaning, in this context, of the word 'enemy' (your adversary in court). They are warned not to neglect the normal requirements of brotherly obligation even though they are engaged in legal conflict.

> If you come across your enemy's ox or donkey wandering off, be sure to take it back to him. If you see the donkey of someone who hates you fallen down under its load, do not leave it there; be sure you help him with it.
>
> (Exod. 23:4–5)

3. *The judges.* Those who must decide the issue before the court must do so with impartiality and incorruptibility, but also with appropriate understanding and compassion.

> Do not deny justice to your poor people in their lawsuits. Have nothing to do with a false charge and do not put an innocent or honest person to death, for I will not acquit the guilty.
>
> Do not accept a bribe, for a bribe blinds those who see and twists the words of the righteous.
>
> Do not oppress an alien; you yourselves know how it feels to be aliens, because you were aliens in Egypt.
>
> (Exod. 23:6–9)

When these paragraphs are set alongside similarly strong injunctions in Leviticus 19:15, Deuteronomy 16:18–20 and Jehoshaphat's admirable brief to his appointed judges in 2 Chronicles 19:4–11, it becomes obvious how concerned the Old Testament is that the manner in which the law is administered should match up to the standard of the content of the law itself. There is a persistent demand that the *processes* of the legal system should be just and, as they say, seen to be just. This corresponds well with a growing awareness in our own day that people, especially the powerless, the poor, the illiterate, the immigrant, the asylum seeker are as often hurt by the cumbersome and complicated *process* of the law, even good law, as they are victims of bad law or deliberate injustice. Legal processes that are delayed, demeaning and discriminatory, or simply unaffordable by the poor, are as bad as active injustice and oppression. In this instance, too, the Old Testament 'has been there before us', which should encourage Christians who are actively concerned for justice in the procedural side of our legal systems. This, after all, is only to apply the ninth commandment, 'You shall not bear false witness', in the sphere to which it originally applied; namely, the protection of the integrity of legal procedures.

Israel's scale of values

We have observed above that there is texture and variation within the law of the Old Testament in terms of the different kinds of law. Not all laws are the same as all other laws in terms of their social function; there are distinctions related to different social contexts, differing kinds of cases, different levels of seriousness and so on. The same is true when we consider the relative moral values expressed within the great variety of law. Not all laws are equally important as all other laws in terms of their moral values. This is not to say that some of the laws did not matter: there is a powerful emphasis especially in Deuteronomy (reflected perhaps in Ps. 119) on 'observing' (paying careful and detailed attention to) *all* God's laws. Nevertheless, even Deuteronomy can propose that the central and most important of God's requirements on Israel can be reduced to a few key phrases: to fear the LORD, walk in his ways, love him, serve him and obey him (Deut. 10:12–13). Micah reduced it still further to three: to do justice, love mercy and walk humbly with God (Mic. 6:8). So it seems appropriate not to try to tackle the whole law as a single solid slab of undifferentiated duties. Rather, we can seek to discern what the primary moral values are within the law. What are its more central priorities? Is there a scale of values inherent in all the variety?

This question occupied the minds of some of the rabbinical schools at the time of Jesus, as is reflected in the Gospel story when a teacher of the law solicited from Jesus his personal viewpoint on the question 'Of all the commandments, which is the most important?' Jesus famously answered with the dual commands – one from Deuteronomy 6:4–5 (total love for God), the other from Leviticus 19:18 (love for one's neighbour as oneself) – adding that 'there is no commandment greater than these'. In other words, here are the primary values, the overriding priorities, that govern the rest of the detailed legislation.

In Mark's version of the encounter the teacher's response is interesting (and emphatically commends itself to Jesus): '"Well said, teacher," the man replied. "You are right in saying that God is one and there is no other but him [Deut. 6:4]. To love him with all your heart, with all your understanding and with all your strength, and to love your neighbour as yourself *is more important than all burnt offerings and sacrifices*"' (Mark 12:32–33; my italics). This is not, of course, a fresh insight. On the contrary, it is an authentically scriptural (Old Testament) perspective. Such expression of moral priorities is found, for example, in the words of Samuel to Saul, 'to obey is better than sacrifice' (1 Sam. 15:22), or of God to Israel through Hosea, 'I desire mercy not sacrifice, knowledge of God rather than burnt offerings' (Hos. 6:6), or of the voice of wisdom, 'To do righteousness and justice is more acceptable to the LORD than sacrifice' (Prov. 21:3). So, with the encouragement of these affirmations of moral prioritization from the Old Testament itself, what scale of values can we discern?

God above all else

Our starting point has to be the words of Jesus himself, that the LORD God matters above all else. No moral imperative ranks higher than the command to love God with the totality of one's whole being. This fundamental principle, enshrined in the Shema ('Hear O Israel . . .'), is further established in the order of the Ten Commandments, which begins with the prohibition on worshipping any other god before (literally, 'before the face of') the LORD. It is given even more stringent social clout in the sharp and uncompromising instructions of Deuteronomy 13. With great realism the text acknowledges that the temptation to worship other gods may come from religious celebrities whose credibility seems remarkably supported by their miraculous powers (vv. 1–5), or it may come from within the bosom of close family and friends (vv. 6–11), or it may come from the pressure of some dominant voice within the local community (vv. 12–18). But no matter what the source, the response is to be the same – ruthless rejection of any alternative to worshiping the one true living God. All other roads lead to idolatry, injustice and eventually death and destruction. Something of the ultimate value and stark choice articulated in this chapter (Deut. 13) is presented with comparable lack of compromise in the teaching of Jesus about the supreme priority of submitting to the reign of God through following Jesus as Lord (see Luke 14:25–27).

Looking again at the Ten Commandments we may detect a scale of values in their order. They begin with God and end with the inner thoughts of a person's heart. In a sense the tenth (against covetousness) and the first (against worshipping any other god than the LORD) correspond to one another. That is because covetousness by its nature puts other persons or things in the position that should be occupied by God alone: 'covetousness which is idolatry' (Col. 3:5, RSV). Then, after God's person, God's name and the unique acknowledgment of God's sovereignty expressed through sabbath observance come the family (through honouring parents), human life, the integrity of sex and marriage, property and the integrity of the system of justice. Now since echoes of the commandments elsewhere do not always follow exactly this order (e.g. Jer. 7:9; Hos. 4:2), we should not place too much weight on it. However, there is certainly a clear transition from those mainly concerned with God (the first three at least, and also the fourth in its Godward dimension) to those mainly concerned with interhuman relationships (the social effects of the fourth, and the remaining six).

Though every commandment is a 'word' of God, and though breaking any of them is a serious offence (tantamount to 'crime' in some ways, as we saw above), this order is not haphazard: the most vital demands are placed first. This probably intentional scale of values is confirmed by Israel's penal law. Flagrant disregard of the first six commandments carried a mandatory death penalty. For the seventh (adultery), the death penalty was available but there is no record of any occasion when it was carried out, and some scholars think that other options were allowed to the aggrieved husband. The eighth (theft) was not sanctioned by the death penalty in normal law (except theft of a person or kidnapping, Exod. 21:16; Deut. 24:7). The ninth (perjury) would only carry a death penalty if one was caught falsely accusing someone of a crime that would result in their execution (Deut. 19:16–21). And it is most unlikely that the tenth commandment was ever the subject of any judicial process. The order of the commandments thus gives some insight into Israel's hierarchy of values. Roughly speaking, the order was God, family, life, sex, property. It is sobering, looking at that order, that in modern society (in its debased Western form at least) we have almost exactly reversed that order of values. Money and sex matter a lot more than human life, the family is scorned in theory and practice, and God is the last thing in most people's thinking, let alone priorities.

Three more features of Israel's scale of values are worth discussing a little further: the priority of life over property, the priority of persons over punishment and the priority of needs over rights.

Life and property

The sanctity of human life is one of the earliest explicit moral values in the Old Testament, based as it is on the creation of human beings in God's image. God's words to Noah make the matter clear:

> for your lifeblood I will surely demand an accounting. I will demand an accounting from every animal. And from each man, too, I will demand an accounting for the life of his fellow man.

> Whoever sheds the blood of man,
>   by man shall his blood be shed;
> for in the image of God
>   has God made man.

(Gen. 9:5–6)

The effect of this unique value of human life can be seen in some almost incidental features of certain Israelite laws. When an ox gores a human being to death, for example, the law requires that the ox itself be stoned. This is a unique Israelite detail in what is otherwise a very common law, found in most other ancient Near Eastern codes. It ties in with the concept of Genesis 9:5 that God holds even animals accountable for the lifeblood of human beings.[26]

But the most outstanding effect of the priority of life over property is that in Israelite law life and property are never measured against each other. That is, no property offence in normal legal procedure was punishable by death.[27] Thus although David's emotional response to Nathan's 'parable' (which David presumably thought was an actual case Nathan was bringing before him for his royal judgment, 2 Sam. 12:1–6) was an angry explosion that the wealthy thief deserved to die, legally the only penalty David could pronounce was the fourfold restitution the law specified (Exod. 22:1). This feature of Israelite law stands in sharp contrast to many ancient law codes where certain thefts by certain people were punishable by death. Indeed, it contrasts with British law until fairly recent times (people were hanged for sheep-stealing in Britain until the nineteenth century). On the other hand, as mentioned above, theft of a *person* for gain (kidnapping) *was* a capital offence in Israel (21:16; Deut. 24:7). Stealing a human *life* was different from stealing *property*.

The other side of this principle is that if you had committed a capital offence with a mandatory death penalty, you could not get off by paying money instead. If a life was forfeit, money would not do. The one could not be measured in terms of the other (see Num. 35:31–34). Again, this contrasts with some ancient Near Eastern codes where many capital offences could be commuted to fines. There the system favoured those who were wealthy enough to afford to 'pay' for their crimes. In the Old Testament the only exception to this rule was in the case of the fatally goring ox. The owner of the 'guilty' ox could ransom his life if the family of the ox's victim agreed, since the homicide was indirect and unintentional (Exod. 21:30). Even the life of a slave was protected in this way, notwithstanding the fact that in other respects he was his master's property (Exod. 21:20–21).

Human life, then, and material property were incommensurable. They were

---

[26] Possibly because it was a common occurrence in the farms and villages of the ancient world, goring by a frightened or ill-tempered ox gave rise to much legislative activity in the attempt to apportion blame and fix penalties and compensation. The blood spilt by unruly oxen has been matched by the ink spilt by investigating scholars. For a survey of the literature on these laws, and the distinctive aspects of Israelite law on the matter, see C. J. H. Wright, *God's Land*, pp. 160–164.

[27] In abnormal cases, like Achan's theft of silver and gold from Jericho in Josh. 7, the matter was a serious violation of a covenant demand in time of war – the 'ban' or destruction of pagan, 'polluted' things.

treated as qualitatively different, not to be equated with one another in judicial procedure. As the old saying goes, people matter more than things.

Persons and punishment

This Old Testament conviction concerning the unique value of human life not only informs the hierarchy of serious offences and the distinguishing of capital and non-capital penalties; it also extends to the offender himself and the nature and extent of the punishment meted out. When we allow ourselves to see beyond the stumbling block that the mandatory death penalty presents for some, there is a humanitarian ethos in Israelite penal law, which is acknowledged by all who have compared it with contemporary ancient Near Eastern collections of law.

The prototype example of God's concern for the rights of the criminal is the case of Cain. In other respects this is a curious case, for God himself waives the death penalty for Abel's murder. But God answers Cain's fear as to how others will treat him, the murderer, by making it explicit that other people will be held accountable to God for their treatment of Cain (Gen. 4:15).

This view that criminals remain human persons with rights protected by God is found in the provisions of Deuteronomy 25:2–3. If corporal punishment is the verdict of a proper court, then it is to be administered under the supervision of the judge (not out of sight in some secret, sadistic dungeon). Furthermore, the punishment is to be clearly specified in relation to the seriousness of the offence ('the number of lashes his crime deserves') – not just a general thrashing. And, most important of all, the punishment has to have a clear maximum limit ('not more than forty lashes'), explicitly so that the offender ('your brother') should not be 'degraded'. He is still a brother, albeit a guilty one. The principle that legal penalties should be specific and proportionate, supervised and subject to maximum limits, is still entirely valid today as a recognition of the continuing human rights and dignity even of convicted offenders. Apart from the death penalty by stoning, the use of a whip appears to have been the only other normal physical punishment in Israelite law. Unlike other ancient Near Eastern codes, which specified amputations, choppings and impalings as punishment for a range of offences (especially sexual), physical mutilation as a judicial penalty is absent from Old Testament law, except for one rather bizarre and relatively unlikely circumstance (Deut. 25:11–12).[28]

No form of imprisonment is prescribed in Israelite law, though it was a

---

[28] There are scholars who believe that 'cut off her hand' was not intended literally, but had symbolic significance in relation to the woman's ability to have children. See C. J. H. Wright, *Deuteronomy*, p. 269.

feature of later monarchic practice. When one thinks of some of the horrific features and long-term effects of our own 'civilized' prison system, it is at least arguable that the bonded labour prescribed by Old Testament law for some offences (e.g. unrepayable theft or debt) was, on humanitarian grounds, preferable to imprisonment. At least a slave was still free to enjoy his own marital and family life, remained within the community, sharing its seasons and festivals, and was engaged in normal, useful work alongside the rest of the community – things imprisonment denies.

There is also no trace in Old Testament law of any gradation of penalties according to the social class and rank of the offended party. In Mesopotamian law an injury to a nobleman would commonly entail a far heavier penalty than an identical injury done to a commoner or slave. In Israel, by contrast, equality before the law for all social groups, including aliens and immigrants, is made explicit in Exodus 12:49, Leviticus 19:34 and Numbers 15:16. Furthermore, substitutionary punishment was excluded. For example in the Code of Hammurabi, if a house collapsed and killed the house-owner's son, then the *son* of the house-builder (not the man himself) was to be put to death. Deuteronomy 24:16 forbade this on principle, and in the law of the goring ox (again!) the penalty is clearly stated to be constant, even if the ox killed a son or daughter (Exod. 21:31).

A study of the penal provisions, particularly in Deuteronomy, shows up some clear and positive principles on which Israelite punishments operated. Taking Deuteronomy 19:18–20 and 25:1–3 as key examples, the following ingredients of punishment can be seen:

- *Retribution.* The offender was to suffer his just deserts, which should be appropriate to the offence. That is the significance and justification of the *lex talionis* ('an eye for an eye' etc.) principle. Contrary to the popular and quite mistaken use of the phrase to mean unlimited vengeance, this was a simple, and almost certainly metaphorical, way of decreeing proportionality in punishment. It was a law of limitation, *preventing* excessive or vengeful punishments. It was a handy way of saying that the punishment must fit the crime.
- *Purging.* Guilt had to be 'wiped away' from God's sight.
- *Deterrence.* 'All Israel shall hear *and fear*'; that is, be afraid to do the same.
- *Restoration.* The offender remained a brother and was not to be degraded.
- *Compensation.* Restitution was made to the injured party – not to the state as a fine.

As an illustration of some of these points, and of the way in which a careful study of particular laws (as opposed to a hasty dismissal of their strangeness) can bring to light values and principles that have abiding relevance, let us take an example that at first sight seems likely to be highly unhelpful – the law prescribing the execution of the rebellious son in Deuteronomy 21:18–21. If we examine the text and context carefully, the following points may be observed:

1. The preceding verses are concerned with the right of the firstborn son, protecting him from the whim of a father who might show favouritism to another child. The law before us is a kind of balance, showing that sons had a reciprocal responsibility to their father and family. There is a balance in the rights of parents and children in respect of each other. Sons should not suffer from the favouritism of a father; but parents should not suffer from the rebellious profligacy of a son.

2. The law presupposes the necessity of family discipline, for the case is brought before the elders only after prolonged parental discipline has been disregarded. The law shows, however, that sometimes even the most diligent parental discipline may founder on the rocks of rebellion.

3. The law is a limitation on the extent of family law. That is, the father did not have the right of life and death over his own children: such a serious matter had to be brought before the whole community, under civil law. Parents can and must handle some things, but others lie beyond their exercise of legitimate power. Lines have to be drawn somewhere.

4. The law therefore recognizes a valid role for the civil law and public authorities in domestic matters when they are serious enough to threaten the rest of the community.

5. Further protection for the son, in spite of his delinquency, is found in the requirement that *both* parents must together bring the charge; the son will not suffer for the malice of a vindictive father alone. 'His father *and* mother' are mentioned twice.

6. The described offence is serious. It is not just a case of an unruly, high-spirited child, but almost certainly of an uncontrollable young adult. The law specifies several offences, including stubbornness, rebellion,[29] persistent disobedience, drunkenness and social delinquency. Such behaviour both squandered the family's substance and was an infectious bad example. If the son in this law was the firstborn son (as in the immediately

---

[29] The words 'stubborn and rebellious' are frequently used elsewhere to refer to Israel's own disobedient response to the LORD. It has been suggested that Deuteronomy deliberately 'preaches' this case in these terms as a way of impressing on Israel what their own behaviour as the LORD's 'son' deserved.

preceding law), then his incorrigible extravagance was endangering the whole family and its future. For if this was how he behaved as a minor, what would become of the family's substance when he inherited it? As Old Testament law reveals elsewhere, the welfare of every family was the concern of the whole community. That is why this case becomes a community problem and no longer just an internal domestic matter. Such behaviour threatened a family in Israel; if not dealt with, it also threatened the whole community.

7. The penalty reflects the seriousness of the offence for Israel. It was a covenant crime, an offence against the fifth commandment, and therefore against God himself. It therefore threatened to bring judgment on the whole covenant community and so had to be purged away. Now of course we are aware that no state today stands in the same theocratic or covenantal relationship with God as did Israel. So the form of the penalty in Israel, reflecting that reality and its 'criminal' implications, cannot of course be advocated for such behaviour today. Nevertheless, the law and its penalty in Israel signals the seriousness of the nature of the offence described (incorrigible, wasteful and destructive antisocial behaviour), and suggests that there are grounds for supporting some degree of severity and deterrence in the law's response to serious young adult criminality.

Needs and rights

Another feature of Israel's law in the Old Testament worth noting is the way it prioritizes human need over strict legal rights and claims. This is another aspect of the general principle that people matter more than things, but it is more subtle. It says that some people's needs and circumstances matter more (generate a greater moral urgency) than other people's legitimate claims. A few examples will illustrate the point:

1. *The need of a refugee slave, as against the claims of his owner (Deut. 23:15–16).* As pointed out elsewhere, this is a highly countercultural law. In all other societies where slavery has operated, the legal rights and claim of the slave-owner take priority. Running away is an offence. Harbouring a runaway is an offence. Israel, however, not only *prohibits* sending the slave back, but *commands* that the slave be allowed to find refuge in any place of his own choosing.[30] The need of the weaker party is given priority over the legal right of the stronger.

---

[30] The phrase echoes YHWH's own freedom to cause his name to dwell in the place of his own choosing. Such is the powerful theological resonance of this remarkable law.

2. *The need of a female prisoner, as against the rights of a soldier (Deut. 21:10–14).* Here is another law, which at first reading wrinkles our noses. We want to say that there should not be wars, and there should not be prisoners, and women should not be captured. Doubtless. But Deuteronomy's legal and pastoral strategy is to deal with the world where such things were realities, and then to mitigate the worst effects for those caught up in them. So the law permitted the victorious soldier to take a woman from among the captives. However, first of all he might only take her as his fully legal wife with all the responsibilities that gave him and the rights it gave her. That might make him pause and consider carefully the implications of his actions. Rape or slavery are ruled out. Secondly, even having made her his wife, he is to give her a full month of adjustment after her traumatic experience before he may exercise the normal sexual right of a bridegroom. It seems that the law, in the midst of the nastiness of war, is trying to privilege the needs of the vulnerable (a woman, a foreigner, a captive) over the customary rights of the powerful (a man, a soldier, a victor, a husband).

3. *The need of a debtor, as against the legal claims of a creditor (Deut. 24:6, 10–13).* The Old Testament commends lending to the poor. And lending requires security; that is, debtors must provide collateral pledges for the loans they receive. Such is economic reality, accepted also in Israel. However, yet again, the law seems to align itself with the weaker party by requiring the creditor to respect the needs of the debtor. On the one hand, there is the debtor's need for daily bread, so the creditor must not deprive him of the means of making it (the domestic millstone). On the other hand, there is the debtor's need for shelter and warmth, so the creditor must not take basic clothing as security. And even the need of the poor for dignity and privacy is to be respected: the creditor is not to barge into the debtor's home, but must remain outside and allow the debtor to choose what he will offer in pledge. Such laws may seem almost petty, but they side with human needs and soften the exercise of legitimate rights and claims.

4. *The need of the landless, as against the legal property of the landowner (Deut. 24:19–22).* The law concerning gleaning in the fields, olive groves and vineyards is also found in Leviticus 19:9–10. Those who possessed land, and had done all the hard work of clearing, ploughing, sowing and harvesting might feel entitled to 100% of the produce of their own labour. But these instructions counteract such an attitude and remind the Israelite landholder that the LORD is the ultimate landlord and reserves the right to insist that all Israelites should 'eat and be satisfied'. So the needs of the landless poor are upheld by granting them freedom to glean, and insisting that the harvesters ensure plenty of gleanings left to be gathered. Once again, human need is brought to the forefront as a moral priority that relativizes the personal benefits of landownership. To these

laws we might add the similar compassionate provision that puts the need of the hungry before the rights of private property – allowing a person to satisfy hunger in the field or vineyard of a neighbour, but within clear limits (Deut. 23:24–25).

Doubtless all of these arrangements were vulnerable to abuse – either by being wrongly exploited by the poor themselves, or by being ignored by the powerful. But the attitude and principle behind them seems clear and important: the law inculcates an ethos in which even the law itself, and the rights and claims it gives to people, must yield to the realities of human need. There is a highly relational and situational dynamic at work within Israel's scale of values as seen in their legal codes. This, of course, reflects exactly what we found to be true in the last chapter in relation to Israel's understanding of righteousness and justice.

Theological reflections

At the beginning of this chapter I insisted on the need to work at understanding Old Testament law from within, rather than imposing on it a dogmatic framework forged in the controversies of the New Testament era, or the later formulations of Christian traditions. However, now that I have completed my far from adequate attempt to survey some aspects of the law as it functioned in Israelite society, let us stand back and reflect theologically on the significance of this material in relation to the whole canon of Scripture, including the New Testament. What theological presuppositions should govern Christian ethical use of Old Testament law? It would be hard to ask a question more open to multiple and mutually contradictory answers. Just documenting the options would fill another chapter (and indeed, chapters 12 and 13 below offer a survey of some of them). All I can reasonably do, therefore, is to set out what seem to me to be guiding assumptions for the way I believe it is appropriate for Christians to bring Old Testament law to bear on their mission and ethics in God's world. What follows, therefore, is a personal perspective, offered in the hope that the reader will imitate the example of the Bereans and eagerly search the Scriptures to see if it rings true (Acts 17:11). The questions to ask are these: Is this approach consistent with the overall witness of the canon? And is it helpful and fruitful in releasing the ethical impact of the Old Testament law in our own moral strivings and dilemmas? Here, then, are some basic presuppositions that govern my own approach as a Christian to handling Old Testament law. This list summarizes some of the key perspectives already articulated elsewhere in the book, particularly in chapters 1 and 2.

Hermeneutical steps in the canonical context

1. *The authority and relevance of the Old Testament for Christians.* I take 2 Timothy 3:15–17 as an axiomatic starting point for canonical reflection on the law: 'from infancy you have known the holy Scriptures, which are able to make you wise for salvation through faith in Christ Jesus. All Scripture is God-breathed and is useful for teaching, rebuking, correcting and training in righteousness, so that the man of God may be thoroughly equipped for every good work.' This text affirms that the Scriptures (by which was meant the Old Testament Scriptures, including without doubt the *tôrâ*) are 'God-breathed'. Because of this divine origin they are both savingly effective and ethically relevant. This New Testament text agrees with the unselfconscious affirmation of dual authorship of the law (human and divine) found in Ezra 7:6 – 'the Law of Moses, which the LORD, the God of Israel, had given'. The question therefore is not *whether* the Old Testament law has authority and relevance for us as Christians, but *how* that given authority is to be earthed and that relevance applied. The question of how we are to understand the meaning of authority in relation to the Old Testament is discussed in more depth in chapter 14 below.

2. *The unity of Scripture.* This is not to affirm a flat identity between the two Testaments, or to overlook the diversity within the Testaments and the crucial developments between them. Rather, I believe that the organic unity and continuity of God's work of revelation and redemption in history, from the call of Abraham to the return of Christ, is the fundamental key to understanding the whole grand-narrative of the biblical canon. That overarching unity of the narrative is a greater reality than the historical eras, covenantal articulations and changing cultural contexts at each stage of its outworking. Therefore, discerning the unity of the narrative exercises hermeneutical priority over isolating its parts. By analogy, one might point to the unity and continuity of a single human life. In trying to understand a human being, that unique, unifying continuity of the living person is of greater importance than the multiple differences of context, understanding, motives, behaviour and so on. that mark each period of the person's life – infancy, childhood, adolescence, adulthood, old age. Of course, there are significant differences between each stage of the story. But it is the totality and unity of the whole story of my life that makes me who I am.

Furthermore, it seems vital to affirm that this story is our story. Being a Christian is to locate oneself by faith within the narrative of the Bible – both looking back in grateful faith to all God has done for our salvation and looking forward with expectant faith to all the story assures us lies ahead for God's people and God's creation. So then, what God said and did in Old Testament Israel matters to us as Christians because it is part of the way we have been saved; it is part of our story and part of the story of the salvation of humanity and the creation itself. Similarly, therefore, what God required of Israel ethically must speak to us also, because of the moral consistency of God and the continuity of the people of God to whom we, along with them, belong.

Having affirmed this basic unity and continuity, we must also, of course, recognize the balancing discontinuity as well, but see it in proper perspective. It seems to me that there is a continuity and discontinuity in biblical *ethics* as regards the *law* that is analogous to the continuity and discontinuity in biblical *theology* as regards *redemption*. In relation to the story of redemption we can see the correspondence between the 'new thing' in Christ and the 'former things'. With Peter we can say, '*this* [the events of Easter and Pentecost] is *that* [what the prophets were talking about]' (Acts 2:16, AV; my italics). In the same way, we know that neither we nor our personal ancestors were literally delivered from slavery in Egypt (discontinuity), but we recognize *the redemptive purpose of the same God*, to whose victory in the cross and resurrection of Jesus we attribute our own redemption (continuity). Thus, we can use the story and metaphors of exodus to describe our own experience of salvation. We did not participate in the story historically (discontinuity), but we certainly share it spiritually and even more fully in Christ (continuity).

In the same way, in relation to the law and ethics, we may not have an ox threshing our corn in our backyard, so we will not feel addressed or bound by the letter of Deuteronomy 25:4 (discontinuity). Nevertheless, we can appreciate the objective of that law and perceive the moral principle at work in it – a working animal should be allowed to feed from what it is producing for your table. So we can understand the Christian application made by Paul in a particular situation in 1 Corinthians 9:7–12, applying the principle of the law to working missionaries. 'Doesn't the Law say the same thing? For it is written in the Law of Moses . . . Surely he says this for us, doesn't he? Yes, this was written for us, because . . .' Paul's hermeneutical assumption is that we can recognize *the moral will of the same God* behind the specific, culture-related Israelite injunction and the principle that he applies to practical rights and responsibilities within the Christian church (continuity).

3. *The priority of grace.* The foundation of biblical faith and ethics in *both* testaments is God's grace and redemptive initiative. The law was not given as a means of salvation, but as a gift of grace to those whom God had already redeemed.[31] This drives us back again to the importance of the narrative

---

[31] Thus I cannot accept a rigid separation of law and grace as a valid way of categorizing the difference between the Old and New Testaments, still less the setting of one

context within which the law is given (or, more correctly, the narrative structure of the whole of what Israel considered its Torah). For that narrative is fundamentally a narrative of grace – the grace of the LORD's faithfulness to his promise, the LORD's compassion for his suffering people, the LORD's righteous judgment on their oppressors and the LORD's sustaining and protecting power in the wilderness. As I emphasized in chapter 1, it is essential to set all our study of Old Testament ethics (including the law) within this framework. Anything else is a distortion, and indeed a betrayal. As the father was instructed to answer his son's enquiry about the meaning of the law, in Deuteronomy 6:20–25, the very meaning of the law is to be found in the 'gospel' – the old, old story of YHWH and his love.

Another way of expressing this is to point out that Old Testament law was covenantal. That is to say, the covenant relationship stood behind and was prior to the law itself. The whole law, especially as summed up in the Decalogue, enshrines both the vertical and the horizontal dimensions integral to the covenant: God's redemptive initiative and Israel's responsive obedience, expressed in love for God and for one another.

This covenant dimension also provides the bridge between the status of the law in the Old Testament and the use made of it, particularly of the Decalogue, in the New. We are not dealing with some universal moral law imposed externally and equally upon Israel and the church. It is rather the continuity of *relationship* between God and God's people and the nature of that relationship which is the constant factor. Although we speak of old and new covenants, in both cases we are dealing with *covenant relationship*, and in both cases it is the prior action of the same God in redemptive grace that calls for our response of love and ethical obedience.

In Christ we are granted that intimate covenant relationship with God to which the Old Testament law pointed. Even the pre-Christ experience of it filled devout Israelites with joy. We need to remind ourselves again (as at the beginning of this chapter) that the ancient Israelite looked on the law not as a burden, but as a gift of grace, a delight, precisely because of the warm and personal relationship with the LORD that it enabled and expressed (see Pss. 19; 119). But also in Christ that part of the promise of the *new* covenant which related to the law is fulfilled in us:

---

against the other – except in terms of the specific argumentation of Paul against a *distorted* view of both. Similarly, while appreciating much that goes by the name 'covenant theology', I prefer not to speak of a so-called 'covenant of works', even hypothetically. I do not believe such a thing ever existed. I am in agreement here with Kaiser Jr, 'God's Promise Plan', pp. 293–295.

I will put my law in their minds
and write it on their hearts.

(Jer. 31:33)

So while we Christians are certainly no longer 'under the law' (Rom. 3:19; 6:14) (we are not bound by the law of the old covenant as a defining mark of our membership of the ethnic community of ancient Israel), we are nevertheless not 'without the law' (1 Cor. 9:21) (as though the law had nothing whatever to say to us about our behaviour). Rather, the power of the indwelling Spirit makes it possible 'that *the righteous requirements of the law* might be fully met in us, who . . . live . . . *according to the Spirit*' (Rom. 8:4; my italics). The indwelling Spirit, far from removing us from any connection with the law, actually enables us to live in the way the law originally intended the Israelites to. And the principal fruit of the Spirit is love, which is the fulfilling of the law, especially of the Ten Commandments (Rom. 13:8–10). For to love God wholly and exclusively and to love your neighbour as yourself constitute the very essence of the law and the prophets. But both of these are ultimately possible only within the freedom of the new covenant relationship in Christ and in the power of the Spirit. Only, in other words, on the basis of God's grace. So the law has abiding theological and ethical validity, as Christ himself affirmed (Matt. 5:17–20). This is not because of what the law is in itself, but because of what it was the expression of, and response to; namely, a redeemed, covenant relationship with God founded upon his initiative of grace.[32]

4. *The mission of Israel.* Much ink has been spilt (and, I might add, much blood, sweat and tears, as well) trying to answer the question (from a Christian perspective) 'Why the law?' The answer would have been much more straight-

---

[32] Elmer Martens, 'Old Testament Land', stresses both the narrative context and the covenant context in handling Old Testament law, and then also emphasizes Jesus and the New Testament as the final context. Each of these 'spiralling' contexts exercises priority over the law and prevents us absolutizing it, or treating it in dogmatic isolation.

The setting of the laws within covenant returns us to the acknowledgment that back of the laws is the covenant, back of the covenant is God's salvific act, and back of God's salvific act is God himself, whose intrinsic holiness colors whatever is said about covenant obligations. (pp. 205–206)

Interpretive decisions on ethics require attention to the biblical theological context, namely: (1) story, (2) covenant, (3) law, and (4) the Christ-event. In other words, in regard to laws, covenant trumps laws, story trumps covenant, and Jesus Christ trumps all. (p. 212)

forward if we had paused to ask the prior question 'Why Israel?' For, to understand the purpose of the *law* it is vital to enquire first about the role of *Israel* in God's purposes. It was, after all, to Israel that God gave this law. This takes us back to the argument developed in chapter 2 concerning the mission of Israel. God created and called Israel to fulfil his purpose of blessing the nations. The covenant with Abram in Genesis 12:1–3 has this as its climax, and the phrase is repeated throughout the book of Genesis. There was a universal goal to the very existence of Israel. God's covenant commitment to Israel was dependent on, and an expression of, God's commitment to the rest of the nations of humanity as a whole. So therefore, what God did in, for, and through Israel was ultimately intended to be for the benefit of the nations. And furthermore, what God *ethically required* of Israel had the same universal breadth of reference. Genesis 18:19 states this clearly, when it links together in one sentence God's election of Abraham, the ethical demand to walk in the way of the LORD by doing righteousness and justice, and the ultimate missional goal – blessing the nations as promised. In other words, the election of Israel, in all its particularity, not only has a universal goal, but also leads to a clear and distinctive ethical agenda in the world for God's people as part of the condition of that goal being accomplished.

If the previous point had a backward perspective (that the law must be set within the context of the narrative of God's historical acts of redemption for Israel), this point has a forward perspective (that the law must be set within the context of God's eschatological mission of blessing the nations).

5. *The function of the law in relation to the mission of Israel.* If this, then, was God's purpose in creating Israel (that they should be the vehicle of his intentions for the nations), the giving of the law must be seen to serve that wider purpose. Exodus 19:1–6 is a key text at this point. Coming at the hinge between the exodus and the giving of the law and making of the covenant, it looks both backwards and forwards. It points back to the initiative of God's redemptive grace ('You have seen what I have done . . .') as the essential context for obedience to the law (as the Decalogue also does). But then it also points forward by giving to Israel an identity and role as a *priestly* and *holy* people in the midst of 'all the nations' in 'the whole earth'. Obedience to the covenant law was thus to enable Israel to be holy; that is, different, distinctive *from* the nations. But at the same time, as God's priesthood, Israel was to be teacher, model and mediator *for* the nations. Keeping the law, then, was not an end in itself for Israel, but was related to their very reason for existence – God's concern for the nations. Deuteronomy 4:5–8 sets Israel's social righteousness in the same context – the public stage of the world of nations. Israel's ethical system would be visible to, and raise admiration and questions among, the rest of the nations.

If we ask, then, whether Old Testament law was given specifically to Israel with particular relevance to them, or whether it was meant to apply to the nations as well in some sense, the answer is both. But this needs careful qualification. The law was not explicitly and consciously applied to the nations. But that does not mean it was irrelevant to them. Rather, the law was given to Israel to enable Israel to live as a model, as a light to the nations, such that, in the prophetic vision, the law would 'go forth' to the nations, or the nations would 'come up' to learn it from the LORD through Israel (Is. 2:2–5). The God who, as their redeemer, gave the law to Israel as his 'special possession' was also known to be the creator and ruler of all nations. The law is based on the assumption of Israel's accountability to the LORD as their covenant sovereign. But behind that stands the axiom of Old Testament creation faith that *all* people are morally accountable to the LORD as the one living God of all creation and history (see Ps. 33:8–15).[33]

6. *Israel and its law as paradigmatic.* Given, then, on the one hand, Israel's role in relation to God's purpose for the nations, and given, on the other hand, the law's function in relation to that mission of Israel, we can see that the law was designed (along with many other aspects of Israel's historical experience) to mould and shape Israel in certain clearly defined directions, within their own historical and cultural context. That overall social shape, with its legal and institutional structures, ethical norms and values and theological rationale, thus becomes the model or paradigm *that was intended* to have a relevance and application beyond the geographical, historical and cultural borders of Israel itself.[34] The particularity of Israel, then, becomes not a *hindrance* to wider application, but actually serves it. There is no need to repeat the explanations

---

[33] Further reflections on the universal relevance of Israel's law, with particular reference to the worship of the living God, ecological responsibility, respect for life, justice and sexual integrity are found in the wide-ranging article by Sidney Greidanus 'Universal Dimension of Law'. Greidanus's point (as my own), is that these are not just our retrospective interpretations of Old Testament law, but can be seen to have an intentional universality within the Old Testament text itself.

[34] R. E. Clements draws attention to this broad adaptability of Old Testament law, which, though he does not use the term 'paradigmatic', is similar in effect to the point I am making. 'What is remarkable in fact is the way in which the Old Testament has provided a system of *tora* – instruction, which has proved to be remarkably adaptable to a vast range of human social and political systems. Societies of dramatically different economic, political and cultural types have found within the Old Testament a richly viable source of social and moral teaching' (Clements, 'Christian Ethics', p. 22).

of my understanding of 'paradigm' (see chapter 2). My point here is that this paradigmatic nature of Israel is not just a hermeneutical tool devised by *us* retrospectively, but, theologically speaking, was part of God's design in creating and shaping Israel in the first place.

So there is, within the Old Testament itself, an awareness that the law given in a unique way to Israel as a unique people had wider relevance for the rest of humanity. That is, we assume that if God gave Israel certain specific institutions and laws, they were based on principles that have universal validity. This does not mean that Christians will try to impose by law in a secular state provisions lifted directly from the laws of Moses. It does mean that they will work to bring their society nearer to conformity with the overall paradigmatic structure of principles underlying the concrete laws of Old Testament society, because they perceive the same God to be both the redeemer and law-giver of Israel, and also creator and ruler of all people. This approach and assumption, then, is concerned with the implication, not just the application, of Old Testament law. It releases the ethical *potential* of the law, without short-circuiting the task of working at *actual* practical applications in varying cultural contexts. It does not guarantee or predetermine the results of such outworking. But it does justify, and indeed necessitate, the task itself.

Ethical steps towards the contemporary context

How, then, are we to go about that task? What are the steps we should take in seeking to move from the world of Old Testament law to the world of contemporary ethical objectives and choices? Consistently with the path taken so far through this chapter, the first three steps below are taken within the world of Old Testament Israel itself, seeking to understand the law we are studying from within. Only then, in the fourth step, do we deliberately step out of that world into our own to wrestle with contemporary relevance.

1. *Distinguish the different kinds of law in the text.* Here we go back to the second major section above, and seek to classify any given law or group of laws we are studying according to the different kinds of laws that existed in Israelite culture. This may not always be entirely clear, and indeed it may seem that some laws will fit more than one category. But that does not greatly matter. The exercise in itself will help us gain greater understanding of the law in its own context. The important thing is that in order to make ethical use of the Old Testament we must first step inside it and understand the law from Israel's own social perspective. It is immediately clear that we do not find a separate, textually isolated, category of 'moral law' as such. But we do find moral motivation, rationale, objectives and values, sometimes expressed and sometimes implied, in every category of law we identify.

2. *Analyse the social function and relative status of particular laws and institutions.* When dealing with any particular law, we need to ask how it related to and functioned within the overall social system of Israel. Is it central or peripheral to the dominant themes and social objectives we find in the rest of the material? Is it a primary expression of key values and priorities, or does it reinforce other such primary legislation? Or is it a modification or a secondary application? This is where the importance of seeing the overall social shape of Israel really counts. It also highlights the importance of recognizing Israel's scale of values, as discussed above. Such enquiry prevents us from treating every text with flat equality and enables us to discern those laws or values that were treated with greater priority in Israel itself. This ought to give us some guidance in our own scale of relative moral values. It will help us to organize and prioritize whatever ethical deductions we may wish to make from specific texts. It also helps us to avoid the tendency to jump straight from any particular legal text to the question 'How does this text (in isolation) apply to modern society?'

Such analytical and descriptive work does not come cheaply. It calls for an awareness of the fields of Old Testament economics, politics, sociology, legal history and so on. But there is no short cut to careful understanding of the historical context of Israel's law, if we are to take seriously the way by which God has given us his Word.[35] In this respect, Old Testament ethics has to take into account the whole social world of Israel in the same way that New Testament ethics now looks not just at the biblical text alone but the whole social, economic and political context of the first Christians.[36]

3. *Define the objective(s) of the law in Israelite society.* Laws in any society are made for a purpose. Laws protect interests. Laws restrict power. Laws try to balance the rights of different and possibly competing groups in society. Laws promote social objectives according to the legislators' vision of what kind of ideal society they would like to see. So, in the light of our understanding of Israelite society, we need to articulate as precisely as possible the objective of any specific law. In other words, we are trying to understand 'Why was this law there?' This can best be done by addressing a number of questions to the laws we are studying and trying to identify and articulate plausible answers. Remembering to keep ancient biblical Israel in focus, such questions might include the following:

---

[35] This is not the place to embark on the range of materials in these fields, but helpful surveys are found in R. E. Clements (ed.), *World of Ancient Israel*; and V. H. Matthews, 'Social-Scientific Approaches'.

[36] See Wayne Meeks, *Moral World of First Christians*.

- What kind of situation was this law trying to promote, or prevent?
- Whose interests was this law aiming to protect?
- Who would have benefited from this law and why?
- Whose power was this law trying to restrict and how did it do so?
- What rights and responsibilities were embodied in this law?
- What kind of behaviour did this law encourage or discourage?
- What vision of society motivated this law?
- What moral principles, values or priorities did this law embody or instantiate?
- What motivation did this law appeal to?
- What sanction or penalty (if any) was attached to this law, and what does that show regarding its relative seriousness or moral priority?

Now of course there are times when the obscurity of some laws defeats even such questioning. We may remain doubtful whether we have really uncovered the objectives or rationale of certain laws. But again that does not greatly matter in the relatively few cases where it may be true. More often the sheer exercise of asking such questions and thinking through the possible answers generates a more nuanced understanding of the purpose of Israel's laws in their own context. And that then enables a much more targeted application of them when we move to the final step.

4. *Preserve the objective but change the context.* Moving at last quite deliberately from the Old Testament world back to our own, we can ask a parallel set of questions about our own context. In the light of the issues we have observed in Israel's social context and how their laws addressed them, we can seek to identify comparable situations, interests, needs, powers, rights, behaviours and so on. that need to be addressed in our own society. Then in that new context (our own contemporary world) we ask how the objectives of Old Testament laws can be achieved. Or we ask how we can bring our own social ethical objectives to point in the same direction. At this point, of course, we cannot avoid getting into the realm of specific policy and action in our world. And there will be room for differences of opinion, and varying political options and moral choices. However, we are now engaging with our context equipped not merely with highly generalized and abstract principles but with much more sharply articulated objectives derived from the paradigm of the society God called Israel to be.

Such a procedure may help to bridge the gap between, on the one hand, an authoritative biblical text we often find cannot be directly applied because it was addressed to a context alien to ours, and, on the other hand, general moral principles we may like to claim to be 'biblical', but which do not possess the intrinsic authority of the biblical text itself. The authority of Scripture is that which authorizes us to develop our ethical stances, policy choices and decision-making in new contexts not directly addressed by the Bible. The authority of the Old Testament for ethics does not predefine every choice we have to make. But the more sharply we can articulate the very particularity of Israel and understand the reasons for the laws they had, the more confident we can be in making 'authorized' ethical choices; that is, choices that are legitimate within the contours and limits of the paradigm God has given us.

The limitations of the law for ethics
Our last reflection on the ethical relevance of the law is more cautionary. There is an awareness in the Old Testament itself that the law is limited in its capacity for sustaining righteousness and justice in society, if there is determination to avoid its demands. This brings some limiting realism to those who would put all the eggs of their concern for social justice in the basket of legislative reform – either by attacking laws they regard as dangerously 'permissive', or by promoting laws they deem morally 'protective'. This is not in the least to deny the value of the work of Christians in this field of legislative reform. We have seen the depths of God's concern, witnessed in the Old Testament, that the laws of any society should reflect justice and compassion. My point is simply that society cannot be preserved or reformed by force of law alone. Gordon Wenham has a helpful discussion of the distinction we need to make between ethical ideals and social legislation.

> In most societies what the law enforces is not the same as what upright members of that society feel is socially desirable let alone ideal. There is a link between moral ideals and law, but law tends to be a pragmatic compromise between the legislators' ideals and what can be enforced in practice. The law enforces a minimum standard of behaviour . . . ethics is much more than keeping the law. Or to put it in biblical terms righteousness involves more than living by the Decalogue and the other laws in the Pentateuch.[37]

In the Old Testament there are three aspects of this awareness. First, just laws may be unjustly used, or simply ignored. Amos 2:6 accused unscrupulous creditors of actions that were probably technically legal. People were being taken into a form of debt-slavery as a 'working pledge' for unpaid debts. The law allowed for this. But it seems this was being imposed for trifling debts and with callous disregard for the poor or their families. Likewise, the creditors Nehemiah tackled (Neh. 5:1–13) were probably using the legal technique of the

---

[37] Wenham, *Story as Torah*, p. 80.

redemption of land from impoverished kinsmen to their own greedy benefit. Nehemiah appealed to their *consciences*, not to a court of law or any legal statute (except that prohibiting the charging of interest, which was making the burden even heavier and reducing people to debt-slavery all the quicker).

Secondly, those with sufficient power and influence could promulgate unjust laws to their own advantage. Oppression can be given a semblance of legality by unscrupulous legislators. Isaiah observed this extra bitter burden that was borne by the oppressed of his day:

> Woe to those who make unjust laws,
>   to those who issue oppressive decrees,
> to deprive the poor of their rights
>   and rob my oppressed people of justice,
> making widows their prey
>   and robbing the fatherless.
>
> (Is. 10:1–2)

The psalmist gives powerful expression to a similar complaint about legalized oppression on the part of corrupt rulers:

> Can a corrupt throne be allied with you –
>   one that brings on misery by its decrees?
>
> (Ps. 94:20)

Thirdly, mere changing of the law or invoking of old laws is an inadequate remedy, once injustice has taken deep root and become structurally ingrained and 'naturalized' in a society. In Jeremiah 34, for example, the wealthy and powerful proved themselves unable to fulfil a promise they had made to obey the ancient law on slave release, even after much prophetic exhortation and an abortive attempt to do so. Presumably, the whole exercise turned out to be too costly to be continued, and their economic heads silenced their fleetingly charitable (and obedient) hearts. This is the only occasion where a prophet appears to have campaigned for the enforcement of a specific statute law in circumstances of social and economic oppression. For the most part, the prophets see only two possibilities before the people: either God's direct judgment on a corrupt and incorrigible society, or else a *spiritual* change of heart, which only God could give (Ezek. 18:31; 36:26–27).

So again we see the prior necessity of experiencing God's grace, redemptive or restorative, if genuine social justice is to be established, maintained or restored. The law by itself cannot achieve those ends. Justice flows from the knowledge of *God*, not merely from knowledge of the *law*.

Further reading

Barr, James, 'Biblical Law and the Question of Natural Theology', in Timo Veijola (ed.), *The Law in the Bible and in Its Environment* (Göttingen: Vandenhoeck & Ruprecht, 1990), pp. 1–22.

Bruckner, James K., 'The Creational Context of Law before Sinai: Law and Liberty in Pre-Sinai Narratives and Romans 7', *Ex Auditu* 11 (1995), pp. 91–110.

Clements, R. E. (ed.), *The World of Ancient Israel: Sociological, Anthropological and Political Perspectives* (Cambridge: Cambridge University Press, 1989).

Gemser, B., 'The Importance of the Motive Clause in Old Testament Law', in *Congress Volume in Memoriam Aage Bentzen*, Supplements to *Vetus Testamentum*, vol. 1 (Leiden: E. J. Brill, 1953), pp. 50–66.

Gerstenberger, Erhard, '". . . He/They Shall Be Put to Death": Life-Preserving Divine Threats in Old Testament Law', *Ex Auditu* 11 (1995), pp. 43–61.

Greidanus, Sidney, 'The Universal Dimension of Law in the Hebrew Scriptures', *Studies in Religion* 14 (1985), pp. 39–51.

Hays, J. Daniel, 'Applying the Old Testament Law Today', *Bibliotheca Sacra* 158 (2001), pp. 21–35.

Hesselink, I. John, 'John Calvin on the Law and Christian Freedom', *Ex Auditu* 11 (1995), pp. 77–89.

Janzen, Waldemar, *Old Testament Ethics: A Paradigmatic Approach* (Louisville, KY: Westminster John Knox, 1994).

Kaiser Jr, Walter C., *Toward Old Testament Ethics* (Grand Rapids: Zondervan, 1983).

Martens, Elmer A., 'How Is the Christian to Construe Old Testament Law?' *Bulletin for Biblical Research* 12 (2002), pp. 199–216.

McBride Jr, S. Dean, 'The Yoke of Torah', *Ex Auditu* 11 (1995), pp. 1–15.

Patrick, Dale, *Old Testament Law* (Atlanta: John Knox, 1985).

Taylor, Robert D., and Ricci, Ronald J., 'Three Biblical Models of Liberty and Some Representative Laws', *Ex Auditu* 11 (1995), pp. 111–127.

Tucker, Gene M., 'The Law in the Eighth-Century Prophets', in Tucker, Petersen and Wilson, *Canon, Theology and Old Testament Interpretation*, pp. 201–216.

Wright, Christopher J. H., *Deuteronomy*, New International Biblical Commentary, Old Testament Series (Peabody: Hendrickson; Carlisle: Paternoster, 1996).

10. CULTURE AND FAMILY

For all that Israel was called to be a holy nation, for all that they could be described in the words of Balaam's oracles as a 'people who live apart / and do not consider themselves one of the nations' (Num. 23:9), it is important to remember that they were not a 'clean slate'. Israel did not live in vacuum-sealed isolation from the rest of humanity. On the contrary, they were an ancient people in a world of nations. They lived at the geographical cross-roads of the already ancient civilizations of the Nile and of Mesopotamia, whose tides of influence ebbed and flowed across them throughout their history. And they lived in the midst of the particular Canaanite or West Semitic culture that bordered the eastern Mediterranean. So there were countless points of common culture, social norms and conventions shared by Israel and her contemporaries. The question posed for our ethical enquiry is, 'How did Israel's religious faith relate to and interact with this social and cultural area of life?' This is a question that exercises the minds of missiologists also (though it is unfortunately more commonly addressed to the New Testament than to the Old, even though the issues are in principle similar). What is the relationship between the gospel (the story of God's saving action and all that it entails) and culture (the ever-changing patterns of historical human existence)?[1]

---

[1] A basic survey of some of the issues of culture, worldviews and the biblical faith is provided by David Burnett, *Clash of Worlds*. Donald Senior and Carroll Stuhlmueller,

Simple answers in so complex a field are perilous, but some broad classification of the spectrum of Israel's responses to surrounding contemporary culture may be attempted. One can discern a range that moves from outright rejection and prohibition of some customs, through toleration with careful regulation of others, to critical affirmation of others, with 'value added' theological interpretation. We shall look at each of these three responses in its Old Testament context and then raise a few pointers to their relevance for Christian ethics. On the way we shall look in detail at one feature of human life common to all cultures – kinship and family, to see how Israel built theology and ethics around the particular cultural manifestation of family that was at the heart of their own society, and how those Old Testament perspectives relate to New Testament and Christian ethics.

Rejection and prohibition

Some practices of ancient cultures contemporary with Israel are portrayed as abhorrent to God and were accordingly prohibited to Israel. The clearest articulation of the requirement that Israel be distinctive from such ways is the double prohibition in Leviticus 18:3, 'You must not do as they do in Egypt, where you used to live, and you must not do as they do in the land of Canaan, where I am bringing you. Do not follow their practices.'

Most of those cultural practices specifically prohibited in the law were connected directly or indirectly with Canaanite religion, and the prohibitions related not only to their inherent wickedness but to their connection with the snare of idolatry and 'other gods'. The adoption of any of the accoutrements of the religion of Canaan was prohibited with uncompromising severity. The unceasing struggle of the prophets over this issue, however, shows how difficult Israel seems to have found it to resist the worship of the old gods of the land.

The social side effects of Canaanite religion come under similar condemnation. The practice of cultic prostitution was outlawed, along with a variety of other kinds of sexual perversion. All kinds of occult practice were prohibited, including spiritism, mediums, witchcraft, necromancy and divination. Probably

---

Biblical Foundations for Mission, offer more historico-critically focused reflections on the engagement of biblical faith and culture in the biblical period itself. David J. Bosch, *Transforming Mission*, carries the issue forward through developing eras of the Christian church and the different paradigms that have emerged for understanding mission in relation to both faith and culture.

the rationale behind the ban on some cultural practices that seem obscure to us now lay in their connection with perverted Canaanite religious cults (e.g. certain forms of cutting the hair or beard, ritual mutilation, cross-dressing etc.). The greatest horror was reserved for the practice of child sacrifice, regarded by Deuteronomy as the worst manifestation of this 'detestable' worship (Deut. 12:31). The range of practices prohibited and the depth of feeling against them can be assessed by reading through the references in the footnote.[2]

First, if Israel absorbed these features of her surrounding culture, rather than resisting and destroying them, Israel would cease to be distinctive. And that would be to forfeit the very reason for their election. As Deuteronomy 7:1–10 makes clear, the command that Israel should reject and destroy the religious culture of Canaan was based first of all on who they (Israel) were – the people called to be holy to the LORD (v. 6). But that in turn was based on what God had done for them – God had redeemed them out of slavery (v. 8). And that act of God, finally, was based upon God's own inexplicable love and faithfulness towards them and their ancestors (vv. 9–10).[3] What they must *not* imagine was that any of this was due to their numerical (or indeed cultural) superiority – quite the opposite. So, when in the course of their history Israel did in fact go the way of the Canaanites, with all the cultural and religious degradation this involved, it was not just a sad cultural decline, but a fundamental theological denial. It denied all Israel were chosen, called and redeemed for.

But secondly, if Israel went the way of the Canaanites by adopting their abhorrent practices, they would expose themselves to the same divine judgment as their present practitioners. The Canaanites were about to be 'vomited out' of the land, such was the divine revulsion at these aspects of their 'culture' (Lev. 18:25). The same standard of judgment would be applied to Israel, and the land would be quite capable of repeating its purgative performance (Lev. 18:28). Israel's holiness and Canaanite practices could not be mixed.

Qualified toleration

Some customs and practices common in the ancient world were tolerated within Israel, without explicit divine command or sanction, but with a developing

---

[2] Exod. 22:18; 23:24; Lev. 18:21–30; 19:26–29, 31; 20:2–6, 22–23, 27; Deut. 12:29–31; 18:9–13; 22:5; 23:1, 17–18.

[3] For a discussion of the remarkable shape of Deut. 7, with destruction of Canaanite religion in its outer framework, and yet the eternal, self-definitive love of God at its heart, see C. J. H. Wright, *Deuteronomy*, pp. 108–119.

theological critique that regarded them as falling short of God's highest standards. The customs in question were then regulated by legal safeguards in such a way as to soften or eliminate their worst effects. In this category one could place for brief discussion, polygamy, divorce and slavery. Probably one could also include monarchy in this bracket also (discussed in chapter 7), as an institution permitted though not commanded by God, and limited by a critique that indicated strong disagreement with the way it was practised in surrounding cultures.

Polygamy

Polygamy is certainly present in the Old Testament, but its extent should not be exaggerated. Examples are almost entirely confined to kings or those in positions of leadership or prestige of some kind. And even in these cases, with a few notable exceptions such as Solomon, mostly bigamy rather than polygamy is evidenced. Monogamy seems to have been the common practice of the populace.

The patriarchs are sometimes held up as examples of polygamy, a fact that causes wry amusement to some when the patriarchal marriages are cited as paragons of monogamous fidelity in the marriage service of the Book of Common Prayer! But we must distinguish between polygamy (having more than one *wife*) and concubinage. The difference may seem immaterial to us, but it was an immense social distinction in the ancient world. A concubine was a slave woman, normally bought like other slaves. The relation of concubine to master was quite different, legally and socially, from that of wife to husband. With that in mind, we realize that, strictly speaking in terms of ancient culture, Abraham and Isaac were both *monogamous*, while Jacob, who actually *wanted* only one wife, ended up with four women in his life (two wives and two concubines) by a combination of trickery and jealousy.

'But it was not this way from the beginning' (Matt. 19:8). These words spoken by Jesus about divorce could equally be applied to polygamy. For the creation narrative clearly implies a monogamous 'one-flesh' relationship between one man and one woman (Gen. 2:24). To this could be added passages in the Wisdom literature that advocate, or at least would seem to presuppose, faithful monogamy (Prov. 5:15–20; 18:22; 31:10–31; Song). And monogamy as the theological and ethical ideal seems clearly presupposed in the way marriage was used as a metaphor for the *exclusive* relationship between the LORD and Israel. Notwithstanding this theological awareness that polygamy was short of ideal, it was tolerated in Israel as a social custom. But there were laws, as we shall now see, that sought to limit polygamy's potentially exploitative effects on women.

As mentioned above, the status of a concubine was far inferior to that of a wife, yet the legal rights of concubines were explicitly laid down in Exodus

21:7–11. A concubine could not be resold by her owner: she was to be treated as only one man's concubine, not a family plaything of father and son. If the man took another concubine, he must not deprive the first one of material provision and sexual rights. Now if these were the legal rights of *concubines*, the rights of *wives* in a polygamous situation cannot have been less. Deuteronomy 21:10–14 likewise protects the rights of a female captive of war who is taken as a wife (whether as a first or as an additional wife is not stated, but it is made clear that she is to be married as a *wife*, not simply taken as a slave). This unfortunate woman was to be treated with humanity and sensitivity and she was not to be treated as a slave. The inheritance law of Deuteronomy 21:15–17 tacitly acknowledges the prime criticism of bigamy, which is that a man cannot love two women equally, or rather that one may end up not being loved at all. It then goes on to protect the unloved wife from the ignominy of having her son, if the firstborn, deprived of his inheritance. The story of Elkanah and his rival wives (1 Sam. 1), although hardly written for the primary purpose of criticizing bigamy, may well have such a critique as a subtheme. Certainly, it is a vivid illustration of the potential agonies bigamy can produce. (Though, of course, Hannah's main suffering was not that she was a second wife, but that she was childless. The taunting presence of the other wife, however, made the distress even worse.)[4]

Divorce

Polygamy, then, was tolerated without explicit approval, but with legal safeguards that were latent criticisms of it. *Divorce*, on the other hand, was also tolerated, but with eventual explicit disapproval. Divorce hardly features in Old Testament law at all, for the reason that, unlike modern Western custom, neither marriage nor divorce was a matter for civil law in biblical Israel. They fell within the 'family law' jurisdiction of the head of a household (see chapter 9 for definitions of these categories of law). A man did not have to 'go to court' to get a divorce. Those laws that do refer to divorce are concerned

---

[4] For many Christians in the West, the issue of polygamy may seem remote. It could be said, however, that the high rate and frequency of divorce in the West amounts to a kind of serial polygamy, which is morally no better (and arguably worse) than parallel polygamy in some cultures. For the African churches, in the midst of cultures where polygamy is much more common and normal, this is a matter that has been considered in great depth, and with a combination of biblical theology and pastoral sensitivity. See the finely argued position laid out by David Gitari, 'Church and Polygamy', which was adopted as the official stance of the Anglican Church of Kenya, and is similar to Christian positions on the matter in other parts of Africa.

either with circumstances where divorce is prohibited or with regulating relationships *after* divorce has already happened. In both cases the protection of the woman seems to be the main point of the law.

The first is Deuteronomy 22:28–29, where a man is prohibited from divorcing a woman he has been obliged to marry as a result of premarital intercourse. The law seems to take the view that for the woman the continued security of belonging within the home of even such a man was preferable to the parlous future that would await a woman divorced in such circumstances (her most likely fate would probably be either prostitution or destitution). The second is the regulation in Deuteronomy 24:1–4, the interpretation of which was a point of controversy between Jesus and the Pharisees. This law does not 'command' divorce; it presupposes that a divorce has happened. What it does require is that a man who divorces his wife must give her a 'bill of divorce'. This would have been for the woman's protection. It was documentary proof that she had been divorced, so neither she nor any future husband could be accused of adultery if she married again. This law also prohibited the first husband from taking her back if her next husband divorced her or died. There were probably ritual or cultural reasons for this limitation,[5] but its social and personal effect was to prevent a woman from becoming the victim of sexual football between feckless men. One might also mention again the case of the female prisoner of war whom an Israelite soldier decides to take as his wife. If the captor-husband later regrets his action, then the woman is to be properly divorced, not sold as a slave. He was not to make a financial profit out of his rash action. In this case, divorce appears as a lesser of two evils for the woman. At least divorce preserved some shreds of dignity and freedom of future choice for her, which would have been denied if she had been sold into slavery (Deut. 21:14).

So then, divorce also was tolerated, within legal limits. But it falls much further short of God's ideal than seems to have been the case with polygamy. On divorce there is the uncompromising attack of Malachi 2:13–16, culminating in the blunt denunciation '"I hate divorce," says the LORD God of Israel'. Nothing as sharply absolute as this, or with such powerful theological argument, is directed at polygamy. Presumably this is because, whereas polygamy is a kind of 'expansion' of marriage beyond the monogamous limit intended by God, divorce is a severing destruction of marriage. Divorce is 'covering oneself with violence', as Malachi puts it. Polygamy multiplies relationships where God intended a single relationship; but divorce destroys that relationship altogether.[6]

---

[5] See Gordon J. Wenham, 'Restoration of Marriage'.

[6] For a helpful survey of these and other issues in sexual ethics in ancient Israel, with a recent bibliography, see J. M. Sprinkle, 'Sexuality, Sexual Ethics'.

Slavery

The Old Testament, like the apostle Paul, receives a large measure of criticism for tolerating *slavery*, which it does. Slavery was such an integral part of the social, economic and institutional life of the ancient world contemporary with Old Testament Israel that it is difficult to see how Israel could have excluded it altogether or effectively abolished it. Nevertheless, two preliminary things can be said at once.

First, slavery in relatively small societies like Israel was qualitatively vastly different from slavery in the large imperial civilizations – the contemporary ancient Near Eastern empires, and especially the later empires of the Greeks and Romans. There the slave markets were glutted with captives of war and displaced peoples, and slaves were put to degrading and dehumanizing labour. And, of course, Israelite slavery was even more different from the ghastly commercialized and massive-scale slave trade that Arabs, Europeans and Americans perpetrated upon Africa. We must put out of our mind pictures such as the Roman galley slaves of *Ben Hur*, or the neck-irons, slave-ships and sugar plantations of modern black slavery when we read the word 'slave' in the Old Testament. It is not even the most helpful translation of the word *'ebed*, which basically meant a bonded worker, and in some circumstances could be a term of high office when applied to royal servants.

In the pastoral–agricultural society of Israel slaves were largely residential, domestic workers. In many cases they would have been debtors working off their debt through bonded labour to their creditor. They complemented, but were not a substitute for, the labour of free members of the household. The head of the household, his own children, other employees, and slaves all worked together. In other words, slave labour was not a means by which free Israelites were released from physical labour, as was the case in classical Greece, for example. Provided they were humanely treated (as the law required), such slavery could be said to be little different *experientially* from many kinds of paid employment in a cash economy. And the evidence shows, as we shall see below, that slaves in Israel had more legal rights and protection than in any contemporary society. Indeed, slaves enjoyed more explicit legal and economic security than the technically free, but landless, hired labourers and craftsmen.

Secondly, slavery in the Old Testament was not simply tolerated with a 'rubber stamp' of uncritical approval. Aspects of Old Testament thought and practice in this area virtually 'neutralized' slavery as an institution and sowed the seeds of its radical rejection in much later Christian thinking. Certainly these aspects, to which we now turn, made Israel unquestionably unique in the ancient world in its attitude to slavery. This is a fact unanimously acknowledged by ancient Near Eastern scholars. Three points are worth noting:

1. *Israel's own origins in slavery.* The first and most influential factor in Israel's theological and legal attitude to slavery was her own *history.* The Israelites never forgot that they started out, in terms of national origin, as a rabble of freed slaves. This in itself is unusual, if not unique, among epics of national origins. Most ethnic myths glorify their nation's ancestral past. Israel, by contrast, looked back to four centuries of slavery in a foreign land, which had become increasingly oppressive, inhumane and unbearable. The experience coloured their subsequent attitude to slavery enormously. On the one hand, Israelites were not supposed to subject one another to slave status or conditions of labour. Such action was incompatible with the equality of being redeemed brothers, slaves of the LORD alone (see Lev. 25:42–43, 46, 53, 55). On the other hand, their treatment of aliens within their own society, whether those aliens were the technically free but landless 'tenant' workers, or actual bought slaves, was to be marked with compassion born of the memory of Egypt, where they themselves had been denied mercy. This principle is explicit in the earliest legal code of the Old Testament, the Covenant Code of Exodus 21 – 23: 'Do not oppress an alien; you yourselves know how it feels to be aliens, because you were aliens in Egypt' (Exod. 23:9; cf. 22:21; Deut. 15:15).

2. *Israel's slave legislation.* In the second place, however, these historically generated attitudes were translated into specific *legislation* that accorded to slaves in Israel a degree of status, rights and protection unheard of elsewhere.

Slaves were included within the *religious* life of the community. They could be circumcised and partake of the Passover (Exod. 12:44). They were to be allowed to join in the feasting and rejoicing of the great festivals (Deut. 16:11–14; note v. 12). Probably most relevant of all, in view of their occupation, was the command that slaves, male and female, be included in the weekly sabbath rest (Exod. 20:10): indeed, it is said to be for their prime benefit – along with working animals – in Exodus 23:12.

This social and religious inclusion of slaves was extended into the realm of the protection of *civil* law. Two laws in the Covenant Code in the book of Exodus deal with a master's treatment of *his own* slaves.[7] That in itself makes them unique in ancient Near Eastern law. In other law codes there were abundant laws concerning assault or murder of *another person's* slaves, but not of your own. How you treated your own slaves was a matter only for yourself, since they were your exclusive property. Not so in Israel. In Exodus 21:20–21

---

[7] The Covenant Code is universally reckoned to be Israel's earliest body of legislation, so Israel's uniquely humane slave laws were not the late product of some slowly developing ethical sensitivity, but were part of the legal expression of her theology from the earliest period.

if a master administered a beating of such severity that it was immediately fatal, the slave was to be 'avenged'. That is the literal meaning of the verb used, and in any other context would mean that the guilty party would be liable to death himself at the hands of his victim's family. Though some commentators are reluctant to accept it, this law's natural sense is that the vicious master was to be charged with the offence by the legal community on behalf of the slave, who had no family to avenge him. Exodus 21:26–27 protected a slave from bodily harm. If it was inflicted, the slave had to be set free.[8] The mention of a 'tooth' shows that it was not just because the slave's work capacity was impaired. There is here a deeper concern for the personal humanity and physical integrity of the slave, which had been assaulted. It should be stressed that these were civil laws, not charitable exhortations, which implies that in such circumstances a slave could appeal to the court of elders against his own master. This too would be a unique right in the ancient world. Yet such a legal appeal by a slave seems to be a possibility Job had in mind when he claimed he had never denied justice to any of his own slaves in any legal complaint they had had against him (Job 31:14).[9]

After six years of service a Hebrew slave had to be given the opportunity of freedom in the seventh year. Since he or she would still not own any land,[10] it is

---

[8]   This is an interesting case because it has a bearing on the so-called *lex talionis* (which I have already mentioned above) that immediately precedes it – the notorious principle of 'eye for an eye, tooth for tooth' etc. The point of that principle, as often pointed out, was not to foster violent vengeance, but precisely the opposite, to limit vengeance. Punishment must be strictly proportionate to the offence. That it was a principle of *proportionality*, not a command to be taken *literally*, is shown here, in that the *actual* penalty for damaging an eye or knocking out a tooth is not the infliction of the same disfigurement on the offender, but rather granting freedom to the victim, which would mean a financial loss to the slave-owner. Physical assault is punished by proportionate loss of income.

[9]   The significance of these laws, the relevance of Job 31, and other aspects of the social and legal status of slaves in Old Testament Israel are discussed more fully in C. J. H. Wright, *God's Land*, ch. 8.

[10] As noted earlier, the word 'Hebrew' in the slave-release laws of Exod. 21:2–6 and Deut. 15:12–18 is probably not just a synonym for 'Israelite', but refers to a landless, rootless and often stateless substratum of society, found throughout the ancient Near East. It accurately described the condition of the Israelites while in Egypt (Exod. 2:11–13) and of David and his outlaws while in the land of the Philistines (1 Sam. 29:3). So the 'Hebrew slave' who was to be freed after six years was landless, and quite different from the Israelite landowner who had mortgaged land because of increasing

unlikely that such 'freedom' would mean much more than a change of employer. Deuteronomy 15:13–14 expands the original law with a generous gift that was a primitive form of unemployment benefit. Proof that slavery was not necessarily oppressive is found in the fact that the law presumes that slaves would often prefer the security of their present residence to the insecurity of freedom and a potentially less benevolent owner (Deut. 15:16–17). The choice of whether to leave or stay, however, rests with the slave, not with the master.

But the most astonishingly unique slave law in the Old Testament is the law of asylum in Deuteronomy 23:15–16. Runaway slaves, far from being punished or sent back, were to be given freedom of residence in a village of their choice. The universal law of the rest of contemporary societies (as indeed of modern societies before slavery was abolished) not only punished runaway slaves but also laid severe penalties on anyone who gave them refuge. Israel's law was the diametrical opposite, one of the most countercultural pieces of Old Testament legislation to be found. Israel's law not only *allowed* runaway slaves freedom; it went beyond that and *commanded* their protection:

> Is it not extraordinary – not to say amusing – that the one society in the ancient Near East that had a law protecting runaway slaves was that society that traced its origin to a group of runaway slaves from Egypt? . . . The point is that Israel has experienced God as the one who is sympathetic to runaway slaves. So this law is not just an ethical or legal principle in defence of human rights, but a reflex of Israel's own religious experience – a fundamental characteristic of Biblical ethics.[11]

So starkly different is this law that some scholars think it can have applied only to *foreign* slaves seeking asylum in Israel. The law does not state that. But even if that were true, the law would still be unique, and would also show that Israel was an attractive society for a slave to seek refuge in. If, on the other hand, this law of asylum applied to slaves within Israel who had run away from oppressive masters, it represents a radical undermining of the institution of slavery itself. Slavery is not treated as sacrosanct under Israelite law. At the very least it can be said that such a law probably presumes that runaway slaves would have been the exception, not the rule. This lends further weight

---

debt and poverty, but who was to be restored to his land and freedom in the jubilee (fiftieth) year (Lev. 25:39–41). For my own position on this distinction (which continues to be a matter of debate among scholars), see C. J. H. Wright, 'Every Seven Years in Israel'.

[11] David J. A. Clines, 'Social Responsibility in the Old Testament', a Shaftesbury Project Working Paper (unpublished), p. 8.

to the view that normally slavery in Israel was not oppressively harsh. It would certainly not have been, if the spirit of the slavery laws of Exodus and Deuteronomy were put into practice.

3. *The slave's created equality.* The third thing to be said about slavery in the Old Testament arises from the remark above about slavery not being sacrosanct. It is that slavery was never viewed as 'natural'. In other words, it was not regarded as a divinely ordered part of creation itself, as though slave and free were different degrees of humanity. The old Akkadian proverb 'Man is the shadow of a god; a slave is the shadow of a man' would not have been acceptable in Israel. In the Bible the first mention of slaves and slavery is in the context of a *curse*. In Genesis 9:25–27 the future slave status of Canaan is attributed to the curse of Noah. Slavery here is seen as something unnatural, fallen and accursed. It is not part of the way God created human beings to live. Nor is it an essential and unchangeable part of the 'nature of things'. On the contrary, slaves are human beings too, and they share that status before God with all other humans.

The highest point of the Old Testament's ethical critique of slavery is found again on the lips of Job as he affirms the created equality of master and slave. Speaking of his own slaves Job says:

> Did not he who made me in the womb make them?
> Did not the same one form us both within our mothers?
>
> (Job 31:15; cf. Prov. 14:31; 17:5)

This gem from the creation ethic comes closer than anything else in the Old Testament to the finality of Paul's assertion that slave and free are one in Christ (Gal. 3:28). And if, in the light of the latter text, the abolition of slavery was not accomplished in Christendom for centuries, let alone by the New Testament church, we can hardly stand in critical judgment on Old Testament Israel for tolerating it with such a high degree of humanity and compassion.[12]

Critical affirmation: the family in the Old Testament

The clearest example of a sociocultural pattern Israel shared with surrounding societies was that of the importance of kinship, and the range of rights

---

[12] For further discussion of the hermeneutical battle that raged over the biblical texts on slavery during the campaign to have it abolished, see Willard M. Swartley, *Slavery, Sabbath, War and Women.*

and responsibilities it conferred on individuals. The family is, of course, a vital basic unit of all human society. In ancient Semitic culture it took the larger form of the 'extended family', a household incorporating several generations vertically and several nuclear families horizontally, plus slaves and resident employees. This sizeable household unit was of prime importance in social structure and cohesion.

Two features of family life in this wider Semitic culture stand out. First, there was the strength of the bonds of kinship and the obligation felt towards them. This was not only so in terms of 'lateral' kinship – the demands of brotherhood. It also had a 'vertical' dimension in two directions. On the one hand, there was a powerful respect for one's ancestors. In some cultures this amounted to veneration, if not actual worship. At any rate, one's present activities were either a credit or a shame to them, and even stronger was the degree of submission to the authority of one's living parents and grandparents. On the other hand, it was of prime importance to preserve the family line into the future by the birth of children, especially sons. One 'survived', in a sense, through one's descendants, or one was 'cut off' by childlessness or the death or destruction of one's posterity.

Secondly, there was the sacredness of family land. The preservation of the ancestral inheritance was vital for two reasons particularly that corresponded to the two directions of the vertical line of kinship. On the one hand, it was the place where one's ancestors were buried, and where you too would eventually be 'gathered to them'. On the other hand, keeping land in the family was vital to the economic survival of the next and succeeding generations. Kinship and land, then, were tightly bound together in this cultural matrix.[13] These features of kinship and land in the ancient world are still found in many traditional societies today where the acids of Western individualism have not eroded robust and broad family networks.

Now, coming specifically to Israel, we find that Israel's kinship structure had three tiers, each of which is reflected in the way Israelite names were recorded. Of these, the first two were of far greater social and economic significance in the everyday life of average Israelites.

1. *The father's house (bêt-'āb).* This was the smallest unit, but still a fairly large group of people. It consisted of all those living within the household of a single living male ancestor, who was known as the 'head of a father's house'. It would thus include his wife or wives, his sons and their wives

---

[13] See Herbert C. Brichto, 'Kin, Cult, Land and Afterlife', and for a critical summary of his views, C. J. H. Wright, *God's Land*, pp. 151–159.

and their sons and wives and unmarried daughters. It would normally therefore have been a three-generational community, and sometimes even four generations, with people marrying relatively young. It would also have included any servants or resident aliens living as part of the household, which would obviously have inhabited a small cluster of dwellings within an allotment of land.

2. *The clan (mišpāḥâ)*. This was a group of related households, named after one of the grandsons of Jacob (i.e. the names of the sons of the tribal ancestors of Israel). A clan often seems to have had a territorial identity as well, and sometimes village names and clan names were identical. The clan functioned as a protective association of families, with a variety of economic, social, judicial and military duties.

3. *The tribe (šēbeṭ/maṭṭeh)*. The tribe was the largest kinship grouping, named after the sons of Jacob (with Joseph subdivided into Ephraim and Manasseh), and the tribes' major significance was in territorial landholding.

Now this kind of socio-economic pattern of family life, or something like it, would to some degree have been true of Israel as an ancient Semitic people within the macroculture of their world, whether or not they had come to regard themselves as the people of YHWH. But, given that they did in fact regard themselves as having that unique covenant relationship with YHWH, and given that the maintenance of that national relationship with YHWH was of paramount importance, the role of the kinship–land basis of society had an even greater significance. Briefly put, the household–land unit was central to the triangle of relationships between God, Israel and the land, outlined in Part One. It will be helpful at this point to revive the original diagram and add the family into the centre.

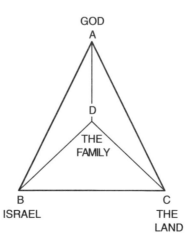

You will remember that the outer triangle represents the three major relationships of Israel's self-understanding. There was the primary covenant relationship between God and Israel (AB), God was the ultimate owner of the land (AC), and the land was given to Israel for an inheritance (CB). Now the family, which will stand as shorthand for what I have described as the extended-family-plus-its-land (the *bêt-'āb*), was the basic, central unit in each of these dimensions. First, it was the basic unit of Israelite social and kinship structure (BD), with important military and judicial functions. Secondly, it was the basic economic unit of Israelite land tenure (CD). We saw some of the implications of this in terms of rights and responsibilities in chapter 3. Thirdly, it was of pivotal importance in the experience of the covenant relationship (AD). It was by belonging within such a family that an individual could claim membership of the covenant people, whether by birth or (as in the case of slaves or resident aliens) by residence. It was by the duty of parental teaching (see Deut. 6:6–9, 20–25; 11:18–21) that knowledge of the covenant and its obligations would be preserved from one generation to another. And it was within the family that some of the primary ritual acts took place, such as circumcision, Passover and the redemption of firstborn sons (Exod. 12; 13). So all three realms – social, economic and theological – were closely bound together (as we have already seen), and all three had the family as their focal point.[14] I shall expand on this covenantal centrality of the family below.

It can at once be appreciated, therefore, how anything that threatened to break up the 'lower triangle' (BCD), the socio-economic fabric of the nation, would *thereby* endanger the national covenant relationship with God. Such a threat would undermine the roots and soil of the covenant; namely, the network of free landowning families. In view of all this it is not at all surprising to find a deep concern in the Old Testament to protect the family, both by affirming with theological support those customs already part of the kinship .culture and by specific protective legislation.

Yet, at the same time, the Old Testament is not blind to the fallenness of all human social forms. The family shares in this fallenness just as much as any individual. So there is an awareness that families, for all their centrality to God's covenantal purpose, could be riddled with evil and cauldrons of oppression. Hence, the phrase '*critical* affirmation' in the title for this section. So in the survey that now follows we shall observe both the positive and the negative things said about the family within different strands of the Old Testament canon: the law and narratives, the prophets and the Wisdom tradition.

---

[14] For fuller detailing of all these dimensions of the family's function within Israel's covenantal life and faith, see C. J. H. Wright, *God's Land*, especially chs. 2–3.

The family in Old Testament law and narrative

a. Family as the context of covenant faithfulness and social stability
Circumcision. The fundamental *sign of the covenant* between the LORD and Israel was circumcision, an act carried out within the family on all male children. Appropriately, therefore, the family, as the focus of this covenant ceremony, was also the prime place for the teaching of the faith, history, laws and traditions of Israel, and circumcision itself became a metaphor for covenant obedience – 'Circumcise your hearts' (Deut. 10:16).

Redemption. A major part of Israel's suffering in the latter stages of their bondage in Egypt was genocidal intrusion into their families. Egypt's state-sponsored campaign to reduce the population by the extermination of male births was part of an oppression that eventually led to the LORD's intervention. In a form of poetic justice the climax of the LORD's plagues upon Egypt was the death of Egypt's firstborn. And in the context of that event two rituals were instituted in Israel that focus on *the family as the key context for the experience and celebration of redemption*:

- *The Passover (Exod. 12).* This annual family ritual both celebrates and re-enacts the exodus and specifically the fact that the LORD spared the firstborn of Israelite families during the night of the final plague. Its social inclusiveness, with careful limitations, is based on the composition of normal Israelite households (Exod. 12:43–49).
- *The Consecration of the Firstborn (Exod. 13:1–16).* That which the LORD had delivered from death belonged to him. But in claiming the firstborn son in every family the LORD effectively claimed the whole succeeding generation. In this way the continuity of the covenant relationship through the generations was symbolized.

Decalogue. In the context of the great liberation of the exodus the Decalogue forms the charter of freedoms and responsibilities for a redeemed people. *Protection of the family* is an essential aspect of its 'second table', including the preservation of parental authority (fifth commandment), of sexual integrity (seventh commandment) and of economic viability (eighth and tenth commandments). Each of these central principles is then reinforced by other groups of laws and institutions:

- *Parental authority* is buttressed by the penalties on cursing or striking a parent (Exod. 21:15, 17; cf. Deut. 27:15) and by the law that makes incorrigible profligacy on the part of a son an offence which parents may bring before the civil courts (Deut. 21:18–21). Parental authority is balanced, however, with responsibility – particularly the responsibility not to show favouritism or deprive a firstborn son within a polygamous family of his rights (Deut. 21:15–17).

- *Sexual integrity* is buttressed not only by the wide range of laws relating to various sexual offences (e.g. Deut. 22:13–30), but also by the prohibitions on marriage between certain degrees of kinship (Lev. 18:6–18; 20:11–14, 19–21). These were not solely to do with sexual ethics, but with providing clear boundaries on sexual relations between the nuclear families living within the larger 'father's house'.

- *Social and economic viability* is buttressed by a remarkable number of mechanisms designed either to prevent families falling into serious economic decline, or to rescue them for a fresh start if they had done so. I mentioned these in chapter 5 above, but they are worth listing again: *The original division of land* was specifically designed to enable every household to have a share. The land division texts in Joshua 13ff. specify that territory was to be allotted 'according to their families'. This broad distribution into family inheritances was then protected by the *law of inalienability*, which prohibited permanent sale of land outside the family (Lev. 25:23). If poverty and/or debt forced a family to sell or offer for sale some of its patrimonial land, the *law of redemption* called for it to be bought back by a kinsman-redeemer within the limits of the *mišpāḥâ*, and *the year of jubilee* provided for land and persons that had been sold for debt to be restored to their *bêt-'āb* (Lev. 25:24–55). The broad purpose of all these mechanisms was to preserve families as participating members in the economic and social community, and thereby to preserve their place within the covenant community as well. For, as explained above, in ancient Israel, kinship and land together played a major role in belonging within the covenant community, such that loss or lack of either family or land, or both, created great vulnerability.

Society. Since the Israelite family was the focus of covenant membership, it had significant functions in the *judicial* realm (both internally in the exercise of family law and externally in the role of family elders in administering local justice). It was also the prime vehicle for the *teaching* of the historical traditions and the requirements of the law (Deut. 6). It was important, therefore, that Israelite households be as socially inclusive as possible. The *worship* of the LORD, whether at the recurring annual festivals, or the triennial tithe, or at the grand reading of the law in the seventh year, was to draw together not only family members, but also the landless (Levites and aliens), the familyless (widows and orphans) and the lowliest of slaves (Deut. 14:27–29; 16:11, 14; 29:10–12). The *social and ethical* duties of an Israelite family extended beyond immediate kith and kin to embrace the needy in the wider community.

Paradigm. So deeply imbedded is the family in Israel's covenantal self-understanding and socioreligious practice that Waldemar Janzen argues that what he calls 'The Familial Paradigm' was the dominant motif in the ethical consciousness of Israel. From a variety of narratives (which he regards as of equal, if not greater, importance to Torah laws) he lists the major components of the familial paradigm as the gift, continuance and enhancement of *life*; the possession of *land*, as the prerequisite of familial viability; and the ethical imperative of *hospitality* – especially to those beyond the kinship boundaries.[15]

b. Family as a context for covenant unfaithfulness and social collapse

Patriarchs at their worst. Even before we encounter Israelite families in the land itself, the Old Testament gives us a realistic portrait of the negative sides of the patriarchal families in Genesis. The catalogue of deception, lies, half-truths, abuse of women, favouritism, jealousy, competiveness, failure and grief is appalling. And that is only the marriages. Add in all the sibling rivalry, parental favouritism, cunning trickery, murderous jealousy, callous deceit, simmering hatred and lingering fear and you could fill a comprehensive casebook on dysfunctional families – just from Genesis alone. A major part of the sharp challenge of Genesis is precisely that it does not conceal the horrendous wickedness and frequent misery and pain that stalked the generations of these proto-Israelite families. While the enormous strength and durability of these families is also apparent, and while the relationship that various key individuals have with God is emphasized, there is no doubt that Genesis 12 – 50 reflects family life in all its fallenness.

And yet God carried on his mission of redemptive blessing for the nations *through* such recalcitrant agents. In fact, if the story of Genesis shows anything, it shows that God's determination to bless 'all families of the earth' will ultimately be *in spite of* human failure and inadequacy, not because of human prowess or success. If God is willing to be known as the God of Abraham, Isaac and Jacob, and their fissiparous families, God can doubtless cope with the rest of us.

Families in rebellion. A number of narratives in the Old Testament recount incidents of serious conflict within key families, or acts of rebellion involving whole families, that disturbed the relationship between God and Israel. I have already commented on the darker side of the patriarchal families in Genesis. Other examples worthy of note would include Aaron and Miriam opposing Moses (Num. 12); the rebellion of Korah, Dathan and Abiram and their whole families (Num. 16); Achan's breaking of the rules of *ḥērem* at Jericho

---

[15] Waldemar Janzen, *Ethics*; see especially ch. 2, 'The Familial Paradigm'.

(Josh. 7); the tragic divisions and violence that engulfed David's family in his later reign.

Compromised loyalty. There is an awareness that the strength of family loyalty could become a rival to that primary covenant loyalty due to the LORD alone. Family ties could be a source of temptation to the worship of other gods – thus breaking the primary and most fundamental bond of Israel's covenantal monotheism. Marriage to non-Israelites was not prohibited on grounds of *ethnic* purity – Moses himself married a Cushite wife and the disapproval of Aaron and Miriam was not echoed by the LORD. Similarly, there is no explicit condemnation of Elimelech's sons for marrying Moabite women, but rather clear approval of Boaz for marrying Ruth as an act of kinsman duty in spite of her foreignness. Marriage with Canaanite women was, however, prohibited on the grounds of the threat posed, not to Israel's ethnic mix, but to their *covenant* faith. Intermarriage would inevitably lead to the intrusion of other gods into family piety (Deut. 7:1–4). This feature of foreign marriages was the undoing of Solomon (1 Kgs. 11:1–6), and the cause of the harsh reforming actions of Nehemiah and Ezra (Ezra 9 – 10; Neh. 10:30; 13:23–27).

Potential source of idolatry. Deuteronomy 13 is one of the starkest chapters in the Old Testament, dealing with the threat of being enticed into the worship of other gods. With immense realism and perception it anticipates that the temptation to go after other gods may come not only from highly plausible but spurious wonder-workers (vv. 1–6), not only from the social pressure of a whole disaffected community (vv. 12–18), but also from within the bosom of one's closest family – 'your very own brother, or your son or daughter, or the wife you love, or your closest friend' (vv. 6–11). Even if so, the enticement is to be resisted with a steely firmness that puts loyalty to the LORD alone above even such familial ties. This was a choice Jesus himself faced – not in the sense that his family wished to entice him into blatant idolatry, but rather that in pressing him to return to his *family* responsibilities they were inadvertently drawing him away from obedience to the will of his *Father*. Jesus promptly highlighted the stark nature of that choice when he redefined his family in terms of those who, like himself, would put the will of his Father above all else (Matt. 12:46–50).

Dismal dynasties. Perhaps the most ambiguous of all family-based institutions in the Old Testament was the royal dynastic principle. The first time it emerges it is greeted with shock, horror and resistance. Gideon's reply to the proposal of the grateful Israelites that he and his descendants should rule over them seems to reject dynastic monarchy as incompatible with the theocratic rule of the LORD (Judg. 8:22–23). Yet, with typical sardonic economy, the Hebrew narrator tells us that Gideon, for all his protests, behaved just like a king – accepting a handsome reward in gold and taking many wives (contra

Deut. 17:17). Furthermore, a son of Gideon actually made the first abortive attempt at monarchy. It was an attempt, however, that included the ruthless murder of seventy other sons of Gideon (Judg. 9) – a less than promising start for the whole idea of monarchy, which is accordingly shelved until the next book of the Bible.

When the monarchy eventually did get established after Saul's disastrous 'reign', the dynastic principle is affirmed by the LORD in his covenant promise to David (2 Sam. 7). This dynastic covenant then becomes the foundation not only for the following centuries of virtually uninterrupted Davidic incumbents on the throne in Jerusalem (Athaliah being the only transient exception), but also for a messianic theology and eschatology we as Christians, on the authority of the New Testament, are happy to endorse in the person of 'great David's greater Son'. Yet it also has to be said that just as the patriarchal families were simultaneously models of faith and obedience at one level, but also of horrific abuse and wickedness at another, the royal households of the two kingdoms of Judah and Israel display every family horror known to humanity: patricide, matricide, fratricide, suicide, adultery, murder, incest, conspiracy, intrigue, betrayal, feuds, hatred and vengeance. It is only the miraculous grace and sovereignty of God that enables this to be a story of redemption at all.

The family in the prophets

a. Championing the family under attack

The positive view of the family in the prophets is implied by their virulent critique of current practices that were destroying families. The prophets attacked the socio-economic forces and judicial corruption that led to dispossession, poverty, debt and apparent loss of covenant inclusion. These were the things that dislocated and destroyed families, and thereby threw ordinary people not only into material poverty and distress but also into a kind of socioreligious limbo in relation to the covenant. Did these dispossessed people really belong to the covenant community any more? If they lacked family and land, were they not to be counted among 'the wicked' and 'cut off'? Not so, said Amos. The poor and dispossessed are 'the righteous', while those whose land and families were prospering on the back of such oppression were 'the wicked'.

> The prophets denounced [these abuses] so vehemently because they saw in them an
> *intrinsic* threat to [the covenant] relationship through the effect they were having on
> the units of landowning households. This familial aspect becomes explicit in such
> texts as Mic. 2:1–3, 8–9; 7:5–6; and Isa. 5:8–10. If . . . the experience of the relationship
> with God was vested in the household units of Israel – just as possession of the land
> was vested in inalienable family inheritances – then the socio-economic forces and

changes which were destroying these family land units would inevitably and 'internally' destroy the nation's relationship with God as well. The theological status of Israel was earthed and rooted in the socio-economic fabric of their kinship structure and their land tenure, and it was this fabric which was being dissolved by the acids of debt, dispossession and latifundium. The prophetic protest against these evils, therefore, must be illumined by the fact that there was an essential link between the social and economic facts of life and the theological self-understanding of Israel. That link was the family.[16]

b. Eschatological vision – a familied future

In several of the prophetic visions of the future messianic age, visions that usually include not only the restoration of God's people, their wholehearted obedience to God and enjoyment of his blessing, but also the renewal of creation and its abundance, the place of the family is prominent. The new creation described in Isaiah 65:17–25 will be a place in which families are safe from infant mortality or early death and the fruit of family labour will not be frustratingly swept away.

The family in the Wisdom tradition

Family relationships constitute one of the major matters of concern to the wise men and women of Israel.

a. Family as the target of strong moral support

Proverbs regards family relationships as of paramount importance for those who desire to act wisely and live well. The opening advice, after the prologue (Prov. 1:1–7) reflects the fifth commandment about honouring parents (Prov. 1:8–9), and this is amplified again and again throughout the book. Similarly, reflecting the seventh commandment, the integrity of marriage is upheld vigorously in the graphic warnings against adultery (Prov. 2:16–19; 5:1–23; 7:1–27). Significantly, in the case of adultery the main point of the warning is the potential disaster adultery will bring upon one's own family – not just from the social disgrace, but also from the loss of standing in the covenant community that would be the consequence of the loss of the family's substance (Prov. 5:9–14). In contrast, the praise of a good wife is notable. The book brings to a climax its praise of wisdom with a portrait, not of a model wise man but of a model wise woman – the 'wife of noble character' in Proverbs 31:10–31. The description, of course, reflects not just on the woman herself, but is a window on some features of the ideal Israelite home and

---

[16]   C. J. H. Wright, *God's Land*, p. 109.

family. Such a home, in Israelite thought, should be not only a place of blessing and security for the husband and children, but also a source of hospitality and generosity for the needy.

b. But what if the family fails?

A characteristic of the Old Testament Wisdom literature is that it incorporates a self-critical element, a kind of literary and theological deconstruction of some of the strong and positive affirmations of the book of Proverbs and, we might add, of the idyllic portrayal of sexual love in marriage in the Song of Solomon.

Ecclesiastes explores the theory that wealth creation is a good thing because you can pass it on to your son and heir. But what if that heir is a fool who squanders all you've worked for? And is it fair anyway that he should get for free from your life of toil what he has not personally worked for (Eccles. 2:18–23)? And to be a workaholic for one's own benefit, with nobody to pass it on to, seems no better (Eccles. 4:7–8). And then, even if you believe it is still a good thing to accrue wealth to pass on, 'some misfortune' can rob you of it so that you depart as naked as you arrived and your heirs get nothing (Eccles. 5:13–15). And while the joys of marriage are all very well in themselves, and to be regarded as a gift of God, do they really count for much in view of the darkness of death that awaits us all (Eccles. 9:7–10)? The author's experience of the other sex had not even had that mitigation, it seems (Eccles. 7:28).

Job raises even sharper questions in the midst of the actual experience of massive bereavement – the loss of his children, his wealth and his health. With pathetic nostalgia he recalls the status he had had in the community when, as an elder with his family and his substance around him, he had been a giant for justice in the land, loved by the poor and respected by all (Job 29; note vv. 5–6). This description matches the picture of the respected husband in Proverbs 31:23 and the social security that comes from having a quiver full of sons (Ps. 127:3–5). But what if you lose the whole lot – sons and substance? The social reality is painted graphically by Job in chapter 30 – disgrace, contempt, marginalizing. The question then is, as the satan was trying to prove, would such loss expose Job's piety as a mere pretence that would not be sustained once he lost his goods? Or, as God was prepared to wager, would Job prove that his faith in God was truly located in God, not merely in the abundant family and fortune God had entrusted to him? Even through the darkness of God's hiddenness and silence Job maintained his integrity under the pressure of the accusations of his friends and his own agonized protests, preserved his faith in God and was finally commended.

The book of Job forces us to ask hard questions about even the best earthly gifts that our Creator God can give – the blessings of family, health and abundance. If they become our security in themselves, then they rapidly become idolatrous and we are vulnerable in times of loss. Perhaps this very thought lies behind the severely relativizing perspective of Psalm 127. Although this psalm celebrates children as a heritage and a reward from the LORD, nevertheless (v. 1), 'Unless the LORD builds the house, / its builders labour in vain' – a sentence which in Hebrew as in English has a double entendre: literal house-building, and the building of a family. For all your genealogy and ancestry, where does your true identity come from? For all your family heritage in persons and property, where does your real security come from?

Christians and culture

We return now, after this survey of the family in the Old Testament, as an example of critical affirmation of a cultural reality, to the opening issue of this chapter – the evaluation of culture in the context of biblical faith. We now have to ask whether the Old Testament's approach to the social and cultural aspects of its own day has anything to teach us as Christians about our response to the societies and cultures in which we live.

The first thing to be said is that the variety of the Old Testament responses to different cultural phenomena rules out simplistic views on our part. We should neither wholly accept the culture of our society as good or at least tolerable, nor should we wholly reject it as irretrievably evil and abhorrent. A discriminating and critical approach is clearly called for. Let us recall the three categories of response Israel seems to have made: total rejection, qualified toleration and critical affirmation.

Total rejection

In the first place, the Old Testament leads us to expect that there will be some aspects of fallen human society that must be rejected as abhorrent to God. The only valid Christian response to them is renunciation and separation. The Old Testament also gives us some clue about how to identify such features. Broadly, one could say that the following four categories in particular were condemned by Israel's legal and prophetic traditions: (1) the idolatrous, (2) the perverted, (3) that which was destructive of persons, and (4) callousness to the poor. Each of these is still powerfully relevant today. So many dimensions of human cultures all over the world manifest some aspect of these four gloomy tendencies of fallen human nature.

Do we not still need the severity of the Old Testament's strictures against the subtle, as well as the blatant, idolatries of our age and cultures? Christians are often as prone as Israel to relegate God unconsciously to salvation and

Sundays, while we serve the golden calves and Baals of materialistic, consumerist culture in 'real life'. Discernment of idolatry is a crucial task, a prophetic responsibility, and frequently a costly undertaking for those who expose the idols of any culture.

Do we not still need the clarity of the Old Testament's exposure of perversion, in an age where every moral value is questioned or turned inside out? It is significant how closely Paul links idolatry with perversion, *not only* in the realm of sexual practice, but also in a whole intellectual climate and in the realm of the perversion of *truth* (Rom. 1:18–32).

Do we not still need the indignant revulsion of the Old Testament at the destruction of the weak and innocent, in such practices as ritual prostitution and child sacrifice? The pornography trade has elements of both in taking over from the economic exploitation of women and children in earlier eras – not that even the latter is by any means eradicated. And what does this dimension of Old Testament sensitivity say to the wholesale destruction of millions of the unborn, sometimes for understandable medical reasons but overwhelmingly, it seems, for mere convenience?

Do we not still need the Old Testament's uncompromising critique of all that oppresses and those who callously 'trample on the heads of the poor' (Amos 2:7; Mic. 3:2–3 is even more bloodcurdling)? If the sin of Sodom was to be 'arrogant, overfed and unconcerned' and callously unhelpful to the poor and needy (Ezek. 16:49), then large sections of the Christian church (and especially in the West) are dwelling at ease, not in Zion, but in Sodom.

No doubt the reader can add his or her own contemporary and local cultural content to what may be regarded as idolatrous, perverted, destructive or callous. Here at least is a framework for the necessarily negative side of our cultural analysis. Israel was called to reject and resist these things. There is surely a battle for the church as well.

Qualified tolerance

In the second place, the experience of Old Testament Israel prepares us to allow for the fact that society is fallen. Even God accepts this fact! That is the point of Jesus' saying that while, from the beginning, God's creation purpose was lifelong marriage, nevertheless he 'allowed' divorce 'for your hardness of heart' (Matt. 19:8, RSV). If divorce could be tolerated within Israel as God's redeemed people, though not without criticism and the teaching of the higher standard, it seems to me we must agree to its being tolerated within secular society. Not that it should pass without criticism and, more than that, working to uphold the highest, absolute standards and to enable people to approximate to them. But the law has to tolerate and legislate for situations that are less than the ethical ideal.

As we saw in the last chapter, Gordon Wenham provides a fine discussion of the difference between what the law prescribes or prohibits, and what society regards as ethically desirable or not:

> In most societies what the law enforces is not the same as what upright members of that society feel is socially desirable let alone ideal. There is a link between moral ideals and law, but law tends to be a pragmatic compromise between the legislators' ideals and what can be enforced in practice. The law enforces a minimum standard of behaviour . . . Or to put it in biblical terms righteousness involves more than living by the Decalogue and the other laws in the Pentateuch . . . Laws generally set a floor for behaviour within society, they do not prescribe an ethical ceiling. Thus a study of the legal codes within the Bible is unlikely to disclose the ideals of the law-givers, but only the limits of their tolerance . . . [the many non-legal exhortations in Old Testament law] indicate that the legislators' ethical ideals are higher than the letter of their laws.[17]

This principle must, then, apply to wider areas of social and political life. Christians are constantly in the position of having to live and work in, and cope with, situations and structures that they know fall short of God's standards. Some things have to be tolerated while we work, like salt or yeast, for change.

Polygamy, for example, may no longer be a live ethical issue in the West, but in other parts of the world it still faces Christians and demands an ethical and pastoral answer. From the perspective of a full biblical ethic we have to insist, of course, that polygamy is morally defective in comparison with God's intention for monogamous marriage. The divorce sayings of Jesus, by regarding as an adulterer a man who divorces a wife and marries another, by implication rule out the taking of other wives as a valid option for Christians. So certainly a Christian may not choose to *become* a polygamist. But what of the situation where a man in a polygamous culture already has several wives, and then becomes a Christian? Are we to say that his only course is to divorce all his wives but one? The Old Testament would surely regard that as replacing a lesser evil with a far greater one – from the wives' point of view. The balance of Old Testament teaching, as we saw, was to regard divorce as a worse evil in God's sight than polygamy. An Israelite might have gone on to give some pragmatic justification for tolerating polygamy. In a society without much in the way of independent gainful employment for women, without welfare benefits for single, divorced or widowed women, and where childlessness was

---

[17] Wenham, *Story as Torah*, p. 80; from ch. 5, 'Ethical Ideals and Legal Requirements'.

deepest shame, he might have argued that it was unquestionably better for every woman to be some man's wife, even if necessary in a polygamous marriage, than to face the alternative – usually either prostitution or the parlous plight of widowhood. Some degree of toleration, combined with a radical and theological critique and proclamation of the higher ideal, seems to be suggested by the light of the Old Testament.[18]

One might also note Paul's handling of a comparable moral problem when he addressed the question of marriage and divorce. Paul commanded that a Christian should not marry an unbeliever. But if one partner in a previously non-Christian marriage *became* a Christian, he or she was not to divorce the unbeliever – unless the latter wished to divorce, in which case Paul granted the believing partner freedom. His principle seems to have been that personal commitments undertaken *before* conversion should be honoured from the new Christian's side. To remain married to an unbeliever was preferable to the newly Christian partner initiating divorce. It is arguable that Paul would have adopted a similar approach and toleration to the converted polygamist (cf. 1 Cor. 7:12–24).

Similarly, though we may have technically abolished slavery (though even that is a dubious claim in view of pockets of continuing slavery around the world), there remain structures of economic and industrial life that fall far short of God's standards for human dignity. Christians have to tolerate these to the extent of being able to work within them and address them. At the same time, however, they must seek to challenge and reform them in the light of the Old Testament's own clear principles of justice, fair trade and compassion for the weakest.

We might even be led to ponder the fact of Israel's toleration of slavery, as to whether it might even have been preferable to other alternatives. Immediately, one has to say this is not in any sense at all an attempt to justify the enslavement of any human being in the normal meaning of that term. No human being has the unqualified right to *own* another human being as a piece of property or to treat him or her as such. But when we look at the main

---

[18] We should note that in African churches, where polygamy remains a live issue, a careful and mature biblical and theological response has been articulated for many decades. A man who is a polygamist when he is converted is not required to divorce his existing wives. To that extent, polygamy is 'critically tolerated'. But a believer who enters polygamous relationships after conversion is put under church discipline (i.e. not admitted to communion). Polygamy, for a Christian, is regarded as sin. And, in line with New Testament teaching, a man with polygamous marriages is not allowed to be in church leadership.

problem in society for which bonded service was Israel's solution, namely debt, we wonder if Israel's solution does not have at least some defensible aspects. The debtor undertook a bond. He was bound to the creditor and worked off his debt through his labour. One could argue that this is at least worthy of sympathetic consideration in comparison with the alternatives in modern societies. Modern responses to unrepayable debt range from bankruptcy, where the creditor may get nothing, which seems unjust, to imprisonment, which benefits nobody and costs society dearly. Indeed, as we saw in the last chapter, considered simply as a legal penalty, it is arguable that time-limited slavery for debt on Israelite terms was more humane than imprisonment on ours. The slave still lived at home. He worked with human company in the 'normal' world. He walked on God's earth under God's sky. Imprisonment denies all these things, and it is interesting (to say the least) that imprisonment is never prescribed as a penalty anywhere in the Torah (though it was practised in the later monarchy). The point of this comparison is not, of course, to advocate the reintroduction of slavery, or to imagine that there are easy alternatives to imprisonment in modern society. It is rather to suggest, given our instinctive recoil from slavery but our easy tolerance of imprisonment, that the Old Testament challenges us to think rather more carefully through the ethical (and not so ethical) aspects of both. We may find we have more to learn from the Old Testament's paradigm than we thought.

Critical affirmation

In the third place, the Old Testament shows that there are aspects of human social and cultural life that can be affirmed positively, though discriminatingly. The church through the ages has done this in a myriad ways. It has, for example, harnessed the arts, music, painting and drama to its own ends. It has taken over pagan festivals and given them a disinfected, Christian content. Ever since the earliest Christians in the New Testament faced the task of enabling the scriptural gospel to take root in Greek soil, the necessity of articulating the gospel in the Greek language and the challenge of relating the gospel to Greek philosophy, it has been the essential nature of Christian mission to engage constructively and creatively with diverse human cultures. Since all human beings are made in God's image, there will always be dimensions of *any* culture that reflect the nature of God, affirm the goodness of creation, embody something of God's moral standards and contribute in some ways to human flourishing. There will, of course be many dimensions of those same cultures, by contrast, that suppress the truth of God, degrade creation, pervert God's standards and collude in human impoverishment. But that should not paralyse our appreciation of the goodness of cultures where it can be identified and affirmed.

Christians and the family

What, then, of the example we took from Israel's social structure, *the family*? Surely here is an 'institution' Christians can affirm in any cultural dress? We know that the family is God-given and surely we must make every effort to support it. Indeed so, but we need to be careful how and where we are applying our biblical insights, and whether our insights really take the *whole* biblical model into account. As we have just seen, biblical material on the family presents a series of paradoxes or ambiguities. This is inevitable because the family closely mirrors the ambiguity of human life itself. That is to say, the human family shares the ambiguity inherent in every human being: made in the image of God and yet at the same time fallen and sinful.

On the one hand, composed of persons made in God's image, the family reflects something of God's own relational self, and is also an appropriate context and vehicle for the worship of God. There is abundant material in the Bible affirming a high view of the family as God's intended, creational context for human lives to begin, for them to be nurtured and shaped according to the values and standards that please God, to learn and express the social and relational skills essential to our humanity, to offer and receive support at many different levels of life and work, abundance and need.

On the other hand, composed of persons who are fallen and sinful, the family can intensify the horrors of human oppression and wickedness, and, when it is endowed with ultimate value or priority, it can become an idolatrous substitute for the true worship of God. There is similarly abundant material in the Bible, as we saw, depicting dysfunctional families, broken and grieving families, and families acting in concerted rebellion against God. The family is recognized as a potential source of the temptation to idolatry, and certainly as a potential rival for that ultimate loyalty due to God alone through Christ.

We ought, therefore, to avoid a naive or simplistic view of 'the Family', and assume that anywhere and everywhere the Bible will happily affirm that it is simply 'a good thing'. It is, of course, like everything else in God's creation, something God created to be 'very good'. But it has the power, like all things human, to be distorted into something very evil. Christians sometimes use the term 'family' as a 'warm-glow' word – similar in its emotive appeal to the word 'community'. We talk of 'family values' and 'community values', and we think we know what they mean. But there can be, of course, as the Bible makes clear, community among thieves and evil-doers. And there can be terrible oppression and injustice deeply inculturated in family patterns. We need to be discerning. We need *critical* affirmation.

In my view, the Old Testament teaching on the family can be ethically applied in two directions: with reference to the family in ordinary secular society, on the one hand, and with reference to the church, especially the local church, as the family or household of God, on the other. To make use again of our different levels of interpretation, in the former case our interpretation needs to be *paradigmatic*; in the latter case, *typological*.

The family in society

Having perceived its centrality in Israel, it would then be easy to champion the family with great zeal as at once the bedrock, bricks and cement of a healthy society. This pro-family stance tends to go along with an attitude that loads the family with great expectations and responsibilities, and is quick to blame families, especially parents, for many of the ills and troubles of society at large. The danger here lies in not seeing the whole Old Testament model of which the family was a functioning part. We need to remember the *whole paradigm*; namely, Israel's overall social, economic and theological system. For, as we have seen, the family in the Old Testament stood at the centre of a conceptual framework that gave it a pre-eminent place and social and economic support within that framework. It was only as part of that larger structure that the family was able to perform its vital role in the moral and religious life of the people. So if we want to assert the importance of the family in society along truly biblical lines, we must also ask serious and critical questions about the nature of society itself.

Many traditional societies today still have patterns of kinship similar to those of biblical Israel. Certain African and Asian cultures will tell us they have no difficulty at all in relating positively to many features of Old Testament family customs and laws. In modern Western society, however, and in cultures that have been (often detrimentally) impacted by Western cultural dominance, there is a much greater sociological difference. Israel was a comparatively simple society, based on a relatively stable kinship network where family ties, both horizontally in the 'present' living generation and vertically in genealogical descent, were all-important. The 'normal' family was an extended household. This cluster of related families, with their servants and other dependants, between them spanned up to four generations under a single head. Such a family was economically largely self-supporting and bound to the collective security of the clan and tribe. This kinship network met most of the social and economic needs of most people.

Modern Western society, as it has developed especially since the Industrial Revolution, has generated a wide plurality of other social bonds quite unrelated to kinship, such as (among others) profession, occupation, sport, regional loyalties, ethnic and religious identities in a plural society. Families are smaller and are often splintered by social mobility. It is no longer 'standard' even for average families to have two parents of both genders. All kinds of societies, associations, charities, government departments and institutions, schools and hospitals, banks and insurance companies and so on have taken over many of the social functions previously vested in kinship networks.

This is another area where serious sociological study needs to be allied to biblical insights and principles. Such work as is being done, both Christian and secular, far from concluding that kinship and family are irrelevant and dispensable in modern society, seems to me rather to point to the urgent necessity of rethinking and refortifying the role of the family in society.[19]

Granted, we cannot load the shrunken nuclear family with the same burdens as the broad-shouldered extended household of old. Nevertheless, the nuclear family is still a fundamental factor in society, just as it was, after all, the basic unit within the extended household. The extended household in Israel was like a molecule formed by the adhesion of several kinship nuclei. It was not an amorphous, free-for-all commune. The extended family in Israel was not, as one writer put it, a dormitory full of double beds. On the contrary, the internal boundaries of legitimate and illegitimate sexual relationships within the close-knit kinship framework were carefully defined in a way that protected very carefully the integrity of the constituent nuclear families (see Lev. 18; 20).

Granted also that no modern society is a redeemed, covenant nation, standing in the same triangular pattern of relationships as did Israel, we can nevertheless allow that pattern to function paradigmatically in this, as in matters considered earlier. Applying it in that way to wider human society, we can still aim towards a pattern of family-in-society that in some sense reflects the Old Testament ideal. This would mean that we work towards the following goals for society. We could seek to ensure that

- families could feel that they have a central social significance and value in the community rather than being statistical pawns of the state machine (the social angle);
- families could enjoy a degree of economic independent viability based on an equitable sharing of the nation's wealth (the economic angle);
- every family could have the opportunity of hearing the message of divine redemption in all its fullness of meaning and the freedom to respond to it and live it out through succeeding generations (the theological angle).

---

[19] A good example of such work, attempting to relate the biblical paradigm of the extended family to the realities of modern society, is Michael Schluter and Roy Clements, *Reactivating the Extended Family*.

Idealistic? Perhaps. But at least it is an idealism based on the overall biblical paradigm. It may also be more realistic than aiming for a morally revitalized society by calling for greater family cohesion, without at the same time tackling the economic pressures and evils that undermine the very thing called for. In other words, although the 'support-the-family' line is admirable as far as it goes, it does not do adequate justice to the whole biblical model unless at the same time we are striving to create social conditions in which family cohesion is economically possible, socially worthwhile and spiritually nourished.

Even less helpful, it seems, is to chant the 'I blame the parents' slogans. Certainly the Bible as a whole places great responsibility on the shoulders of parents. That is unquestionable, and needs to be reasserted in every generation. As well as the laws and the exhortations of Wisdom to that effect, there were the sad examples of the sons of Eli (1 Sam. 2:12 – 3:18) and of Samuel (1 Sam. 8:1–3). And the law recognizes the problem of stubborn incorrigibility among delinquent young adults (Deut. 21:18–21). But when Israel began to fall apart morally, spiritually, economically and politically in the later centuries of the monarchy, you do not find the prophets blaming the families for the social ills of the nation. Rather, the reverse. They condemned those whose greed, oppression and injustice were *destroying* families. The destructive and divisive effect of poverty and debt and the sheer powerlessness of ordinary families in the face of ruthless economic greed was later poignantly expressed in the plea of distraught parents to Nehemiah: 'We have had to borrow money to pay the king's tax on our fields and vineyards . . . we have to subject our sons and daughters to slavery . . . *but we are powerless*, because our fields and our vineyards belong to others' (Neh. 5:4–5; my italics).

That is a cry with modern echoes.

The New Testament and the family of God

Moving finally to the New Testament we find the same ambiguity about the family, rendered even more sharply defined by the claims of Christ, the demands of the kingdom of God and the eschatological era in which we live.

Jesus and the family

It is clear from the Gospels that Jesus had a positive appreciation of the family, both in terms of marriage, children and the responsibilities of parenthood.[20] There are, for example, the narratives of Jesus' own birth and childhood in Matthew and Luke. Luke particularly emphasizes the role of Mary,

---

[20] A very helpful survey of the different perspectives on the family in each of the Gospels is provided by S. C. Barton, 'Family'.

mother of Jesus, both in his Gospel narrative and at the beginning of Acts (1:14). Luke preserves the ambivalent narrative of Jesus as a boy in the temple, an action in which he seems to put his heavenly Father's house or business above his parents' anxiety, but immediately follows it with the observation that as he grew up in Nazareth Jesus was obedient to his earthly parents (Luke 2:49–51). Then there is also Jesus' presence at the wedding in Cana, and his remarkable gift to the couple in their embarrassment (John 2).

As regards Jesus' teaching we could include his strong affirmation of marriage in his teaching on divorce (Mark 10:2–12; Matt. 5:31–32; 19:1–9), and his affirmation of the fifth commandment's duty to parents in rebuke to those who had sought to evade it under a cloak of piety (the Corban issue, Mark 7:9–13; Matt. 15:3–6).

Furthermore, many of the healing miracles of Jesus were compassionate responses to the family members of those who implored him on their behalf; for example especially those who asked him to heal children, and Simon's request for his mother-in-law. And even on the cross his compassion for his mother overrode his own agony for a moment (John 19:26–27).

On the other hand, the Gospels show clearly that following Jesus meant a radical reassessment of family ties. Discipleship could inject serious disruption into the whole social and economic sphere of family and household. Mark has scarcely brought Jesus onto the scene when he portrays him calling his first disciples. These men promptly leave their family businesses, including their father and his business, and follow Jesus. This may be portrayed in countless Christian sermons as an act of admirably radical commitment, which we should be willing to emulate. But their action was also one that undoubtedly would have been seen as socially scandalous and morally irresponsible in the culture of the time. The fact was that, even for Jesus, the breaking in of the kingdom of God in his own person meant he had to subordinate his own family to the imperative of proclaiming its arrival. So also all who would dare to follow him and believe his message must put the kingdom of God above all else, including even family duties where necessary. Indications of this priority of kingdom over family include the following:

- His words to his mother and brothers, deliberately distancing himself from their demands and identifying his true family as those who do the will of God (Mark 3:31–35). The question 'Who are my mother and my brothers?' was a remarkably shocking response to their summons. It must have sounded like he was virtually disowning his own kin. We know that of course Jesus did *not* do that, but in this stark way he presented the reality of 'kinship' with himself in the kingdom of God as a higher priority than human kinship obligations.

- Similarly shocking was his reply to the man who wanted to become a disciple but asked first to go and bury his father. Such filial piety was, and still is in many cultures today, possibly the highest social and religious priority expected of any son. Jesus' famous riposte 'Let the dead bury their dead' implies not only that the demands of discipleship and the urgency of the kingdom must come before the highest human duty, but also that those who refuse to act according to that priority have excluded themselves from the life of the kingdom and are virtually dead (Luke 9:59–60).
- The same stark clash of priorities is expressed in the demand that, in comparison with love for Jesus, the disciple's love for his parents and family must be regarded as hatred – a characteristic form of Hebrew hyperbole or comparative negation (Matt. 10:37; Luke 14:25–26). It is put in the same category as taking up the cross and not loving one's own life. With such radical and uncompromising demands, it is no wonder Jesus anticipates that his coming, far from bringing 'peace on earth', would first of all bring 'a sword' – a critical division between his followers and his enemies that would run through families and households just as much as through the rest of the community (Matt. 10:34–36; Luke 12:49–53). Hatred and persecution for the sake of Christ would be no respecter of family bonds (Mark 13:12–13). The history of Christian mission and martyrdom through the ages has proved him right.
- Such radical detachment from family commitments and securities for the sake of Christ and the kingdom of God, however, would find compensation in a whole new experience of 'family' – the family of God in Christ. Jesus' promise that those who have left home, or family, or possessions for the kingdom will receive a hundredfold such blessings is made in the context of his demand that the rich young ruler give up his wealth and follow Jesus, and Peter's almost tentative claim that he and his fellow disciples had done just that (Matt. 19:16–30; Mark 10:17–31; Luke 18:18–30). This brings me naturally to my final point.

The church as the family of God

It was indeed the experience of the early church that the new experience of 'family' in Christ, in terms of spiritual fellowship and its social and material expression, replaced, for some, the loss of natural family securities that accompanied their profession of loyalty to Christ. Yet, at the same time, the early Christian movement did not set itself against the normal forms of family life in society, but rather sought to sustain and redeem them under the lordship of Christ.

'We are his household (*oikos*)', says the letter to the Hebrews, addressing Christian readers (3:2–6). The writer is referring to Numbers 12:7, where the term refers to the people of Israel as the household of God with Moses as chief steward. This is one of the many places in the New Testament where language and pictures originally applied to ancient Israel are used of the Christian church, justified by the typological relationship that exists between them, focused on Jesus the Messiah. The expression 'house of Israel' was common in the Old Testament, as was the idea of Israel as the 'house of the the LORD (in contrast to their plight when they had been in Egypt, the 'house of bondage'). The 'house of God', of course, also commonly referred to the temple in Jerusalem. But occasionally it was used figuratively of the whole people and land of Israel combined. As such they constituted the household, the family, the inheritance, of God.[21] The point of the metaphor was that Israel was not just a nation or a collection of individuals, but a community with a sense of family oneness, a household belonging to God.

The background and content of the metaphor derive from the nature of the actual Israelite family, which we have already looked at in some detail. Two of its features may be emphasized in this context. First, it was a centre of *worship and teaching*, and was therefore a vital agent in maintaining the continuity of the traditions and faith of the nation from generation to generation. Secondly, it was the place *of inclusion, belonging and protection* for the individual. It was where individuals found the substance and experience of their status as members of the covenant people of God. That was the major reason for the special care commanded for widows, orphans and strangers – those who lacked the natural inclusion and protection of a household.

In the New Testament the Christian church saw itself as the inheritor of the title 'House of Israel', the family of God. This terminology could be applied both in the sense of the whole church (corresponding to the nation of Israel)[22] and in the sense of the smaller local church communities (corresponding to the Israelite extended family household). The second is of greater interest to us here. The use of family and household imagery for the local Christian churches was, of course, greatly facilitated by the historical fact that many of them originated as converted households and met in homes:

> What could be conveyed by the idea of the family of God had, in fact, already come into being in the early Christian community through the house churches. The household as a community . . . formed the smallest unit and basis of the congregation. The house churches mentioned in the NT (Acts 11:14; 16:15, 31, 34;

---

[21] E.g. Jer. 12:7; Hos. 8:1; 9:15; Mic. 4:2.

[22] E.g. Luke 1:33; Eph. 2:19; Heb. 3:3–6; 8:8–10; Gal. 6:10.

18:8; 1 Cor. 1:16; Phm. 2; 2 Tim. 1:16; 4:19) no doubt came into being through the use of homes as meeting places.[23]

Accordingly, the two features of the old Israelite family mentioned above are both seen to be operative in the New Testament local church family. First, it was the place of *worship and teaching*. Homes were used for the preaching of the gospel (Acts 5:42; 20:20). The Lord's Supper was celebrated there (Acts 2:46) and baptism was administered (1 Cor. 1:16; Acts 16:15). So the letters of Paul to his churches envisage them as living, learning and worshipping together in a 'household' spirit. Indeed, Paul operates the correspondence between church and family life in reverse, when he insists that those who exercise authority within the pastoral and teaching life of the *church* family must have proved themselves capable of managing their *own* household (1 Tim. 3:4–5, cf. 3:15).

Secondly, the local church was also the place of *belonging and inclusion*. From an ethical point of view this is perhaps the feature to emphasize here. Christians are born into, and so belong within, the family of God. Therefore, in company with the other members among whom God has placed us, we share the responsibilities and privileges of family membership. Among the responsibilities comes the obligation to share the family's 'substance', in the social and economic demands of genuine *koinōnia* fellowship, which I discussed in chapter 6. This also extended to a more general sense of mutual obligation within the family, as summed up by Paul: 'Therefore, as we have opportunity, let us do good to all people, especially to those who belong to the family of believers' (Gal. 6:10). The pervasive New Testament ethical emphasis on 'love for the brethren' is another expression of the 'family first' motif.

The primary privilege is, of course, that of full inclusion within the family of God, such that those who belong to the church through faith in Jesus the Messiah share in all the blessings of the promised inheritance. The Christian believer, Jew or Gentile, is no longer, like the guest or resident alien, a 'parafamily' person (*paroikos*), but has been given the status of a blood relative (Eph. 2:19).

But another important function of the church family was seen to be the provision of a kind of spiritual and even physical compensation, in cases where the natural human family ties of a member had been disrupted as a result of his or her response to the gospel. This disruption of natural family relationships was also something foreseen in the Old Testament and commented on by Jesus himself.

---

[23] Goetzmann, 'House', p. 250.

The way in which the Gospels take up Micah's prophecy of the end-time (Mic. 7:6 = Matt. 10:35f.; Luke 12:53) indicates that the primitive community had to reckon with the disruption of the family for the sake of the Gospel. Those who take this upon themselves are promised 'now in this time' new 'houses and brothers and sisters and mothers and children' (Mk. 10:29f.; Matt. 19:29; Lk. 18:29f.). The place of the disrupted family is taken by the family of God, the Christian community.[24]

One has to ask whether many local church families are sufficiently aware of this dimension of their reason for existence. Are they providing that social care and inclusion for those who, perhaps through very costly deliberate choice, come to them in circumstances that correspond to the widow, the orphan and the stranger of the Old Testament?

Once again, then, we find that social, economic and cultural aspects of ancient Israel's life feed through typologically into our understanding of the New Testament people of God. But having done so, they do not end there. Rather, we see that they then issue forth into new and perpetually relevant ethical principles for Christian living. In this context it is, therefore, interesting to notice that one of the paramount blessings commonly discovered by churches that experience a renewal of their spiritual life is a revival of a truly biblical fellowship. There is a rediscovery of the true social nature and function of the church as the household of God and of the privileges and responsibilities it entails. It is satisfying to realize that this has a depth and richness that owes much to the Old Testament soil in which the New Testament church had its roots and from which it drew its ethical nourishment – even if many of those in today's church who are enjoying this rediscovery are, as yet, unaware of those origins.

Further reading

Barton, S. C., 'Family', in J. B. Green and S. McKnight (eds.), *Dictionary of Jesus and the Gospels* (Downers Grove: InterVarsity Press; Leicester IVP, 1992), pp. 226–229.

Bendor, S., *The Social Structure of Ancient Israel: The Institution of the Family (Beit 'Ab) from the Settlement to the End of the Monarchy*, Jerusalem Biblical Studies, vol. 7, ed. E. Katzenstein (Jerusalem: Simor, 1996).

Brichto, Herbert C., 'Kin, Cult, Land and Afterlife – a Biblical Complex', *Hebrew Union College Annual* 44 (1973), pp. 1–54.

Gitari, David, 'The Church and Polygamy', *Transformation* 1 (1984), pp. 3–10.

---

[24] Ibid.

Goetzmann, J., 'House', in Colin Brown (ed.), *New International Dictionary of New Testament Theology*, vol. 2 (Carlisle: Paternoster, 1976), pp. 247–251.

Janzen, Waldemar, *Old Testament Ethics: A Paradigmatic Approach* (Louisville, KY: Westminster John Knox), 1994.

Matthews, V. H., 'Family Relationships', in Alexander and Baker, *Dictionary of the Old Testament: Pentateuch*, pp. 291–299.

Mott, Stephen Charles, *A Christian Perspective on Political Thought* (Oxford: Oxford University Press), 1993.

Perdue, Leo G., Blenkinsopp, J., and Collins, J. J., *Families in Ancient Israel* (Louisville, KY: Westminster John Knox), 1997.

Schluter, Michael, and Clements, Roy, *Reactivating the Extended Family: From Biblical Norms to Public Policy in Britain* (Cambridge: Jubilee Centre), 1986.

Sprinkle, J. M., 'Sexuality, Sexual Ethics', in Alexander and Baker, *Dictionary of the Old Testament: Pentateuch*, pp. 741–753.

Swartley, Willard M., *Slavery, Sabbath, War and Women: Case Issues in Biblical Interpretation* (Scottdale, PA: Herald), 1983.

Wright, Christopher J. H., 'What Happened Every Seven Years in Israel? Old Testament Sabbatical Institutions for Land, Debts and Slaves', *Evangelical Quarterly* 56 (1984), pp. 129–138, 193–201.

———, *God's People in God's Land: Family, Land and Property in the Old Testament* (Grand Rapids: Eerdmans, 1990; Carlisle: Paternoster, rev. ed., 1996).

———, 'Family', in Freedman, *Anchor Bible Dictionary*, vol. 2, pp. 761–769.

11. THE WAY OF THE INDIVIDUAL

The individual in community

We arrive now in the final chapter of this section, at the point where some might have expected me to begin; namely, Old Testament personal ethics, the moral demand God makes upon the individual in the whole course of his or her life and daily living. This order has been quite deliberate. It is my contention, as noted in chapter 2, that the individual aspects of Old Testament theology and ethics cannot be appreciated apart from an understanding of the community God called into being in his election and redemption of Israel. That is why I have devoted the foregoing chapters to the social aspects of Israel as a nation before narrowing the focus to the individual. In fact, the distinction between social and personal ethics is not always helpful or appropriate in the Old Testament, for individual ethics are 'community-shaped'.

Those of us who are Westerners have to undergo a certain reorientation in our habitual pattern of ethical thought in this matter if we are to see things from an Old Testament perspective. We tend to begin at the individual level and work outwards. Our emphasis is to persuade people individually to live a certain kind of life according to this or that moral standard. If only enough individuals would live up to these standards, then, almost as a by-product, society itself would be improved or at least maintained as a healthy, happy, safe environment for individuals to pursue their own personal goodness. Our emphasis is to say, *this* is the kind of person you must be; *that* is the kind of society that lies as a bonus in the background.

In traditional cultures not yet eroded by Western individualism, however, the pattern of ethical thinking tends to start the other way round. The way the community understands itself governs what is acceptable or unacceptable individual behaviour. This is certainly the way the Old Testament works. It says, here is the kind of society the LORD God wants. This God's desire is for a holy people, a redeemed community, a model society through whom God can display a prototype of the new humanity whom he intends to create. God wants a community that will reflect God's own character and priorities, especially marked by justice and compassion. Now if *that* is the kind of society God wants, *this* is the kind of person you must be if you belong to it. Individual ethics are thus derived from the theology of the redeemed people of God. Put another way, individual ethics in the Old Testament, just as much as social ethics, are *covenantal.* The covenant was established between God and Israel as a *people*, but its moral implications affected every *person* within it.

This feature of Old Testament ethics is wholly in accord with the ethical emphasis of the New Testament. Much of the ethical instruction there is given in the context of the nature of the community God has called into being in Christ. Individuals are called to ethical behaviour in the context of the whole church, living, learning and worshipping together and serving Christ in the world. Thus, for example, the great ethical chapters of Ephesians 4 – 6 begin with the call to 'live a life worthy of the calling you have received'. From the preceding chapters this means the calling to be a member of God's new society, the miracle of social and spiritual reconciliation God has created through Christ. The *personal* moral standards of the later chapters are asserted on the basis of membership of the redeemed *community* expounded in the earlier ones.

So, one possible way to assemble a substantial quantity of the moral requirements of God upon the individual would be to work through the foregoing chapters on Israelite society and produce appendices containing the logical moral implications for the individual. For example, if God desired a society characterized by economic equality and compassion, then it required the individual Israelite to forgo selfishness and resist the temptation to cash in unjustly on the misfortunes of a neighbour. If God wanted a society founded on justice and ordered by known and upheld laws, then it was up to individual judges to act impartially and incorruptibly. And so one could go on through the whole spectrum of social characteristics, drawing out their individual entailments.

Since readers can make their own deductions, however, they would find it tedious to wade through lengthy lists of fairly obvious results. The only point I want to establish here is this matter of perspective. In biblical ethics it is the nature of the *community* God seeks (and will, in the eschatological vision, ultimately create) that governs the kind of *person* God approves. Social and personal are inseparable in Old Testament ethics.[1]

Personal responsibility

However, having made that point, I carefully stress that this does not mean that such a community-orientated ethic in any way replaces, let alone diminishes, the moral responsibility of the individual. The obligation of an individual oarsman to pull his weight is no less, just because the object of the exercise is for the whole crew to win races and fulfil the expectations of their coach. Likewise, for all its emphasis on the corporate aspect of God's moral demand, the Old Testament never loses sight of, never waives, the obligation on the individual to live uprightly before God. The first questions in the Bible, addressed to Adam and Eve, assume personal accountability: 'Where are you? . . . Who told you? . . . What have you done?' (Gen. 3:9–13). But the same questions address every human individual whom Adam and Eve represented. Similarly, God's question to Cain 'Where is your brother?' (Gen. 4:9) extends its claim to every individual, for each of us carries responsibility, under God, for fellow human beings. Such Godward accountability for our own behaviour and for our treatment of one another is the essence of being human. We humans are the creatures, unique among all the rest, whom God holds personally and individually answerable for our conduct. For we are individually made in God's image – addressable by God and accountable to God. That is a fundamental dimension of what it means to be a human being, a person, an individual.

As the story of the Old Testament moves forward, we find the same attention paid to the conduct of individuals. The story begins with the faith and obedience of an individual, Abraham. Indeed, the ethical nature of Abraham's obedience is stressed as the reason for the continuation of the covenant. When God renews it with Isaac he says he is doing so 'because Abraham obeyed me and kept my requirements, my commands, my decrees and my laws' (Gen. 26:5). The patriarchal (ancestral) narratives are models of the power, providence and patience of God in the lives of individuals, which would in due course be so manifest and necessary in the history of the nation.

At Sinai the covenant that had been made with the individual Abraham for

---

[1] More detailed reflections on the way Old Testament ethics is governed by, and derives authority from, its presentation of the people God created (among other things, of course) are found in the final section of chapter 14 below.

the sake of his descendants is renewed and expanded with the whole nation of those descendants. But it is then applied to every individual. The essence of the covenant relationship is corporate: 'I will be your God; you will be my people.' Here 'you' and 'your' are plural. But the primary demand of the covenant is addressed to the individual, with a singular 'you': 'You shall have no other gods before me.'

The same individual thrust is true of the rest of the Ten Commandments, and indeed of a substantial number of the detailed laws of the Pentateuch. The earliest law code, the 'Book of the Covenant' (Exod. 21 – 23), operates legislatively on the unmistakable ground of individual responsibility and liability before the law. Indeed, as we saw in chapter 9, vicarious or collective forms of punishment, which excused or diminished the individual's liability, were legally excluded in the realm of normal, human judicial procedure (Exod. 21:31; Deut. 24:16). It is well known among scholars that the Hebrew text of Deuteronomy oscillates between addressing Israel in the second person ('You'), in the plural and in the singular. This is no longer thought to be an indication of different documents or authors within the text, but a stylistic way of showing that God's moral claim upon his people's behaviour addressed both the whole community and also every individual within it.

Moving from the law to the prophets, it is, of course, obvious that the primary calling of the prophets was to address the nation, or nationally representative individuals, such as kings and other leaders. However, in the midst of this social and corporate task the prophets did not hesitate to confront individuals with the moral challenge of the word of God addressed to specific individual acts. Deborah rebuked Barak for his lethargy (Judg. 4:8–9). Samuel challenged Saul regarding his disobedience (1 Sam. 15:22–23). Nathan confronted David with his adultery and murder (2 Sam. 12:1–10). Elijah denounced Ahab for injustice and murder (1 Kgs. 21:17ff.). Isaiah, having failed to get Ahaz to trust in God, rebuked him for his faithless disobedience (Is. 7:1–13). Jeremiah opposed the false prophets, collectively (Jer. 23:9–40) and individually (Jer. 28), and mercilessly exposed the individual greed and oppression of King Jehoiakim (Jer. 22:13–19).

Ezekiel has often been credited with the introduction of his insight on individual responsibility as though it were something new in the ethical thought-world of Israel (Ezek. 18). This is because he condemns the idea that the generation in exile could blame all their suffering on the sins of their fathers, and counter-argues, in his famous words, 'it is the person who sins who will die' (Ezek. 18:4). But the view that Ezekiel 'invented' the doctrine of individual responsibility has been abandoned by those who have looked more closely both at the true relationship between corporate and individual in Israelite thought, and at what Ezekiel was actually arguing.

On the one hand, the fact that Israel had a strong concept of corporate solidarity did not mean, as some scholars in the past had maintained, that Israel had no understanding of individual responsibility prior to the exilic period. The individuality of the early legal texts (e.g. the Book of the Covenant, as we saw), centuries before Ezekiel, proves that. It is clear that in the courts of Israel individuals were held individually liable for their actions, and punished or vindicated accordingly.[2]

On the other hand, Ezekiel was involved in an 'evangelistic' exercise (see the ending of Ezek. 18). For this purpose he needed to clear away false notions that were being used as a pretext to avoid responsibility. The exiles were blaming their fate on previous generations. They were trying to argue that it was all very unfair that God had now let his judgment fall on *their* generation, after so many generations of wickedness before them. *They* were being made to suffer innocently for the sins of others, they protested. But Ezekiel denies the premise. They were not the innocent children of wicked parents. They themselves were fully responsible for their own behaviour, which was so unquestionably wicked that they deserved God's judgment in their own right. They must face up to their own guilt and responsibility. So Ezekiel begins by refuting a popular proverb (18:2) and then lays out a complex generational case study that embodies a doctrine of personal ethics consistent with Deuteronomy 24:16. The thrust of Ezekiel's case study is also to make clear that just as each generation will stand or fall according to its moral response to God's law, so can each individual. To turn from righteousness to wickedness is to court disaster. But – and this is the wonderful evangelistic gospel of the chapter – when wicked people turn from wickedness and demonstrate their repentance with a radical ethical change of life, then they will find God's forgiveness and their life will be spared. Ezekiel's sermon certainly gives a new depth and challenge to personal responsibility, and he certainly sets out clearly the life or death issues involved in personal moral choices and habits. But his argument is a *development* of well-established Old Testament faith, not a radical *innovation*.

---

[2] Early anthropological studies of ancient Israel propounded concepts of communal responsibility and corporate personality that have largely been exposed as based on a priori assumptions. There was a reaction against such views in the 1960s and 1970s, but they still tend to get resuscitated – especially when the idea is touted yet again that Ezekiel, on the basis of Ezekiel 18, was the 'inventor' of individual responsibility. For counter-arguments, see George E. Mendenhall, 'Relation of the Individual to Political Society'; J. Roy Porter, 'Legal Aspects of the Concept of "Corporate Personality"'; John W. Rogerson, 'Hebrew Conception of Corporate Personality'.

Models of morals

We move on now from the general considerations of the last two sections to something more specific. For the Old Testament provides us with a number of models of the kind of personal ethical life pleasing to God (and of the opposite). It is not the multitude of actual individuals who populate the pages of Old Testament history that I have in mind, though these constitute a rich quarry for personal moral lessons, as every Sunday school teacher knows. Rather, my concern now is with the character portraits that occur in various forms, giving an identikit picture of the typical qualities of the righteous person. These reflect what Waldemar Janzen calls the classic 'paradigms' of behaviour in ancient Israel.[3] Janzen uses the word 'paradigm' in a slightly different way to me. Whereas I use it mainly to describe the total structure of Israel as presented to us in the Old Testament, Janzen uses the term to speak of the patterns of ideal behaviour that, he believes, governed the ethical decision-making of Israelites. And these paradigms – or portraits of the ideal family, or ideal priest, king or prophet – were shaped mainly by the narratives.

Gordon Wenham, in his suggestive study of the rhetorical strategy of Genesis, also concludes that a model of ethical behaviour is being presented through the variety of stories:

> Thus out of the stories of Genesis we can build up a catalogue of the virtues as they are perceived by the author, an identikit picture of the righteous. He or she is pious, that is prayerful and dependent on God. Strong and courageous, but not aggressive or mean. He or she is generous, truthful and loyal, particularly to other family members. The righteous person is not afraid to express emotions of joy, grief or anger, but the last should not spill over into excessive revenge, rather he should be ready to forgive. Finally righteousness does not require asceticism: the pleasures of life are to be enjoyed without becoming a slave to them.[4]

To complete the line of thought suggested here by Janzen and Wenham, we shall consider a number of such 'paradigmatic' portraits of model behaviour in the Old Testament. First, there is the world of the wise – a world very much concerned with patterns (and consequences) of human choices. Then we shall look at several individuals who present case studies of ethical and unethical behaviour – either in moral self-defence or for a wider apologetic. And finally, we shall go to worship with ancient Israel and observe how

---

[3]   Waldemar Janzen, *Ethics*.
[4]   Wenham, *Story as Torah*, p. 100.

ethical criteria were on prominent display to challenge those who thought to come into the courts of the Holy One of Israel.

The wise person

The Wisdom literature of the Old Testament, for all its international connections and assimilations, stands firmly within the mainstream of Israel's Yahwistic faith. As its theme verse insists, 'The fear of the LORD is the beginning [or first principle] of wisdom' (Prov. 9:10).[5] The Wisdom literature has a deep social concern, like the law and the prophets, but the bulk of its sayings are directed at the individual. These proverbs are collected to inform, forewarn, correct and guide the individual Israelite in that path of life which is both pleasing to God and in his or her own best interests.

Although the prevailing interest of Proverbs appears to be anthropocentric (concerned about the affairs of human life), there is an interesting and indirect God-centredness underlying it. So many of the *human* character traits, behaviour patterns and moral values commended in the Wisdom texts do in fact reflect the known character of *God*, as described elsewhere in the Old Testament. In this respect the personal ethics of Proverbs bear out the point made in chapter 1 about Old Testament ethics embodying a strong element of imitation of the ways of God himself. A few examples will sketch in the outlines of this particular model. I shall begin in each case with some feature of the LORD as God, and then observe how the Wisdom model for human life reflects that:

'*God created man in his own image. Male and female he created them.*' Human sexuality is a dimension of the image of God in human life, and is therefore infinitely precious. The wise person therefore avoids any abuse of it, especially the destructive consequences of seduction and adultery (Prov. 2:16–22; 5; 6:20–35; 7). Instead, the wise choice is to find continually fresh delight and joy within faithful marriage (5:15–19; 31:10–31; cf. Song).

God is the divine parent (cf. Deut. 32:6, 18). The parent–child relationship is used as a figure for God's relationship to his people. So we find that a lot of the teaching in Proverbs is cast in a 'father-to-son' form, which has a divine–human ambiguity about it. That is, on the surface it speaks out of that human relationship (though it may reflect other forms of authority under the parental guise – e.g. of the king, or court), but the voice of the 'father' in the text clearly also reflects the voice of God in the warnings and advice being given. But there is nothing ambiguous about the authority expected of human fathers and mothers, or the discipline and punishment affirmed as a function,

---

[5] For this way of reading the text, see Henri Blocher, 'Fear of the Lord'.

not a denial, of familial love (Prov. 13:24; 15:5; 19:18; 22:15). Conversely, humility and obedience are required of the 'wise son' (13:1, 18). The sage feels the joys and pains of parenthood as keenly as God feels for his wayward people (10:1; 17:21; 19:26; 23:24–25).

God is righteous, both as king and as judge. So Proverbs has plenty to say to the individuals who find themselves in either of those offices. Political and judicial justice matter as much to the sage as to the law-giver and prophet (Prov. 16:10, 12–15; 17:15; 18:5; 20:8, 26; 22:22; 28:3, 16; 29:14; 31:1–9). Here is an area where the social and moral health of the wider community depends very much on the integrity and commitment of individuals and the decisions they make.

God is love. The LORD's unmerited kindness and infinite faithfulness were keynotes in the praises of Israel. Such qualities are to be reflected in human friendships. One of the most attractive features of the wise person as com-mended by the book of Proverbs is the quality of his or her friendships, the subtlety and maturity of his or her social skills. The wise person knows the values of tact (15:1), confidentiality (11:13), patience (14:29), honesty (15:31–32; 27:6), forgiveness (17:9), loyalty (17:17; 18:24), considerate behaviour (25:17; 27:14) and practical help (27:10). Conversely, the wise person also knows the dangers of bought friendship (19:4), of gossip (20:19), anger (22:24–25), flattery (27:21) and misplaced sympathy (25:20). These are all down-to-earth practical ways in which the command of the law to 'love your neighbour as yourself', as a reflection of the love of God for us and of our love for God, is dressed in the everyday clothes of individual ethics.

God is compassionate and generous. The history of Israel, including the delivery from slavery and the gift of the land, proved both of these. Indeed, it was in the wake of the exodus that God proclaimed the definition of his own name and character: 'Yahweh, Yahweh, the compassionate and gracious God . . .' (Exod. 34:6). Practical concern for the poor was therefore laid on the shoul-ders of every Israelite. Many of the sayings of the sage concerning wealth and poverty and economic justice have a thoroughly modern relevance (Prov. 11:24–25; 14:31; 17:5; 19:17; 21:13; 22:9, 16).[6]

God is a worker. God has transmitted something of his own infinite skill in creation (see Prov. 8) in a finite degree to human beings made in God's own image. Human beings also, therefore, are workers by nature and design. Accordingly, the virtues and rewards of work are set before the individual in

---

[6] See above, chapter 5, for further discussion of the response to poverty that we encounter in Israel's Wisdom literature, and the different ways in which scholars have evaluated it.

Proverbs. These positives are contrasted with the laziness of 'sluggard'. This latter figure is portrayed vividly in tragicomic colours. But he is more than a laughing stock. His deliberate, habitual and absurdly rationalized laziness is a denial of his humanity and an insult to his Maker (Prov. 12:11; 14:23; 18:9; 22:13; 24:30–34; 26:13–16; 28:19).

God speaks. This is one of the chief and most distinctive features of the *living* God of Israel, and surely one of God's highest gifts to humanity is the boundless power of verbal communication. Words matter deeply to the authors of Proverbs, for they see words as powerful vehicles of good or evil, just as much so as actual deeds. So there is a lot of advice and warning for the wise person about his or her use or abuse of words (Prov. 12:19, 22; 13:3; 14:5; 15:2, 23; 18:6–8, 20–21).

God is sovereign. God has given each person freedom and responsibility in his or her moral decisions and choices, but in the end it will be God's will that counts (Prov. 16:1–2, 9; 19:21; 21:1–2, 30–31). The essence of wisdom, there-fore, is to accept the paradox of this ultimately incomprehensible truth, and to seek God's guidance in the humility of commitment and obedience (3:5ff.; 16:3). This, in a great variety of shapes, is the meaning of the pervasive message 'seek wisdom'. Conversely, 'the fool' in Proverbs is not intellectually defective (he may be very clever indeed). Rather, the fool is the person whose life is lived deliberately, boastingly – even scoffingly – without reference to God. Wisdom and folly in the Old Testament are not primarily intellectual concepts, but moral and spiritual. Wisdom is to choose to live within the will and guidance of the sovereign God. Folly is to think you can live in defiance of both.

Before leaving the model of the wise person, let us observe that the beauti-ful portrait which brings the book of Proverbs to a conclusion and climax sums up all these characteristics in the feminine dress of the 'wife of noble character' (Prov. 31:10–31). She exemplifies sexual integrity (vv. 11–12), paren-tal care (v. 15), productive and profitable work (vv. 16–19), compassion and generosity (v. 20), support of the judicial role of her husband (v. 23), whole-some speech (v. 26), and the fear of the LORD (v. 30). She reflects, in other words, the Lord she worships.

The moral apologia

Job

The Wisdom literature includes Job. That powerful reflection on the relation-ship between personal morality and undeserved suffering furnishes us with another example of the paradigm of personal ethics – the moral apologia, or self-defence. Job, of course, defends his own moral uprightness all the way through the book. His whole case is that his suffering has not been brought about by his own wickedness. He resists the increasingly manipulative attempts of his friends to get him to confess to sins he knows he has not committed, in order to escape the pain of a punishment he knows he has not deserved. This, he claims, is the integrity he will never surrender.

But the climax of Job's case comes in Job 31 – a chapter of superb poetic and ethical power, in which Job invokes a long series of self-curses in support of his claim to have led an upright life. Because of the curse formula of the speech, the ethical points are necessarily framed in the negative. Job is rehearsing the kinds of deeds he has *not* been guilty of, the kind of person he has *not* been, and inviting God to inflict various stereotypical disasters upon him if he is not speaking the truth. That is the nature of the self-curse formula of the chapter. But the negatives can easily be processed into positive prints, snapshots of the kind of person Job actually was, or was claiming to be. In summary, Job's list includes the following comprehensive claims. In his own self-defence, he claims to have

- disciplined himself against lust (v. 1);
- refrained also from actual adultery (vv. 9–12);
- been honest in trade (vv. 5–6);
- acted with justice in relation to his slaves (vv. 13–15);
- been generous and compassionate to all classes of the poor (vv. 16–23);
- avoided idolatry, whether in the form of materialism or of astrology (vv. 24–28);
- controlled his thoughts and tongue (vv. 29–30);
- shown hospitality (vv. 31–32);
- been willing to make open confession of sin (vv. 33–34);
- treated both land and labourers properly, including just payment (vv. 38–40).

Two things are worthy of comment. One is the breadth of moral behaviour included in this remarkable listing. It extends from the thoughts of the heart, through spoken words, private actions, sexual and family affairs, to economic, judicial, social and public conduct. Clearly, personal ethics in the thinking of the author of this book covered a very wide range of life: inward and outward, private and public, seen and unseen. The other noteworthy point is the role played by God in the moral reasoning. God is all-seeing (4), and evaluates every act (6, 14). God is the creator of all human beings and therefore the protector of everyone's equal rights, including slaves (15). God holds the sanction of judgment upon wrongdoing (23), especially on idolatry, which is disloyalty to him (28). In short, God is inescapable, and the whole of life is lived before God and under his moral inspection. As another sage had said:

> Death and Destruction lie open before the LORD –
>   how much more the hearts of men!
>
> (Prov. 15:11)

Samuel

A second example of this moral self-defence is found on the lips of Samuel in his farewell speech when he hands over political power to Saul (1 Sam. 12:2–5). It is much shorter and refers only to the sphere of social morality, as was appropriate to the occasion. Samuel was handing in the accounts for his public leadership. So he asked for public testimony of his incorrupt tenure of office. Samuel's list of questions and the people's response exonerated him from the charges of

- theft or extortion (personal profit from public office), and
- bribery (personal profit from judicial power).

This short passage indicates the qualities of integrity in public office that were expected even then. Indeed, it was the failure of Samuel's own sons to maintain Samuel's standards that triggered the successful bid for kingship (1 Sam. 8:1–5).

Ezekiel

A third list of virtues and vices that might be included here is the repeated list in Ezekiel 18. It is not so much a particular individual's moral apologia as an outline of the typical features of righteousness and wickedness as they had been manifested by succeeding generations. It is set up as a case study by Ezekiel, who uses all his training as a priest to set out a moral-legal case. Again the list is specific, and it overlaps with Job and Samuel at several points. According to Ezekiel, the sins that the paradigmatic righteous person avoids include the following:

- idolatry (6a)
- adultery and other sexual offences (6b)
- oppression of the poor, such as by failing to return pledges taken for debt (7a)
- robbery (7b)
- failure to feed the hungry and clothe the naked (7c)
- lending for exorbitant profit through usury (8a)

- failure to judge fairly in lawsuits (8b)
- violence and murder (10)

We note again how the Old Testament intermingles what we tend to keep in separate compartments as 'private' and 'public' morality. Ezekiel would have had no patience with the curious modern idea that people's private sexual life and infidelities have no bearing on their public integrity or trustworthiness. Also noteworthy is the point that failure to do positive good is also a sin. The complacent attitude every pastor battles with 'Of course I'm a Christian; I never do anyone any harm' would have been curtly dismissed by Ezekiel. It was not enough, in defining the righteous person, to say, 'He does not commit robbery' (18:7), without adding, 'but gives his food to the hungry and provides clothing for the naked' (18:16). Here is a clear foreshadowing of the moral teaching of Jesus himself, which is even more explicitly echoed by Paul: 'He who has been stealing must steal no longer, but must work, doing something useful with his own hands, that he may have something to share with those in need' (Eph. 4:28).

The acceptable worshipper

Other lists of virtues and vices in the prophets are found in those contexts where the prophets are addressing the matter of worship and ethics. Too often the prophets observed people whose lives lacked ethical integrity coming to worship, people who presumed to perform the rituals of worship while living in blatant wickedness. But for the prophets there could be no peaceful coexistence between sacred rites and social wrongs. There was no shortage of religion and ritual in Amos's day, but the rampant social injustice made a blasphemous mockery of it. Amos said so and was thrown out (Amos 4:4–5; 5:21–27; 8:5–6). Isaiah echoed the same note (Is. 1:10–17). Both prophets injected short lists of positive social ethics into their case:

> Stop doing wrong,
>   learn to do right!
> Seek justice,
>   encourage the oppressed.
> Defend the cause of the fatherless,
>   plead the case of the widow.

> (Is. 1:16–17)

> Seek good, not evil,
>   that you may live.
> Then the LORD God Almighty will be with you,

> just as you say he is.
> Hate evil, love good;
>> maintain justice in the courts.

(Amos 5:14–15)

The shortest and yet most comprehensive positive list comes in Micah 6, and once again comes in the context of a reflection on what constitutes acceptable worship. Having heard God's indictment of his people in 6:1–5, Micah wonders what will be appropriate as a sacrifice fit for repentance: 'With what shall I come before the LORD?' After questioning the adequacy of any offering, even of his own firstborn, he utters the memorable declaration, inescapably individual in its challenge and relevance,

> He has showed you, O man, what is good.
> And what does the LORD require of you?
> To act justly and to love mercy
>> and to walk humbly with your God.

(Mic. 6:8)

Jeremiah was sent to the very gate of the temple, there to confront the approaching worshippers with the moral demands of the God of the covenant whom they claimed to worship and whose protection they presumed upon. Jeremiah outlines the kind of practical behaviour that would be evidence of true repentance and contrasts it with what they are actually doing. The details of his indictment, providing again the typical characteristics of the unrighteous, include (Jer. 7:1–11)

- oppression of the alien, the orphan and the widow
- shedding innocent blood
- idolatry
- presumptuous false security and complacency
- theft
- adultery
- perjury

Isaiah 58 contrasts a merely ritual fasting with the ethics of true repentance. True repentance will bear practical fruit, in another typical list:

> Is not this the kind of fasting I have chosen:
> to loose the chains of injustice
>> and untie the cords of the yoke,

> to set the oppressed free
>> and break every yoke?
> Is it not to share your food with the hungry
>> and to provide the poor wanderer with shelter –
> when you see the naked, to clothe him,
>> and not to turn away from your own flesh and blood?

(Is. 58:6–7)

It is not hard to detect echoes of the Decalogue in these passages (similarly in Hos. 4:1–2). Indeed, some scholars think that the Ten Commandments were used in public liturgy as part of the 'entrance requirements' for those coming to worship. If this cultic use of the Decalogue was indeed practised, then Jeremiah was reawakening people to the demands of what may have become a toothless ritual. Certainly, whether or not the Decalogue was used in this way, we do have two other clear examples of 'entrance requirement' liturgy, in Psalms 15 and 24.

> LORD, who may dwell in your sanctuary?
>> Who may live on your holy hill?
> He whose walk is blameless
>> and who does what is righteous . . .

(Ps. 15:1–2)

The psalm goes on to outline the acceptable worshipper as a person who

- speaks the truth from the heart;
- avoids hurtful action, words and thoughts;
- shows proper discrimination in his associations;
- is loyal to his word, even to his own cost;
- is uncorrupted by the lure of money, either through usury or judicial bribery.

Psalm 24 is more succinct, and brackets outward act and inward motive in the memorable phrase 'He who has clean hands and a pure heart' (Ps. 24:4).[7]

These are only the most obvious examples of a theme that runs throughout the Psalms, and indeed many parts of the Old Testament: acceptable worship is inseparably linked with acceptable living. The liturgy of Israel is

---

[7] On the interesting links between Israel's worship and the ethical assumptions of a psalm such as Psalm 15, see R. E. Clements, 'Worship and Ethics'.

saturated with moral contrasts. The tone is set in the very opening psalm. For all the depth of the psalter's corporate awareness, the dividing line of right-eousness and wickedness, blessedness and judgment meets the steps of every individual: 'Blessed is the *person* who . . .' It is in worship that the demands of the covenant between the LORD and the whole nation confront afresh every individual, even in the secret places of the heart and in relation to sins hidden from public view or detection.

Exposing even the hidden sins of individuals was probably the function of the list of curses in Deuteronomy 27:14–26. Here is a list that left no loophole for the popular excuse 'It's all right so long as nobody finds out.' Again, the contents of that list are significant, tying in with the other lists we have noted, both in general intention and in some specific details. Deuteronomy 27 includes curses upon the following:

- idolatry
- dishonour to parents
- removal of boundary stones (economic fraud)
- leading the blind astray (social callousness)
- withholding justice from alien, orphan or widow
- sexual offences, including adultery, bestiality and incest
- secret murder
- accepting bribery for 'judicial murder'
- general failure to keep the law

It is also in worship that ethical perspectives are sharpened and readjusted to see things from God's point of view, rather than through the confusion and frustration of outward appearances. This is the experience profoundly described in Psalm 73. The poet is scarcely able to hold on grimly to his per-sonal moral integrity and his belief in God's moral justice in the face of the prosperity of the wicked and suffering of the righteous (vv. 1–16). But when he went to *worship* in the sanctuary (v. 17), his insight and moral assurance were restored by a fresh vision of God's ultimate purposes. Worship and ethics are inseparably linked in Israel's faith and worldview.

Another way of recognizing the importance of worship in the formation of Israel's ethical worldview is to recall that it was in the context of worship that the great stories of Israel's past were recounted. These were the narra-tives that infinitely repeated and underscored the character of the LORD. These were the narratives that thereby entered into the consciousness of Israel as a powerfully shaping and sustaining ethical force. We tend to focus more than we probably ought on the *law* of the Old Testament when, in the everyday experience of the people, it was more likely the regular experience of *narrative-in-worship* that orientated their ethical compass and provided both internal and community-validated values and sanctions.[8]

Failure and forgiveness

To see things from God's perspective is, of course, much more uncomfortable when your gaze is directed at yourself. For then that awareness of personal sin, failure and inadequacy becomes acute. This brings us to one of the most profound and important ethical features of the Old Testament, and one of its central contributions to the faith and ethics of biblical religion, Jewish and Christian – the awareness of human ethical failure combined with the amazing grace of divine forgiveness.

We have had occasion to reckon with the effects of the fall in all the areas of social ethics considered in the earlier chapters of this book. Sin is undoubtedly portrayed as having its effect in the social realm, and in the accumulating processes of history. We now discover that the Old Testament is no less radical and comprehensive in the way it describes the effect of sin upon every aspect of personal human life as well. The verdict of Genesis on humanity could scarcely be more total: 'every inclination of the thoughts of his heart was only evil all the time' (Gen. 6:5); 'every inclination of his heart is evil from childhood' (Gen. 8:21). The universality of these affirmations is both generic (all human beings without exception are sinners) and specific (every aspect of the individual's personality is affected by sin).

Thus the sage enquires rhetorically, expecting no hands raised in answer,

> Who can say, 'I have kept my heart pure;
> I am clean and without sin'?
>
> (Prov. 20:9)

So Old Testament ethics stand on a foundation of realism. Without lessening the great moral absolutes of God's demand, they take full account of our human moral predicament, ranging from sheer frailty and weakness to outright obstinate rebellion. Jeremiah, who perhaps had closer prolonged contact with wickedness than many another, saw the penetration of evil to the depths of man's constitution:

---

[8] Among the scholars who have particularly focused on the ethical power of narrative, in addition to Janzen and Wenham, mentioned above, see, e.g., Bruce C. Birch, 'Old Testament Narrative and Moral Address'; and 'Moral Agency'.

> The heart is deceitful above all things
>   and beyond cure.
>   Who can understand it?

(Jer. 17:9)

He also saw that sin could not be erased by one's own effort:

> Can the Ethiopian change his skin
>   or the leopard its spots?
> Neither can you do good
>   who are accustomed to doing evil.

(Jer. 13:23)

> Although you wash yourself with soda
>   and use an abundance of soap,
>   the stain of your guilt is still before me.

(Jer. 2:22)

But such realism need not lead to despair. Awareness of sin and failure is not the paralysis of ethics in the Old Testament. Knowing your sin does not *stop* you walking in the way of the LORD; it simply tells you where you have to *start* from, before you can set foot on it. That starting point was God's objective provision of atonement and the subjective experience of forgiveness. In the Old as well as the New Testament, gospel precedes ethics. So we can see that the detailed provisions of the elaborate Levitical sacrificial system had its ethical significance. Not only did it enable the Israelite to receive cleansing for past misdeeds, through the atoning blood of sacrifice; it also thereby reassured the repentant worshipper of continuing inclusion within the covenant people of God. And that was the only position in which the word and will of the LORD could be known and obeyed in the future.

But Israel also knew that God's redeeming power transcended the rituals of sacrifice. The LORD's essential character as the saving and forgiving God is a reality to which appeal can be made even when no sacrifice is available or possible. Even the bleak verdicts of Genesis, quoted above, are set in the context of God's miraculous deliverance of Noah, the prototype of redemption. Jeremiah, for all his pessimism, looked forward to the new covenant when, God promises,

> I will forgive their wickedness
>   and will remember their sins no more.

(Jer. 31:34)

Ezekiel too could see the transforming power of God replacing hearts of stone that were calloused in evil with hearts of flesh, reborn and filled with his Spirit (Ezek. 36:25–27; 37:1–14).

Again it is the psalmists who reveal most deeply the meaning of repentance, forgiveness and the ethical freedom and joy that issues from them. Both Psalms 25 and 32 pray for forgiveness of sins, the latter after deep conviction and confession. And both psalms link the experience of forgiveness to the expectation of both guidance and ability in the ethical sphere. It is the *repentant and forgiven sinner* whom God enables to live as pleases him:

> he instructs sinners in his ways.
> He guides the humble in what is right . . .

> (Ps. 25:8–9)

> you forgave
>   the guilt of my sin . . .
> I will instruct you and teach you in the way you should go . . .

> (Ps. 32:5, 8)

Perhaps no-one knew this better than David. Though David could be called 'a man after God's own heart',[9] he nevertheless descended to the lowest depths of deception, violence, lust and evil. Yet, as king, he was supposed to give moral guidance to his people, by example and instruction. But how could such a flawed character lead others? Only by the supernatural grace of a forgiving, cleansing, renewing God:

> Create in me a pure heart, O God,
>   and renew a steadfast spirit within me . . .
> *Then* I will teach transgressors your ways,
>   and sinners will turn back to you.

> (Ps. 51:10, 13; my italics)

The ethical power of forgiveness is discussed by Stanley Hauerwas, another scholar who stresses the importance of the narrative tradition in the

---

[9] 'A man after God's own heart' probably does not so much mean 'someone whom God was specially fond of' (a kind of favouritism the English phrase seems to suggest, but the Bible elsewhere denies, about God), but rather, someone who will carry out God's will and purpose ('heart' being the Hebrew for purposeful intentions, not primarily for emotions).

Bible for shaping the ethical life of the community, and thereby the ethical life of the individual:

> The moral use of the scripture, therefore, lies precisely in its power to help us remember the stories of God for the continual guidance of our community and individual lives . . . The narrative of scripture not only 'renders a character' [sc. God] but renders a community capable of ordering its existence appropriate to such stories. Jews and Christians believe this narrative does nothing less than render the character of God and in so doing renders us to be the kind of people appropriate to that character . . .
>
> The question of the moral significance of scripture, therefore, turns out to be a question about what kind of community the church must be to be able to make the narratives of scripture central for its life . . .
>
> Scripture has authority for Christians because they have learned as a forgiven people they must also be able to forgive [which separates us from the world which lives by power and thinks it needs no forgiveness] . . . Being a community of the forgiven is directly connected with being a community sustained by the narratives we find in scripture, as those narratives do nothing less than manifest the God whose very nature is to forgive.[10]

But let us give the final word to Isaiah. For it was to people whom he had accused of being filled with the blood of wickedness and oppression, people whose worship was a wearisome, sickening abomination to God, that he addressed the breathtaking invitation of God's saving 'reasonableness':

> 'Come now, let us reason together,'
>   says the LORD.
> 'Though your sins are like scarlet,
>   they shall be as white as snow;
> though they are red as crimson,
>   they shall be like wool.'

(Is. 1:18)

But this saving word of gospel is at once followed by the inescapable ethical challenge

> 'If you are willing and obedient,
>   you will eat the best from the land;

---

[10] Hauerwas, *Community of Character*, pp. 66–69.

> but if you resist and rebel,
>> you will be devoured by the sword.'
>>>>>> For the mouth of the LORD has spoken.
>>>>>>>> (Is. 1:19–20)

In the same book of Isaiah we find the great vision that ultimately the focus of atonement will not be a place or an object, but a person, the Servant of the LORD. We see this mysterious figure, in the climactic description of his rejection and triumph, Isaiah 52:13 – 53:12, suffering vicariously, victoriously and effectively, for sins not his own but ours. For in God's redemptive purpose,

> the LORD has laid on him
>> the iniquity of us all . . .
> It was the LORD's will to . . .
> [make] his life a guilt offering . . .

>>>>>> (Is. 53:6, 10)

Here is the Calvary of the Old Testament. Here, too, is the essential basis of the unity of gospel and ethics, of faith and life, in both Testaments; namely, the sovereign grace and mercy of God. For the cross of the Messiah is the gateway, not only to life, but to living.

Further reading

Birch, Bruce C., 'Old Testament Narrative and Moral Address', in Tucker, Petersen and Wilson, *Canon, Theology and Old Testament Interpretation*, pp. 75–91.

———, 'Moral Agency, Community, and the Character of God in the Hebrew Bible', *Semeia* 66 (1994), pp. 23–41.

Blocher, Henri, 'The Fear of the Lord as the "Principle" of Wisdom', *Tyndale Bulletin* 28 (1977), pp. 3–28.

Clements, R. E., 'Worship and Ethics: A Re-examination of Psalm 15', in Graham, Marrs and McKenzie, *Worship and the Hebrew Bible*, pp. 78–94.

Hauerwas, Stanley, *A Community of Character: Toward a Constructive Christian Social Ethic* (Notre Dame: University of Notre Dame Press), 1981.

Janzen, Waldemar, *Old Testament Ethics: A Paradigmatic Approach* (Louisville, KY: Westminster John Knox, 1994).

Mendenhall, George E., 'The Relation of the Individual to Political Society in Ancient Israel', in J. M. Myers, O. Reimherr and H. N. Bream (eds.), *Biblical Studies in Memory of H. C. Alleman* (Locus Valley, NY: J. J. Augustin, 1960), pp. 89–108.

Muilenburg, J., *The Way of Israel: Biblical Faith and Ethics* (New York: Harper, 1961).

Porter, J. Roy, 'The Legal Aspects of the Concept of "Corporate Personality" in the Old Testament', *Vetus Testamentum* 15 (1965), pp. 361–380.

Rogerson, John W., 'The Hebrew Conception of Corporate Personality: A Re-examination', *Journal of Theological Studies* New Series 21 (1970), pp. 1–16.

Wenham, Gordon J., *Story as Torah: Reading the Old Testament Ethically* (Edinburgh: T. & T. Clark, 2000).

PART THREE

STUDYING OLD TESTAMENT ETHICS

12. A SURVEY OF HISTORICAL APPROACHES

The question of what authority the scriptures of the Hebrew Bible have for Christians and how they should be used for ethics is, and always has been, difficult and divisive. Although moral issues raised by contemporary life are in some ways unprecedented, few fundamental questions have not in principle been raised within the Christian community since the earliest years. It is instructive (and sometimes properly humbling) to give thought to that great stream of tradition within which we stand, rather than fondly imagine we are the first generation to face the challenge the Old Testament sets before us as Christians. Just because we recently invented the word 'hermeneutics' does not mean we are the first to wrestle with what we are pleased to call 'hermeneutical issues'.

This chapter offers nothing more than a mere sketch of some key points in the history of Christian interpretation of the Old Testament. Vast tracts of ancient, medieval and early modern biblical scholarship are omitted. I shall dip only briefly into some representative approaches to the ethical use of the Old Testament in the early church, the church at the time of the European Reformation and among a few contemporary strands of Christian confessional approaches to biblical interpretation. In the next chapter I shall survey the variety of approaches to Old Testament ethics within the wider world of contemporary scholarship, concentrating mainly on the past quarter century.

The early church

In a brief but stimulating article Richard Longenecker suggested three major positions or traditions of biblical hermeneutics (specifically on handling the Old Testament) in the early centuries of the church and that these three approaches have continued to be influential all through Christian history.[1] His classification provides a useful starting point and grid for my survey.

Marcion

No writings of Marcion have survived, so he is known only through those who opposed him, especially Irenaeus and Tertullian. Writing in the mid second century AD, his starting point was Galatians, which he understood as directed against Judaism and all things Jewish. The revelation of God in Jesus was totally different from the work of the Jewish creator God. He thus saw a radical discontinuity between the Jewish Scriptures and the Christian New Testament. The Hebrew Bible had no relevance or authority for Christians and should be regarded as having no place in Christian Scripture – along with several parts of the New Testament, which he judged to be seriously infected with Jewish concerns. Not surprisingly, any ethical authority of the Old Testament for Christians is rejected a priori. Marcion's radical rejection of the Hebrew Scriptures was itself rejected by the church. His attack, however, was indirectly one of the factors that led to the clarification and defining of the canon of Christian Scripture, with the Old Testament firmly included in that canon.

The Alexandrian fathers

Christian scholarship at Alexandria flourished from the late second to mid third century. The most notable figures there were Clement and Origen, Origen being the more prolific and influential. Origen distinguished between the 'letter' and the 'spirit' of the Old Testament, with priority given to the spiritual meaning and purpose of the text. He did not deny the historical and literal meaning of the Old Testament, but argued that often the literal sense of a story or command was simply *impossible* and concluded that the Spirit must have *intended* the reader to look for a hidden spiritual meaning. The Word could use historical stories to teach spiritual truths, but could also weave into the narrative things that did not happen, or into the law things that could not be obeyed. The reader is thereby forced to seek the higher sense worthy of God.[2]

Origen also made a distinction between two parts of the law – the ceremo-

---

[1] R. N. Longenecker, 'Three Ways of Understanding'.

[2] See Froehlich, *Biblical Interpretation*, pp. 62–64.

nial and the moral (though in his commentary on Romans he listed six ways in which Paul talks about law!). The first part came to an end in Christ, but the second was retained and amplified by Christ. This distinction, subsequently expanded by the identification of a third category, namely Israel's civil or judicial law, has remained as a major hermeneutical framework for handling Old Testament law right down to the present day.

Since the main characteristic of the Alexandrian school was the belief that there was a spiritual meaning already there, intentionally hidden in the text of the Old Testament by the Spirit, they had to devise a method for getting at this hidden meaning and expounding it. The allegorical method of exegesis and interpretation was their solution. Though it has become that for which Alexandria is most famous, it should be remembered that this allegorical method was essentially just a tool, and was later discarded or modified by the heirs of their tradition. The more important legacy of Alexandria in relation to Old Testament hermeneutics was the presupposition of continuity and harmony between the testaments. The Hebrew scriptures, since they had come from the same Spirit who had inspired the New Testament, must also have Christian spiritual significance. This led to a fairly static conception of the Bible, with little weight given to historical development between the testaments.

The Antiochene fathers

The rival school of Antioch flourished in the fourth and fifth centuries, and includes such names as Chrysostom, Theodore of Mopsuestia, Theodoret, and Diodore of Tarsus in its broad tradition.

Whereas Alexandria subordinated the literal, historical sense of the Old Testament to a higher, moral and spiritual sense (the *allēgoria*), Antioch gave priority to history, and looked for higher principles only secondarily. They used the term *theōria* or *anagōgē* for such secondary principles. They strongly and vociferously rejected the allegorical methods of Alexandria, and also questioned the twofold division of the law that stemmed from there.

Chrysostom argued that a whole new dynamic had entered the world with the arrival of the gospel in Christ. In the light of that, he did not accept that the Old Testament law had ongoing moral authority for Christians. Even things that had been allowed by the law in the Old Testament could be rejected by Christians because of the newness of life in Christ. He applied this argument to slavery – being one of the earliest to suggest that although the Old Testament allowed it, that fact did not of itself justify the practice for Christians, who must take Galatians 3:28 into consideration.[3]

---

[3] See Longenecker, 'Three Ways of Understanding', p. 27.

Diodore of Tarsus, in his commentary on the Psalms, however, did see the ethical value of the Old Testament, provided it is carefully grounded in historical reality and a literal reading of the text. He refused all allegory.[4] Theodore of Mopsuestia in his commentary on Galatians emphasizes the two covenants, through Moses and through Christ, and sets up a very clear law–gospel contrast.[5]

The Antiochene school thus emphasized the historical development within the Scriptures and the importance of redemptive fulfilment of the Old Testament in the New. This led to a less static and more dynamic approach to biblical authority, in which Old Testament perspectives could be set aside in the light of the 'new thing' of the incarnation and kingdom of God in Christ. Both Alexandria and Antioch believed in the continuity between the Testaments, but whereas Alexandria saw sameness and made the Old Testament say Christian things, Antioch saw development and allowed the New Testament to override the Old where necessary.

Longenecker suggests, then, that these three attitudes and approaches to the Old Testament have surfaced in different traditions in the church ever since. Though officially rejected by the church, the ghost of Marcion has haunted the hermeneutical house down through the ages, making its appearance in the antinomian tendencies of the radical wing of the Reformation, the ahistorical existentalism of Bultmann and kindred spirits, and (for very different theological reasons) in modern Dispensationalism. And those are only the theological movements. Many churches are in practice Marcionite in their abysmal neglect of the scriptures Jesus himself used, refusing to read them in worship even when lectionary provision is made for it. Small wonder there is such confusion over whether and how the Old Testament has anything ethical to contribute to the Christian's resources for practical living.

The influence of Alexandria lives on in Calvin and the Reformed tradition – not in its allegorical treatment of the Hebrew Bible, which Calvin definitely rejected in favour of a careful historico-grammatical exegesis. Rather, it is seen in the commitment to the unity and continuity of the Testaments, such that the Old Testament is read as unquestionably Christian scripture to be interpreted and obeyed in the light of Christ. Its influence can be seen in the Puritans' emphasis on the 'third (moral) use' of the law in the Christian's life. A static kind of unity is pushed to its ethical extreme in the theonomist movement (see below), which asserts that the moral authority of the Old Testament applies with as much force for Christians as the law did for Israel,

---

[4] See Froelich, *Biblical Interpretation*, p. 82.

[5] Ibid., pp. 98ff.

since it is God's law for all time for all humanity. Whereas, however, the Alexandrians made Hebrew law relevant by allegorizing it, theonomists wish to make it relevant by literal application as far as possible.

The Antiochene antipathy to allegory surfaced again in Luther's bold rejection of medieval scholastic theology. Luther was also more Antiochene than Calvin in allowing the new wine of the gospel to dispense with the old wineskins of the Old Testament wherever he sensed a conflict. Where Calvin sought consistency and harmony, Luther was content with a very free and sometimes inconsistent handling of the Old Testament ethically, which arose from his dynamic and ebullient glorying in the primacy of the gospel as over against the law. As for modern examples of the Antiochene spirit, I think I would point to the heirs of the radical Reformation, such as those Mennonites who are concerned and active in social issues, who stress a radical discipleship and have a strongly New Testament, messianic orientation in both theology and ethic, while emphasizing the importance of the distinctiveness of the people of God, which is a value most strongly inculcated in the Hebrew scriptures. So we turn now to these great minds of the Reformation.

The Reformation era

Luther

Martin Luther, as a biblical expositor, inherited the medieval tools of exegesis, which included the allegorical method among others that had been developed in the Western church, particularly in North Africa. The early editions of his Galatians commentary show that Alexandrian influence. However, he came to reject entirely (in principle, if not always consistently in practice) the allegorical method, and swung to a much more Antiochene approach – theologically as well as exegetically. This, of course, was directly related to his own experiential rediscovery of the New Testament gospel. The tremendous experience of liberation by the gospel from the burdens of conscience, which he felt were imposed upon him by the law and wrath of God, led Luther to a fundamentally Christocentric and gospel-centred approach to everything, including biblical hermeneutics. This entailed a dynamic, historically differentiated, use of the Old Testament. On the one hand, Luther never relinquished the Old Testament as essential to the Scriptures and the Christian faith, but, on the other hand, he certainly subordinated it to the New Testament and his own understanding of grace and salvation. This led to a not always consistent use of the Old Testament. Sometimes he can teach certain duties from Old Testament laws and stories; while at other times he can urge Christians to be free from certain scruples (e.g. in relation to monastic vows) precisely because they (vows) *are* in the Old Testament, and Christians need not behave like Jews![6]

Luther saw the Old Testament law as having had a civil use: like a hedge it functioned as a political restraint upon human sin in Israelite society. He also saw its spiritual use: like a mirror it exposes sin and thus drives us in terror and condemnation to repentance and the gospel. This second use, for Luther, is its primary purpose as far as Christians are concerned. There is debate over whether Luther ever accepted a 'third use' of the law; namely, as a moral guide for Christian living now, with ethical authority over believers. It seems that he rejected such moral authority for the law, in the sense of Christians being bound to obey it. And yet, in *practice*, he made extensive use of the Old Testament in his *catechisms* when dealing with the requirements of Christian behaviour. Much of his teaching there is based on the Decalogue. He 'de-judaizes' the commandments and freely reinterprets them in Christian terms, but the assumption is clearly that the Ten Commandments still function authoritatively in guiding Christian behaviour, even though Luther insists that the Christian is not bound – even by the Decalogue. So when it comes to the grounds for finding moral authority in Old Testament law, Luther locates it in natural law. That is, at those points where the Christian is bound by moral authority in the law, it is not by the law qua given by Moses, but by the law as simply reflecting the wider moral will of God in creation.

Fundamentally, however, for Luther the law precedes, and stands in final contrast with, the gospel (as remains the case for Lutheran theology and ethics ever since). The Antiochene model is there; the new events of salvation history in Christ override and supersede all that went before. Thus Luther can be free in handling not only the laws but also the narratives of the Old Testament. He can engage in curious defence of the morally questionable actions of great heroes of the Old Testament (e.g. Abraham's lying to Abimelech about Sarah), if he can show that they were acting out of faith in God's promise. In that sense, grace covers a multitude of sins in more ways than one.

Calvin

Calvin represents a swing of the pendulum towards a more Alexandrian approach to the Old Testament, *not* in the sense of allegorical exegesis (which Calvin renounced as much as Luther), but in seeing the unity and continuity of

---

[6] A very helpful discussion of this feature of Luther, with illustrations and full bibliographical detail, is provided by D. F. Wright, 'Ethical Use of the Old Testament'. See also G. O. Forde, 'Law and Gospel'; Bloesch, *Freedom for Obedience*, chs. 7–8.

the testaments. Calvin affirmed a single covenant of saving grace – the Abrahamic promise – running throughout the Bible. So he saw the gospel of grace also in the Old Testament and made great efforts to display a greater harmony and consistency between the law and the gospel.

Calvin took very seriously Christ's affirmation of the continuing validity of the law and the prophets (Matt. 5:17ff.), so he not only accepted the 'third use' of the law, but regarded it as in fact the most important. The law functions as a practical guide for Christian conduct, to shape and prepare us for good works in response to saving grace. So, whereas Luther, though he was aware of the threefold use of the law, affirmed that the principle use was the second (i.e. to accuse, condemn and terrify us so that we are driven to Christ), Calvin emphasized the third use (to guide and train us morally):

> The third and principal use [of the moral law], which pertains more closely to the proper purpose of the law, finds its place among believers in whose hearts the Spirit of God already lives and reigns . . . Here is the best instrument for [believers] to learn more thoroughly each day the nature of the Lord's will to which they aspire, and to confirm them in the understanding of it . . . And because we need not only teaching but also exhortation, the servant of God will also avail himself of this benefit of the law: by frequent meditation upon it to be aroused to obedience, be strengthened in it and be drawn back from the slippery path of transgression.[7]

The law, in fact, provided 'a perfect pattern of righteousness', which applied in all ages, not just to Israelites. Its historical and contextual particularity was, of course, to be taken into account, but that did not destroy its relevance to the people of God of later ages. Even Christ did not *add* to the law, but rather 'he only restored it to its integrity'.[8]

With this more positive perspective, Calvin argues that the way to derive benefit from the law (and he is principally expounding the Decalogue) is to look for the *purpose* of each commandment. He constantly seeks a positive use, somewhat in the same way Jesus often went to the heart of a matter by seeing the *point* of a law – why it was given and for whose benefit. Likewise, Calvin regards it as legitimate to expand the force of the literal words themselves by presupposing that any law prohibits the opposite of what it commands, or commands the opposite of what it prohibits.

One can detect, therefore, a difference between Luther's and Calvin's handling of the law that is almost as much psychological or intuitive as

---

[7] Calvin, *Institutes* 2.7.12.

[8] Ibid., 2.7.13; 2.8.7.

theological. Whereas Luther often sees what the law *prohibits*, in order to emphasize its role as a 'killer' from which one must flee to the grace of the gospel, Calvin looks for what the law *promotes*, using it as a model or primer that he applies to all kinds of issues of Christian living in the world of his day. When either of these approaches (both of which can claim New Testament precedent) is taken to extremes, they can, of course, become unbalanced in opposite ways. Thus, the danger of Lutheranism is a slide into practical Marcionism or antinomianism, while the danger of Calvinism has always been a slide into legalism. But neither of these extremes can be charged against Luther or Calvin themselves.

In the *Institutes* Calvin is mainly expounding the Decalogue. However, in his *Commentaries on the Last Four Books of Moses* he comments not only on the Ten Commandments themselves, but on all the other laws he arranges in relation to their connection with the Ten Commandments.[9] He makes a further distinction in these latter laws between 'Exposition' (laws that simply clarify or apply the main thrust of the Decalogue commandment, and therefore belong to the essence of the law and share the continuing moral validity of the Decalogue) and 'Political Supplements' (civil or ceremonial provisions that were applicable to Israel). This last category of laws need not be imposed in the laws of other societies, so long as the basic purpose of the Decalogue is preserved. Thus, for example, in his handling of the eighth commandment (against stealing) he includes in the 'Exposition'

- prompt payment of wages (Lev. 19:11, 13; Deut. 24:14–15; 25:4);
- care and impartiality for aliens (Exod. 22:21–24; Lev. 19:33–34; Deut. 10:17–19);
- honesty in weights and measures (Lev. 19:35–36; Deut. 25:13–16);
- no removal of boundary markers (Deut. 19:14);
- duties in respect of pledges for loans (Exod. 22:26–27; Deut. 24:6, 10–13, 17–18);
- laws against taking interest (Exod. 22:25; Lev. 25:35–38; Deut. 23:19–20);
- recovery of lost possessions (Exod. 23:4; Deut. 22:1–3);
- restitution for theft (Num. 5:5–7);
- denunciation of bribery and corruption (Exod. 23:8; Lev. 19:15; Deut. 16:19–20);
- prohibition on partiality, for or against the poor (Exod. 23:3, 6).

He then includes in the category of 'Political Supplements'

---

[9] J. Calvin, *Four Last Books of Moses.*

- gleanings for the poor (Lev. 19:9–10; 23:22; Deut. 24:19–22);
- the sabbatical year (Exod. 21:1–6; Deut. 15:1–18);
- the jubilee and redemption regulations (Lev. 25);
- a ban on destroying fruit trees in war (Deut. 20:19–20);
- exemptions from military service for certain categories of people (Deut. 20:5–8);
- the levirate marriage duty (Deut. 25:5–10).

The question obviously arises in relation to Calvin's categorizing as to how and why certain laws are assigned to his two sub-Decalogue categories, and no easy answer can be given. The point is, however, that he is refusing to allow that only the Ten Commandments themselves are of any relevance to Christians. The principles they express are also to be found in other laws, laws that stand to a greater or lesser degree in relationship to the Ten Commandments. Thus, while a modern state may differ greatly in its civil and political arrangements from the specific laws of Israel, that does not matter, provided the modern laws serve the same purpose and safeguard the same basic principles. What matters is that the 'general equity' (Calvin's own phrase) that characterizes Israel's civil law should be preserved even if the literal form is no longer binding. If the essential principle of the Decalogue commandment is taken seriously, then matters of practical justice, fair treatment of the poor, protection of boundaries and so on. will fall into place with appropriate legislation, just as they did in Israel.[10] To this extent, then, Calvin took the authority of the Old Testament law very seriously, and sought to show its relevance from a wider perspective than just the Ten Commandments. He was not, however, a 'theonomist' in the contemporary sense of seeking to apply the whole Old Testament law as it stands to post-biblical societies. The modern theonomist movement, since it stands closest to the Reformed theological worldview, often claims Calvin as patron saint. But there is no doubt that Calvin would not have endorsed theonomy's assertion of literal application of Old Testament law in modern society, since he explicitly distinguished between permanent moral or natural law and temporary political laws.[11]

---

[10] See D. F. Wright, 'Calvin's Pentateuchal Criticism'; and his further discussion in 'Ethical Use of the Old Testament'.

[11] For a helpful critique, from within the Reformed tradition itself, of the theonomists' claim to Calvin, pointing out significant differences of approach and exegesis, see W. Robert Godfrey, 'Calvin and Theonomy'. The theonomist approach is examined further below.

The Anabaptists

The radical wing of the Reformation produced a remarkable variety of writings – remarkable in view of the pressures and prejudice they faced. It is harder to make general classifications of their position on a given subject than one can do for a single Reformer, like Luther or Calvin, but there are some significant common features. On the matter of biblical interpretation and the specific ethical use of the Old Testament, we can point to certain areas of broad agreement between the Anabaptists and the mainline Reformers before we identify key areas of disagreement.[12]

The Anabaptists were in full agreement with the other Reformers that the Bible was the authoritative word of God; that it could be understood clearly by the common person; that interpretation was to be free from bondage to ecclesiastical tradition; that special hermeneutical techniques were necessary to elucidate certain difficulties; and that in the end the Bible was meant to be obeyed. However, disagreement focused on three major matters:

1. *The scope of biblical relevance.* The question was whether the Bible as a whole (Old and New Testament) was to be applied to public, civil life or whether the New Testament applied only to Christian personal behaviour and not to civil matters. The Reformers' position generally was that the Old Testament law could be related to civil affairs (thus permitting them to apply Old Testament sanctions and penalties in judicial and military matters), whereas the teachings of Christ were essentially for personal relationships between Christians. The Anabaptists asserted that the rule of Christ should govern the whole of life, including civil life also. So for Anabaptists, since the New Testament (on their understanding) governed civil life, and since the New Testament had superseded the Old Testament, this had the effect of rejecting, or at least relativizing, the authority of the Old Testament for civil life and government. Anabaptists could not accept, therefore, the extensive (and often oppressive) use of Old Testament sanctions and justification for state actions that were approved by mainline Reformers.

2. *The nature of the church and its relation to the state.* The mainline Reformers are sometimes called 'magisterial' because of their conviction that the church and state were bound together in the purposes of God, and that the reformation of the church was part of the responsibility of the civil magistrate. Though they advocated different patterns of how that relationship should work, the mainline Reformers were commonly committed to a broadly theocratic understand-

---

[12]   A most helpful and illuminating collection of essays on Anabaptist biblical hermeneutics is provided by Willard Swartley (ed.), *Biblical Interpretation*.

ing of 'Christendom'. The Anabaptists, on the other hand, regarded the church as the separated and gathered community of true believers, clearly and visibly distinct from all secular institutions and certainly not part of the state. They rejected the 'Christendom' notion, and along with it the theocratic presuppositions derived from the Old Testament. The church was precisely *not* a nation state like Israel in the Old Testament, and therefore should not behave as if she were. This distinction is seen in two fundamental Anabaptist convictions:

a. *Baptism.* For the Reformers, infant baptism was part of Christian citizenship in a Christian state, and was justified partly through affirming its equivalence to Old Testament circumcision. To refuse it, or deny its validity by 'rebaptism', was, in the religio-political context of sixteenth century Europe, tantamount to sedition or rebellion against the foundations of the state itself. For the Anabaptists, baptism was clearly commanded in the New Testament only for believers, had nothing to do with civil citizenship, and therefore the Old Testament was irrelevant to the question. The strength of Anabaptist conviction on this matter, coupled with the intense heat and severe cost of the controversy, probably led to a sharper devaluation of the Old Testament than would have been intended otherwise. That is, since the mainline Protestants justified infant baptism on Old Testament grounds, and then ruthlessly persecuted and slew Anabaptists for rejecting it (again justifying their action on Old Testament grounds), it is hardly surprising to find the Anabaptist counter-polemic seeking to undermine the Old Testament foundations of their enemies' aggressive position.

b. *Pacificism.* The Reformers argued that since civil authority was appointed by God, Christians were bound to obey the state government, which included bearing arms on behalf of the state in war. Again, the Old Testament was widely used in support of the legitimacy of war in certain circumstances. The major tradition of the Anabaptists (though some groups took an opposite and extreme view) took Jesus' teaching on non-violence with total seriousness and therefore argued that Christians could not participate in violence or war. Again, since this was an issue so dear to them and so anathema to their opponents, it affected the hermeneutical argument. In order to highlight Christ's non-violence, they had to put the Old Testament and its wars in the shadows – either by careful relativizing in relation to Christ, or by a less careful rejection of Old Testament authority, which led in some cases to the charge of Marcionism.

So we can see that in the Reformation era to a considerable degree the question of the ethical authority and use of the Old Testament was affected by the prior question of ecclesiology, particularly the vexed question of the church's relation to the state. It is possible to point to a comparable dynamic today. The extent to which Christian groups are prepared to use the Old Testament at all, or, if they are, the use to which they put it is certainly partly affected by how they understand the nature of the church and its role in society in general.

It is also interesting to note that the Anabaptist relegation of the Old Testament was partly a reaction to what they perceived as the continuing legalism and 'Erastianism' of the mainline Protestant movement. This was also true, though in a very different ecclesiastical climate, of the origins of Dispensationalism, as we shall see below.

3. *The absolute priority of obedience to Christ.* This could probably be regarded as the guiding principle of Anabaptism in many respects. Christianity was a personal, spiritual experience of salvation through Jesus and thereafter of simple committed discipleship. What Jesus said, must be done. This could sometimes lead to a new kind of literalism and legalism of its own, but it certainly meant that the Old Testament was decidedly secondary to the New in moral priority. (Again, there were exceptions, such as Thomas Müntzer and Jan of Leyden, who resorted to Old Testament apocalypticism as justification for violence and other excesses.) Sometimes this prioritizing of Jesus and the New Testament led to virtual Marcionism, and indeed, when coupled with claims for direct contemporary revelations of the Spirit, could lead to the abandoning of even the New Testament as well among some on the radical spiritualist wing of the movement. But among the more careful and significant exegetes and leaders the clearly dominant position was that the advent of Christ and the New Testament relativized the Old.

Menno Simons, an Anabaptist leader with the most enduring legacy (in the Mennonite communion), held the Old Testament in high regard, but believed that Christ enables Christians to go far beyond it.

> According to Menno, Jesus Christ really did bring something new. The Old Covenant was displaced by the radical newness of Christ's kingdom. The mainline reformers stressed the continuity of the two testaments; for them there was really only *one covenant in two dispensations*. This principle enabled them to justify infant baptism by analogy to its Old Testament counterpart, circumcision. They also found in the Old Testament a pattern for church–state relationships. The Anabaptists denied the legitimacy of this appeal to the Old Testament by pointing to the *normative* status of the New Covenant.[13]

---

[13] Timothy George, *Theology of the Reformers*, p. 276 (his italics).

Menno's superior evaluation of the New Testament was but the corollary of his basic affirmation – the centrality of Jesus Christ ... When Christ came he fulfilled the Law and enabled man to 'realize' fully what God wanted of him. Menno says that men can now go beyond the Old Testament Law, for they are directed to Christ. Moses served his day, now Christ has given a new commandment ... Menno was fully aware of the ethical issues which stemmed from his theological concerns. His statements about warfare and the use of the sword grew out of his position of seeing the difference between the Old and New Testaments. Any vindictive approach to a person is ruled out because the New Testament forbids revenge, and the law of love must motivate the believer. Christ's command is too clear to be ignored, and wherever the Old Testament stipulations are not in accord with the teachings of Jesus and the apostles they must give way.[14]

Menno, like some other Anabaptists (e.g. Pilgram Marpeck[15]), insisted that the Old Testament was still part of Christian scripture, and made extensive use of it for devotional and spiritual exhortation. But the overwhelming priority in moral authority was given to the New Testament.

These hermeneutical debates of the Reformation era over the ethical authority and use of the Old Testament are fascinatingly relevant and alive today, though thankfully shorn of the vitriol and bloodshed that accompanied them in the sixteenth century. Should we ascribe to the Old Testament equivalent moral authority to the New, or a relativized and secondary authority, or none at all? Does obedience to Christ *endorse* the Old Testament or *relegate* it? These questions live on in the selection of contemporary approaches to which we now turn.

Some contemporary confessional approaches

Dispensationalism
Dispensationalism traces its roots to J. N. Darby (1800–82) in nineteenth century England, though the premillennialism, which it also espouses, has a much longer history in the church. Darby found himself frustrated and

---

[14] Poettker, 'Menno Simons' Encounter with the Bible', pp. 70–71.

[15] See H. W. Klassen, 'Pilgram Marpeck's Theology'. Klassen asks whether Marpeck was a Marcionite, and concludes that he was not. Though he stressed the discontinuity of the old and new covenants, he placed a high value on the devotional use of the Old Testament.

depressed with the ineffective legalism of Anglican church life at that time. It was ineffective because although it was deeply moralistic in theory, it was abysmally lax in practice. A conversion-type experience liberated Darby into an experience of the grace of God and a realization of the fullness of the Gospel in Christ. This simultaneously engendered a strong antipathy to 'works', and thence also to what he perceived to be an over-reliance on the Old Testament in the church's moralizing.[16]

Darby went on to develop a system of biblical understanding that stemmed from his desire to preserve the utter priority of grace over law. The most straightforward way to do this, in a sense, is to separate them altogether. Darby and those who followed his lead[17] did this by arguing that God's dealings with human beings in the course of redemptive history have proceeded by entirely separate dispensations. The precise number of these varies in different dispensationalist schools, but the most fundamental divide is between the dispensation of the law through Moses and the dispensation of grace (the present age) through Christ. The next most significant will be the millennial earthly reign of Christ. This entails also a complete separation between national (ethnic) Israel and the church. God deals with them differently, and the distinction will be preserved eternally. The moral teaching of the Old Testament law was only intended for, and relevant to, the dispensation before Christ, and will be the standard again in the millennial age when Christ reigns on earth among a converted Jewish nation. But in the age of the church it has no continuing authority. In the twentieth century dispensationalism has softened somewhat under the onslaught of so-called covenant theology, and is prepared to recognize that there was grace in the Old Testament also and that salvation was never simply by keeping the law. But its hermeneutical and eschatological system has remained largely intact.

Norman Geisler has provided a helpful statement of a dispensationalist approach to biblical ethics.[18] He points out that all Christians, including theonomists, know that Christians are not bound to obey every single law in the Pentateuch, since in practice they do not do so and do not urge that others should. 'So even those who claim that Christians are still under the Old Testament Law do not agree that every point is still applicable. The question then is not whether the Mosaic Law is still in force, but *how much* of it is still

---

[16] Daniel P. Fuller, *Gospel and Law*, provides a full account of Darby's pilgrimage and the development of his theological system, followed by an exegetically very thorough examination and critique of the conflict between these opposing systems.

[17] Most influentially, the author of the notes in *The Scofield Bible*.

[18] Norman L. Geisler, 'Dispensationalism and Ethics'.

binding on Christians' (p. 7). Geisler dismisses the attempt to preserve some part of the law as authoritative by distinguishing between moral, civil and ceremonial categories, arguing that such a distinction is not borne out by the New Testament. He cites a list of New Testament passages where the law, as a whole, is regarded as at an end, or that Christians are no longer under it:[19] 'According to Paul, with the Law it is either all or nothing at all. So on the one hand, if any of the Law is binding on Christians, then all of it is, but even theonomists cringe at this suggestion. On the other hand, if some of the Mosaic Law does not apply to Christians then none of it does. This is precisely what Paul argues in Galatians' (p. 9).

Geisler is well aware that many Old Testament laws are quoted in the New Testament, along with other uses of the Old Testament there. But he insists that the force of the texts as authoritative law is not carried over. Rather, it is the principles that are being applied, sometimes (as in the case of the sabbath or adultery) with significant modifications in the actual law: 'There are many similar moral principles in both Old and New Testaments, but it by no means follows that there are the same laws' (p. 10), and certainly not the same penalties. So the Old Testament can provide guidance on social holiness and personal righteousness, but it cannot be applied either theocratically or theonomically today. The law of Moses was never intended as a guide for civil government other than in Old Testament Israel. For civil government among the rest of the nations God has given the unwritten 'natural law' of general revelation: 'From this discussion it should also be clear that the law of God (divine revelation) is not the basis for civil law today. God does not presently rule the world's governments by divine law. He desires that they be ruled by civil law based on natural law. Divine law is only for the church. Natural law is for the whole world (Rom 2:12–14)' (p. 10).

It is clear from Geisler's discussion in this article that his main target is the theonomists and their insistence on applying the laws of the Old Testament (including their penalties) as rigorously as possible in modern society.[20] He is not denying the relevance of the moral principles exemplified in the Old Testament, but is rejecting its authoritative normativity as law. This is apparent also in his later monograph on Christian ethics, which examines different

---

[19] Geisler cites Jas. 2:10; Rom. 6:14; 2 Cor. 3:7, 11; Eph. 2:15; Rom. 10:4; Gal. 3:25; Heb. 7:11; 8:1–2.

[20] Theonomist reconstructionism is similarly the main target of H. Wayne House and Thomas Ice (eds.), *Dominion Theology*. House and Ice include helpful chapters setting out a dispensational view of the law, especially in chs. 6, 'Are Christians under the Mosaic Law?', and 7, 'Should the Nations Be under the Mosaic Law?'

ethical stances in relation to specific contemporary issues.[21] In that book Geisler makes plenty of use of Old Testament texts in framing what he regards as appropriate Christian responses. So in practice he seems to assume the moral *relevance* of the Old Testament, while theologically declining to accord it normative *authority*.

In evaluating the dispensationalist approach to Old Testament ethics we can first of all express a positive appreciation for the emphasis on the priority of grace, and for the proper insistence on the centrality of Christ and on the theology of fulfilment we find in the New Testament, in any Christian interpretation of the Old Testament.

However, in my view the approach is flawed by the theological questionability of the whole dispensationalist scheme. I find dispensationalism seriously inadequate because of its severance of the Old from the New Testament redemptively, its denial of the organic spiritual continuity between Israel and the church through the Messiah, and its overemphasis on the contrast between law and grace. These major distinctives of the theology of dispensationalism appear to demote the Old Testament in a way that makes its ethical use more or less redundant. My impression is that Geisler himself is somewhat exceptional in paying the attention he does to the moral value of the Old Testament. On the whole, the teaching that Old Testament law has no relevance to the present dispensation of the church leads to a kind of practical Marcionism. If the law will not apply again until the millennium, the task of finding out what it might mean to us now hardly seems worth the effort. On such a view, the New Testament offers sufficient moral authority and guidance without the Old. It is also my impression that the premillennial eschatology of dispensationalism has a heavily dampening effect on the relevance of the Old Testament to social ethics in the present context. Since the realization of justice and peace will be features of the millennial earthly reign of Christ, they need not be the focus of Christian striving here and now. The primary (if not the only) task of the church is evangelism, conceived as rescuing souls from a perishing world order. Inevitably, this produces a sceptical (and sometimes hostile) assessment of the value of Christian involvement in the social, economic, political, educational and legal structures of the present world order. The Old Testament, therefore, with its obvious strong concern for such issues, suffers corresponding neglect. Dispensationalists are aware of this criticism, but some argue that such negative pietism is not intrinsic to the dispensational system. There is a place for Christian social involvement, but not on the scale, or with the expectations, of the reconstructionist agenda. And for

---

[21] Norman L. Geisler, *Christian Ethics*.

dispensationalists such social involvement is generated via the New Testament and the Great Commission: it does not take its authority or its shaping from the Old Testament.

> Dispensationalists are often accused of being defeatist, just sitting around waiting for the rapture. It is unfortunate but true that pietism has infected many in the dispensational camp. However, social and cultural impotence is not organic to dispensationalism. The believer is called to a ministry of exposing evil during the night (Ephesians 5:11) . . . If dispensationalists are not properly involved in issues today, it is not inherent to their theology; rather it is unfaithfulness to their calling.[22]

Theonomism

At the polar opposite extreme from the dispensationalist demotion of the Old Testament as regards ethical authority lies the theonomist exaltation of the Old Testament as the permanently valid expression of God's moral will for all societies. The difference could be expressed at its simplest by saying that whereas dispensationalists say that *no* Old Testament law is morally binding since the coming of Christ, unless specifically *endorsed and recommended* in the New Testament, theonomists argue that *all* Old Testament laws are perpetually morally binding, unless explicitly *abrogated* in the New Testament. Theonomists have the same essentially 'all-or-nothing' approach to the law as dispensationalists do, except that whereas to the question 'How much of the Old Testament law is authoritatively binding for Christians?' the dispensationalists answer, 'None of it,' the theonomists answer, 'All of it – and not just for Christians.'

The theonomist movement has emerged from the Reformed wing of the church, and claims legitimate descent from the teaching of Calvin, the Westminster Confession of Faith and the Puritans. These claims are strongly resisted by other Reformed scholars who do not accept the validity either of theonomist hermeneutics or of reconstructionist social and political prescriptions, and who say that Calvin and the classic Reformed theologians were by no means theonomist in the modern sense of the word.[23]

The movement emphasizes the essential unity and continuity of the Old and New Testament and espouses a form of covenant theology. Based on

---

[22] House and Ice, *Dominion Theology*, pp. 241, 243.

[23] The most thorough critique of theonomy, which pays attention to its theology, eschatology, ethical agenda and historical roots, comes from a symposium of Reformed 'cousins' from the faculty of Westminster Theological Seminary, William. S. Barker and W. Robert Godfrey (eds.), *Theonomy*.

that, they argue that the Mosaic law was given by God as divine revelation not merely for the guidance of Israel, but to provide a perfect model of justice for all societies – ancient and modern. The ceremonial aspects of the law have been fulfilled by Christ and are therefore not binding on Christians – though theonomists argue that they *would be*, were it not for Christ having fulfilled them for us (to this extent theonomists accept differentiation within the law). But all the rest of the law is binding, including its penalties. Laws that older traditions had regarded as 'civil' and distinguished from 'moral' laws are thus included by theonomists in their 'moral and binding' category. Civil authorities in all societies are thus obligated to enforce the laws and penalties of the Mosaic law. Consequently, modern states are in a state of sin and rebellion to the extent that they fail to do so. Enforcing the Mosaic law, for theonomists, would include a mandatory death penalty for certain sexual offences, rebellious young people and so on. On the penalty for sabbath-breaking there are differences of opinion.

'Christian Reconstructionism' is the name chosen by the leaders of the movement who believe that the church should be preparing to reconstruct society and to exercise rightful 'dominion' (another favourite term in theonomic vocabulary). Such dominion would mean instituting a theocratic government that would embody the lordship of Christ in every realm of society. The optimism of this vision easily degenerates into triumphalism. Theologically it is closely allied to a postmillennialist eschatology. Postmillennialism characterizes and shapes reconstructionism as much as premillennialism does dispensationalism. The founding father of the movement is Rousas Rushdoony, but its growth has largely been due to the theological writings of his disciple Greg Bahnsen and the popularizing, and more economics-inclined writing and speaking, of Gary North.[24]

A helpful starting point for getting to grips with the theonomist approach to Old Testament ethics is Bahnsen's companion article to Geisler's in *Transformation*.[25] In this article he sets out his case that the general continuity of the moral standards of the Old Testament applies legitimately to the socio-political realm as much as to personal, family or ecclesiastical ethics. Bahnsen

---

[24] Rousas Rushdoony, *Institutes of Biblical Law*. This is probably Rushdoony's most significant work, out of his enormous output. It is an exposition of the Decalogue as the blueprint for society. Greg Bahnsen's major contributions have been *Theonomy in Christian Ethics* and *By This Standard*. An extensive, annotated bibliography of the prolific writings of these and other members of the theonomist, reconstructionist camp is provided by House and Ice (eds.), *Dominion Theology*, pp. 425–444.

[25] Greg Bahnsen, 'Christ and the Role of Civil Government'.

argues that the standing civil laws of the Old Testament are God's revealed model of perfect social justice for all societies (though he allows for necessary modifications to accommodated changing cultures).[26] He justifies the non-applicability of those laws that made Israel distinctive symbolically from the nations on the grounds that the New Testament redefines the people of God to include Gentiles as well as Jews, so the old marks of separation are no longer necessary, though their *point* (separation from ungodliness) is still a Christian concern. He stresses the importance of Matthew 5:17 and other New Testament texts pointing to the abiding importance of the law, much as dispensationalists point to texts that speak of its 'end'.

In evaluating theonomism's approach to the ethical authority of the Old Testament, one can begin, as with dispensationalism, with some (probably more) words of positive appreciation. I have nothing but applause for theonomists' concern to restore the validity and authority of the Old Testament as an integral part of the whole canon of Christian scripture to the life and witness of the church. There is no doubt that a contributory factor to the social ineffectiveness and moral confusion of the modern church is the practical Marcionism that besets it. Anything that corrects that imbalance is to be welcomed, but one fears that the perceived extremism of the reconstructionist platform may well reinforce rather than reform popular depreciation of the Old Testament.

Secondly, I agree with the theonomists' premise that the Old Testament law was given by God for a purpose that had a wider ethical relevance than solely the shaping of Israel. Nothing less satisfies the assertion of 2 Timothy 3:16 that 'all Scripture is God-breathed *and profitable*' (my trans.). I have argued for such wider relevance throughout this book.

Thirdly, it is my view that the Reformed, covenantal understanding of the unity of the testaments and of the fulfilled, redefined nature of Israel in the New Testament[27] is a more adequate framework for biblical interpretation than dispensationalism, so again I find myself in agreement with one theological premise of theonomy.

Fourthly, one appreciates the overriding desire to see the lordship of Christ recognized and realized in all of life on earth, though I confess a theological

---

[26] 'Standing law' is Bahnsen's way of distinguishing 'policy' imperatives clearly intended to have continuing force over time for all classes of people from those equally clearly specific to individuals in unique historical contexts (e.g. the command to Abraham to sacrifice Isaac, or to Joshua to invade Canaan).

[27] I have explored some of the implications of this as regards the mission and ethics of Jesus himself in Christopher J. H. Wright, *Knowing Jesus*.

rejection of the postmillennial framework in which reconstructionists expect it and a more subjective rejection of the triumphalist rhetoric with which some reconstructionist writers portray it.

In spite of sharing some of theonomy's theology and concerns, however, there are various criticisms to be made:[28]

1. *Misplaced emphasis on statute law.* From the perspective of the sociology of law it is arguable that theonomists misunderstand the function of statue law, especially in ancient societies. In biblical ancient Israel and contemporary cultures law was not always in the form of hard and fast statutes intended to be applied to the letter in formal courts. It seems, rather, that judges operated more informally with precedents and paradigms guided by *tôrâ* (which means guidance or instruction) and their own wisdom, experience and integrity. The fabric of Israel's judicial system included local elders, Levitical priests, individual 'circuit judges' like Samuel. After Jehoshaphat's reform, there were also royally appointed judges in fortified towns and an appeal court in Jerusalem (2 Chr. 19), but much judicial activity still happened at village level. The emphasis was on the imperative to do justice and act fairly without bribery or favouritism, but much was left to the discretion and judgment of those responsible (Deut. 16:18–20; 17:8–13).[29]

2. *Obsession with penalties.* The theonomists' preoccupation with enforcing the *penalties* of Old Testament law for (assumed) equivalent modern offences attaches too much importance to the literal (and literary) form of the biblical penalties and fails to reckon with two points. First, in many cases it is probable that the penalty specified was a *maximum* penalty that could be reduced at the discretion of the elders or judges handling the matter. This is clear in the law governing the use of the whip as punishment (Deut. 25:1–3). Forty strokes was the *maximum* penalty; the law assumes that fewer than that, at the judges'

---

[28] Two recent books provide extensive and illuminating critiques of theonomist (or reconstructionist, or dominion) theology and proposals. House and Ice, *Dominion Theology*, is from a dispensationalist perspective, and so confronts theonomism head-on at every level – theologically, exegetically, eschatologically, ethically and socially. Barker and Godfrey (eds.), *Theonomy*, is perhaps even more telling in that it attacks theonomy from the same theological perspective on which it is founded. The points I make above are supplementary to the major exegetical and hermeneutical arguments of the latter volume.

[29] On the administration of justice in Israel and the ancient Near East and the role of written law within it, see Boecker, *Law and Administration of Justice*, pp. 21–52; and Gordon J. Wenham, 'Law and the Legal System'. See also chapter 9 above.

discretion, would be normal. The fact that in a few specific cases the law pro-hibits any reduction of penalty (for deliberate murder, Num. 35:31; idolatry, Deut. 13:8; and false testimony in court, Deut. 19:19–21) suggests that lesser penalties *were* permissible in other cases. Wenham has suggested that the death penalty for adultery may have been allowed to be commuted to monetary compensation, though would-be adulterers should not count on it (Prov. 6:32–35).[30]

Secondly, what is important about the penal system of Israel's law is the scale of values it reflects rather than the literal prescriptions themselves. As we saw in chapter 9 above, careful study of Israel's penology shows that the range of offences for which the death penalty was applied were to do with the central concerns of protecting the covenant relationship and the family/household unit within which that relationship was preserved and experienced. The gradation of penalties also shows a clear priority of human life over property, of needs over rights, and other priorities that challenge the some-times distorted values of our modern judicial systems. It is certainly possible to set the scale of moral values reflected in Israel's penalties over against those of our own society and then to observe our shortcomings and suggest reforms in order to bring our own system of law and justice more in line with biblical priorities. But this need not take the form, as it does in theonomist agendas, of seeking to reimpose Old Testament penalties as they stand. This point seems to be reinforced theologically by the fact that in the New Testament it appears that neither Jesus nor Paul wanted to apply the full weight of the Old Testament penal system, for adultery or for false teaching.

3. *Overemphasis on the importance of law.* It seems to me that theonomy over-states the importance of the Pentateuchal laws within the overall balance of the Old Testament canon. Now it is obvious that the Torah (as a whole; it should always be remembered that the word includes narratives as well as law codes) has a foundational role, and is celebrated in the Psalms and held up against the people of Israel by the prophets. Nevertheless, it seems significant that the historical narratives and prophetic texts (and certainly the Wisdom lit-erature) do not often quote specific laws or call for their implementation, or for specific penalties to be enforced. Not as often, that is, as one would expect if the written, 'standing law' had had quite the central importance in Israel's everyday social affairs as theonomists imply. In fact, if the law was as definitive as theonomists claim, then the narratives portray apparent inconsistencies – the most notorious being the lack of capital punishment on either Cain or David. It is arguable that a truly prophetic response to the needs of society

---

[30] Wenham, 'Law and the Legal System', p. 35.

would not place quite the emphasis that theonomy does on law and punishment. The Old Testament seems aware of the limitations of that approach.[31]

4. *Political and economic bias.* The theonomist agenda seems oddly selective in what it says modern civil rulers *must* apply and enforce from Old Testament law and what it says they *must not.* According to Bahnsen, the realm of the economic marketplace is out of bounds for civil rulers, legislatively or coercively, on the grounds that Old Testament law did not prescribe such intervention: 'Outside those areas where God's law prescribes their intervention and application of penal redress, civil rulers are not authorized to legislate or use coercion (e.g. the economic marketplace).'[32]

But surely the Pentateuchal law, by any criterion, is deeply concerned about the economic marketplace and prescribes a whole raft of mechanisms designed to preserve or restore economic justice: in relation to the distribution of land, the payment of workers, lending and debt, alleviation of poverty and so on (see chapter 5 above). By whom were these economic laws and mechanisms supposed to be administered within Israel if not by the civil authorities (the elders)? By whom was coercion to be brought to bear on those who tried to evade them, if not the civil authorities? What was Nehemiah, the civil governor, doing when he confronted the illegal interest-taking nobles on behalf of the debt-impoverished farmers, if not intervening in the economic marketplace (Neh. 5)? To argue that because Old Testament law does not prescribe explicit *penalties* related to infringement of its economic legislation, therefore modern civil authorities are *excluded* from any form of intervention in the economic marketplace betrays both the inadequacy of theonomism's preoccupation with penalties and also, in my view, its ideological bias towards unfettered, free-market economic capitalism.

The Jubilee Centre

In terms of theological and social influence, theonomism is predominantly a North American phenomenon. It has not made significant inroads in Britain. However, that is not to say that Britain lacks Christians committed to a biblical social agenda with strong Old Testament roots. The Jubilee Centre in Cambridge has been active for more than two decades in bringing a biblical perspective to the public arena of social policy, legislation and reform. Its work has been recognized both in Parliament and the secular media. While it shares some of the hermeneutical foundations that theonomists espouse, the Jubilee Centre is not theonomist in its fundamental theology nor in the way it

---

[31] See my comments on the limitations of the law at the end of chapter 9 above.

[32] Bahnsen, 'Christ and the Role of Civil Government', part 1, p. 25.

seeks to influence public policy. It certainly does not follow a 'reconstruction-ist' or 'dominion' agenda or advocate Old Testament penalties in contemporary legislation. The director, Michael Schluter, originally in collaboration with Roy Clements and later with the backing of a wider team, has provided the theological and biblical basis for the Centre's various programmes aimed at social reform in Britain.[33]

Prominent in their theological position is their use of the Old Testament as a normative authority for Christian social ethics. On the basis of New Testament texts such as Matthew 5:17–20 and 2 Timothy 3:16–17, they argue that Christians are obliged to search the Old Testament scriptures for ethical guidance and that to confine the relevance of Old Testament law to Israel BC is fundamentally misguided. However, they are dissatisfied with the proposal that the only way to move from Old Testament text to modern context is by way of a miscellaneous list of derived intermediate principles. The problems they perceive regarding such a 'list of principles' approach include the following: How does one determine the 'right' principle when different interpreters derive different principles from the same text or texts? Deriving principles involves a process of abstraction and generalization, the so-called ladder of abstraction. How far 'up the ladder' should one go, and what steps are appropriate for coming back down again into concrete proposals in our own modern context? How do we organize or prioritize our derived principles if they come into conflict with each other in a complex moral situation? How can we avoid our selection of derived principles being nothing more than a subjective statement of our own biases tangentially linked to the biblical text?

Schluter and Clements argue that the only way to avoid these difficulties (or at least to mitigate them) is the holistic approach, which regards the whole social system of Israel as a normative model.[34] That is, rather than take

---

[33] Some of their published theological work is referred to below. Much of it still exists as unpublished papers, or as biblical/theological sections in specific, issue-related publications available from 3 Hooper Street, Cambridge, CB1 2NZ, UK.

[34] The fullest statement of their position is set out in Michael Schluter and Roy Clements, *Reactivating the Extended Family*. In this they give a concise survey of Israel's kinship system and the political and economic structures that went along with it. Then they set out their hermeneutical method of moving from that descriptive work into normative ethics. Finally, they move on to concrete proposals for social reform in Britain that would, in their view, be a starting point for bringing society more into line with the objectives and priorities of the biblical paradigm. I reviewed this work in Christopher J. H. Wright, 'Kin Deep', *Third Way* 10.1 (January 1987), pp. 29–32.

isolated laws and attempt to derive moral principles from them, we need to see how individual laws and whole categories of law, as well as the many social, economic and political institutions of Israel, *functioned* together. God did not just give arbitrary laws to an otherwise 'neutral' community; God *created* that community, moulding them out of an unpromising crowd of escaped slaves into a people with distinctive structures of social life in relation to the historical and cultural context in which they lived. It is this total community that was to serve as God's model for the nations. Therefore, any principles we derive from different parts of the model must be integrated and be consistent with the whole. So, for example, the law banning interest will not be generalized merely into an abstract principle about curtailing greed, but will be understood in relation to Israel's system of land tenure and economic objectives, which in turn are bound up with the importance and role of the extended families, which in turn relates to other features of Israel's judicial and social life. Since so much of Israel's law has to do with creating or restoring a community of justice and compassion in family and societal life, the Jubilee Centre team use the term 'Relationism' to describe the social ethical system they wish to build from this biblical base.[35]

By advocating this method, they claim to avoid some of the problems inherent in taking as a starting point for Christian social ethics either a creation mandate approach or a kingdom of God approach, while preserving the essential truths of both.[36] In their work they endorse and carry further the concept, which I developed in the first edition of the present book, of Israel and its law as a 'paradigm'. It is this overall paradigm, the social shape of Israel in all its dimensions, that acts as a guiding, organizing and prioritizing control on our expression and application of derived principles. Thus, while they share the theonomists' insistence on the relevance and normativity of the Old Testament and its law, they do not share the reconstructionist agenda of enforcing Old Testament laws and penalties through modern legislation. Nevertheless, they are prepared to step out of the world of biblical research into the complex world of actual social policy and legislation. They are prepared, that is, not only to go up the ladder of abstraction, but to come down again with concrete proposals in the public arena. Not everyone will agree

---

[35] The Jubilee Centre has launched a campaign under the banner of 'Relationism' to bring relational concerns much more into focus in the course of public, policitical, economic and social policy-making. Their proposals are set out in Michael Schluter and David Lee, *R Factor*. The biblical and hermeneutical foundations of the whole project are set out in C. Townsend and J. Ashcroft, *Political Christians in a Plural Society*.

[36] See Michael Schluter and Roy Clements, 'Jubilee Institutional Norms'.

with the specifics of all their agenda. Nor do they expect everyone to, still less do they wish to compel them to. The point is that there comes a time to move from principles to practice, from questions to answers, from debate to action, and the Jubilee Centre at least seeks to do these things from a clearly stated hermeneutical approach to the biblical text.

Messianic Judaism

Finally, it is worth noting the approach of a unique and growing Christian group that is often overlooked, but by its very identity ought to have something to offer on a Christian approach to the Old Testament law; namely, Messianic Jews. There have always been Jewish believers in Jesus as Messiah, since the days of the New Testament itself, of course. Paul, in Romans 9 – 11, accords high theological significance to their existence (himself included) as the believing remnant prophesied in the Scriptures. Over the centuries the tendency has been that those few Jews who became Christians simply assimilated into the predominantly Gentile churches. There really was little other option. However, since the Second World War not only has the number of Jewish believers in Jesus as the Messiah increased dramatically, but also there has emerged the movement known as Messianic Judaism. Numbering approximately 100,000 in America and several thousands in other parts of the world (including the modern state of Israel), Messianic Jews are Christian believers who wish to preserve and affirm their identity as Jews and to live and worship in culturally Jewish ways.[37]

One might have thought that Jewish believers committed to preserving their Jewish heritage and choosing to live their lives as far as possible in accordance with the Torah would adopt a more or less theonomist approach to the Hebrew Bible. But this is not the case. As regards the Torah (understood as it is within Orthodox Judaism to be both the written law of the Tanakh [Hebrew Bible, Old Testament] and the oral rabbinic law) the Messianic Jewish position is that Jewish believers *may* observe Torah as a matter of choice.[38] Thus they may observe the kāšrût (food laws), the sabbath and annual festivals, circumcise their children and so on. There may be two

---

[37] On the history, background and contemporary significance of Messianic Judaism, see Arthur F. Glasser, 'Messianic Jews'; Walter Riggans, Covenant with the Jews; David H. Stern, Messianic Jewish Manifesto.

[38] To the question whether Messianic Jews should keep the Torah as understood in Orthodox Judaism, David H. Stern, Messianic Jewish Manifesto, describes a spectrum of different answers, from absolute yes to absolute no. Stern seems personally to favour the position that it is desirable but not essential to do so.

valid reasons for such an observant lifestyle. It may be a matter of ethnic and cultural identity. The Messianic Jew is saying, 'I *am* a Jew, so let me live as one.' Or it may also be a matter of evangelistic integrity, choosing, with Paul (1 Cor. 9:20), to live a Jewish lifestyle within a Jewish context in order to avoid unnecessary offence while witnessing to Jesus. But such laws are not *binding*. The Messianic Jew may choose to keep these laws and customs and to do so enthusiastically, but he or she is not obliged to, nor are they in any way linked to his or her salvation, which is exclusively grounded in the Messiah's sacrifice on the cross.

However, Messianic Judaism argues further that in the light of the New Testament the very idea of Torah must be redefined. It cannot be confined to (though it still includes) the Old Testament Torah, but now encompasses for the Christian 'the Torah of the Messiah'.[39] This includes not only the specific commands of Jesus, but also the total way of obedience and practical holiness to which Christians are called in the New Testament. But then, the full understanding of New Testament moral teaching actually requires knowledge of Old Testament law, which forms the basis for so much of it. Thus Messianic Judaism agrees that the Old Testament law retains its moral authority for believers, but that it must be set within its total Christian canonical context as part of the new Messianic Torah of the New Covenant.[40] As regards specific application of Old Testament laws in social ethics, the view seems to be that even though they may not be literally binding, they do provide a primary guide as to how God wants people to live. In other words, when necessary cultural and historical adjustments have been made, the law still retains its moral force in principle by way of concrete example.[41]

---

[39] Ibid., pp. 146ff. See also Juster, *Jewish Roots*, ch. 3.

[40] Stern is so concerned about the importance of a right Christian understanding of the abiding relevance of the Torah that he devotes a lengthy chapter of his book to it. 'The lack of a correct, clear and relatively complete Messianic Jewish or Gentile Christian theology of the Law is not only a major impediment to Christians' understanding their own faith, but also the greatest barrier to Jewish people's receiving the Gospel' (p. 125).

Lamenting the lack of interest in the law among Christians in general he goes on: 'It means, first, that most Christians have an overly simplistic understanding of what the Law is all about; and, second, that Christianity has almost nothing relevant to say to Jews about one of the three most important issues of their faith. In short, *Torah* is the great unexplored territory, the *terra incognita* of Christian theology' (p. 126).

[41] I have not been able to find published material on social ethics from Messianic Jewish sources, but gather the above comment from conversations with some members of the community in Britain.

Further reading

Anderson, J. N. D., *Morality, Law and Grace* (London: Tyndale, 1972).

Bahnsen, Greg, *Theonomy in Christian Ethics*, rev. ed. (Phillipsburg: Presbyterian & Reformed, 1984).

————, *By This Standard: The Authority of God's Law Today* (Tyler: Institute for Christian Economics, 1985).

————, 'Christ and the Role of Civil Government: The Theonomic Perspective', *Transformation* 5.2, 5.3 (1988), part 1, pp. 24–31; part 2, pp. 24–28.

Barker, William. S., and Godfrey, W. Robert (eds.), *Theonomy: A Reformed Critique* (Grand Rapids: Academie, 1990).

Bloesch, D. G., *Freedom for Obedience: Evangelical Ethics in Contemporary Times* (New York: Harper & Row, 1987).

Forde, G. O., 'Law and Gospel in Luther's Hermeneutic', *Interpretation* 37 (1983), pp. 240–252.

Froehlich, K., *Biblical Interpretation in the Early Church* (Philadelphia: Fortress, 1984).

Fuller, Daniel P., *Gospel and Law, Contrast or Continuum? The Hermeneutics of Dispensational and Covenant Theology* (Grand Rapids: Eerdmans, 1980).

Geisler, Norman L., 'Dispensationalism and Ethics', *Transformation* 6.1 (1989), pp. 7–14.

————, *Christian Ethics: Options and Issues* (Grand Rapids: Baker; Leicester: IVP, 1989, 1990).

George, Timothy, *Theology of the Reformers* (Nashville: Broadman; Leicester: Apollos, 1988).

Glasser, Arthur F., 'Messianic Jews – What They Represent', *Themelios* 16.2 (1991), pp. 13–14.

House, H. Wayne, and Ice, Thomas (eds.), *Dominion Theology: Blessing or Curse?* (Portland: Multnomah, 1988).

Juster, Daniel, *Jewish Roots: A Foundation of Biblical Theology for Messianic Judaism* (Rockville: Davar, 1986).

Klassen, H. W., 'The Relation of the Old and New Covenants in Pilgram Marpeck's Theology', in Swartley, *Essays on Biblical Interpretation*, pp. 91–105.

Longenecker, R. N., 'Three Ways of Understanding Relations between the Testaments: Historically and Today', in G. F. Hawthorne and O. Betz (eds.), *Tradition and Interpretation in the New Testament: Essays in Honor of E. Earle Ellis for His Sixtieth Birthday* (Grand Rapids: Eerdmans, 1987), pp. 22–32.

Poettker, H., 'Menno Simons' Encounter with the Bible', in Swartley, *Essays on Biblical Interpretation*, pp. 62–76.

Riggans, Walter, *The Covenant with the Jews: What's so Unique about the Jewish People?* (Eastbourne: Monarch), 1992.

Rushdoony, Rousas, *Institutes of Biblical Law* (Phillipsburg: Presbyterian & Reformed, 1973).

Schluter, Michael, and Clements, Roy, *Reactivating the Extended Family: From Biblical Norms to Public Policy in Britain* (Cambridge: Jubilee Centre, 1986).

————, 'Jubilee Institutional Norms: A Middle Way between Creation Ethics and Kingdom Ethics as the Basis for Christian Political Action', *Evangelical Quarterly* 62 (1990), pp. 37–62.

Schluter, Michael, and Lee, David, *The R Factor* (London: Hodder & Stoughton, 1993).

Stern, David H., *Messianic Jewish Manifesto* (Jerusalem: Jewish New Testament Publications, 1988).

Swartley, Willard (ed.), *Essays on Biblical Interpretation: Anabaptist-Mennonite Perspectives* (Elkhart, IN: Institute of Mennonite Studies, 1984).

Townsend, C., and Ashcroft, J., *Political Christians in a Plural Society: A New Strategy for a Biblical Contribution* (Cambridge: Jubilee Centre, 1994).

Wenham, Gordon J., 'Law and the Legal System in the Old Testament', in Kaye and Wenham, *Law, Morality and the Bible*, pp. 24–52.

Wright, D. F., 'The Ethical Use of the Old Testament in Luther and Calvin: A Comparison', *Scottish Journal of Theology* 36 (1983), pp. 463–485.

————, 'Calvin's Pentateuchal Criticism: Equity, Hardness of Heart and Divine Accommodation in the Mosaic Harmony Commentary', *Calvin Theological Journal* 21 (1986), pp. 33–50.

13. CONTEMPORARY SCHOLARSHIP: A
BIBLIOGRAPHICAL ESSAY

As I observed in the preface, the two decades since the publication of *Living as the People of God* in 1983 have seen a remarkable upsurge of interest in the ethical dimension of the Old Testament, although there were stirrings of renewed reflection on the topic in the 1970s. This chapter aims to provide a very selective guide to the past quarter century of literature in the field. Inevitably, this is a personal selection of what I have found interesting or useful, and cannot claim to be an exhaustive bibliography of everything that could be included. At least it will provide determined students of the subject with some bibliographical pump-priming for their own further research. The content is arranged in a broadly chronological sequence, indicated by the dates in bold type, but where an individual scholar's work spans a number of years, it is usually discussed together in one place.

Walter Brueggemann. Spanning the whole quarter century is the massive work of Walter Brueggemann, one of the most prolific advocates of unleashing the ethical power and challenge of the Old Testament. His handling of the text has an almost 'kerygmatic' force, as he constantly strives to see how the great themes of biblical theology address modern issues. He finds in the narratives of Israel, in the message of the prophets, in the passion for justice on the land and so on powerful material that exposes the dynamics of human relationships (personal, social and international), and calls for new ways of bringing God's Word into a missional engagement with contemporary realities. It would be impossible to survey in this space Brueggemann's enormous and endlessly fertile output, even though, remarkably enough, he has never produced a book explicitly on the subject of Old Testament ethics per se. Earlier chapters in this book witness my own debt to his insights. Among his earlier most seminal works were *The Land* (**1977**) and *The Prophetic Imagination* (1978). A helpful collection of a number of his essays that indirectly bear on Old Testament social ethics was edited by Patrick D. Miller Jr. in 1999, *A Social Reading of the Old Testament*. And, of course, many ethical insights and implications can be found in the distinctive approach of his *magnum opus*, *Theology of the Old Testament* (1997).

Apart from Brueggemann's own writings, his stimulation of what might be called 'applied Old Testament theology' can be seen in the series of monographs published by Fortress Press, Overtures to Biblical Theology, which Brueggemann has edited since his own first in the series (*The Land*, 1977). Many of these, while not directly intending to tackle Old Testament ethics, are fruitful and suggestive in a wide variety of ethical directions. The 1980s saw some fine volumes in the series.[1]

John Barton. Barton has made significant contributions to the field of Old Testament ethics throughout our period. He reopened interest in the field in **1978**[2] with some critical reflection on earlier attempts to produce systematic and synchronic accounts of Old Testament ethics, along the lines of comparable earlier work in Old Testament theology. Walther Eichrodt's classic model for structuring Old Testament theology included a major section on the

---

[1] The following volumes are worthy of note as studies of Old Testament themes with ethical relevance: Phyllis Trible, *God and the Rhetoric of Sexuality* (1978); Phyllis Trible, *Texts of Terror* (1984); Walter Harrelson, *Ten Commandments and Human Rights* (1980); J. P. M. Walsh, *Mighty from Their Thrones* (1987); John G. Gammie, *Holiness in Israel* (1989).

[2] Apart from the short reflections offered by Davidson in 1959 (Robert Davidson, 'Old Testament Contribution') and by Fletcher in 1971 (V. H. Fletcher, 'Shape of Old Testament Ethics'), the warm-hearted short summary of biblical ethics by James Muilenburg (*Way of Israel*, 1961) and the rather mixed collection by Crenshaw and Willis in 1974 (J. L Crenshaw and J. T. Willis (eds.), *Essays in Old Testament Ethics*), John Barton's article of 1978, 'Understanding Old Testament Ethics', with its significant sequel of scholarly work in the field by Barton himself, was the first serious work in English on the specific and explicit subject of Old Testament ethics to appear since 1929 (W. B. Greene, 'Ethics of the Old Testament'), as far as I am aware. This was the reason for the remark my supervisor made when I enquired about doing research in the field of Old Testament ethics in the early 1970s, to the effect that nothing had been written on it for fifty years (in English).

ethical teaching of the Old Testament as well.[3] Johannes Hempel likewise, one of the very few to write on Old Testament ethics in the mid-twentieth century, while obviously fully aware of the historical-critical issues of biblical scholarship, sought to present an overview of what could be seen as Old Testament ethics as a whole.[4] Barton refers to both of these (Eichrodt and Hempel), and the whole approach they represent, in two perceptive critiques ('Understanding Old Testament Ethics', 1978; and 'Approaches to Ethics in the Old Testament',1983).[5] Barton argues that, in contrast to the systematic, synchronic approach, we can only satisfactorily make progress in the discipline of Old Testament ethics if we take into account all the sociological, chronological and traditio-critical depths and nuances of the material. We need to distinguish between three different areas of investigation: (1) what some Israelites historically believed and did at various times, (2) what certain Old Testament authors and traditions held regarding what Israelites should believe or do, and (3) what kinds of behaviour the Old Testament, considered as a canon of Scripture, may be said to condemn or endorse. We cannot assume that our construction of the last of these (the 'official' canonical ethic) would have coincided with popular ethics in Israel – in theory or practice – at any given time. Yet neither can we reduce Old Testament ethics merely to a descriptive history of Israel's behaviour, any more than Old Testament theology can be reduced to a history of Israel's religion. We can discern an 'ethos' or 'general thrust' of the moral worldview of ancient Israel. Israelites seem to have believed that there was a pattern of life that could be lived in the presence of God and that was pleasing to God, and this pattern of life had a number of constant factors through the whole period. 'The [Old Testament] law affords an insight into the contours of God's own ideal will for his people and for all mankind.'[6] Barton lists at least three fundamental elements in this 'ethos': (1) obedience to the divine will, (2) conformity to a pattern of natural order, and (3) imitation of God. Barton's distinctive approach to natural law, and the sense in which he uses the phrase in relation to the Old Testament, was further elucidated in 'Natural Law and Poetic Justice' (1979).

Barton returned to the growing debate on Old Testament ethics with his methodological contribution to a symposium on the subject in 1994–5.[7]

---

[3] Walther Eichrodt, 'Effect of Piety on Conduct'.

[4] Johannes Hempel, *Ethos Alten Testaments*.

[5] A similar critique with reflections on critical method in the field of Old Testament ethics was made in 1979 by H. McKeating, 'Sanctions against Adultery'.

[6] Barton, 'Approaches to Ethics', p. 128.

[7] John Barton, 'Basis of Ethics'.

Finally, in 1998 he produced the short book on the subject that summarized the insights and perspectives he has been developing in several articles over twenty years, *Ethics and the Old Testament*. Barton argues that a substantial proportion of the ethical material in the Old Testament conforms to what he calls 'natural law' – not in the technical sense as developed in philosophical ethics since Aristotle, but in the sense of a general human awareness of right and wrong. This basic moral sense is based on the realities of the way the world works. It was found throughout the ancient world and shared by Israel. In addition to this 'natural law', there were ethical values specifically grounded in the direct commandments of YHWH, to which obedience was the only proper response. And undergirding these values and commandments were the motivational factors that revolve especially around the imitation of YHWH in his character and past actions but also include future consequences, whether 'natural' or divine blessing or punishment. Barton includes a reflective chapter on the Old Testament's contribution to the ethics of ecology, sex and property. A most interesting feature of this book is the way Barton treats what most commentators on Old Testament ethics regard as problems (their specificity and variety). He sees these features of the ethical material in the Old Testament, on the contrary, as the major factor in its vitality and longevity. It is precisely the Old Testament's passion for the concrete *particular* (especially through stories), as opposed to philosophical *principles*, that gives it such moral force. Barton builds on the work of Martha Nussbaum on Greek tragedy in developing this approach. In 2003 a helpful republication of John Barton's earlier work in this field, with an introduction, appeared: *Understanding Ethics: Approaches and Explorations* (Louisville: Westminster John Knox, 2003).

Apart from these few articles by Fletcher, Barton and McKeating and the collection by Crenshaw, the 1970s were a barren decade for Old Testament ethics. This coincided with the apparent collapse of the Biblical Theology movement, and its effects on biblical ethics. A mood of uncertainty and introspection seemed to have settled on biblical theology, with scholars repeatedly asking whether such a 'thing' really existed at all and if so, how it was to be defined. In the same way, and presumably for the same reasons, few seemed inclined to offer either accounts of 'biblical ethics' as a whole or accounts of Old Testament ethics or New Testament ethics respectively. On the other hand, sociological or (in the more recent terminology) social-scientific approaches to the Old Testament came more into vogue, bearing fruit that often seemed ambiguous, heavily freighted with ideology, and yet (if handled with care) ethically stimulating.

Norman Gottwald. One of the earliest figures in the contemporary upsurge of sociological study of the Old Testament is also one of the more controversial. Norman Gottwald's overtly Marxist reading of the Hebrew Bible (*The Tribes of Yahweh*, **1979**) has been heavily criticized precisely for its heavy dose of ideological theory, though other examples from various liberationist or advocacy stances could be given. Gottwald sees ethical relevance in the Old Testament, not in the sense that there is any revelation of God with ethical norms inherent in the literature as Scripture, but rather in its portrayal of the historical struggle of Israel. According to Gottwald's sociological theory, Israel is a remarkable historical case study of a people committed to a great experiment in social freedom, equality and justice. This social experiment generated a supporting and sanctioning religion, mono-Yahwism. Any ethical authority that the literary deposit of this historical phenomenon may have lies in the realm of historical precedent and contemporary challenge, not in the spiritualizing idealism of claiming YHWH as our own God. Gottwald's sociological positivism and critical methodology have not gone unchallenged in the wider world of Old Testament scholarship, and they will certainly be unacceptable to those committed to any view of divine authority in Scripture. But in my view (as discussed in chapter 2 above) he has made two significant contributions to Old Testament ethics: first, by establishing the importance of studying Israel as a total social organism, so that we no longer simply try to quarry out ethical 'gems' from isolated texts, but rather see the relevance of all Israel tried to be and achieve in their historical context; and second, by showing in considerable depth and detail the extent to which Israel was distinctive from surrounding Canaanite culture, in social, economic, political and religious terms (though this view is also challenged in certain schools of recent Old Testament historiography).

John Goldingay. Goldingay opened the new decade with his *Approaches to Old Testament Interpretation* (**1981**). This wide-ranging book (which was revised and updated, with even more extensive bibliographies in 1991) is not specifically on Old Testament ethics, but it has a chapter, 'The Old Testament as a Way of Life', that tackles some of the problems inherent in Old Testament ethics, and offers helpful perspectives on how the Old Testament functions ethically for Christian readers. Goldingay wishes to affirm the normative authority of the Old Testament, as an integral part of the canon of Scripture, in Christian ethics. But he also sees the importance of formulating derived or intermediate principles (sometimes called 'middle axioms') as a way of moving from the specifics of the ancient text to the specifics of our modern context. Otherwise, the 'specificness' (his term) of the Old Testament commands (not to mention its stories and other genres) could induce a kind of ethical paralysis in which one is so aware of the cultural and historical particularity of Israel's laws that one despairs of finding any modern relevance at all, let alone a normative ethic. Against such a negative view, Goldingay points out that, even in ordinary secular life, the specificity of a command to its particular context need not spell irrelevance to other contexts, since it can be the concrete expression of some general principle that is being applied in the context of the original command and will be relevant to other contexts also. There are also human constants that survive cultural discontinuities, as well as the moral consistency of God himself. As well as discussing the problem of the specificity of Old Testament commands, Goldingay tackles the diversity and apparent limitations of Old Testament moral standards. These features also necessitate making use of broader derived principles as a form of bridge from the texts themselves to the world in which we have to make our ethical decisions.

However, in exploring the necessity of some such procedure, Goldingay warns against making the derived principles themselves the locus of authority. It is the text of Scripture itself that remains normative:

> If we are concerned with interpreting the Bible itself, it is nevertheless not these hypothetical principles which are normative or canonical. The Bible itself remains the norm. The principles we find in it are part of our interpretation, not the object of our interpretation. They are limited by our blind-spots, and can be the means of missing aspects of the whole message of Scripture or of evading the meaning of the text itself, rather than of serving it.[8]

This is an important caveat. But it might seem to impale us on a dilemma: on the one hand, we have an authoritative text we cannot apply directly, or which does not address the specific contemporary moral problem that confronts us, while on the other hand we have derivative moral principles which we are doubtless helpful but have no intrinsic authority. Nevertheless, it seems to me that we have no alternative but to derive intermediate mechanisms of some kind, or else the Bible will be ethically gagged and bound. In this book (in chapter 2 and, in relation to Old Testament law, in chapter 9) I have argued the case for recognizing the constructive nature of the biblical paradigm, as that which binds together into a coherent structure the various principles or axioms (or whatever other term is used) that we discern in the text. The vital thing, however, is that we constantly submit those intermediate means – call them paradigms, principles, axioms, or whatever – to revision in the light of the biblical text itself. The text remains the final authority, in the light of which our ethical affirmations must be as *semper reformanda* (always subject to reform) as our ecclesiology or theology.

---

[8] Goldingay, *Approaches*, p. 55.

In later work (*Theological Diversity and the Authority of the Old Testament*, 1987) Goldingay examines the importance of historical *context* in understanding and relating Old Testament laws and narratives. The Bible itself shows how changing contexts called forth different responses and different priorities, and we ought not merely to flatten all that diversity into alleged timeless truths, except in cases where the Bible itself explicitly offers an abiding truth or imperative on the basis of a historical incident. As a case study in this, Goldingay traces the idea of 'the People of God' through its long historical journey in the Old Testament. He shows how each major period found the people of God in sometimes radically different forms, and facing new challenges and ethical tasks, as they move from the ancestral wandering clan, through theocratic nation, institutional state, afflicted remnant to the post-exilic community of promise. There is continuity and yet obvious diversity as well, and ethical principles drawn from the texts that relate to any one of these periods must take into account the interwoven patterns of this whole historical tapestry. As Goldingay explores this continuity in diversity, he makes it clear that he sees definite ethical challenges and resources for the Christian church in such a study of just one theme of the Hebrew canon.[9]

In the same book (*Theological Diversity*), chapter 5, Goldingay puts forward what he calls the 'pastoral strategy' of Deuteronomy. After surveying the book's behavioural values and theological perspectives, he points out that apparent moral tensions between high ethical ideals, on the one hand, and some laws that appear less than ethical to us, on the other hand, may be resolved if we recognize this 'pastoral strategy'. We need to appreciate that the legislator was concerned both to set out the highest possible standards of covenant loyalty and behaviour, and yet at the same time to take into account the reality of a sinful, rebellious people and their ambient culture. You have to start where people are – then as now. So the law necessarily made concessions to the facts of human sin and of undesirable aspects of historical culture. In noting this, Goldingay takes his cue from the way Jesus handled the divorce controversy. Jesus contrasted the creation ideal with the Mosaic permission. Yet both of the texts Jesus quoted, of course, are part of the same Torah. The Bible itself, therefore, gives us precedent for moral evaluation and relativizing of some texts in the light of others. But it is only the text of Scripture that can do this, not our own claims to some higher ethical stance.

The authority of the Old Testament, therefore, in Goldingay's view, is not

---

[9] Goldingay, *Theological Diversity*, ch. 3. The insights and structure of this chapter of Goldingay's book underlie my own discussion of the relationship between the people of God and political authorities in chapter 7 above.

simply flat and even and equal in every text. While the whole text has its canonical authority, some parts are clearly prescriptive in a way that moves quickly towards application now, while others are more in the nature of case studies of God's engagement with Israel in situations of greater or lesser obedience to God's will:

> Thus either the Bible's statements tell us how to live, or (when they do not do this) these actual statements are the model for and the measure of our attempts to state how we are to live. This means we do not ignore the particularity of biblical commands (and apply them to our own day as if they were timeless universals). Nor are we paralysed by their particularity (and thus unable to apply them to our day at all). We rejoice in their particularity because it shows us how the will of God was expressed in their context, and we take them as our paradigm for our own ethical construction.[10]

John Rogerson. Like John Barton, John Rogerson ('The Old Testament and Social and Moral Questions', **1982**), also relates Old Testament morality to a natural order. He finds much in common between Israelite law and the laws and other moral texts of contemporary ancient Near Eastern societies, and thus sees the moral norms of Israel as reflecting that natural morality of the time. This is not the same as 'natural law' in the dogmatic or philosophical sense, since it is clearly historically conditioned. But the modern Christian (or non-Christian) can still learn from these ancient texts when we observe their moral consensus and weigh it up in its historical context. There are principles, but they are not timeless or unique to Israel. However, if we are to take the Old Testament's moral demands seriously *as Christians*, we have to do so in the light of the Old Testament's imperatives of redemption. We are reminded by it of our total dependence on God, our constant need for his grace, and our need for the vision of his kingdom that the Bible alone supplies.

Thomas Ogletree. In **1983** Ogletree produced his stimulating book *The Use of the Bible in Christian Ethics*. As the title suggests, Ogletree does not aim to write a comprehensive or descriptive biblical ethics, but to open up a dialogue between the biblical text and modern understandings for the moral life. He surveys consequentialist, deontological and perfectionist conceptions of ethics, and concludes that none is sufficient by itself to account for the complexity of human ethical awareness. He proposes a synthesis grounded in historical contextualizing, and finds this synthesis supported by a representation

---

[10] Goldingay, *Approaches*, p. 55.

of classic biblical themes from both testaments. He confines his biblical survey to the Pentateuch and eighth-century prophets in the Old Testament and the Synoptic Gospels and Paul in the New Testament. Without underestimating the rich diversity of the biblical materials, he finds a broad thematic unity in the Bible, a unity that resides in the unfolding identity of the people of God. This enables him to work from the particularity of their historical context to the particularity of our modern context, since 'the significance of the biblical texts cannot be confined to the past, to the original intentions of their authors, or to the initial contexts of their production' (p. 9). Ogletree, then, sets Old Testament ethics (or that portion of the material he chooses to discuss) firmly within the broader field of canonical biblical ethics. And while he would not attach quite the same degree of normative authority to the biblical text per se as Goldingay, or Kaiser, Wright and Janzen (see below), he certainly affirms the central place the Bible must have in Christian ethical construction and decision.

Walter C. Kaiser, Jr. The first edition of my own work *Living as the People of God*, retitled *An Eye for an Eye* in the USA emerged in **1983** – a somewhat intuitive attempt to set out a way of understanding the ethical thrust of the Old Testament in general terms and then to illustrate a suggested method in several applied areas. In the same year Walter Kaiser produced his much more wide-ranging work *Toward Old Testament Ethics*. At the time, both authors were quite unaware of the other's interest and work in the field.

Kaiser devotes a major first section of this work to a survey of the field itself, its definition, scope and methodological problems, and also a classification of such approaches as were advocated in various scholars' work on biblical ethics in general. After an exegetical survey of the major sections of the law, he organizes his material around the central theme of holiness, and then proceeds with an exposition of the second table of the Decalogue. Finally, he tackles some of the moral difficulties frequently raised by readers of the Old Testament.

Kaiser is thus among those who affirm two things about the Old Testament: first, that it can be handled in some systematic, unified way, in spite of its manifest diversity; and second, that it does still hold moral authority for the Christian. On both counts, he finds much current writing on the subject deficient. In an article in 1992 ('New Approaches to Old Testament Ethics') Kaiser regrets the absence of a sense of coherence or a central principle in writing on Old Testament ethics over the previous decade or two, such as characterized the work of Eichrodt. Kaiser is well aware of the reasons for this, as expressed by many of Eichrodt's critics, and by John Barton in relation to Old Testament ethics in particular. But Kaiser points out that even where a scholar like Barton is willing to see several dominant motifs (such as conformity to natural order, obedience to divine will, imitation of God), he (Barton) does not see these as normative or prescriptive for us. There is, in other words, says Kaiser, a marked resistance to a deontological understanding of ethics in treatments of the Old Testament.

In the same article Kaiser also regrets the effect on ethics of the paradigm shift in Old Testament hermeneutics from concern for author intention to theories of reader response. While there is much to learn and great potential in the newer literary criticism, it can undermine any objective authority the text was believed to embody for normative ethics. Some practitioners of a reader-response approach to the text, of course, would say that no such thing as objectivity exists anyway. There is certainly a shift from attempting to explicate some kind of objective, cognitive understanding of the text to a more subjective, intuitive stance: 'More and more, the Bible functions in modern thought as a catalyst suggesting ways in which former communities faced problems, but imposing no categories, no norms, or principles of its own – especially in an objective, cognitive, or regulative way.'[11] There is little scope here for a revelation-based authority in actual ethical decision-making.

Kaiser himself wants to insist on the moral authority of the Old Testament and does so first by calling for a fresh appreciation of the classic division of the law into moral, civil and ceremonial categories.[12] This ancient scheme (partly perceived by Origen, given clear shape by Calvin, enshrined for Anglicans in Article 7 of the Thirty-Nine Articles of Religion and for the Reformed tradition in the Westminster Confession of Faith, and influential until comparatively recent years[13]) has fallen into disfavour. The main attack upon it is, first, that it serves no exegetical purpose, in that it is impossible to make clear divisions into such categories when actually studying Old Testament legal texts; and second, that it is foreign to the thought of either Old or New Testament.[14] However, it could be argued against the first point that it was never intended as an *exegetical* tool, but as a self-consciously post-biblical hermeneutical means of applying the law in a Christian context. And

---

[11] Kaiser Jr, 'New Approaches', p. 295.

[12] Walter C. Kaiser Jr, 'God's Promise Plan'.

[13] E.g. it is the framework of Norman Anderson's discussion of the role of the law for Christian ethics in Anderson, *Morality, Law and Grace*, pp. 118ff.

[14] I myself joined in the attack in my earliest wrestling with the task of applying Old Testament law in 'Ethics and the Old Testament', *Third Way* 1.9–11 (May–June 1977), articles subsequently reprinted as a booklet, *What Does the Lord Require?* (Nottingham: Shaftesbury Project, 1978).

against the second point, Kaiser shows that there is more evidence than one might think for an awareness of some such distinction in the minds of New Testament authors. Indeed, the Old Testament itself prepares the way for such distinctions when some of the prophets clearly set up priorities, as between the sacrificial and other ritual laws, on the one hand, and the demands of social justice, on the other (and not only the prophets: Prov. 21:3). In calling for a fresh understanding and application of this way of handling the law, Kaiser is waging a polemic against the 'all-or-nothing' banner of the theonomist-reconstructionist school: that is, either the whole law applies today, or none of it does at all. This position is critiqued in chapter 12 above.

Having reinstated the idea of moral law, Kaiser is keen not to confine it merely to the Ten Commandments alone, as has often been done. Rather, there is a breadth of moral *principles* that inform the whole core and meaning of the Torah, and can be drawn on as we seek to apply them to contemporary issues. The law was given not solely for Israel but purposely to be of moral relevance to the nations, as the prophets implicitly affirm in their moral evaluation of the nations' behaviour. Kaiser advocates a 'ladder of abstraction' approach,[15] in which the precedents of Old Testament law are applied to modern situations by way of intermediate moral principles.[16]

In affirming the moral authority of the Old Testament mediated through moral principles derived from the text, Kaiser nevertheless declines to see Israel as a *model* for the nations.[17] This again is because he resists the theonomist scheme, particularly as advocated by Greg Bahnsen, in which the expression 'Israel as a model' is used to imply fairly literal and total application of Israel's law, including its penalties in the civil realm. However, in my view, the expression need not be taken in the theonomists' fashion, but can be a useful means of encapsulating the relevance to contemporary ethics of Israel as a total society. It was Israel as a whole community that was to be 'a light to the nations'. It was Israel as a holy nation that was to be a priesthood in the midst of the nations. As we saw in chapters 2 and 9, I believe there are ways that we can use the idea of Israel as a model in applying Old Testament laws and institutions paradigmatically that avoid the theonomists' extreme while preserving their commendable enthusiasm for the abiding ethical relevance of the law.

---

[15] This is a term and a method also used by Michael Schluter and the Jubilee Centre in their application of biblical materials to social issues, as discussed in chapter 12 above.

[16] Kaiser has developed these ideas further. Kaiser Jr, *Rediscovering the Old Testament*, pp. 155–166.

[17] Kaiser Jr, 'God's Promise Plan', pp. 296–297.

R. E. Clements. Like several others already mentioned, Ronald Clements ('Christian Ethics' and the Old Testament', **1984**) also recognizes the historically contextual limits on the ethical material of the Old Testament and observes how even phrases that have passed into the fundamentals of the Christian ethical tradition (such as 'Love your neighbour as yourself') come in contexts that are 'occasional' and sometimes syntactically incidental. It is questionable, in Clements's view, whether the Old Testament gives us, in its own words and by its own intention, any timeless moral principles. Nevertheless, Clements is impressed with the breadth and durability of Old Testament moral insights. 'Overall, the Old Testament literature appears to be feeling its way towards the formulation of universal principles of morality' (p. 17). Certain moral priorities and demands are so repeatedly apparent that they achieve a 'sense of "primacy" as regards importance [which] readily lends itself to a sense of "principle", as regards universal applicability' (p. 17). Clements also observes how the long history of Israel in the Old Testament period gave ample opportunity for the fundamental insights and values of their society to be tested and refined in an amazing variety of historical situations. Since Israel had to adapt and yet preserve essentials, the norms and values they expressed, through law, prophecy, narrative, worship and wisdom, likewise manifest that quality of adaptability: 'The Old Testament has provided a system of *tora*-instruction, which has proved to be remarkably adaptable to a vast range of human social and political systems. Societies of dramatically different economic, political and cultural types have found within the Old Testament a richly viable source of social and moral teaching' (p. 22).

R. E. Clements is also the editor of a major symposium of essays on social dimensions of the Old Testament, *The World of Ancient Israel* (1989). While not directly addressing ethical questions, there is a rich source of raw material here for the (stout-hearted) student of Old Testament ethics. It is also a most helpful quarry for further bibliographical resources.

Richard Bauckham. More renowned as a New Testament scholar, Bauckham contributed a short but very helpful volume to the study of biblical ethics, with strong emphasis on the Old Testament, *The Bible in Politics* (**1989**). He offers a helpful hermeneutical guide to ethical reading of the Old Testament (and the New), with particular focus on the sociopolitical realm. Bauckham espouses an approach similar to my own in handling the paradigmatic significance of ancient texts for contemporary relevance, and includes a fine study of the ethics of Leviticus 19.

Robert R. Wilson. In contrast to the attempts of Goldingay and Kaiser (and myself) to argue for the possibility of deriving universal moral norms from the Old Testament material, Robert Wilson argues that the material cannot bear such weight. In his contribution to the Festschrift for Brevard Childs ('Approaches to Old Testament Ethics', **1988**) Wilson points out how the narratives of the Deuteronomic historians appear quite inconsistent in applying Torah norms to some of the central characters in Israel's history (e.g. David). So, Wilson asks, if Pentateuchal laws did not exclusively govern the ethical evaluation even of biblical authors, why should they be considered binding on us in any direct way? Better known for his sociological work on the Old Testament (especially on the prophets), Wilson later brought his sociological insights to bear on what he saw as conflicting ethical agendas within Israelite society ('Ethics in Conflict', 1990). He also contributed a further methodological essay on Old Testament ethics ('Sources and Methods in the Study of Ancient Israelite Ethics'), to the *Semeia* symposium of 1994.

Bruce C. Birch. In the same Festschrift for Brevard Childs (**1988**) Bruce Birch takes a rather more positive line in his contribution 'Old Testament Narrative and Moral Address'. Birch emphasizes particularly the power of biblical narrative. While it cannot function prescriptively or normatively for the Christian, it can help to shape the Christian's moral identity and character. The Old Testament narratives have moral power in exposing reality, shattering or transforming worldviews and challenging the reader to respond. They therefore have to be read as wholes within their canonical context, and not just by the methods of historical criticism. This perspective builds on Birch's earlier work along with **Larry Rasmussen** (1978; revised 1989).[18] There again, while arguing that the Old Testament cannot be prescriptive or normative for the Christian, Birch affirms that it shares in the primacy of the whole Bible as a moral resource for Christian decision-making and for the church's moral response to the world.

The canonical approach also underlies Birch's own monograph *Let Justice Roll Down* (1991). Birch claims that this is not strictly a book on Old Testament ethics, but is about the role the Old Testament can play and the resources it can provide in shaping Christian ethical behaviour and choices. This, of course, raises the question of definition (what is meant by 'Old Testament ethics'?), to which we shall return in chapter 14. Birch surveys each major section of the Old Testament canon in turn, summarizes the main theological themes found in each, and then assesses what that section has to offer for the ethical task facing the Christian and the church in the modern world. All this is comprehensive, informative, theologically suggestive and

---

[18]   Bruce C. Birch and Larry L. Rasmussen, *Bible and Ethics*.

(with its ample bibliographical footnotes) very welcome for students of the field of Old Testament ethics, even though it is not finally clear what actual moral *authority* the Old Testament bears for the Christian. It has *power*, but not *authority*:

> Authority is not a property inherent in the Bible itself . . . it is a recognition of the Christian community over the centuries of experience that the scripture is a source of empowerment for its moral life in the world . . . Often the authority of Scripture is as much in its modeling of a process as in its mediating of a content. In attending to the discernment of God's will by the biblical communities we become sensitized to God's will in our own time.[19]

Well, yes. But we could do with more help in the hermeneutical steps by which we move from the one to the other.

In the following decade, having emphasized the importance of biblical *narrative* and the biblical *canon* in shaping Christian ethics, Birch went on to add a third significant dimension – the role of the *community* of God's people. Within this community developed that distinctive understanding of the identity, character and actions of YHWH that shaped the ethical faith, thought and praxis of Israel. Birch explored these dimensions of Old Testament ethics, with particular attention to the book of Exodus, in two fine articles, 'Moral Agency, Community, and the Character of God in the Hebrew Bible' (1994) and 'Divine Character and the Formation of Moral Community' (1995).

Stanley Hauerwas. In his emphasis on canon, narrative and community Birch owes much, on the one hand, to the tradition of Brevard Childs and his canonical approach to the Old Testament, and, on the other hand, to Stanley Hauerwas and his emphasis on the role of narratives in shaping communities. The prolific work of Hauerwas in the 1980s (especially *A Community of Character*, 1981; *Peaceable Kingdom*, 1983; and *Resident Aliens*, 1989) can be seen to have influenced many in the following decade, including, for example, Waldemar Janzen and Mary Mills.

Hauerwas also stressed the importance of the community as the locus for the formation of ethical character and behaviour. Neither in ancient Israel nor for the contemporary Christian is ethics simply a matter of moral choices made by the autonomous rational individual – that peculiar abstraction of enlightenment modernity. Individuals are shaped within communities, and

---

[19] Birch, *Let Justice Roll Down*, p. 34.

communities are shaped by their stories (both in the sense of their actual history and the story they tell to affirm their identity and aspirations). Birch and others who have followed Hauerwas in recognizing the place of narrative and community in ethics, however, have gone much further than him in study-ing the actual text and traditions of Israel. For one double-sided criticism that has been made of Hauerwas's writing is that although it has an inspir-ational and prophetic quality, it has, on the one hand, a somewhat idealized view of Christian community that most local churches do not aspire to, and lacks, on the other hand, detailed exegetical engagement with texts of the Scriptures for whose narrative shape he claims such a high regard.

Christopher J. H. Wright. In 1990 the fruit of my own doctoral research, completed thirteen years previously, at last saw the light of publication, in *God's People in God's Land* (1990; rev. ed. 1996). This study of the economic ethics of ancient Israel built on the seminal work of Gerhard von Rad on Israel's theology of land.[20] It established the strong theological links between land, covenant and family in Israel's economic structures; surveyed the twin themes of divine gift and divine ownership of the land; explored the ethics of property rights and responsibilities; and critically assessed the common view that a man's wife, children and slaves were regarded as mere chattels in Israel. In concluding discussions at the end of each main part the relevance of the material for Christian social ethics is touched upon, in ways more expansively handled in the present book, especially chapters 3, 5 and 6 above.

In the years following the publication of *Living as the People of God* (1983) my interest and work in the field of Old Testament ethics generated several articles that carried forward its method in different areas. They were published as a collection of essays, *Walking in the Ways of the Lord*, in 1995. Most of the contents of *Walking in the Ways of the Lord* have been incorporated into this book.

Terence E. Fretheim. In 1991 Fretheim offered the helpful contribution 'The Reclamation of Creation'. Fretheim wishes to challenge the traditional habit among critical scholars of reading Genesis in the light of Exodus; that is, on the understanding that the creation traditions in Genesis emerged within an Israel that had already experienced YHWH through their (Israel's) redemptive history. Fretheim argues for the canonical and theological import-ance of the fact that Genesis comes first in affirming the priority of God's work in the world and among the nations *before* the emergence of Israel. This

---

[20] G. von Rad, 'Promised Land'.

means that the intention of God's redemptive work is not confined to Israel but has universal impact. The Song of Moses in Exodus 15 celebrates God's redemption in history overcoming anticreational forces of chaos (historically symbolized in Egypt). He stresses the missiological integration of the Abrahamic and Sinaitic covenants. Sinai is meant to enable Israel to fulfil its vocation as the people of God in the service and restoration of creation. The law, therefore, has its roots in creation faith, not merely in the exodus, even though it is obviously motivated and empowered by that historical event. 'Israel now joins God in seeking to keep right what God has put right and to extend that rightness into every sphere of daily life . . . Sinai reiterates for those redeemed the demands of creation.'[21]

I warm to Fretheim's combination of missiological and ethical understanding of the thrust of the Old Testament. He pays attention equally to the universality of the creation theme and the particularity of Israel's election, redemption and vocation in the midst of the nations. As the structure of many of the chapters in the present book demonstrates, it is also my conviction that we must constantly bind creational and redemptive ethical values together in considering any topic in relation to the Old Testament Scriptures.

Brevard Childs. In **1992** Childs included a section on biblical ethics within his *Biblical Theology of the Old and New Testaments* ('The Shape of the Obedient Life', pp. 658–716). He surveys the methodological problems inherent in the task of producing what might be called 'Old Testament Ethics' (some of which are explored in chapter 14 below). He is particularly scathing of the attempt to reduce the subject merely to sociological examination of Israel (or, more usually, of an 'Israel' reconstructed by the sociologist), and argues (as one expects from Childs) for a broad canonical approach:

> Rather than suggest that the route of Old Testament ethics is to pursue far more radically the application of sociology in reconstructing small areas of Israelite culture, I would argue that the task of Old Testament ethics is to acknowledge this canonical corpus as a theological construct which is only indirectly related to an historical and empirical Israel, and to pursue rigorously the theological witness of Israel, the people of God . . . The route of a radical sociological approach will never produce a normative ethic for the Christian faith, but only confirm the initial assumptions of cultural and theological relativism.[22]

---

[21] Fretheim, 'Reclamation of Creation', pp. 362–363.

[22] Childs, *Biblical Theology of the Old and New Testaments*, p. 676.

Waldemar Janzen was the next to attempt a monograph specifically on our subject, *Old Testament Ethics* (**1994**). Following in the footsteps of Hauerwas, Birch and others, Janzen argues that narrative is a much more formative genre for ethics than law. Even within the law itself, Janzen disputes the common idea that the Decalogue was somehow intended to be a comprehensive summary of required behaviour. He sees it rather as illustrative and representative of key areas. Janzen proposes that there were certain normative paradigms of behaviour in biblical Israel, shaped by stories and other genres (including commandments). Janzen uses 'paradigm' in a somewhat different sense from my own. Whereas I use it to describe either the total conceptual matrix of Israel's faith, or the concrete model by which Israel was to be an exemplar to the nations, Janzen uses it in a more subjectively. Israelites made their ethical decisions and directed their ethical behaviour under the influence of internalized portraits of ideal behaviour. These mental paradigms were built up by many complex factors – not excluding the laws, but more dominated by narratives – into a composite picture of what it meant to be a 'good Israelite' in different circumstances. Janzen lays out the profiles of what he regards as the primary ethical paradigms of the Old Testament: the royal paradigm, priestly paradigm, prophetic paradigm, the wisdom paradigm and familial paradigm. Of these, the last underlies the others and holds them together through a common emphasis on life, land and hospitality.

The Year **1995** was particularly rich for connoisseurs of Old Testament ethics, with a menu of three multi-authored volumes and several monographs on biblical ethics that included substantial Old Testament contributions:

1. The journal *Semeia* devoted the whole of issue 66 to the subject *Ethics and Politics in the Hebrew Bible* (**1994–5**). In the methodological section **John Barton** ('The Basis of Ethics in the Hebrew Bible') repeated and strengthened his classification of Old Testament ethics as a combination of obedience to God's will, natural law and imitation of God – perspectives he had first suggested in 1978 and 1983. As mentioned above, this in turn prepared the way for his 1998 monograph *Ethics and the Old Testament*. Further methodological essays were offered by **Eryl W. Davies** ('Ethics of the Hebrew Bible') and **Robert Wilson** ('Sources and Methods'). Both of these in my view, however, are rather sketchy and disappointing. More satisfying is the contribution of **Bruce Birch** mentioned above, 'Moral Agency, Community, and the Character of God in the Hebrew Bible'.

2. A Sheffield colloquium produced the volume *The Bible in Ethics* (**1995**).[23]

---

[23] John W. Rogerson, Margaret Davies and M. Daniel Carroll (eds.), *Bible in Ethics*.

Again, **Bruce Birch** has a stimulating contribution on the ethical aspects of the theology of Exodus (mentioned above). **Philip R. Davies**, 'Ethics and the Old Testament', however, offers a strikingly negative assessment by comparison. The basic element of Old Testament ethics, which he takes to be blind obedience to the deity's commands (a debatable assumption in itself, as we shall see in chapter 14 below), is unacceptable to Davies on the grounds that it is not really ethical at all. For Davies, to engage ethically with the Bible will in very many cases mean resisting it (p. 173). The same hostile assessment of the ethical values (and value) of the Old Testament is found in **Cheryl Exum**'s contribution to the symposium, 'The Ethics of Biblical Violence against Women'. These are discussed more fully in chapter 14.

3. Also in **1995**, **Cyril Rodd** edited the symposium *New Occasions Teach New Duties?* His own thoughtful contribution, 'The Use of the Old Testament in Christian Ethics' (matched, incidentally, with an equally helpful article by Howard Marshall, 'The Use of the New Testament in Christian Ethics'), surveys the difficulties we have in handling the Old Testament ethically. Rodd argues that often we are very selective in what we commend; sometimes we ignore what we don't or can't approve of; and at other times we impose upon the Old Testament a range of ethical concerns that are more modern than biblical. Rodd assesses four representative attempts to solve these issues (those of John Rogerson, Richard Bauckham, John Goldingay and me). He concludes that all have been unsuccessful in the final analysis, though probably acceptable to those who share their respective assumptions or confessional stances. This article is clearly preparatory for Rodd's major work, *Glimpses of a Strange Land*, published six years later (2001; see below).

William C. Spohn. The abundance of **1995** continued with Spohn's *What Are They Saying About Scripture and Ethics?* Like other titles in the series this monograph surveys the current state of the field and gives a lot of attention to the hermeneutical and methodological questions. In his final chapter, however, Spohn presents his own perspective, summarizing the essential aspect of biblical ethics as 'responding love'. He sees Jesus as the 'concrete universal' and, in discussing the way we move by analogy from that model (Jesus) as a paradigm to the choices and decisions we have to make in our own world, adopts a comparable position to my own on the nature of biblical paradigms.

Moshe Weinfeld. Another major monograph in **1995** was Weinfeld's *Social Justice in Ancient Israel and in the Ancient near East.* Weinfeld first revisits some well-trodden ground in defining these terms. Then he relates them to Israel's historical kings, the eschatological king and then to sabbatical and jubilee concepts. He also explores the impact of Israel's perception of themselves as servants of YHWH, and of the land as YHWH's. This wide-ranging and informative book is noted more fully in chapter 8 above.

Norman Habel. Yet another **1995** monograph moves from social justice to economic conflict. Normal Habel returned to the theme of the land, explored in different ways by Brueggemann and me, in *The Land Is Mine*. Strongly influenced by more recent social-scientific approaches to the Old Testament, which claim to detect the all-pervasive role of ideology and class interests within the biblical texts, Habel surveys the theme of the land through six different blocks of tradition: land as source of wealth (the royal ideology); land as conditional grant (the theocratic view of the Levites); land as family lots (the household ideals found in the book of Joshua); land as YHWH's personal portion (the prophetic ideology found strongly in Jeremiah); land as 'sabbath bound' (the priestly perception); and land as host country (the immigrant ideology of the patriarchal texts). While his analysis is fascinating, and has the merit of covering a wide range of relevant texts, it seems to me that Habel sees conflicting ideologies in what others might regard as complementary perspectives. In this he anticipates the work of David Pleins, discussed below. A further criticism would be that Habel pays little attention to the canonical order of the traditions as found in the Hebrew Bible (he discusses the royal ideology first and the patriarchal traditions last, for example). The result of this is that he can present as 'valid' ideology attitudes and practices towards the land which are themselves clearly set under critique and judgment within their canonical context (as the monarchic practices certainly are – both in the historical and in the prophetic texts).

James T. Bretzke produced his extensive *Bibliography on Scripture and Christian Ethics* in **1997**. Apart from its comprehensive coverage, this is useful for drawing attention to many works of Roman Catholic Moral Theology that include biblical discussions but are not commonly listed in bibliographies of biblical studies. As well as the major sections on Old and New Testament ethics, Bretzke includes topical sections on issues such as ecology, economics, justice, liberation, medicine, politics, sex, racism, war and peace.

Tom Deidun. Whether the Bible can be used for such contemporary issues at all, however, is the question Deidun addresses in his lengthy article 'The Bible and Christian Ethics' (**1998**), effectively pouring cold water on the whole attempt to use the Old Testament (or the Bible as whole) in any authoritative way for Christian ethics. Deidun surveys the methodological and hermeneutical problems that attend the task (the cultural distance, the Bible's diversity of contexts, the situational specificity of ethical statements in the Bible, the variety of literary genres etc.) – apparently unaware of the discussion of precisely these challenges by John Goldingay in 1981 and 1991. He then surveys some of the standard attempts to handle biblical ethics, classifying them into prescriptive approaches, principles/ideals approaches and response/relational approaches. None of these approaches satisfies Deidun. Behind them all he finds a nostalgia for authority, which he suspects is in need of subversion in principle and ultimately impossible to satisfy in practice. So in the end Deidun cheerfully dispenses with both method and authority altogether and advocates instead 'a recommended non-method', which means a very free, creative and unprogrammatic reading of biblical texts. There is a refreshing (or infuriating, depending on your predisposition) splash of postmodernity about Deidun's proposal, but its inbuilt provisionality leaves one wondering what value there might be in reading the Old Testament at all, in preference to any other selection of religious or secular texts that might nourish our imagination. Nevertheless, Deidun's article clearly catches a current mood, and is explicitly cited with approval in Cyril Rodd's major book, *Glimpses of a Strange Land* (2001; see below).

J. Gary Millar. A very different spirit pervades the close ethical reading of Deuteronomy offered by Millar, *Now Choose Life* (**1998**). While Millar surveys the field of Old Testament ethics, highlighting the major contributions of the past century, and draws attention to the methodological difficulties inherent in the discipline, he is not paralysed by them. He shows what can be done when an Old Testament book is studied in depth with ethical questions in mind, paying close attention to the literary and theological dynamic of the book itself. Millar argues that the motif of 'journey' is key to Deuteronomy – not merely as a geographical feature of the opening chapters, but as a theological and ethical thread running through the whole book. Israel is called to constant decision (another key ethical category explored by Millar), through being a people on the move. There is thus a sense in which Deuteronomy challenges the people of God with a constantly changing ethical demand – not in the sense of a change in the moral character of God, but because the covenant relationship with God must be lived out in constantly changing circumstances and contexts. Millar provides helpful exegetical surveys of the major legal blocks of Deuteronomy, and also explores themes in the book that have been given little attention hitherto, such as his chapters 'Ethics and the Nations' and 'Ethics and Human Nature'.

Eryl W. Davies. In **1999**, just in time for the start of the fourth millennium (roughly speaking) since Abraham, Eryl Davies re-emphasized the importance of the concept of the imitation of God – a dimension of ethical reflection and behaviour that seems to be implied in God's insistence that Abraham should 'walk before me and be blameless' (Gen. 17:1), and that, furthermore, he should teach his own household and descendants to 'keep the way of the LORD by doing righteousness and justice' (Gen. 18:19). Davies's article 'Walking in God's Ways' (1999) surveys the theme through several strands of the Old Testament canon (with greater and lesser conviction), and is helpfully detailed in its textual discussion. It is, however, roundly critiqued by Cyril Rodd,[24] who, somewhat excessively in my view, rejects the notion of 'imitation of God' as a feature of Old Testament piety or ethics (the issue is discussed in chapter 1 above with reference to other scholars who have used the phrase 'imitation of God').

Mary E. Mills. Even if we allow imitating or reflecting YHWH as a dimension of Old Testament ethics, we still have to ask, *what kind of God* is this Yahweh? What is it that is to be imitated? Davies, Barton and others, including myself, point to the motivational clauses in Old Testament laws. These motivational clauses often pick out especially YHWH's *character* as compassionate and just, and his historical *action* in liberating Israel from oppression in Egypt. These are repeatedly held up in the text as model and motivation for Israel's own social behaviour to be marked by reflective compassion and justice. But YHWH is a complex *character* in the Old Testament texts and his *actions* are many and varied. YHWH's very omnipresence in the text generates a huge variety of images and metaphors and behaviours that are all ascribed to him. Are all of these dimensions of YHWH to be factored in to this concept of the imitation of God? And would we want them all to be? Mary Mills, *Images of God in the Old Testament* (**1998**), lists the variety of images and metaphors along with what she sees as their often conflicting and competing messages about the identity of God. But she concludes without much comment beyond a rather unhelpful kind of shrug that implies, 'This is what you get; take your pick.'

Mary Mills entered more directly into the field of Old Testament ethics from the perspective of the Old Testament as literature and the insights of the burgeoning field of newer literary criticism. In *Biblical Morality* (**2001**) she explores nine sections of Old Testament narrative, with three being given respectively to each of the major factors in narrative art – character, plot and setting. In each section she observes the moral complexities woven into the narratives and how they are usually patient of very diverse ethical

---

[24] In *Glimpses*, pp. 69–76.

evaluation. Her book offers many helpful summaries of the views of a wide range of scholars on all aspects of critical study of Old Testament narratives, but I wish she had wrestled more with the ethical depths of the texts themselves.

David Penchansky. Returning to the matter of the imitation of God, we face again the question of what kind of God we are called upon to reflect. On this issue, David Penchansky is much more provocative. In his book *What Rough Beast?* (**1999**) he picks out six narratives in which the character of YHWH appears to be enigmatic at best and vicious at worst: the 'fall' of Adam and Eve (Gen. 3); the death of Uzzah (2 Sam. 6); David's census (2 Sam. 24); the execution of Aaron's sons (Lev. 10); the attack on Moses (Exod. 4); and Elisha's curse on the youngsters who jeered him (2 Kgs. 2:23–25). What are we to make of such narratives, and what can we infer about the theology or ethics of those who told them and then included them in the Scriptures? In Penchansky's hands the stories reveal YHWH (in Penchansky's own words) as insecure, irrational, vindictive, dangerous, malevolent and abusive. Penchansky's discussion is at times profound, but also at times (in my view) tendentious and speculative. There is certainly a desperate seriousness about these biblical stories (and others like them), but part of the problem lies precisely in Penchansky's chosen method, which is to ask his readers (as, we are told, he asks his students), 'If all you knew about God you knew from this passage, how would you describe the divine being?' But of course, this is precisely *not* all we know about God. There is a hugely wider canvas in the biblical canon within which these strange stories have found their place, to be heard and wrestled with in the light of everything else we know. None is easy to handle. But to isolate them and then attempt to describe the character of God exclusively on the basis of these narratives seems a very odd approach to the Scriptures.

Walter Brueggemann. So is YHWH God simply too diverse to be coherently identified, let alone imitated? Not according to Brueggemann. Also in **1999**, and in the same volume as Eryl Davies's resuscitation of the imitation of God, Brueggemann argues that, notwithstanding the plurality and diversity of the Old Testament's testimony, the God of Israel, as given to us 'on the lips of Israel', has a coherence of identity and character. Brueggemann insists that there is a

> family kinship of all these utterances when set over against alternative accounts of reality, ancient or modern . . . 'God' in the Old Testament is identifiable, known by characteristic actions that are recognizable from one context to another, known by

direct utterance treasured and passed on, known by moves that can be placed in the text and on the lips of the witnesses.[25]

R. E. Clements. Brueggemann's phrase 'on the lips of Israel' directs our attention to the traditions of worship in the Old Testament as a somewhat neglected witness to Israel's ethical understanding and aspirations. Since worship is a response to the presence, character and action of God, it is appropriate to link it here with the matter of the imitation of God as a factor in biblical ethics. In the same year (**1999**) two contributions focused on Israel's worship, with interesting ethical implications. First, Ronald Clements, 'Worship and Ethics', affirms the strongly didactic nature of this psalm in which 'the people identify themselves as a group of loyal worshippers of the LORD God and declare their solidarity in embracing a conscientious and socially responsible standard of conduct' (p. 85). The values they express in worship reflect both upon YHWH and upon themselves. Worship and ethics are inseparable.

Timothy M. Willis. Secondly, Timothy Willis, in 'Eat and Rejoice before the Lord', observes how the passages prescribing Israel's round of worship and festivals all *presume* the experience of YHWH's blessing – they are not means by which blessing can be squeezed from a reluctant deity. That is, in Israel you were to worship YHWH *because* he had blessed you, not *in order* to get him to bless you. However, having received and given thanks for such blessings, the appropriate response was not merely celebration, but *ethical* obedience in the horizontal realm of social relations. Response to God's blessings 'spills over into the everyday lives of the worshippers . . . In particular, they should "celebrate" their blessing by imitating the way Yahweh provides for them in the way they provide for those who depend on them' (p. 292).

Carol J. Dempsey. The first decade of the twenty-first century has begun as promisingly as the final one of the twentieth. In **2000** Carol Dempsey offered a survey of ethical themes from the prophetic books, *Hope Amid the Ruins*. She explores the areas of creation and covenant, of Torah and relationships, of worship and hope. Dempsey claims not only to present the ethical perspectives of the prophetic texts themselves, but also to evaluate them from the standpoint of contemporary ethical insights. Thus she finds much in the prophetic books she feels must be open to ethical question. This includes, for example, the prophetic concept of retributive punishment or the use of

---

[25] Brueggemann, 'Role of Old Testament Theology', pp. 78–79.

violence (especially under the metaphor of sexual abuse) as a divine response to Israel's unfaithfulness. Unfortunately, much of Dempsey's discussion simply raises rather than addresses such questions. Her final chapter widens the survey to explore what the ethics of the prophets have to say to the ecological and cosmic concerns that engage Christian and secular reflection.

Gordon J. Wenham. In 2000 Gordon Wenham added to his fine commentaries a volume on the ethical power of Old Testament narrative. In *Story as Torah* he employs the tools of rhetorical criticism to explore the ethical values of Genesis and Judges, and draws stimulating conclusions on the relationship between laws, stories and ethics.

J. David Pleins. Two volumes in 2001 draw this survey to a close, with every indication that the field of Old Testament ethics will continue to generate major contributions well into the future. The massive work by David Pleins *The Social Visions of the Hebrew Bible* takes very seriously the sociological approach to the Old Testament, which has more than a century of history and now tends to be referred to as the 'social-scientific' approach. He is aware that texts both reflect and conceal complex histories of social struggle, of interests and advocacy, of competing ideologies and alternative visions. Conscious of this he nevertheless examines each main section of the Hebrew canon – law, narrative, prophets, poetry and wisdom – and explores the social and ethical visions to be found therein. The work is ambitious in scope and achievement. Pleins does not minimize the complexity and diversity, but concludes that this polyvalent nature offers a range of 'checks and balances in biblical ethics'. Thus

> the legal material points the way to an ethics of obligation . . . prophetic voices foster an ethics of conscience and advocacy for society in its brokenness . . . the narrative voice, in turn, can be mined for an ethics of scrutiny . . . the wisdom voice, by contrast, offers an ethics of consequence . . . the voice of worship provides us with an ethics of disposition.[26]

This leads Pleins to a fairly positive and optimistic assessment of the contribution that the Old Testament can make to our present ethical concerns, even though he is more accommodating of the multiple whims of scholarship across all the forms of Old Testament criticism than seems advisable or necessary, in my view. Like Habel and others he is inclined to detect ideological conflict and textual contradiction (the *Social Visions* of his title is deliberately

---

[26] Pleins, *Social Visions*, pp. 530–531.

and significantly plural) where one might more charitably posit complementary perspectives. Nevertheless, Pleins believes that the Old Testament has much to offer for contemporary Christian ethical reflection on social ethics.

Cyril Rodd. By contrast, the major work Cyril Rodd offers, after a lifetime of interest and engagement in the field of Old Testament ethics, has a depressingly negative tone. His book *Glimpses of a Strange Land* (2001) is, on the one hand, simply masterly and majestic in the sweep of its coverage. In every chapter are historical surveys of scholarship on a range of issues from the imitation of God to concern for nature. These are extraordinarily helpful and informative for any student looking for what whole rafts of scholars have said about Old Testament perspectives on adultery, murder, economics, the poor, war, animals, nature, women and so on. Rodd's coverage of topics and of relevant literature is admirably comprehensive and thoroughly researched. On the other hand, the book has a curiously subversive and deconstructive feel in relation to its own subject matter.

The problem is that Rodd believes that most scholars have read into the Old Testament modern ethical interests that were not really there in ancient Israel; that they have been highly selective in what they extract from the Old Testament for contemporary ethical advocacy; and that they have ignored some of the concerns that were of major importance in Israel itself, such as honour and ritual purity. We have not, in other words, according to Rodd, paid sufficient attention to how culturally strange the world of Old Testament Israel was in comparison with our own (hence his title). Often we simply do not know enough about Israel's cultural worldview to make confident assertions about the ethics inherent in a given narrative, law or prophecy. And furthermore, much that took place in the Old Testament under the apparent command or approval of the God portrayed there strikes us as odd at best and morally indefensible at worst. For all *our* great concern about contemporary ethical issues such as war, the plight of the poor, ecological damage and the oppression of women, Rodd argues that for ancient Israel these things were scarcely ethical issues at all. Such things, so troubling for us, were for them simply sad but accepted manifestations of how the world is. In fact, Rodd suspects that much of what *we* regard as ethical issues were not so in Israel, and much of what *they* were passionately concerned about would be either morally neutral or questionable to us. There is no doubt that much of Rodd's argument here does effectively and justifiably expose shortcomings in the way some people have used the Old Testament in Christian ethics, and his cautions need to be heeded (though in my view Israel was not so untroubled by such things as poverty and war as Rodd implies).

This leads Rodd in conclusion to reject all attempts of those who seek to

build some kind of bridge from the Old Testament to the modern world on
the assumption that the Bible constitutes a normative, revealed authority for
ethics. This assumption, for Rodd, simply cannot stand the weight of problems, exceptions and evasions it generates. So although Rodd is detailed and
fair in summarizing the work of scholars like Birch, Janzen, Goldingay,
Bauckham and me, who have tried to build such a bridge, he finds our work
doomed to failure in the end. Rather, in line with Deidun (see above), whom
he quotes approvingly, Rodd's view (which we shall come back to in the next
chapter) is that we must *abandon* the twin concepts of revelation and authority
altogether: 'The first requirement is to abandon the propositional view of revelation, and with it the belief in the Bible as an external authority. We need to
leave the Old Testament where it is, in its own world – or rather worlds, for it
stretches across different periods of history and contains the ethics of many
different human groups. Then we can go to visit it . . .' and in our glimpses of
this strange land we will find that the Bible can 'offer assistance in our attempt
to solve the many puzzling moral questions which face us today',[27] though
how it will now do so, or what value such assistance will have, remains a
mystery.

So, as I draw this chapter to a close, we have come back to the issue with
which the last chapter began. It seems that at the beginning of the third
Christian millennium the question of the authority of the Old Testament for
Christians is as live and controversial as it was at the beginning of the first millennium. Inevitably, therefore, we must turn to it again in the next and final
chapter.[28]

---

[27] Rodd, *Glimpses*, pp. 327–329.

[28] Since this chapter is something of an annotated bibliography in itself, I have not
     included a further reading section here. All the works referred to in the chapter are to
     be found in the bibliography at the end of the book.

14. HERMENEUTICS AND AUTHORITY IN OLD TESTAMENT ETHICS

Can the job be done? In spite of the doubts expressed by those referred to in the opening words of the preface, it seems clear that the discipline of Old Testament ethics is alive and well. But the sheer diversity of approaches scanned in the last two chapters might make us wonder if the job of presenting a coherent account of whatever we understand by those three words 'Old Testament ethics' can actually be done at all. If, however, having taken stock of the vast array of scholarship now available, we are still bold enough to plunge recklessly onward, surrounded by so great a cloud of witnesses, with the intention of making our own humble contribution to the field of Old Testament ethics, there are at least three challenges that await us.

Our first task is to 'get there' – that is, to project ourselves by some means into the world of Israel of the Old Testament, and to ask ethical questions of the environment we find ourselves in. How we go about doing that raises methodological questions. Then, secondly, we have to 'get back here from there'; that is, to ask how we in our world should respond to what we have been confronted with in our exploration of the biblical world. At this point we shall unavoidably be faced with some ideological questions. That is because the nature of whatever we choose to bring back will to some extent be governed by the eyes with which we explored the biblical world, who we took along as our guide, what we think we saw, what we took to be of value and what our own contextual priorities are. We did not go as neutral observers and we shall not return as such. Thirdly, and finally, we shall have to answer the question as to whether and how anything we bring back from the world of

Old Testament Israel carries ethical authority in our own day. And this raises the question of what we mean by 'authority' in the first place, and how it functions in biblical ethics. To these three tasks I now give some attention.

Getting there from here: methodological problems

Setting out to explore the ethical world of the Old Testament confronts us with several methodological difficulties. By now these are getting rather well worn. It seems to be an entrance requirement for the guild of aspiring writers on Old Testament ethics to be able to rehearse all the difficulties inherent in the task.[1] Some have made the rehearsal a substitute for any substantive offering of the real thing, or an excuse for not offering one at all. I shall therefore try to be brief in summarizing them.

It all boils down to what we mean by the phrase 'Old Testament ethics'. Broadly, it can have three possible points of reference. First, it could refer to the historical task of describing how Israelites *actually* behaved in Old Testament times. Secondly, it could refer to the still broadly descriptive but more canonical task of outlining what Old Testament texts tell us about how some Israelites thought the rest of the Israelites *should* have behaved (but often did not), and why. And thirdly, it could refer to the more normative or prescriptive task of affirming what Old Testament texts might tell *us* about how *we* ought to behave. Each of these distinct endeavours generates its own questions.

The descriptive question: What ethical behaviours characterized ancient Israel?

It might seem a straightforward task – just read the Old Testament and jot down how Israelites behaved. It is a lot more complicated than that. We have to ask, which Israelites? Where? At what period of history? And according to whom? ('whom' meaning both according to which biblical writers and according to which contemporary scholars). This immerses us in the task of the critical reconstruction of the history of Israel in Old Testament times. As noted in chapter 13 in the work of David Pleins, social-scientific approaches to the texts and history of the Old Testament are enjoying great popularity at present. So the job of extracting straightforward information about 'how Israelites behaved' at any given point in their chequered history is nothing if not controversial. And 'critical reconstruction' raises its own thorny issues.

---

[1] See the survey of scholarship in chapter 13 above.

For the further such reconstruction takes us away from the narrative of the canonical text itself, the more we have to ask whether we are observing the ethics of the reconstructors or of the reconstructed, and whether either truly reflects the ethics of actual ancient Israelites.

The canonical question: What do Old Testament texts tell us about how the Israelites should *have behaved?*

Again, this might seem straightforward at first sight. We have the law, roundly declaring what Israelites were to do and not to do. We have the narratives with their subtle moral evaluations, occasionally explicit but more often generated through fine literary art and engagement of the reader in the authors' perspectives. We have the prophets beaming a merciless spotlight on the moral failures of successive generations of Israelites, and in the process painting an alternative ethical vision against the background of the negative realities they expose. We have the worship of Israel, filled with ethical assumption or comment. And we have the wisdom of Israel putting its arm around the shoulders of society with moral warning and advice regarding a wide range of behaviour, choices and attitudes.

All these textual traditions are there to be mined for their ethical evaluation of the society these texts emerged from. But texts have authors, collectors and promoters. And these agents have contexts, agendas and conflicts. So another layer of questions is exposed. Who wrote or promoted these particular texts? In whose interests did they do so? What links are there between ethical exhortation and social, political or economic advocacy? That is, when a text purports to tell Israelites that this is how they should or should not behave, in whose interest was it to persuade them thus? What vision (or visions) of society fuelled the canonical articulation of ethical values? And again, scholars answer such questions with bewildering variety. Some find a whole political agenda of struggle for an egalitarian society in Israel's scriptures and the religious sanction they gave to that project (e.g. Gottwald). Others, operating with a more acidic hermeneutic of suspicion, find most of the ethical rhetoric of the Old Testament aimed at preserving a fairly patriarchal and hierarchical status quo. Furthermore, as Pleins also shows, there is such a range of material in the canon that we have to ask if it makes sense to think of any 'official' or 'unitary' position that deserves the label '*Old Testament* ethics'. We may hope to speak of coherence in the canonical ethic, but certainly not of uniformity.

The normative question: What do Old Testament texts tell us *about how we ought to behave?*

Here the question is, when we finally get 'there' and have attained some measure of answers to the first two questions that we can live with, what is the freight we want to bring back home when we set off to return from 'there' to 'here'? What is the ethical teaching of the Old Testament that Christians need to attend to? In what sense, if any, does it function authoritatively for us now?

Actually, of course, as we saw in the surveys of the last two chapters, this question is as old as the New Testament itself and has been the focus of much theological wrestling ever since. Some of the main difficulties in making Christian ethical use of the Old Testament have been well summarized by John Goldingay, as mentioned in chapter 13,[2] and need only be listed here.

1. *There is the specific nature of Old Testament laws and teachings.* They are not given to us as timeless moral truths but within local cultural contexts or to particular individuals or groups. So if they are to speak ethically to us at all we have several hermeneutical steps to take to get from there to here. And even that assumes these specifics were intended to speak to later generations, including our own, which may not be true in every case, or at least can only be true in some cases very indirectly.[3]

2. *There is the diversity of the material* – not only in the sense that there is a great deal of it and in many different literary genres, but also in the sense that even within the Old Testament there is room for different ethical perspectives, expanded or modified laws, allowance for new situations creating new duties and so on. We are listening, not to a single voice, not even to a single choir in harmony, but to several choirs singing different songs with some protest groups jamming in the wings.

3. *And there are the ethical limitations of the material.* On the one hand, many things happen, or are advocated, in the Old Testament that bother us ethically and we wonder how to cope with the suspicion of feeling ethically superior to something we find in what purports to be the Word of God. On the other hand (and partly to help the last problem while making it even more complicated), the Old Testament is BC, and so is limited by being chronologically prior to the fuller revelation of God in the person of Jesus Christ.

So then, we shall need a method that takes account of each of the above three challenges. *First*, in response to the descriptive question, an account of

---

[2] John Goldingay, *Approaches*. There is also a good survey of methodological and hermeneutical problems in Kaiser Jr, *Toward Old Testament Ethics*, chs. 3–4.

For comments on both scholars and their work, see chapter 13 above.

[3] John Barton, *Ethics*, has helpful things to say on the benefits of the particularity of the ethical resources of the Old Testament, especially in ch. 1.

Old Testament ethics must take seriously the historical, cultural and social realities of the worlds of ancient Israel. We need to 'be there' somehow, while recognizing the partial and provisional nature of all historical knowledge. At the same time, to engage in *Old Testament* ethics, as distinct from a piece of purely descriptive anthropology or ethnography of biblical Israel, we must give the final say to the scriptural texts that express the ethical values we are studying, not to the critically reconstructed world *behind* the text.[4] Similarly, for example, while it is vital to understand the social world of ancient Corinth in the midst of first-century Graeco-Roman macroculture, we derive the relevant portion of our New Testament ethics from Paul's letters to the church in Corinth, not from the historical reconstruction of its environment, even though the latter will help us better understand the former.

Secondly, in response to the canonical question, we must be sensitive to the enormous diversity of texts in the Hebrew Scriptures and the multiple contexts and agendas that produced them. As we listen to any given text we must ask 'Whose voice is this?' as well as 'What is it saying?' And yet, on the other hand, we must respect the massive ethical phenomenon of the canon itself. These texts come to us bound together and making their collective claim upon us as the scriptures of the community of faith for generations. There is (or at least, I believe there is) an organic unity, a broad harmony that holds this vast and varied edifice together. So the task of Old Testament ethics has a legitimate synthetic and synchronic dimension, as well as having its analytic and diachronic homework to do.

Thirdly, in response to the normative question, we must respect the per se voice of the Old Testament, to use Christopher Seitz's phrase.[5] That is, we must allow it to say what it says 'warts and all', and refrain from sprinkling our moral disinfectant around its earthiness or wreathing its human characters in stained-glass hagiography. Yet at the same time we receive the Old Testament as the Bible of Jesus Christ and his church. Since it renders to us the God whom we acknowledge and worship as the Holy One of Israel, the God and Father of our Lord Jesus Christ, it is ultimately the Old Testament that claims and judges us, not we who judge, convict or exonerate it.

That, at any rate, is how it seems to me. To be sure, the methodological problems of Old Testament ethics are daunting, but they need not deter us from ever making the attempt. One can only try, as I have done in offering this present volume – and leave others to judge the results.

---

[4] Recall the critique of attempts to build biblical ethics merely upon sociological reconstruction, by Brevard Childs, in chapter 13, n. 22.

[5] Christopher Seitz, *Word without End.*

Getting back here from there: ideological problems

The task of constructing an adequate Old Testament ethics is rendered diffi-cult not merely by methodological complexity, but also by fundamentally differ-ing ideological, philosophical or theological approaches to the material under study. This goes beyond the recognition of tensions within the biblical material itself. Such tensions and varied perspectives within the canon are acknow-ledged on all sides. Indeed, Philip Wogaman argues that these inner tensions are vital to the dynamic of biblical ethics and that when we handle them we must hold on to both poles of each tension, not try to resort exclusively to one or the other.[6] More fundamental questions, however, are answered differently by different scholars (and sometimes in diametrically opposite ways). These different answers then lead to some seemingly irreconcilable divergence over what the ethical value of the Old Testament is or might be (or is not at all, in some opinions). The survey of scholarship above has already hinted at some of these scholarly presuppositions and the effect they have on the conclusions drawn. My own selection of controversial presuppositions can be summarized by enquiring what answers are given by any scholar (or school of thought) to the following questions: Does the biblical God exist, or not? Does the Old Testament carry any form of authority by virtue of divine revelation, or not? Is the Old Testament ethically relevant to our modern world, or not?

God or not?

Does it matter if a scholar believes in God or not? Or, to be more precise, does it matter if he or she believes in the objective reality of the deity pre-sented to us on the pages of the Old Testament as the LORD? In theory one might want to say that it should not. At least for the first two tasks described above (the mainly descriptive tasks of portraying the social and ethical world of ancient Israel and analysing their sacred canonical scriptures) one would expect that critical objectivity would be sufficient to arrive at conclusions that would then have to stand or fall by their acceptance in the academy of histor-ical and textual research. Certainly, this is the assumption one would like to make if I, as a Christian believer, were to attempt to research and write on the ethics of, say, certain Hindu or Buddhist scriptures, or the Quran. In theory I would hope to be able to do so with reasonable diligence and fairness to the

---

[6] See Wogaman, *Christian Ethics*, ch. 1, 'The Biblical Legacy of Christian Ethics', pp. 2–15. The particular tensions Wogaman finds in the Bible and discusses are Revelation vs. Reason; Materialism vs. the Life of the Spirit; Universalism vs. Group Identity; Grace vs. Law; Love vs. Force; Status vs. Equality.

sources. While recognizing the fact that I do not share the same faith stance or confessional worldview of any of those texts, I would aim at an informed and sympathetic presentation of their ethical teaching that would be accorded some credibility by those who do stand in those faith traditions.

Yet in practice whether scholars believe in the biblical God or not does seem to affect significantly the posture and the outcome of their scholarship in this area. Simply to highlight the point by the most extreme contrasts: on the one hand, we hear the passionate appeal of Christopher Seitz that we must read the Old Testament as those who know the God of its pages, the Holy One of Israel, as the Father of Jesus Christ, and therefore our God and Lord.[7] Or we hear the rhetoric of Walter Brueggemann reminding us that the task of Old Testament theology (and surely therefore also of Old Testament ethics) is to 'give a particular account of reality with this God as agent and as character at its center . . . a Holy Character who is given us on the lips of Israel'. Indeed, Brueggemann goes on, scholarship that refuses to admit this reality is '"tone deaf" to the voice of the text . . . for when the Holy Character is deleted from the calculus of meaning, not much that matters remains.'[8]

On the other hand, Philip Davies, writing from the claimed objectivity of discourse that constitutes his vision of the university,[9] and from a cheerful personal atheism, gives notice that in his understanding of academic study of biblical texts, gods will not be allowed to wander unchallenged around the vocabulary. His assessment of the ethical worth of the Old Testament turns this refusal to accept any deity (least of all the one offered in the Old Testament) into a virtue. Since he considers that the alleged moral teaching of the Old Testament is essentially blind obedience to arbitrary divine commands, he finds such teaching to be unethical in principle:

---

[7] See Christopher Seitz, *Word without End*.

[8] Brueggemann, 'Role of Old Testament Theology', pp. 78, 83.

[9] This stance of alleged neutrality is itself suspect, of course, and not innocent. Brueggemann has Philip Davies in mind when he writes,

> there are many scholars who discount the God-speech of Israel in the name of 'disinterested' scholarship, who refuse theological questions on the ground of 'history', who are themselves advocates and not more than advocates . . . Skepticism is not particularly high ground in intellectual activity. It simply advocates Enlightenment rationality, an increasingly doubtful stance for interpretation. See, e.g., the odd use of the term 'disinterested' by P. R. Davies, *Whose Bible is it Anway?* (JSOTSup, 204: Sheffield, Sheffield Academic Press, 1995), p. 1.

(Brueggemann, 'Role of Old Testament Theology', p. 80)

The Old Testament is not much of a resource for ethics because it usually resorts to invoking obedience to commands, be they from a deity, a prophet or a parent . . . I would find myself personally opposed to that point of view. For although I do not believe in gods, I believe they are symbols of authority which claim absolute power (or more precisely instruments by which some other agent claims authority). And I reject such symbols, and such authority.[10]

Philip Davies goes on to find little of any ethical value in most sections of the Old Testament canon. On the prophets, for example, he comments:

It is precisely where many biblical scholars see the high ethical watermark of the Old Testament that I fail to see coherence, foundational principles or ethical reflection. One finds Zion theology, the holiness of the god, the hatred of the god, the marital status of the god, the vengeance or inscrutability of the god, his monopoly, authority and much else being used as a reason for doing what the prophet says: much religion, little ethics and not a lot of consistency.[11]

On the ethics of Leviticus: 'This society represents the values of that least ethical community, the totalitarian state, with its big brother, the all-holy uncompromising sacrifice-consuming despot as the invention of a fascist clique. The idealized society of Leviticus is no Utopia except for the ritually pure and the utterly obedient, a haven of hierocracy.'[12] 'Disinterested objectivity' is hardly the first phrase that comes to mind to describe such comments.

Or one can leave open the question of whether there is an objectively real God of some kind, but inject plenty of clear blue water between 'the real God' and the literary construct of the Old Testament deity. This similarly leaves one free to subject the biblical text to some scorching ethical critique. Thus Cheryl Exum, writing in the same volume as Philip Davies, offers a trenchant survey of the metaphorical use of sexual abuse in the prophetic portrayals of YHWH's judgment on Israel, as an angry husband against an unfaithful wife.[13] It is not explicit in the article whether or not Exum herself 'believes in God', but it is clear that whatever God she might believe in, it is not this one. She comments, 'I think it important to recognize that God is a

---

[10] P. R. Davies, 'Ethics and the Old Testament', pp. 165, 167.

[11] Ibid., p. 172.

[12] Ibid., p. 170.

[13] This is a matter of considerable importance that cannot be tackled here, but deserves serious study by those more sympathetic to the theological stance of the texts than Exum.

character in the biblical narrative (as much a male construct as the women in biblical literature) and thus not to be confused with anyone's notion of a "real" god.'[14] Exum would doubtless agree with Davies that in many cases the most responsible way to engage ethically with the Bible is to resist it.[15]

It does appear, then, that what you find in the landscape of the Old Testament when you 'get there' very much depends on whom you take with you and through whose eyes you view it.

Revealed or not?

Clearly, if you do not believe in the existence of a god of any kind, then the notion of some form of authority within the text on the grounds that it has been revealed by the one living God is nonsense or worse. But even for those whose personal faith is not apparent in their writing, the idea of canonical authority and revelation can be dismissed as ethically problematic. Thus, Cheryl Exum comments, 'I prefer doing away with the notions of canon and biblical authority altogether. Because the Bible is an important part of our cultural heritage, it would be presumptuous to suggest that we can casually dispense with it. But I see no reason to privilege it.'[16]

As we saw in chapter 13, this is certainly the conclusion Cyril Rodd comes to at the end of his major survey of the ethical dimensions of the Old Testament. In his view it is the ideas of divine revelation and its correlative, textual authority, that are themselves the real problem. It is impossible, he argues, simultaneously to deal honestly with the material in the Old Testament as responsible ethical readers (which means we find ourselves selecting and rejecting among the laws and narratives on the basis of ethical standards we assume to be right but that conflict with what we read in the text) and to maintain the traditional concepts of revelation and authority. So it is the latter that must be abandoned. Furthermore, it is impossible to hold on to the concepts of revelation and authority and find a viable method of making the material relevant to ourselves, in spite of all the attempts that have been made by books like this one:

> If you start with revelation there is no way in which a coherent and plausible method can be devised . . . So long as some divine influence on the moral teaching of the Old Testament is retained it is impossible to explain how the Old Testament can offer authoritative guidance to those faced by very different ethical dilemmas today.

---

[14] Exum, 'Biblical Violence', p. 264.
[15] P. R. Davies, 'Ethics and the Old Testament', p. 171.
[16] Exum, 'Biblical Violence', p. 264.

We reject some biblical demands out of hand (e.g. to stone adulterers or homosexuals).

> If, then, we choose to accept that the Old Testament is divine revelation and its ethics possesses authority given by God, we find ourselves up against insuperable problems. This in itself convinces me that to begin with revelation, and to look for authority, constitutes the problem which can only be solved when this is abandoned.[17]

It is unclear to me how the problem is solved by this abandonment. If there is no 'divine influence' in the reality we know as the Scriptures, and if they hold no kind of authority, then why should I bother reading them at all for any kind of ethical benefit, other than the stimulation of my imagination by contemplating the strangeness of it all?

At the other end of the spectrum is the position advocated by Walter Kaiser. Writing with a strong conservative presupposition of the revealed and authoritative nature of the Bible as a whole, Kaiser finds a primarily deontological flavour in Old Testament ethics; that is, it flows to us as a priori commandments of God for our responsive obedience. Accordingly, Kaiser focuses mainly on the law as the place where those commandments most obviously impinge upon us – revealed and sanctioned by the holiness of God. But it seems to me to be a misleading tendency to equate the terms 'revealed and authoritative' too exclusively with the category of command. According to traditional understanding of biblical revelation, it is not only commands that were revealed, nor only commands that carried divine authority. There is a great deal more in the Old Testament for our ethical reflection and construction than the laws. And if we do choose to operate hermeneutically with some assumption of divine revelation and authority inherent in the *whole* canon, then we have to ask in what sense the terms applied just as much to narrative and poetry (and even to genealogy) as to laws.

Then Eryl Davies adds what seems to me to be another confusion. Commenting favourably on John Barton's concept of 'natural law' in the Old Testament, he argues that if we accept the validity of this concept it will mean a corresponding reduction in the place we give to revelation. This is because he sees natural law (in Barton's usage) as based on a *rational* approach to life, drawn from universal observation. If such rational observation undergirds some of the Old Testament's ethics, then, according to Eryl Davies, the place of *revelation* is reduced. But why should revelation and rationality be contrasted in this way? In biblical thinking surely both alike come from God.

---

[17] Rodd, *Glimpses*, pp. 323–325.

However, Eryl Davies is of the view that 'the tendency to regard the ethics of the Hebrew Bible as exclusively revelational may need to be reconsidered, for it may well be that Scripture bears witness to principles of right conduct which are rationally discoverable'.

He then goes on to link revelation to command, in the way I have just questioned, and argues that a non-revelational approach would be more congenial to a secular age:

> In an age that is becoming increasingly secular in outlook, the emphasis upon the place of reason in making moral judgments would probably be very appealing. Unlike revealed law, which demands unconditional obedience to divine commands, natural law evinces a deliberative approach to the formation of the moral norm and provides rational justification for the ethical imperative.[18]

But surely Old Testament motive clauses do exactly this all the time; that is, they present rational and persuasive reasons for obeying the law. Both the law itself and the rational justification are contained within the biblical understanding of revelation. And surely also the Wisdom tradition combines in its ethical construction the category of divinely revealed wisdom with devout human rational reflection, without posing any dissonance between them. Eryl Davies seems to create both an unnecessary (and certainly unbiblical) disjunction between revelation and rationality on the one hand, and an unhelpful (and equally unbiblical) equation of revelation with command on the other.

It seems to me that we need a broader understanding of revelation and also a more flexible understanding of authority. And the first step towards that greater breadth and flexibility will be to stop talking as if the only form of authoritative utterance is command. I shall return to this question of authority in the final section.

Relevant or not?
Having 'got there' into the world of Old Testament Israel, and having surveyed some of the ethical values in their (critically reconstructed historical) behaviour and in their (critically analysed, sourced, deconstructed and stitched together again) scriptures, do we actually expect or intend to bring back anything of relevance to the world in which we live and move and have our ethical being? What is this material *for*? What use can be made of it by Christians engaged with the world around us? Again all kinds of ideological or theological assumptions determine the answers.

---

[18] E. W. Davies, 'Ethics of the Hebrew Bible', pp. 49–50.

At one end of the spectrum stands the view that stresses the direct divine revelation of the Old Testament and its consequent abiding relevance for all time. Basically, whatever God said to Israel, God says to us. The strongest expression of such conviction is known as theonomism (or sometimes reconstructionism, when it become a social or political platform). In chapter 12 I surveyed and critiqued this position, along with its opposite within the conservative ranks – dispensationalism (the view that none of the Old Testament holds authority over Christians because we live in a different dispensation of grace through the coming of Christ).

A paradoxical example of a very different kind of relevance is the massive sociological study of Norman K. Gottwald, *The Tribes of Yahweh*. The paradox is that, on the one hand, Gottwald has no time for the idea that YHWH the God of Israel is alive and well and living in a church near you. He dismisses attempts to draw a *religious* line from the Old Testament to modern society as 'the mystifying idealistic and supernaturalistic dregs of biblical theology'.[19] The religion of Israel per se has no relevance to us. But, on the other hand, what Gottwald regards as the great *social* experiment of early Israel is enormously relevant. Israel, according to Gottwald's sociological reconstruction, emerged out of a social revolution in early Iron Age Palestine, and attempted to create a broadly egalitarian society with dispersion of political power, economic benefit flowing to families rather than to kings, and a range of social, judicial and military arrangements designed to protect the vision. The peculiar religion of YHWH was a kind of feedback loop that sanctioned and reinforced the social system. YHWH was the kind of god he was because of the kind of society Israel was trying to be. In the modern world we may not need their god any more, but we could still use their social ideals. So Gottwald sees continuing ethical potential in Israel's society, but no continuing ethical potential in Israel's religion.

The two major works on Old Testament ethics published in 2001, listed in chapter 13, take fascinatingly different positions on the question of the contemporary relevance of the material they survey. As already noted, Cyril Rodd, *Glimpses of a Strange Land*, is sceptical of most attempts to make the Old Testament relevant today. Apart from his rejection of revelation and authority (as outlined above), his main reason is that the major ethical issues with which we wrestle today were simply not perceived as ethical issues for Israel. On the contrary, what usually happens is that commentators on these issues (e.g. war, animal rights, the environment, women, the poor etc.) have made up their minds on the basis of other (non-biblical) grounds on what their ethical

---

[19] Gottwald, *Tribes of Yahweh*, p. 702.

agenda will be in relation to them. Then they enlist the spurious help of sparse or highly selective Old Testament texts, texts that nearly always did not originally mean what the commentators allege. Meanwhile, the issues that were of real concern to ancient Israel (purity, honour, the stability of the wider community) rarely feature in modern discussion of ethics at all. Even those issues that appear at first sight to be immediately relevant in both worlds (e.g. adultery) actually meant something different in ancient Israel.

Basically, Rodd is persuaded that the cultural gap between the ancient biblical world and our contemporary world is just too unbridgeable for much ethical freight to be safely or validly conveyed from one side to the other. I find that many of Rodd's cautions and qualifications are wise and need to be taken fully into account. We do, indeed, need to be wary of the temptation of forcing 'relevance' out of inappropriately selected proof-texts. But I also feel that he sometimes falls prey to making sweeping a priori generalizations about Israel's cultural strangeness and I cannot finally share his methodological paralysis. It is worth pointing out that there was also a significant historical and cultural gap between the worlds of early biblical Israel and that of the first century AD – the world of the New Testament. Yet the writers of the New Testament documents, taking their lead presumably from Jesus himself, seem to have worked with principles of ethical authority and relevance inherent in their ancient texts, even though they faced many of the same hermeneutical challenges in handling the Hebrew scriptures as we do. I shall return to Rodd once more in my final consideration of biblical authority below.

J. David Pleins, *The Social Visions of the Hebrew Bible*, works on a similar scale to both Rodd and Gottwald, but without the negativity of the former or the monolithic ideological advocacy of the latter. He surveys the social and ethical visions he finds embedded in each of the major sections of the Hebrew scriptures: the law, the narratives, the prophets, poetry and wisdom. He uses the tools of historical and social-scientific criticism, and exposes what he regards as conflicting social interests and agendas, not only between the different literary genres, nor even the different historical eras, but also within single books or collections in the canon. However, rather than regarding this variety as irredeemably contradictory, he feels it is a valuable ethical contribution to contemporary issues 'to offer up as a ground for ethical reflection the very tensions that infused the communities whose insights are extended to us in the pages of the Hebrew Scriptures'.[20] So at the end of each chapter he points out some contemporary relevance of his findings, and in a concluding

---

[20]   Pleins, *Social Visions*, p. 517.

chapter, 'Diverse Visions in a Canonical Context', summarizes the various ethical responses called forth by the material he has surveyed.

I could go on. Ideological and theological conflict also arises over the question of unity or not. Is there such a thing as 'an overall ethical thrust of the Old Testament'? Or are there only many and varied and sometimes competing perspectives? This in principle is the same question that exercises those who attempt to grapple with something that could be called 'Old Testament Theology'. And there is considerable ideological fission over whether the Old Testament bears a message that is fundamentally 'a good thing' or not. Some seek to interpret the texts from within a tradition that basically honours the material as in some sense divine in ultimate origin and scriptural in its canonical function in the communities of faith. Others find themselves so repelled by features of the biblical world and texts that their reading strategy is fairly consistently hostile, sceptical or subversive – a strategy they would, of course, regard as having ethical integrity within their own worldview.

I choose to stand alongside what I understand to be the position of the writers of the New Testament vis-à-vis the scriptures they already had. That is, I believe that the God we meet in the pages of the Old Testament is the God and Father of Jesus Christ, the God worshipped as the triune God by the church. I accept the affirmation of 2 Timothy 3:16 that all Scripture is *theopneustos* – breathed out by that God. This means that the Old Testament scriptures share in some way in the authority that is ultimately God's, and that they are 'profitable'; that is, relevant and applicable to ethical issues of our world (as much as to Timothy's world), as well as being able to make us 'wise to salvation through faith in Christ Jesus'.

It is one thing, however, to make these grand affirmations; it is another to unpack what they mean. Particularly, I wrestle with the question of the authority of the Old Testament. If we are going to come back here from there with anything more than a fascinating slideshow of glimpses of the strange land we have visited, we must be able to affirm that there is something about the texts we study that compels our attention, something that demands an appropriate response, something that validates certain ethical actions and choices and condemns others. To that final challenge I now turn.

The question of authority

Can the job of Old Testament ethics be done in such a way that the end product carries any kind of authority? What authority is inherent in the Old Testament itself for Christians? This matter of the ethical authority of biblical texts is inadequately tackled, in my view, in much of the critical scholarship I surveyed in chapter 13 above. Many scholars are willing to talk about the *power* of the text without really coming to grips with the question of its *authority*. The question is whether the Old Testament carries, for Christians, an authority that *requires* us to hear and respond to its texts as the Word of God. In much writing on the subject, it is fair to say, the *challenge* of the Old Testament texts is certainly there, and can be eloquently expressed. Yet it seems somehow ungrounded in any view of prescriptive normativity. If the Old Testament text is not telling us what we ought to do directly (and it usually isn't), is there any way in which it is telling us what to do at all? And how can we find that out and articulate it?

One major difficulty is with the connotations of the word 'authority' itself. As observed above, it seems to be associated most often in people's minds with the issuing of commands, based on a military model of authority. Certainly, those who explicitly reject the idea of biblical or Old Testament authority in the moral realm usually do so on the grounds that commands, and obedience to commands, are an inadequate, even infantile, basis for ethics. They are not going to be bossed around by the despotic god they perceive in the Old Testament. So in rejecting commands they reject authority.

But even for those of us who gladly affirm our acceptance of 'biblical authority', the association of *authority* primarily with *command* does not sit comfortably with the material in our hands. The bulk of the Old Testament is *not* command – either in the sense of issuing commands to its first readers or to future generations of readers. Much of the Old Testament is narrative, poetry, prophecy, song, lament, vision and so on. What is the authority latent in those forms of utterance? And furthermore, the commands clearly there in the Old Testament, in considerable number, were not originally addressed to us. They were commands given a very long time ago to people in a very different kind of world to the one we inhabit. So if we pursue the military model of authority, going to the Old Testament for commands for marching orders for today's problems could be compared to scouring the orders issued by Allied Command in the Second World War for guidance in running the 'war on terrorism'. Ours is a different world.[21]

---

[21] It should be clear from the rest of this book (and especially chapter 9) that I am *not* suggesting here that there is no way ancient commands in the Old Testament can be relevant and authoritative for us. On the contrary I affirm that they can, when handled by the paradigmatic method I have advocated. My point here is, on the one hand, that we cannot locate authority in a *direct* use of Old Testament commands as if they were simply *addressed to us* just as they stand, and, on the other hand, that the great bulk of our Old Testament texts are *not* in fact in the form of command at all, and yet we claim they have authority.

One very helpful distinction was made by Oliver O'Donovan when he pointed out the difference between *authority* and *claim* in any biblical command.[22] If I am on a crowded street and hear a policeman call out, 'Move back!', I see his uniform and recognize his *authority* in giving such a command. His public imperative speech is authorized. But I also have to decide whether or not he is addressing *me*. If not, his command has no *claim* on my obedience – not because it has no authority (it has), but because I am not the one addressed. However, I also recognize that the authority of the command *would* claim me if I were in a comparable situation to the person actually addressed. So biblical commands carry authority because of the one who gave them, the one whose divine authority we acknowledge. They claimed the obedience of those to whom they were given in their own historical context. But whether or not they claim *my* obedience depends on many other factors.

Authority as the predicate of reality

We are still, however, operating with a military model of authority and I believe we need to widen our understanding of the word considerably. Here, again, I am indebted to Oliver O'Donovan. In his majestic apologia for evangelical biblical ethics, *Resurrection and Moral Order*, O'Donovan argues that authority is a dimension of reality which constitutes sufficient and meaningful grounds for action. The created order itself, by its reality, provides an authority structure within which we have freedom to act (both in the sense of permission to act and a wide range of legitimate options for our action).[23] Authority is not just a matter of positive directives; it is also legitimating permission. Authority authorizes; authority grants freedom to act within boundaries. Thus the authority of my driving licence (or my bishop's licence) is not to order me every day where I must drive or what sacred service I must render. Rather, the authority of those documents functions to authorize me to make such choices for myself. They give me freedom and authority to drive where I wish, or to take services, preach, baptize and so on. In those contexts I am an *authorized* person, liberated by, while still subject to, the authority of the realities that stand behind those documents (the laws of the land and the road; the canons of the church).

Authority, then, is the predicate of reality, the source and boundary of freedom. Now, as O'Donovan argues, the created order itself as a reality is

---

[22] Oliver M. T. O'Donovan, 'Interpretation of Biblical Ethics'.

[23] I have discussed this insight of O'Donovan's further in relation to the authority of Scripture in an age of historical and cultural relativism, in C. J. H. Wright, *Walking in the Ways of the Lord*, ch. 2.

also a structure of authority. A physical brick wall, for example, by its simple real existence constitutes an authority. You have freedom to act on this side of it, or on that side of it. But your freedom ends when you attempt to run through it at high speed. It exerts its authority rather abruptly. Gravity as a force in the physical universe is an authority built into the way the universe exists. For us humans gravity authorizes an immense freedom of action on and above the surface of the planet. But it also sets limits to that freedom. You may freely choose to step off a cliff, but the authority of gravity will decree it to be the last free choice you make. Reality kicks in!

Now, how do these considerations help our understanding of the authority of the Old Testament (or indeed of the Bible)? If authority is the predicate of reality, then the authority of the canon of Scripture is that it brings us into contact with reality – or rather several connected realities, each of which has its own instrinsic authority. Reading and knowing the Scriptures causes us to engage with reality. That, in turn, functions to authorize and to set boundaries around our freedom to act in the world. If this all sounds extremely vague and abstract, it is time to explore what those realities are and what kind of ethics they generate. I have four realities in mind, which are rendered to us by the Old Testament scriptures. In these texts we encounter the reality of this God, the reality of this story, the reality of this word, and the reality of this people.[24]

The reality of this God
It is becoming increasingly important in any talk of 'God' to be clear whom we are talking about. 'God' is merely an Anglo-Saxon monosyllable that in its origins would more commonly have been plural – 'gods', the generic term for the deities of northern Europe. The Bible introduces us to the very specific, named and biographied God known as YHWH, the Holy One of Israel (and other titles), the one called Father by Jesus Christ and worshipped as Lord by Israelites, as Father, Son and Holy Spirit by Christians. This is not a generic 'god' at all.

> Everything depends on our confession of God. The covenanting God of the Bible is not to be understood according to the general category 'god.' Making a theoretical

---

[24] I was stimulated in this direction also by the observation of Gustafson that the Bible offers us a 'revealed reality rather than a revealed morality' (Gustafson, 'Changing Use', p. 140). I would want to add that the nature of the revealed reality in the Bible is of such a kind (or rather is of a unique kind of its own, *sui generis*) that a revealed morality is implicit within it as its authority predicate. But I take the point Gustafson is making: the Bible is not primarily concerned to give us a moral code but to introduce us to the living Person of God.

case that this God is unique is not necessary; it is enough to note that in the Bible this God makes a break with all cultural definitions and expectations and stands distant from the other gods who are preoccupied with their rule, their majesty, their well-being in the plush silence of heaven.[25]

While the Bible does insist that much has been disclosed about this God through the natural world around us (which is, in fact, this God's creation), it is fundamentally the texts of the canon of Scripture in both testaments that bring us knowledge of this God. Not only is the LORD the God 'enthroned on the praises of Israel' (Ps. 22:3); he is the God rendered to us by the lips and pens of Israel.[26] The LORD is the reality to which the Old Testament scriptures testify. His, therefore, is the authority they share, because our primary access to the LORD's divine reality is through these scriptures. This 'rendering of God' in the Old Testament includes both his identity and his character. Each has its authority and impact on ethics.

God's identity

'You were shown these things [the exodus and Sinai experiences]', declares Moses in the rhetoric of Deuteronomy, not so that you might grasp the philosophical construct called monotheism, but so 'that you might know that . . . *YHWH* is God in heaven above and on the earth beneath; there is no other' (Deut. 4:35, 39, RSV). The big issue was not merely the singularity of deity (though that is important later in Deut. 6:4–5), but the *identity* of the God who had done these spectacular things. It was not just a matter of knowing God, but of knowing YHWH to be God and knowing God to be defined, identified and recognized only as YHWH.

This links to the importance of the disclosure of the divine name itself. It is not just a vocable of mysterious pronunciation: 'When Yahweh divulges his name, he identifies himself as the God already known to the fathers and promises a future in which he will continue to be recognized . . . Yahweh has an identity which includes a specific biography by which he is recognized in the present and anticipated future.'[27] He is the living God, and the proper response on encountering him is humility, worship and obedience – as Moses discovered but Pharaoh rejected (Exod. 5:2). YHWH 's unique reality as God carries its own authority and that authority calls for appropriate response.

---

[25] Brueggemann, *Social Reading*, pp. 43–44.

[26] It will be evident that I am indebted here to the fascinating study of Dale Patrick, *Rendering of God*.

[27] Ibid., p. 44.

This was the essence of the challenge Elijah laid before Israel on Mount Carmel. The only god worthy of service is one that is real. Whichever god demonstrates his reality is therefore the one to serve. 'If YHWH is God, follow him.' The ensuing recognition of YHWH's reality and identity as God carried its own implications for action.

Similarly, in the worship of Israel, the acknowledgment of YHWH carries within it an ethical authority, for it is impossible for YHWH to be enthroned on the praises of Israel but be ignored in the practice of Israel. They tried it, but the prophets pointed out that flagrant rebellion in the moral and social realm was tantamount to 'forgetting' YHWH; that is, not acknowledging him at all, no matter how fervent their praises.

So the reality of the identity of YHWH implies the authority of an ethics of worship and response. Inasmuch as we encounter the reality of this God in the pages of the Old Testament we encounter that authority also.

God's character

YHWH is without question a character, a *dramatis persona*, in the great drama of the Old Testament – that much is richly demonstrated by Dale Patrick's work. Indeed, as *the* character YHWH is portrayed in hugely more depth and complexity than any of the human cast, simply because he participates in far more storylines throughout more generations than Methuselah had hot dinners. Given the enormous time span of the literature (the number of different generations over which it came into existence), it is surprising that the character of YHWH is portrayed with such consistency. Yet that consistency, of course, is not lacking in surprise. YHWH is constant, but not predictable or safe:

> The identity of the biblical God is not rigid or static. Rather, he is a persona whose
> identity emerges as dynamic, surprising and occasionally paradoxical, requiring of the
> reader a dialectical process of recognition. When a depiction borders on
> inconsistency, the interpreter must grasp it as a surprising manifestation of the one
> already known. When a depiction is polemical, the interpreter must recognize that
> the identity of Yahweh involves elements of paradox.[28]

Or, as Brueggemann puts it, referring to Patrick's work, the Old Testament introduces us to this 'Holy Character who is given us on the lips of Israel, who exhibits some constancy, but whose constancy is regularly marked by disjunction and tension'.[29]

---

[28] Ibid., p. 59.
[29] Brueggemann, 'Role of Old Testament Theology', p. 81.

At this point, of course, I could go into a long list of the qualities and traits that the Hebrew scriptures apply to YHWH. Such an exercise for a rainy day would be duly instructive and improving. When, however, Moses asked the LORD to show himself to Moses, God was content to utter a very few of the personality items on his CV, but they became the few that were enduringly linked to the name of YHWH in the narratives, prophecy, praise and prayer of Israel ever after. ' YHWH, YHWH, the compassionate and gracious God, slow to anger, abounding in love and faithfulness, maintaining love to thousands, and forgiving wickedness, rebellion and sin. Yet he does not leave the guilty unpunished; he punishes the children and their children for the sin of the fathers to the third and fourth generation' (Exod. 34:6–7).

When this foremost characterization of YHWH is encountered in the Old Testament, it likewise exudes an authority that calls for the response of reflective attitudes and behaviour. It is here that the 'imitation of God' (for all its limitations as a phrase – see chapter 1) is most at home. Deuteronomy 10:14–19 is the clearest positive example. If YHWH is the kind of God who cares for the weak and loves the alien, then you should do likewise. Paradoxically, Jonah's disgruntled reaction to God's gracious response to the repentant Ninevites stands in ironic contrast to his own quotation of the Exodus text as a reason for his original rejection of the mission. 'I knew that's what you would go and do,' Jonah complains, 'because that's the kind of God you are – compassionate and gracious, and it makes life difficult for us prophets of doom' (Jonah 4:1–2; my paraphrase).

So the reality of YHWH's character implies the authority for an ethic of imitation and reflection of that character in human behaviour. We ought to behave in certain ways because that is what YHWH is like, and that reality is sufficient authority.

Some more philosophically minded readers may question if I have not committed the 'naturalistic fallacy' – the point of which is to say that no set of natural facts by themselves generates an obligation. The colloquial rendering of this fallacy is, you can't get an *ought* from an *is*. If God is simply a 'fact', that does not in itself produce ethical obligation. My answer, which I learned a long time ago from Keith Ward when he lectured in ethics at Cambridge, is that God is not a *natural* fact. Rather, God's reality is *sui generis*, and the essence of God's transcendently unique reality does indeed generate ethical obligation for human beings. The reality of the biblical God inescapably claims us and demands response. God's reality therefore predicates God's authority.

That needed to be said before moving on to our next point. Because if you can't get an *ought* from an *is*, how much less can you get an *ought* from a *has been*. Yet I am now going to affirm that the very nature of the story rendered to us in the Bible predicates an authority to which we must respond.

The reality of this story

That the Old Testament tells a story needs no defence. The point is much greater, however. The Old Testament tells its story as *the* story or, rather, as a part of that ultimate and universal story that will embrace the whole of creation, time and humanity within its scope. In other words, in reading these texts we are invited to embrace a metanarrative, a worldview that, like all worldviews and metanarratives, claims to explain the way things are, how they have come to be so, and what they ultimately will be.

The story that engages us in the Old Testament answers the fundamental worldview questions 'Where are we?' 'Who are we?' 'What's gone wrong?' 'What's the solution?' Taking them in order, we inhabit the earth, which is part of the creation of the one living God, the LORD. We are human persons made by this God in God's own image, one of God's creatures but unique among them in spiritual and moral relationship and responsibility. What has gone wrong is that, through rebellion and disobedience against our creator God, we have generated the mess we now see around us at every level of our lives, relationships and environment. The solution has been initiated by God through the choice and creation of a people, Israel. Through this people God intends eventually to bring blessing to all nations of the earth, and ultimately to renew his whole creation.

Now the reality of this story is such that it includes us in its scope, for it points to a universal future that embraces the nations. This is the story, the story of God, Israel and the nations, taken up without question (though again, not without surprise) in the New Testament. This is the story that stretches from Genesis to Revelation, not merely as a good yarn, or even as a classic of epic literature, but fundamentally as *a rendering of reality* – an account of the universe we inhabit and of the new creation we are destined for. We live in a storied universe.

And once again, such a rendering of reality carries its own intrinsic authority. For if this is truly the way things are, if this is how they have become so, and if this is where they are going, then there are all kinds of implications for how we ought to respond personally and collectively. At the very least one has to say that if the story ends in the reality of a final moral judgment by this God, as the Bible story insists, then human moral choices matter now.

In Old Testament terms, the story had a past and a future and both were important in shaping ethics.

The past

Israel's celebration of its past is legendary. It was the very stuff of their existence, for it rendered to them not only their own identity and mission, but also that of the LORD, their God:

> Sing to the LORD, praise his name;
>> proclaim his salvation day after day
> Declare his glory among the nations,
>> his marvellous deeds among all peoples.

(Ps. 96:2–3)

The name, salvation and glory of the LORD were all bound up with 'his marvellous deeds'. The LORD was known through what he had done, and Israel knew that to preserve the LORD's identity they must tell the story – whether to themselves or to the nations. For in telling the story stood the rendering of the God who was its prime character. So they told the story as a bulwark against idolatry (Deut. 4:9ff.). They told the story as an explanation and motivation for the law (Deut. 6:20–25). They told the story as a rebuke, to themselves (Pss. 1; 5; 106; Amos 2:9–16; Mic. 6:1–8), or to the LORD himself (Pss. 44; 89). They told the story as a comfort and anchor for hope (Jer. 32:17–25).

As a motivation for observing the law, this reminder of the past focused especially on the exodus, of course, as the great model par excellence of the redeeming love and power of the LORD. As such it generated an ethic of gratitude that was to be earthed in acts of comparable justice and compassion in Israel's horizontal relationships in the community (Exod. 22:21; 23:9). The blessings experienced in the story are realities that carry authority. 'Give to him [the released slave] as the LORD your God has blessed you. Remember that you were slaves in Egypt and the LORD your God redeemed you. That is why I give you this command today' (Deut. 15:14–15).

The future

But the story Israel told also had an anticipated future right at its beginning. The call of Abraham included the promise that through his descendants God intended to bring blessing to all the nations of the earth. That vision shone with greatly varying degrees of clarity or obscurity at different eras of Israel's life, but there is in many places an awareness of the nations as spectators both of what God did in and for Israel, and of how Israel responded positively or negatively (Deut. 4:5–8; 29:22–28; Ezek. 36:16–23; see further chapter 7 above). Ultimately, Israel existed *for the sake of* the nations. So there is a teleological thrust to Israel's story. Here is a God with a mission and a people with a mission, to be a light to the nations so that ultimately all flesh will see the glory of the LORD (cf. Is. 40:5). Such a vision, a prophetic reality even if not yet a historically realized one, undoubtedly generated a range of ethical responses. For if this is the future guaranteed by the faithfulness of God, what should be the impact on the way Israel should live now (Is. 2:1–5; note verse 5)? The question remains authoritative for us too. For we share the same vision of the future. To the eyes of faith this biblical future is a reality, 'the substance of things hoped for', and thereby also contains an ethic-generating authority for those who live in its light.

So the reality of this story, rendered to us on the pages of the Old Testament, carries authority for an ethic of gratitude in view of God's actions for Israel in the past, and an ethic of missional intentionality in view of God's purposes for humanity in the future.

The reality of this word

Revelatory word

There is a revelatory claim intrinsic to the Old Testament scriptures. It is possible, of course, with Cyril Rodd and many before him, to deny the claim – either in the sense that these texts are actually revelatory of God, even if God's reality is accepted, or to deny that there is any god there to be revealed, so the textual claim is fatuous anyway: there is no reality of which they speak. However, in seeking what as Christians we may regard as the authority of the Old Testament, there can be no doubt that it is bound up with the reality of this word from this God. In these texts, we confess, the real God really spoke and still speaks, and the reality of God's person and God's word constitutes an authority that grants freedom and sets boundaries, as the very first story of divine–human encounter (Genesis 2 – 3) illustrates with such profound simplicity.

Disclosure is at the heart of Israel's faith:

> You were shown these things . . . so that you might know . . .
>
> (Deut. 4:32–40)

> He has shown you, O man, what is good . . .
>
> (Mic. 6:8)

> He has revealed his word to Jacob, his laws and decrees to Israel.
> He has done this for no other nation.
>
> (Ps. 147:19)

> I have not spoken in secret, from somewhere in a land of darkness;
> I have not said to Jacob's descendants, 'Seek me in vain.'
> I, the LORD, speak the truth; I declare what is right.
>
> (Is. 45:19)

The very heart of Israel's creedal faith is addressed to their ears (in explicit contrast to their eyes – 'you saw no form') as something to be heard and heeded – a disclosure of reality that is both propositional and relational: '*Hear,*

O Israel, the LORD our God, the LORD is one; and you shall love the LORD your God with all your heart, with all your soul and with all your strength' (Deut. 6:4–5; my trans.).

This last text, though in a class of its own, is one of many which seem to me to pull the rug from under the strange idea that revelation in the Bible is personal but not propositional (the subtext being that propositions are somehow cold, abstract and less than personal or relational, which has always struck me as very odd in view of one rather relational use of the word 'propose'). It is hard to imagine a more propositional form of utterance than Deut. 6:4, though the context supplies plenty of other candidates (4:39, for example, or 7:9, or supremely the identity card of the LORD, Exod. 34:6–7). Do the Psalms not bristle with revelatory propositions like 'The earth is Yahweh's and everything in it' (Ps. 24:1)? And the prophets would be left with rather thin books if their propositional disclosures of the LORD's reality were removed. No, in the Old Testament we hear a word that declares, affirms, proposes and states, in no uncertain terms. But, as the seamless flow in Deuteronomy 6:4–5 makes clear, the disclosure of reality immediately predicates an authority within which relationships and ethics can flourish. 'The LORD is . . . and you shall love . . .' There is no dichotomy between the statement and the response. The same is true of the lavish sprinkling of the simple proposition 'I am the LORD' through the commands of Leviticus 17 – 26. The well-worn observation that God's revelatory disclosure is typically and simultaneously indicative and imperative is no less true for being well worn. It is not a case of a 'revealed reality *rather than* a revealed morality', but a revealed reality *that by its very nature* carries a revealed, but fundamentally responsive and relational, morality.

Now this familiar combination brings us to the *covenantal* nature of Israel's relationship with God and of the authority of 'this word' within it. As we saw earlier, the idea of an authoritative revelation is most often linked (by those who don't like it much) with the direct commands of God. And then this 'revelation–command–obedience' combination is frequently relegated to an inferior brand of ethics for which the technical word is 'heteronomy' (obedience to the laws of another; i.e to an external authority source). Words like 'arbitrary' seem to pop out of the subconscious thesaurus and bond with 'commands', just as the word 'blind' so often does with 'obedience'. Or, in another discourse stable, the boo-words include 'external', 'codes' and 'legalism'. Over against such derogatory colouring of the whole vocabulary of command and obedience we need to set the covenantal dynamic of Old Testament faith and ethics.[30]

---

[30] See also the reflection on this matter by Richard J. Mouw, 'Commands for Grown-Ups'.

The essence of the covenant relationship as portrayed in the texts of the Old Testament is that it is emphatically relational, not mechanical, arbitrary or blind. This God has acted in this story for the good of this people. The whole relationship is based upon the constantly affirmed realities of the LORD's love, faithfulness to his promise, redeeming power, gracious patience, providence and protection. Predicated upon such realities, the obedience of Israel is framed as a response of love, gratitude, praise and continued blessing. The Israelite was urged to feel, 'I do what YHWH wants because that is what I most want too. The relationship between us makes such choices and behaviour natural and joyful.' That, at least, is the ideal hope of the covenant. Furthermore, since, as we saw, authority is the source as well as the boundary of freedom, obedience to God's law is seen as fulfilling, satisfying, a delight, and indeed the hallmark of personal freedom:

> I will walk about in freedom,
>> for I have sought out your precepts.
>>> (Ps. 119:45; cf. of course, Pss. 1 and 19)

Covenantal obedience in relationship to such a God is, simply, the way to life and to living (Deut. 30:11–20).

Furthermore, the covenantal nature of Israel's obedience means that it is precisely *not* blind. First, obedience is constantly justified and enlightened on the basis of the wide range of motivational and rationale-providing clauses in the law itself. In line with my definition of authority, these clauses typically point to some *reality* (of God, for example, or of the story so far, or of the nature of life in the land), and then say, 'Because this is so, this is the authority for what you are being told to do, or not do.' In fact, the narrative framework of the Torah (with its past and future orientation) makes this implicit point: the authority of this whole law rests on the reality of this God and this story. And secondly, Israel's obedience is not blind, because it is actually presented as *consenting*, at least in intent. In more than one context Israel is presented as making the free, informed and deliberate *choice* to submit to the LORD as covenant Lord, even, on one occasion, in the face of some sceptical dissuasion (Exod. 24:24:7; Deut. 5:27–29; 26:17; Josh. 24:14–24). In other words, the authority of the LORD was an authority freely chosen and submitted to by Israel – not a blind or servile obedience to arbitrary commands. With the hindsight of history, Israel's promise to obey the LORD may have been optimistic (isn't our own?), but it was certainly not blind, coerced or arbitrary.

This seems to me to answer Cyril Rodd's categorical assertion that obedience to authority is not only an inadequate basis for ethics but is actually impossible. You only submit to authority because you choose to (unless, of course, the authority takes the form of coercion – which is ethically bankrupt anyway; and so, compelled obedience to superior force is not chosen obedience to an accepted authority). But, Rodd seems to say, when you choose to submit to an authority, your act of choice constitutes your real authority, or rather, it effectively sets you above the authority you say you are submitting to. You become your own authority when you choose (or claim) to be obeying an external authority:

> It is my firm conviction that no external authority is possible for thoughtful human beings. However much they may assert, and believe, that they are subject to such an authority, ultimately the decision to accept it as an authority has been made by them. They *choose* – even if the internalised norms and values which come from the culture in which they were nurtured greatly influenced their decision. In the final analysis, my own decision has to be decisive for me . . . There can be no authority external to me, only power which imposes itself upon me.[31]

Taken to its conclusion the logic of Rodd's last sentence would make all ethics finally solipsistic; that is, self-referential in the sense that my own ego is my only authority.

But I think the clue, and the fallacy, is in the word 'thoughtful'. The opening sentence seems to mean that the individual rational human self is the final authority, which has been the classic Enlightenment stance. This confusingly treats human reason, which is simply the faculty through which we recognize and assent to authority, as if it were in itself the source of that authority – which it is not. The authority remains objectively distinct from our human rational capacity to discern it. When I choose to accept the authority of God as the supreme reality, I do not thereby place myself, and the rationality by which I make that choice, above the reality and authority of God. My rationality is simply the means of making that recognition, just as my will is the means of acting accordingly and responsively. To say there is no objective authority external to yourself just because you have to choose rationally to accept it, is like saying there is no objective world external to yourself because you have to open your eyes to see it.

There also seems to be a contradiction between Rodd's assertion that there can be no authority external to myself and his acceptance that people's choices are affected by 'internalized norms' from the nurturing culture. What are these 'norms'? Are they simply the collected edition of millions of individual choices people have made on the basis of being their own authority? And if

31 Rodd, *Glimpses*, p. 325.

so, why do they frequently manifest a high degree of commonality and longevity? And if each of us is effectively his or her own final authority, is there any sense in talking of norms at all? Does ethics not then become, not merely autonomous (as distinct from heteronomous), but potentially anarchic?

Furthermore, can I even be a consistent moral authority for myself, if there is no authority external to myself that in some way governs or 'norms' my choices and behaviour over time? For why should any choice made in the past exercise moral authority over me in the present? Last year I chose to make a promise. But this year I choose to ignore it. Who or what is to question the validity of the second choice if there is no authority external to myself that normatively instructs me that promises should be kept as a matter of integrity?

Performative word

Secondly, the reality of this word is not only revelatory; it is performative. God does things with words.[32] The fresh appreciation of this dimension of speech-act in divine utterance (as indeed in many forms of human speech) is welcome, but hardly new. Isaiah 55:10–11 has a thing or two to say about the performative power of this word of this God. The amazing fecundity of this word is that it both *refers* to reality and *generates* reality. Therein lies its double authority. These texts speak of the reality of God, creator of the universe, redeemer of Israel, already creating a new heaven and a new earth. But the same texts also deliver to us the love and justice, the will and demands, the judgment and promise of this God in such a way that we cannot escape their ethical force field.

As Psalm 33 so richly reflects in its majestic exaltation of the word of the LORD, this is a world-transforming word that puts the world to rights (vv. 4–5). It is a world-creating word that calls the world into being (vv. 6–9). It is a world-governing word that runs the world's history according to plan (vv. 10–11). And it is a world-watching word that calls the world universally to account (vv. 13–15). This is the authority structure, rendered to us in the text of the Old Testament, which makes righteous rejoicing, hope-filled fear and patient trust the only appropriate responses to such a word (vv. 1–2, 18–22),

---

[32] This deliberately echoes the title of J. L. Austin's book *Doing Things with Words* (Oxford: Clarendon, 1962), a seminal text on the illocutionary force of words in many forms of human utterance, such as promise, threat, contract etc. It has inspired a whole genre of 'speech-act' study of the performative function of many biblical texts. For a helpful recent appreciation, see Richard S. Briggs, 'Uses of Speech-Act Theory', and with particular emphasis on the importance of 'self-involving' reading of biblical texts, Richard S. Briggs, 'Getting Involved'.

and warns those who rely on anything as paltry as huge armies that they have simply lost touch with reality (vv. 16–17).

So then, the reality of this word, delivered to us in the scriptures of Israel, carries authority for an ethic of covenantal obedience for us as for Israel, for we know the One who said these things (Heb. 10:30).

The reality of this people

The fourth reality that the Old Testament scriptures render to us is that of the people of Israel. Whatever may be our historical reconstruction of the process of their emergence in late Bronze Age, early Iron Age Palestine,[33] the fact remains that they did emerge. Ancient Israel, with their distinctive view of their own election, history and relationship to the LORD their God, is a historical reality of enormous significance to the history of the rest of humanity. We would know about them to some degree, of course, from the material remains of their existence and the references to them in the literature of other contemporary nations. But essentially, it is the Hebrew Bible that renders this people to us, just as it renders to us this God, the Holy One of Israel.

Now it is clear that for the Israelites themselves the simple reality of their existence as a people constituted an authority for mandating certain forms of ethical behaviour and condemning others. To be an Israelite was to belong to a community of ethical norms. Positively, the concept of holiness was a community ethic with a wide range of implications – social, economic, familial, political, agricultural, judicial, commercial, ritual, etc. (as seen clearly in Lev. 19, for example). Negatively, the conviction that certain things 'are not done in Israel' (even when they actually were) points to the ethical normativity of simply being 'this people'.

Theologically, of course, we could point to many dimensions of the significance of Israel's election, such as the missional purpose of God for the nations that is the bottom line of the promise to Abraham, and we could point to their faith that witnessed to the reality of the God they worshipped and whose worship they bequeathed to us. But my point here is simply this. When we are considering what ethical authority the Old Testament carries, part of it lies in its witness to the reality of this people as a historical phenom-

---

[33] The guild of Old Testament historians remains as divided as ever over their reconstruction of the process by which Israel emerged. For recent surveys of the debate, and particularly the archaeological battleground, see John J. Bimson, 'Origins of Israel'; William G. Dever, 'Biblical and Syro-Palestinian Archaeology'; *What Did the Biblical Writers Know?*; V. P. Long, D. W. Baker, and G. J. Wenham (eds.), *Windows into Old Testament History*.

enon. The phenomenon of Israel carried its own ethical authority for those who belonged to that people in the Old Testament period itself. But more than that, the role and mission laid on Israel of being a priesthood in the midst of the nations (Exod. 19:4–6), of being a light to the nations (Is. 42:6; 49:6 etc.), an exemplar of social righteousness to the watching nations (Deut. 4:6–8) – all of these gave the ethics of Israel a wider authoritative relevance than in their own society alone. As discussed in chapter 2 above, Israel was intended to function as a paradigm for others. As I have argued, this is not a hermeneutical ruse imposed upon the Old Testament retrospectively by us, but was part of the intentionality of election from the beginning. Israel's particularity serves their universal significance. Their concrete existence in history functions not in spite of its particularity but precisely through and because of it to disclose the kind of ethical behaviour, attitudes and motivation God requires universally in human communities.

So, the reality of this people, rendered to us in the Old Testament scriptures, generates an ethic of paradigm and analogy, in which we assume the moral consistency of God and ask, 'If this is what God required of them, what, in our different context, does God require of us?'

What I have argued in this chapter, then, is that the authority of the Old Testament for us as Christians lies, in part, in its witness to some fundamental realities. Those realities then generate authority that governs our responsive behaviour. The detailed working out of that response is the task of hermeneutics and ethical construction, such as this book has attempted to offer in a selection of areas. In summary, we could tabulate the discussion above as follows.

The reality of	*Predicates the authority of*
• this God	• an ethic of worship and response (to his identity)
	• an ethic of imitation and reflection (of his character)
• this story	• an ethic of gratitude and mission
• this word	• an ethic of covenantal obedience
• this people	• an ethic of paradigm and analogy

Conclusion

It remains only to point out that these four features of the Old Testament are affirmed as realities also for Christian believers in the New Testament. They are all, in fact, focused on Jesus in such a way that their authority and ethical relevance is not only sustained, but also enhanced and transformed for those who are 'in Christ'.

For in Jesus we meet this God. The New Testament typically addresses the issue of 'Jesus and God' not so much in the categories of ontology but of identity and character, as well as function. Jesus is the one who explicitly shares the identity and character of YHWH and who ultimately accomplishes what only YHWH could.[34] So to know Jesus as Saviour and Lord is to enter a realm of ethical response and imitation that reflects Israel's to YHWH.

In Jesus we have the climax of this story, and the guarantee of its ending. This story is also our story, for if we are in Christ, then, according to Paul, we are also in Abraham and heirs according to the promise. Our future is the future promised by God to Abraham, achieved by Jesus and to be enjoyed by the whole of redeemed humanity from every nation, tribe, people and language (Rev. 7:9–10). Our lives also, then, are to be ethically shaped by the gratitude that looks back and the mission that looks forward.

In Jesus we have heard God's final word, the Word made flesh. The disclosure of God, rendered to us in the Old Testament, is now completed by the disclosure rendered to us through the New Testament portrait and interpretation of Jesus of Nazareth. There are, of course, discontinuities and developments, but the New Testament authors were in no doubt that behind the Word that came to them with Jesus stood the same God whose word they had received in the scriptures they already possessed: 'We know the One who said . . .' (Heb. 10:30; my trans.) both identifies the speaker and affirms the abiding relevance of his original words.

In Jesus we have become part of this people, sharing the comprehensive range of identity and responsibility that was theirs. For through the cross and the gospel of the Messiah Jesus we have become citizens of God's people, members of God's household, the place of God's dwelling (Eph. 2:11 – 3:13). Such an identity and such a belonging generate an ethical responsibility in the church and the world, which the New Testament spells out in some detail.

So then, the *authority* of the Old Testament is mediated to us through the *reality* of these things. As we read the Old Testament, in the light of Christ, we are called to respond across the range of our whole ethical environment to these great life-sustaining truths. This is the God we worship, this is the story we are part of, this is the Word we have heard, and this is the people we belong to. In view of these realities and the authority they predicate, how should we then live?

---

[34] See, e.g., N. T. Wright, *Jesus*; and Richard J. Bauckham, *God Crucified*.

Further reading

Barton, John, *Ethics and the Old Testament* (London: SCM, 1998).

Briggs, Richard S., 'Getting Involved: Speech Acts and Biblical Interpretation', *Anvil* 20 (2003), pp. 25–34.

Brueggemann, Walter, 'The Role of Old Testament Theology in Old Testament Interpretation', in Ball, *True Wisdom*, pp. 70–88.

Brueggemann, Walter, *A Social Reading of the Old Testament: Prophetic Approaches to Israel's Communal Life*, ed. Patrick D. Miller Jr. (Minneapolis: Fortress, 1994).

Davies, Eryl W., 'Ethics of the Hebrew Bible: The Problem of Methodology', *Semeia* 66 (1995), pp. 43–53.

Goldingay, John, *Approaches to Old Testament Interpretation: Updated Edition* (Leicester: Apollos, 1991).

O'Donovan, Oliver M. T., 'Towards an Interpretation of Biblical Ethics', *Tyndale Bulletin* 27 (1976), pp. 54–78.

Patrick, Dale, *The Rendering of God in the Old Testament*, Overtures to Biblical Theology, vol. 10 (Philadelphia: Fortress, 1981).

Rodd, Cyril, *Glimpses of a Strange Land: Studies in Old Testament Ethics* (Edinburgh: T. & T. Clark, 2001).

Seitz, Christopher, *Word without End* (Grand Rapids: Eerdmans, 1998).

APPENDIX: WHAT ABOUT THE CANAANITES?

It is impossible, in my experience, to teach on the topic of Old Testament ethics or on other aspects of the Old Testament foundations of the Christian faith, without this question arising as soon as hands go up at the end of the lecture. It takes various forms. If the emphasis of the teaching has been on the central purpose of Israel's election – namely, that they were called into existence in order to be the means of God's blessing the nations – then the questioner usually wonders how the existence of the Israelites was any kind of blessing to the Canaanites. Does the conquest narrative not stand in an impossibly deconstructive relationship with the promise of blessing? If the teaching focused on the warmer dimensions of the ethics of the Old Testament texts – such as justice, compassion, care for the poor and needy – the questioner wonders how this can be squared with the commands to eradicate the Canaanites (the difficulty being most acute in the book of Deuteronomy, which contains both emphases virtually side by side). If the teaching highlighted the character of the LORD as the God of justice and compassion whose sovereign rule over the world, in history, in the present, and in the ultimate future, is based on those great foundations, the questioner wonders whether that is a perspective the Canaanites would have found quite so self-evident.

Clearly, then, the biblical narratives of the conquest of Canaan are most troubling to sensitive readers, and rightly so.[1] How can we handle them as

---

[1] This is so whether the events took place just as the Bible describes them, or whether

Christians, in relation to our convictions about God's will to bless the nations, God's compassion and God's justice? This question cries out for a very thorough investigation, with full attention to its biblical, theological, ethical and missiological dimensions. All I can offer in this limited appendix are a few broad perspectives. I do not claim that they 'solve' the problem, but I have found them helpful at least in setting the problem within the wider context of other biblical considerations.

No contradiction between ultimate blessing and historical judgment

God declared to Abraham that his purpose in calling him was that all nations on the earth would find blessing. This is repeated six times in Genesis and is clearly a central dimension of Israel's election (as we saw especially in chapter 2 above). Israel was to be the means of blessing to the nations. How, then, could God use them to bring such suffering on the Canaanites? It is important to see the blessing of the nations as God's ultimate (eschatological) purpose. It does not mean that God would therefore have to 'be nice' to everybody or every nation, no matter how they behaved. God remains the moral judge of all human action, and it is an equally essential part of the biblical testimony that God acts within history in judgment upon the wicked. As I shall argue more fully below, that is how the conquest of Canaan is plainly interpreted.

So God's ultimate purpose of blessing all nations does not eliminate his prerogative to act in judgment on particular nations within history, any more than parents' long-term and loving desire for their children to flourish prevents them from necessary acts of discipline or punishment in the meantime. On the

---

(as in the view of some scholarly reconstructions of the emergence of Israel in Palestine) the biblical texts are, on the one hand, rhetorically exaggerated beyond events on the ground, or, on the other hand, retrospective idealizations of what should have happened. This is not the place to address the complex arguments among biblical historians and archaeologists over 'what really happened' in the process by which Israel came into visible historical existence in the land of Canaan: whether it was a conquest, or a slow settlement, or an internal revolution, or some mixture of all of these; whether indeed there ever was such a fundamental distinction between Israelites and Canaanites as the Old Testament so rhetorically portrays. My own conviction is that a process of events did take place to which the narratives of Joshua reliably, though necessarily selectively, refer. For detailed surveys of the current state of scholarship, see John J. Bimson, 'Origins of Israel'; William G. Dever, *What Did the Biblical Writers Know?*; V. P. Long, D. W. Baker and G. J. Wenham (eds.), *Windows into Old Testament History*.

contrary, it requires such acts. This was equally true for Israel. The covenantal commitment God made through Abraham, renewed at Mount Sinai, bound him to his own promise to Israel, that he, the LORD, would for ever be their God and they would be his people, and he would accomplish his purpose for them and through them. But that ultimate and overarching commitment to bless Israel did not prevent God from taking action on particular generations of Israelites within history. Those who are unrepentantly wicked face the wrath of God – including within the covenant nation itself in Old Testament times. Long-term blessing and historical wrath are not in opposition to one another. Indeed, it is precisely because of that unique covenantal relationship that God had with Israel, that he acted in punishment on their sin (Amos 3:2). So it is with humanity at large. God's intention to bless all nations will be accomplished (as Rev. 7 gloriously anticipates), but that does not exclude God's freedom to use human agents and human history as the vehicle of his moral judgment in the meantime. Psalm 47 remarkably anticipates that eventually all nations can be summoned to praise and applaud the LORD for what he has done – even in those events that included the conquest of nations. Ultimately, the history of Israel will be the subject of praise among the nations – for whose ultimate saving benefit it happened. Deuteronomy 32:43, and its use by Paul in Romans 15:7–12, points in the same direction.

The conquest of Canaan a limited event

The conquest narratives describe one particular period of Israel's long history. Many of the other wars that occur in Old Testament narrative had no divine sanction, and some were clearly condemned as the actions of proud and greedy kings, or military rivals. Sometimes questioners accuse 'the whole Old Testament' of being full of wars of extermination, all commanded by this vicious god, YHWH. That is a caricature of the canon. The events described in Joshua took place largely within a single generation, even though Judges shows that the aftermath went on for quite some time. It is placed within the category of *ḥērem* – that specific form or warfare in which YHWH is the chief protagonist and the enemy is 'renounced' or 'devoted' to him. Some of the later wars also had this characteristic, but many are not explicitly so described.

A conventional rhetoric of warfare in the ancient Near East

We do need to allow for the exaggerated language of warfare. Israel, like other nations of the ancient Near East whose documents we possess, had a rhetoric of war that often exceeded reality on the ground. Even in the Old Testament itself this phenomenon is recognized and accepted. It is well known, for example, that the book of Joshua describes the conquest in rhetorically total terms – all the land is captured, all the kings are defeated, all the people without survivors are destroyed (e.g. Josh. 10:40–42; 11:16–20). Yet the book of Judges (whose final editor must have been aware of these accounts in Joshua) sees no contradiction in telling us that the process of subduing the inhabitants of the land was far from completed and went on for some considerable time. So even in the Old Testament itself, rhetorical generalization is recognized for what it is. We need, therefore, in reading some of the more graphic descriptions, either of what was commanded to be done, or recorded as accomplished, to allow for this rhetorical element. This is not to accuse the biblical writers of falsehood, but to recognize the literary conventions of writing about warfare.

The conquest described as an act of God's punishment

The conquest should not be portrayed as random genocide or 'ethnic cleansing'. Nor is it right to argue that there is an irreconcilable contradiction between Israel's celebration of their own release from oppression in Egypt and Israel's 'oppression of the Canaanite nations' a generation later.[2] The action of Israel against the Canaanites is not placed in the category of oppression, but of divine punishment operating through human agency. It is consistently described as an act of God's moral punishment on a degraded society.

The wickedness of Canaanite society is anticipated in Genesis 15:16, where God tells Abraham that his descendants will possess the land of his temporary residence, but not immediately, 'for the sin of the Amorites has not yet reached its full measure'. This seems to say that the nature of Amorite/Canaanite society in Abraham's day was not yet so wicked as to justify God acting in such comprehensive judgment upon it (as he would do, for example, on Sodom and Gomorrah). But that time would come.

The wickedness of Canaanite society is more explicitly described in moral and social terms in Leviticus 18:24–25; 20:22–24; Deuteronomy 9:5; 12:29–31. It includes the sexual promiscuity and perversion particularly associated with fertility cults, and also the callousness of child sacrifice. It is surely significant that Leviticus uses a dramatically vivid term for God's reaction to the degradation of the Canaanites. Several times we are told that the land itself will 'vomit

---

[2] As Knierim does: *Task of Old Testament Theology*, p. 97.

them out'. This speaks of something that is not merely an 'abomination' to God, but also repulsive and disgusting, so much so that he can no longer 'stomach' it. This interpretation is accepted in the New Testament (e.g. Heb. 11:31 speaks of the Canaanites as 'the disobedient', implying that they were morally aware of their sin but chose to persist in it – as the Bible affirms of all human beings).

There is a huge moral difference between arbitrary violence and violence inflicted within the moral framework of punishment. This is true in human society as much as in divine perspective. Whatever our view of corporal punishment in any form, there is clearly (in my view, at least) a categorical difference between smacking a child (say) as an explained punishment for unacceptable behaviour that has been clearly forbidden and wanton physical assault on a child for no reason at all or out of sheer cruelty. Again, whatever one's views on capital punishment, there is likewise a moral difference between the execution of a criminal convicted as guilty within a system of law and random murder of an innocent person. We may not agree with either smacking or execution, and good arguments can be put forward for rejecting both, but among those good arguments cannot be the idea that such forms of punishment are simply morally indistinguishable from violent child cruelty or indiscriminate murder.

So the consistent biblical affirmation that the conquest constituted an act of God's punishment on a wicked society, using Israel as the human agent, must be taken seriously (by those who wish to take the Bible's own testimony seriously) and not be dismissed as self-serving disinfectant for the poison of Israel's own aggression.

God threatened to do the same to Israel – and did

The Old Testament claims that in the conquest God used Israel as the agent of his punishment on the Canaanites. God warned Israel that if they behaved in the same way as the Canaanites, God would treat Israel as his enemy on the same terms as the Canaanites, and inflict the same punishment on them by using other nations (Lev. 18:28; Deut. 28:25–68). The land that had vomited out the Canaanites would be perfectly capable of repeating its expurgation if Israel indulged in the same repulsive Canaanite practices. The same YHWH who acted in moral judgment on Israel's enemies would act in precisely the same way on Israel itself.

In the course of Israel's long history in Old Testament times God repeatedly did so. He thus demonstrated his moral consistency in international justice. It was not a matter of favouritism (taking Israel's side no matter what).

If anything, the Old Testament argues that Israel's status as God's elect people exposed them all the more to God's moral judgment and historical punishment than any of the surrounding nations, including those they conquered (cf. Amos 3:2). Indeed, we might point out that far more generations of Israelites felt the hand of the LORD's anger at the hands of their enemies (including some Canaanite ones in the early years) than the generation of Canaanites that experienced the judgment of the LORD at the hands of the Israelites. It is simply a distortion of the Old Testament to say (as many questioners allege, in my teaching experience) that 'God is always for Israel, and all the other nations get nothing but judgment'. Have they never read the pre-exilic prophets or the Deuteronomistic History (especially 1–2 Kings)?

Fairness a slippery concept

Was God fair to judge the Canaanites in this way? On the one hand, is the catalogue of their wickedness any worse than many other societies, ancient or modern, upon whom God has neither rained the fire and brimstone of Sodom and Gomorrah, nor inflicted invading armies as the arm of his judgment? Why them and not others? And on the other hand, was it fair to inflict the Israelites on that particular generation of Canaanites, when presumably at least the previous one was not noticeably more righteous or less deserving of punishment.

These are awkward questions, but they do point to the problem of any kind of fairness within human history in a fallen world. John Goldingay, in an interesting discussion of precisely this matter,[3] points out that it may be thought equally unfair that the Israelite generation of the exile were punished in that way when previous generations in Judah were just as wicked – a point the exiles themselves did not hesitate to hurl in the LORD's face, posing a major pastoral and evangelistic challenge of theodicy for Ezekiel (see Ezek. 18). But, in its historical manifestation, God's judgment has to fall sometime. And some people will be 'there' at that time. Others will not. If that is not 'fair', it seems also to be unavoidable – unless God were to suspend *all* demonstrations of his justice within history. This is one reason why the Bible increasingly points towards the final 'reckoning' when God will act to put things right ultimately, so that justice prevails and reigns throughout the cosmos, in a way that will be universally fair (something that cannot be achieved within the limitations of history and the ambiguities of all historical

---

[3] Goldingay, 'Justice and Salvation', especially pp. 178–186.

events). In the meantime – within the provisional and penultimate events of history – God 'harnesses unfairness' (Goldingay's phrase) within the accomplishment of his wider, longer-term purpose of salvation for the world.

To Goldingay's interesting discussion I would add a further reflection on what might be called the intrinsic and extrinsic nature of 'fairness'. If I am punished for what I have manifestly done wrong, that is intrinsically fair. I cannot complain it is unfair as far as I am concerned. However, if others are *not* punished for the same thing, I feel that is unfair, extrinsically. My punishment is fair. Their impunity seems unfair. The Bible clearly affirms that the punishment of the Canaanites at the time of the conquest was intrinsically fair and just – as far as they were concerned. God acted with moral justification (according to the witness of the Bible). It does not directly address the question of any apparent unfairness if other nations further afield were left unpunished in the same way. What it does do, however, is to affirm that *in the end* God remains the ultimate judge of all humanity – nations and individuals. So whatever may or may not happen within the flow of history, nothing will get swept under the carpet and escape the just verdict of 'the judge of all the earth' who will surely, as Abraham affirmed, 'do justice'; that is, deliver and execute his own just verdict (Gen. 18:25).[4]

It might be worth observing the curious fact that we do not usually reflect on fairness and unfairness in relation to God's blessings, even though they are apparently as randomly and 'unfairly' distributed as his punishments – in this life. We are not so inclined to respond with 'That's not fair' when we enjoy gifts and blessings that others do not. On the other hand, we are inclined to protest if others receive what we consider unwarranted bounty at God's hand, if we only got what is 'fair' – as Jesus exposed so trenchantly in the parable of the workers in the vineyard and the 'unfair' generosity of the owner. All in all, then, we might be wise to be cautious in our assessment of what is fair or unfair in God's dealings with humanity in history, recognizing the ambiguity of the terms, and our own rather warped and flawed perspectives.

The conquest anticipated the final judgment

Like the stories of Sodom and Gomorrah and the flood, the story of the conquest of Canaan stands in the Bible as a 'prototypical' narrative. The Bible affirms that ultimately, in the final judgment, the wicked will face the awful

---

[4] John Goldingay's above-mentioned article also includes a helpful discussion of this verse, and the dynamic meaning of the Hebrew terms *mišpāṭ* and *ṣĕdāqâ*.

reality of the wrath of God, in exclusion, punishment and destruction. There will then be the final vindication of God's ethical justice. But at certain points in history, such as the conquest, God has demonstrated the power of his judgment. The story of Rahab, set in the midst of the conquest narrative, also demonstrates the power of 'repentance' and faith, and God's willingness to spare his enemies when they choose to identify with God's people. Rahab thus enters the New Testament hall of fame – and faith (Heb. 11:31; Jas. 2:25).

I am well aware that these considerations only scratch the surface of some very deep issues in relation to the conquest narratives. Furthermore, the conquest of Canaan is only one of a whole raft of issues in the Old Testament where modern readers pin their ethical question marks (to put it mildly). There are many other tales of violence. There are violent forms of speech, metaphor and symbolism, some particularly disturbing to women. There are curses and prayers of vengeance. The bibliography below offers help in these areas, but there is room for further reflection in what might be called moral defence of the Old Testament (a task some would deem sorely needed, and others would deem impossible and even unethical in principle). If this sounds faintly like the promise (or threat) of another book, that is perhaps because I hope it is.

Further reading

Craigie, Peter C., *The Problem of War in the Old Testament* (Grand Rapids: Eerdmans, 1978).

Goldingay, John, 'Justice and Salvation for Israel and Canaan', in Wonil et al., *Reading the Hebrew Bible for a New Millennium*, pp. 169–187.

Cowles, C. S., Merrill, E. H., Gard, D. L., Longman III, T., and Gundry, S. (eds.), *Show Them No Mercy: Four Views of God and Canaanite Genocide* (Grand Rapids: Zondervan, 2003).

Houston, Walter, 'War and the Old Testament', *Modern Churchman* 28 (1985), pp. 14–21.

Kaiser Jr, Walter C., *Hard Sayings of the Old Testament* (Downers Grove: InterVarsity Press, 1988).

Kidner, Derek, 'Old Testament Perspectives on War', *Evangelical Quarterly* 57 (1985), pp. 99–112.

Knierim, Rolf P., 'On the Subject of War in Old Testament and Biblical Theology', in Wonil et al., *Reading the Hebrew Bible*, pp. 73–88.

Lind, Millard C., *Yahweh Is a Warrior: The Theology of Warfare in Ancient Israel* (Scottdale: Herald, 1980).

Longman III, Tremper, and Reid, Daniel G., *God Is a Warrior* (Grand Rapids: Zondervan; Carlisle: Paternoster, 1995).

Niditch, Susan, *War in the Hebrew Bible: A Study in the Ethics of Violence* (Oxford: Oxford University Press, 1993).

Thompson, Alden, *Who's Afraid of the Old Testament God?* (Grand Rapids: Zondervan, 1989).

Waldow, H. E von, 'The Concept of War in the Old Testament', *Horizons of Biblical Theology* 6 (1984), pp. 27–48.

Wenham, John W., *The Enigma of Evil: Can we Believe in the Goodness of God?* (Leicester: IVP, 1985; Carlisle: Paternoster, 1997).

BIBLIOGRAPHY

Alexander, T. D., *From Paradise to the Promised Land: An Introduction to the Pentateuch*, 2nd ed. (Grand Rapids: Baker Academic; Carlisle: Paternoster, 2002).

———, 'Book of the Covenant', in Alexander and Baker, *Dictionary of the Old Testament: Pentateuch*, pp. 94–101.

Alexander, T. D., and Baker, D. W. (eds.), *Dictionary of the Old Testament: Pentateuch* (Downers Grove: InterVarsity Press; Leicester: IVP, 2003).

Allen, L. C., 'Micah's Social Concern', *Vox Evangelica* 8 (1973), pp. 22–32.

Alt, Albrecht, 'The Origins of Israelite Law', in *Essays on Old Testament History and Religion* (Oxford: Blackwell; Garden City: Doubleday, 1966), pp. 81–132.

Andersen, F. I., 'The Social-Judicial Background of the Naboth Incident', *Journal of Biblical Literature* 85 (1966), pp. 46–57.

———, 'Israelite Kinship Terminology and Social Structure', *Bible Translator* 20 (1969), pp. 26–39.

Anderson, B. W., 'The Earth Is the Lord's: An Essay on the Biblical Doctrine of Creation', *Interpretation* 9 (1955), pp. 3–20.

Anderson, J. N. D., *Morality, Law and Grace* (London: Tyndale, 1972).

Bahnsen, Greg, *Theonomy in Christian Ethics*, rev. ed. (Phillipsburg: Presbyterian & Reformed, 1984).

———, *By This Standard: The Authority of God's Law Today* (Tyler: Institute for Christian Economics, 1985).

———, 'Christ and the Role of Civil Government: The Theonomic Perspective', *Transformation* 5.2, 5.3 (1988), part 1, pp. 24–31; part 2, pp. 24–28.

Bailey Wells, Jo, *God's Holy People: A Theme in Biblical Theology*, JSOT Supplement Series, vol. 305 (Sheffield: Sheffield Academic Press, 2000).

Ball, Edward (ed.), *In Search of True Wisdom: Essays in Old Testament Interpretation in Honour of Ronald E. Clements* (Sheffield: Sheffield Academic Press, 1999).

Ball, Jim, 'Evangelicals, Population and the Ecological Crisis', *Christian Scholars Review* 28 (1998), pp. 228–253.

Barker, P. A., 'Sabbath, Sabbatical Year, Jubilee', in Alexander and Baker, *Dictionary of the Old Testament: Pentateuch*, pp. 695–706.

Barker, William. S., and Godfrey, W. Robert (eds.), *Theonomy: A Reformed Critique* (Grand Rapids: Academie, 1990).

Barr, James, 'Man and Nature – the Ecological Controversy and the Old Testament', *Bulletin of the John Rylands Library of the University of Manchester* 55 (1972), pp. 9–32.

――――, 'Biblical Law and the Question of Natural Theology', in Timo Veijola (ed.), *The Law in the Bible and in Its Environment* (Göttingen: Vandenhoeck & Ruprecht, 1990), pp. 1–22.

――――, *Biblical Faith and Natural Theology* (Oxford: Clarendon Press, 1993).

――――, *The Concept of Biblical Theology: An Old Testament Perspective* (London: SCM, 1999).

Barton, John, 'Understanding Old Testament Ethics', *Journal for the Study of the Old Testament* 9 (1978), pp. 44–64.

――――, 'Natural Law and Poetic Justice in the Old Testament', *Journal of Theological Studies* 30 (1979), pp. 1–14.

――――, 'Approaches to Ethics in the Old Testament', in John W. Rogerson (ed.), *Beginning Old Testament Study* (London: SPCK, 1983), pp. 113–130.

――――, 'The Basis of Ethics in the Hebrew Bible', *Semeia* 66 (1994), pp. 11–22.

――――, *Ethics and the Old Testament* (London: SCM, 1998).

――――, 'Canon and Old Testament Interpretation', in Ball, *True Wisdom*, pp. 37–52.

――――, *Understanding Old Testament Ethics: Approaches and Explanations* (Louisville, KY: Westminster John Knox, 2003).

Barton, S. C., 'Family', in J. B. Green and S. McKnight (eds.), *Dictionary of Jesus and the Gospels* (Downers Grove: InterVarsity Press; Leicester: IVP, 1992), pp. 226–229.

Bauckham, Richard J., *Jude, 2 Peter*, Word Biblical Commentary (Waco: Word, 1983).

――――, 'First Steps to a Theology of Nature', *Evangelical Quarterly* 58 (1986), pp. 229–244.

――――, *The Bible in Politics: How to Read the Bible Politically* (London: SPCK; Louisville, KY: Westminster John Knox, 1989).

――――, 'Jesus and Animals i) What Did He Teach? ii) What Did He Practise?' in Linzey and Yamamoto, *Animals on the Agenda*, pp. 33–60.

――――, *God Crucified* (Carlisle: Paternoster; Grand Rapids: Eerdmans, 1999).

Baum, Gregory, 'Exodus Politics', in van Iersel and Weiler, *Exodus*, pp. 109–117.

Bendor, S., *The Social Structure of Ancient Israel: The Institution of the Family (Beit 'Ab) from the Settlement to the End of the Monarchy*, Jerusalem Biblical Studies, vol. 7, ed. E. Katzenstein (Jerusalem: Simor, 1996).

Biggar, Nigel, and Hay, Donald, 'The Bible, Christian Ethics and the Provision of Social Security', *Studies in Christian Ethics* 7 (1994), pp. 43–64.

Bimson, John J., 'The Origins of Israel in Canaan: An Examination of Recent Theories', *Themelios* 15.1 (1989), pp. 4–15.

Birch, Bruce C., 'Old Testament Narrative and Moral Address', in Tucker, Petersen and Wilson, *Canon, Theology and Old Testament Interpretation*, pp. 75–91.

――――, *Let Justice Roll Down: The Old Testament, Ethics, and Christian Life* (Louisville, KY: Westminster John Knox, 1991).

————, 'Moral Agency, Community, and the Character of God in the Hebrew Bible', *Semeia* 66 (1994), pp. 23–41.

————, 'Divine Character and the Formation of Moral Community in the Book of Exodus', in Rogerson, Davies and Carroll, *Bible in Ethics*, pp. 119–135.

Birch, Bruce C., and Rasmussen, Larry L., *Bible and Ethics in the Christian Life*, rev. ed. (Minneapolis: Augsburg, 1989).

Bishop, Stephen, 'Green Theology and Deep Ecology: New Age or New Creation?' *Themelios* 16.3 (1991), pp. 8–14.

Blauw, Johannes, *The Missionary Nature of the Church* (New York: McGraw Hill, 1962).

Blocher, Henri, 'The Fear of the Lord as the "Principle" of Wisdom', *Tyndale Bulletin* 28 (1977), pp. 3–28.

Block, Daniel I., *The Gods of the Nations: Studies in Ancient near Eastern National Theology*, 2nd ed. (Grand Rapids: Baker; Leicester: Apollos, 2000).

Bloesch, D. G., *Freedom for Obedience: Evangelical Ethics in Contemporary Times* (New York: Harper & Row, 1987).

Blomberg, Craig L., *Neither Poverty nor Riches: A Biblical Theology of Material Possessions* (Downers Grove: InterVarsity Press; Leicester: Apollos, 1999).

Bloom, A., 'Human Rights in Israel's Thought', *Interpretation* 8 (1954), pp. 422–432.

Boecker, Hans-Jochen, *Law and the Administration of Justice in the Old Testament and Ancient East* (Minneapolis: Augsburg, 1980).

Bosch, David J., *Transforming Mission: Paradigm Shifts in Theology of Mission* (Maryknoll: Orbis, 1991).

Boyce, Richard Nelson, *The Cry to God in the Old Testament* (Atlanta: Scholars Press, 1988).

Bretzke, SJ, James T., *Bibliography on Scripture and Christian Ethics*, Studies in Religion and Society, vol. 39 (Lewiston: Edwin Mellen, 1997).

Brichto, Herbert C., 'Kin, Cult, Land and Afterlife – a Biblical Complex', *Hebrew Union College Annual* 44 (1973), pp. 1–54.

Bridger, Francis, 'Ecology and Eschatology: A Neglected Dimension', *Tyndale Bulletin* 41.2 (1990), pp. 290–301.

Briggs, Richard S., 'The Uses of Speech-Act Theory in Biblical Interpretation', *Currents in Theology and Mission* 9 (2001), pp. 229–276.

————, 'Getting Involved: Speech Acts and Biblical Interpretation', *Anvil* 20 (2003), pp. 25–34.

Bruckner, James K., 'The Creational Context of Law before Sinai: Law and Liberty in Pre-Sinai Narratives and Romans 7', *Ex Auditu* 11 (1995), pp. 91–110.

Brueggemann, Walter, *The Land* (Philadelphia: Fortress, 1977).

————, *The Prophetic Imagination* (Philadelphia: Fortress, 1978).

————, *Theology of the Old Testament: Testimony, Dispute, Advocacy* (Minneapolis: Fortress, 1997).

————, 'The Role of Old Testament Theology in Old Testament Interpretation', in Ball, *True Wisdom*, pp. 70–88.

Brueggemann, Walter, *A Social Reading of the Old Testament: Prophetic Approaches to Israel's Communal Life*, ed. Patrick D. Miller Jr. (Minneapolis: Fortress, 1994).

Burge, Gary M., *Whose Land? Whose Promise? What Christians Are Not Being Told about Israel and the Palestinians* (Carlisle: Paternoster; Cleveland, OH: Pilgrim, 2003).

Burnett, David, *Clash of Worlds* (Eastbourne: Monarch, 1990).

———, *God's Mission, Healing the Nations*, rev. ed. (Carlisle: Paternoster, 1996).

Calvin, J., *Commentaries on the Four Last Books of Moses Arranged in the Form of a Harmony*, trans. C. W. Bingham, 4 vols. (Edinburgh: Calvin Translation Society, 1852–5).

Carroll R., M. D., 'Wealth and Poverty', in Alexander and Baker, *Dictionary of the Old Testament: Pentateuch*, pp. 881–887.

Chalcraft, David J. (ed.), *Social-Scientific Old Testament Criticism: A Sheffield Reader* (Sheffield: Sheffield Academic Press, 1997).

Chapman, Colin, *Whose Promised Land?* Rev. ed. (Oxford: Lion, 1989).

Chester, Andrew, 'The Concept of Peace in the Old Testament', *Theology* 92 (1989), pp. 466–481.

Childs, Brevard S., *Biblical Theology of the Old and New Testaments: Theological Reflection on the Christian Bible* (Minneapolis: Fortress, 1992).

Chirichigno, Greg, 'A Theological Investigation of Motivation in Old Testament Law', *Journal of the Evangelical Theological Society* 24 (1981), pp. 303–313.

Clements, R. E., *God and Temple: The Idea of Divine Presence in Ancient Israel* (Oxford: Blackwell; Philadelphia: Fortress, 1965).

———(ed.), *The World of Ancient Israel: Sociological, Anthropological and Political Perspectives* (Cambridge: Cambridge University Press, 1989).

———, 'Christian Ethics and the Old Testament', *Modern Churchman* 26 (1984), pp. 13–26.

———, 'Worship and Ethics: A Re-examination of Psalm 15', in Graham, Marrs and McKenzie, *Worship and the Hebrew Bible*, pp. 78–94.

Clines, David J. A., 'Ethics as Deconstruction, and the Ethics of Deconstruction', in Rogerson, Davies and Carroll, *Bible in Ethics*, pp. 77–106.

———, *The Theme of the Pentateuch*, 2nd ed. (Sheffield: Sheffield Academic Press, 1997).

Cowles, C. S., Merrill, E. H., Gard, D. L., Longman III, T., and Gundry, S. (eds.), *Show Them No Mercy: Four Views of God and Canaanite Genocide* (Grand Rapids: Zondervan, 2003).

Craigie, Peter C., *The Problem of War in the Old Testament* (Grand Rapids: Eerdmans, 1978).

Crenshaw, J. L., and Willis, J. T. (eds.), *Essays in Old Testament Ethics* (New York: Ktav, 1974).

Curran, Charles E., and McCormick SJ, Richard A. (eds.), *The Use of Scripture in Moral Theology*, vol. 4, Readings in Moral Theology (New York: Paulist Press, 1984).

Davidson, Robert, 'Some Aspects of the Old Testament Contribution to the Pattern of Christian Ethics', *Scottish Journal of Theology* 12 (1959), pp. 373–387.

Davies, Eryl W., 'Ethics of the Hebrew Bible: The Problem of Methodology', *Semeia* 66 (1995), pp. 43–53.

———, 'Walking in God's Ways: The Concept of *Imitatio Dei* in the Old Testament', in Ball, *True Wisdom*, pp. 99–115.

Davies, G. I., 'The Destiny of the Nations in the Book of Isaiah', in Jacques Vermeylen (ed.), *The Book of Isaiah* (Leuven: Leuven University Press, 1989), pp. 93–120.

Davies, Philip R., 'Ethics and the Old Testament', in Rogerson, Davies and Carroll, *Bible in Ethics*, pp. 164–173.

Davies, W. D., *The Gospel and the Land: Early Christianity and Jewish Territorial Doctrine* (Berkeley: University of California Press, 1974).

Dearman, John Andrew, *Property Rights in the Eighth-Century Prophets: The Conflict and Its Background* (Atlanta: Scholars Press, 1988).

Deidun, Tom, 'The Bible and Christian Ethics', in Bernard Hoose (ed.), *Christian Ethics: An Introduction* (Collegeville, MN: Liturgical Press, 1998), pp. 3–46.

Dempsey, Carol J., *Hope Amid the Ruins: The Ethics of Israel's Prophets* (St. Louis: Chalice, 2000).

Dever, William G., 'Biblical and Syro-Palestinian Archaeology: A State-of-the-Art Assessment at the Turn of the Millennium', *Currents in Research: Biblical Studies* 8 (2000), pp. 91–116.

———, *What Did the Biblical Writers Know and When Did They Know It?* (Grand Rapids: Eerdmans, 2001).

Diamond, A. S., 'An Eye for an Eye', *Iraq* 19 (1957), pp. 151–155.

Duchrow, Ulrich, and Liedke, Gerhard, *Shalom: Biblical Perspectives on Creation, Justice and Peace* (Geneva: WCC Publications, 1987).

Dyrness, William A., 'Environmental Ethics and the Covenant of Hosea 2', in Robert L. Hubbard Jr, Robert K. Johnston and Robert P. Meye (eds.), *Studies in Old Testament Theology* (Dallas: Word, 1992), pp. 263–278.

Eichrodt, Walther, 'The Effect of Piety on Conduct (Old Testament Morality)', in *Theology of the Old Testament*, vol. 2 (London: SCM, 1967), pp. 316–379.

Ellison, H. L., 'The Significance of the Old Testament Today', *Churchman* 74 (1969), pp. 231–238.

Elsdon, Ron, *Green House Theology: Biblical Perspectives on Caring for Creation* (Tunbridge Wells: Monarch, 1992).

Englehard, David H., 'The Lord's Motivated Concern for the Underprivileged', *Calvin Theological Journal* 15 (1980), pp. 5–26.

Exum, J. Cheryl, 'The Ethics of Biblical Violence against Women', in Rogerson, Davies and Carroll, *Bible in Ethics*, pp. 248–271.

Fager, Jeffrey A., *Land Tenure and the Biblical Jubilee*, JSOT Supplements, vol. 155 (Sheffield: JSOT Press, 1993).

Fensham, F. Charles, 'Widow, Orphan and the Poor in the Ancient near Eastern Legal and Wisdom Literature', *Journal of Near Eastern Studies* 21 (1962), pp. 129–139.

Fletcher, V. H., 'The Shape of Old Testament Ethics', *Scottish Journal of Theology* 24 (1971), pp. 47–73.

Forde, G. O., 'Law and Gospel in Luther's Hermeneutic', *Interpretation* 37 (1983), pp. 240–252.

Forster, G., *Christian Ethics in the Old Testament* (Nottingham: Grove Ethics Books, vol. 35, 1980).

Freedman, D. N. (ed.), *Anchor Bible Dictionary*, 6 vols. (New York: Doubleday, 1992).

——, 'Divine Commitment and Human Obligation: The Covenant Theme', *Interpretation* 18 (1964), pp. 419–431.

Fretheim, Terence E., 'The Reclamation of Creation: Redemption and Law in Exodus', *Interpretation* 45 (1991), pp. 354–365.

Froehlich, K., *Biblical Interpretation in the Early Church* (Philadelphia: Fortress, 1984).

Fuller, Daniel P., *Gospel and Law, Contrast or Continuum? The Hermeneutics of Dispensational and Covenant Theology* (Grand Rapids: Eerdmans, 1980).

Gammie, John G., *Holiness in Israel* (Minneapolis: Fortress, 1989).

Gamoran, H., 'The Biblical Law against Loans on Interest', *Journal of Near Eastern Studies* 30 (1971), pp. 127–134.

Geisler, Norman L., *Christian Ethics: Options and Issues* (Grand Rapids: Baker, 1989; Leicester: IVP, 1990).

——, 'Dispensationalism and Ethics', *Transformation* 6.1 (1989), pp. 7–14.

Gemser, B., 'The Importance of the Motive Clause in Old Testament Law', in *Congress Volume in Memoriam Aage Bentzen*, Supplements to *Vetus Testamentum*, vol. 1 (Leiden: E. J. Brill, 1953), pp. 50–66.

George, Timothy, *Theology of the Reformers* (Nashville: Broadman; Leicester: Apollos, 1988).

Gerbrandt, Gerald Eddie, *Kingship According to the Deuteronomistic History* (Atlanta: Scholars Press, 1986).

Gerstenberger, Erhard, 'Covenant and Commandment', *Journal of Biblical Literature* 84 (1965), pp. 38–51.

——, '". . . He/They Shall Be Put to Death": Life-Preserving Divine Threats in Old Testament Law', *Ex Auditu* 11 (1995), pp. 43–61.

Gillingham, Sue, 'The Poor in the Psalms', *Expository Times* 100 (1988), pp. 15–19.

Gimsrud, Ted, and Johns, Loren L. (eds.), *Peace and Justice Shall Embrace: Power and Theopolitics in the Bible: Essays in Honor of Millard Lind* (Telford, PA: Pandora, 1999).

Gitari, David, 'The Church and Polygamy', *Transformation* 1 (1984), pp. 3–10.

Glasser, Arthur F., 'Messianic Jews – What They Represent', *Themelios* 16.2 (1991), pp. 13–14.

Gnanakan, Ken, *God's World: Biblical Insights for a Theology of the Environment* (SPCK International Study Guides, London: SPCK, 1999).

Gnuse, Robert, 'Jubilee Legislation in Leviticus: Israel's Vision of Social Reform', *Biblical Theology Bulletin* 15 (1985), pp. 43–48.

——, *You Shall Not Steal: Community and Property in the Biblical Tradition* (Maryknoll: Orbis, 1985).

——, *No Other Gods: Emergent Monotheism in Israel*, JSOT Supplement Series, vol. 241 (Sheffield: Sheffield Academic Press, 1997).

Godfrey, W. Robert, 'Calvin and Theonomy', in Barker and Godfrey, *Theonomy*, pp. 299–312.

Goetzmann, J., 'House', in Colin Brown (ed.), *New International Dictionary of New Testament Theology*, vol. 2 (Carlisle: Paternoster, 1976), pp. 247–251.

Goldingay, John, *Theological Diversity and the Authority of the Old Testament* (Grand Rapids: Eerdmans, 1987).

———, *Approaches to Old Testament Interpretation: Updated Edition* (Leicester: Apollos, 1991).

———, 'Justice and Salvation for Israel and Canaan', in Wonil et al., *Reading the Hebrew Bible*, pp. 169–187.

Gossai, Hemchand, *Justice, Righteousness and the Social Critique of the Eighth-Century Prophets*, American University Studies, Series 7: Theology and Religion, vol. 141 (New York: Peter Lang, 1993).

Gottwald, Norman K., *The Tribes of Yahweh: A Sociology of the Religion of Liberated Israel 1250–1050 BCE* (Maryknoll: Orbis, London: SCM, 1979).

———, 'Theological Education as a Theory–Praxis Loop: Situating the Book of Joshua in a Cultural, Social Ethical, and Theological Matrix', in Rogerson, Davies and Carroll, *Bible in Ethics*, pp. 107–118.

Gowan, Donald E., 'Wealth and Poverty in the Old Testament: The Case of the Widow, the Orphan, and the Sojourner', *Interpretation* 41 (1987), pp. 341–353.

Graham, M. P., Marrs, R. R., and McKenzie, S. L. (eds.), *Worship and the Hebrew Bible* (Sheffield: Sheffield Academic Press, 1999).

Greenberg, Moshe, 'Some Postulates of Biblical Criminal Law', in M. Haran (ed.), *Yehezkel Kaufmann Jubilee Volume* (Jerusalem: Magnes, 1960), pp. 5–28.

———, 'Mankind, Israel and the Nations in the Hebraic Heritage', in J. Robert Nelson (ed.), *No Man Is Alien: Essays on the Unity of Mankind* (Leiden: E. J. Brill, 1971), pp. 15–40.

Greene, W. B., 'The Ethics of the Old Testament', *Princeton Theological Review* 27 (1929), pp. 153–193.

Greidanus, Sidney, 'The Universal Dimension of Law in the Hebrew Scriptures', *Studies in Religion* 14 (1985), pp. 39–51.

Gustafson, James M., 'The Changing Use of the Bible in Christian Ethics', in Charles E. Curran and Richard A. McCormick SJ (eds.), *Readings in Moral Theology* (New York: Paulist Press, 1984), pp. 133–150.

———, 'The Place of Scripture in Christian Ethics: A Methodological Study', in Curran and McCormick, *Use of Scripture in Moral Theology*, pp. 151–178.

Habel, Norman C., 'Wisdom, Wealth and Poverty: Paradigms in the Book of Proverbs', *Bible Bhashyam* 14 (1988), pp. 26–49.

———, *The Land Is Mine: Six Biblical Land Ideologies* (Philadelphia: Fortress, 1995).

Halpern, Baruch, *The Constitution of the Monarchy in Israel* (Missoula: Scholars Press, 1980).

Hamilton, J. M., *Social Justice and Deuteronomy: The Case of Deuteronomy 15*, Society of Biblical Literature Dissertation Series, vol. 136 (Atlanta: Scholars Press, 1992).

Hammershaimb, E., 'On the Ethics of the Old Testament Prophets', Supplements to *Vetus Testamentum* 7 (1959), pp. 75–101.

Hanks, Thomas D., *God So Loved the Third World: The Biblical Vocabulary of Oppression* (Maryknoll: Orbis, 1983).

Hanson, Paul D., *The People Called: The Growth of Community in the Bible* (San Francisco: Harper & Row, 1986).

Harrelson, Walter, *The Ten Commandments and Human Rights* (Minneapolis: Fortress, 1980).

Hauerwas, Stanley, *A Community of Character: Toward a Constructive Christian Social Ethic* (Notre Dame: University of Notre Dame Press, 1981).

———, *Peaceable Kingdom* (Notre Dame: Notre Dame University Press, 1983).

———, *Resident Aliens* (Nashville: Abingdon, 1989).

Hawking, Stephen, *A Brief History of Time: From the Big Bang to Black Holes* (London: Bantam, 1988).

Hay, Donald A., 'Christians in the Global Greenhouse', *Tyndale Bulletin* 41.1 (1990), pp. 109–127.

Hays, J. Daniel, 'Applying the Old Testament Law Today', *Bibliotheca Sacra* 158 (2001), pp. 21–35.

Hempel, Johannes, *Das Ethos Des Alten Testaments*, Beihefte zur Zeitschrift für die alttestamentishe Wissenschaft 67, rev. ed. (Berlin: Töpelmann, 1964).

Hendrickx, Herman, *Social Justice in the Bible* (Quezon City: Claretian Publications, 1985).

Hesselink, I. John, 'John Calvin on the Law and Christian Freedom', *Ex Auditu* 11 (1995), pp. 77–89.

Hobbs, T. R., 'Reflections on "the Poor" and the Old Testament', *Expository Times* 100 (1988–9), pp. 291–293.

Holwerda, David E., *Jesus and Israel: One Covenant or Two?* (Grand Rapids: Eerdmans; Leicester: Apollos, 1995).

Hoppe OFM, Leslie J., *Being Poor: A Biblical Study* (Wilmington, DE: Michael Glazier, 1987).

House, H. Wayne, and Ice, Thomas (eds.), *Dominion Theology: Blessing or Curse?* (Portland: Multnomah, 1988).

Houston, Walter, '"and Let Them Have Dominion . . ." Biblical Views of Man in Relation to the Environmental Crisis', *Studia Biblica* 1 (1978), pp. 161–184.

———, 'War and the Old Testament', *Modern Churchman* 28 (1985), pp. 14–21.

———, '"You Shall Open Your Hand to Your Needy Brother": Ideology and Moral Formation in Deut. 15:1–18', in Rogerson, Davies and Carroll, *Bible in Ethics*, pp. 296–314.

———, 'The King's Preferential Option for the Poor: Rhetoric, Ideology and Ethics in Psalm 72', *Biblical Interpretation* 7 (1999), pp. 347–368.

Hughes, Dewi, *God of the Poor: A Biblical Vision of God's Present Rule* (Carlisle: OM Publishing, 1998).

Jacobs, Mignon R., 'Toward an Old Testament Theology of Concern for the Underprivileged', in Wonil et al., *Reading the Hebrew Bible*, pp. 205–229.

Janzen, Waldemar, 'Land', in Freedman, *Anchor Bible Dictionary*, vol. 4, pp. 144–154.

————, 'The Theology of Work from an Old Testament Perspective', *Conrad Grebel Review* 10 (1992), pp. 121–138.

————, *Old Testament Ethics: A Paradigmatic Approach* (Louisville, KY: Westminster John Knox, 1994).

Jenson, P., *Graded Holiness: A Key to the Priestly Conception of the World*, JSOT Supplements, vol. 106 (Sheffield: Sheffield Academic Press, 1992).

Johnston, P., and Walker, P. W. L. (eds.), *The Land of Promise: Biblical, Theological and Contemporary Perspectives* (Leicester: IVP; Downers Grove: InterVarsity Press, 2000).

Juster, Daniel, *Jewish Roots: A Foundation of Biblical Theology for Messianic Judaism* (Rockville: Davar, 1986).

Kaiser Jr, Walter C., *Toward Old Testament Ethics* (Grand Rapids: Zondervan, 1983).

————, *Toward Rediscovering the Old Testament* (Grand Rapids: Zondervan, 1987).

————, *Hard Sayings of the Old Testament* (Downers Grove: InterVarsity Press, 1988).

————, 'The Old Testament Promise of Material Blessings and the Contemporary Believer', *Trinity Journal* 9 (1988), pp. 151–170.

————, 'God's Promise Plan and His Gracious Law', *Journal of the Evangelical Theological Society* 33 (1990), pp. 289–302.

————, 'New Approaches to Old Testament Ethics', *Journal of the Evangelical Theological Society* 35 (1992), pp. 289–297.

————, *Mission in the Old Testament: Israel as a Light to the Nations* (Grand Rapids: Baker, 2000).

Kapelrud, A. S., 'New Ideas in Amos', Supplements to *Vetus Testamentum* 15 (1966), pp. 79–113.

Kaufman, Stephen A., 'A Reconstruction of the Social Welfare Systems of Ancient Israel', in W. Boyd Barrick and John R. Spencer (eds.), *In the Shelter of Elyon* (Sheffield: JSOT Press, 1984).

Kaye, B. N., and Wenham, G. J. (eds.), *Law, Morality and the Bible: A Symposium* (Leicester: IVP, 1978).

Kidner, Derek, 'Old Testament Perspectives on War', *Evangelical Quarterly* 57 (1985), pp. 99–112.

Kim, Wonil, Ellens, Deborah, Floyd, Michael, and Sweeney, Marvin (eds.), *Reading the Hebrew Bible for a New Millennium: Form, Concept, and Theological Perspective* (Harrisburg, PA: Trinity Press International, 2000).

Klassen, H. W., 'The Relation of the Old and New Covenants in Pilgram Marpeck's Theology', in Swartley, *Essays on Biblical Interpretation*, pp. 91–105.

Kline, M. G., *The Structure of Biblical Authority* (Grand Rapids: Eerdmans, 1972).

Knierim, Rolf P., *The Task of Old Testament Theology: Substance, Method, and Cases* (Grand Rapids: Eerdmans, 1995).

————, 'On the Subject of War in Old Testament and Biblical Theology', in Wonil et al., *Reading the Hebrew Bible*, pp. 73–88.

Knight, Douglas A., and Meyers, Carol (eds.), 'Ethics and Politics in the Hebrew Bible', *Semeia* 66 (Atlanta: Society of Biblical Literature, 1994).

———, 'Political Rights and Powers in Monarchic Israel', *Semeia* 66 (1994), pp. 93–117.

Kraftson-Hogue, Michael, 'Toward a Christian Ecological Ethic: The Lesson of Old Testament Israel's Dialogic Relations with Land, History and God', *Christian Scholars Review* 28 (1998), pp. 270–282.

Kuhn, Thomas S., *The Structure of Scientific Revolutions*, 2nd ed. (Chicago: University of Chicago Press: 1970).

Lang, B., 'The Social Organization of Peasant Poverty in Israel', *Journal for the Study of the Old Testament* 24 (1982), pp. 47–63.

———, *The Hebrew God: Portrait of an Ancient Deity* (New Haven: Yale University Press, 2002).

Leggett, D. A., *The Levirate and Goel Institutions in the Old Testament with Special Attention to the Book of Ruth* (Cherry Hill: Mack, 1974).

Lemche, Niels Peter, 'Habiru, Hapiru', in Freedman, *Anchor Bible Dictionary*, vol. 3, pp. 6–10.

Liechty, Daniel, 'What Kind of Political Power? The Upside-Down Kingdom in Millard Lind's Reading of the Hebrew Bible', in Gimsrud and Johns, *Peace and Justice Shall Embrace*, pp. 17–33.

Lind, Millard C., 'The Concept of Political Power in Ancient Israel', *Annual of the Swedish Theological Institute* 7 (1968–9), pp. 4–24.

———, *Yahweh Is a Warrior: The Theology of Warfare in Ancient Israel* (Scottdale: Herald, 1980).

Lindars, Barnabas, 'Imitation of God and Imitation of Christ', *Theology* 76 (1973), pp. 394–402.

Linville, Mark D., 'A Little Lower Than the Angels: Christian Humanism and Environmental Ethics', *Christian Scholars Review* 28 (1998), pp. 283–297.

Linzey, Andrew, *Animal Theology* (London: SCM, 1994).

———, *Animal Gospel* (London: Hodder & Stoughton; Louisville, KY: Westminster John Knox, 1998).

Linzey, Andrew, and Yamamoto, Dorothy (eds.), *Animals on the Agenda: Questions about Animals for Theology and Ethics* (London: SCM, 1998).

Loewe, Raphael, *The Position of Women in Judaism* (London: SPCK, 1966).

Lohfink SJ, Norbert F., *Great Themes from the Old Testament* (Edinburgh: T. & T. Clark, 1982).

———, *Option for the Poor: The Basic Principle of Liberation Theology in the Light of the Bible* (Berkeley: BIBAL Press, 1987).

———, *God of Israel and the Nations: Studies in Isaiah and the Psalms*, trans. Everett R. Kalin (Collegeville, MA: Liturgical Press, 2000).

Long, V. P., Baker, D. W., and Wenham, G. J. (eds.), *Windows into Old Testament History: Evidence, Argument and the Crisis of 'Biblical Israel'* (Grand Rapids: Eerdmans, 2002).

Longenecker, R. N., 'Three Ways of Understanding Relations between the Testaments:

Historically and Today', in G. F. Hawthorne and O. Betz (eds.), *Tradition and Interpretation in the New Testament: Essays in Honor of E. Earle Ellis for His Sixtieth Birthday* (Grand Rapids: Eerdmans, 1987), pp. 22–32.

Longman III, Tremper, and Reid, Daniel G., *God Is a Warrior* (Grand Rapids: Zondervan; Carlisle: Paternoster, 1995).

Lovelock, James E., *Gaia: A New Look at Life on Earth* (Oxford: Oxford University Press, 1979).

Malchow, Bruce V., 'Social Justice in the Wisdom Literature', *Biblical Theology Bulletin* 12 (1982), pp. 120–124.

———, 'Social Justice in the Israelite Law Codes', *Word and World* 4 (1984), pp. 299–306.

Marak, Krickwin C., and Aghamkar, Atul Y. (eds.), *Ecological Challenge and Christian Mission* (Delhi: ISPCK, 1998).

Marshall, J. W., 'Decalogue', in Alexander and Baker, *Dictionary of the Old Testament: Pentateuch*, pp. 171–182.

Marshall, Paul, *Thine Is the Kingdom: A Biblical Perspective on the Nature of Government and Politics Today* (Basingstoke: Marshall, Morgan & Scott, 1984).

Martens, Elmer A., *God's Design: A Focus on Old Testament Theology*, 2nd ed. Grand Rapids: Baker; Leicester: Apollos, 1994).

———, 'How Is the Christian to Construe Old Testament Law?' *Bulletin for Biblical Research* 12 (2002), pp. 199–216.

Martin-Achard, Robert, *A Light to the Nations: A Study of the Old Testament Conception of Israel's Mission to the World*, trans. John Penney Smith (Edinburgh: Oliver & Boyd, 1962).

Mason, John, 'Biblical Teaching and Assisting the Poor', *Transformation* 4.2 (1987), pp. 1–14.

Mason, Rex, *Propaganda and Subversion in the Old Testament* (London: SPCK, 1997).

Matthews, V. H., 'Family Relationships', in Alexander and Baker, *Dictionary of the Old Testament: Pentateuch*, pp. 291–299.

———, 'Social-Scientific Approaches', in Alexander and Baker, *Dictionary of the Old Testament: Pentateuch*, pp. 787–793.

Mays, James L., 'Justice: Perspectives from the Prophetic Tradition', in David L. Petersen (ed.), *Prophecy in Israel: Search for an Identity* (London: SPCK Philadelphia: Fortress, 1987), pp. 144–158.

McBride Jr, S. Dean, 'The Yoke of Torah', *Ex Auditu* 11 (1995), pp. 1–15.

McCarthy, D. J., 'Notes on the Love of God in Deuteronomy and the Father–Son Relationship between Yahweh and Israel', *Catholic Biblical Quarterly* 27 (1965), pp. 144–147.

McConville, J. Gordon, *Law and Theology in Deuteronomy*, JSOT Supplements, vol. 33 (Sheffield: JSOT Press, 1984).

McDonagh SSC, Sean, *To Care for the Earth: A Call to a New Theology* (London: Geoffrey Chapman, 1986).

———, *The Greening of the Church* (Maryknoll: Orbis; London: Geoffrey Chapman, 1990).

McKeating, H., 'Sanctions against Adultery in Ancient Israelite Society, with Some Reflections on Methodology in the Study of Old Testament Ethics', *Journal for the Study of the Old Testament* 11 (1979), pp. 57–72.

McKenzie, D. A., 'Judicial Procedure at the Town Gate', *Vetus Testamentum* 14 (1964), pp. 100–104.

McKenzie, J. L., 'God and Nature in the Old Testament', *Catholic Biblical Quarterly* 14 (1952), pp. 18–39, 124–145.

————, 'The Elders in the Old Testament', *Biblica* 40 (1959), pp. 522–540.

Meeks, Wayne, *The Moral World of the First Christians* (Philadelphia: Westminster; London: SPCK, 1986).

Mendelsohn, I., *Slavery in the Ancient Near East* (Oxford: Oxford University Press, 1949).

Mendenhall, George E., 'The Relation of the Individual to Political Society in Ancient Israel', in J. M. Myers, O. Reimherr and H. N. Bream (eds.), *Biblical Studies in Memory of H. C. Alleman* (Locus Valley, NY: J. J. Augustin, 1960), pp. 89–108.

Mettinger, Tryggve N. D., *King and Messiah: The Civil and Sacral Legitimation of the Israelite Kings* (Lund: Gleerup, 1976).

Middleton, J. Richard, and Walsh, Brian J., *Truth Is Stranger Than it Used to Be: Biblical Faith in a Postmodern Age* (London: SPCK; Downers Grove: InterVarsity Press, 1995).

Millar, J. Gary, *Now Choose Life: Theology and Ethics in Deuteronomy* (Leicester: Apollos, 1998).

Miller Jr, Patrick D., 'The Gift of God: The Deuteronomic Theology of the Land', *Interpretation* 23 (1969), pp. 454–465.

————, 'The Place of the Decalogue in the Old Testament and Its Law', *Interpretation* 43 (1989), pp. 229–242.

Mills, Mary E., *Images of God in the Old Testament* (Collegeville, MN: Liturgical Press; London: Cassells, 1998).

————, *Biblical Morality: Moral Perspectives in Old Testament Narratives*, Heythrop Studies in Contemporary Philosophy, Religion and Theology, ed. Laurence Paul Hemming (Aldershot, UK: Ashgate, 2001).

Mills, Paul, *Interest in Interest: The Implications of the Old Testament Ban on Interest for Today* (Cambridge: Jubilee Centre, 1989).

Moss, R., *The Earth in our Hands* (Leicester: IVP, 1982).

Mott, Stephen Charles, 'The Contribution of the Bible to Economic Thought', *Transformation* 4.3–4 (1987), pp. 25–34.

————, *A Christian Perspective on Political Thought* (Oxford: Oxford University Press, 1993).

Mouw, Richard J., *When the Kings Come Marching In: Isaiah and the New Jerusalem* (Grand Rapids: Eerdmans, 1983).

————, 'Commands for Grown-Ups,' in Curran and McCormick, *Use of Scripture*, pp. 66–77.

Muilenburg, J., *The Way of Israel: Biblical Faith and Ethics* (New York: Harper, 1961).

Murray, Robert, *The Cosmic Covenant: Biblical Themes of Justice, Peace and the Integrity of Creation* (London: Sheed & Ward, 1992).

Nahmani, H. S., *Human Rights in the Old Testament* (Tel Aviv: J. Chachik, 1964).

Napier, B. D., 'Community under Law: On Hebrew Law and Its Theological Presuppositions', *Interpretation* 7 (1953), pp. 26–46.

Nash, James A., *Loving Nature: Ecological Integrity and Christian Responsibility* (Nashville: Abingdon, 1991).

Nasuti, Harry P., 'Identity, Identification, and Imitation: The Narrative Hermeneutics of Biblical Law', *Journal of Law and Religion* 4 (1986), pp. 9–23.

Nicholson, E. W., 'The Decalogue as the Direct Address of God', *Vetus Testamentum* 27 (1977), pp. 422–433.

Niditch, Susan, *War in the Hebrew Bible: A Study in the Ethics of Violence* (Oxford: Oxford University Press, 1993).

Northcott, Michael S., *The Environment and Christian Ethics* (Cambridge: Cambridge University Press, 1996).

North, R., *Sociology of the Biblical Jubilee* (Rome: Pontifical Biblical Institute, 1954).

O'Donovan, Oliver M. T., 'Towards an Interpretation of Biblical Ethics', *Tyndale Bulletin* 27 (1976), pp. 54–78.

——, *Resurrection and Moral Order: An Outline for Evangelical Ethics* (Leicester: IVP, 1986).

——, *The Desire of the Nations: Rediscovering the Roots of Political Theology* (Cambridge: Cambridge University Press, 1996).

Ogletree, Thomas, *The Use of the Bible in Christian Ethics* (Minneapolis: Fortress, 1983; Oxford: Blackwell, 1984).

Orlinsky, Harry M., 'The Biblical Concept of the Land of Israel: Cornerstone of the Covenant between God and Israel', in L. A. Huffman (ed.), *The Land of Israel: Jewish Perspectives* (Notre Dame: Notre Dame University Press, 1986), pp. 27–64.

Otto, Eckart, *Theologische Ethik des Alten Testaments* (Stuttgart: W. Kohlhammer, 1994).

Patrick, Dale, *The Rendering of God in the Old Testament*, Overtures to Biblical Theology, vol. 10 (Philadelphia: Fortress, 1981).

——, *Old Testament Law* (Atlanta: John Knox, 1985).

——, 'God's Commandment', in Linafelt and Beal, *God in the Fray*, pp. 93–111.

Penchansky, David, *What Rough Beast? Images of God in the Hebrew Bible* (Louisville, KY: Westminster John Knox, 1999).

Perdue, Leo G., Blenkinsopp J., and Collins, J. J., *Families in Ancient Israel* (Louisville, KY: Westminster John Knox, 1997).

Petrie, Alistair, *Releasing Heaven on Earth* (Grand Rapids: Chosen Books, 2000).

Phillips, Anthony J., *Ancient Israel's Criminal Law: A New Approach to the Decalogue* (Oxford: Blackwell; New York: Schocken, 1970).

Plant, Raymond, *Politics, Theology and History* (Cambridge: Cambridge University Press, 2001).

Pleins, J. David, 'Poverty in the Social World of the Wise', *Journal for the Study of the Old Testament* 37 (1987), pp. 61–78.

——, 'Poor, Poverty', in Freedman, *Anchor Bible Dictionary*, vol. 5, pp. 402–414.

————,'How Ought we to Think about Poverty? Re-thinking the Diversity of the Hebrew Bible', *Irish Theological Quarterly* 60 (1994), pp. 280–286.

————,*The Social Visions of the Hebrew Bible: A Theological Introduction* (Louisville, KY: Westminster John Knox, 2001).

Poettcker, H., 'Menno Simons' Encounter with the Bible', in Swartley, *Essays on Biblical Interpretation*, pp. 62–76.

Porter, J. Roy, 'The Legal Aspects of the Concept of "Corporate Personality" in the Old Testament', *Vetus Testamentum* 15 (1965), pp. 361–380.

Poythress, Vern S., *Science and Hermeneutics: Implications of Scientific Method for Biblical Interpretation* (Grand Rapids: Academie; Leicester: Apollos, 1988).

Rad, G. von, 'The Promised Land and Yahweh's Land', in *The Problem of the Hexateuch and Other Essays* (New York: McGraw Hill; London: SCM, 1966), pp. 79–93.

Reimer, David J., 'Ṣdq', in VanGemeren, *New International Dictionary of Old Testament Theology and Exegesis*, vol. 3, pp. 744–769.

Reventlow, Henning Graf, 'The Biblical and Classical Traditions of Just War', in Reventlow and Hoffman, *Politics and Theopolitics*, pp. 160–175.

Reventlow, Henning Graf, and Hoffman, Yair (eds.), *Justice and Righteousness: Biblical Themes and Their Influence*, JSOT Supplement Series 137 (Sheffield: JSOT Press, 1992).

Reventlow, Henning Graf, Hoffman, Yair, and Uffenheimer, Benjamin (eds.), *Politics and Theopolitics in the Bible and Postbiblical Literature*, JSOT Supplement Series vol. 171 (Sheffield: JSOT Press, 1994).

Reviv, Hanoch, *The Elders in Ancient Israel: A Study of a Biblical Institution* (Jerusalem: Magnes, 1989).

Ridder, Richard R. de, *Discipling the Nations* (Grand Rapids: Baker, 1975).

Riggans, Walter, *The Covenant with the Jews: What's so Unique about the Jewish People?* Eastbourne: Monarch, 1992).

Ringe, S. H., *Jesus, Liberation, and the Biblical Jubilee: Images for Ethics and Christology* (Philadelphia: Fortress, 1985).

Rodd, Cyril, 'The Family in the Old Testament', *Bible Translator* 18 (1967), pp. 19–26.

————,'The Use of the Old Testament in Christian Ethics', in Rodd, *New Occasions Teach New Duties?* pp. 5–19.

————(ed.), *New Occasions Teach New Duties? Christian Ethics for Today* (Edinburgh: T. & T. Clark, 1995).

————,*Glimpses of a Strange Land: Studies in Old Testament Ethics* (Edinburgh: T. & T. Clark, 2001).

Rogerson, John W., 'The Hebrew Conception of Corporate Personality: A Re-examination', *Journal of Theological Studies* New Series 21 (1970), pp. 1–16.

————,'The Old Testament View of Nature: Some Preliminary Questions', *Oudtestamentische Studiën* 20 (1977), pp. 67–84.

————,'The Old Testament and Social and Moral Questions', *Modern Churchman* 25 (1982), pp. 28–35.

————, 'Discourse Ethics and Biblical Ethics', in Rogerson, Davies and Carroll, *Bible in Ethics*, pp. 17–26.

Rogerson, John W., Davies, Margaret, and Carroll, M. Daniel (eds.), *The Bible in Ethics: The Second Sheffield Colloquium*, JSOT Supplement Series vol. 207 (Sheffield: Sheffield Academic Press, 1995).

Rushdoony, Rousas, *Institutes of Biblical Law* (Phillipsburg: Presbyterian & Reformed, 1973).

Schluter, Michael, and Clements, Roy, *Reactivating the Extended Family: From Biblical Norms to Public Policy in Britain* (Cambridge: Jubilee Centre, 1986).

————, 'Jubilee Institutional Norms: A Middle Way between Creation Ethics and Kingdom Ethics as the Basis for Christian Political Action', *Evangelical Quarterly* 62 (1990), pp. 37–62.

Schluter, Michael, and Lee, David, *The R Factor* (London: Hodder & Stoughton, 1993).

Schnabel, Eckhard J., 'Israel, the People of God, and the Nations', *Journal of the Evangelical Theological Society* 45 (2002), pp. 35–57.

Schofield, J. N., '"Righteousness" in the Old Testament', *Bible Translator* 16 (1965), pp. 112–116.

Scobie, C. H. H., 'The Place of Wisdom in Biblical Theology', *Biblical Theology Bulletin* 14 (1984), pp. 43–48.

————, 'Israel and the Nations: An Essay in Biblical Theology', *Tyndale Bulletin* 43.2 (1992), pp. 283–305.

Seitz, Christopher, *Word without End* (Grand Rapids: Eerdmans, 1998).

Selman, M. J., 'Law', in Alexander and Baker, *Dictionary of the Old Testament: Pentateuch*, pp. 497–515.

Senior, Donald, and Stuhlmueller, Carroll, *The Biblical Foundations for Mission* (London: SCM, 1983).

Shepherd, J. J., 'Man's Morals and Israel's Religion', *Expository Times* 92 (1981), pp. 171–174.

Siker, Jeffrey S., *Scripture and Ethics: Twentieth-Century Portraits* (New York: Oxford University Press, 1997).

Simkins, Ronald A., *Creator and Creation: Nature in the Worldview of Ancient Israel* (Peabody: Hendrickson, 1994).

Simon, U., 'The Poor Man's Ewe Lamb . . . Judicial Parable', *Biblica* (1967), pp. 207–242.

Sloan Jr, R. B., *The Favorable Year of the Lord: A Study of Jubilary Theology in the Gospel of Luke* (Austin: Schola, 1977).

Spanner, Huw, 'Tyrants, Stewards – or Just Kings?' in Linzey and Yamamoto, *Animals on the Agenda*, pp. 216–224.

Sparks, Kenton L., *Ethnicity and Identity in Ancient Israel: Prolegomena to the Study of Ethnic Sentiments and Their Expression in the Hebrew Bible* (Winona Lake: Eisenbrauns, 1998).

Spohn, William C., *What Are They Saying About Scripture and Ethics?* 2nd ed. (New York: Paulist Press, 1995).

Sprinkle, J. M., 'Sexuality, Sexual Ethics', in Alexander and Baker, *Dictionary of the Old Testament: Pentateuch*, pp. 741–753.

Stackhouse, M. L., 'What Then Shall We Do? On Using Scripture in Economic Ethics', *Interpretation* 41 (1987), pp. 382–397.

Stamm, J. J., and Andrews, M. E., *The Ten Commandments in Recent Research* (London: SCM, 1967).

Stein, S., 'The Laws on Interest in the Old Testament', *Journal of Theological Studies* New Series 4 (1953), pp. 161–170.

Stek, John H., 'Salvation, Justice and Liberation in the Old Testament', *Calvin Theological Journal* 13 (1978), pp. 112–116.

Stern, David H., *Messianic Jewish Manifesto* (Jerusalem: Jewish New Testament Publications, 1988).

Strickland, Wayne G. (ed.), *The Law, the Gospel and the Modern Christian: Five Views* (Grand Rapids: Zondervan, 1993).

Swartley, Willard M., *Slavery, Sabbath, War and Women: Case Issues in Biblical Interpretation* (Scottdale, PA: Herald, 1983).

———— (ed.), *Essays on Biblical Interpretation: Anabaptist-Mennonite Perspectives* (Elkhart, IN: Institute of Mennonite Studies, 1984).

Taylor, Robert D., and Ricci, Ronald J., 'Three Biblical Models of Liberty and Some Representative Laws', *Ex Auditu* 11 (1995), pp. 111–127.

Thompson, Alden, *Who's Afraid of the Old Testament God?* (Grand Rapids: Zondervan, 1989).

Townsend, C., and Ashcroft, J., *Political Christians in a Plural Society: A New Strategy for a Biblical Contribution* (Cambridge: Jubilee Centre, 1994).

Trible, Phyllis, *God and the Rhetoric of Sexuality* (Minneapolis: Fortress, 1978).

————, *Texts of Terror* (Minneapolis: Fortress, 1984).

Tucker, Gene M., 'The Law in the Eighth-Century Prophets', in Tucker, Petersen and Wilson, *Canon, Theology and Old Testament Interpretation*, pp. 201–216.

Tucker, Gene M., Petersen, David L., and Wilson, Robert R. (eds.), *Canon, Theology and Old Testament Interpretation: Essays in Honor of Brevard S. Childs* (Philadelphia: Fortress, 1988).

Tuckett, Christopher M., 'Paul, Scripture and Ethics: Some Reflections', *New Testament Studies* 46.3 (2000), pp. 403–422.

Ucko, Hans (ed.), *The Jubilee Challenge: Utopia or Possibility: Jewish and Christian Insights* (Geneva: WCC Publications, 1997).

Van den Toren, Benno, 'God's Purpose for Creation as the Key to Understanding the Universality and Cultural Variety of Christian Ethics', *Missiology: An International Review* 30 (2002), pp. 215–233.

van Iersel, B., and Weiler, A. (eds.), *Exodus – a Lasting Paradigm, Concilium*, vol. 189 (Edinburgh: T. & T. Clark, 1987).

VanGemeren, Willem A. (ed.), *New International Dictionary of Old Testament Theology and Exegesis*, 5 vols. (Grand Rapids: Paternoster, 1996).

Voegelin, E., *Israel and Revelation* (Baton Rouge: Louisiana State University, 1956).

Waldow, H. E. von, 'Social Responsibility and Social Structure in Early Israel', *Catholic Biblical Quarterly* 32 (1970), pp. 182–204.

————, 'The Concept of War in the Old Testament', *Horizons of Biblical Theology* 6 (1984), pp. 27–48.

Walker, P. W. L. (ed.), *Jerusalem Past and Present in the Purposes of God*, rev. ed. (Carlisle: Paternoster, 1994).

Walsh SJ, J. P. M., *The Mighty from Their Thrones: Power in the Biblical Tradition*, Overtures to Biblical Theology, vol. 21 (Philadelphia: Fortress, 1987).

Walzer, Michael, *Exodus and Revolution* (New York: Basic, Books, 1985).

Weinfeld, Moshe, *The Promise of the Land: The Inheritance of the Land of Canaan by the Israelites* (Berkeley: University of California Press, 1993).

————, *Social Justice in Ancient Israel and in the Ancient near East* (Jerusalem: Magnes; Minneapolis: Fortress, 1995).

Weinfeld, W., 'The Origin of Humanism in Deuteronomy', *Journal of Biblical Literature* 80 (1961), pp. 241–249.

Weir, J. Emmette, 'The Poor Are Powerless: A Response to R. J. Coggins', *Expository Times* 100 (1988), pp. 13–15.

Wenham, Gordon J., 'Law and the Legal System in the Old Testament', in Kaye and Wenham, *Law, Morality and the Bible*, pp. 24–52.

————, *The Book of Leviticus*, New International Commentary on the Old Testament (Grand Rapids: Eerdmans, 1979).

————, 'The Restoration of Marriage Reconsidered', *Journal of Jewish Studies* 30 (1979), pp. 36–40.

————, *Story as Torah: Reading the Old Testament Ethically* (Edinburgh: T. & T. Clark, 2000).

Wenham, John W., *The Enigma of Evil: Can we Believe in the Goodness of God?* (Leicester: IVP, 1985; Carlisle: Paternoster, 1997).

White, Lynn, 'The Historical Roots of Our Ecologic Crisis', *Science* 155 (1967), pp. 1203–1207.

Whybray, R. N., *Wealth and Poverty in the Book of Proverbs*, JSOT Supplements 99 (Sheffield: Sheffield Academic Press, 1990).

Wilkinson, Loren, 'New Age, New Consciousness and the New Creation', in W. Granberg-Michaelson (ed.), *Tending the Garden: Essays on the Gospel and the Earth* (Grand Rapids: Eerdmans, 1987), pp. 6–29.

————(ed.), *Earthkeeping in the Nineties: Stewardship of Creation*, rev. ed. (Grand Rapids: Eerdmans, 1991).

Willis, John T., 'Old Testament Foundations of Social Justice', in Perry C. Cotham (ed.), *Christian Social Ethics* (Grand Rapids: Baker, 1979), pp. 21–43.

Willis, Timothy M., ' "Eat and Rejoice before the Lord": The Optimism of Worship in the Deuteronomic Code', in Graham, Marrs and McKenzie, *Worship and the Hebrew Bible*, pp. 276–294.

Wilson, Robert R., 'Approaches to Old Testament Ethics', in Tucker, Petersen and Wilson, *Canon, Theology and Old Testament Interpretation*, pp. 62–74.

————, 'Ethics in Conflict: Sociological Aspects of Ancient Israelite Ethics', in Susan

Niditch (ed.), *Text and Tradition: The Hebrew Bible and Folklore* (Atlanta: Scholars Press, 1990), pp. 193–205.

———, 'Sources and Methods in the Study of Ancient Israelite Ethics', *Semeia* 66 (1995), pp. 55–63.

Wiseman, D. J., 'Law and Order in Old Testament Times', *Vox Evangelica* 8 (1973), pp. 5–21.

Wogaman, J. Philip, *Christian Ethics: A Historical Introduction* (Louisville, KY: Westminster John Knox, 1993).

———, *Christian Perspective on Politics*, 2nd ed. (Louisville, KY: Westminster John Knox, 2000).

Wonil, Kim, Ellens, Deborah, Floyd, Michael, and Sweeney, Marvin (eds.), *Reading the Hebrew Bible for a New Millennium: Form, Concept, and Theological Perspective* (Harrisburg, PA: Trinity Press International, 2000).

Woods, John A., *Perspectives on War in the Bible* (Macon: Mercer University Press, 1998).

Wright, Christopher J. H., 'The Israelite Household and the Decalogue: The Social Background and Significance of Some Commandments', *Tyndale Bulletin* 30 (1979), pp. 101–124.

———, *Living as the People of God: The Relevance of Old Testament Ethics* (in the USA, *An Eye for an Eye*) (Leicester: IVP; Downers Grove: InterVarsity Press, 1983).

———, 'What Happened Every Seven Years in Israel? Old Testament Sabbatical Institutions for Land, Debts and Slaves', *Evangelical Quarterly* 56 (1984), pp. 129–138, 193–201.

———, 'Family', in Freedman, *Anchor Bible Dictionary*, vol. 2, pp. 761–769.

———, 'Jubilee, Year Of', in Freedman, *Anchor Bible Dictionary*, vol. 3, pp. 1025–1030.

———, *Knowing Jesus through the Old Testament* (London: Marshall Pickering; Downers Grove: InterVarsity Press, 1992).

———, 'Biblical Ethics: A Survey of the Last Decade', *Themelios* 18.2 (1993), pp. 15–19.

———, *Tested by Fire: Daniel 1–6 in Today's World* (London: Scripture Union, 1993).

———, 'Leviticus', in Gordon J. Wenham, J. Alec Motyer, Donald A. Carson and R. T. France (eds.), *New Bible Commentary: 21st Century Edition* (Leicester: IVP; Downers Grove: InterVarsity Press, 1994), pp. 121–157.

———, *Walking in the Ways of the Lord: The Ethical Authority of the Old Testament* (Leicester: IVP; Downers Grove: InterVarsity Press, 1995).

———, *Deuteronomy*, New International Biblical Commentary, Old Testament Series (Peabody: Hendrickson; Carlisle: Paternoster, 1996).

———, *God's People in God's Land: Family, Land and Property in the Old Testament* (Grand Rapids: Eerdmans, 1990; Carlisle: Paternoster, rev. ed., 1996).

———, ''ab', in VanGemeren, *New International Dictionary of Old Testament Theology and Exegesis*, vol. 1, pp. 219–223.

———, ''ereṣ', in VanGemeren, *New International Dictionary of Old Testament Theology and Exegesis*, vol. 1, pp. 518–524.

————, 'nhl', in VanGemeren, *New International Dictionary of Old Testament Theology and Exegesis*, vol. 3, pp. 77–81.

————, *The Message of Ezekiel*, The Bible Speaks Today (Leicester: IVP; Downers Grove: InterVarsity Press, 2001).

Wright, D. F., 'The Ethical Use of the Old Testament in Luther and Calvin: A Comparison', *Scottish Journal of Theology* 36 (1983), pp. 463–485.

————, 'Calvin's Pentateuchal Criticism: Equity, Hardness of Heart and Divine Accommodation in the Mosaic Harmony Commentary', *Calvin Theological Journal* 21 (1986), pp. 33–50.

Wright, N. T., *Jesus and the Victory of God* (London: SPCK, 1996).

Zimmerli, Walther, *The Old Testament and the World* (London: SPCK, 1976).

INDEX OF SCRIPTURE REFERENCES

INDEX OF NAMES

INDEX OF SUBJECTS